CLINICAL CHILD PSYCHOLOGY

CLINICAL CHILD PSYCHOLOGY
An Introduction to Theory, Research, and Practice

Edited by

STEVEN I. PFEIFFER, Ph.D.

Department of Pediatrics
Department of Psychiatry
Child Development Center
Ochsner Clinic and
Alton Ochsner Medical Foundation
New Orleans, Louisiana

GRUNE & STRATTON, INC.
(Harcourt Brace Jovanovich, Publishers)
ORLANDO   SAN DIEGO   NEW YORK
LONDON   TORONTO   MONTREAL   SYDNEY   TOKYO

Library of Congress Cataloging in Publication Data
Main entry under title:

Clinical child psychology.

Bibliography: p.
Includes index.
1. Clinical child psychology—Addresses, essays,
lectures.   2. Child psychotherapy—Addresses, essays,
lectures.   3. Child mental heallth servvices—Addresses,
essays, lectures.   I. Pfeiffer, Steven I. [DNLM:
1. Child Psychology.   2. Psychology, Clinical—in infancy
& childhood. WS 105 C641]
RJ503.3.C55   1985   618.92'89   84-22395
ISBN 0-8089-1680-7

Grune & Stratton, Inc.
Orlando, FL 32887

Distributed in the United Kingdom by
Grune & Stratton, Ltd.
24/28 Oval Road, London NW 1

Library of Congress Catalog Number 84-22395
International Standard Book Number 0-8089-1680-7
Printed in the United States of America

85 86 87   10 9 8 7 6 5 4 3 2 1

CONTENTS

PREFACE

This volume introduces the reader to the major concepts, research findings, and professional issues influencing the practice of clinical child psychology. A number of sociocultural, political, economic, and professional forces have contributed to recent changes in the field of clinical child psychology. This volume reflects these transformations and paradigm shifts, and suggests future directions for all those concerned with the health care of children.

The authors who have contributed to this book are eminently qualified to address their particular topics. All have made significant contributions in their respective specialties and are actively engaged in providing health care services to children, youth, and families. The selection of contributors and themes was based on a desire to provide an eclectic orientation to a biopsychosocial perspective of human behavior.

It is my intention that this volume will be an invaluable addition to the library of all health care professionals concerned with promoting the mental health and human potential of children—psychologists, psychiatrists, pediatricians and family practice physicians, nurses, social workers, teachers, child care workers, and all other practitioners in fields related to health care.

I wish to thank all those who devoted their time and energies to this volume. First, to all of the contributors; to Marion Stafford and the Medical Editing Department of the Alton Ochsner Medical Foundation; and to my colleagues, students, and patients for their encouragement of this undertaking. And a special thanks to my wife and children who supported this endeavor with patience and humor.

CONTRIBUTORS

HOWARD S. ADELMAN, Ph.D.
Professor of Psychology and Director of Fernald Laboratory & Clinic
Department of Psychology
U.C.L.A.
Los Angeles, California

ERNEST M. BERNAL, JR. Ph.D.
Professor of Education
California State University
San Bernardino, California

VALERIE J. COOK, Ph.D.
Associate Professor of Psychology
Department of Psychology & Human Development
George Peabody College
Vanderbilt University
Nashville, Tennessee

STEPHEN T. DeMERS, Ed.D.
Associate Professor
Department of Educational and Counseling Psychology
University of Kentucky
Lexington, Kentucky

JUDY L. GENSHAFT, Ph.D.
Associate Professor and Director
School of Psychology Training Program
Ohio State University
Columbus, Ohio

BERTHA G. HOLLIDAY, Ph.D.
   Associate Professor of Psychology
   Department of Psychology & Human Development
   George Peabody College
   Vanderbilt University
   Nashville, Tennessee

GEORGE W. HOWE, Ph.D.
   Assistant Professor of Psychology & Human Development
   George Peabody College
   Vanderbilt University
   Nashville, Tennessee

ALAN E. KAZDIN, Ph.D.
   Professor of Child Psychiatry and Psychology
   Department of Psychiatry
   University of Pittsburgh School of Medicine
   Research Director, The Children's Psychiatric Treatment Service
   Western Psychiatric Institute and Clinic
   Pittsburgh, Pennsylvania

ROBERT L. MARION, Ph.D.
   Associate Professor
   Department of Special Education
   College of Education
   University of Texas
   Austin, Texas

JACK A. NAGLIERI, Ph.D.
   Assistant Professor, School of Psychology Training Program
   Ohio State University
   Columbus, Ohio

GARLAND F. NIQUETTE
   Doctoral Candidate
   Department of Educational and Counseling Psychology
   University of Kentucky
   Lexington, Kentucky

STEVEN I. PFEIFFER, PH.D.
Clinical Child/Pediatric Psychologist
Departments of Pediatrics and Psychiatry
Ochsner Clinic and Alton Ochsner Medical Foundation
Adjunct Assistant Professor of Psychology
Tulane, University
New Orleans, Louisiana

J. CONRAD SCHWARZ, PH.D.
Professor of Psychology
Graduate Training Program in Clinical Psychology
University of Connecticut
Storrs, Connecticut

ANDREA STARRETT, M.D.
Developmental Pediatrician
Director, Child Development Center
Department of Pediatrics
Ochsner Clinic and Alton Ochsner Medical Foundation
New Orleans, Louisiana

WILLIAM E. STILLWELL, PH.D.
Professor and Director of Graduate Study
Department of Educational and Counseling Psychology
University of Kentucky
Lexington, Kentucky

LINDA TAYLOR, PH.D.
Lecturer in Psychology and Assistant Director of the
Fernald Laboratory and Clinic
Department of Psychology
U.C.L.A.
Los Angeles, California

BENNETT I. TITTLER, PH.D.
Director, Psychology Internship
Greater Lynn Community Mental Health Center
Union Hospital
Lynn, Massachusetts

JUNE M. TUMA, Ph.D.
Professor of Psychology
Department of Psychology
Louisiana State University
Baton Rouge, Louisiana

GORDON ULREY, Ph.D.
Assistant Clinical Professor of Psychiatry and Pediatrics
University of California, Davis Medical School
Sacramento, California

CLINICAL CHILD PSYCHOLOGY

June M. Tuma

1

Child Mental Health in Perspective

The understanding of the child's situation in today's society has reached new heights, yet significant problems of research methodology, methods of remediation, and erratic social policy still mitigate against optimism for future mental health services to children. Traditionally, child mental health professionals have been characterized as having three psychological and scientific perspectives: (1) *A developmental perspective*. Professionals serving children must have an understanding of the normal as well as deviant processes of development in children and youth; (2) *An empirical perspective*. Empirical experience provides the basic criteria for development of clinical services to children and in research with children and youth; and (3) *The psychosocial perspective*. Sensitivity to, and understanding of, the intrapsychic and sociocultural forces affecting the psychological and social development and growth of children and youth are essential.

The principles of understanding the child and subsequent interventions in the potential multitudinous problems of children and youth have always been the same. Research findings that encompass an expanded view of the child's development to include the child's own influence, changes in social policy, and current findings about the effects of the changing societal trends, have, however, posed some issues that have far-reaching implications for the child mental health professionals. In addition, the fluctuating governmental policies, coupled with the in-

CLINICAL CHILD PSYCHOLOGY
ISBN 0–8089–1680–7

1

creased governmental influence on the treatment and evaluation services to children and youth create additional problems and difficulties in defining areas of research, training, and service efforts.

An adequate evaluation of the status of child mental health professionals today involves analysis of the forces that determine the child's development, those that influence the professions, the effects of social policy on the role of the professions and services to children and youth, and finally, a consideration of the ethics and professional guild issues impinging on child mental health professionals.

THE DEVELOPING CHILD AS AN AREA OF SCIENTIFIC INQUIRY

The study of the child in the United States began as a child study movement just before the beginning of this century. The approach of the time has recently been compared to a sociobiological approach to children's behavior (White, 1979). Early work consisted mainly of social statistics, journal accounts of the condition of children, arguments about social action, editorials, etc. Even in the beginning, mainstream American psychology was committed to the scientific method; in the basis of being unscientific in methodology, it ignored the early movement that concerned the betterment of children and youth in this country. During the 1920s and 1930s the child development movement was housed in institutes and child study centers. By the 1950s this movement moved into psychology departments (Sears, 1975), where it achieved a measure of seriousness in its empirical studies and research. The study of the child has achieved full circle by today, with some prominent developmental psychologists insisting that the proper concern of psychologists is to develop programs and policy for children.

It was not until the 19th century that specific psychopathologies of children were recorded (Harms, 1967; Veith, 1964). The text of Benjamin Rush, written in 1812, was the first American reference to specific disorders of children (Rubenstein, 1948). During this early period, organic causes were viewed as mediating mechanisms for psychopathology and the basic treatment was physiologic. Only the major disorders were considered pathology at the time. There was no theory of childhood disorder or even of childhood development.

During the 20th century many advances have been made. The rights of children and women were advanced (Key, 1909), and psychoanalytic theory was elaborated and gained wide acceptance. With this theoretical advance, the developing child was represented in detail. Adolf Meyer (Klein, 1944) proposed a dynamic emphasis and innovative practices that influenced the "mental hygiene" movement in the United States. Interest in juvenile delinquents and interdisciplinary work with children and their families began with William Healy (Healy & Bronner, 1936). Mental hospitals began admitting children, and the guidance movement and orthopsychiatry originated and thrived. Objective measures of human characteristics were developed as were concepts of mild and moderate disorders in children. There was also a renewed emphasis on the major disorders along different lines of inquiry. Child psychotherapy and residential treatment of children were improvised. During this period, the search for determinants of disordered behavior had become increasingly thorough, detailed, and systematic.

The current views changed from those at the beginning of the century in a number of different ways, characterized as follows: (1) One of the major developments has been the recognition of various environmental influences in the development of disordered behavior in childhood. The mother's role, especially, has been emphasized, perhaps inappropriately (Kessen, 1979). Mother's impact on her child was stimulated by both Meyer's (Klein, 1944) early investigations of his patient's home life and from psychoanalytic interest in the child's early life. This environmental emphasis became extreme and only recently is being tempered by other considerations.

Nonenvironmental elements have recently been shown to contribute to disordered behavior in children. Temperamental differences in children (Thomas & Chess, 1977) have tempered the exclusive interest in the maternal role. Recent findings on the biological state and competencies of the newborn and studies on genetic factors in behavior have further cautioned researchers and practitioners about placing too much emphasis on environmental factors.

Recent work has also emphasized a more complex analysis of environmental factors, different from the psychoanalytic theorist's exclusive emphasis on parental influence. More recent work emphasizes the impact of economic and other factors on family functioning and its subsequent influence on the child's development. Studies of families of young adult schizophrenics have led to scrutiny of the family and the larger community as environmental influences of significant proportion. The availability of mental health services through community mental health agencies in recent times has highlighted the multiplicity of problems previously not investigated, e.g., the altered socialization process in children of culturally deprived families, lag in the growth of language dependent functions in socially and culturally disadvantaged children. These problems have generated interest in early cognitive development and have spurred programs of cognitive stimulation, interest in determination of the timing and the nature of the environmental impact that will facilitate the emergence of one or another function related to disadvantaged children. The idea that certain critical periods might exist in early human development for certain functions or classes of functions to appear according to norms has been gaining popularity.

(2) The cumulative impact of deleterious conditions in a child's life has been stressed more recently. Previously, it was tempting to attribute dysfunction to the crucial event, parental divorce, ill-timed surgery, or a gross change in living conditions, etc. Now, consideration of the relative impact of the duration of negative influence, the child's previous resources, and their timing relative to various emerging functions or degree and nature of conflict resolution and the existence of compensatory factors is the mode. The concept of a single trauma as a determinant of dysfunction has fallen in disfavor. Development is presently viewed as a process whereby each solution of a developmental task is built upon successful completion of a previous one (Bronfenbrenner, 1979; Rie, 1971).

(3) The cumulative impact concept brings into importance the dual concept of multiplicity and interaction of determinants. The child's problem is not held now to be consequent upon an error of upbringing, a given habit, or any single stroke of misfortune except where the impact is so overwhelming and the affected emerging evaluation is altered or remains incomplete. Problems are thus not attributed to either endowment or environmental factors, but rather, the interaction in the form of mutual impact of child and caretaker.

(4) During this century, it is increasingly common to search for the nature of the identifiable causal relationships. The search is now for mechanisms of interpersonal and intrapsychic factors by means of which determinants yield their effects, and the conditions under which they do so. These explanations represent progressively more detailed descriptions of sequences of events since they are clearly the result of more extensive and more systematic observations of childhood behavior.

(5) The most important change during this century is perhaps in the conceptualization of child psychopathology that recognizes the uniqueness of childhood and of the differences among developmental levels with respect to a growing array of specifiable functions. Different functions will thus be affected by disruptive influences at different points in a child's development; emergent functions are more likely to be affected than well-established and integrated functions; the nature and range of dysfunction is partly contingent on the timing and duration of deleterious influences; gross categorizations of psychopathology may fail to acknowledge the uneven development of various functions (though excessive interest in circumscribed dysfunction may, in turn, fail to identify more subtle and less obviously related manifestations); and environmental conditions for optimal development demand change rather than

constancy to maintain harmony with constant change in the child (Bronfenbrenner, 1979). With these and other implications of the developmental perspective, attention seems finally to be directed to those issues
that are of specific relevance to childhood and to the evolution of concepts of child psychopathology (Wenar, 1982).

The Changing View of the Child

The child at birth is active and competent. In recent years, a dramatic
change has occurred in our view of the child. The child is not viewed
as a passive participant in development, but as an active and influential
partner in promoting his or her own growth and development. Even
infants are no longer thought of as passive creatures with limited sensory
perceptual and social capacities, awaiting the imprint of the adult world.
Instead, we recognize that infants possess a wide range of perceptual,
cognitive, and social capacities. Infants can localize sound and discriminate sounds of different loudness and duration (Bartoshuk, 1964;
Brackbill, 1970; Hammond, 1970), discriminate among different pitches
of sound (Leventhal & Lipsett, 1964), are sensitive to brightness changes
immediately after birth (e.g., Sherman, Sherman & Flory, 1936), can
detect movement (Haith, 1966), and can follow a visual stimulus (Greenman, 1963). Although visual acuity is not fully developed at birth, it
improves rapidly during the first year of life (Cohen, DeLoache, & Strauss,
1978). At 4 months of age, the infant can focus as well as an average
adult (Haynes, White, & Held, 1965), and at a very early age he/she can
distinguish colors and hues (Bornstein, Kessen, & Weiskopp, 1976) and
can discriminate among patterns (Fantz, 1961). Furthermore, infants
have depth perception as soon as they can crawl (Gibson & Walk, 1960)
as young as $1^{1}/_{2}$ months of age (Campos, Langer, & Krowitz, 1970) and
possess the capacity to judge size constancy. Infants can discriminate
among a variety of odors (Lipsett, Engen, & Kaye, 1963) and spatial
location of doors (Reiser, Yonas, & Wikner, 1976) and are selectively
responsive to different gustatory stimuli (Crook & Lipsett, 1976; Desor,
Maller, & Turner, 1973; Jensen, 1932; Nisbett & Gurwitz, 1970).

The child's behavior is organized. The behavior is not a disorganized
bundle of responses, reflexes, and reactions; instead, organization is
evident in the child's behavior. Even infant responses such as sucking,
looking, and sleeping are highly structured response patterns.

The child's behavior has multiple causes. Current views stress that biological-genetic factors as well as situational-environmental factors play
an important role in shaping the course of development. This interplay
between biology and environment is evident in a host of ways including

the role of nutrition in cognitive development, the effects of drugs on children's learning, and the influence of hormones on sex-role development.

The effects that biological factors play on development have always been of importance to psychologists, both in the study of developmental processes and evaluation of intellectual and behavioral characteristics. The current understanding of the chemical processes and multiple gene interactions involved in genetic transmissions on the modification of phenotypes through environmental factors had modified the genetic study of such characteristics. Phenotypical appearance, transmission, and survival of genetically based characteristics depend on a variety of factors including dominant, sex-linked genes and interaction with other genes. Such factors as age of mother, intrauterine environment, physiological condition, and postnatal experiences also influence the phenotypical expression of the genotype.

The genetic explanation in the development of social behavior and intelligence has not been explained by biologists (Hetherington & Parke, 1979). There are some advances, however, in the study of twins and adoption. These studies suggest that genetic factors play a role in the development of many physical and physiological characteristics (Matheny, 1975; Nichols & Bromon, 1974; Wilson, 1974), in intelligence (Burt, 1966; Scarr-Salpatek, 1971), sociability (Buss, Plomin, & Willerman, 1973; Gottesman, 1963; Shields, 1962), and emotional responsiveness (Petrie, 1967). They also play a role in preference for certain types and levels of stimulation, and in some form of psychopathological and deviant behavior. These disorders and phenotypical manifestations of these generic predispositions are also influenced by environmental and experiential factors. Even characteristics strongly influenced by heredity are modified by environment, which permits an understanding of the emergence of individual differences.

Intellectual Factors

Even though intellectual factors are heavily weighted by genetic factors (Matheny, 1975; Nichols & Bromon, 1974; Wilson, 1974), environmental factors play a greater role on achievement tests than on intelligence tests (Burt, 1966). Studies on adoption show that environment affects children's IQ scores as well (Scarr-Scalpatek, 1971).

Personality. Genetic factors apparently affect personality characteristics less than intellectual factors. Methodologic difficulties in definition and measurement of personality traits, however, make this conclusion tentative. One dimension of personality, sociability, or introversion-extroversion appears to have a hereditary component, however. Studies show more similarity in identical than fraternal twins, for instance (Buss, Plomin, & Willerman, 1973; Freedman & Keller, 1963; Gottesman, 1963; Scarr, 1969; Shields, 1962), and sociability has been found to be stable over time (Kagan & Moss, 1962; Schaeffer & Bayler, 1963).

Twin studies also indicate that preference for different types and amounts of stimulation has a heredity component (Bushsbaum, 1973). Studies on stimulus-reducers and stimulus-augmenters (Petrie, 1967) link the nervous system to stimulation and also relate to certain personality types. For example, psychopaths have been linked to reducers and neurotics to augmenters (Sykrzypek, 1969). Aggressive, acting-out, antisocial children were more likely than neurotic children to seek stimulation (DeMyer-Gapin & Scott, 1977). Stimulus seeking has been attributed to differences in rates of transmission of neural impulses that are, at least in part, genetically determined (Quay, 1979; Wheeler, 1974).

Activity, another form of stimulus-seeking, is influenced by heredity, as shown by twin studies (Scarr, 1966; Willerman & Plomin, 1973) and comparisons of activity levels of children and parents (Willerman & Plomin, 1973). Activity level appears to be a relatively stable characteristic (Halverson & Waldrop, 1976) into adolescence (Kagan & Moss, 1962; Neilon, 1948) and maturity (Tuddenham, 1959).

Parent-Child Interaction

The role of environmental factors in temperament includes the responsiveness of parents to the temperamental variations in their infants and to their stimulus preferences. Depending on the responses, the same temperamental genotype may be manifested in different personality characteristics in children. Difficult children (Chess, Thomas, & Birch, 1968; Graham, Rutter, & George, 1973; Thomas & Chess, 1977; Thomas, Chess, & Birch, 1968; Thomas, Chess, Birch, Hertzig, & Korn, 1963) are identifiable in the earliest months of life, characterized by biological irregularities in sleep, feeding, and elimination; inflexibility, avoidance of or distress in response to new experiences; slow adaptability to new situations; nonfastidiousness; and negative moods, including extremes of fussiness and crying. These children are more likely to manifest behavior disorders as adults than more malleable children.

Two factors have been suggested to account for the higher incidence of behavior disorder: the difficult child is less adaptable to environmental demands and more prone to psychological damage, and more likely to elicit different or adverse responses from the social environment. These children are often the targets of parental irritability, and parents are more likely to take out their own stresses on these difficult children. The child's temperament thus puts the child at higher risk of encountering adverse experiences in interacting with his or her environment rather than of being a direct cause of psychological disorder (Thomas, et al., 1963; Thomas & Chess, 1977).

Deviant behavior. There are genetic factors in a wide variety of deviant behaviors (neuroticism, depression, hysteria, suicide, alcoholism, manic-depressive psychosis, psychopathic personality, childhood behavior disorders, and crime). Schizophrenia has received the greatest research attention, however, based on evidence concerning concordance rates of twins.

Children of emotionally disturbed or mentally retarded parents or those being raised in a particularly stressful environment are of current concern. Recent findings show that even if children are removed from their schizophrenic mothers, they have a greater than average probability of developing problems (Heston, 1966; Mednick, Schulsinger, & Schulsinger, 1975). Studies of the salient life experiences for high risk children are currently being pursued and intervention programs for high risk children (Bell, Mednick, Raman, Schulsinger, Sutton-Smith, & Venables, 1975) have been implemented with some success.

Children play an active role in modifying and altering adult behavior even in infancy. A very recent development involves the child's influence on the responses of other people. The early unidirectional view of development under which adults influence children but children do not alter adult behavior is no longer considered valid. A bidirectional view of child development is now widely accepted, with children playing an influential part of their own social and cognitive development.

Not only is it important for the social environment to be responsive to the infant (Reingold, 1956), but the infant must learn that the control of the social environment is to some measure manipulable (Lewis & Goldberg, 1969) for normal development. Recent research on the effects of institutionalization, for example, has related the apathetic, passive, and withdrawn infants to an unalterable environment (Finkelstein & Ramey, 1977). The infant, in this situation, simply stops trying to have any effect on others. Further, mothers who attend to and stimulate their infants in response to infant signal (vocalization or a distress call), had more developmentally advanced infants (Yarrow, Rubinstein, & Pedersen, 1975). In addition, complexity of toys and variety of play materials and household objects available to the infant are significantly related to a variety of measures of infant development (Yarrow, et al., 1975). It has also been demonstrated that children affect adults' behavior in situations immediately following misbehavior and/or administration of punishment (Parke & Sawin, 1975).

The family has been recently viewed as a process of interdependent mutual shaping. This view gives the children a role in shaping parents' behavior as well as vice versa. Childrearing practices are influenced by constitutional dispositions of the child as well, with the active, irritable, demanding son often found to receive increasingly more severe methods of control from mothers, particularly in one-parent families (Bell, 1968). The role of the child's behavior in battered child cases has recently been investigated with findings that the behavior of the child contributes to parental violence (Gil, 1970; 1975; 1978; 1979; 1981).

The child thus has considerable power in the determination of his/her development. The influence of genetics and temperament, as well as learning, plays a role in this phenomenon.

The child is embedded in a variety of social systems and settings in which the members shape each other's behavior. These range from smaller immediate settings and systems, such as the family or peer group in which the child has considerable influence, to larger or more remote systems, such as school, community, or greater society over which the child has less control. Once the child is viewed in the larger context of social systems, even this bidirectional view of development inadequately accounts for all factors. It may be more accurate to think of development as being multidirectional, rather than a bidirectional process. The nature of the interactions, stresses, and supports encountered in social systems influences development (see Bronfenbrenner, 1979). Bronfenbrenner is a major critic of study of the child apart from the environments in which he or she lives or the processes through which these environments affect the course of development. Bronfenbrenner introduced four propositions that specify the properties of the ecological environment that foster processes of human development: (1) experimentation with progressively more complex activity under direct guidance; (2) engagement in activities learned without guidance; (3) third parties in the setting supportive rather than undermining activities engaged in in interaction with the child; and (4) fostering an increase in developmental potential as a function of the number of supportive links between that setting and other contexts involving the child or persons responsible for his or her care. He thus includes dyadic relationships in the first two propositions, but acknowledges the importance of other persons and systems; for example, the nuclear family is a three-person system, yet, most investigations of people in the child's life other than mother have tended to use the dyadic paradigm of study by simply substituting the third person, e.g., father for mother in the analytic model (Lamb, 1976). The interactions are thus never investigated.

Some recent data appear to support this proposition: Parent-child interaction increases with the newborn when the spouse is present (Parke,

1978); when father is supportive of mother, the latter more effectively feeds the baby, whereas marital conflict is associated with inept feeding on part of mother (Pederson, 1976). Hetherington, Cox, and Cox (1976, 1978) found that after divorce if father continued to be supportive of mother's role as parent, mother's relation with child was more harmonious and the child's adjustment was relatively unimpaired. If conflict between the divorced parents continued, the mother-child dyad and behavior of the child deteriorated. They found that in the single-parent family, other stresses such as economic reverses, task overload with outside employment, and lack of support systems result in a change in family function for the single mother and her children.

The impact of the child's experience from one setting to another, has been researched only meagerly (Elder, 1974; Elder & Rockwell, 1978; Scarr-Salpatek & Williams, 1972). One study serves as a model of how one setting, the school, can interdigitate with the home, community, and other people in the school context (Smith, 1968). Since the developing child spends a great deal of time in the school, the school setting is probably the context most closely connected to the home. However, circumstances of school location, segregated classes, teacher socioeconomic-based value systems and the like, make it even more isolated (Bronfenbrenner, 1979).

Knowledge of the influence of multiple factors in child development has led to consideration of those factors as they influence disordered behavior in children. Assessment of childhood deviations is presently more complex and inclusive than ever before and interventions are attempted at multiple levels of the child's life. Attention to prevention of high-risk children and families, to more detailed study of the effects of the more prevalent incidence of divorce, working mothers, single-parent families, and socioeconomic status has become increasingly important in the training of mental health professionals, in mental health treatment planning, and in social policy activities. Many of these factors also affect ethical and guild considerations in the treatment of the pathological child.

MENTAL HEALTH SERVICES TO CHILDREN

Estimates of the number of emotionally disturbed children in the United States vary. The Joint Commission on the Mental Health of Children (1969) estimated that 0.6 percent of all children suffer from psychoses, 2 to 3 percent from severe disorders, and 8 to 10 percent from emotional disturbances requiring some treatment. A survey of 25 catchment areas yielded similar estimates (Sowder, 1975). A larger estimate was given by the President's Commission on Mental Health (1978). They estimated that 5 to 15 percent of all children and adolescents, or 3 to 9 million children, require some type of mental health service.

Despite the problems inherent in epidemiological surveys, including technical problems of definition and sampling (Gould, Wunsch-Hitzig, & Dohrenwend, 1981; Sowder, 1979), all estimates agree that the number is great. Knitzer (1982) settles on an estimate of approximately 3 million (about 5 percent of the population) seriously disturbed children and adolescents. Of this number, approximately one third of them are served in the mental health system (Knitzer, 1982). This estimate is derived from data indicating that in 1976, 655,000 children and adolescents under 18 years received some kind of care through traditional mental health agencies (Rosen, 1979) and that 348,954 children 3 to 18 years old had been identified by the schools as seriously disturbed in 1980-1981 (Department of Education, 1982).

Inequity of service apparently is the norm, with the most disturbed children often the least likely to get help (Knitzer, 1982). Sowder (1975), for example, discovered that 30 percent of the children judged to be seriously emotionally disturbed were receiving services as compared to 38 percent of the less seriously disturbed children.

Types of Mental Health Services for Children

When a referral is made by a family to seek help for emotional problems of their child, they have three choices. They can choose among the public, the private, or the medical center mental health facilities depending on their financial situation. It is widely held that children of all ages should have access to three kinds of services: nonresidential, residential, and therapeutic case advocacy (e.g., Knitzer, 1982).

Nonresidential services. Early intervention efforts, traditional diagnostic and outpatient services, and intensive programs in the home and community are the three types of nonresidential services essential to provide adequate mental health care to children.

(1) Early intervention efforts involve both parents and children. These interventions include parent counseling; consultation to help agencies identify and cope with children's problems; telephone hotlines offering parents or adolescents support, advice, or referrals; preventive services that keep children out of restrictive residential placements; and programs to prevent emotional problems in particularly vulnerable children such as those with multiple handicaps or mentally ill parents.

(2) Outpatient therapies perhaps reach more children than any
     other mental health service (Sowder & Burt, 1980). Sowder
     reports that in 1975, 54 percent of children in outpatient ther-
     apy were in individual therapy, 34 percent in family therapy,
     8 percent in group therapy, 3 percent in drug therapy, and 4
     percent in other psychiatric treatment. This compares with sim-
     ilar results of treatment of children by clinical child psychol-
     ogists (Tuma & Pratt, 1982). Outpatient services can be pro-
     vided on an individual basis, to an entire family, or to groups
     of children of similar ages or with comparable problems.

          The hallmark of therapy is that it usually occurs in an office
     setting; rarely at the child's home. In-home treatment, how-
     ever, can be particularly important when families are in crisis
     or have a young troubled child, when parents rather than chil-
     dren are the primary clients, or when families are disorganized
     and unwilling or unable to go to the therapist.

          Contrary to common belief, outpatient therapy continues
     six months or less. In fact, one study found that children at
     the University of California at Davis were seen a median of 4.8
     visits per year. The goals of therapy are for children to talk,
     play, or learn to behave in different ways and to cope more
     effectively with crises or chronic problems (Reisman, 1973).
     Common settings include community mental health centers,
     child guidance centers, or family service agencies. Current es-
     timates indicate that there are 590 federally assisted community
     mental health centers now operating (President's Commission
     on Mental Health, 1978). These centers are accessible, however,
     only to about 43 percent of the population. Some states also
     fund mental health centers (Knitzer, 1982), and schools are a
     source of outpatient therapy. Their role in therapy provision
     is, however, ambiguously mandated and often suffers fiscal
     restraints.

(3) Intensive services in the home or community provide services
     to the child at home, avoiding placement in institutions or other
     residential settings. These programs operate out of the com-
     munity mental health centers and provide a mixture of less
     traditional services and therapy and usually have an emphasis
     on specialized treatment modalities. For example, they may be
     short term and oriented around crises (e.g., sudden death,
     diagnosis of a life-threatening illness), or they may provide
     treatment combining therapy with educational and recreational
     activities. They may also offer multiple services to disturbed
     children with numerous problems and a history of unsuccessful

experiences with one or more "helping" systems. These services have successfully reduced children's need for more restrictive care, and should be given priority in efforts to reform mental health care for children (Knitzer, 1982). Few such services now exist, in part because arbitrary funding restrictions make it easier to use dollars for costly out-of-home placement.

Residential services. These usually provide inpatient care in psychiatric hospitals or the psychiatric units of general hospitals, and specialized care in residential treatment centers. In 1975–1976, the National Institute of Mental Health estimated that there were over 331 residential centers in the United States with a capacity of 18,000 beds, distributed unevenly throughout the country (Witkin, 1977). Inpatient psychiatric hospitals were designed to care for seriously ill children (children who are suicidal, engage in bizarre behavior, endanger lives of others, hear voices), while residential treatment centers provide carefully structured, therapeutic programs of treatment, education, vocational training, and family involvement to children whose behavior is less impaired but still requires their removal from home.

New approaches that include therapeutic group and foster homes and crisis beds reflect a mounting concensus that children who need residential programs should be able to move from more restrictive institutional settings to small facilities closer to their homes and preferably within their communities. In spite of this increasing awareness, traditional residential treatment and costly inpatient care remain the most readily available "help" for too many disturbed children; even though inpatient care is frequently inappropriate, the quality of residential treatment varies greatly, and the efficacy of residential treatment is still undocumented (Knitzer, 1982).

Therapeutic case advocacy. This type of mental health service offers disturbed children and their families a spokesperson to help work with various agencies and get needed services delivered in an appropriate, coordinated, and sensitive fashion. It is not recognized nor funded as a mental health service for children. It is, however, potentially a powerful way of reaching those greatly in need and hard to serve, including severely disturbed children and adolescents and those from "disorganized" families that lack the abilities to navigate through the maze of available educational and social service programs. Such families and children need one person they can trust and count on for effective advocacy on their behalf (Knitzer, 1982; Shore, 1979).

This kind of advocacy goes beyond the untrained advocate and case management because it requires knowing not only what services are available but also how to work with the various systems involved to ensure that quality services are provided (Knitzer, 1982).

Manpower for Mental Health Services to Children

Trained staff members are needed to design and provide responsive mental health services for children and adolescents. The pool of trained professionals is very limited, however. Of the 28,000 psychiatrists in this country, a little more than 10 percent are child psychiatrists. These psychiatrists are not evenly distributed around the country and several states have no or few child psychiatrists (President's Commission on Mental Health, 1980).

The American Psychological Association estimates that although children under 18 make up about 30 percent of the population (based on 1970 census data), less than one percent of psychologists are devoted primarily to serving children (VandenBos, Nelson, Stapps, Olmedo, Coates, & Batchelor, 1979). The estimte is that there are about 500 psychologists in the United States who specialize in serving children. No specific data are available on the number of specially trained psychiatric social workers or psychiatric nurses, but there is no reason to believe patterns are very different from those described for psychiatrists or psychologists.

States estimate they can meet only 5 to 50 percent of the need for teachers for the 300,000 emotionally disturbed children identified and served in 1979, while there are some 700,000 such children who are still unserved (Grosenick & Huntze, 1980).

The number of specially trained people working with children and adolescents in residential settings is growing, but the need for such child case workers is still greater than the supply (Joint Commission on Mental Health of Children, 1969; Vanderver, 1976).

To complicate matters, some trained providers choose not to work with seriously disturbed children or they may be trained only in the most traditional mental health services (Toth & Kenealy, 1981). Moreover, children under the care of public agencies are seldom brought to these trained professionals.

Knitzer (1982) stressed the need for innovative programs with committed staff reflecting new ways to respond to troubled children and families. She found some. Almost all reach beyond the therapist's office to provide case advocacy for children and families caught between numerous caring systems and help families with needs for food, child care, and shelter. "The majority are nonresidential and place a strong emphasis on working with parents, even training them as paraprofessional therapists" (Knitzer, 1982, p. 17).

PSYCHOLOGICAL SERVICES TO CHILDREN

Roles and Goals of Clinical Child Psychology

The Practice of Clinical Child Psychology

Clinical child psychology is concerned with understanding and improving functioning in the immature human. In its scientific function, the profession is concerned with children in general, but in its clinical function, it is concerned with the child in particular. The clinical child psychologist endeavors to use the best knowledge and techniques available to improve the lot of individuals in distress, while also striving through research to increase the knowledge and sharpen the techniques needed for improved intervention in the future.

The practice of clinical child psychology, like clinical psychology in general, utilizes findings and techniques from many branches of psychology, such as abnormal psychology, personality and social psychology, learning theory, and psychological testing but also relies heavily on developmental psychology. The activities of the clinical child psychologists include a variety of service functions, as well as research, training, consultation, and supervision (Tuma, 1982b; Tuma & Grabert, 1983).

The clinical child psychologist, in the quest to improve the lot of the child, is primarily interested in treatment and assessment. Consultative and research functions, while important to the psychologist, appear to place third and fourth in priority of service and practice (Tuma, 1976; Tuma & Grabert, 1983). There is some variability in the way psychologists spend their time, dependent on work setting. For example, members of the Section on Clinical Child Psychology spend half of clinical time on intervention and one third on assessment (Tuma & Pratt, 1982). In contrast, in settings where more emergent kinds of referrals occur, the emphasis shifts somewhat. A survey of the members of the Society of Pediatric Psychology (Section 5, Division 12, APA) showed that members spent 40 percent of their time on assessment, while they spent 45 percent on treatment (Tuma & Cohen, in press). Tuma and Grabert (1983) compared internship training settings for clinical child and pediatric psycholgists and found that priorities of service and training reflected these differences between the traditional and medical work settings. Another comparison is illuminating: a survey of Division 12 members (Garfield & Kurtz, 1976) found that respondents spend 24 percent of their time in diagnosis and assessment. This suggests that psychologists serving children spend proportionately more time in assessment activities than those who also serve adults.

Characteristics of the client populations of clinical child psychologists reveal that service to children and adolescents is distributed differentially across age and socioeconomic groups. The children seen by clinical child psychologists tend to be nonminority children, predominately within the five to ten year age group, members of the middle socioeconomic group, and who present with rather minor behavioral or emotional problems (Cerreto & Tuma, 1977; Tuma & Pratt, 1982). These data further underscore Knitzer's (1982) analysis of underservice to minority and poor children.

Typical services offered to children today are similar to those of previous years. Assessment techniques most frequently used by clinical child psychologists are intelligence scales, projective tests, drawing tests, achievement tests, and the Bender Gestalt Test (Tuma & Pratt, 1982). Behavioral assessment and objective techniques, while used, are endorsed by about only a third of those surveyed (Tuma & Pratt, 1982), indicating that at least in assessment with children, traditional techniques currently are found to be of continuing utility.

The popularity of the Wechsler scales has been shown consistently by others (Brown & McGuire, 1976; Lubin, Wallis, & Paine, 1971; Sundberg, 1977). The Rorschach has also been the most popularly administered personality assessment technique over the years (Brown & McGuire, 1976; Klopfer & Taulbee, 1976; Lubin, Wallis, & Paine, 1971; Reynolds & Sundberg, 1976; Sundberg, 1977; Zubin, Eron & Schumer, 1965), especially for those clients over 9 years of age (Brown & McGuire, 1976). In fact, in 1976, Brown and McGuire found that the Wechsler Intelligence Scale for Children (WISC), Rorschach, and the Bender Gestalt are the five most popular means of personality assessment across age groups.

Orientation preferences of today's clinical child psychologists illuminate some of the trends in the area predicted by Iscoe (1974) and Cummings (1974). While psychodynamic and behavioral theories are the predominant influences in clinical child psychology practice (Tuma & Pratt, 1982), neither appears to be the dominant influence in clinical child psychology practice (Tuma & Cawunder, 1983). Each is claimed to some degree by about half of the respondents to a survey. These data contrast with a heavier emphasis on behavioral than psychodynamic traditions found in a survey of members of the Society of Pediatric Psychology (Tuma & Cohen, in press).

These latter data are seen to support the more emergent role functions of the psychologist in medical settings. The diversity of orientation preferences of the sample appears to indicate that flexibility is the rule

in assessment and treatment of the child's mental and behavioral problems. Although traditional assessment techniques appear more useful across age groups, behavioral assessment techniques are apparently more useful with the 0–6 year old child (Brown & McGuire, 1976).

Clinical child psychologists choose treatment modalities according to the age of the child also (Tuma & Pratt, 1982). Parental counseling, play therapy, and behavior therapy are preferred for the preschool age groups, while play therapy is predominant in the school age group (individual, family, and behavior therapy assume secondary positions). Individual therapy is most frequently utilized with adolescents but family therapy and parent counseling are also frequently utilized (Tuma & Pratt, 1982).

The activities and techniques used by the clinical child psychologist have implications for the training appropriate to prepare one for that practice. Specialized training in assessment techniques especially geared for the child population (achievement tests, child intelligence scales, drawing techniques) and in child treatment modalities (parent counseling, play therapy, individual, and behavior therapy as it applies to children) is essential. These techniques are different from those used with adult populations. It is obvious that unless graduate training programs offer courses and supervision in such techniques, students will be ill-informed and will develop insufficient skills to serve the child population.

Current training programs are inadequate in preparing psychologists to address the needs of children. Respondents to the above mentioned survey (Tuma & Pratt, 1982) noted the inadequacies of the graduate training programs they attended, denoting especially deficits in child-related courses (developmental psychology, clinical child psychology, skill course in assessment and therapy), experience with a wide variety of children, and adequate supervision of clinical work with children. Roberts (1982), Fischer (1978) and Mannarino and Fischer (1982) also found that child programs are inadequate in number and in their offerings. Training standards for clinical child psychology are unformulated (Tuma, 1982a; Wohlford, 1979).

The information obtained from these surveys supports the notion that an inconsistency between training and practice currently exists. Training in the techniques most widely utilized in practice with the child population was not available in many respondent graduate training programs and they were forced to supplement training in various ways. Many have expressed concern about the manner in which psychologists are being trained to deliver services to children (Tuma, 1981; Wolford, 1979).

The Practice of Pediatric Psychology

The large number of psychologists working in medical settings (Tuma & Pratt, 1982) encompasses primarily those employed in departments of psychiatry and departments of pediatrics, although some are in other medical departments, e.g., neurology, family medicine. While those in the departments of psychiatry are involved with mostly the traditional role of the psychologist, including assessment, treatment, and diagnosis, with some consultation to other areas of medicine, those in the departments of pediatrics are involved in an entirely new and different endeavor. Since 1967, the psychologist involved with pediatrics has been referred to as a pediatric psychologist (Wright, 1967). The pediatric psychologist is any psychologist who works with children in a medical/pediatric setting, dealing with nonpsychiatric clinical entities (Christopherson & Rapoff, 1980).

The pediatric psychologist has been described as an offshoot of clinical child psychology (Tuma, 1975). Most present-day pediatric psychologists work in medical schools (Tuma & Cohen in press). These psychologists work in close cooperation with pediatricians on problems that are of mutual interest to the pediatrician and to the psychologist. The major commitment of the psychologist is to the development of methods, philosophy, and training guidelines for the practice of clinical child psychology in relation to the practice of pediatrics (Tuma, 1982b). Since pediatric psychologists function within a pediatric setting, treatment procedures are not geared to long-term involvement, but work within a limited time framework (Tuma, 1982b; Wright, 1979). The involvement has many preventive components since approximately a half of the general pediatrician's time is spent on well-child visits.

The psychosocial or behavioral problems most frequently encountered by pediatricians are negative behaviors (e.g., disobedience, temper tantrums, demanding, whining, crying behavior) and toileting problems (e.g., encopresis, enuresis, toilet training) (Bergman, Dassel, & Wedgwood, 1966; Mesibov, Schroeder, & Wesson, 1977). Pediatricians are not well trained to handle these problems, thus, his/her reliance on pediatric psychologists (Brazelton, 1974; Christopherson & Rapoff, 1979).

Wright (1975) outlines a number of physical health problems that are in the purview of the pediatric psychologist. These include specific physical diseases and also the effects of hospitalization, surgery, and dentistry. Wright estimates that from one third to one half of all children's hospital patients have highly significant behavioral concomitants to their physical illnesses. Attention to these problems at early stages can prevent further complications and development of more serious problems later.

The preventive role also involves the psychologist teaching pediatricians principles of health care delivery that can minimize the problems imposed by hospital and health care procedures. A related issue involves medical compliance. It has been estimated that up to 93 percent of patients fail to follow their doctors' orders. This is perhaps the best documented example of health-related behavior (Becker & Maiman, 1975). The implications of this patient behavior relate to reduced efficacy of medical care, reduced cost effectiveness of care, introduction of bias in clinical therapeutic research trials, and increased dissatisfaction with health care in general (Becker & Maiman, 1975; Ruley, 1978). The misuse of medications can also lead to other complications such as emergence of resistant strains of organisms and/or result in recurrent infection as well as increase the risk of accidental poisoning when medicine accumulates in homes with young children (Mattar & Yaffe, 1974; Ruley, 1978).

The Practice of Clinical Child Psychologists in the Schools

Approximately 10 percent of clinical child psychologists work in school settings (Tuma & Pratt, 1982). Clinical child psychologists employed in the schools as school psychologists, along with those trained in school psychology, have increasingly designed interventions that attempt to resolve problems that are first apparent in the school and that, if remediation is prompt, will prevent further problems from developing. These problems include parent education and training, bibliotherapy (Henry, 1981), home-based contingency systems (Broughton, Barton, & Owen, 1981), school intervention of children of separation and divorce (including intervention with children who are affected by the other children's reactions to separation and divorce) (Drake & Shellenberger, 1981), child abuse (O'Block & Billimoria, 1981) and neglect (Kline, Cole, & Fox, 1981), and liaison within the child's ecological system (Plas, 1981).

Bronfenbrenner (1980) encourages the psychologist in the schools to expand his/her role in researching and initiating programs for parent involvement in the child's principle learning environment. This role expansion would encourage parents to be directly involved in the child's education and in the planning stages of innovative programs and new curriculum design. He also proposes that the school psychologists should use strategies to involve community resources and local industry in the educational process. This approach would serve to reduce the child's social isolation from the world of adults.

Particularly as a result of the activities of behavior therapists, who construe their method as a process of learning, unlearning, and relearning, psychological activities in the schools are increasing. These psychologists have expanded their activities from the psychological problems usually encountered in clinical settings to the difficulties children experience with acquisition of such academic subject matter as reading, impulse control problems, and hyperactive behavior in the classroom.

Since 1964 psychologists have been very influential in designing remediation for reading deficiencies (Staats & Butterfield, 1965; Staats, Minke, Finley, Wolf, & Brooks, 1954; Staats, Minke, Goodwin, & Landeen, 1967; Rybac & Staats, 1970). Token reinforcement techniques (Dalton, Rubino, & Hislop, 1973; Ferster, 1967; Lovitt & Curtiss, 1969) have been helpful in facilitating reading acquisition and enhancing retention of what has been learned. Reading tutoring programs (Heimen, Fischer, & Ross, 1973; Schwartz, 1977; Staats & Butterfield, 1965) have also recently been found to be successful. These remedial programs use both verbal praise and tangible objects as reinforcers.

Although the primary cause of language deficits is the subject of impassioned discussions (Ross, 1981) because some theorists claim that language is an innate capacity that is relatively independent of experience, psychologists have applied behavioral principles to help the child compensate for and overcome deficits in language (Carr, Schreibman, & Lovass, 1975; Harris, 1975; Lovaas, 1977; Risley & Wolf, 1967). Nonverbal approaches have been worked out (deVilliers & Naughton, 1974; Permack, 1970) as have techniques to extend rudimentary speech (Wheeler & Sulzer, 1970) by using imitation techniques (Baer & Sherman, 1964) and planned generalization (Bauermeister & Jemail, 1975; Harris, 1975).

An area of increasing concern in the schools involves deficits in attention. Skills in selective attention have been developed in children by techniques to treat overexclusive attention (Lovaas & Schreibman, 1971; Lovaas, Schreibman, Koegel, & Rehm, 1971; Schreibman, 1975) and overinclusive attention (Hagen & Hale, 1973; Pelham & Ross, 1977; Siegel, 1968; Tarver, Hallahan, Kauffman, & Ball, 1976). Teaching the child to control impulses (Douglas, 1972; Palkes, Steward, & Kahana, 1968; Ross, 1964) and treating the hyperactive child (since both poor impulse control and hyperactive behavior are often associated with learning disabilities) by teaching task-oriented behavior (O'Leary, Pelham, Rosenbaun, & Price, 1976; Patterson, Jones, Whittier, & Wright, 1965) and self-instruction (Bornstein & Quevillon, 1976; Friedling & O'Leary, 1979) have also proven useful.

Clinical child psychologists have also been involved with daycare and early childhood education. Clinical child psychologists as well as developmental and school psychologists have flocked into daycare and Head Start programs as researchers, program evaluators, and diagnosticians. Federal funding demanded research and program evaluation to monitor results of the programs. In spite of the early positive results of the children in Head Start programs, findings show that these gains dissipated quickly as the children proceeded into the elementary school grades (Greenblatt, 1977; Lazar & Darlington, 1982; Zigler & Berman, 1983). However, the programs did provide opportunities for psychologists to gain insights into preventive aspects of early childhood education by exposing children at an earlier age to evaluation and referral for remediation efforts in the intellectual, cultural, and educational spheres.

Psychologists were influential in the planning of early childhood education (Greenblatt, 1977) both in its federal legislative phase and its implementation. As the program was launched, increasing numbers were also involved as consultants to the programs and were also indirectly involved by virtue of increased referrals from the administrators and teachers of the program as needy children were identified in the process of their participation in the program.

SOCIAL POLICY CONSIDERATIONS FOR CHILD MENTAL HEALTH

Social policy established by our governing bodies affects children profoundly and also affects the manner in which psychologists conduct research on and provide services for children. The physical and intellectual development of millions of children is indirectly affected when Congress allocates money for food stamps; court policies involving custody decisions or the treatment of juvenile offenders have a profound psychological effect in some manner, for better or for worse, in affecting the kind of adults that children will become. The mental health professionals bear the brunt of Congressional legislation and more recently, have become more involved in influencing the formation of social policies.

Policy makers often do not have the expertise about children to make the wisest policies that affect them. Obversely, the mental health professional may not be politically astute, but does have power to affect this country's direction in the social arena.

With the numerous potential stresses of family life affecting child rearing practices, the future of the child is increasingly coming into the public, as well as the scientific view. Child advocates of various kinds seek legislation for services to children.

Most of the social policy concerns of this decade are similar to those that have occurred historically: the rights of children and especially their rights for adequate and appropriate mental health services. This section will cover funding for research, children's services, the delivery of mental health services by state mental health, juvenile justice, and educational systems and will also consider legislation, advocacy, and the rights of children.

Social Policy for Research on Children

How government has involved itself in research on children and the influence of federal funding policies on the direction, scope, topics, and quality of research on children is of interest to child mental health professionals (Kiesler, 1979). Although there is no federal policy for research on children, decisions about research are made by several divisions of the Office of Management and Budget, various congressional committees, intraagency departments, and external advisory groups. This fact of scattered responsibility for programs among federal and state agencies makes tracking of data on funding trends, categories, and functions difficult.

A survey by the Social Research Group (Nielson, Hurt, & Berkeley, 1978) indicates that nearly 5,000 projects and $474 million are supported by the federal government. The amount for basic, applied, evaluation, and policy research on children is approximately a quarter to a third of this, or approximately $130 million. The largest proportion of these funds is for education research and development, with approximately as much for health research for children (approximately one third of all funds for research on children).

Apparently, the federal government prefers applied to basic research and the physical and biological to the behavioral and social sciences (Kiesler, 1979). The survey (Nielson et al., 1978) shows a ratio of applied to basic research of about 2 : 1; the same ratio holds in psychology and the social sciences (Kiesler & Turner, 1977). Behavioral and social scientists conducting research on children fare less well than do other scientists who conduct research on children (Kiesler, 1979).

Policy Areas of Research Funding

The general areas of research support are education, health, welfare, and science. In practice, government programs loosely fit a problem-oriented model (Cohen, March, & Olsen, 1972), usually within the dominant preoccupation with important social and political problems of the time. It is rare that programs consider how research can help children in general or consider scientific issues. From year to year with the changing selection of social problems, funds are reallocated for children's research from one policy area to another (Crecine & Linett, 1977; Kiesler, 1979).

Federal Needs and Research and Development Funding

Research funding is influenced unduly by national crises and acute political pressures on the federal establishment.

A large proportion of research on children falls within the mental health and health policy areas and shares a history with biomedical research (see Strickland, 1972). Before World War II most biomedical research and basic research was carried on in hospitals and universities with private support, and the federal government supported less than 15 percent of all research and development expenditures in health and basic science. Problems of testing and placement of personnel during World War II led to the establishment of an Office of Scientific Research and Development in 1941 to initiate and support research related to the defense effort. This move enabled the United States to reach world prominence in defense, atomic energy, medicine, and the sciences by the end of the war.

After the war the government continued to support scientific research. The National Institutes of Health (NIH), National Institute of Mental Health (NIMH), and National Science Foundation (NSF) evolved in part from these forces to mobilize for the future and from scientific interest in research.

Other agencies have been started. The National Institute of Child Health and Human Development (NICHD) was established during the Kennedy era of new frontiers. This agency was mandated to take a broader look at child health in the context of human development (Steiner, 1976).

Advocacy and Professional Groups

Childhood became a social issue during the period from approximately 1880 to 1917 (Bremner, 1970, 1971; Platt, 1969). It was during this period that social reformers attached new concepts of what a child is, what a child needs, and what a child deserves to their organized efforts on behalf of social justice, subsidized expertise, and government intervention. Among their demands were child labor laws, university education, children's hospitals, the pasteurization of milk, and public playgrounds. They succeeded not only in improving the welfare of children but in stimulating the development of specialized and professional experts on children. Implicit and explicit pressures from the new professions contributed to the partitioning of government programs for children and to de facto research policies.

During the 19th century and through the first decade of this century, political activists lobbied on behalf of mothers and children for a children's policy. Through this effort Congress, in 1912, established the Children's Bureau, "to investigate and report upon all matters pertaining to the welfare of children and child life among all classes of our people." In 1913, the Bureau carried out the first major federal study of causes of infant mortality. In general, the Bureau offered flexible and multiple services, but it did not survive. By the 1960s it had been moved from the department of Labor to the Department of Health, Education and Welfare (DHEW) and demoted. It has continued to administer traditional programs in child welfare and foster care alongside the huge Head Start program within the Office of Child Department. As the new children's professions devised their own associations and government programs, the Children's Bureau saw its demise. Specialization contributed to de facto policy and the fragmentation of children's services and research. Research programs flourished where areas of expertise could be identified to carry them out, child psychiatry and clinical psychology for the study of disturbed children, pediatrics for research on childhood disease, developmental psychology from understanding normal and abnormal growth.

Another factor at work is that the professionals who gained greater status or whose credentials were more difficult to obtain also acquired greater control of federal research and development programs. The American Medical Association is the most powerful of professional groups, and physicians surely control the bulk of biomedical research. Psychiatrists, the mental health professionals with the money and prestige, also hold the most prominent positions in the National Institute of Mental Health. In education, professors in schools of education and elsewhere usually receive more of the resources to study elementary and secondary education than do teachers. When the dominant providers of services to children in a policy area are of high prestige, the more likely it is that research funds in that area are awarded noncompetitively.

Research Policy and Knowledge

Research influences the way people think and shape government policy for children's programs and research. The obverse is also true: Government policies affect research directions. A prime example of how this works is the stimulation of scientific interest in heredity-environment issues with the institution of the Kennedy-Johnson programs on stimulating children's early environments.

Government support of research may have improved the quality of research on children. Modern advances of knowledge in the area of children's needs and problems are significant, and these required perseverance, patience, stimulating research environments, and continuing financial support. Federal agencies have contributed more than money; they have taken special responsibility for particular lines of research. "Had our political organizations been less mission oriented, less attuned to their constituencies, and less likely to parcel sponsorship of research among themselves, perhaps much less would have been accomplished" (Kiesler, 1979, p. 1015).

FUNDING FOR CHILDREN'S SERVICES

The President's Commission on Mental Health (PCMH, 1978) explicitly addressed children's needs. The commission identified children and adolescents as needing unique services, ascertaining that for this population "mental health care was inadequate or nonexistent." It endorsed the principle that every child has a basic right of opportunity to achieve full potential, and that mental health services can be essential to the realization of that potential. The PCMH noted the alarming numbers of children who suffered from indifference, neglect, and abuse throughout this country: "Many American children grow to adulthood with mental disabilities which could have been addressed more effectively earlier in their lives through appropriate prenatal, infant and early childhood development care programs," all of which are areas of concern to which psychology has made significant contributions. During the past two decades there has been a dramatic increase in drug and alcohol abuse, and a threefold increase in the suicide rate among adolescents. Troubled children and adolescents, particularly if they are from racial minorities, are too often placed in various facilities such as foster homes, special schools, or mental and correctional institutions without adequate prior screening or subsequent follow-up (Cummings, 1979; Knitzer, 1982). These children are then shuttled from one service to another, each adding its own label, resulting in increased confusion and despair that sets the pattern for adult disability (Knitzer, 1982).

Noting that there are too few trained professionals available that are necessary to deliver the unique services needed by children, the PCMH in 1978 called for efforts to increase the number of mental health professionals trained to work with children and adolescents with the provision that programs include training in supervision, administration, and consultation as well as diagnosis and treatment. In addition to recommending the training of mental health professionals, the commission called for a periodic, comprehensive, developmental assessment to be available to all children, with consent of parents and with maximal parental involvement in all stages of the process. When children are candidates for out-of-home placement, there should be adequate prior evaluation as well as family counseling and support through the situation. Finally, and most importantly, there is a specific charge to the Secretary of DHEW to review existing Federal programs that pertain to health and mental health services for infants and children, and design a coordinated national plan to make available comprehensive services for all children. Out of this charge has grown the proposed Youth Mental Health Service Systems Initiative, dubbed the "Most in Need Program." During the past 15 years, several programs designed to address the service needs of children and adolescents have not been successful. The Community Mental Health Centers Act (1963) mandates children's services as 1 of 12 essential services, but this has never been fully implemented (Knitzer, 1982). Since 1971, $12 million has been renewed annually for these services, with grants going directly to the 10 regions. Some regions follow the guidelines in funding grants; others do not. Although the intent of legislation and of the attendant regulations is usually met, widespread noncompliance with the guidelines all too often renders children's services ineffective or less than adequate. At other times, the selection of what is funded seems to be arbitrary.

Pilot projects in Early and Periodic Screening, Diagnosis and Treatment (EPSDT) anticipated by several years the PCMH's emphasis on early detection, evaluation, and treatment. These programs, funded by NIMH, were of demonstrable value in terms of the early identification of problems in children and youth, but a frustrating aspect of the EPSDT projects was the lack of available treatment once the diagnosis had been made. Growing out of these projects was the most comprehensive Child Health Assessment Program (CHAP), which originally proposed both early detection and therapeutic intervention in children's health and mental health. Unfortunately, in spite of vigorous advocacy by its proponents, CHAP suffered defeat at the hands of the 1978 Congress. Although organized psychology (APA) was originally one of the program's proponents, once the mental health component was erased from the proposed legislation, psychologists had to take a stand in opposition to CHAP because it set a precedent that mental health services were not an indispensible part of comprehensive health services for children (Cummings, 1979).

In the area of training, Congress authorized 6 million more for the fiscal year 1979 than was requested in the President's budget. The money was targeted for underserved populations and public facilities with the intent that trainees or those who have concluded their training be placed in underserved areas. In the fiscal year 1982, the target population was almost exclusively in training child mental health specialists, indicating that Congress perhaps was at last cognizant that the need for services to children is paramount in this country. Clinical training continues to be the most important training in the NIMH, with 80 percent of the training budget as opposed to only 20 percent for research training. Of the millions of children and adolescents in the United States under 18 years of age who suffer from mental health problems, most do not receive the services they need (Kramer, 1976). The magnitude of this problem has not been addressed by any proposed legislation sponsored by the administration. Rather, there has been identified a group of people who demonstrate severe mental health problems and who constitute only 15 percent of the needy population, or 1.5 to 2 million individuals under age 18. It is to this population that the administration addresses its proposed Child and Youth Mental Health Services Systems Initiative, also known for the reason just delineated as the Most in Need Program. in Need Program.

As written, the program was to be launched in the fiscal year 1980 with a modest $7 million (cutback from an original $10 million), increasing to $22 million in fiscal year 1981, and $37 million in fiscal year 1982 (Klerman, 1978). (These figures vary because of the uncertain determination of an economy-minded Congress.)

The Most in Need Program does not constitute a new categorical mental health services program but is instead "a program of improved systems management, planning, knowledge synthesis and dissemination" (Klerman, 1978). It is to be managed by NIMH with the cooperation of the Public Health Service and other parts of DHEW, with contracts going to states and territories for a variety of activities designed to improve the availability of services to the most in need. As conceived, the proposal presents a host of coordination, implementation, and linkage problems, many of which have been of concern to the Office of Management and Budget in its review. Further, by concentrating on children who are psychotic, autistic, chronic, or "grossly maladaptive," the program addresses the most intractable problems and ignores the childhood population for whom intervention can be the most fruitful (Cummings, 1979; Knitzer, 1982). Finally, the concept is heavily tilted toward the medical model and psychiatry, and away from the most innovative contribution (i.e., ecological, preventive, consultative, and educational) that could be made by psychology (Cummings, 1979; Knitzer, 1982).

The Youth Mental Health Services Systems Initiative falls pitifully short of the goal of the President's Commission on Mental Health that there be availability of mental health services for all troubled children and adolescents. An analysis of the implementation of mental health services by states has recently been reported (Knitzer, 1982), and shows that because of budget restraints, the already inadequate state and federal response to children's needs is diminishing.

State Mental Health System Service Delivery

Knitzer (1982) indicates that public agencies with responsibility for disturbed children and adolescents are allocating funds for these children too late and often inappropriately. The most appropriate preventive or intensive community-based services are in scarce supply. Currently, funds are allocated more for costly institutional and residential care. Services to children in their own homes and communities are not provided and large numbers of children remain unserved or inadequately served.

Knitzer (1982) surveyed all 50 states and the District of Columbia and found mental health services for children and adolescents a scarce commodity. Those who receive care receive inappropriate care (Joint Commission, 1969). Knitzer calls these unserved children "unclaimed" by the public agencies with responsibility to serve them.

Many children who are placed in inpatient care centers should never have been admitted to the institutions or have remained there too long (Knitzer, 1982).

Even though evidence shows that intensive nonresidential services in the community benefit children without isolating them and are cost effective, almost half of the states surveyed (18 of 44) were working to increase residential care and were not working to create almost nonexistent nonresidential services. Once children are hospitalized, their special needs are not met by states. Some states (22) now differentiate between children and adolescents in procedures for voluntarily admitting minors to psychiatric institutions, but only six states routinely mandate child-specific reviews (Knitzer, 1982). Only 17 provide children and adolescents the right or access to counsel in voluntary admission proceedings.

The role of the federal government does not provide guidance to the states. Most federal funds encourage medically oriented inpatient care while steadily decreased funds are allocated for community-based services. Only about 17 percent of community mental health center funds is spent on children (NIMH, 1981). Most amazingly, no funds at all are provided for troubled children under the new Alcohol, Drug Abuse, and Mental Health Block Grant (Knitzer, 1982).

Knitzer (1982) stresses that children need programs that work with children in their own homes and communities, involve parents in their children's treatment, show sensitivity to children's ages, developmental levels, strengths and weaknesses and cultural heritage, and allow children to move easily from one setting to another, if necessary, by advocating on their behalf with other agencies.

"Many of the seriously troubled children and adolescents needing mental health services will cost the states money, if not in one way then in another. In the absence of mental health services, these children have or will become the fiscal responsibility of other systems, like child welfare, juvenile justice, or special education. Some will probably require costly long-term institutional care throughout their lives. The public policy choice is not whether to spend money but how" (Knitzer, 1982, p. x).

The Juvenile Justice System and Mental Health Service Delivery

Children who are charged with status offenses or delinquent acts and show a range of emotional or behavioral disorders pose a complex and unsolved challenge for the juvenile justice and mental health systems. No comprehensive national data exist regarding the number of children within the juvenile justice system who have serious emotional or behavioral problems or need mental health services (Knitzer, 1982). State data are spotty. For example, Pennsylvania estimates 30 percent of all adjudicated delinquents may have severe emotional problems (Pennsylvania Office of Mental Health, 1982); a New York study of a sample population of children within the state's juvenile justice facilities found 58 percent had at least one psychiatric diagnosis (Knitzer, 1982).

According to a recent survey of state officials, there is no clear pattern to how children in the juvenile justice system receive the few services they do get. Generally, they get them through mental health facilities, juvenile correctional facilities, and services purchased by juvenile correctional facilities (Turney, 1980). In the Tuma and Pratt (1982) survey, there were no data to reflect psychologists in these settings. Psychologists in private practice and other settings serve these children either through referral to their facilities or through consultation to the juvenile justice system.

Children in detention often need mental health services. A recent New Jersey study examined the psychiatric or psychological evaluations of 68 children who were in detention and shelter care facilities (Wood & Moore, 1981). According to the evaluation 5 to 10 percent of these children had serious mental disturbances, and 70 percent had behavior or personality disorders. The services provided for delinquents largely are limited to diagnostic evaluations or special programs serving only delinquent children: some programs are offered through the courts (Sobel, 1979). There are no data on systematic examination of the quality of these services, numbers of children served, or benefits to the children and adolescents.

Joint monitoring of programming would be ideal because children often move back and forth between mental health and juvenile justice facilities. New York State has developed joint programs of teams of psychologists, mental health nurses, and social workers, who provide assessments, treatment plans, referrals for children in juvenile justice facilities, and consultation and training for staff of these programs (Knitzer, 1982). Recruitment of these teams is by the Department of Mental Health and the Division of Youth, jointly. Long-term therapy is not provided but they do provide up to three counseling sessions to stabilize a child's behavior or prepare him or her for a move to a different facility. Teams are affiliated with and supervised by regional children's psychiatric centers (described in Knitzer, 1982).

One group of juveniles in the juvenile justice system has received a good deal of attention—"violent" children. These children represent a small proportion of those housed in juvenile justice institutions, but are highly visible because of behavior viewed as dangerous. Several states (Massachusetts, New York, Colorado, Wisconsin, Oregon, North Carolina) have established programs for this group of children (Agee, 1979; Ahearn, 1980; Cocozza & Hartstone, 1977, 1978a, 1978b; Oregon Department of Human Resources, 1979). These programs are typically small inpatient programs within designated regions of the state. They usually offer long-term treatment to serious offenders through an intensive, structured program (for example, in Colorado, these were defined as rapists or murderers). Follow-up of most of these programs revealed no further contact with the law upon release (Neilson, Engle, & Latham, 1979). Some of these programs are within the states' maximum security training school (e.g., North Carolina) and often follow Project Re-Ed, a psychoeducational program developed by Nicholas Hobbs (1982). These programs were often controversial and most have been abandoned in spite of the success at follow-up.

In spite of inadequate data, it is obvious that children and adolescents in the juvenile justice system are in need of mental health services and that they do not receive them. At least one suggestion appears in the literature for improved services to this population of children and adolescents. Knitzer (1982) suggests that each state should ensure that mental health agencies work closely with the juvenile justice system, especially with those children in detention facilities or training schools. She further suggests that states make frequent assessment of transfers between juvenile justice and mental health institutions and create mechanisms to prevent misuse of such transfers and to protect the rights of juveniles. One last suggestion is that states assess the adequacy of state policies regarding evaluations and crisis mental health services available through juvenile or family courts.

Education and Mental Health Service Delivery

In 1975 landmark federal legislation was enacted guaranteeing children with handicapping conditions the right to a free appropriate education. The Education for All Handicapped Children Act, Public Law 94-142 (Education for All Handicapped Children Act, 1975; U.S. Department of Education, 1982) explicitly includes seriously disturbed children in its mandate. Federal regulations under the act define serious emotional disturbance as a

. . . condition exhibiting one or more of the following characteristics over a long period of time and to a marked degree, which adversely affects educational performance: (a) An inability to learn which cannot be explained by intellectual, sensory or health factors; (b) an inability to build or maintain satisfactory interpersonal relationships with peers and teachers; (c) inappropriate types of behavior or feeling under normal circumstances; (d) a general pervasive mode of unhappiness or depression; or (e) a tendency to develop physical symptoms of fears associated with personal or school problems.

"Emotional disturbance," includes children who are schizophrenic. It does not include children who are socially maladjusted, unless it is determined that they are seriously emotionally disturbed (Knitzer, 1982). It requires that for each disturbed child, as for all other handicapped children, an Individualized Education Program (IEP) be prepared detailing the specific educational and related services to be provided. The law further provides that handicapped children be educated in the least restrictive setting appropriate to their needs, and spells out the due process protections that must be available for children and their parents. The passage of this legislation probably marks the single most significant policy commitment to handicapped children this country has made (Knitzer, 1982). Prior to the law's enactment children with handicapping conditions were too often denied schooling, and parents had no resources to compel schools to serve such children.

Implementation of this key piece of legislation on behalf of severely disturbed children has been limited, however, for the following reasons: (1) In the 1980 to 1981 school year, according to the latest federal data, 348,954 seriously disturbed children ages 3 to 21 received special education under the mandates of P.L. 94-142 and P.L. 89-313 (Department of Education, National Center for Educational Statistics, 1982). Using prevalent estimates that two percent of the total child and adolescent population has emotional problems serious enough to warrant specialized treatment, this still reflects less than one third of all potentially eligible children (Kaskowitz, 1977). (2) Seriously disturbed adolescents are especially likely to receive inappropriate services or no services at all. They are often expelled, suspended from school, given shortened school days, or placed on homebound instruction (Grosenick & Huntze, 1980). Under P.L. 94-142 and Section 504, a number of courts has ruled that when a behavior problem is linked to the child's handicapping condition, the child is entitled to an appropriate education and the full protections of P.L. 94-142, instead of exclusion and the district's disciplinary procedures (*S-1 vs. Turlington*, 1981; *Stuart vs. Nappi*, 1978; *Howard S vs. Friendswood Independent School District*, 1978; *Doe vs. Koger*, 1979). (3) Children living in group homes or returning from residential settings such as hospitals or residential treatment centers are often refused services by schools. This is especially true for children living in group homes outside their original school districts. For example, one school district refused to serve children who were living in a specialized group home within the area but were originally from outside the district. The State Department of Mental Health funded the group home, but the state would not pay the local school system to educate the children. The children's original school district also refused to pay (Knitzer, 1982). (4) Disturbed children in mental health hospitals or correctional facilities are likely to be untrained or be excluded from education programs, despite evidence of great need. For example, a study of the inpatient population at a psychiatric hospital in the District of Columbia found that on the average the children and adolescents were five years below grade level regardless of diagnosis, age, length of stay, family responsibility, or other factors (Knitzer, 1982). Psychiatric hospitals do not always inform children or parents of the children's educational rights.

Implementation of the law has been hindered by substantial confusion in four areas.

First, it is unclear how severe children's disturbances must be for them to be covered by P.L. 94-142. One study reported that different states may or may not cover children with mild, moderate, or severe difficulties. It is estimated that only 20 percent of the troubled children served under 94-142 are seriously disturbed (Grosenick & Huntze, 1980). Further, the law explicitly excludes children who are "socially maladjusted" but not seriously emotionally disturbed from its mandate. Yet clinicians agree that any distinction between these children and other disturbed children is meaningless. Initially, the exclusion of socially maladjusted children was made to guard against the needless labeling of poor and minority children. In practice socially maladjusted children often get disciplined or expelled. For example, a significant proportion of the children identified as needing mental health care in a major class action lawsuit in North Carolina was viewed by the school as disruptive and no specialized education planning had been done for them (*Willie M vs. Hunt,* 1979).

Second, although disturbed children may need psychotherapy to learn, the obligation of schools to provide or pay for therapy is uncertain. The law requires schools to provide those educational and related services needed to ensure a child's learning. But neither the law nor the regulations clarify whether therapy is a related service and, if so, under what conditions. It is also unclear if there are any circumstances under which parents can be charged for such services. As a result, schools and states are avoiding the issue (Knitzer, 1982). Children who could benefit from psychotherapy are not getting it.

Third, there is confusion about the responsibility of schools to pay for residential treatment when children and adolescents cannot be served in regular or special local schools. Parents, advocates, and state officials have expended a lot of energy resolving these disputes, while the children generally have gotten nothing. Some schools have sought to pay only for the educational costs of such placements. Other schools have tried to escape any obligation by arguing the children needed placement for no educational reason and, thus, that the placements are not covered under the law's mandates. No clear standards have emerged for determining when public day programs versus residential programs would be appropriate. Rather, such a determination has been treated by courts as an individual factual issue heavily dependent on the testimony of experts (Knitzer, 1982).

There are at least two additional concerns about the law's effect on children and adolescents who need mental health services. Partially because of the law's emphasis on diagnosis and evaluation, as a prerequisite to a student's entrance . . . many school psychologists are being asked to function exclusively as testers. Any time they otherwise might have had to consult with teachers or counsel students has been eliminated or greatly reduced. Further, the emphasis on serving severely handicapped children has meant fewer schools have tried to develop mental health programs focusing on early intervention (Knitzer, 1982).

To contain the costs of psychological services, some school districts are developing these services themselves. They are using staff who are less well trained than those in existing mental health programs, such as community mental health centers. In other districts, schools are not referring children for services (Knitzer, 1982).

Affirmative steps to address these implementation problems are few. State departments of education often have not identified staff to work intensively to ensure that disturbed children receive an appropriate education and related services.

The needed training programs to help teachers cope with the most disturbed children or to increase the pool of specially educated teachers who could serve troubled children and adolescents have also not been developed by states. Grosenick and Huntze (1980) emphasize the need for teachers for emotionally disturbed children. However, institutions of higher education are training between 1 and 10 percent of the teachers needed to work with the most severely disturbed population and 5 to 50 percent of the teachers needed for the board spectrum of emotionally disturbed children already identified by the schools (Grosenick & Huntze, 1980).

Manpower shortages are inflated also by the fact that even trained teachers do not stay on the job for long (Grosenick & Huntze, 1980). The attrition rate for teachers of disturbed children is higher than for any other category of handicaps. Over a five-year period was a 53 percent loss of personnel in behavior disorders (Grosenick & Huntze, 1980).

A fourth problem of implementation concerns the monitoring of the quality of education available for children and adolescents in hospitals or the extent to which hospitals comply with P.L. 94-142. These items receive low priority from departments of education and mental health (Knitzer, 1982).

According to Knitzer (1982), states can provide better mental health services through the educational system. She suggests that each state should increase training and support services for teachers, clarify policies regarding the fiscal responsibility of educational agencies for educating children and adolescents in out-of-home placements, and establish high-level interagency or legislative committees to resolve problems between educational and mental health agencies in funding, staffing, and certifying intensive day treatment services. She further recommends the establishment of state-level liaison efforts among state children-serving agencies to facilitate the pooling of fiscal, staff, and program resources and insure the development of appropriate nonresidential and residential services for seriously disturbed children and adolescents under the care of any state agency, and to establish cross-agency mechanisms for definition of gaps in services and monitoring quality of care.

LEGISLATION, ADVOCACY, AND THE RIGHTS OF CHILDREN

Children are different from adults in judgment, maturity, independence, and self-reliance. All societies define expectations of when the child is no longer considered to be a child and other age limits of what is expected of children, e.g., when the child must go to school and when he or she can stop. Societal decisions on these matters are based on the religious, technological, social, economic, cultural, and political development of the specific society. From these decisions, services and social programs are made available to children and youth.

These assumptions about the role and rights of children and youth in any society may not assure that the best services and programs are provided, however. As an example of how this works, Shore and Mannino (1976) traced some of the forces in this country that have inhibited the growth of mental health services for children and youth since their inception two centuries ago. They list five factors: (1) Resistance to the idea that children and youth are separate and autonomous individuals. The idea that children are different from adults and have special needs and require different approaches from adults did not develop in western thought until 200 years ago. (2) The primacy of politics as the major force for social change in the United States is imperative since children cannot vote and are not organized politically, they have meager political power; (3) defense of family privacy in the nuclear family unit; (4) belief in the importance of parental control over children; (5) suspiciousness in the United States of the role of government especially in family life and the care of children. All five of these forces influenced the strong opposition in the early 1900s to the passage of child labor laws aimed at protecting children from severe exploitation.

Psychological knowledge is slowly playing an increasing role in influencing social policy recently. The first significant use of psychological research data in a Supreme Court decision was only in 1954, however. This was in the case of *Brown vs. Board of Education* (1954) on desegregation of schools. In recent history, psychologists have been involved more in all three branches of the government with influence on development of national and social policy with regard to children and youth. Data are used in amicus briefs or by psychologists serving as expert witnesses in courts in the judicial branch. Psychological data have been used in presentations at congressional committee hearings and by congressional staff in drafting legislation in the legislature. Influence in the executive branch is apparent also since two of the three directors of Child Development have been psychologists.

Rights of Children

Rights are inherent guarantees and are owned by the person. Rights of the individual are important for legislation and program design. Programs must not violate the rights of individuals. If a consensus on children's rights can be reached, those working with children and youth can be held accountable. One of the most important developments toward consensus in this country was the 1969 Joint Commission on the Mental Health of Children, which defined a number of rights of children: the right to be wanted, to be born healthy, to live in a healthy environment, to obtain satisfaction of basic needs, to receive continuous loving care, to acquire the intellectual and emotional skills necessary to achieve individual aspirations and to cope effectively in our society, and to receive care and treatment through facilities that are appropriate to children's needs and that keep them as closely as possible within their normal social setting.

The judicial system is also interested in rights of patients. In the area of adult mental health, the courts recently have upheld and defended the rights of mental patients as well as defined some new rights, e.g., the right to treatment. In recent years, the courts have also ensured that the rights are implemented in programs in accordance with the latest and best available professional standards (e.g., the case of *Wyatt vs. Aderholt* [1974]).

Courts have addressed the rights of children and youth in the 1948 decision in *Haley vs. Ohio,* which stated that the rights guaranteed to adults also apply to children. The courts' application is far from unidirectional, however. Major struggles surround two issues: (1) When do parental rights conflict with the rights of children and youth, and how can these conflicts be resolved in the best interests of children and youths? (2) What are the developmental issues? Our research, for example, makes it unclear in what important ways children differ from adults so that special protections need to be built in to ensure their rights, e.g., how long and in what ways should children be considered dependent? What protection is needed against misuse of the doctrine of the "best interests of the child"? The struggles can be best illustrated nationally by contrasting the Supreme Court decisions in 1967 *re Gault* where due process for youths charged with delinquency was affirmed, with the recent decision *Ingraham vs. Wright* (1967), in which the right of the public schools to administer corporal punishment was upheld. The APA contributed an amicus brief describing the research data on the effects of punishment in producing long-lasting changes in behavior.

The Rights of Children in Residential Care

The President's Commission on Mental Health (1969) defined a number of rights of children, one of which was to receive care and treatment through facilities that are appropriate to children's needs and that keep them as closely as possible within their normal social setting. However, children sometimes need residential confinement at which time legal rights also come into play. Current efforts are being made to define these rights and to develop ways to enforce these rights and to strengthen the mental health statutes (Knitzer, 1982). However, the rights of children have lagged behind. Often attention is placed on how a person can be admitted to psychiatric hospitals and retained there. The courts contribute by their rulings. For example, the United States Supreme Court held that due process does not require a formal or quasi-formal hearing prior to commitment, emphasizing the authority of parents over minor children, although the two named plaintiffs were both in state custody (*Parham vs. J.R.* 1979). Guidelines for hospitalizing minors have recently been proposed (American Psychiatric Association, 1982). However, states do not follow them. Knitzer (1982) reports that at least 13 states allow minors to be voluntarily admitted to psychiatric hospitals upon the request of a parent or guardian with no provision for the minor to object or for the objection of another on the minor's behalf. Most states, in addition, do not require mandatory review of care of hospitalized children and adolescents nor for the appropriateness of their continued stay in the hospital. Twenty-two states treat older adolescents differently from children in their voluntary admission procedures. Typically, this involves giving adolescents either the right to apply for admission on their own or to object to the admission. Yet in 13 states, parents can still admit minors of any age to psychiatric hospitals.

Once the child is admitted, most states do not require child-specific reviews. In 24 states children and adolescents are subjected to the same reviews as adults, while 19 have no statutory requirements for periodic reviews of voluntary admissions. Only six states require child-specific reviews (Knitzer, 1982).

Rights of access to appointed counsel or to a mental health advocacy service, rights to education while confined, rights to interagency services are unevenly respected by the states (Knitzer, 1982). There is a great need for tangible ways to assure that children receive the services they are supposed to and have some place to go if their rights are violated.

Legislation and Advocacy

The Joint Commission on the Mental Health of Children (1969) recommended an organized system of child advocacy throughout the nation in an effort to stimulate national political action and to commit the country to a broadly based and soundly conceived program for children and youth. An advocate in this regard is defined as "someone who will insist that programs and services based on sound child development knowledge be available to every child as a public utility" (Joint Commission on the Mental Health of Children, 1969, p. 9). Knitzer (1976) clarified the many different types of such advocacy: case advocacy, class action litigation, monitoring, legislative advocacy, and administrative advocacy. The efforts at advocacy continue to be fragmented, disorganized, and for the most part ineffective (Knitzer, 1982).

Child advocates could have profound significance in advancing the cause of children and youth in the United States. It has been suggested that the President should deliver an annual message to Congress and the citizenry on the state of children, youth, and families in the United States, outlining the progress made each year and making specific proposals for further legislation (Knitzer, 1982).

A second suggestion is that all congressional legislation be systematically reviewed as to its possible effect on children, youth, and families in the United States. This is a large order, since it is a rare piece of legislation that does not have some impact on families and children. Although some believe that family impact studies may be premature because of the limits of our current knowledge, others (e.g., Shore, 1979) believe that at least efforts should be made to undertake such studies on a pilot basis.

Shore (1979) also believes there is a need for continuous monitoring and coordination to ensure that new legislation does not cancel out or conflict with other legislation or produce unintended and undesirable effects. In our history, there is evidence that the juvenile court, a well-intended program, can be destructive to children (Shore, 1979). Also in some recent child abuse activity, professionals eager to protect children from harm have separated a child from his or her family, only to find a placement destructive to the child's growth and development (Knitzer, 1976).

Any comprehensive national policy on children, youth, and families similar to that in many other countries will need psychological data for planning, implementing, monitoring, and evaluating such a policy. The psychological data, in turn, will also be orchestrated with data from other social sciences to develop a sound comprehensive national program for children and youth. Knitzer (1982) outlines coordination of efforts of child advocates, professionals, local, state, and federal mental health advocates with governmental officials to create a visible advocacy presence.

ETHICS AND PROFESSIONAL GUILD ISSUES

WHO IS THE CLIENT?

When a child is brought in for treatment, it is usually the parent who decides to bring him/her, without consulting the child. Sometimes, others are involved, as for example, when the school (teacher and/or principal) suggests to parents that the child needs help. Usually, the problems that concern parents and other third parties are not related to the child's discomfort or unhappiness, but rather they relate to the adult's discomfort or unhappiness with the child and/or behavior. These problems usually take the form of misbehavior, noncompliance, excessive shyness, and the like; the kind of behaviors the child is not aware of as "problems." Thus, we might wonder, who is the client? The child or the referring adult(s)?

Parents notoriously neglect preparation of their child for psychological consultation and evaluation. Often the child is not even told about the appointment until the last minute and certainly not the reason for it. Parents will sometimes tell the child that they have a "doctor's appointment," which, depending on the child's prior experience with doctors, might set up negative expectations about the appointment that have deleterious effects on the possibility of a congenial and cooperative interview with the child. If asked, parents usually confess to difficulties in explaining the nature of their concerns to their child, often because of their own biases about psychological problems and the implications of them. It is helpful if the therapist or agent for the therapist makes specific suggestions to the parent about how to prepare the child for the upcoming interview.

Despite the nature of the child's preparation for the interview, the child often will be unaware of any problem with his/her own behavior. The child will deny any unhappiness or conflict about any area of his/her life. The typical response of the child is "Everything is just fine." When this kind of response is obtained, and it is the most frequent one from most children and adolescents, the therapist is in a dilemma. Again, who is the client? The child does not own any problem; the parent does, however. Should then the therapist offer to see the parent about the child's problem or should there be some arrangement to convince or force the child to come in for intervention? Usually, the adults, the parents, and the therapist consult with each other and establish the decision to seek treatment after evaluation and set up the goals of treatment. Too often, the child is not involved in this process. The child undergoes the interview and the psychological evaluation if it is needed, and then is excused from the process until the parent announces the next appointment. Reisman (1973) and others (e.g., Tuma & Sobotka, 1983) suggest that the child should be an integral part of the total process from an explanation of the reasons for the visit to involvement in the feedback session concerning the evaluation and recommendations, to the establishment of the goals of treatment. This appears to be a wise course to follow, given some evidence that treatment is doomed to failure unless the child takes an active part at least by participating in setting up the goals of the intervention (e.g., Seagull & Noll, 1982).

The course the therapist must follow is clear if we remember the principles for child therapists, noted by Ross in 1974: (1) The child has the right to be told the truth; (2) the child has the right to be treated with personal respect; (3) the child-client has the right to be taken seriously; and (4) the child has the right to meaningful participation in decision-making that applies to his or her life. If the therapist relates to the child in the manner required when these rights are respected, the child will usually be amenable to the project and show cooperation. This manner of treatment is different than in most other areas of the child's experience. In daily life, respect does not often come to the child; children are not often taken seriously; do not often participate in decision-making; the truth is not even always shared with them. Parents, in their effort to socialize the child, often engage in the "don'ts" of proper behavior; teachers in their efforts to teach the child, insist on group cooperation, discipline, and direct the child in daily assignments.

Even if the evaluating mental health professional follows these principles, however, sometimes the child will not want to cooperate, will want to refuse treatment when it is suggested. When then, is the proper decision? The usual rule that is followed, and is espoused by most child advocates (e.g., Shore, 1979), is that adults must act in the "best interests" of the child. Do we respect the child's right to refuse help even though it may mean that the child will struggle through a stressful childhood? Or, should we set our goals on helping the child "adjust" to reality at home, which may contribute to the problem? Should the problem be dealt with in a family therapy format that eliminates the issue of "identified patient?"

Looking at the issue from the other side of the coin reveals just as perplexing a problem. Can we allow the child to override adult judgments by refusing therapy, although we are respecting the child's right to self-determination? If so, are we violating the parents' right to seek help for their child? What about the therapist's judgment? Should the child's refusal be respected when the professional recommendation is clearly for the necessity for treatment?

As Koocher (1976) notes, the therapist is ethically bound in this kind of situation to respect the best interests of the child-client, but also is paid to be a parental agent who has the legal responsibility for their children's welfare. The solution to this problem is not clear or simple but remains for the therapist to consider all variables in making the final recommendation. It has been suggested in such cases an independent child advocate who is neither paid by the patients nor therapist evaluate the circumstances and evaluate the treatment plan in line with the child's best interests (Knitzer, 1982; Koocher, 1976; Shore, 1979).

The Ethics of Treatment

Of the 10 principles contained in the Ethical Standards of Psychologists (American Psychological Association, 1981), principles 5, 6, and 7 are most frequently confusing ones for the child mental health professional. These principles are concerned with confidentiality, client welfare, and the professional relationship.

Perhaps the most confusing principle involves confidentiality. Most psychologists have no confusion about confidentiality as it pertains to treatment of adult clients. However, in the case of treatment of the child, because of the dependence of the child on parents, and the legal and financial responsibility of the parent, this issue is not clear to many professionals. Information obtained during the course of treatment of the child is often revealed without thought to parents. Justification is based on the best interests of the child in most cases.

However, if confidentiality is not assured to most children and adolescents by the therapist, communication cannot be open. Children, like adults, are reluctant to reveal aspects of themselves to a therapist who they know reports directly to the parents. The child also surmises that the therapist reveals information to others, e.g., teachers, and even strangers. Careful negotiation about confidentiality with the child client assures a trusting and open relationship with the child. It is useful to state the confidentiality principle to the child such that only those items the child wants the therapist to reveal or confront the parent about are revealed to them. All other areas are assured to be held confidentially. Of course, if some information is revealed by the child during the course of therapy where there is imminent danger to an individual or society, principle 7a will still apply, and the therapist is free to divulge this information to the parents or others. In less crucial matters, where the child may reveal information about which it is nevertheless important for the parent to be informed, the therapist simply has to explain to the child that that information is important enough to be relayed to the parent(s). In this instance, the therapist asks the child for permission to reveal. If the child refuses, the therapist has to risk disruption in the relationship by informing the child that he/she will be required to tell the parent(s). Such situations are rare, however, and most therapists will never have to confront such a dilemma.

Principle 6 also causes some professionals confusion. This principle requires that the child be made fully aware of the purposes of the interview, testing, or evaluation, and of the ways the information will be used. Most mental health professions assume that if the parent is informed, this principle is met. However, if the rights of the child are respected as outlined in a previous section (Ross, 1974), the child will also be informed. The honoring of this principle with the child as well as the parent has the advantage of promoting the relationship between therapist and child.

Often the child evaluation and/or therapy sessions will be recorded in some manner (videotape or audiotape). Principle 7 requires that the client be informed about all aspects of the potential relationship that might affect the client's decision to enter the relationship. This includes recording of sessions. Child therapists often assume that the persons that need to be informed to satisfy this principle are the parents. However, because of the importance of respecting the child's rights, the child should also be apprised of the plans to record.

When considering the ethical principles as they apply to children, it appears that conducting therapy with children is more complex than with adults. At times, treating material confidentially is similar to straddling a fence; the parent is curious about what occurs in therapy with the child and, in some cases, demands information; on the other hand, the therapist wishes to protect the child's privacy. It is necessary to inform the parent(s) about how the information obtained by association with the child will be handled. Most parents can relate to the necessity of privacy; most can accept an explanation that the child may wish to reveal to them (which is permissible) what therapeutic activities have transpired but that they should respect the child's decision if the child does not wish to. Children are about equally divided between those who wish to reveal to their parents the therapeutic events and those who remain mute concerning their treatment. In any case, it is better to leave the jockeying for information between the parent and child rather than to be the conveyor of information about the child without the child's knowledge.

Sometimes the same therapist will work with the parents in a parent counseling or similar arrangement. This situation is a complex one; the therapist has to protect the privacy of the child client at the same time that the same issues are discussed in the parent sessions. The therapist in this situation has to have considerable skill in being able to address these issues from two sides of the professional situation. In so doing, the parental concerns are addressed from the perspective of the parent behavior, observations, feelings, etc., rather than bringing in confidential information from therapy sessions with the child.

SUMMARY

➤ Today, we understand a great deal about the child's competence in the world, even from birth. However, when the normal development of the child is disrupted, remediation efforts are not maximally efficacious because of problems along several fronts: availability of mental health services, training availability and funding of child mental health professionals, inequities in social policy as it relates to issues concerning family and children, and problems in ethical and guild issues.

The study of the child has evolved during this century from a sociobiological approach to children's behavior that was chiefly concerned with accounts of the condition of children with appeals for social action to a highly scientific and empirical field. Much has been learned about children's normal and abnormal development during this time period. However, because of continued problems in connecting deleterious conditions affecting children, there is presently a call for mental health professionals to return to efforts for developing programs and influencing social policy while armed with more extensive knowledge about the children's reactions to the conditions in which they find themselves today.

Since the beginning of the century, several changes have occurred in the current view of the child. Environmental factors in the development of disordered behavior in childhood, although tempered by considerations of effects of temperament and interaction with other environmental factors other than the family, are considered to be of primary importance. The concept of a single trauma as a determinant of dysfunction has fallen in disfavor, and the interaction of mutual impact of child and caretaker has attracted interest. Also during this century, the identified causal relationships of interpersonal and intrapsychic factors are being studied more vigorously by systematic observations of childhood/family behavior in a search for the nature of the effects of these causal relationships. Perhaps the most important change is the concept of child psychopathology that recognizes the uniqueness of childhood and the impact of experiences on specifiable functions in interaction with the developmental level of the child.

The study of the child has yielded significant findings of an active and competent being, even at birth, such that infants are recognized as possessing a wide range of perceptual, cognitive, and social capacities. This behavior is organized and has multiple causes of biological-genetic factors as well as situational-environmental factors that play an important role in shaping the course of development. Environmental factors are seen now to affect social behavior, intelligence, personality, and activity levels. Likewise, parent-child interactions are beginning to be studied from the perspective of the influence of the child on parents in addition to the more traditional view that parents affect children. Deviant behaviors are studied from the perspective of the possible genetic factors as well as more environmental ones of having emotionally disturbed or mentally retarded parents or being raised in a particularly stressful environment. A bidirectional and even a multidirectional view is presently being entertained with the acknowledgment that children play an influential part in their own social and cognitive development. Social systems are also studied for their impact on child development, resulting in an ecological perspective in the study of the child.

Knowledge of the expanding influence of multiple factors in the development of the child has yielded consideration of those factors as they influence disordered behavior in children. Assessment, intervention, and prevention efforts are increasingly focused on the multiple impacts of the various factors important for normal childhood development.

Approximately 15 percent of all children and adolescents in our country are in need of mental health services. Only about one third of them are served in the mental health system, with service more likely to go to those who are less seriously disturbed. Services available to children include nonresidential, residential, and therapeutic case advocacy. Nonresidential services are available to only about 43 percent of the population. Residential services are unevenly distributed throughout the country and tend to be used inappropriately and with dubious efficacy. Therapeutic case advocacy, which would insure that children and their families have appropriate, coordinated, and sensitive services, has not been supported widely although the need for such services is obvious.

Manpower for mental health services to children continues to be in short supply. There are not enough psychiatrists, psychologists, social workers, child care workers, or teachers of emotionally disturbed children. It has been estimated, for example, that less than 1 percent of psychologists in this country devote time primarily to serving children.

Those entering the child mental health profession encounter difficulties in finding training programs devoted to serving children. They then become disillusioned because of inadequate funding for services to children in spite of national recognition that children are one of the groups of unserved and underserved in this nation. The situation has not improved during the last decade.

The practice of clinical child psychology includes traditional assessment and intervention techniques as well as newer techniques of family therapy, public services, program planning, consultation and evaluation research, and the integration of research into treatment and prevention programs. Although some have previously predicted the demise of traditional techniques of assessment and treatment, the evidence seems to show that with the diversity of considerations of the proper development of the child, the clinical child psychologist must be flexible in the application of techniques suitable to the individual child such that he/she must be child oriented, rather than theory or technique oriented.

Settings in which child mental health professionals practice include primarily medical settings and private practice offering mental health services. However, recent trends show the need for psychologists attached in a more integral manner to pediatric and family medicine practices and hospitals, and also in the schools. Moreover, psychologists are in short supply in mental health centers and traditional child guidance centers, indicating that poor and minority children received less than their share of mental health services.

Treatment and assessment are the traditional interests of the clinical child psychologist. Consultation and research, while important, take secondary positions in both the practice of psychologists and in internship training centers. Currently, psychologists serving children appear to spend more clinical time in assessment rather than intervention than do psychologists who serve adults. The clients of the clinical child psychologist tend to be nonminority children, predominately within the 5- to 10-year age group, members of the middle socioeconomic groups, and those who suffer relatively minor problems. Techniques of assessment and treatment vary with the age of the child. Drawings and intelligence and achievement tests especially designed for use with children are frequently useful with children. Parental counseling, play therapy, and behavior therapy are preferred for the preschool age group, whereas play therapy is predominant in the school age group. At adolescence, individual therapy appears most useful.

In contrast with the clinical child psychologist who practices in mental health facilities, the pediatric psychologist practices predominately in pediatric settings, stresses an interdisciplinary liaison with pediatrics, and espouses a philosophy of practice procedures to emphasize preventive and limited time framework. The nature of the problems of referred children is related to concommitants of illness, hospitalization, and medical care. The primary goal of pediatric psychologists is preventive.

The psychologist in the schools also displays numerous differences from the one in the more traditional work settings. In the schools, the psychologist is on the front line of emerging problems, especially as they relate to the social system of the school where the child spends most of the time. The school psychologist's focus, like the pediatric psychologist's, is thus prevention and early intervention. The activities of school psychologists with children with behavioral or learning problems result in less referrals to outside agencies and thereby avoid a number of problems inherent in gaining mental health services for school children. New approaches designed by those of an ecological persuasion and which involve the parent in the child's school offer much promise. However, the bulk of most school psychologists' activities presently encompasses determining eligibility for placing students with learning disabilities and problems into special education programs.

Since governmental policies, rules, laws, and programs affect the lives of most children and their families, child mental health professionals must be concerned with an attempt to influence social policy. Although social policy appears to be episodic, following the dominant preoccupation with social and political problems of the time, programs supported by the government deeply affect service delivery to children.

One of the primary concerns of mental health specialists is how the government supports research. Administrative responsibility for distributing research funds is scattered among numerous governmental agencies. Behavioral and social scientists conducting research on children appear to fare less well than do other scientists. Research in the past has been unduly influenced by national crises and acute political pressures, setting research directions. However, research itself influences the way people think and shape government policy for children's programs and research.

Funding for children's services has been deficient in the past. In 1978, the President's Commission on Mental Health explicitly addressed children's needs, endorsing every child's basic right of opportunity to achieve full potential, which can include mental health services. They called for increased training support for mental health professionals, periodic review of the children being treated, and the availability of comprehensive services for all children. However, programs designed to answer this mandate suffered implementation problems, concentrated on intractable problems, and ignored the childhood population for whom intervention can be most fruitful.

Funding for services is allocated inappropriately, often to costly institutional and residential care, and too late. A recent analysis of all 50 states shows that more than two thirds of children in need are not getting the services and also found that some children were inappropriately placed. Children's rights have not been respected, and funding was either inadequate or inappropriately spent.

Children who come to the attention of the juvenile justice system and who also manifest emotional and behavioral disorders pose a complex and unsolved challenge for both this system and the mental health system. Because of poor records, we do not even know how many children within this system need mental health services. Furthermore, the few services they get are haphazardly arranged with no efforts for joint monitoring by both systems.

Although the landmark 1975 federal legislation 94-142 was enacted guaranteeing children with handicapping conditions the right to a free appropriate education, problems of interpretation and implementation have hindered the promised provision of services to these children. Confusion in three areas has especially been noted: (1) It is unclear how severe children's disturbances must be for them to be covered by P.L. 94-142; (2) although disturbed children may need psychotherapy to learn, the obligation of schools to provide or pay for therapy is uncertain; (3) there is confusion about the responsibility of schools to pay for residential treatment when children and adolescents cannot be served in regular or special local schools.

The rights of children are important for legislation and program design. Consensus on children's rights has never been reached, but an important development was made by the 1969 Joint Commission on the Mental Health of Children who defined a number of rights of children. One of these included the right to receive care and treatment through facilities that are appropriate to children's needs and that keep them as closely as possible within their normal social setting. Major struggles surrounding the legislation for children's rights include (1) conflicts between rights of parents versus rights of children and youth, and (2) definition of developmental issues that differentiate between rights of adults and children.

The Joint Commission also recommended that an organized system of child advocacy throughout the nation to ensure that programs and services are based on sound child development knowledge be available to every child as a public utility. We are presently only at the beginning of recognizing the full implication of the lack of this kind of service.

Ethical issues surrounding the treatment of the child are different from those that concern treatment of adults. Particularly important are issues surrounding the child's informed consent to treatment. Most children do not come to treatment of their own choice but at the bidding of parents or other adults. The child mental health professional is often placed in the position of choosing between being the parent's agent or the child's agent with all the implications for confidentiality, consent to treatment, inclusion in goal-setting, etc. Residential treatment of the child presents perplexing problems with violation of children's rights due to lax state and federal regulations of protection of their rights.

REFERENCES

Agee, VA. *Treatment of the violent incorrigible adolescent.* Lexington, Mass: Lexington Books, 1979

Ahearn, FL. *A study of the regional adolescent programs: Success and failure.* Boston, MA: Boston University School of Social Work, April 24, 1980

American Psychiatric Association. Guidelines for the psychiatric hospitalization of minors. *American Journal of Psychiatry,* 1982, *139,* 971–974

American Psychological Association. *Ethical standards of psychologists.* Washington DC: Author, 1981

Baer, DM, & Sherman, J. Reinforcement control of generalized invitation in young children. *Journal of Experimental Child Psychology,* 1964, *1,* 37–49

Bartoshuk, AK. Human neonatal cardiac responses to sound: A power function. *Psychonomic Science,* 1964, *1,* 151–152

Bauermeister, JJ, & Jemail, JA. Modification "electric mutism" in the classroom setting: A case study. *Behavior Therapy*, 1975, *6*, 246–250

Becker, MH, & Maiman, LA. Sociobehavioral determinants of compliance with health and medical care recommendations. *Medical Care*, 1975, *13*, 10–24

Bell, B, Mednick, S, Raman, AC, Schulsinger, F, Sutton-Smith, B, & Venables, P. A longitudinal psychophysiological study of three year-old muuritian children. Preliminary report. *Developmental Medicine and Child Neurology*, 1975, *17*, 320–324

Bell, RW. A reinterpretation of the direction of effects in studies of socialization. *Psychological Review*, 1968, *75*, 81–95

Bergman, AB, Dassel, SW, & Wedgwood, RJ. Time-motion study of practicing pediatricians. *Pediatrics*, 1966, *38*, 254–263

Bornstein, MH, Kessen, W, & Weiskopp, S. The categories of hue in infancy. *Science*, 1976, *191*, 201–202

Bornstein, PH, & Quevillon, RP. The effects of self-instructional package on overactive preschool boys. *Journal of Applied Behavior Analysis*, 1976, *9*, 179–188

Brackbill, Y. Continuous stimulation and arousal level in infants: Additive effects. *Proceedings, 78th Annual Convention, American Psychological Association*, 1970, *5*, 271–272

Brazelton, TB. Anticipatory guidance. *Pediatric Clinics of North America*, 1974, *21*, 533–544

Bremner, RH. (Ed.). *Children and Youth in America:* Vol. 1, 1600–1865. Cambridge, Mass: Harvard University Press, 1970

Bremner, RH. (Ed.). *Children and Youth in America: A documentary history:* Vol. 2, 1836–1932. Cambridge, Mass: Harvard University Press, 1971

Bronfenbrenner, U. Contexts of child rearing. *American Psychologist*, 1979, *34*, 844–850

Bronfenbrenner, U. Ecology of childhood. *School Psychology Review*, 1980, *9*, 294–297

Broughton, SF, Barton, ES, & Owen, PR. Home-based contingency system for school problems. *School Psychology Review*, 1981, *10*, 26–36

Brown, vs. Board of Education, 347, U.S. 483 (1954)

Brown, WR, & McGuire, JM. Current psychological assessment practice. *Professional Psychology*, 1976, *7*, 475–484

Burt, C. The genetic determination of differences in intelligence: A study of monozygotic twins reared together and apart. *British Journal of Psychology*, 1966, *57*, 137–153

Bushsbaum, M. Visual and auditory SER in MZ and DZ twins. Paper presented at the 81st meeting of the American Psychological Association, Montreal, August, 1973

Buss, AH, Plomin, R, & Willerman, L. The inheritance of temperaments. *Journal of Personality*, 1973, *41*, 513–524

Campos, JJ, Langer, A, & Krowitz, A. Cardiac responses on a visual cliff in prelocomotor human infants. *Science*, 1970, *170*, 196–197

Carr, EG, Schreibman, L, & Lovass, OI. Control of echolalic speech in psychotic children. *Journal of Abnormal Child Psychology*, 1975, *3*, 331–351

Cerreto, MC, & Tuma, JM. Distribution of DSM-II in children. *Journal of Abnormal Child Psychology*, 1977, *5*, 147–155

Chess, S, Thomas, A, & Birch, HG. Behavioral problems revisited. In S Chess & H Birch (Eds.), *Annual progress in child psychiatry and development*. New York: Brunner/Mazel, 1968

Christophersen, ER, & Rapoff, MA. Behavioral problems in children. In GM Scipien, MU Barnard, MA Chard, J Howe, & PH Phillips (Eds.), *Comprehensive pediatric nursing* (2nd ed.). New York: McGraw-Hill, 1979

Christophersen, ER, & Rapoff, MA. Pediatric psychology: An appraisal. In BB Lahey & AE Kazdin (Eds.), *Advances in clinical child psychology*, New York: Plenum Press, 1980

Cocozza, J & Hartstone, E. *The Bronx Court-Related Unit: Evaluations and recommendations.* Albany, NY: Department of Mental Hygiene, March, 1977

Cocozza, J, & Hartstone, E. *A descriptive profile of youths admitted to the Bronx Court-Related Unit.* Albany, NY: Council on Children and Families, June, 1978(a)

Cocozza, J, & Hartstone, E. *Treatment effectiveness: The level of improvement experienced by youths while on the Bronx Court-Related Unit.* Albany, NY: Council on Children and Families, June, 1978(b)

Cohen, LB, DeLoache, JS, & Strauss, MS. Infant visual perception. In J Osofsky (Ed.), *Handbook of infancy.* New York: Wiley, 1978

Cohen, MD, March, JG, & Olsen, JP. A garbage can model of organizational choice, *Administrative Science Quarterly,* 1972, *17,* 1–25

Community Mental Health Centers Act of 1963, P. L. 88–164

Crecine, JP, & Linett, R. *An empirical examination of a budgetary argument for a separate department of education.* Unpublished manuscript, Carnegie-Mellon University, 1977

Crook, CK, & Lipsitt, LP. Neonatal nutritive sucking: Effects of taste stimulation upon sucking rhythm and heart rate. *Child Development,* 1976, *47,* 518–522

Cummings, NA. Funding for childrens' services. *American Psychologist,* 1979, *34,* 1037–1039

Cummings, ST. Is traditional clinical child psychology obsolete? In GJ Williams & S Gordon (Eds.), *Clinical child psychology: Current practices and future perspectives.* New York: Behavioral Publications, 1974

Dalton, AJ, Rubino, CA, & Hislop, MW. Some effects of token rewards on school achievement of children with Downs Syndrome. *Journal of Applied Behavior Analysis,* 1973, *6,* 251–259

DeMyer-Gapin, S, & Scott, TJ. Effects of stimulus seeking in anti-social and neurotic children. *Journal of Abnormal Psychology,* 1977, *86,* 96–98

Department of Education, National Center for Education Statistics. *The condition of education.* 1982 Edition. Washington, DC: U.S. Department of Education, 1982

Desor, J, Maller, O, & Turner, R. Taste in acceptance of sugars by human infants. *Journal of Comparative and Physiological Psychology,* 1973, *84,* 496–501

de Villiers, JG, & Naughton, JM. Teaching a symbolic language in autistic children. *Journal of Consulting and Clinical Psychology,* 1974, *42,* 111–117

Doe vs. Koger, 480 F. Supp. 225 (N.D. Ind. 1979)

Douglas, VI. Stop, look and listen: The problem of sustained attention and impulse control in hyperactive and normal children. *Canadian Journal of Behavioral Science,* 1972, *4,* 259–281

Drake, EA, & Shellenberger, S. Children of separation and divorce: A view of school programs and implications for the psychologist. *School Psychology Review,* 1981, *10,* 54–61

Education for All Handicapped Children Act. P. L. 94-142, U.S.C. §§ 1401, *et seq.,* 1975

Elder, GH, Jr. *Children of the great depression.* Chicago: University of Chicago Press, 1974

Elder, GH, Jr, & Rockwell, RC. Economic depression and post-war opportunity: A study of life patterns in hell. In RA Simmons (Ed.), *Research in community and mental health.* Greenwich, Conn: Jai Press, 1978

Fantz, RL. The origin of form perception. *Scientific American,* 1961, *204,* 66–72

Ferster, CB. Arbitrary and natural reinforcement. *Psychological Record,* 1967, *17,* 341–347

Finkelstein, NW, & Ramey, CT. Learning to control the environment of infancy. *Child Development,* 1977, *48,* 806–819

Fischer, CT. Graduate programs in clinical child psychology and related fields. *Journal of Clinical Child Psychology,* 1978, *7,* 87–88

Freedman, DG, & Keller, B. Inheritance of behavior in infants. *Science,* 1963, *140,* 196–198

Friedling, C, & O'Leary, SG. Effects of self-instructional training on second and third-grade hyperactive children: A failure to replicate. *Journal of Applied Behavior Analysis,* 1979, *12,* 211–219

Garfield, SL, & Kurtz, R. Clinical psychologists in the 1970's. *American Psychologist,* 1976, *31,* 1–9

Gibson, EJ, & Walk, RR. The "visual cliff," *Scientific American,* 1960, *202,* 2–9

Gil, DG. *Violence against children: Physical child abuse in the United States.* Cambridge, Mass: Harvard University Press, 1970

Gil, DG. Unravelling child abuse, *American Journal of Orthopsychiatry,* 1975, *45,* 346–356

Gil, DG. Societal violence and violence in families. In JM Eekelaar & SN Katz (Eds.), *Family violence.* Toronto: Butterworths, 1978

Gil, DG. *Beyond the jungle.* Cambridge: Schenkman Publishing Co., 1979

Gil, DG. The United States versus child abuse. In LH Pelton (Ed.), *The social context of child abuse.* New York: Human Sciences Press, 1981

Gottesman, II. Genetic aspects of intelligent behavior. In N Ellis (Ed.), *Handbook of mental deficiency: Psychological theory and research.* New York: McGraw-Hill, 1963

Gould, S, Wunsch-Hitzig, R, & Dohrenwend, B. Estimating the prevalence of childhood psychopathology: A critical review. *Journal of the American Academy of Child Psychiatry,* 1981, *20,* 462–476

Graham, P, Rutter, M, & George, S. Temperamental characteristics as predictors of behavior disorders in children. *American Journal of Orthopsychiatry,* 1973, *43,* 328–399

Greenblatt, B. *Responsibility for child care.* San Francisco: Jossey-Bass, 1977

Greenman, GW. Visual behavior of newborn infants. In AJ Solnit & SA Provence (Eds.), *Modern perspectives in child development.* New York: Hallmark, 1963

Grosenick, J, & Huntze, SL. National needs analysis in behavioral disorders: Severe behavior disorders. Columbia, MO: Department of Special Education, University of Missouri-Columbia, 1980

Hagen, JW, & Hale, GA. The development of attention in children. In AD Pick (Ed.), *Minnesota symposia on child psychology,* Vol. 7. Minneapolis: University of Minnesota Press, 1973

Haith, MM. The response of the human newborn to visual movement. *Journal of Experimental Child Psychology,* 1966, *3,* 235–243

Haley vs. Ohio, 332, U.S. 596 (1948)

Halverson, CF, & Waldrop, MF. Relations between preschool activity and aspects of intellectual and social behavior at age $7^1/_2$. *Developmental Psychology,* 1976, *12,* 107–112

Hammond, J. Hearing and response in the newborn. *Developmental Medicine and Child Neurology,* 1970, *12,* 3–5

Harms, E. *Origins of modern psychiatry.* Springfield, Ill: Charles C Thomas, 1967

Harris, SL. Teaching language to nonverbal children—with emphasis on problems of generalization. *Psychological Bulletin,* 1975, *82,* 565–580

Haynes, H, White, BL, & Held, R. Visual accommodation in human infants. *Science,* 1965, *148,* 528–530

Healy, W, & Bronner, A. *New light on delinquency and its treatment.* New Haven, Institute of Human Relations, Yale University, 1936

Heiman, JR, Fischer, MJ, & Ross, AO. A supplementary behavioral program to improve deficit reading performance. *Journal of Abnormal Child Psychology,* 1973, *1,* 390–399

Henry, SA. Current dimensions of parent training. *School Psychology Review,* 1981, *10,* 4–14

Heston, L. Psychiatric disorders in foster-home reared children of schizophrenic mothers. *British Journal of Psychiatry,* 1966, *112,* 819–825

Hetherington, EM, Cox, M, & Cox, R. Divorced fathers. *Family Coordinator*, 1976, *25*, 417–428

Hetherington, EM, Cox, M, & Cox, R. The aftermath of divorce. In JH Stevens, Jr, & M Matthew (Eds.), *Mother-child, father-child relations*. Washington, DC: National Association for the Education of Young Children, 1978

Hetherington, EM, & Parke, RD. *Child psychology: A contemporary viewpoint* (2nd ed.). New York: McGraw-Hill, 1979

Hobbs, N. *The troubled and troubling child: Re-education and mental health education and human services programs for children and youth*. San Francisco, Calif: Jossey-Bass, 1982

Howard, S vs. Friendswood Independent School District, 454 F. Supp. 634 (S.D. Texas, 1978)

Ingraham vs. Wright, 489, F.2d 248, 259–60, N.20 (5th Cir. 1974)

In re: *Gault*, 387, U.S. 1 (1967)

Iscoe, I. Is clinical child psychology obsolete? Some observations on the current scene. In GJ Williams & S Gordon (Eds.), *Clinical child psychology: Current practices and future perspectives*. New York: Behavioral Publications, 1974

Jensen, K. Differential reactions to taste and temperature stimuli in newborn infants. *Genetic Psychology Monographs*, 1932, *12*, 363–479

Joint Commission of Mental Health of Children. *Crisis in child mental health: Challenge for the 1970's*. New York: Harper & Row, 1969

Kagan, J, & Moss, HA. *Birth to maturity*. New York: Wiley, 1962

Kaskowitz, DH. *Validation of state counts of handicapped children*. Estimation of the number of handicapped children in each state. (Vol. 2), Menlo Park, Calif: Stanford Research Institute, 1977

Kessen, V. The American child and other inventions. *American Psychologist*, 1979, *34*, 815–820

Key, E. *The century of the child* (Engl. Rev.). New York: Putnam, 1909

Kiesler, SB. Federal policies for research on children. *American Psychologist*, 1979, *34*, 1009–1016

Kiesler, SB, & Turner, CM (Eds.). *Fundamental research and the process of education*. (Final report to the National Institute of Education by the Committee on Fundamental Research Relevant to Education, Assembly of Behavioral and Social Sciences.) Washington, DC, National Academy of Sciences, 1977

Klein, DB. *Mental Hygiene*, New York: Holt, 1944

Klerman, GL. *Implementation plan for the child and youth mental health services systems initiative*. Washington, DC: U.S. Department of Health, Education and Welfare, 1978

Kline, DF, Cole, P, & Fox, P. Child abuse and neglect. The school psychologist's role. *School Psychology Review*, 1981, *10*, 65–71

Klopfer, WG, & Taulbee, ES. Projective tests. In *Annual review of psychology*. Palo Alto, Calif: Annual Reviews, 1976

Knitzer, JE. Child advocacy: A perspective. *American Journal of Orthopsychiatry*, 1976, *46*, 200–216

Knitzer, J. *Unclaimed children: The failure of public responsibility to children and adolescents in need of mental health services*. Washington, DC: Children's Defense Fund, 1982

Koocher, GF. A bill of rights for children in psychotherapy. In GP Koocher (Ed.), *Children's rights and the mental health professions*. New York: John Wiley, 1976

Kramer, M. *Report to the President's biomedical research panel*. Washington, DC: U.S. Government Printing Office, 1976

Lamb, ME. *The role of the father in child development*. New York: Wiley, 1976

Lazar, I, & Darlington, RB. Lasting effects of early education, *Monographs of the Society for Research in Child Development*, 1982, *47* (2–3), 1–151

Leventhal, AS, & Lipsett, LP. Adaptation, pitch discrimination, and sound localization in the neonate. *Child Development*, 1964, *35*, 759–767

Lewis, M, & Goldberg, S. The acquisition and violation of expectancy: An experimental paradigm. *Journal of Experimental Child Psychology*, 1969, *7*, 70–80

Lipsett, LP, Engen, T, & Kaye, H. Developmental changes in the olfactory threshold of the neonate. *Child Development*, 1963, *34*, 371–376

Lovaas, OI. *The autistic child: Language development through behavior modification*. New York: Irvington, 1977

Lovaas, OI, & Schreibman, L. Stimulus overselectivity of autistic children in a stimulus situation. *Behavior Research and Therapy*, 1971, *9*, 305–310

Lovaas, OI, Schreibman, L, Koegel, R, & Rehm, R. Selective responding by autistic children to multiple sensory input. *Journal of Abnormal Psychology*, 1971, 77, 211–222

Lovitt, TC, & Curtiss, KA. Academic response rate as a function of teacher- and self-imposed contingencies. *Journal of Applied Behavior Analysis*, 1969, *2*, 49–53

Lubin, R, Wallis, R, & Paine, C. Patterns of psychological test use in the United States: 1935–1969. *Professional Psychology*, 1971, *2*, 70–74

Mannarino, A, & Fischer, CT. Survey of graduate training in clinical child psychology. *Journal of Clinical Child Psychology*, 1982, *11*, 22–26

Matheny, AP. Concordance for Piagetian-equivalent items derived from the Bayley mental test. *Developmental Psychology*, 1975, *11*, 224–227

Mattar, ME, & Yaffe, SJ. Compliance of pediatric patients with therapeutic regimens. *Postgraduate Medicine*, 1974, *56*, 181–188

Mednick, SA, Schulsinger, H, & Schulsinger, F. Schizophrenia in children of schizophrenic mothers. In A Davies (Ed.), *Child personality and psychopathology* (Vol. 2). New York: Wiley, 1975

Mesibov, GB, Schroeder, CS, & Wesson, L. Parental concerns about their children. *Journal of Pediatric Psychology*, 1977, *2*, 13–17

National Institute of Mental Health. *8th annual report on child and youth activities*. Washington, DC: Author, 1981

Neilon, P. Shirley's babies after fifteen years: A personality study. *Journal of Genetic Psychology*, 1948, *73*, 175–186

Neilson, G, Engle, T, & Latham, S. *Through the looking glass: A short term follow-up study of adolescents released from secure treatment*. Portland, Or: Secure Treatment Facility, June, 1979

Neilson, C, Hurt, M, Jr, & Berkeley, M. *An analysis of trends in federal RDD&E for children and youth: FY' 75–77*. Washington, DC: George Washington University, Social Research Group, 1978

Nichols, PH, & Bromon, SH. Familial resemblance in infant mental development. *Developmental Psychology*, 1974, *10*, 442–446

Nisbett, R, & Gurwitz, S. Weight, sex and the eating behavior of human newborns. *Journal of Comparative and Physiological Psychology*, 1970, *73*, 245–253

O'Block, FR, & Billimoria, A. National survey of involvement of school psychologists with child abuse. *School Psychology Review*, 1981, *10*, 62–64

O'Leary, KD, Pelham, WE, Rosenbaun, A, & Price, GH. Behavioral treatment of hyperkinetic children: An experimental evaluation of its usefulness. *Clinical Pediatrics*, 1976, *15*, 510–515

Oregon Department of Human Resources. *Procedures for admission to the child and adolescent secure treatment program at Oregon State Hospital*. Portland, Ore: Department of Human Resources, 1979

Palkes, H, Stewart, M, & Kahana, B. Porteus maze performance of hyperactive boys after training in self-directed verbal commands. *Child Development*, 1968, *39*, 817–829

Parham vs. JR., 442 U.S. 584 (1979)

Parke, RD. Children's home environments: Social and cognitive effects. In I Altman & JF Wohlwill (Eds.), *Children and the environment*. New York: Plenum, 1978

Parke, RD, & Sawin, D. Infant characteristics and behavior as elicitors of maternal and paternal responsibility in the newborn period. Paper presented at the biennial meeting of the Society of Research in Child Development, Denver, 1975

Patterson, GR, Jones, R, Whittier, J, & Wright MA. A behavior modification technique for the hyperactive child. *Behavior Research and Therapy*, 1965, *2*, 217–226

Pederson, FA Mother, father, and infant as an interaction system. Paper presented at the meeting of the American Psychological Association, Washington, DC, September, 1976 1976

Pelham, WE, & Ross, AO. Selective attention in children with reading problems: A developmental study of incidental learning. *Journal of Abnormal Child Psychology*, 1977, *5*, 1–8

Pennsylvania Office of Mental Health. *Pennsylvania State Mental Health Plan*. Harrisburg, Pa: Office of Mental Health, 1982

Permack, DA. A functional analysis of language. *Journal of the Experimental Analysis of Behavior*, 1970, *14*, 107–125

Petrie, A. *Individuality in pain and suffering*. Chicago: University of Chicago Press, 1967

Plas, JM. The psychologist in the school community: A liaison role. *School Psychology Review*, 1981, *10*, 72–81

Platt, A. *The child savers: The invention of delinquency*. Chicago: University of Chicago Press, 1969

President's Commission on Mental Health Task Panel Reports, Vols. I–II. Washington, DC: U.S. Government Printing Office, 1978

President's Commission on Mental Health, Task Panel Reports. Washington, DC: U.S. Government Printing Office, 1980

Quay, HC. Psychopathic behavior: Reflections on its nature, origins and treatment. In F Weizmann & I Uzgiris (Eds.), *The structuring of experience*. New York: Plenum, 1979

Reingold, HL. The modification of social responsiveness in institutional babies. *Monographs of the Society for Research in Child Development*, 1956, 21 (No. 63)

Reiser, J, Yonas, A, & Wikner, K. Radial localization of odors by human newborns. *Child Development*, 1976, *47*, 856–859

Reisman, JM. *Principles of psychotherapy with children*. New York: Wiley, 1973

Reynolds, WM, & Sundberg, ND. Recent research trends in testing. *Journal of Personality Assessment*, 1976, *40*, 228–233

Rie, HE. Historical perspective of concepts of child psychopathology. In HE Rie (Ed.), *Perspective in child psychopathology*. New York: Aldine-Atherton, 1971

Risley, T, & Wolf, M. Establishing functional speech in echolalic children. *Behavior Research and Therapy*, 1967, *5*, 73–88

Roberts, MC. Clinical child psychology programs: Where and what are they? *Journal of Clinical Child Psychology*, 1982, *11*, 13–21

Rosen, B. Distribution of child psychiatric services. In JD Nopshitz (Ed.), *Handbook of basic child psychiatry*, Vol. IV. New York: Basic Books, 1979

Ross, AO. Learning theory and therapy with children. *Psychotherapy: Theory, Research and Practice*, 1964, *1*, 102–108

Ross, AO. The rights of children as psychotherapy patients. Paper presented at the American Psychological Association Meeting, New Orleans, Louisiana, September 1, 1974

Ross, AO, *Child behavior therapy*. New York: Wiley, 1981

Rubenstein, E. Childhood mental disease in America: A review of the literature before 1900. *American Journal of Orthopsychiatry*, 1948, *18*, 314–321

Ruley, EJ. Compliance in young hyperactive patients. *Pediatric Clinics of North America*, 1978, *25*, 175–182

Ryback, D, & Staats, AW. Parents as behavior therapy-technicians in treating reading deficits (Dyslexia). *Journal of Behavior Therapy and Experimental Psychiatry*, 1970, *1*, 109–119

S-1 vs. Turlington, 635 F. 2d 342 (5th Cir. 1981)

Scarr, S. Genetic factors in activity motivation. *Child Development*, 1966, *37*, 663–673

Scarr, S. Social introversion-extraversion as a heritable response. *Child Development*, 1969, *40*, 823–832

Scarr-Salapatek, S. Unknowns in the IQ equation. *Science*, 1971, *174*, 1223–1228

Scarr-Salapatek, S, & Williams, M. The effects of early stimulation on low-birthweight infants. *Child Development*, 1972, *43*, 509–519

Schaeffer, WW, & Bayler, N. Maternal behavior, child behavior and their intercorrelations from infancy through adolescence. *Monographs of the Society for Research in Child Development*, 1963, *28* (Serial No. 87), 1–27

Schreibman, L. Effects of within-stimulus and extra-stimulus prompting on discrimination learning in autistic children. *Journal of Applied Behavior Analysis*, 1975, *8*, 91–112

Schwartz, GJ. College students as contingency managers for adolescents in a program to develop reading skills. *Journal of Applied Behavior Analysis*, 1977, *10*, 645–655

Seagull, AA, & Noll, RB. Beyond informed consent: Ethical and philosophical considerations in using behavior modification or play therapy in the treatment of enuresis. *Journal of Clinical Child Psychology*, 1982, *11*, 44–49

Sears, RR. *Young ancients revisited: A history of child development*. Chicago: University of Chicago Press, 1975

Sherman, M, Sherman, IC, & Flory, CD. Infant behavior. *Comparative Psychology Monographs*, 1936, *12* (No. 4)

Shields, J. *Monozygotic twins brought up together and apart*. London: Oxford University Press, 1962

Shore, MF. Legislation, advocacy, and the rights of children and youth. *American Psychologist*, 1979, *34*, 1017–1019

Shore, MF, & Mannino, FV. Mental health services for children and youth: 1976. *Journal of Clinical Child Psychology*, 1976, *5*, 21–25

Siegel, AW. Variables affecting incidental learning in children. *Child Development*, 1968, *39*, 957–968

Smith, MB. School and home: Focus on achievement. In AH Passow (Ed.), *Developing programs for the educationally disadvantaged*. New York: Teachers College Press, 1968

Sobel, SB. One day in court: The clinician's role in preventing delinquency. *Journal of Clinical Child Psychology*, 1979, *8*, 137–139

Sowder, BJ. *Assessment of child mental health needs*, Vol. I-VIII. McLean, Va: General Research Corp., 1975

Sowder, BJ. *Issues related to psychiatric services for children and youth: A review of selected literature from 1970–1979*. Bethesda, Md: Burt Associates, 1979

Sowder, BJ, & Burt, MR. *Utilization of psychiatric facilities by children and youth*. Bethesda, Md: Burt Associates, Inc., 1980

Staats, AW, & Butterfield, WH. Treatment of nonreading in a culturally deprived juvenile delinquent: An application of reinforcement principles. *Child Development*, 1965, *36*, 925–942

Staats, AW, Minke, KA, Finley, JR, Wolf, MM, & Brooks, LOA. Reinforcer system and experimental procedure for the laboratory study of reading acquisition. *Child Development*, 1954, *35*, 209–231

Staats, AW, Minke, KA, Goodwin, W, & Landeen, J. Cognitive behavior modification: "Motivated learning" reading treatment with sub-professional therapy -technicians. *Behavior Research and Therapy*, 1967, *5*, 283–299

Steiner, G. *The children's cause*. Washington, DC: Brookings Institution, 1976

Strickland, SP. *Politics, science, and dread disease*. Cambridge, Mass: Harvard University Press, 1972

Stuart vs. Nappi, 443 F. Supp. 1235 (D. Conn. 1978)

Sundberg, ND. *Assessment of persons*. Englewood Cliffs, NJ: Prentice-Hall, 1977

Sykrzypek, GJ. Effects of perceptual isolation and arousal on anxiety, complexity preference and novelty preference in psychopathic delinquents. *Journal of Abnormal Psychology*, 1969, *74*, 321–329

Tarver, SG, Hallahan, DP, Kauffman, JM, & Ball, DW. Verbal rehearsal and selective attention in children with learning disabilities: A developmental lag. *Journal of Experimental Child Psychology*, 1976, *22*, 375–385

Thomas, A, & Chess, S. *Temperament and development*. New York: Brunner/Mazel, 1977

Thomas, A, Chess, S, & Birch, HG. *Temperament and behavior disorders in children*. New York: New York University Press, 1968

Thomas, A, Chess, S, Birch, H, Hertzig, M, & Korn, S. *Behavioral individuality in early childhood*. New York: New York University Press, 1963

Toth, E, & Kenealy, E. Maxmizing private and public funding: A successful experiment. Paper presented at the 33rd annual Meeting, American Association of Psychiatric Services for Children, Spring, 1981

Tuddenham, RD. The constancy of personality ratings over two decades. *Genetic Psychology Monographs*, 1959, *60*, 3–29

Tuma, JM. Pediatric psychologist? . . . Do you mean clinical child psychologist? *Journal of Clinical Child Psychology*, 1975, *4*, 9–12

Tuma, JM. (Ed.). *Directory: Practicum and internship training resources in pediatric psychology*. Galveston, TX: Society of Pediatric Psychology, 1976

Tuma, JM. Crisis in training pediatric psychologists. *Professional Psychology*, 1981, *12*, 516–522

Tuma, JM. Proposal for conference on professional training of clinical child psychologists. *Journal of Clinical Child Psychology*, 1982, *11*, 1–7 (a)

Tuma, JM. Training in pediatric psychology. In JM Tuma (Ed.), *Handbook for the practice of pediatric psychology*. New York: Wiley, 1982 (b)

Tuma, JM, & Cawunder, P. Orientation and practice patterns of members of professional child psychology societies and divisions. *The Clinical Psychologist*, 1983, *36*, 73–76

Tuma, JM, & Cohen, R. Pediatric psychology: An investigation of factors relative to practice and training. *Journal of Pediatric Psychology*, in press

Tuma, JM, & Grabert, J. Internship and postdoctoral training in pediatric and clinical child psychology: A survey. *Journal of Pediatric Psychology*, 1983, *8*, 245–260

Tuma, JM, & Pratt, JM. Clinical child psychology practice and training: A survey. *Journal of Clinical Child Psychology*, 1982, *11*, 27–34

Tuma, JM, & Sobotka, K. Traditional therapies with children. In TH Ollendick & M Hersen (Eds.), *Handbook of child psychopathology*. New York: Plenum, 1983

Turney, KV. *The provision of intensive mental health services to adjudicated delinquents: A survey of state practices*. Cambridge, Mass: Harvard Law School, 1980

U.S. Department of Education, Office of Special Education and Rehabilitation Services. *To assure the free appropriate public education of all handicapped children, fourth annual report to Congress on the implementation of Public Law 94-142: The Education for All Handicapped Children Act*. Washington, DC: U.S. Department of Education, 1982

VandenBos, GR, Nelson, S, Stapps, J, Olmedo, E, Coates, D, & Batchelor, W. *APA input to NIMH regarding planning for mental health personnel development.* Washington, DC: American Psychological Association, 1979

Vanderven, K. A compendium of training programs in the child care professions in the U.S. and Canada. *Child Care Quarterly,* 1976, *5*(4)

Veith, I. The infancy of psychiatry. *Bulletin of the Menninger Clinic,* 1964, *28,* 186–197

Wenar, C. Developmental psychopathology: Its nature and models. *Journal of Clinical Child Psychology,* 1982, *11,* 192–201

Wheeler, AJ, & Sulzer, B. Operant training and generalization of a verbal response form in a speech deficient child. *Journal of Applied Behavior Analysis,* 1970, *3,* 139–147

Wheeler, CA. The relationship between psychopathy and the weak automatization cognitive style. *FCI Research Reports,* 1974, *6,* (No. 2)

White, SH. Children in perspective. *American Psychologist,* 1979, *34,* 812–814

Willerman, L, & Plomin, R. Activity level in children and their parents. *Child Development,* 1973, *44,* 854–858

Willie, M vs. Hunt, 484 F. Supp. 278 (D.M.d. 1979)

Wilson, RS. Mental development in the preschool years. *Developmental Psychology,* 1974, *10,* 580–588

Witkin, MJ. *Residential treatment centers for emotionally disturbed children 1975–76.* Mental Health Statistical Note No. 135. Washington, DC: National Institute of Mental Health, July, 1977

Wohlford, P. Clinical child psychology: The emerging specialty. *The Clinical Psychologist,* 1979, *33,* 25–29

Wood, L, & Moore, C. *Beneath the labels: Children in detention and shelter care.* Newark, NJ: Association for Children of New Jersey, 1981

Wright, L. The pediatric psychologist: A role model. *American Psychologist,* 1967, *22,* 323–325

Wright, L. Outcome of a standardized program for treating psychogenic encopresis. *Professional Psychology,* 1975, *6,* 453–456

Wright, L. Health care psychology: Prospects for the well-being of children. *American Psychologist,* 1979, *34,* 1001–1006

Wyatt vs. Aderholt, 503, F.2d, 1305 (5th Cir. 1974)

Yarrow, LJ, Rubenstein, JL, & Pedersen, FA. *Infant and environment: Early cognitive and motivational development.* Washington, DC: Hemisphere, 1975

Zigler, E, & Berman, W. Discerning the future of early childhood intervention. *American Psychologist,* 1983, *38,* 894–906

Zubin, J, Eron, L, & Schumer, F. *An experimental approach to projective techniques.* New York: Wiley, 1965

Howard S. Adelman
Linda Taylor

2

Toward Integrating Intervention Concepts, Research, and Practice

There is a wealth of literature concerning psychological and educational interventions for children. The prevailing trend has been to present each approach as unique. Relatively little analysis has been done of significant commonalities and differences among various approaches to psychotherapy, behavior change, remediation, schooling, parenting, and other interventions.

Our intent is to present tentative frameworks and concepts for analyzing psychological and educational practices. Such analysis and model building provide a valuable basis for identifying the "active ingredients" of effective approaches and for developing new strategies. They also can provide a foundation for conceiving and investigating a comprehensive model of the general nature of intervention.

The discussion that follows is organized around three topics (1) the essence of intervention, (2) basic underlying considerations in intervening with children, and (3) major elements of intervention practices.

WHAT IS INTERVENTION?

In the context of psychological and educational practices for children, intervention generally is defined with reference to its altruistic objectives. "Intervention is a general term that refers to the application

CLINICAL CHILD PSYCHOLOGY
ISBN 0–8089–1680–7

57

of professional skills to maintain or improve a child's potential for on-going healthy development" (Suran & Rizzo, 1979, p. 79). Intervention is involvement "in ongoing systems interacting with these (systems) in such a way as to help them (the systems) function better" (Sundberg, Tyler, & Taplin, 1973, p. 136).

Adopting a neutral stance, Ford and Urban (1963) state that psychotherapeutic intervention is designed to alter (1) responding mechanisms, (2) situational events that elicit a particular behavior, or (3) the individual's response repertoire through learning. They recognize, however, that such actions do raise such controversial questions as "What behavior should be changed?", "Changed to what?" and "Who should choose?"

Also avoiding presumptions of altruism, Rhodes and Tracy (1972, p. 28) define intervention with children as "any directed action upon the deviance predicament between child and community." They stress that intervention always implies (1) a trained socially sanctioned intervener, (2) an intervention target, (3) a set of assumptions, attitudes, and perceptions about deviance that make up the world view of society, (4) a set of specific rituals and structured contacts between the intervener, the intervenee, and their cultural binding, and (5) a circumscribed set of contracts between the power structures and the intervener-intervenee contacts.

A recent trend has been to conceive psychological intervention in terms of its emphasis on solving problems (e.g., Ozer, 1980; Spivak, Platt, & Shure, 1976). In defining intervention as a problem-solving approach, Urban and Ford (1971) specify 12 sequential components: (1) initial recognition of a difficulty, (2) identification (specification) of the problem, (3) analysis of the problem, (4) summary restatement of the problem, (5) selection of objectives that are to be affected, (6) depiction of the criteria (values) by which solutions will be judged, (7) consideration of possible solutions, (8) testing proposals against criteria, (9) selection of a single final solution, (10) operation planning (how it is to be done and who is to do it), (11) implementation (actuation) of the solution, and (12) subsequent evaluations.

When attempting to identify the essential components of a comprehensive definition of intervention, it is useful to refer to a dictionary description. *Webster's Third New International Dictionary* (1976) states intervention is "the act of intervening . . . interference that may affect the interests of others." To intervene is "to enter or appear as an irrelevant or extraneous feature . . . to occur, fall, or come between . . . by way of hindrance or modification . . . to interfere." What the definition implies is that as much as professionals may intend interventions to have positive outcomes, by definition there is a distinct possibility that an intervention may be irrelevant or a hindrance. The definition also describes the interference nature of interventions.

The definition does not clarify other important components that are implied by common use of the term in fields such as psychology, education, and public health and welfare. In such fields, intervention seems to refer to planned actions that are intended to produce desired changes in existing conditions of a person or environment, often with the condition identified as a problem in need of correction, improvement, or prevention.

Thus, as an aid in theory building and analysis, we propose that (1) actions (interferences), (2) changes (outcomes), and (3) conditions be viewed as primary facets in defining intervention. An adequate general definition of intervention must also incorporate references to whether or not the actions and changes that occur are intended and whether or not the conditions to be changed are problematic. The focus on intentionality guarantees that unplanned actions and unintended changes, such as positive and negative "side effects," are not ignored. The inclusion of nonproblematic conditions provides a reminder about the relevance of actions and changes related to such matters as positive growth and enrichment. It should be noted that conditions can refer broadly to any system including a person, organization, institution, society, and so forth (Adelman & Taylor, 1983).

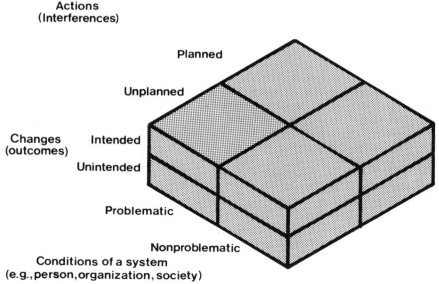

Fig. 2-1. Essential features of a definition of intentional intervention.

In sum, as a broad working definition, intentional intervention can be viewed as encompassing the planned (and unplanned) actions that result from a desire to produce changes in existing problematic or non-problematic conditions of a system (person, environment, or interaction of both). Such actions may or may not produce changes, and resultant changes may include unintended outcomes (Figure 2-1). From this perspective, any formal psychological and educational program is an intervention. Whenever individuals or groups seek help, they are requesting an intervention. When society mandates that a person be treated, intervention is occurring.

The above definition is meant to be one aid in analyzing interventions. It can be used, for instance, in systematically formulating such basic intervention questions as: What are the bases for the actions? How do the actions produce change? What is the nature of the changes produced?

BASIC UNDERLYING CONSIDERATIONS IN INTERVENING WITH CHILDREN

For purposes of this discussion, we attempt to capture the essence of some of the most basic concerns that arise in connection with psychological and educational interventions, especially for children, by focusing on two basic considerations: (1) what are the logical or rational bases for intervention and; (2) who makes the major decisions about intervention rationale, objectives, and effectiveness.

Rational Bases for Intervention

Intentional interventions are rationally based. That is, underlying such activity there is a rationale, whether or not it is explicitly stated. It consists of views derived from theoretical, empirical, and philosophical sources. The rationale shapes an intervention's purposes and procedures. It provides guidelines regarding the nature of the intervention's aims and practices. While rationales direct intervention, it is rare to find them systematically formulated and explicitly stated.

Rossi, Freeman, and Wright (1979) suggest that interventions are based on a set of hypotheses drawn from causal and predictive studies, from logical theories, and from clinical impressions. With regard to instruction, Bruner (1966, p. 1) has stated that intervention reflects "a theory of how growth and development are assisted by diverse means." With regard to psychotherapy Howard and Orlinsky (1972, p. 617) indicate that the activity implies "some conception of *human nature* or personality (the 'material' to be worked with), *human fulfillment* (the ideal to be sought), *human vulnerability* (psychopathology), of *therapeutics,* and of the therapeutic *profession.* Taken together, they comprise . . . the Therapeutic Belief-Value Complex".

In general, philosophical and theoretical concepts and data are amalgamated into an intervention rationale. They may be drawn from a variety of disciplines and fields, such as basic and applied psychology, the biological sciences and medicine, education, sociology, philosophy, and social welfare. A rationale can reflect a general orientation or "model" of the causes of problems, of tasks to be accomplished, and/or of the appropriate outcomes and processes of intervention.

With regard to models of cause, three basic orientations can be seen to underlie a great deal of intervention research and practice: the disordered or "ill" person (medical) model; the lack of developmental readiness or slow maturation model; and an interactional model emphasizing the interplay between person and environment.* In clinical child psychology, the prevailing orientation has been a tendency to see locus of casuality as centered in the child, i.e., disordered and slow maturation. However, with increasing acceptance of the role environmental factors can play in causing problems, there has been greater emphasis on environmental deficits and defects either as the locus of causality or as accounting for a significant portion of the interplay of person and environmental variables (e.g., Bandura, 1982; Bowers, 1973; Deci, 1980; Gordon, 1973; Mischel, 1973).

For those interveners who favor one or the other of these causal models, their rationale for choosing tasks, outcomes, and procedures may be based on their preferred causal model. Others may ignore causal factors and design interventions primarily in terms of their rationale for correction. Still others respond in terms of models that incorporate specific orientations toward both cause and correction. In this last connection, based on an analysis of different patterns of attributions of responsibility for problems and for solutions, Brickman and his colleagues have identified four general orientations to helping—moral, medical, compensatory, and enlightenment orientations (Brickman, Rabinowitz, Karuza, Coates, Cohn, & Kidder, 1982).

Adherence to any particular model both guides and limits the nature

---

*Urban and Ford (1971) list a representative sample of 10 models used to explain behavioral dysfunctions. i.e., the somatogenic model, the trauma model, the Pavlovian model, frustration theory, conflict theory, anxiety theory, tension model, need-satisfaction models, the psychosomatic model, and the sociogenic model.

of subsequent intervention activity and undoubtedly has major ramifications for intervention outcomes.† For example, as Brickman et al. (1982, p. 368) suggest, "each set of assumptions has characteristic consequences for . . . competence, status, and well-being . . . the wrong choice . . . will undermine effective helping and coping."

Who Decides—Parents, Child, Clinicians, or Society?

What is finally incorporated into a particular rationale is dependent largely upon who is doing the incorporating and the forces influencing that person or persons. Concern about this matter is reflected in the extensive critical discussion of society's ability to exercise control through psychological and educational interventions (e.g., Beauchamp & Childress, 1979; Coles, 1978; Feinberg, 1973; Hobbs, 1975; Illich, 1976; Kittrie, 1971; Laing & Esterson, 1970; Robinson, 1974; Rogers, 1977; Szasz, 1969). At one extreme are those who state that society must put its needs before those of individuals in order to maintain itself; at the other extreme are those who espouse the view that activities that include coercion and invasion of privacy jeopardize individuals' rights and are never justified. For many persons, however, neither extreme is acceptable, and thus the matter becomes a complex ethical and legal dilemma.

Without agreeing or disagreeing with a particular position, one can appreciate the importance of the debate in raising public consciousness. Specifically, it serves to heighten awareness that: (1) no society is devoid of some degree of coercion in dealing with its members (e.g., no right or liberty is absolute); (2) interventions can be used to serve the vested interests of subgroups in a society at the expense of other subgroups and individuals (e.g., loss of freedoms and rights, coercion, invasion of privacy); and (3) consent and due process of law are central to the protection of individuals when there are conflicting interests at stake (e.g., about who or what should be blamed for a problem).

However, if individuals (especially children, minorities, and the poor, who are particularly vulnerable) are to be adequately protected from abuse by those with power to exercise control over them, there must be greater awareness of when conflicts in interest are likely to occur. It is

---

†Interventions and their underlying rationales, of course, also, are affected by pragmatics, absence of data, and other factors not very rationally or ethically rooted, such as conceptual deficiencies, inconclusive data, personal biases, and societal biases. Space precludes discussing these "inappropriate biasing factors" here. The interested reader may refer to Adelman and Taylor, 1983; Hobbs, 1975; Lee and Temerlin, 1970; Mercer, 1973; Szasz, 1969; Weiss, 1972.

in this connection that understanding the topic of "who decides" is essential. Our efforts in this area have led us to attempt to identify the range of "interested parties" and to distinguish helping relationships from socialization, particularly as they apply to understanding intervention practices for children.

The importance of understanding that intervention practices are of concern to a variety of persons and groups who often have conflicting interests has been alluded to for many years in the "mental health" field (e.g., see Krause, 1969; Parloff, Kellman, & Frank, 1954; Smith, 1963). For instance, Strupp and Hadley (1977) propose that there are three "interested parties" involved in intervention decision making: the client, society, and the intervener. In our work (Adelman and Taylor, 1983), we have distinguished the interested parties in terms of two, not mutually exclusive, groups.

Directly Involved Interested Parties

Persons or systems to be changed. Individuals referred by self or others or an identified setting (such as the child referred for therapy or the classroom to be changed).

Interveners. Those who, in addition to their own rationale may base their activity on the stated desires or interpreted needs of subscribers, the person or systems to be changed, or both.

Subscribers. Private individuals or representatives of organized bodies who underwrite the cost of intervention for themselves or others (such as parents arranging therapy for their child or a school referring a child for related services).

Indirectly Involved Parties (i.e., Those Whose Influence Has the Potential to Produce a Major Impact on the Intervention)

Primary environmental influences. Family, friends, employers, teachers, coworkers, local representatives of funding sources.

Secondary and tertiary environmental influences. Governmental agents related to health, education, welfare, and law enforcement; professional and lay organizations; theorists, researchers, and instructors (i.e., those who lobby for, underwrite, study, evaluate, and teach about intervention).

While it may thus appear at first glance that the intervener is the only party concerned with intervention rationales, this is not the case. Sophisticated or not, directly involved or not, with or without control, each of the interested parties is likely to have beliefs and values about causes, corrections, and what constitutes progress. For example, even if a teacher and parents agree that a child should be in therapy, they each may have very different ideas about the nature of the problem and how it should be approached and both may differ from the intervener's viewpoint, to say nothing of the child's perspective.

Given the range of concepts, data, and general orientations from which "interested parties" can make choices, the questions arise: How greatly do rationales differ? Who decides what theory, data, and philosophy should be incorporated into any specific rationale? How are such decisions made? Because rationales for currently prominent interventions are not systematically formulated, these questions are not easily studied.

Concerns related to the major interested parties and factors that differentiate helping relationships and socialization are represented in Figure 2-2 and highlighted below.

First, the various parties probably use different criteria in evaluating the need for and effectiveness of interventions (e.g., the client's, the society's, the profession's, and the intervener's view of what is a problem and what is progress may differ).

Second, the matter of whose criteria are used and whose interests are being served should be recognized as the key to differentiating helping from social control. That is, we propose that only when the client agrees his or her interests are served is it proper to designate the intervention as a helping relationship. In contrast, when the intervention is designed to serve society's interests, it probably is better viewed as socialization.‡ When clients' and society's interests do not coincide, this distinction takes on a critical significance. For example, if a child resists practices intended to facilitate positive social development, the intervention may undergo subtle transformations until it encompasses processes designed solely to control behavior.

Third, in helping, client consent for and control over intervention

---

‡The term socialization has both positive and negative connotations. From a positive perspective, parents and teachers are seen as trying to facilitate the development of pro-social values and skills so that children will be able to function appropriately and effectively in society. From a negative perspective, the majority are seen as trying to use political and economic pressures and institutions such as schools and mental health facilities to control those who threaten established values, policies, customs, and so forth.

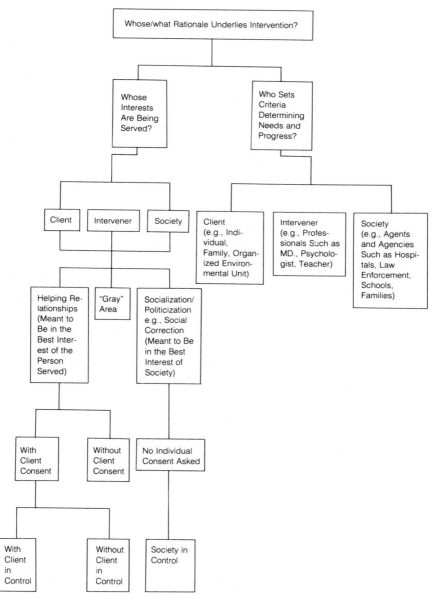

Fig. 2-2. Basic concerns related to whose interests are served and who sets criteria.

is seen as the desired state of affairs. In this connection, two points should be particularly noted. (1) Client control of intervention is by definition a matter of ensuring that key decisions are made collaboratively with no action proceeding without the client's specific approval. (In contrast, socialization presumes general consent under implied "social contracts," i.e., individual consent is not seen as necessary, and control is in the hands of the socializing agent.) Although this collaboration is more difficult when working with children, it is especially relevant. Such collaboration in itself may enhance the effectiveness of the intervention (Croghan & Freutiger, 1977). (2) Interveners often presume that clients with problems, especially children, do not have the competence to know what is in their long-range interests. This presumption bypasses several critical issues related to determination of competence and society's overly paternalistic stance toward children. Decisions about incompetence and who should act for those judged as incompetent continue to be defined primarily by legislation and court action, and the bases for such decisions remain controversial (Biklen, 1978; Melton, 1981). With regard to mental health treatment, what scant research there is suggests that once individuals reach age 14 their decision making ability is comparable to adults, and even nine-year-olds have shown adequate competence to participate effectively in treatment planning (Weithorn & Campbell, 1982).

Fourth, we recognize there are many times when others must attempt to help even though consent of the individual has not been given. When "help" proceeds without client consent and control, the intervention is seen to fall into a "gray" area (Murphy, 1974). At such times, an intervener wittingly or unwittingly may be acting more as a societal agent (e.g., socializing a problem "citizen") than as an agent of the client.

Fifth, even when a client provides consent and exercises a degree of control, the intervener is in a very powerful position. Obviously, this is especially true for children. Interveners, such as psychologists and teachers, almost always have a significant degree of control over those they treat and teach. Thus, in many situations where they mean to establish helping relationships, interveners find themselves operating in a gray area.

Sixth, while not represented in Fig. 2-2, it should be stressed in this context that research suggests that even the illusion of choice and control can enhance attainment of intervention objectives; conversely, the perception that one has no choice can hinder intervention processes and outcomes (Perlmuter & Monty, 1977; 1979). Research also suggests that directive, controlling intervention procedures are incompatible with restoring a sense of self-determination and control over one's life and can undermine such percepts (Deci, 1980).

Summary

The nature and scope of the forces shaping a particular intervention (e.g., intended processes and outcomes) often are hard to identify. As we have highlighted, interventions explicitly or implicitly reflect (1) philosophical and theoretical ideas and (2) standards regarding need and progress that are determined by various interested parties. In many instances, the intervention has been influenced by major sociocultural and political-economic actions. (This is why evaluative research of intervention programs often has significant political overtones. While research findings cannot resolve the philosophical and political questions at issue, data can be a useful aid in policy making.)

These, then, are the type of underlying considerations that must be understood if one is to appreciate the forces shaping decisions about the elements that constitute an intervention. We now turn to a discussion of the nature of the major elements themselves.

MAJOR ELEMENTS OF INTERVENTION

The focus in this section is on nine major elements of systematic intervention: (1) focal point of intervention, (2) intervention models, (3) phases, (4) major tasks related to clinical services, (5) types of interveners, (6) intervener facilitation, (7) time of intervention, (8) level of intervention, and (9) degree of disruptiveness/restrictiveness. While not exhaustive, these elements and the way they are conceived here suggest commonalities among interventions and concepts for analyzing the general nature of intervention.

Focal Point of Intervention

As has been widely discussed, the prevailing orientation in dealing with problems associated with children is to focus intervention on the individual (e.g., Hobbs, 1975; Rhodes & Tracy, 1972). This underlying bias or perspective is not surprising. Psychologically, there is a tendency for observers to attribute causes of problems to stable dispositions within the person (Jones & Nisbett, 1972). The fact that those experiencing a particular problem are a minority (i.e., most other people don't have the problem) becomes supporting evidence for observers' belief that the cause must be within the person. Prevailing social and political forces have been identified as furthering this bias or perspective (Hobbs, 1975). The almost inevitable result has been that the greatest portion of the problem-oriented literature on psychological intervention assumes the object of change is the person. Although this bias strongly affects interventions with adults, it seems to play an even stronger role in mental health and special education programs for children. Ironically, even those who adopt an "innocent child" view (i.e., the position that children's problems are the result of their ecological environment), often adopt intervention strategies focused on changing the child.

A smaller portion of the problem-oriented literature emphasizes that in many cases individuals should not be viewed as behaving inappropriately (e.g., Goodwin, 1973; Hobbs, 1975; Kelly, Snowden, & Munoz, 1977; Kessler & Albee, 1975; Laing & Esterson, 1970; Rhodes & Tracy, 1972). Instead, environments such as home, school, and society are seen as establishing standards and limiting choices in ways that result in a child's behavior being labeled as inappropriate. From this perspective, the proper intervention is one that changes the environment in appropriate ways to accommodate either a specific person or a wider range of individual differences, as contrasted with changing the individual (Fig. 2-3).

Given the range of ways interveners discuss "changing the environment," it is important to clarify the differences between environmental changes designed to accommodate rather than change individuals. Instructing parents and teachers to be more discriminating in their use of reinforcement contingencies is not the same as helping them see implications of offering additional options whenever appropriate and feasible, such as more choice in what a child can do and how the child can do it. It also is not the same as helping them understand the impact of appropriately changing their expectations regarding acceptable behavior, performance, and rate of progress (Nicholls, 1979). While this example involves what we have designated as the primary or immediate environment (e.g., home, classroom), often what appears to be a unique problem may be an indication of a more widespread malaise. An unhealthy milieu affecting more than a few individuals suggests the need for changes in the larger environment such as the neighborhood, school, and even the total society.

Rather than emphasizing person or environment, change on the part of both may represent an appropriate or necessary solution. It certainly is a more satisfactory compromise than an intervention that might force a child to accommodate to an inappropriate or "pathological" situation. Furthermore, even if it is a child who is the primary object of change, concomitant changes that make the environment more supportive and accommodating often are warranted.

Clearly, decisions in selecting the focal point of intervention are

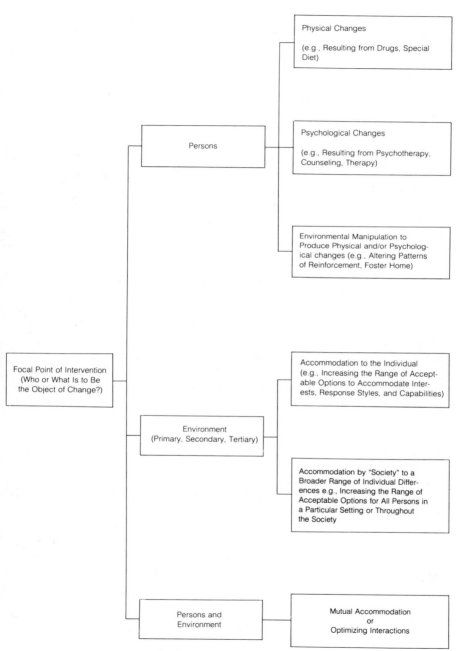

Fig. 2-3. Options related to focal point of intervention.

shaped profoundly by the decision makers and by the criteria and rationale they use. The critical question in this context is "Who should determine such matters and on what basis or rationale?" This question once again highlights the political nature of the decision making and underscores the concerns over the "political power balance" among involved parties.§

Intervention Models

A reasonably good starting point for identifying important similarities and differences among psychoeducational interventions is to classify them with regard to whether persons, environments, or both are the intended object of change. Within each of these three intervention groupings, we make additional distinctions as follows:

Person Models

· Commonalities and contrasts between person change models can be highlighted by classifying them as either therapy- or behavioral-oriented. Therapy-oriented approaches have their roots in medical, psychotherapeutic, and pedagogical concepts. They emphasize the need to increase client understanding (i.e., to bring unconscious or nonconscious thoughts, feelings, and motives into awareness) and may focus on personality as well as behavior changes. These approaches include the idea that prescriptions should be based on diagnostic testing designed to analyze psychodynamic and organic functioning. With regard to treatment processes, the literature stresses such modalities as verbal interchanges and physical activities, and such concepts as rapport building, acceptance, collaboration, choice and responsibility, awareness and insight, directiveness and nondirectiveness, transference relationships, catharsis, altering expectations, learning to cope, and so forth (e.g., Frankl, 1959; Freud, 1969; Klein, 1932; Moustakas, 1973; Perls, Hefferline, & Goodman, 1951; Rogers, 1951).

Behavioral-oriented approaches are based on behavior modification concepts, particularly those associated with operant conditioning, cognitive behavior modification, and operationism (see Chapter 7). Such approaches emphasize that what is to be changed is some observable

---

§For instance, when a child's behavior or performance is identified as deviant, it is likely that those representing normative behavior have the greatest power and make the decisions. This may lead to good and just actions. However, power is not necessarily to be equated with objectivity and competence in making decisions. Power imbalances are typical between teachers and students, parents and their children, and psychologists employed to intervene with children.

behavior. The process by which change is accomplished is systematic application of techniques derived from learning theory and experimental research, especially work related to operant and respondant conditioning and modeling, e.g., shaping and desensitization. In general, the reason for insisting that the behavior changed must be observable is based on the belief that intervention effectiveness cannot be evaluated stringently unless more than one person can agree that the frequency, rate, intensity, duration, or pattern of behavior has been affected (cf. Mahoney, 1974; O'Leary, 1972).

The increasing emphasis on cognitive behavior modification during the 1970s has led to a rapprochement between therapy-oriented and behavior-oriented approaches. This has been necessary in order to address the problems of (1) applying extrinsic reinforcements to thoughts, self-evaluations, and a variety of overt behaviors that are not very accessible to therapists, and (2) increasing a client's assumption of responsibility for maintaining and generalizing behavior changes. The major shift in such work has been to expand behavioral orientations to emphasize cognitive variables as mediators of behavior and behavior change (e.g., Bandura, 1977), thus the term cognitive behavior modification (Mahoney, 1974; Meichenbaum, 1977). Basic components of the resultant cognitive-behavior approaches include self-monitoring, self-evaluation, and self-reinforcement (Kanfer, 1980).

Goldfried (1980) has suggested a growing trend of rapprochement among the varying person-oriented, psychological intervention approaches. To advance this synthesis, he proposes investigation of clinical strategies and principles of change common to different orientations, e.g., providing clients with new, corrective experiences and offering direct feedback. Limits and barriers to such a trend have included political, social, and economic factors (Frank, 1972; 1976; Messer and Winokur, 1980; 1981; Norcross, 1981; Parloff, Waskow, & Wolfe, 1978; Sundland, 1977).

Environmental and Interactional Models

Currently, interventions focused on changing the environment to accommodate children manifesting problems can be conceived as involving four nonmutually exclusive strategies: (1) rearranging physical and social-environmental variables, (2) individualizing intervention (i.e., designing it to accommodate the developmental differences of specific clients), (3) personalizing intervention (i.e., not only accommodating developmental but also motivational differences), and (4) introducing special supportive services (e.g., placement in special institutions or classrooms, use of additional personnel.

Due to the influence of community and environment-oriented psychologists and of the ecology movement, transactional and reciprocal change strategies have been gaining acceptance in recent years. Reciprocal change models refer to approaches that stress transactional procedures and mutual accommodation; that is, the approaches encompass a series of reciprocal person and environment change procedures. For example, family therapists commonly elicit changes whereby parents alter aspects of family rules or physical setting to accommodate their child's desires (e.g., for increased self-determination, privacy) and the child agrees to change in ways that cause less distress to the family.

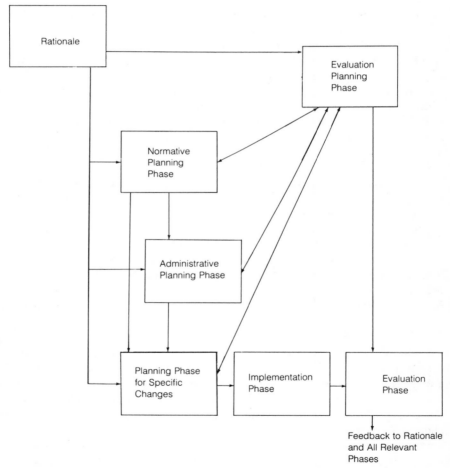

Fig. 2-4. The process of planning, implementing, and evaluating intervention.

General Phases of Intervention

A general classification of intervention models provides a framework for delineating one range of factors that may influence intervention outcomes. The complexities of psychoeducational interventions, however, are even more involved than these models can highlight. Appreciation of the complex nature of systematically planned and implemented intentional interventions also requires an understanding of the general phases of such activity. Elsewhere, Adelman (1974) has presented a framework discussing seven phases and detailing sequential activities involved in each (see Fig. 2-4).

Figure 2-4 illustrates most vividly that intentional intervention requires planning. Planning may be unilateral or participatory in nature and can provide ways to ensure that implementation is dynamic, innovative, and purposeful rather than static and reactive. As the following sections are intended to convey, planning represents an attempt to organize an intervention's content and procedures in ways that are consistent with the underlying rationale and incorporate appropriate evaluation.

Conceiving intervention in terms of phases is viewed as consistent with a general systems theory approach (Bertalanffy, 1968). The scope of systematic activity implied by such a schema is considerably greater than that which currently is implemented and evaluated by most psychologists and educators (Bergin & Lambert, 1978; Weiss, 1972).

Major Tasks Related to Clinical Services

Given the broad definition of intervention we have adopted, any psychoeducational activity (e.g., assessment, treatment, instruction, enrichment) can be viewed as an intervention. The most compelling and visible manifestations of such interventions are the specific programs and services that are offered by professionals. These may be designated as intervention tasks. For example, with reference to services provided for children in clinics and remedial settings, we have identified six major interrelated tasks (Fig. 2-5).

Figure 2-5 shows how we conceive the relationship between the six tasks. Such a formulation highlights the sequence and the connections between the various tasks, all of which may be needed to produce effective change.

Since each task has a comprehensive rationale and extensive planning and evaluation requirements associated with it, we can describe only the essence of each below.

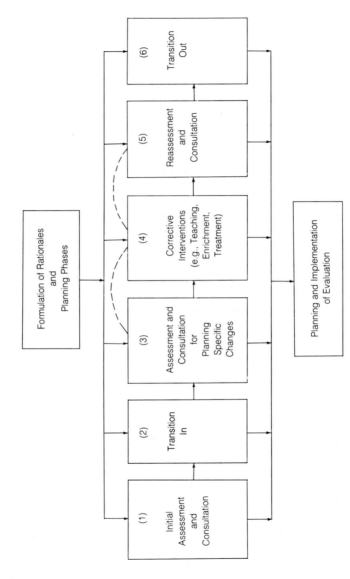

Fig. 2-5. Major tasks related to services for learning problems.

Initial Assessment and Consultation

Although assessment often is seen as an activity separate from intervention, in practice assessment almost always is an intervention. It underscores the existence of problems and is the initial step leading to decisions regarding placement and treatment. When someone is experiencing a problem, there is an immediate need for assessment and consultation to determine the following: (1) the general scope of the problem (severity and pervasiveness), (2) the appropriate focal point of the intervention (person, environment, person-environment interaction), and (3) what general types of corrective steps might be appropriate, such as changes in the environment to accommodate an individual, changes in a specific aspect of a person-environment interaction, or special forms of therapy, schooling, and tutoring to change individuals. It is important to stress that the immediate focus of initial assessment and consultation is on the general nature of the services needed, such as individual therapy to improve basic social skills, and not on a specific prescription, such as a detailed plan to be carried out by a therapist. It also should be noted that diagnostic classification may occur in the process of such assessment but is not a logical necessity (Adelman, 1979).

Transition Into Corrective Interventions

Once a decision has been made to pursue a service alternative, the task focus shifts to implementing the decision. However, in implementing intervention decisions, significant practical and psychological barriers usually confront the involved parties. When asked to make changes, most individuals are anxious, and for some the step from decision making to successfully initiating a chosen intervention proves to be altogether too difficult. Such instances indicate the need for transition steps encompassing such activities as (1) clarifying procedures for making application and financial arrangements, (2) arranging visits to potential services to discuss and demystify as much of the intervention features as is feasible and to develop positive expectations, (3) personalizing contact to provide support and assurance when needed, and (4) monitoring and facilitating the initial implementation in order to identify any selection (screening and placement) errors and to mediate any initial adjustment problems. In other words, the task is to implement procedures that lead to an effective beginning. Research on intervention outcomes supports the importance of clarifying children's expectations about treatment (Day & Reznikoff, 1980).

Assessment and Consultation for Planning Specific Changes

Corrective interventions are shaped by ongoing assessment and decision-making processes. The initial focus is on assessing the present status of the child or environment to be changed and deciding on initial objectives. Subsequent emphasis is on refining plans based on feedback and new assessment data. The intent is to guide daily intervention actions toward systematic accomplishment of intended outcomes.

Formulating specific objectives is most appropriately accomplished at the time an intervention is initiated and by those who implement it. Those involved in implementing an intervention are in the best position to assess changes and to formulate daily plans. Essentially, what occurs is that the intervener initiates the best approach feasible based on the intervention rationale and whatever preliminary data appear appropriate and useful, and monitors intervention impact as data for planning subsequent steps.

Of course, in most instances where children are involved, planning is done with reference not only to assessment data, but with regard to the desires of parents, clinicians, program administrators, the state, and sometimes the child. Moreover, since conditions change regularly during intervention, there usually are ongoing consultations with specific interested parties and mechanisms for arriving at mutual agreements.

Corrective Interventions

While there is a wide range of specific corrective services in terms of orientations and methods, the types can be categorized as treatment, instruction, and enrichment. As conceived by social learning theory (Bandura, 1977; 1982), the activities involved in such services include facilitation of direct and vicarious experiences, logical verification, and verbal and other forms of social persuasion. Simply stated, once such services and activities are planned, the task becomes that of implementing them in order to accomplish the intended outcomes.

Although types of services and activities can be conceptually contrasted, in practice such distinctions may be very hard to demonstrate (e.g., in situations where a child is hospitalized for psychiatric problems, treatment, teaching, and enrichment all may be included). Each type of activity may be needed to some degree where severe psychoeducational problems exist. However, the need for, the value of each, and the impact of various combinations cannot be investigated without making distinctions among them. This, in turn, may help to increase understanding of causality, e.g., at least with reference to the gross distinction between whether a problem stems from deficiencies within the child or from deficiencies in the environment.

Reassessment and Consultation

After corrective interventions have been implemented beyond an appropriate "transition in" period, there is a need to reconsider such matters as the appropriateness of the selection decision. If problems are occurring at this stage, how can the difficulties best be understood and dealt with? Is progress adequate? If goals are reached, what is the next step? In essence, decisions are made about whether an intervention should be continued, changed, or discontinued. The data used are a combination of daily evaluations and an updating of the type of information gathered during initial assessment and consultation.

Transition From the Intervention

An intervention may be discontinued because it was inappropriate, insufficient, or because goals were achieved. Once this decision is made, the next task focuses on the same administrative, practical, and psychological concerns that arise during initial assessment and consultation and transitions into the intervention. For example, when it is decided that a child will leave a special institutional placement, the range of services appropriate as a next step is carefully considered. Once a decision is made, the intervention focus shifts to anxiety related to the transition and anticipation of specific activities the child needs to master to succeed in the next situation (e.g., "survival skills"). Often appropriate are plans for ongoing support until children are successfully assimilated into the new milieu.

Types of Interveners

In appreciating the full range of available interveners for psycho-educational concerns, one can see the continuum as beginning with persons with no special training, such as parents and friends, and proceeding through volunteers and paraprofessionals to professionals with highly specialized training and experience. With recent interest in community psychology and self-help groups, natural and informal "helpers," always a part of the community fabric, again are being recognized as socially sanctioned interveners (Cowen, 1982). Natural helpers in the society may be neighbors, friends, or relatives (Caplan & Killilea, 1976; Collins,

1973; Illich, 1976). Informal helpers include neighborhood business people and nonpsychoeducational professionals, such as recreational youth leaders and pediatricians. Such helpers may informally intervene or may participate in formally organized activities, e.g., self-help groups.

The political climate of the sixties and seventies (e.g., as reflected in such legislation as the Community Mental Health Act of 1964) sanctioned widespread training of paraprofessionals to increase availability of helpers (Gershon & Biller, 1977; Guerney, 1969; Karlsruher, 1974; Sobey, 1970). Many of these paraprofessional programs have been developed around the concept that people are best understood and helped by those who have experienced and solved similar problems. For example, children and adolescents who have had problems learning or those who have belonged to juvenile gangs are recruited to be peer tutors and counselors (e.g., Allen, 1976).

The professionals directly involved in psychoeducational interventions represent a wide spectrum. For example, mental health professionals include clinical psychologists, child psychiatrists, community mental health workers, social workers, and marriage counselors; and are involved in clinics, hospitals, mental health centers, counseling centers, welfare agencies, correctional institutions, and private practice. School professionals, of course, also are involved on a large scale in psychoeducational interventions for children both in regular and spcial education settings.

When the "general practitioner" and the regular second line resources are unable to provide a satisfactory intervention, specialists usually are considered necessary. Unfortunately, those who can deal with particularly complex problems and exceptional populations are a very limited group and the costs related to the services they provide make them relatively inaccessible to many who need their services. This limited accessibility means that although theoretically there is a large number of interveners, in practice, some children have very few, if any, options.

Intervener Facilitation

Systematic implementation of intervention is accomplished by planning and initiating transactions that realistically account for the current status of the child and his or her environment. Deciding on appropriate means involves identifying a wide range of alternative actions and selecting those that are consistent with the underlying intervention rationale and that anticipate interfering factors. Such activities may take the form of direct or vicarious experiences, reasoning, and verbal and other forms of social persuasion. If intervention is to be facilitated optimally, the intervener must use an appropriate range of methods to achieve a motivational and developmental match with the child. The plan must also avoid or minimize iatrogenic effects.[||]

Methods

Experienced interveners usually do not consider manipulating one procedure at a time. They usually have some overall method or implementation plan that guides selection of certain procedures and rejection of others.

For our purposes, intervention *methods* are defined as the regular, systematic, and orderly use of *tools* and *techniques,* based on a general *model* of intervention. A model is an overall pattern or plan that guides the course of intervention. It usually incorporates both content and the kinds of procedures (tools and techniques) to be pursued. For example, some models stress person changes in terms of personality and motivation and others primarily stress learning new behaviors and skills.

"Tools" are the specific instruments or types of actions-experiences-materials used to implement an intervention. For example, the concept includes activities such as role playing and other simulations, exercises, group discussions, and media and materials such as videotapes and self-help books.

Techniques are viewed as the way in which tools (e.g., materials, activities, tasks) are developed and used. For instance, the same activity can be pursued under different degrees of guidance and support by varying the amount of cueing and prompting. More specifically, with regard to immediate intent, techniques can be viewed as planned variations in the characteristics of a tool or the way it is applied. These variations are designed to increase attraction and accessibility and decrease avoidance and distraction. That is, the intent is to enhance motivation (attitudes, commitment, approach, follow-through), sensory intake (perceptual search and detection of external stimuli intended to initiate action and provide feedback), processing and decision making

---

[||]Iatrogenesis, comes from *iatros,* the Greek word for "physician," and *genesis,* meaning "origin." As used here, iatrogenic means any negative consequence resulting from an intentional intervention (Illich, 1976).

(evaluation and selection of stimuli and feedback), and output (practice application, and demonstration). (See Adelman & Taylor, 1983, for an outline summarizing techniques as categorized above.)

Motivational and Developmental Match

Psychological and educational interventions often are described as starting from "where the client is." In a common sense way, this maxim presents the essence of what is involved in facilitating intervention. For many interveners, this phrase simply means not initially requiring responses beyond current developmental levels (e.g., Hunt & Sullivan, 1974; Miller, 1981). For some, the phrase may mean matching current motivational levels, e.g., clarifying with the child with goals or changes he or she desires. For a few, the idea is understood to mean there is a need to match both motivation and development (i.e., to personalize intervention). This last position seems the most comprehensive.

In general, decisions about intervener methods are guided by a desire to establish a set of environmental opportunities (e.g., tasks, activities, settings) that maximize the likelihood of a good motivational and developmental match. Such a match is seen as appropriately challenging the client's assimilated way of adapting to environmental circumstances (Hunt, 1961). This leads to accommodative growth and learning, i.e., developing new ways to cope. With regard to the concept of the match, diverse areas of psychological research (e.g., on conceptual matching, perceived choice, attributions, expectations) converge in underscoring the importance of considering this factor as a key consideration in intervention planning (e.g., Friend & Neale, 1972; Hunt, 1975; Prentice-Dunn, Wilson & Lyons, 1981; Tobias, 1976).

Efforts to establish and maintain an optimal match are complicated by continuous changes resulting from experience and maturation. Further complications arise because of the varying degrees of understanding, access, and control interveners have over relevant environmental circumstances. Because of such complications, procedures to establish and maintain an optimal match are based on trial and appraisal. Some direction is provided by knowledge of the general trends and stages of human and organizational development and functioning. Further direction is provided when the intervener has acquired specific knowledge about particular objects of intervention as the result of assessment. Ideally, then, procedures are planned with reference to both a general and specific knowledge base. From a psychological perspective, the relevant knowledge base includes theory and data on major facets of functioning such as motivation, attention, information processing, decision making, and interpersonal dynamics.#

In evolving a motivational and developmental match, the initial focus of most interventions is one of minimizing nonfacilitative anxiety and establishing an appropriate (facilitative/constructive) interpersonal relationship and pattern of communicication between client and intervener. This initial focus can be viewed as providing a bridge between the establishment of a promising environment and the development of a working agreement and procedures for ongoing decision making (Adelman & Taylor, 1977; 1983). In addition, of course, the need for the intervener to focus on anxiety, relationship, and communication continues throughout the period of intervention. The importance of these concerns has made them central topics in the literature on helping relationships (e.g., Brammer & Shostrom, 1982; Kanfer & Goldstein, 1980).

Overcoming Iatrogenic Effects

Iatrogenic effects refer to problems that result from the methods used by interveners, i.e., negative effects such as errors in identification, self-fulfilling prophecies, increases in dependency, or somatic residual effects. Our only purpose here is to highlight the need to anticipate such effects and plan steps to minimize them. The importance of doing so relates both to intervention efficacy and ethical considerations. For this brief presentation, identification of three sources of negative effects must suffice. These are technical deficiencies, interpersonal dynamics, and misuse of intervention procedures.

Technical deficiencies. These probably have been discussed more than any other type of procedural concern. The most frequently cited examples of these deficiencies are the use of assessment procedures that have poor reliability and validity and lack appropriate norms for use as standards (e.g., Cronbach, 1970). Technical deficiencies related to prevailing assessment practices play a major role in generating problems in

---

#Depending on the intervener's orientation, these areas of functioning encompass such topics as the role of realistic goals, choice, commitment, incentives, curiosity, strivings for competence, schedules of reinforcement, negative consequences, feedback, expectation and set, intensity and vividness, cues, stimuli covariation, life circumstances, active participation, massed vs. distributed practice. overlearning, memory and assimilated schemata, group dynamics in informal and formal settings, sense of community, task focus vs. ego-oriented communication, leadership styles, and so forth.

identification and placement (e.g., false negative and false positive errors) and also are responsible for many of the problems that have been encountered in planning specific changes and evaluating the efficacy of interventions. In planning, generally the major recourse open to the intervener is to be cautious, especially avoiding methods that are extremely deficient, and to develop strategies to minimize inevitable negative effects.

Interpersonal dynamics. Interveners, of course, rely heavily on interpersonal dynamics to produce desired outcomes. These dynamics may also produce undesired effects that represent serious problems to be overcome, i.e., the intervener must plan how to avoid or eliminate them. In general, problems that result from interpersonal dynamics of intervention require the intervener's vigilance in watching for signs of their occurrence and planning strategies to counter them.

Examples of negative dynamic phenomena discussed in the literature are dependency, transference, countertransference, and resistance (Brammer & Shostrom, 1982; May, 1967; Rapaport, 1960; Rogers, 1951; Schuldt, 1966), the expert trap and the rescue/drama triangle (Adelman & Taylor, 1978; 1983; Karpman, 1968), and reactions to change (Baldridge, 1972; Bennis, Benne, & Chin, 1969; Haley, 1977; Lippitt, Watson, & Westley, 1958; Sarason, 1982). Another common experience with children and adolescents is realizing that some really don't want to engage in a particular intervention and may initiate a variety of avoidance strategies. We have designated these types of devious and deviant reactions to unwanted intervention as protective reactions (Adelman, 1982[##]). Given this understanding of its source, the behavior is dealt with as an iatrogenic effect and not treated as evidence of the severity and/or pervasiveness of the condition that is the focus of intervention.

Misuse of intervention procedures. Examples of these include: (1) prematurely applying inadequately validated procedures (Adelman, 1978; Adelman & Compas, 1977; Elinson, 1967; Ward & Kassebaum, 1972; Weiss, 1975); (2) allowing the limitations of currently available assessment (e.g., diagnostic and evaluation) procedures to limit the nature and scope of interventions (Cohen, 1972; Sjoberg, 1975); (3) inappropriately restricting choices and participation (Bierman, 1969; Ellsworth, Maroney, Klett, Gordon, & Gunn, 1971; Moss & MacIntosh, 1970; Rosenshine, 1971); (4) inappropriately gathering and using information (An-

---

[##]Adelman, HS. Anti-involvement attitudes toward corrective interventions; A neglected phenomena, 1982, unpublished manuscript.

astasi, 1966; Mercer, 1972; Wasserstrom, 1976; Willingham, 1967); and (5) inappropriately assigning the locus of causality to an individual when it is environmental (e.g., societal) factors that are responsible (Ryan, 1971). The negative consequences of such misuses involve the whole spectrum of practical and ethical iatrogenic concerns. The primary recourse for dealing with such problems is planning ways to avoid creating them. For this to occur, however, interveners must be aware of the forces that perpetuate such misuses, and they must be committed to combatting them.

Time of Intervention

In discussing the time of intervention, three simple categories have been chosen: prevention or before the need exists; early intervention or as soon after appearance of the need as is feasible; and remedial intervention after the need has existed for a while. Others have proposed similar categorizations (e.g., Caplan, 1964; Wagenfeld, 1972). Our review of the literature confirms that interveners generally recognize the desirability of prevention and early intervention (e.g., Caplan, 1964; Cowan, Gardner, & Zax, 1967), but they also recognize that such activity is not yet feasible on a large scale for most psychological problems (Cowen, 1982). Most intervention thus occurs after a problem has become fairly well established. This state of affairs is understandable given current knowledge and methodology (Kessler & Albee, 1975; Simon, 1972; Wagenfeld, 1972). For example, an important component in systematic and precise prevention efforts is an understanding of etiology; unfortunately, research has yet to provide satisfactory evidence as to the cause of many psychological problems. Another important component in such preventive efforts would be the availability of predictive procedures. Satisfactory tools for large scale predictive assessment, however, have yet to be developed (e.g., Adelman, 1978).

Without a comprehensive understanding of etiology and without satisfactory large scale screening procedures for prediction and "early identification" of psychological problems, early intervention generally has been targeted toward specific individuals, and thus has been applied on a relatively small scale. That is, individually oriented early intervention activity has been found appropriate only for that relatively small group of individuals with the most serious psychological problems. These types of problems usually are identified by general practitioners, teachers, parents, and friends without special assessment procedures. Group-oriented early interventions, while not necessarily based on the assessment of individuals, still are shaped by views as to the causes of the current and anticipated problems that the programs intend to reduce or eliminate. Such interventions also have been limited by current understanding of etiological factors. Data related to the efficacy of such early interventions as Head Start, parent training, and comprehensive physical, psychosocial, and education "health" maintenance programs are either equivocal and controversial or yet to be gathered (e.g., Austin, 1976; Hobbs, 1975; Zigler, Abelson, Trickett, & Seitz, 1982).

Finally, it should be noted that this categorization of time and intervention tends to emphasize a problem orientation and thus raises the usual concerns over such a "pathological" bias, e.g., interventions that view clients as deficient/defective. A very different time perspective arises when the focus shifts to "positive mental health" (Jahoda, 1958). The emphasis becomes one of providing programs for health maintenance, maximizing growth, actualization, and competence, for which there are no clear time boundaries.

Level of Intervention Focus

The notion that psychological and educational problems can be conceptualized hierarchically has been discussed directly or implied by numerous writers (e.g., Adelman, 1971; Bruner, 1966; Carkhuff & Berenson, 1967; Hewett, 1968; Maslow, 1954; Quay, 1973; Sundberg et al., 1973). For example for purposes of this discussion, the focus of intervention activity can be conceptualized as being on one or more of three hierarchical levels: on current tasks and interests (e.g., current personal and social problems, acquisition of competence in an area of current interest); on the prerequisites needed in order to function effectively on current tasks and interests (e.g., beginning skills and attitudes involved in social relating, working cooperatively, following directions); and on behaviors and underlying problems that may be interfering with performance and learning on the above levels (e.g., emotional and neurological disorders).

Conceiving intervention in terms of levels has numerous important implications. For instance, such a perspective points to the need for reliable and valid assessment to identify the appropriate level for intervention, as well as specific prescriptions at any level. Also implied is that once effective help is provided at a lower level, assistance may be required at the next higher level. More generally, such a perspective has led to suggestions that interventions be conceived in sequential and hierarchical terms (Adelman, 1971; Hewett, 1968). For example, once a child's phobic avoidance of others has been reduced he or she will probably need support in acquiring age appropriate social skills.

Degree of Disruptiveness/Restrictiveness

By definition, the impact of all interventions is disruptive of the "natural" course of events. By implication, such disruptions may be restrictive of choices and options. Treatment activities such as psychiatric hospitalization and special remedial school placement clearly are seen as disruptive and usually restrictive. The disruptive nature of many teaching and enrichment activities (e.g., public school programs, sex education, human relations training, assertiveness and effectiveness training) has not been so evident. Indeed, such activities have become a focal point for concern only when participation has become a compulsory part of being in an organization, when negative side effects have been widely experienced, or when the activity has taken on fad-like proportions and attracted entrepreneurs with little training and experience (Rogers, 1977).

Since all interventions can be an appropriate avenue for change and to this end are intended to be disruptive, it is clear that disruption per se is not the issue. What is of concern is how to accomplish desired changes with no more disruption and restriction of options than is absolutely necessary. Most interveners probably would agree that interventions should be guided by a principle of least intervention needed (Kanfer & Goldstein, 1980). For example, a child who can receive equivalent help at an outpatient child guidance clinic should not be in a residential psychiatric hospital; similarly a child whose reading problem can be corrected by a regular classroom teacher should not be placed in a remedial class; a family whose decision-making needs can be met by a short interview and consultation should not undergo extensive assessment. Recent trends in both mental health and education reflect a desire to adhere to this principle, e.g., establishment of community mental health centers and "mainstreaming" of exceptional children.

The dilemma remains one of how to match the person to the correct type and degree of intervention, while at the same time balancing the rights of the client and the needs of society (Kittrie, 1971). Strongly associated with this dilemma is the confusion over what problems and tasks require certain approaches and the lack of demonstrated effectiveness of many psychological and educational interventions. Periodically, the lack of demonstrated effectiveness has led to frustration on the part of many professionals and the general public, and this frustration has been a force for needed change in the nature and scope of interventions. Too often, however, the resultant changes have been naive fads rather than sound innovations, and thus have used limited valuable resources and disappointed the consumers and general public. While efforts to implement the principle of least restrictive/disruptive intervention have yielded new approaches, the innovations, for the most part, have not been effective. Consequently, this appears to be another example of a valuable principle that is beyond the field's ability to operationalize satisfactorily at this time.

CONCLUDING COMMENTS

The purpose of this chapter has been to introduce ways to think about psychological and educational interventions systematically and in general terms so that common ideas and concerns can be highlighted. There are distinct practical advantages to be gained from a systematic understanding of general concepts that underlie a variety of apparently discrete theories and practices.

Given the lack of satisfactory theory and research data and, in general, the limited state of knowledge regarding the phenomenon under discussion, no one theory or intervention is in a good position to claim it provides the definitive approach. As a result, many people would argue that an "eclectic" perspective seems to be reasonable. However, it is important to distinguish between naive, professional, and scholarly eclectism. Naive eclectism is seen as pulling together whatever feels intuitively right or seems to work, without concern for a set of systematically related underlying principles. It is the tendency to indiscriminately adopt and casually use newly encountered viewpoints, concepts, and techniques that results in a negative view of eclectism by some professionals. Such an approach, at the very least, is likely to compound the current lack of systematic understanding and inconsistency in carrying out interventions and, at the worst, may result in negative side effects that could have been anticipated and prevented. That is, naive eclectism probably maintains the status quo by adapting to and suffering with the problems that result from limited knowledge.

Professional/empirical eclectism results from years of experience in a field. As a result of their experience, professional practitioners have encountered and tried many procedures. They differentiate among those practices that never seem to work for them and thus should be avoided and those that are likely to be useful in a particular situation. In some instances, professionals develop a philosophical (as contrasted with a theoretical) stance and try to use only those practices that fit their philosophy.

By way of contrast, scholarly eclectism is based on systematic investigation and theoretical and philosophical analyses used to evolve a set of procedures that is comprehensive, integrated, and consistent. Such an approach not only may avoid the pitfalls noted above, but can have an heuristic value that helps advance knowledge. In effect, scholarly eclectism is not really eclectism, but model building in the best tradition of efforts to advance the field.

Understanding conceptual, ethical, and methodological concerns is essential to wise decision making related to intervening with children with problems. This understanding provides a basis for selecting among procedures and for decisions that are made. Such understanding also raises concerns regarding the appropriate relationship of means to ends, the desirability of specific ends, the processes by which ends and means of any given intervention are decided upon, and the degree to which planning should be participatory rather than unilateral. Of even greater importance, however, is the potential for refining research and theory and thus advancing the understanding of clinical interventions for children.

ACKNOWLEDGMENT

Some material in this chapter is adapted from H. Adelman and L. Taylor, *Learning Disabilities in Perspective* (1983) and is presented here with the kind permission of the publisher, Scott, Foresman & Co.

REFERENCES

Adelman, HS. The not so specific learning disability population. *Exceptional Children*, 1971, *37*, 528–533

Adelman, HS. Competency-based training in education. Monograph published by ERIC (ED090214), 1974

Adelman, HS. Predicting psychoeducational problems in childhood. *Behavioral Disorders*, 1978, *3*, 148–159

Adelman, HS. Diagnostic classification of LD: A practical necessity and a procedural problem. *Learning Disabilities Quarterly*, 1979, *2*, 56–62

Adelman, HS, & Compas, B. Stimulant drugs and learning problems. *Journal of Special Education*, 1977, *11*, 377–416

Adelman, HS, & Taylor, L. Two steps toward improving learning for students with (and without) "learning problems". *Journal of Learning Disabilities*, 1977, *10*, 455–461

Adelman, HS, & Taylor, L. Learning problems and the Fernald laboratory: Beyond the Fernald techniques. Presented at the World Conference of the Council for Exceptional Children, Stirling, Scotland, 1978

Adelman, HS, & Taylor, L. *Learning disabilities in perspective*. Glenview, Ill: Scott, Foresman & Co., 1983

Allen, VL. (Ed.). *Children as teachers: Theory and research on tutoring.* New York: Academic Press, 1976

Anastasi, A. (Ed.). Testing problems in perspective. (Twenty-fifth anniversary volume of topical readings from the invitational conference on testing problems.) American Council on Education, 1966

Austin, GR. *Early childhood education: An international perspective.* New York: Academic Press, 1976

Baldrige, VJ. Organizational change: The human relations perspective versus the political systems perspective. *Educational Researcher,* 1972, *1,* 4–10, 15

Bandura, A. *Social learning theory,* Englewood Cliffs, NJ: Prentice-Hall, 1977

Bandura, A. Self-efficacy mechanism in human agency. *American Psychologist,* 1982, *37,* 122–147

Beauchamp, TL, & Childress, JF. *Principles of biomedical ethics.* New York: Oxford University Press, 1979

Bennis, WG, Benne, KD, & Chin, R. (Eds.). *The planning of change.* (2nd ed.). New York: Holt, Rinehart & Winston, 1969

Bergin, AE, & Lambert, MJ. The evaluation of therapeutic outcomes. In SL Garfield & AE. Bergin (Eds.), *Handbook of psychotherapy and behavior change: An empirical analysis* (2nd ed.), New York: Wiley, 1978

Bertalanffy, L. von. *General systems theory: foundations, development, applications.* New York: Braziller, 1968

Bierman, R. Dimensions of interpersonal facilitation in psychotherapy and child development. *Psychological Bulletin,* 1969, *72,* 338–52

Biklen, D. Consent as a cornerstone concept. In J. Mearig & Associates (Ed.), *Working for children: Ethical issues beyond professional guidelines.* San Francisco: Jossey-Bass, 1978

Bowers, KS. Situationism in psychology: An analysis and a critique. *Psychological Review,* 1973, *80,* 207–336

Brammer, LM, & Shostrom, EL. *Therapeutic psychology* (4th ed.). Englewood Cliffs, NJ: Prentice-Hall, 1982

Brickman, P, Rabinowitz, VC, Karuza, J Jr, Coates, D, Cohn, E, & Kidder, L. Models of helping and coping. *American Psychologist,* 1982, *37,* 368–384

Bruner, JS. *Toward a theory of instruction.* New York: Norton & Co., 1966

Caplan, G. *Principles of preventive psychiatry.* New York: Basic Books, 1964

Caplan, G, & Killilea, M. (Eds.). *Support systems and mutual help: Multidisciplinary explorations.* New York: Grune & Stratton, 1976

Carkhuff, R, & Berenson, B. *Beyond counseling and therapy.* New York: Holt, Rinehart, & Winston, 1967

Cohen, DK. Politics and research: Evaluation of social action programs in education. In C Weiss (Ed.), *Evaluating action programs: Readings in social action and education.* Boston: Allyn & Bacon, 1972

Coles, GS. The learning disabilities battery: Empirical and social issues. *Harvard Educational Review,* 1978, *48,* 313–340

Collins, AH. Natural delivery systems: Accessible sources of power for mental health. *American Journal of Orthopsychiatry,* 1973, *43,* 36–42

Cowen, EL. Help is where you find it: Four informal helping groups. *American Psychologist,* 1982, *37,* 385–395

Cowen, EL, Gardner, EA, & Zax, M. *Emergent approaches to mental health problems.* New York: Appleton-Century-Crofts, 1967

Croghan, LM, & Fruetiger, AD. Contracting with children: A therapeutic tool. *Psychotherapy: Theory, Research and Practice,* 1977, *14,* 32–40

Cronbach, LJ. *Essentials of psychological testing* (3rd ed.). New York: Harper & Row, 1970

Day, L & Reznikoff, M. Social class, the treatment process, and parent's and children's expectations about child psychotherapy. *Journal of Clinical Child Psychology,* 1980, *9,* 195–198

Deci, E. *The psychology of self-determination.* Lexington, Mass: Lexington Books, 1980

Elinson, J. Effectiveness of social action programs in health and welfare. In *Assessing the effectiveness of child health services* (Report of the Fifty-sixth Ross Conference on Pediatric Research). Columbus: Ross Laboratories, 1967

Ellsworth, RB, Maroney, R, Klett, W, Gordon, H, & Gunn, R. Milieu characteristics of successful psychiatric treatment programs. *American Journal of Orthopsychiatry,* 1971, *41,* 427–441

Feinberg, J. *Social philosophy.* Englewood Cliffs, NJ: Prentice-Hall, 1973

Ford, DH, & Urban, HB. *Systems of psychotherapy: A comparative study.* New York: John Wiley and Sons, Inc., 1963

Frank, JD. *Persuasion and healing* (2nd ed.). Baltimore: Johns Hopkins Press, 1972

Frank, JD. Restoration of morale and behavior change. In A Burton (Ed.), *What makes behavior change possible?* New York: Brunner/Mazel, 1976

Frankl, V. *Man's search for meaning.* Boston: Beacon Press, 1959

Freud, S. *An outline of psychoanalysis.* Rev. Ed. New York: Norton, 1969

Friend, R, & Neale, J. Children's perceptions of success and failure: An attributional analysis of the effects of race and social class. *Developmental Psychology,* 1972, *7,* 124–128

Gershon, M, & Biller, HB. *The other helpers: Paraprofessionals and nonprofessionals in mental health.* Lexington, Mass: Lexington Books, 1977

Goldfried, MR. Toward the delineation of therapeutic change principles. *American Psychologist,* 1980, *35,* 991–999

Goodwin, L. Bridging the gap between social research and public policy: We have a case in point. *Journal of Applied Behavioral Science,* 1973, *9,* 85–114

Gordon, IJ. On early learning: The modifiability of human potential. In P Satz & JJ Ross (Eds.) *The disabled learner: Early detection and intervention.* Rotterdam University Press, 1973

Guerney, BG, Jr. (Ed.). *Psychotherapeutic agents: New roles for nonprofessionals, parents, and teachers.* New York: Holt, Rinehart & Winston, 1969

Haley, J. *Problem solving therapy.* San Francisco: Jossey-Bass, 1977

Hewett, PM. *The emotionally disturbed child in the classroom.* Boston. Allyn & Bacon, Inc., 1968

Hobbs, N. *The futures of children: Categories, labels and their consequences.* Report of the Project on Classification of Exceptional Children (Vol. 1). San Francisco: Jossey-Bass, 1975

Howard, KI, & Orlinsky, DE. Psychotherapeutic processes. In P Mussen & MR Rosenzweig (Eds.), *Annual Review of Psychology* (Vol. 23). Palo Alto: Annual Reviews Inc., 1972

Hunt, DE. Person-environment interaction: A challenge found wanting before it was tried. *Review of Educational Research,* 1975, *45,* 209–230

Hunt, DE, & Sullivan, EV. *Between psychology and education.* Chicago: Dryden Press, 1974

Hunt, JMcV. *Intelligence and experience.* New York: Ronald Press, 1961

Illich, I. *Medical nemesis.* New York: Pantheon Books, 1976

Jahoda, M. *Current concepts of positive mental health.* New York: Basic Books, 1958

Jones, E, & Nisbett, R. The actor and the observer: Divergent perceptions of the causes of behavior. In EE Jones, DE Kanouse, HH Kelley, RE Nisbett, S Valens, & B Weiner. *Attribution: Perceiving the causes of behavior.* Morristown, NJ: General Learning Press, 1972

Kanfer, FH. Self-management methods. In FH Kanfer & AP Goldstein (Eds.), *Helping people change* (2nd ed.). New York: Pergamon Press, 1980

Kanfer, FH, & Goldstein, AP. (Eds.) *Helping people change.* (2nd ed.), New York: Pergamon Press, 1980

Karlsruher, AE. The nonprofessional as a psychotherapeutic agent: A review of the empirical evidence pertaining to his effectiveness. *American Journal of Community Psychology*, 1974, *2*, 61–77

Karpman, S. Script drama analysis. *Transactional Analysis Bulletin*, 1968, *7*, 39–43

Kelley, JG, Snowden, LR, & Muñoz, RF. Social and community intervention. In MR Rosenzweig & LW Porter (Eds.), *Annual review of psychology*, Vol. 28. Palo Alto: Annual Reviews Inc., 1977

Kessler, M, & Albee, GW. Primary prevention. In MR Rosenzweig & LW Porter (Eds.), *Annual review of psychology* (Vol 26). Palo Alto: Annual Reviews Inc., 1975

Kittrie, NN. *The right to be different: Deviance and enforced therapy*. Baltimore: Johns Hopkins Press, 1971

Klein, M. *The psychoanalysis of children*. London: The Hogarth Press, 1932

Krause, MS. Construct validity for the evaluation of therapy outcomes. *Journal of Abnormal Psychology*, 1969, *14*, 524–530

Laing, RD, & Esterson, A. *Sanity, madness, and the family*. Baltimore: Penguin, 1970

Lee, SD, & Temerlin, MK. Social class, diagnosis, and prognosis for psychotherapy. *Psychotherapy: Theory, Research and Practice*, 1970, *7*, 181–185

Lippitt, R, Watson, J, & Westley, B. *The dynamics of planned change*. New York: Harcourt, Brace & Co., Inc., 1958

Mahoney, MJ. *Cognition and behavior modification*. Cambridge, Mass: Ballinger Pub. Co., 1974

Maslow, AH. *Motivation and personality*. New York: Harper, 1954

May, R. *Psychology and the human dilemma*. Princeton: D. Van Nostrand, 1967

Meichenbaum, D. *Cognitive behavior modification: An integrative approach*. New York: Plenum Press, 1977

Melton, GB. Effects of a state law permitting minors to consent to psychotherapy. *Professional Psychology*, 1981, *12*, 647–654

Mercer, JR. *Labeling the mentally retarded: Clinical and social system perspectives on mental retardation*. Berkeley: University of California Press, 1972

Mercer, JR. IQ: The lethal label. *Psychology Today*, 1973, *6*, 44–47, 95–97

Messer, SB, & Winokur, M. Some limits to the integration of psychoanalytic and behavior therapy. *American Psychologist*, 1980, *35*, 818–827

Messer, SB, & Winokur, M. Therapeutic change principles: Are commonalities more apparent than real? Comment section. *American Psychologist*, 1981, *36*, 1547–1548

Miller, A. Conceptual matching models and interactional research in education. *Review of Educational Research*, 1981, *51*, 33–84

Mischel, W. Toward a cognitive social learning reconceptualization of personality. *Psychological Review*, 1973, *80*, 252–283

Moss, RH, & MacIntosh, S. Mulitvariate study of the patient-therapist system: A replication and extension. *Journal of Consulting and Clinical Psychology*, 1970, *35*, 298–307

Moustakas, C. *Children in play therapy*. New York: Jason Aronson, 1973

Murphy, J. Incompetence and paternalism. *Archiv fur Rechts-und-sozialphilosophie*, 1974, *50*, 465–486. As cited in TL Beauchamp & JF Childress, *Principles of biomedical ethics*. New York: Oxford University Press, 1979

Nicholls, JG. Quality and equality in intellectual development: The role of motivation in education. *American Psychologist*, 1979, *34*, 1071–1084

Norcross, JC. All in the family? On therapeutic commonalities. Comment section. *American Psychologist*, 1981, *36*, 1544–1545

O'Leary, KD. The assessment of psychopathology in children. In HC Quay & JS Werry (Eds.), *Psychopathological disorders of childhood*. New York: Wiley, 1972

Ozer, MN. *Solving learning and behavior problems of children: A planning system integrating assessment and treatment.* San Francisco: Jossey-Bass, 1980

Parloff, MB, Kelman, HC, & Prank, JD. Comfort, effectiveness, and self-awareness as criteria of improvement in psychotherapy. *American Journal of Psychiatry,* 1954, *3,* 343–351

Parloff, MB, Waskow, IE, & Wolfe, BE. Research on therapist variables in relation to process and outcome. In SL Garfield & AE Bergin (Eds.), *Handbook of psychotherapy and behavior change: An empirical analysis* (2nd ed.). New York: Wiley, 1978

Perlmuter, LC, & Montey, RA. The importance of perceived control: Fact or fantasy? *American Scientist,* 1977, *65,* 759–765

Perlmuter, LC, & Monty, RA. (Eds.) *Choice and perceived control.* Hillsdale, NJ: Erlbaum Associates, 1979

Perls, FS, Hefferline, RF, & Goodman, P. *Gestalt therapy.* New York: Julian Press, 1951

Prentice-Dunn, S, Wilson, D, & Lyman, R. Client factors related to outcome in a residential and day treatment program for children. *Journal of Clinical Child Psychology,* 1981, *10,* 188–190

Quay, HC. Special education: Assumptions, techniques, and evaluation criteria. *Exceptional Children,* 1973, *40,* 165–170

Rapaport, D. The structure of psychoanalytic theory: A systematizing attempt. *Psychological Issues,* 1960, *2,* 1–158

Rhodes, WC, & Tracy, MC. *A study of child variance: Intervention.* (Vol. 2). Ann Arbor: University of Michigan Press, 1972

Robinson, DN. Harm, offense, and nuisance: Some first steps in the establishment of an ethics of treatment. *American Psychologist,* 1974, *29,* 233–238

Rogers, CR. *Client-centered therapy.* Boston: Houghton Mifflin, 1951

Rogers, CR. *On personal power: Inner strength and its revolutionary impact.* New York: Delacorte Press, 1977

Rosenshine, B. Teaching behaviors related to pupil achievement: A review of research. In I Westbury & AA Bellack (Eds.), *Research in classroom processes: Recent developments and next steps.* New York: Teachers College Press, 1971

Rossi, PH, Freeman, HE, & Wright, SR. *Evaluation: A systematic approach.* Beverly Hills: Sage Publications, 1979

Ryan, W. *Blaming the victim.* New York: Random House, 1971

Sarason, SB. *The culture of the school and the problem of change* (2nd ed.) Boston: Allyn & Bacon, Inc., 1982

Schuldt, JW. Psychotherapists' approach-avoidance responses and clients' expressions of dependency. *Journal of Counseling Psychology,* 1966, *13,* 178–183

Simon, WB. Some issues in the logic of prevention. *Social Science and Medicine,* 1972, *6,* 95–107

Sjoberg, G. Politics, ethics and evaluation research. In M Guttentag & EL Struening (Eds.), *Handbook of evaluation research* (Vol. 2). Beverly Hills: Sage Publ, 1975

Smith, MB. Personal values in the study of lives. In RW White (Ed.), *The study of lives.* Englewood Cliffs, NJ: Prentice-Hall, 1963

Sobey, F. *The nonprofessional revolution in mental health.* New York: Columbia University Press, 1970

Spivak, G, Platt, J, & Shure, N. *The problem solving approach to adjustment.* San Francisco: Jossey-Bass, 1976

Strupp, HH, & Hadley, SM. A tripartite model of mental health and therapeutic outcomes with special reference to negative effects in psychotherapy. *American Psychologist,* 1977, *32,* 187–196

Sundberg, ND, Tyler, LE, & Taplin, JR. *Clinical psychology: Expanding horizons.* Englewood Cliffs, NJ: Prentice-Hall, Inc., 1973

Sundland, DM. Theoretical orientations of psychotherapists. In AS Gurman & AM Razin (Eds.), *Effective psychotherapy: A handbook of research.* New York: Pergamon, 1977

Suran, BG, & Rizzo, JV. *Special children: An integrative approach.* Glenview, Ill: Scott, Foresman & Co., 1979

Szasz, TS. Psychiatric classification as a strategy of personal constraint. In TS Szasz (Ed.), *Ideology and insanity.* New York: Doubleday, 1969

Tobias, S. Achievement treatment interactions. *Review of Educational Research,* 1976, *46,* 61–74

Urban, HB, & Ford, DH. Some historical and conceptual perspectives on psychotherapy and behavior change. In AE Bergin & SL Garfield (Eds.), *Handbook of psychotherapy and behavior change.* New York: Wiley & Sons, Inc., 1971

Wagenfield, MO. The primary prevention of mental illness: A sociological perspective. *Journal of Health and Social Behavior.* 1972, *13,* 195–203

Ward, D, & Kassebaum, GG. On biting the hand that feeds: Some implications of sociological evaluations of correctional effectiveness. In C Weiss (Ed.), *Evaluating action programs: Readings in social action and education.* Boston: Allyn & Bacon, 1972

Wasserstrom, R. The legal and philosphical foundations of the right to privacy. Unpublished manuscript, University of California at Los Angeles, 1976

Webster's Third New International Dictionary. Springfield, Mass: GC. Merriam Co., 1976

Weiss CH. (Ed.). *Evaluating action programs: Readings in social action and education.* Boston: Allyn & Bacon, Inc., 1972

Weiss, CH. Evaluation research in the political context. In EL Struening & M Guttentag (Eds.), *Handbook of evaluation research* (Vol. 1). Beverly Hills: Sage Publications, 1975

Weithorn, LA, & Campbell, SB. Informed consent for treatment: An empirical study of children's capacities. *Child Development,* 1982, *53,* 413–425

Willingham, WW. (Ed.). Invasion of privacy in research and testing (Proceedings of a symposium sponsored by the National Council on Measurement in Education). Published as a supplement to the *Journal of Educational Measurement,* 1967, *4,* 1

Zigler, E, Abelson, WD, Trickett, PK, & Seitz, V. Is an intervention program necessary in order to improve economically disadvantaged children's IQ scores. *Child Development,* 1982, *53,* 340–348

J. Conrad Schwarz

3

Childhood Psychopathology

CLASSIFICATION, EPIDEMIOLOGY, AND PROGNOSIS

How Shall Deviancy Be Called?

Childhood psychopathology is one of a number of labels applied to deviant behavior in children. Others include psychological disturbance, mental disease, mental disorder, psychiatric disorder, psychological disorder, emotional disorder, behavioral disorder, or simply, abnormality. Does it make a difference which of these terms we use? Yes and no. No, because they are synonyms that denote the same deviant behavior patterns, and yes, because they have differences in connotative meaning. Each has slightly different connotations with regard to the nature and cause of the deviance, connotations that arise from the history of the meaning of the term.

First, I will consider the connotations with regard to the nature of the problem. Labels that include "psycho-" suggest that the problem is in the mind, a mental problem. However, the connotations of psycho-have changed. Since psychology has been defined as the science of behavior, psycho- now connotes a focus on behavior. The term "emotional" suggests that it is the emotions that are out of regulation, and the term "behavior" suggests that behavior is deregulated. Historically, the terms "ill," "diseased," and "pathological" have all suggested suffering and discomfort, but since the rise of medical science in the 1th century, they have come to connote biological infection. More recently, "pathological" and "diseased" have come to denote any deviation from a normal or healthy condition of mind, body, or society (Stein, 1982). The term "psychopathology" is thus generally taken to mean behavioral abnormality, while, according to its historical connotations, it may suggest to some ears biological infection of the organ of mind, that is, the brain.

The tension between professional disciplines over labels is centered on their connotations with regard to the causes of behavioral deviance. Labels have become a weapon in the struggle for professional pre-eminence and legitimacy as providers of service for a fee (Schacht & Nathan, 1977). Regardless of true cause, labels that, in the mind of the public, connote biochemical cause or dysfunction (whether by infection, heredity, or exogenous physical-chemical insult) tend to favor the medically trained as service providers; labels that connote socially acquired behavioral dysfunction tend to favor as service providers professionals with training in social-behavioral therapies. Jurisdictional disputes and the struggle for professional hegomony and the right to third party payment fuel the controversy over labels. Since many childhood behavioral disorders seem to have multiple causes (for example, infantile autism and childhood schizophrenia) and since the nature of the treatment is not always dictated by the cause, the controversy over the connotations of labels cannot be resolved on the weight of the evidence. In this chapter the terms psychopathology and behavior disorder will be used interchangeably to refer to deviant or abnormal patterns of behavior.

The Judgment of Behavioral Deviancy in Children

What standards are typically used in judging behavioral deviancy versus normalcy in children? Why do we sometimes find disagreement among observers?

The diagnostic labeling process for children typically begins in the home or school. The child's behavior calls attention to itself for one of three reasons: it is noxious and troublesome to others; it evokes empathetic concern in others because of the child's discomfort; or it evokes concern because of anticipated future discomfort to the child or others given the future implications of the current behavior pattern (e.g., retarded performance).

Typically, after the preliminary judgment of parents and teachers that a child is behaviorally deviant, the opinion of a school counselor or of a family physician is sought. Their concurrence may then result in referral to a clinical child psychologist or psychiatrist. This professional hierarchy of specialized training in and knowledge of childhood disorders also defines the hierarchy of power as labelers of disorder (Ullmann & Krasner, 1975) and as controllers of disposition and treatment. The legal status and public respect accorded the clinical psychologist and the psychiatrist cause others to accept the labels that these professionals apply and increase the likelihood that their (and not others') recommendations will be followed. Once a child has entered the diagnostic hierarchy, concurrence in the judgment of deviancy at each level facilitates movement toward contact with the most expert and powerful labelers.

Reliability of Diagnosis

Disagreement about the presence of significant deviancy often occurs between observers at the same and at different levels in the hierarchy. These differences arise from two basic causes, differences in the samples of behavior viewed by different observers, and divergent evaluative reactions to the same behavior.

Situational specificity of behavior is a source of unreliability in diagnosis. Although children's behavior has some generality across settings, and especially the behavior of children severely disturbed or under considerable stress (Hetherington, Cox, & Cox, 1979b), most children show variation in their typical response as a function of the context. This variation can result in disagreement about deviancy between parents, teachers, and mental health professionals. Children who are devils at home can be angels in the psychologist's office, at least for the first few visits (Lobitz & Johnson, 1975). The children of strict, punitive parents often toe the mark at home but, to the dismay of their parents, may terrorize permissive and insecure teachers. Miller (1964) examined agreement about the presence of symptoms in children between parents, teachers, and clinicians, using the Q-sort method. He found that the greatest average agreement (.60) occurred between parents and that the largest number of symptoms were reported by parents. On the average, the greatest average agreement between parents and teachers was .35, between parents and clinicians .37, and between teachers and clinicians .24. Parents, of course, observe the child in the same situation and also have spent more time with the child than any other class of observer. Their judgments are probably the most valid for the child's behavior in the home setting.

The context in which the behavior occurs also influences judgments about its deviancy. For example, a child who is very active and equally so at the Boys' Club, at home, and in school, may be viewed as perfectly normal by the Boys' Club staff, as full of energy by his parents, and as hyperactive and deviant by the teacher in the school context where sedentary behavior and sustained attention to a single task are demanded.

For example, Klein and Gittelman-Klein (1975) found that of 155 subjects who were judged hyperactive in the classroom, only 25 percent were judged hyperactive at home.

Divergent Evaluative Reactions

Another source of diagnostic disagreement, especially among individuals at different levels of the diagnostic hierarchy is differences among observers in evaluative frameworks. Divergence may result from differences in tolerance, values, knowledge, and training. Often because of differences in tolerance, or what Kanner (1960) calls "annoyance threshold," one of the parents may believe their child to be normally active and aggressive while the other sees pathology. In fact, in one study (Shepherd, Oppenheim, & Mitchell, 1966) it was found that the symptoms of children brought to a mental health clinic did not differ significantly from those of a control group of randomly selected children; however, the parents of the clinic children were less able to cope with misbehavior and more likely to consult others with their problems. Parents' standards for assessing deviancy in children can vary greatly because they often lack age-appropriate norms for behavioral development. Some parents are distressed because their 4-year-olds do not listen to reason and will not confess misdeeds, behaviors seldom seen until age 8 or 9. Technical knowledge about behavioral development, both normative and prognostic, is evoked when evaluating children's behavior. Behaviors that are normal in an adult (working rather than attending school, wearing make-up, being sexually active) are judged as deviant in children. Behaviors that are considered normal in a 6-month-old (such as wetting the bed, drinking from a bottle, and crying when the caretaker leaves the child's sight) are considered deviant in a 5-year-old. The age-appropriateness of behaviors is thus a major consideration when judging childhood behavior. Technical knowledge about the longitudinal correlates of behavior plays a part in determining judgments of deviancy and the urgency of intervention.

Diagnostic Classification: Issues and Controversy

When one mentions diagnostic controversy, the system of classification that comes to mind is that embodied in the American Psychiatric Association's *Diagnostic and Statistical Manual of Mental Disorders,* third edition (APA, 1980). It is important to keep in mind that DSM-III represents only one of several systems for assessing and diagnosing childhood psychopathology. Other systems include psychodynamic assessments of the causes, meaning, and function of a child's deviant behavior, and behavioral-analytic assessment of the deviant behavior in terms of its stimulus antecedents and consequent reinforcing events. Systems of assessment are not mutually exclusive and each is designed to serve best a particular set of functions. Behavior-analytic assessment contributes little to decisions about the use of psychoactive drugs or to the development of epidemiological data on the incidence of various types of disorder, and psychiatric classification contributes little to the planning of behavioral treatment programs. As Robert Spitzer has stated, "Classifications (and I would add, assessment systems) are man-made, are always for one or more specific purposes, and continually need to be tested and revised based on further knowledge" (1982).

What have been the specific objections to the use of psychiatric classification as an assessment system? Among the most frequently reiterated are the following: Each child is unique. The use of DSM-III forces one to put in the same category children who are very dissimilar. Categorizing and labeling supports the medical model (cf. Albee, 1969). Categorizing is a crude and primitive form of assessment and stigmatizes children (cf. Hobbs, 1975). In the following section I will first look at psychiatric assessment from the perspective of measurement and then consider the purposes served by classification.

Classification as Measurement

There are two major types of measurement, categorical and continuous. In categorical measurement people or objects are grouped together by kind, that is, qualitatively. In continuous measurement, people or objects are grouped together by amount of or degree of a potentially variable property, that is, quantitatively. Psychiatric classification is categorical measurement; people are legitimately grouped together into the same category when each possesses all of the defining properties of the category (Stevens, 1958). The key term here is "defining properties." For example, I may define a category in terms of the following three properties: fits of rage at least weekly, intermittent anxiety or depression, and absence of hallucinations. The label for the category is arbitrary; however, it typically reflects some of the properties, as, for example, the label "enraged personality disorder" that I could give this hypothetical syndrome. If an individual possesses these three behavioral properties or criteria, he qualifies for the enraged personality disorder category regardless of other behaviors he may exhibit and other categories for which his behavior may also qualify. An individual may fit more than one category, for example, being both male and a Democrat. Irrelevant to category membership is the individual's level of self-esteem, activity, work record, etc.; these are not defining properties of the category. Often continuous measurement is used to assess defining properties of category membership, for example, anxiety, a symptom that occurs in degree.

Both categorical and continuous measurements of behavior must be reliable to be useful, that is, repeatable operations must lead to similar judgments with regard to category membership or placement on the continuum of amount. Reliability, in turn, requires repeatable samples of behavior, objective procedures for abstracting behavior, and objective rules for proceeding from behavioral abstractions to category membership or placement on the quantitative continuum.

When psychiatric classification of children is viewed from this perspective, those children whose behaviors fit a particular category need not be identical; they need only possess the behavioral attributes chosen to define the category; they may vary in every other respect. If a clinician assigns a category label to the behaviors of a child when the behavior does not possess all of the defining properties of the category, the clinician is misusing the system. Furthermore, a child may qualify for two or more diagnostic labels, provided that the categories are not defined as mutually exclusive.

The Utility of Classification

Categorical classification of psychopathology serves three functions: communication, prognosis, and research. To the extent that a classification system is shared by others, it can serve as a nomenclature or taxonomy, a set of labels each of which stands for a different pattern of behavioral symptoms and serves as an economical method of communicating about the client's behavior. A few words then can stand in place of paragraphs of behavioral description. To serve this function well, the system needs as many categories as there are distinctive patterns of behavior, but not so many that the system is unwieldy and therefore not widely employed. In addition to broad coverage, assignment to categories must be reliable. There is a trade-off between reliability and coverage. When categories are defined with sufficient rigor to yield high agreement among observers, the behavior of many individuals does not fit any category; with loosely defined categories the behavior of more individuals can be categorized, but with less agreement among observers about the appropriate category (Blashfield, 1973).

Walter Mischel, a leading proponent of the situational specificity of behavior, recently endorsed the utility of classification for processing information with the following statement, "Categorizations are an inevitable, fundamental, and pervasive aspect of information processing, one that is built into our cognitive economics . . . (they) are the foundation of efficient information processing and thought" (1979, p. 744). He then added, "Categorizing at the middle level of abstraction minimizes both parsimony—a few broad categories are formed—and richness—there are many features common to members of each particular category" (p. 745). These statements acknowledge both the utility of classification for processing information and the trade-off between the utility of, and the degree of detail in the system of classification (Pfeiffer, 1980).

When category membership has correlates in addition to those that define membership, a category label has value beyond its shorthand communication function. These correlates may include other behaviors that are probable concomitants of the syndrome, a probable future course for the disorder in the absence of treatment, the likely response to various therapies, and information about prevention in the future. The more useful the predictions that can be made from category membership, the more valuable is knowledge of category membership. The prognostic value of categories arises from empirical research. Studying the life course and response to treatment of individuals with a common behavioral syndrome builds knowledge about the prognostic correlates of that category. Categories are often subdivided when other properties (behavioral or biochemical) prove to be predictive of treatment response, prevention, or prognosis. Since categories are man-made, they will continue to evolve to accommodate new empirical knowledge, and the new categories, in turn, may lead to the discovery of previously unknown correlates of category membership. Later in this chapter the demographic and prognostic correlates of major categories of childhood disorder are examined.

Research is necessary to increase the useful correlates of diagnostic categories. This accrual of knowledge is facilitated when researchers studying a given category of disorder use the same criteria for the selection of subjects. Uniform selection criteria permit comparisons between studies conducted in different settings and independent replication of results. Because the descriptions of categories in the earlier edition of the *Diagnostic and Statistical Manual* (DSM-II, APA, 1968) lacked sufficient detail, research was impeded. Feighner, Robins, Guze, Woodruff, Winokur, and Munoz (1972) published research criteria for selected disorders that yielded high diagnostic agreement and these criteria, in part, served as a model for defining categories of disorder in the new edition, DSM-III (APA, 1980). The researcher needs a precise definition because he or she is highly motivated to include only those individuals whose behaviors exactly fit the category. Erroneous inclusion of subjects reduces the likelihood of finding significant relationships between category membership and other variables. The clinician, on the other hand, is often motivated to include individuals in a category when clearly they do not fit the criteria. The clinician may need a label for shorthand communication and no category fits perfectly, or the clinician may wish to justify the use of a particular therapy, for example, drug therapy for hyperactivity. Thus, the researcher is biased toward underinclusion and the clinician toward overinclusion. It is the need to put every person's behavior into an existing category that results in erroneous and misleading classification.

However, the psychiatric classification system is not of equal value to all mental health professionals. Beyond its communication value, it is of little use to behavior modifiers, family therapists, Gestalt therapists, psychoanalysts, and therapists who take a transactional view. On the other hand, categorization may be of great value to researchers pursuing the antecedants of specific disorders, whether social, genetic, or biochemical in nature; to psychopharmacological therapists and researchers; and to epidemiologists. Some constructs are better suited to the discovery of one class of determinants than another.

Those professionals whose descriptive and predictive needs have not been met by the psychiatric classification system have developed or advocated the development of alternative systems. A case in point is McLemore and Benjamin (1979), who recently advocated that psychologists develop their own interpersonal nosology based on Benjamin's structural analysis of social behavior. Such a system, they assert, would be more useful in planning psychotherapeutic interventions than the psychiatric system, whereas the later system, they concede, may be more useful for decisions regarding hospitalization and medication. Similarly, within the field of special education, a system has evolved for classifying childhood disorders, a system tailored to the needs of educational settings and only partially overlapping with the psychiatric system (see Forness & Cantwell, 1982). Also, among family therapists there seems to be a growing interest in family diagnosis (see reviews by Fisher, 1976; Kelsey-Smith, & Beavers, 1981; Ksacke, 1981). While considerable commonality exists with respect to the dimensions of family structure and function deemed in need of assessment (Fisher, 1976), the techniques of assessment in use are extremely diverse and, for the most part, informal and lacking in validation (Ksacke, 1981). A few tentative steps have been taken toward developing descriptive taxonomy of family types (Kelsey-Smith & Beavers, 1981); however, no system is as yet widely shared, a condition that, when achieved, will accelerate the accrual of useful correlates of category membership. Other systems of diagnosis and assessment may thus be of greater utility to some professionals than the system deemed most useful to the American Psychiatric Association. Whether psychiatric classification is useful to a given professional depends on whether he or she needs to communicate about the syndromes of behavior described therein or to make predictions (prognoses, treatment decisions) in the domain of the correlates established for those syndromes.

Development of the Psychiatric Classification System of Childhood Disorders

The classification system for childhood disorders currently endorsed by the American Psychiatric Association and embodied in DSM-III (APA, 1980) (see abstract in Table 3-1) was preceded by several other comprehensive classification systems. These included prior editions of the *Diagnostic and Statistical Manual,* DSM-I (1952), DSM-II (1968), the classification guide proposed by the committee on Child Psychiatry of the Group for the Advancement of Psychiatry (GAP Report No. 62, 1966), and the system developed by Rutter, Shaffer, and Shepherd (1975) for the World Health Organization. How did these systems originate, how and why do they change?

The development and evolution of classification systems perhaps can be understood best in terms of their functions, namely, the communication function (nomenclature, nosology, taxonomy) and the knowledge function (etiology, prevention, prognosis, and treatment). Categories and accompanying labels are created to facilitate communication about patterns of disordered behavior that occur frequently in the experience of practicing clinicians: the greater the frequency, the greater the need to communicate succinctly. Categories and subcategories also are created when there is a behavioral, or physical basis for distinguishing between groups of individuals whose patterns of deviant behavior are likely, on the basis of research or clinical experience, to have distinctive prognoses and/or positive responses to specific treatments. For example, in 1943 Kanner published a paper in which he described the common behavioral characteristics of 13 children who from a very early age exhibited a lack of emotional attachment to others, peculiar communication deficits, and cognitive features that led him to differentiate them from retarded children. The defining attributes of a new syndrome (category) labeled "early infantile autism" were proposed. In a later paper, Eisenberg and Kanner (1956) reported prognostic correlates of membership in this category based on longitudinal observation of 100 children who fit the category. The category label presently carries prognostic information. Someday more effective treatment or prevention for this distinctive behavioral syndrome may be discovered. The current classification system, then, is a collection of the categories of syndromes as originally defined or as subsequently modified by clinicians and researchers over several decades.

High-speed computers have been enlisted recently in the task of discovering potentially useful categories of disorder. Syndromes are being redefined on the basis of empirical analysis of symptom data from very

Table 3-1
Outline of DSM-III Classification System of Disorders Usually First Evident in Infancy, Childhood, or Adolescence Grouped by Area of Predominant Disturbance

Intellectual
  Mental Retardation

Behavioral (Overt)
  Attention Deficit Disorder
      With Hyperactivity
      Without Hyperactivity
      Residual Type
  Conduct Disorder
      Socialized Nonaggressive Type
      Socialized Aggressive Type
      Undersocialized Nonaggressive Type
      Undersocialized Aggressive Type
      Atypical Conduct Disorder

Emotional
  Anxiety Disorders of Childhood or Adolescence
      Separation Anxiety Disorder
      Avoidant Disorder of Childhood or Adolescence
      Overanxious Disorder
  Other Disorders of Infancy, Childhood, or Adolescence
      Reactive Attachment Disorder of Infancy
      Schizoid Disorder of Childhood or Adolescence
      Elective Mutism
      Oppositional Disorder
      Gender Identity Disorder of Childhood

Physical
  Eating Disorder
      Anorexia Nervosa
      Bulimia
      Pica
      Rumination Disorder of Infancy
  Stereotyped Movement Disorders
      Transient Tic Disorders
      Chronic Motor Tic Disorder
      Tourette's Syndrome
      Atypical Stereotyped Movement Disorder
  Other Disorders With Physical Manifestations
      Stuttering
      Functional Enuresis
      Functional Encopresis
      Sleepwalking Disorder
      Sleep Terror Disorder

Developmental
  Pervasive Developmental Disorders
      Infantile Autism, Full Syndrome, Residual State
      Childhood Onset Pervasive Developmental Disorder
      Atypical Pervasive Developmental Disorder
  Specific Developmental Disorders (Axis II)
      Developmental Reading Disorder
      Developmental Arithmetic Disorder
      Developmental Language Disorder, Expressive Type Receptive Type
      Developmental Articulation Disorder
      Mixed Specific Developmental Disorder
      Atypical Specific Developmental Disorder

Other Diagnostic Categories That Often Will be
Appropriate for Children or Adolescents
      Organic Mental Disorders   Somatoform Disorders
      Substance Use Disorders   Personality Disorders
      Schizophrenic Disorders   Psychosexual Disorders
      Affecting Disorders   Adjustment Disorders
      Schizophreniform Disorders   Psychological Factors Affecting Physical
                                       Condition
  Anxiety Disorders

Adapted from American Psychiatric Association (1980). © 1980 American Psychiatric Association. Reprinted by permission of the publisher.

large samples (see Achenbach & Edelbrock, 1978). The paradigm for this research is as follows: Data on the presence-absence or degree of many symptoms (100 or more) is gathered on a large, representative sample of behaviorally disordered individuals. The 100 or more symptoms are reduced by factor analysis to a smaller number of independent symptom dimensions (10 to 20). The scores of each individual on the symptom dimensions are used as input for a cluster analysis, a statistical algorithm that searches for groups or clusters of individuals with similar profiles of symptom intensity (see Blashfield, 1980). The generality of the clusters discovered in one sample is assessed by repeating the analysis on an independent sample. Clusters that consistently appear in new samples are considered stable and generalizable. The pattern of symptoms that define membership in a cluster becomes the criteria that define membership in a category or syndrome.

The outcome of an empirical search for syndromes with the paradigm described above depends heavily on two factors, the adequacy of the data on symptoms and the composition of the sample of children studied. Ideally, one would prefer highly reliable symptom information based on observation in multiple contexts. The range of symptoms assessed and their redundancy in the total pool of symptom dimensions determine the number of symptom factors that will result. If one fails to ask about hallucinations, or asks only one question, a factor representing hallucinatory behavior will not emerge from the analysis even though this may be an important and independent dimension. Factor analysis cannot rise above the limitations of the input variables. Stated in the vernacular of the data cruncher this means "Garbage in, garbage out." A parallel problem exists with respect to the sample of children. If there are no psychotic children or only one or two in the sample studied, no cluster of children with a psychotic behavior profile will emerge. Thus, rare syndromes, such as infantile autism, which has an incidence of 4 in 10,000, are not likely to be discovered via cluster analysis unless the sample is preselected for severe behavioral disturbance.

The search for syndromes of childhood disorder on the grand scale of the above paradigm has just begun. However, it was foreshadowed by an early cluster-analytic study by Jenkins (1966) that employed 500 child guidance clinic cases and 90 symptom dimensions unreduced by factor analysis. Recently, Edelbrock and Achenbach (1980) have presented four separate empirically derived classification systems of childhood disorders, one each for males and females from 6 to 11 years and from 12 to 16 years, based on replicated profiles of factor scores. Children's factor scores were obtained by factor analyzing parent ratings on 113 symptoms, separately for each age-by-sex subgroup. The profile types were derived from cluster analyses with samples of 250 or more from a total of over 2,683 children, equally divided among clinic-referred and nonreferred cases. A second group of investigators (Nuechterlein, Soli, Garmezy, Devine, & Schaefer, 1981; Soli, Nuechterlein, Garmezy, Devine, & Schaefer, 1981), using the same paradigm and with case history information from over 300 clinic cases, has generated via cluster analysis separate classification systems for male and female children. These empirically derived systems, which show both similarities and differences, are likely to influence the next revision of the Diagnostic and Statistical Manual, just as Jenkins' study (1966) seems to have influenced DSM-II and DSM-III.

Jenkins' cluster analysis yielded five syndromes: two inhibited groups, the shy-seclusive and the overanxious-neurotic, and three aggressive groups, the hyperactive-distractible, the undomesticated, and the socialized delinquent. Two of the three anxiety disorders of childhood in DSM-III seem to be fashioned after Jenkins' inhibited groups (see Table 3-1). The DSM-III avoidant disorder of childhood parallels Jenkins' shy-seclusive group with symptoms of excessive timidity and absence of peer friendships, and the DSM-III overanxious disorder parallels Jenkins' overanxious-neurotic group with symptoms of unrealistic worry, inferiority feelings, and nervousness. Jenkins' hyperactive-distractible group is parallel to attention deficit disorder with hyperactivity from DSM-III. Jenkins' undomesticated and socialized delinquent groups parallel the two most prevalent types of conduct disorder described in DSM-III, the undersocialized aggressive type and the socialized nonaggressive type, respectively.

A significant change between DSM-II and DSM-III has been the de-emphasis of the diagnostic significance of the symptom of hyperactivity reflected in the deletion of hyperkinetic reaction and the inclusion of attention-deficit disorder with hyperactivity. This change may have been in response to numerous factor analytic studies (see review by Quay, 1979) showing that hyperactivity correlates with symptoms of conduct disorder (e.g., assaultive, tantrum prone, disobedient, destructive, imprudent, uncooperative, attention seeking), and that hyperactivity is not well correlated with other symptoms that suggest attention deficit (e.g., short attention span, poor concentration, daydreaming, inattention).

Empirical examination of the concurrence of symptoms in large numbers of disordered children thus suggests new syndromes that may prove more useful to practicing clinicians and researchers alike. These new syndromes, then, become part of the nomenclature recommended by the knowledgeable and influential members of the profession and endorsed by the profession as a whole.

Criticisms of the Structure and Content of the DSM-III Classification of Childhood Disorders

One of the major structural changes from DSM-II to DSM-III has been the introduction of a multiaxial diagnostic system. After identifying the clinical syndrome that may be descriptive of the child's behavior (on Axis I), the clinician is urged to describe on Axis II the client's personality features in terms of more enduring personality traits, personality disorders, and/or specific developmental disorders, and on Axis III any physical disorders or conditions that may also be present. These three axes constitute the official diagnostic assessment. Also suggested for use in special clinical and research settings are Axis IV, Severity of Psychosocial Stressors, and Axis V, Highest Level of Adaptive Functioning in Past Year.

In concert with other experts in psychopathology, Rutter and Shaffer (1980) in general praised the multiaxial framework of diagnosis. However, speaking from the perspective of epidemiologists, they have objected to the placement of mental retardation on the same diagnostic axis with emotional and conduct disorders. Separate axes, they believe, would have encouraged more complete recording. Because of this missed "opportunity," they fear that the statistics on mental retardation as it occurs in children with other psychiatric disorders will remain difficult to interpret. They also point out that specific developmental disorders, such as language delay, are not stable in children, and therefore do not fit well with the other features to be recorded on Axis II. Rutter and Shaffer are discomforted by the fact that the judgement of psychosocial stress (Axis IV) is so subjective. They seem to prefer that the manual provide empirical data on the risk-factor associated with potentially significant events, such as divorce or the death of a sibling. Regarding Axis V, Rutter and Shaffer believe that specifying the premorbid level of adjustment, rather than the highest level in the previous year, would be more meaningful in cases of disorders of more than a year's duration.

From DSM-II to DSM-III there has been a major increase (50%) in the number of listed disorders and especially in syndromes prevalent in childhood. Several critics of DSM-III have objected to the fact that many of the new syndromes of childhood are only mildly handicapping, but now, by virtue of their inclusion, they are labeled as "mental disorders" (Garmezy, 1978b; Rutter & Shaffer, 1980; Schacht & Nathan, 1977). The most frequently cited examples include developmental articulation disorder, developmental reading disorder, avoidant disorder, and oppositional disorder. Schacht and Nathan (1977) raised the possibility that financial, rather than scientific or clinical consideration, motivated the inclusion of these syndromes, and they objected to the assumption that such disorders are "medical conditions." Garmezy (1978b) objected to the inclusion of disorders such as oppositional and avoidant disorder on several grounds: that they are poorly validated as syndromes, that they are not sufficiently handicapping to be considered mental disorders, and that to label these and other mild deviations from the typical developmental path as "mental disorder" may have an unwarranted stigmatizing effect on the child. Rutter and Shaffer (1980) agree with Garmezy that the aforementioned disorders do not meet the "handicapping condition" criterion for mental disorders. They also agree with Garmezy in attacking any discriminatory use of classification; however, they do not reject classification merely because it has the potential to be misused. They express doubts along with Garmezy about the validity of the finer diagnostic distinctions among childhood disorders attempted by DSM-III. For example, they question whether oppositional disorder can be discriminated from conduct disorder in terms of etiology, course, or response to treatment. Spitzer (1982) responded to critics of DSM-III that the larger number of diagnostic categories was required to meet the clinician's and researcher's need for greater specificity in describing behavioral syndromes, and that syndromes were included on the basis of studies that supported the validity of these distinctions. Despite these controversies, all critics seem to agree that the greater specificity in diagnostic criteria and the delineation of the correlates of classifications are significant advances over DSM-II.

Epidemiology of Childhood Psychopathology

There are two major questions to be answered in this section: How prevalent are psychopathological disorders in children? and What are the demographic and prognostic correlates of various types of disorders? The term *prevalence* refers to the number of cases existing in a given population at a given period or point in time. The term *incidence* refers to the number of new cases that have emerged in a given time period. Designating an individual's behavior as disordered, that is, promoting it to casehood, requires the conversion of a continuously distributed characteristic, degree of adjustment, into a categorical (dichotomous) designation, adjusted versus maladjusted. If maladjustment were equally distributed in all countries and in all communities within countries, the results of studies of the prevalence of maladjustment would still differ because of variation between studies in sampling error methods of case finding, sources of diagnostic information, the symptoms indicative of maladjustment as a continuous variable, and the point at which the continuous variable is dichotomized into adjusted and maladjusted cases. Relying predominantly on teachers' reports to locate probable cases, for example, leads to under-reporting of emotional as opposed to conduct disorder, because teachers are more sensitive to and aware of symptoms of conduct disorder, which tend to disrupt the classroom. In comparison with teachers, parents report more symptoms of emotional disorder such as depression, worry, and fear (Emery, 1982; Yule, 1981), and adolescent children themselves report more of the latter symptoms than do either parents or teachers (Rutter, Graham, Chadwich, & Yule, 1976). Rutter, Tizard, and Whitmore (1970) found only seven percent overlap between the lists of children identified as candidates for disorder on the basis of teachers' reports versus parents' reports of symptoms. With regard to dichotomizing the distribution, some studies count mild cases whereas others report only cases of moderately or greater severity (e.g., Rutter et al., 1970). Some studies merely count the number of maladaptive symptoms reported as the index of pathology, dichotomizing it arbitrarily, (e.g., Pringle, Butler, & Davie, 1966, whose decision yielded 12 percent disorder); whereas, others designate cases as fitting specific syndromes of disorder (e.g., Rutter et al., 1970, whose strategy yielded 6.8 percent disorder). To rely solely on institutional or clinic records introduces massive error, since some community surveys (Rutter et al., 1970) indicate that as much as 90 percent of moderately severe childhood psychopathology goes untreated, and also because the availability and cost of psychiatric services vary widely among communities and countries.

Judging from studies that used more adequate methods, the prevalence of childhood psychopathological disorder of a moderate to severe degree appears to lie between 6 percent and 12 percent, with disorder being slightly more prevalent among males through early adolescence and thereafter slightly more prevalent in females (see reviews by Achenbach & Edelbrock, 1981; Eme, 1979; Graham, 1979; Yule, 1981). Richman, Stevenson, and Graham (1975) found a seven percent rate of moderate to severe problems with the rates about equal for males and females in a study of 800 3-year-olds from an outer London borough where initial screening was based on parent interviews. In a similar study in the United States, Behar and Stringfield (1974) found higher rates of disorder in preschool-aged males than females. In the National Child Development Study of 6.5- to 7-year-olds in England, Scotland, and Wales, teachers' symptom ratings yielded a maladjustment designation for 16 percent of boys and 8 percent of girls (Pringle et al., 1966).

The most thorough epidemiological study of children in middle childhood was conducted by Rutter and his colleagues on the Isle of Wight off the south coast of England (Rutter, Graham, & Yule, 1970; Rutter, Tizard, Yule, Graham, & Whitmore, 1976). All 2199 10- and 11-year-olds in this community of 100,000 were screened for disorder by parent and teacher questionnaires, and then candidates for disorder were assessed individually with psychometric tests and psychiatric interviews. The overall rate of psychopathology corrected for screening error was 6.8 percent (Rutter et al., 1970). Emotional disorders were slightly more common in girls, and conduct disorders were very much more common in boys. A comparative study of the prevalence of disorder in inner-city London (Yule, 1981) yielded estimates of psychopathology in 10-year-olds that were double those of the Isle of Wight.

A follow-up and reassessment of psychopathology was conducted on the Isle of Wight when the 10- and 11-year-old children reached 14 years. Methodology similar to that of the earlier study was used, with the exception that more emphasis was placed on interviews with the children. This study yielded a prevalence rate of 7.7 percent handicapping disorder. The rate of conduct disorder was more than three times as high for males as females and the rates of emotional disorder were about equal for males and females, yielding an overall double rate of psychiatric disorder for males as compared with females. The great majority of cases that had continued from the earlier assessment were male, whereas the sex ratio for new cases was equal. The new cases were less likely to be associated with scholastic difficulties or family factors such as broken homes. Interviews from a randomly selected control group from the 14-year-old cohort indicated that parent and teacher screening procedures missed a great deal of self-reported feelings of misery that represented seemingly transient conditions. If added to the nontransient disorders, these conditions would raise the prevalence rate to 21 percent. These prevalence figures for adolescents (13 to 14 years) are comparable to those of Leslie (1974) from an industrial town in North England: severe disturbance equaled 6.2 percent for males and 2.6 percent for females; moderately and severely disturbed equaled 28 percent for males and 13.6 percent for females.

Age of Onset

The New York Longitudinal Study followed 141 middle and upper-middle class predominantly Jewish children from birth through age 10. After the age of 3, there was a sharp rise to a peak at 4 to 6 years in the incidence of children referred for psychiatric consultation and confirmed to have at least mild disturbance (42 of 141) (Thomas, Chess, & Birch, 1968, p. 43), a finding that is congruent with the Berkeley Growth Study (MacFarlane, Allen, & Honzik, 1954). The reported lag-time from onset of symptoms to professional consultation was less than a year for 65 percent of the males and 75 percent of the females.

Problems in peer relations were most frequently brought to professional attention between 4 and 6 years of age, problems of discipline between 4 and 7 years, and problems of learning between 6 and 9 years of age. Scores from the annual assessment of the child's temperament from year 1 through year 5 were not predictive of disorder until age 3; only one of nine temperament variables assessed from parental interview during years 1 and 2 (activity at year 1) was predictive of later disorder (Thomas et al., 1968, chap. 5). These data from a highly educated set of parents with professional services readily available suggest that the majority of deviant patterns of childhood disorder have their onset quite early in childhood but are poorly predicted from temperament in infancy.

Epidemiology of Problem Behaviors

The most comprehensive study of the prevalence of childhood behavior problems conducted in the United States was that of Achenbach and Edelbrock (1981). A total of 2,600 parents completed ratings of their child on 113 behavior problems and 20 social competency items. Half of the children were assessed at intake into outpatient mental health services (referred group), and half were normal controls selected randomly from neighborhoods with demographic equivalence to the referred group. Each group contained 50 males and 50 females of each age from 4 through 16 years. The reported prevalence of each problem was analyzed for the effects of clinic status, age, sex, race, and socioeconomic status (SES). Racial differences were minimal; however, there were significant tendencies for lower SES children to have higher frequencies of behavior problems. There were numerous gender and age differences on specific items that will be discussed below. There was a general tendency for behavior problems to decline somewhat with age; but there was no overall difference between males and females in the total number of problem behaviors reported, a result that is congruent with a similar survey of the parents of 236 randomly selected 7- to 12-year-old children from Louisville, Kentucky (Miller, Hampe, Barrett, & Noble, 1971). As concluded by Achenbach and Edelbrock:

> Most of the problems reported more frequently for lower SES children and for boys were undercontrolled, "externalizing" behaviors, whereas the problems reported more frequently for girls tended to be either overcontrolled, "internalizing" behaviors or problem behaviors not clearly classifiable as undercontrolled or overcontrolled. (p. 64)

Optimal discriminative accuracy between clinic-referred and nonreferred children was achieved with a cutoff score corresponding to the 90th percentile of total behavior problems. Assuming that only a small percentage of the children in the control group who could be referred to a clinic in fact have been referred (cf. Rutter, Tizard, & Whitmore, 1970), and assuming that some of the children in the referred group are normal and should not have been referred, 10 percent is a good estimate of the number of behaviorally disordered children in the United States.

Age Differences in Problem Behavior

Table 3-2 lists those problem behaviors that exhibited large and moderate declines and those that exhibited small, moderate, and large increases in frequency between 4 and 16 years of age. The problems that decline with increasing age suggest that children become less impulsive, less oriented toward immediate gratification, and more conforming to social norms with increasing age; they also become less dependent and less impulsively aggressive. Those problems that increase in frequency with age indicate increased rebellion and resistance to authority as well as increased depression, withdrawal, and somatization with the approach and onset of adolescence.

Sex Differences

Table 3-3 lists those problems that yielded significant sex differences. Listed on the left are problems for which the frequency of occurrence was higher in males and on the right those with higher frequencies in females. The male and female subgroups are further subdivided into those showing equal sex difference for clinic-referred

Table 3-2

Problem Behaviors Exhibiting Significant Change in Prevalence Between 4 and 16 Years of Age

Decrease with Age		Increase with Age	
Effect Size	Problem Behavior	Effect Size	Problem Behavior
Large Decrease		Large Increase	
15	Whining	13	Alcohol & drugs
8	Wets bed	10	Truancy
6	Daytime wetting	4	Poor school work
6	Too dependent	4	Hangs around w/ child in trouble
6	Demands attention	4	Secretive
5	Cries a lot	4	Swearing
5	Fears		
5	Nightmares	Moderate Increase	
5	Picking	3	Runs away from home
4	Encopresis	2	Headaches
4	Speech problem	2	Overweight
4	Thumb-sucking	2	Dizzy
4	Does not eat well		
4	Talks too much		
4	Destroys own things	Small Increase	
4	Shows off	1	Unhappy, sad, depressed
		1	Sleeps much
Moderate Decrease		1	Underactive
3	Prefers younger children	1	Likes to be alone
3	Easily jealous	1	Sexual preoccupation
3	Hyperactive		
3	Plays with sex parts in public		
2	Plays with sex parts too much		
2	Unusually loud		
2	Poor peer relations		
2	Destroys others' things		
2	Attacks people		
2	Disobedient at home		

Derived from data presented in Achenbach and Edelbrock (1981).

and nonreferred children (main effect for sex) and those showing greater sex difference for clinic-referred children (main effect of sex plus interaction of sex and referral). In no case was the sex difference for nonreferred children greater than the sex difference for referred children. This table displays the greater excess of externalizing behaviors and in particular aggressive behaviors in males. It appears that the more

Table 3-3
Problem Behaviors Exhibiting Significant Sex Differences

Higher Prevalence in Males		Higher Prevalence in Females	
Effect Size	Problem Behavior	Effect Size	Problem Behavior
Clinic males equal to or moderately higher than nonclinic males		Clinic females equal to or moderately higher than nonclinic females	
3	Shows off	1	Overweight
2	Bragging	1	Bites fingernails
2	Teases a lot	1	Behaves like opposite sex
2	Disobedient at school	1	Easily jealous
2	Can't concentrate	<1	Fears
2	Destroys own things	<1	Nightmares
1	Destroys others' things	<1	Worrying
1	Impulsive	<1	Shy & timid
<1	Cruel to others	<1	Self-conscious
<1	Attacks people	<1	Moody
<1	Threatens people	<1	Too dependent
<1	Temper tantrums	<1	Thumb-sucking
<1	Steals outside home	<1	Wishes to be opposite sex
<1	Hangs around w/ child. in trouble	<1	Runs away from home
<1	Prefers older children	<1	Headaches
<1	Encopresis	<1	Skin problems
Clinic males much higher		Clinic females much higher	
2	Sets fires	1	Cries a lot
1	Swearing	1	Feels unloved
1	Fighting	1	Stomachaches, cramps
1	Hyperactive	<1	Aches & pains
1	Poor school work	<1	Lonely
<1	Cruel to animals	<1	Unhappy, sad, or depressed
<1	Vandalism	<1	Sulks a lot
		<1	Screams a lot
		<1	Sexual preoccupation
		<1	Overeating

*Derived from data presented in Achenbach and Edelbrock (1981).

serious of these aggressive behaviors are more likely to result in a clinical referral. Females, on the other hand, show an excess of internalizing behaviors, specifically dysphoric feelings, and of somatic complaints. However, the excess of females over males in exhibiting internalized problem behaviors seems less marked than the excess of males over females exhibiting externalizing problem behaviors. The results are consistent with Quay's (1972) conclusion that, in both referred and non-referred populations, boys are consistently reported to score higher on the conduct disorder dimension than girls, while girls attain higher scores on the emotional disorder dimension.

Age By Sex Differences

The Achenbach and Edelbrock (1981) study is the first with a sample of sufficient size and age range from which conclusions could be drawn about sex differences in symptoms over age. Listed in Table 3-4 are the

Table 3-4
Sex by Age Interaction in the Frequency of Problem Behaviors Among Clinic-Referred Children

| | Frequency Per 100 Clinic Referred Cases | | | |
| | Before Age 10 | | After Age 11 | |
Behavior Problem	M	F	M	F
Decrease in Sex Difference with Age				
Males Initially Higher				
Disobedient at home	92	82	84	86
Disobedient at school	70	52	66	58
Hangs around kids who get in trouble	32	15	45	47
Impulsive	80	61	75	64
Attacks people	42	26	51	46
Swears	40	21	51	46
Females Initially Higher				
(None)				
Increase in Sex Difference with Age				
Males Subsequently Higher				
Acts too young	68	59	56	40
Bragging	65	53	67	46
Females Subsequently Higher				
Lonely	49	51	35	52
Feels unloved	57	66	49	71
Headaches	19	26	31	46
Stomachaches, cramps	24	31	25	45
Runs away from home	8	6	12	32
Screams a lot	49	48	31	54
Secretive	47	48	66	69
Moody	61	63	58	76
Sulks a lot	47	54	40	61
Suspicious	23	22	28	42
Sexual preoccupation	5	10	12	25

Derived from data presented in Achenbach and Edelbrock (1981).

behavior problems from among the 113 studied that showed different age trends for male and female clinic-referred children. There were six problems for which referred males had markedly higher frequencies of endorsement than referred females before age 10 but not after age 10. These problems were all of an externalizing or undercontrolled nature, and all six showed marked decline in frequency for males with increased age. There were no problems for which referred females had markedly higher rates than males before age 10 as opposed to after age 10. However, there were 11 problem behaviors for which females had markedly higher rates of endorsement than males after age 10 than before, and these problems were primarily of an internalizing nature.

This evidence of a sex by age interaction in the data of Achenbach and Edelbrock (1981) concurs with the conclusions of Eme (1979) from his recent review of sex differences in child psychopathology. Eme noted that the greatest predominance in the incidence of psychopathology in males versus females occurred at the youngest ages with continued predominance until adolescence and then an equalizing during adolescence, followed by the predominance of females over males after adolescence.

Epidemiology and Prognosis of Specific Syndromes

This section reviews the prevalence and the demographic and prognostic correlates of the more prevalent and severe syndromes of childhood disorder. Data on the prevalence, change in incidence with age, sex ratio, and the correlation of prevalence with SES of major disorders are presented in Table 3-5.

Conduct Disorders

It can be seen in Table 3-5 that conduct disorders are the most prevalent form of disorder in childhood. Figures from the Isle of Wight and inner London studies indicate a three or four to one prevalence ratio of males to females for conduct disorders, and these figures agree with those of Jenkins (1966) for clinic-referred cases in the United States. Quay's review (1972) of studies on nonclinic samples in the United States also yielded congruent conclusions on sex differences in conduct disorder. Studies using cluster analytic (Jenkins, 1966; Soli et al., 1981) and factor analytic methods (Brady, 1970; Collins, Maxwell, & Cameron, 1962; Quay, 1964) suggest two major subtypes of conduct disorder: an *undersocialized aggressive* type with symptoms of fighting, disobedience, defiance, destructiveness, vengefulness, and temper outbursts, and poor interpersonal relationships with peers and adults; and a *socialized non-aggressive* type with symptoms of stealing in the company of others, truancy from school, bad companions, staying out overnight, and disobedience. While these sets of symptoms tend to be somewhat indepen-

Table 3-5

Disorders of Childhood, Prevalence, Change in Incidence with Age, Sex Ratio, and Prevalence by Socioeconomic (SES) Level

Disorder	Prevalence				Change in Incidence with Age	Sex Ratio Male/Female	SES Correlation with Prevalence
	Inner City Age 10–11	Small Town Age 10–11	Small Town Age 14	General			
Conduct Disorder							
Undersocialized Aggressive Socialized Delinquent	8.0%	4.0%	3.6%		Decrease Increase after age 10	3/1 4/1	Slightly Negative Negative
Emotional Disorders							
Anxiety, Depression, Phobias	5.0%	2.5%	5.0%		Increase after age 10	1/1 childhood 1/1.5 late adolescence	Unrelated
Specific Reading Retardation		3.7%			Little or none	3.3/1	Negative
Mental Retardation				U.S. 2.5%	Little or none	1/1	Negative
Hyperactivity		.1–1.6%		U.S. 1–6%	Decrease	5/1 to 8/1	Negative
Childhood Psychoses							
Autism		0.04%			Decrease to zero by age 3	4/1	Slight Positive
Childhood Schizophrenia		0.01%			Begins about 8–10 and increases after puberty	2/1 early 1/1 later	Negative

dent in males, they are more likely to covary in females (Collins et al., 1962; Soli et al., 1981). The symptoms of the undersocialized aggressive type tend to decrease in the general population with age, whereas the symptoms of the socialized nonaggressive type tend to increase with the onset of adolescence (Achenbach & Edelbrock, 1981; Loeber, 1982). Congruently, in clinic populations, the former type are younger than the latter (Jenkins, 1966; Soli et al., 1981). The family correlates of these two syndromes obtained by Jenkins indicate that the undersocialized aggressive syndrome is associated with maternal rejection and neglect in the preschool years and the socialized nonaggressive syndrome in males with later family disorganization and paternal neglect, the latter conditions especially being inversely related to social class.

Conduct disorders are persistent, with many cases continuing on into adulthood in the form of criminal behavior and antisocial personality (Loeber, 1982). Robins (1966) has shown that childhood conduct disorder leads to a future that includes pervasive antisocial problems, greater risk of a prison term, much time spent on public welfare, and a high chance of death by homicide. Olweus (1979) reviewed 16 studies on the stability of aggressive behavior, a major symptom in conduct disorder, and noted that marked individual differences in habitual aggression level manifest themselves as early as three years of age. The degree of stability observed for aggression was only slightly lower than that found for intelligence. Gersten, Langner, Eisenberg, Simcha-Fagen, and McCarthy (1976) found in the Manhattan Family Study that conflict with parents becomes stable at about age 6 and antisocial behavior at about age 10. On the Isle of Wight, conduct problems observed at age 10 were likely to persist into adolescence if the child was also perceived as hyperactive by the parents; if not, only about 10 percent persisted (Schachar, Rutter, & Smith, 1981). Paternite and Loney (1980) on the other hand, provide evidence that among hyperactive males, aggressiveness in childhood is more strongly associated with poor adolescent outcome than is hyperactivity. Although not all children with conduct disorder become antisocial adults, several studies indicate that most antisocial adults exhibited symptoms of conduct disorder during childhood (Robins, 1979).

Given the above evidence for stability, it is not surprising to find that conduct disorder is very refractory to therapeutic intervention (cf. McCord, 1979). In her review of follow-up studies, Robins (1979) noted that children who had attended child guidance clinics in Dallas, St. Louis, and Australia for conduct disorder were worse off as adults than former clients with other childhood symptoms. Also in three follow-up studies of adolescents treated for conduct disorder, respectively 62 percent, 66 percent, and 100 percent remained impaired 2 to 6 years after, whereas, of adolescents treated for neurotic symptoms, respectively, 45 percent, 26 percent, and 9 percent remained impaired. Furthermore, Robins notes that none of the programs of prevention instituted for school-age children at high risk for delinquency has been effective in lowering delinquency rates; however, adoption in infancy has been shown to be effective.

Emotional Disorders

Emotional disorders are the second most prevalent type of disorder with anxiety disorder constituting about two thirds of the disorder in this category. Specific animal and situational phobias (e.g., fear of dogs, fear of the dark) constituted most of the remaining third in the Isle of Wight study (Yule, 1981). Studies in the United States indicate that school phobia has a per year incidence of 1 percent or less of the child population (Kennedy, 1965; Miller et al., 1971). Social phobias are extremely rare in childhood, commonly beginning around early adolescence; and agoraphobia does not appear until mid-adolescence (Marks & Gelder, 1966). Cases of obsessive-compulsive disorder and hysterical or dissociative disorder, which are rare in adulthood, are extremely rare in childhood (Judd, 1965; Rae, 1977; Robins & O'Neal, 1953). The syndrome of depression was also extremely rare at ages 10 and 11 in the Isle of Wight (three cases in 2,199 children); however, by age 14 depression had shown a fivefold increase in prevalence in the same cohort but was still at a prevalence rate of less than 1 percent (Yule, 1981). Overall, emotional disorders were slightly more prevalent in females than males in the Isle of Wight, a finding congruent with observations in the United States (cf. Quay, Sprague, Shulman, & Miller, 1966). Peterson (1961) also found in the United States that boys exceed girls in problems on the emotional disorder (anxiety-withdrawal) dimension until about third grade (8 to 9 years of age) when girls' scores become higher. However, both Rutter (1979) in England and Edelbrock and Achenbach (1980) in the United States observed a significant number of disturbed preadolescent males with symptoms of both emotional and conduct disorder. On the Isle of Wight they constituted 27 percent of psychiatrically disturbed boys, and in the United States study they formed a reliable cluster (Depressed-Social Withdrawal-Aggressive) in a hierarchical cluster analysis for boys (but not for girls) aged 6 to 11 years. This cluster included 8 percent of the clinically referred boys. Although conduct disorder is much more prevalent in males, many of these conduct disordered males have concurrent symptoms of emotional disorder. Puig-Antich (1982) asserts that in many instances the conduct disorder emerges after and is secondary to the depressive symptoms.

Contrary to the low prevalence of the syndrome of clinical depression, depressive symptoms have a high prevalence in early childhood and a pattern of gradual decline with age, according to Lefkowitz and Burton (1978). Using data from Werry and Quay (1971) on children from 5 to 8 years, Lefkowitz and Burton found an average prevalence for 16 depressive symptoms (e.g., feelings of inferiority, lack of emotional expression, chronic sadness) to be 22 percent in males and 18 percent in females. Since children typically recover from a phase of depression and withdrawal and show normal responsiveness in several weeks (Hetherington & Martin, 1979; Rutter, 1971), such depressive symptoms do not meet rigorous diagnostic criteria for the syndrome "depressive disorder" as defined for adults (Cytryn, McKnew, & Bunney, 1980; Lefkowitz, 1980). Furthermore, the extant longitudinal data argue against the permanence of depressive symptoms in children and against their manifestation in adulthood as depressive or manic depressive illness (Welner, 1978). Congruently, Shaffer (1974) found not one case of completed suicide in children under 12 years of age in the United Kingdom over a 7-year period, and manic episodes are never observed in children under 12 years of age (Loranger & Levine, 1978). Thus childhood depression is seldom prodromal to adult depressive illness, except possibly in a small minority of the rare cases that meet adult diagnostic criteria (Poznanski, Krahenbuhl, & Zrull, 1976) as yet not followed to adulthood.

A similar state of affairs exists for children's fears: young children show a high prevalence of irrational fears, and the total number of fears present declines with age. Specific fears are normative at a given developmental stage; without specific treatment they disappear and are often replaced by the normative fear of the next developmental stage (Jersild & Holmes, 1935; Miller, Barret, & Hampe, 1974). Most of these fears are not considered phobias because of their age or stage specificity. Miller et al. noted in a survey of treatment studies that the prognosis for school phobia is good during early childhood and poor during adolescence and that in general, phobias in children under age 10 arise and dissipate rapidly. Nonetheless, animal phobias in adults, although rare, are reported to have had their onset in early childhood, whereas social phobias and agoraphobia (which are more common especially in women) typically have their onset in early or mid-adolescence (Marks, 1969).

As noted above, Robins (1979) concluded from her review of followup studies that emotional disorders of childhood have a more favorable prognosis than conduct disorders. She noted that symptoms such as tics, shyness, fears, hypersensitivity, nervousness, irritability, and insomnia occurred as frequently during childhood for normal adults as for neurotic adults. Across social class, the amelioration of symptoms of isolation and anxiety (but not of antisocial behavior) was noted with improving environment in middle and late childhood (Langner, Gersten, & Simcha-Fagan, 1983). Not all of these emotional problems disappear, however. In the Isle of Wight Study, nearly half of those diagnosed as having emotional disorders at age 10 still had problems at follow-up at age 14, with equal persistence of disorder in males and females (Yule, 1981). In a long-term follow-up study of neurotic children (24 phobic and 18 other neuroses) seen before age 13 at a child psychiatric clinic, 40 percent received a specific diagnosis as young adults, thus indicating an unfavorable prognosis for childhood neuroses (Waldron, 1976). Data from the Manhattan Family Study (Gersten et al., 1976) indicate that neurotic-like anxiety declines from age 6 onward. Also up to middle adolescence, early childhood neurotic symptoms appear to be nearly outgrown and thus to have little prognostic significance. However, in middle adolescence, when less normative or age-appropriate, neurotic anxiety showed greater continuity and prognostic significance. When neurotic and conduct disorder disturbances were assessed at age 14 through 16 years, they had equal predictive power (.46) to ratings at years 19 through 21. Gersten et al. suggest that the greater predictive power of conduct disorder noted in reviews may be due to the selection of neurotic children from the preadolescent period before the stability of neurotic symptoms has yet emerged.

Specific Reading Retardation and Mental Retardation

Specific reading retardation (defined at 10 and 11 years of age by Yule [1981] as 2.3 years below the expected reading level as predicted from age and IQ) runs a close third in prevalence, just behind emotional disorder. Not only was the rate over three times greater in males, on the Isle of Wight one third of all children with specific reading disability also had conduct disorder. Mental retardation, another correlate of other psychiatric disorders, is also fairly high in prevalence relative to other psychiatric disorders.

When the primary diagnostic criterion of mental retardation is a deviation IQ below 70 on a test like the Wechsler Intelligence Scale for Children-Revised (WISC-R), approximately 2.5 percent of the population is expected to score in this range. Since IQ test scores in adulthood are quite stable and are moderately predictable from IQ scores at age 2 (at correlations of about .50), and are even more highly predictable from IQ test scores at age 9 (at correlations of about .75), it is evident that the prognosis for mental retardation diagnosed in the preschool year and after is very poor. The prognosis for specific reading disability seems equally poor. When children with specific reading disability at age 10 to 11 on the Isle of Wight were followed up at age 14, it was found that they had made little progress in the intervening years. If anything, the

brighter dyslexic children had made even less progress than the backward readers, and their spelling was even more impaired than their
reading (Yule, 1981).

Hyperactivity

Attention deficit disorder with hyperactivity, the diagnosis that in
DSM-III replaces hyperkinetic syndrome, has core symptoms of chronic
hyperactivity, short attention span, marked distractibility, emotional lability, and impulsivity. The prevalence of hyperactivity as a syndrome
appears to be both variable as a function of social-ecological conditions
within communities and uncertain because of the divergence in diagnostic practices among investigators. According to Ross and Ross (1982),
hyperactivity is virtually nonexistent in children from Tokyo, Salt Lake
City, primitive Pacific cultures, and Chinese-American children in New
York City. These data suggest a strong influence of ethnicity on prevalence rates, an influence that goes beyond diagnostic differences between investigators. In the Isle of Wight study, where stringent British
diagnostic standards were used, only three children of 2,177 in the 10-
and 11-year-old cohorts were assigned to the hyperkinetic syndrome
(Rutter et al., 1970), a prevalence rate of about 0.1 percent; by comparison between 1 percent and 6 percent of elementary school children
in the United States have been judged to be hyperactive (Lambert, Sandoval, & Sassone, 1978). The higher rate of 6 percent derives when the
judgement of the teacher, the parent, or the physician is accepted as
diagnostic; when all three must concur in the judgement of hyperactivity,
the rate drops to about 1 percent. From 1 percent to 2 percent of United
States elementary school children receive drug treatment for hyperactivity (Ross & Ross, 1982). In a later analysis of data from the Isle of
Wight, children were judged "pervasively hyperactive" when both parent
and teacher reported hyperactivity, and on this basis, 2 percent were so
designated (Schachar, Rutter, & Smith, 1981). The sex ratio of males to
females was three to one (Schachar et al., 1981). In the United States,
sex ratios of from five to one to nine to one, males over females, have
been found (Lambert et al., 1978).

There is general agreement that the specific behaviors symptomatic
of attention deficit with hyperactivity decline in frequency with increasing age (cf. Achenbach & Edelbrock, 1981). However, due to the social
tolerance accorded young children, it is often not until middle childhood
that the dyscontrol of the hyperactive child is labeled as a clinical entity
(Ross & Ross, 1982; Jenkins, 1966). By adolescence only 43 percent of
a group of 57 boys previously diagnosed as hyperactive were still hyperactive; however, 80 percent of this group at adolescence manifested

learning, behavioral, or emotional problems (Sassone, Lambert, & Sandoval, 1981).

Among residents in the East Bay area of San Francisco, Lambert et al. (1978) found that hyperactivity, strictly defined, was overrepresented at the low occupational level, underrepresented at the middle, and proportionately represented at the high occupational level. Schachar et al. (1981) reported that pervasive hyperactivity was twice as prevalent on the Isle of Wight in the lowest social class, and, relative to situational hyperactivity and unsociability, was specifically predictive of other behavioral and emotional problems for children only in the two lowest social classes. Sandberg, Wieselberg, and Shaffer (1980) also found that children from inner London rated by teachers as hyperactive and conduct disordered were significantly lower in social class, and higher in the frequency of broken homes and of one-parent households. In the United States it has been observed that children who are both hyperactive and aggressive are lower in SES than those who are just hyperactive (Milich, Loney, & Landau, 1981).

Ratings and behavioral measures of activity level in the preschool years are predictive of school-age hyperactivity. Campbell, Schleifer, and Weiss (1978) reported that maternal ratings of activity at age 4 were predictive to age 6, and behavior in the nursery school at age 4 predicted teacher ratings of classroom behavior at age 7; hyperactive nursery school children who left their table most during structured activities were more often out of seat and off task in school at age 7. Halverson and Waldrop (1976) also found evidence of consistency in activity level from 2 to 7 years of age in a nonclinic sample.

In the elementary school years hyperactivity is very stable in the absence of medication or other treatment. Although motor hyperactivity tends to decline at adolescence, the attention deficit may persist into adulthood (Ross & Ross, 1982). In a follow-up study from the Worcester Clinic (Shirley, Baum, & Polsky, 1940–41) "neurotic" symptoms were found to be associated with good outcome, whereas restlessness and inattention—symptoms commonly described in hyperactive children—were associated with poor outcome.

Loney and her colleagues (Loney, Laughorne, Paternite, Whaley-Klahn, Blair-Broeker, and Hacker, 1976; Paternite & Loney, 1980) have found that unfavorable adolescent outcome for hyperactive boys (in terms of severity of both hyperactivity and aggression) was related to high aggression at referral, lower SES, and having had a less controlling father; the level of hyperactivity at referral was not predictive of adolecent status. Thus, while hyperactivity tends generally to decrease with age, improvement in hyperactivity and other associated maladaptive symptoms is limited in children of low SES and children with accompanying aggressive symptoms, a combination that is itself more prevalent at lower levels of SES.

The prognosis for adult social adjustment for children who are hyperactive is poor. One of the first long-term follow-up studies (Menkes, Rowe, & Menkes, 1967) indicated that adults who had been hyperactive as children have persisting abnormalities of personality that are often associated with criminal behavior and in a few cases with psychosis. A host of studies have now shown that hyperactive children exhibit antisocial problems at adolescence and adulthood (see review by Ross & Ross, 1982). Recently, Borland and Heckman (1976) demonstrated that hyperactive males, as adults, have lower levels of occupational achievement than their brothers. Treatment with stimulant drugs, although effective in reducing hyperactivity in childhood, does not improve the poor academic achievement of the hyperactive child (Weiss, Minde, Werry, Douglas, & Nemeth, 1974).

Childhood Psychoses

The two most prevalent psychoses of childhood (excluding organic brain syndromes) are infantile autism and childhood schizophrenia. Their combined prevalence is about 100 times less than that of conduct disorder.

Infantile Autism

The best epidemiological study of infantile autism (Lotter, 1966, 1967, 1978) yielded a prevalence rate of 4.5 per 10,000 or about four hundredths of 1 percent in children between 8 and 10 years of age. Lotter observed a 20 percent overrepresentation of cases in the higher social classes relative to the lower.

Several adequate longitudinal studies that have followed infantile autistic children into adolescence and young adulthood indicate that less than 25 percent make a satisfactory community adjustment (DeMyer, Barton, DeMyer, Norton, Allen, & Steele, 1973; Eisenberg & Kanner, 1956; Rutter & Lockyer, 1967). A high percentage (40 percent to 70 percent) at follow-up are living in institutions (Lotter, 1978). Among autistic children of school age, less than 10 percent are in the grade appropriate to their age. Prognosis is closely tied to measured intelligence and the communication skill evident at 5 years of age. Eisenberg and Kanner (1956) noted that the likelihood of a favorable adolescent outcome was nil if the autistic child was not using language for purposes of communication by age 5; whereas, about half of those with useful language at age 5 made a satisfactory community adjustment. Rutter and Lockyer (1967) found that autistic children matched on the basis of sex, age, and measured IQ with nonpsychotic clinical cases had less favorable outcomes than the controls with respect to employment and equal outcome with regard to the percent still institutionalized (44 percent). The best predictor of social adjustment for both the autistic and the retarded was measurd IQ. Thus, the retardation present in most cases at initial diagnosis tends to persist even with treatment. Rutter and Lockyer (1967) noted that children with average intelligence at the time of diagnosis made progress, whereas those who were retarded deteriorated, probably because of institutionalization. The best outcome occurred for those children who had attended schools where they had received an unusual amount of individual attention.

According to Lovaas, Koegel, Simmons, and Long (1973), whether infantile autistic children retain the modest improvement achieved with behavior modification (including in some case, language acquisition) depends on the nature of the environment to which they are discharged. In the hands of parents who continue to apply learning principles, slight further gains are made, whereas, in a custodial setting all gains are quickly lost. Kanner, Rodriguez, and Ashenden (1972) noted that the small group of autistic children who recovered did not make substantial social progress until the adolescent years, and that all had succeeded in avoiding institutionalization, a factor that could be causal in, rather than merely a correlate of, their favorable adjustment. A recent report by Schopler, Mesibov, and Baker (1982), although providing few details on level of adjustment, indicated that the TEACCH program has achieved a remarkably low rate (8 percent) of institutionalization for individuals with infantle autism both over and under 17 years of age.

Childhood Schizophrenia

Childhood schizophrenia appears to be even more rare than infantile autism. Graham (1979) reported that the admission rate for schizophrenia in children aged 10 to 15 years was approximately 1 per 100,000 for both sexes in England and Wales. If only 1 in 10 children with schizophrenia was admitted to the hospital, the prevalence would still be only 1 per 10,000 or one hundredth of one percent. Kolvin's (1971) data from England indicate that the incidence of childhood schizophrenia begins to rise sharply after age 12. Schizophrenic children were also found to be more likely to come from lower than upper class backgrounds, and Kolvin also found that 10 percent of the children's parents were also schizophrenic compared with the population base rate of 1 percent. Kolvin found a 2.5 : 1 predominance of childhood schizophrenia in boys versus girls. However, Miller (1974) reports that the incidence of schizophrenia in girls rises with age until the ratio becomes about equal in adult schizophrenia.

In part because of its rarity, there are few well-documented long-term follow-up studies of childhood schizophrenia. Some follow-up studies (such as that of Bender, 1973) lump together children with infantile autism and children with symptoms of adult schizophrenia under the label "schizophrenic children." The excellent follow-up study by Eggers (1978) included 57 individuals (25 males and 32 females), all of whom met adult criteria of schizophrenia and none of whom had organic brain disease, mental retardation, or disorders of speech development. In 11 cases the onset of psychosis was between 7 and 13 years of age and in the remaining 46, between 10 and 13 years of age. (Over a 35-year period neither hallucinations nor delusions were observed in any child under 7 years of age.) The onset of the psychosis was acute in 36 percent of the younger group and in 82 percent of the older group with a prodromal period of depression and anxiety of two to three weeks' duration. On long-term follow-up (the average length was 15 years), the outcome proved to be more favorable than is usually assumed. In all, 51 percent made a good postpsychotic adjustment; 17 percent, a fair adjustment; and 32 percent had a very poor social adaptation or no remission. Outcome was unrelated to frequency of psychotic episodes, the nature of the psychotic symptoms, the presence of disturbed family relations, or the family history of psychiatric illness. Outcome was most strongly associated with premorbid personality, being more favorable in those who had been sociable, warmhearted, and harmonious and less favorable in those who had been insecure, timid, and introverted. Low intelligence was associated with poor outcome. Disturbance in the family was uncorrelated with outcome. Only 4 of 57 remained free of delusions and hallucinations through the period of follow-up, with these symptoms developing in some cases as much as 5 to 8 years after the onset of the disorder. The modal symptoms pattern (77 percent) was paranoid-hallucinatory.

To summarize, in order from most prevalent to least are: conduct disorder, emotional disorder, specific reading retardation, mental retardation, hyperactivity, and childhood psychoses. In order by rate of decrease in incidence with age are infantile autism, attention deficit with hyperactivity, and conduct disorder. Increasing in incidence with age to at least age 16 is delinquency-rebellion; and beyond age 16, emotional disorder and schizophrenia. The disorders that show the sharpest declines in incidence with increasing age (infantile autism, hyperactivity, conduct disorder) have the greatest surfeit of males over females, whereas those that tend to increase in incidence with age into adulthood (emotional disorders and schizophrenia) either have an equal sex ratio or a surfeit of females over males. Clearly more prevalent in the lower social classes are mental retardation, specific reading disability, schizophrenia, and conduct disorder. The only disorder that appears to be more prevalent in the upper social classes is infantile autism.

ETIOLOGICAL INFLUENCES

Hereditary Influence on Childhood Psychopathology

Knowledge of the influence of hereditary factors on a particular pattern of childhood disorder exists at varying levels of specificity. The first level of specificity is to establish at a high level of likelihood that susceptibility to a disorder is influenced by genetic factors. The second level is to establish with reasonable certainty the mode of inheritance of the susceptibility to the disorder, for example whether a single dominant or recessive gene, or perhaps multiple genes convey increased susceptibility to the disorder. (Increased susceptibility as used here means an increase in the probability of developing a particular disorder over the population base rate.) The highest level of specificity is to establish the biochemical and/or psychological mechanisms or pathways by which the genes influence susceptibility to a particular disorder. For most behavioral disorders there is at least some evidence of genetic influence on susceptibility and, for several, very strong evidence of genetic influence, e.g., schizophrenia (Kessler, 1980) and bipolar depression (Cadoret & Winokur, 1975; Mendelewicz & Rainer, 1977). The mode of inheritance has been established for only a few behavior disorders, e.g., Huntington's chorea; however, for many others specific models of genetic transmission have been eliminated as possibilities even though none of the remaining models have conclusive support (cf. Pauls & Kidd, 1982). Only for some rare forms of mental retardation, such as phenalketonuria (PKU), which is due to an enzyme deficiency, and a few other rare behavioral disorders, do we have conclusive identification of the mechanism by which the genotype contributes to the development of the behaviorally aberrant phenotype.

To have a genetic or heritable component, a disorder must run in families, that is, be more common in the biological relatives of an affected individual (a proband) than in the general population of unrelated individuals. Although a necessary condition of heritability, running in families is not a sufficient condition, since family members often share correlated physical (e.g., interuterine) and social environments. Adoption studies can provide strong evidence of heritability, because genetic and social environmental influences are separated when the adopted individual is reared in a social environment not shared with biological relatives. Greater concordance for disorder between the adopted proband (or index case) and nonrearing biological relatives than between the adopted proband and the rearing nonbiological relatives is evidence for a genetic factor in the susceptibility to development of a given disorder. In the cotwin method, the concordance rates between identical (monozygotic, MZ) twin pairs who share identical genes are compared with those of same-sex fraternal (dizygotic, DZ) twin pairs, who, like regular siblings, share 50 percent of their genes on the average. The cotwin method permits inferences about the probable role of genetic factors in susceptibility to a given disorder, provided that one assumes that the environments of identical and fraternal twins are equally similar. Studies that have empirically addressed this latter assumption have shown it to be robust (Loehlin & Nichols, 1976; Lytton, 1977; Scarr, 1968). Differences between MZ twins reared together reflect environmental influences within families, and differences between DZ twins reflect environmental and genetic influences.

The common disorders of adulthood have been much more extensively investigated from a genetic standpoint than those of childhood. For some disorders of childhood, those that continue unabated into adulthood, it can be argued that data on heritability derived from adult subjects are pertinent to related childhood disorders. For those childhood disorders that are not correlated with adult disorder, e.g., shy-avoidant disorder, the evidence of heritability is rather indirect because studies using the cotwin method or adoption method have not yet been done.

Hyperactivity

According to Ross and Ross (1982) no really adequate adoption or cotwin studies have been done on hyperactivity in children. The best evidence of elevated familial concordance comes from a study using a proband-sibling design. Since hyperactivity diminishes by adolescence, investigators using a proband-parent design must rely on parents' retrospective reports of their own childhood hyperactivity, reports that are prone to errors such as assimilative projection. Welner, Welner, Steward, Palkes, and Wish (1977) observed that one quarter of the brothers of hyperactive males were also hyperactive, a figure that was three times higher than that for the brothers of control males. Other studies report increased rates of alcoholism, antisocial disorders, and hysteria in the adult relatives of hyperactive children (Cantwell, 1972; Morrison, 1980; Morrison & Stewart, 1971). A recent study (Stewart, deBlois, & Cummings, 1980) suggests that these higher rates of psychiatric disorder in adult relatives of the hyperactive child are held in common with the conduct-disordered child and are not specific to the hyperactive children. Moreover, in adult relatives the association of hyperactivity with psychiatric disorder (especially antisocial personality) was restricted to those hyperactive children who were also aggressive, noncompliant, and antisocial. Although no methodologically sound cotwin studies have been done on hyperactivity per se, several studies of normal twins (Scarr, 1966; Vandenberg, 1962; Willerman, 1973) suggest that there is a substantial genetic component to the variation in activity level observed in the general population of children and adults. Ross and Ross (1982, p. 71) concluded their more detailed review of genetic factors in hyperactivity with this statement:

> Although the foregoing data concerning genetic transmission are far from conclusive, they are compelling enough to justify the consideration of a genetic influence operating in combination with environmental factors. (p. 71)

Stuttering, Tourette Syndrome, and Dyslexia

Stuttering (speech disfluency), which according to Pauls and Kidd (1981) occurs in all known cultures and affects about 1 percent of the population, definitely runs in families, and, like hyperactivity, is at least three times more prevalent in males than females. Also, like hyperactivity, studies of concordance between parent and child pose some problem because the majority of parents will have overcome their childhood stuttering behavior. Based on a study of 600 clinically-diagnosed stutterers and self-reported stuttering of their relatives, Pauls and Kidd conclude that the overall pattern of occurrence of stuttering within families is definitely nonrandom. Furthermore, the pattern can be explained by genetic transmission of susceptibility and sex-modified interaction with the environment. Kidd and his associates also observed that the severity of stuttering was not related to the frequency or distribution of stuttering among relatives, and therefore concluded that severity is environmentally influenced or modified by other genes and not related to the transmitted factors that predispose to stuttering (Kidd, Oehlert, Heimbuch, Records, & Webster, 1980). While definite proof is thus not yet at hand, all available evidence suggests that susceptibility to stuttering is genetically transmitted (Pauls & Kidd, 1981).

Tourette syndrome, a behavior with childhood onset and primary symptoms of multiple motor and phonic tics and compulsions, also is more prevalent in males than females. Evidence reviewed by Pauls and Kidd (1981) suggests that Tourette syndrome also may be of primarily genetic origin. The pattern of effects found in a family study of Tourette syndrome (Kidd, Prusoff, & Cohen, 1980) was the same as the pattern found for stuttering. The sex difference in prevalence is related to the transmission of susceptibility to multiple tics, since relatives of female patients are more frequently affected. However, cultural-environmental models of transmission cannot be ruled out by the present evidence.

Pauls and Kidd (1981) also reviewed evidence for the heritability of specific reading disability (developmental dyslexia), a disorder characterized by difficulties in learning to read despite conventional instruction and adequate opportunity in children of normal intelligence. In the largest family study involving 116 probands and 391 first degree relatives (Hallgren, 1950), 77 percent of the probands were male and 23 percent female, figures that agree well with those of Yule (1981) and many other more recent studies. Hallgren found that 47 percent of the male and 36 percent of the female first-degree relatives (i.e., parents and siblings) were also affected. Segregation ratios calculated by Hallgren, based on several Mendelian models, suggested that dyslexia was an autosomal dominant trait with sex-modified expression. In a study of specific reading disability using the cotwin method, Bakwin (1973) found a concordance rate of 84 percent in 31 pairs of MZ twins and 29 percent in 31 pairs of DZ twins. Linkage studies by Smith, Pennington, Kimberling, and Lubs (1979) suggest that one type of dyslexia may be caused by some genotypes at a single genetic locus. Pauls and Kidd (1981) conclude from their review that at least part of the reason for the observed family clustering of specific reading disability is an underlying genetic mechanism. Although the mode of genetic transmission is not known with certainty, the model most often proposed is an autosomal dominant with reduced and sex-modified penetrance.

Conduct Disorder

There is extensive evidence that conduct disorder, delinquency, and antisocial behavior tend to run in families (Glueck & Glueck, 1950, 1968; Robins, West, & Herjanic, 1975; Stewart et al., 1980; see also the review of family factors in conduct disorder by Hetherington & Martin, 1979). For example, Stewart et al. (1980) found antisocial personality and alcoholism to be more common in the natural fathers of aggressive and antisocial boys attending a child psychiatric clinic than in the fathers of other clinic boys. While environmental factors may play a more prominant role than genetic factors in the development of antisocial behavior (Rosenthal, 1975), the evidence that genetic factors also have a significant influence is now extensive.

Although few studies have examined genetic influence in conduct-disordered children, those studies on adults with conduct disorders are relevant to children since the conduct disorders observed in childhood, more so than emotional disorders, tend to persist into adulthood (Robins,

1979). Furthermore, nearly all antisocial adults have exhibited conduct disorder in childhood (Roff, 1974). Studies using the cotwin method to examine concordance rates for psychopathology and criminal behavior (reviewed by Christiansen, 1977; and Rosenthal, 1975) indicate that, across studies, concordance rates for MZ twins are two to three times higher than those of DZ twin pairs. Three studies using the adoption method provide evidence of genetic influence on adult conduct disorder: two of these were on criminal behavior (Crowe, 1974; Hutchings & Mednick, 1977) and one on antisocial personality (psychopathy) (Schulsinger, 1977). Schulsinger found double the rate (14 percent) of psychopathic spectrum disorders (psychopathy, criminality, alcoholism, drug abuse, and hysterical character) in the biological relatives of psychopathic (index) adoptees than in the adoptive relatives of index adoptees (8 percent), the adoptive relatives of control adoptees (5 percent) or the biological relatives of control adoptees (7 percent). Hutchings and Mednick (1977) demonstrated that independent contributions to the prediction of an adopted child's criminality are made by the criminality of both the biological father and the adoptive father as well as by the social class of the adoptive father.

Gorenstein and Newman (1980) have proposed that conduct disorder and hyperactivity are part of a broader constellation of disinhibitory syndromes, which include psychiatric disorders such as alcoholism, psychopathy, hysteria, and impulsive personality as single manifestations of the same diasthesis modified by differential early life experiences. They convincingly array empirical and clinical support for their proposition that these disinhibitory syndromes are behaviorally and genetically related. Another line of argument is that both conduct disorder and hyperactivity are simply reactions to scholastic failure (Miller, et al. 1971; Ross, 1980). The sex ratios are explained by the fact that boys are both more likely to have reading difficulty and more likely to respond aggressively to the stress of failure. If true, the genetic component in hyperactivity and conduct disorder may be due, in part, to the heritability of specific reading disability. Other lines of reasoning suggest that high activity level (Patterson, Littman, & Bricker, 1967) and mesomorphic body build (Glueck & Glueck, 1950), both of which are under genetic influence, may contribute to the development of an aggressive-antisocial interpersonal style. It seems likely that several genetic factors contribute to the susceptibility to develop conduct disorder.

Emotional Disorder

In their review of family influences, Hetherington and Martin (1979) note that surveys consistently have shown that anxious-withdrawn children tend to come from homes in which a high proportion of parents have similar types of symptoms when compared to the general population. Johnson and Melamed (1979) cite several studies indicating a comparable state of affairs for phobic children. Furthermore, Hetherington and Martin (1979) note that married couples have greater similarity in the presence or absence of neurotic disorders, suggesting that some degree of assortative mating occurs with respect to neurotic disorders. In a more systematic family pedigree study, Noyes et al. (1978) observed a higher rate of anxiety neurosis in the blood relatives of neurotics than in nonblood relatives (18 percent versus 3 percent). Schwartz and Johnson (1981) cite several studies linking childhood depression to elevated rates of depression in the parents, and caution that, while the frequency of parental depression appears to be fairly high, it is not clear whether it is higher in families of children displaying other types of psychiatric problems.

Prospective and folllow-back studies between childhood and adulthood indicate that childhood emotional disorders (anxiety, phobias, depression) are poorly predictive of adult disorder. While current evidence then suggests moderate genetic influence in susceptibility to adult anxiety, agoraphobia, and obsessive disorders (Carey, 1982; Carey & Gottesman, 1981) as well as to adult affective disorders (Cadoret & Winokur, 1975; Mendelewicz & Rainer, 1977), these data may have no bearing on the heritability of roughly analogous disorders in childhood. Studies using the cotwin method with samples of normal twins suggest that fear of strangers in infants and toddlers is influenced by genetic factors (Freedman, 1971; Plomin & Rowe, 1979) and that several problem behaviors of childhood, including shyness, tension, and emotionality may be influenced by genetic factors (O'Connor, Foch, Sherry, & Plomin, 1980). Thus, while family studies and cotwin studies on normal children admit the possibility of genetic influence in childhood emotional disorder, the dearth of studies on preadolescent children using either the cotwin method or the adoption method leaves open the question of genetic influence on childhood emotional disorders.

Infantile Autism

Evidence recently summarized by Hanson and Gottesman (1976) supports the view that early-onset childhood psychosis (primarily infantile autism) is both phenomenologically and genetically distinct from late-onset childhood psychosis (primarily childhood schizophrenia). Most supportive of this thesis is Rutter's (1974) summary of data on the frequency of cases with onset in each year from birth to age 14. Frequency of onset decreases as a sharply deccelerated function from 2 years to 6 years, with no cases observed from 6 to 7 years of age, and only a few at 4 to 6 years, the time when one might expect an increase in new cases identified as children enter school. Frequency of onset begins to accelerate markedly between 10 and 14 years in a function that seems continuous with the adult distribution for schizophrenia, a distribution that peaks in the young adult years. The second line of evidence of discontinuity between early and late onset childhood psychosis is the marked difference in the nature of the evidence for genetic influence. Like adult schizophrenics, late-onset childhood psychotics have elevated rates of schizophrenia among parents and siblings; whereas, early-onset childhood psychotics (before age 5) have rates of schizophrenia in parents and siblings that are not significantly different from general population values. Third, the symptoms of early-onset childhood psychotics more closely resemble those of psychotic and severely retarded children with known brain damage; whereas the symptoms seen in late onset cases closely parallel those of adult schizophrenia.

Although Hanson and Gottesman (1976) favor the position that biological, probably congenital but not genetic, factors are involved in the etiology of early-onset psychosis, two genetic models are possible: rare mutations and polygenetic inheritance. However, they believe that the sibling rates of concordance are too low to support polygenetic inheritance. Folstein and Rutter (1977) recently observed a family history of speech delay in 25 percent of families with autistic children and a 2 percent rate of autism among siblings, a rate 50 to 200 times the general population rate for autism. In a careful assessment of 11 pairs of identical twins and 10 pairs of fraternal twins where at least one twin in each pair was autistic, four identical and no fraternal pairs were found to be concordant for autism. The four concordant identical pairs showed no evidence of brain injury, but in 12 of the 17 discordant pairs, brain injury seemed probable or possible for the autistic twin. Folstein and Rutter concluded that early infantile autism, the principle early-onset psychosis, may be caused by an inherited cognitive abnormality, by brain injury, or by both. The new data on elevated rates of sibling concordance and language delay in the families of autistic children (see Minton, Campbell, Green, Jennings, & Samit, 1982) are also compatible with a social environmental influence in autism; however, Folstein and Rutter do not favor that interpretation.

Childhood Schizophrenia

The data supporting genetic influence in schizophrenia are more extensive than those for any major psychiatric disorder. Family studies of schizophrenia show a risk of about 5 percent to 10 percent in first-degree relatives of individuals diagnosed as schizophrenic compared with the general population risk of about one percent (Plomin, DeFries, & McClearn, 1980). Five well-controlled studies using the cotwin method published since 1966 (Gottesman & Shields, 1976) yielded concordance rates of .46 for MZ twins and .14 for DZ twins when combined in a weighted average. The departure of the concordance rate from unity for the MZ twins also suggests that within-family environmental influences play a major role. Similarly, disparate MZ and DZ twin concordance rates have been noted for childhood schizophrenia as well as higher MZ than DZ concordance with respect to age of onset (Kallman & Roth, 1956).

Several studies using the adoption method also provide clear support for a genetic role in susceptibility to the development of schizophrenia (see Kessler, 1980, for a review). A study by Wender, Rosenthal, Kety, Schulsinger and Welner (1974) of Danish adoptees born to schizophrenic parents (index adoptees) and control adoptees in blind interviews had different rates of psychopathology with those of index adoptees being higher. The study also indicated that the experience of being reared by an adoptive parent with schizophrenic disorder does not increase the risk of schizophrenia unless a genetic predisposition to the disorder is already present. Rosenthal, Wender, Kety, Schulsinger, Welner, and Reider (1975) found that the correlation between child psychopathology and the quality of parent-child relationship was highest for the two groups of adoptees with normal (nonschizophrenic) biological parents, one reared by normal adoptive parents and the other by adoptive parents in the schizophrenic spectrum; the correlation was significantly lower for children of schizophrenic biological parents reared either by natural parents or by nonschizophrenic (normal) adoptive parents. These latter groups with a schizophrenic biological parent showed the more severe psychopathology. Rosenthal et al. concluded that the rearing environments appeared to play a relatively greater role in producing normal or psychopathological behavior in individuals without a genetic loading for schizophrenia than it did for individuals with such loading.

Studies of concordance in twins as a function of severity of schizophrenic disorder in the index twin (Gottesman & Shields, 1976), and tests of extreme monogenetic models and extreme polygenetic models with known risk rates at different degrees of family relationship (Matthysse & Kidd, 1976), indicate that individuals who develop schizophrenia are mixed with regard to the genetic makeup that has contributed to the development of their disorder, and to the strength of the genetic predisposition to develop schizophrenic disorder.

Sex Differences in Psychopathology

In the area of sex differences, one typically finds a great variation within each sex and extensive overlap of the male and female distributions of scores on personality and behavioral variables. However, a new debate has arisen over whether the disparate placement of the male and female distributions on some dimensions of social responsiveness, interest, and cognitive ability represents socially or biologically mediated differences between the sexes (Block, 1976; Maccoby & Jacklin, 1974). Empirical evidence strongly indicates an effect of prenatal hormones on sex-dimorphic behaviors such as physical energy expenditure and childhood rehearsal of parenting, even though gender identity itself apparently depends upon sex of rearing parent rather than prenatal hormones (Ehrhardt & Meyer-Bahlburg, 1979). Evidence from research on neonatal and infant gender differences in the frequency of various spontaneous behaviors, stimulus preferences, and memory encoding of stimuli (see McGuiness & Pribram, 1979) also suggests sex-related predispositional differences of potential relevance to later social behavior. These data show continuity with sex differences beyond infancy noted in recent reviews (Eagly, 1978; Frodi, Macaulay, & Thome, 1977; Hall, 1978, 1984; Hoffman, 1977).

Although the expectancies leading to social fear and hopelessness are undoubtedly products of social learning, the differential sex ratios for social anxiety and depression may be a function of predispositional differences between the sexes in the value of social approval and disapproval; females may care more about the potential loss of relationships than males do, and developmental changes at puberty may accentuate these concerns. Substantial differences between the sexes in the prevalence of certain disorders may thus reflect, in addition to specific environmental and genetic influences, a contribution of innate predispositional differences between sexes that in most instances is reinforced by congruent sex-stereotypic socialization.

Eme (1979) concluded from his review of sex differences in childhood psychopathology that disorder was more prevalent in males before adolescence and in females after adolescence. Then he lucidly summarized the evidence on both the nature and the nurture sides of the arguments put forth to account for age by sex interaction. The popular view has been that males experience more stress from cultural expectations and demands during childhood than do females, and that with adolescence, culturally induced conflicts abate for males and increase for females. Eme suggests that the evidence for a strictly cultural explanation for this interaction is not convincing. Furthermore, a devil's advocate could select aspects of the cultural experience that support the reverse, that is, greater female stress in childhood (e.g., lower status of female children and greater restriction of freedom) and increased stress for postadolescent males (e.g., greater cultural demands for initiation in courtship and for economic self-sufficiency). Eme suggests that the age-by-gender interaction is more complex and better explained by an interaction between genetically determined average predispositional differences between males and females (some of whom are later maturing) and age-related cultural pressures.

It has been argued that males are more aggressive because parents and other socializing agents are more permissive of aggression in males than females. Less rather than greater permissiveness toward the young males' aggressiveness seems to be the case. In an observational study of 15 preschool classrooms, Serbin, O'Leary, Kent, and Tonick (1973) found that even after controlling for sex differences in the frequency of aggression, teachers made disciplinary responses to a higher proportion of the incidents of aggression by boys (82 percent) than of those by girls (23 percent), and their responses to boys included a higher proportion of loud reprimands. Serbin (1980) suggested that this attention itself might raise the rate of aggression in boys and account for the sex difference in boys. Serbin's explanation leaves two facts unexplained: the first is the declining rates of aggression and noncompliance with age in boys and the second is the higher rate of noncompliance in boys than in girls from the first year of life (Smith & Daglish, 1977). More parsimonious is the proposition that boys are more strongly disposed than girls to respond to frustration with increased arousal and activity, which, in an aggressive form, often relieves frustration (Patterson, Littman, & Bricker, 1967). Through continuing socialization pressure, aggression is later molded into more socially acceptable forms of assertion. On the basis of his and others' research, Bronfenbrenner (1961b) suggested that strong discipline carries a risk of oversocialization for girls, with consequent inhibition and passivity; for boys, the greater risk is undersocialization resulting from discipline that is not firm enough.

Miller et al. (1971) noted the discrepancy in the sex ratio of problem behavior between their study, where it was 1 : 1 and congruent with the study of Achenbach and Edelbrock (1981) who also used parental reports, and the majority of studies of clinic populations where there is a 3 : 1 excess of boys over girls. They offered the following explanation: Since boys in their sample had greater variance in problem scores and greater academic disability and immaturity than girls, the basic problem is in the boys' failure to learn. Boys, they suggest, are more likely to respond to failure with aggression, hyperactivity, and antisocial behavior, whereas, girls are more likely to respond to failure with social withdrawal, sensitivity, and fear. "Since children are more often referred when they become problems to adults, boys are more likely to be referred for treatment" (p. 21). This explanation is consistent with the fact that, not only do clinics have an excess of males over females, but so also do surveys of child disorder in which teachers rather than parents are the informants (e.g., Werry & Quay, 1971).

Academic failure may be only one of any number of stressors that could yield patterns of disturbance that diverge for males and females. In a recent review of the effects of discord and divorce on children, Emery (1982) noted that when clinic or teacher-rated samples were used, disturbance was found only in boys; however, when nonclinic and parent-rated samples were used, discord was related to disturbance in both boys and girls. Furthermore, marital turmoil was related to externalizing (undercontrol) symptoms in boys and to internalizing (overcontrol) symptoms in girls in nonclinic studies of both intact (Block, Block, & Morrison, 1981; Whitehead, 1979) and divorced (Hess & Camara, 1979) families. Thus, various forms of psychological stress may yield divergent patterns of response in male versus female children.

The Influence of Brain Damage on Childhood Psychopathology

The topic of the effect of brain damage on childhood psychopathology is fraught with problems of inference similar to those associated with the genetic interpretation of familial concordance data: correlation does not necessarily mean causation, since the values of the two correlated variables could be controlled by a third, unmeasured variable. For example, Pond (1961) has argued that socioeconomic privation, acting through lack of self-care and medical access, can cause pregnancy and birth complications (PBCs). Socioeconomic privation, acting through stress on the caretaker and resulting in poor childrearing methods, can also cause conduct disorder. A correlation between PBCs and conduct disorder may thus exist because of the third variable, socioeconomic privation, even when there is no direct causal connection between PBCs and conduct disorder; they simply co-occur under conditions of socioeconomic privation. Nearly all of the empirical data on brain damage and childhood psychopathology is correlational, and only rarely are there assessments of the functioning of the children prior to brain injury. The alleged brain injury is often inferred from pre-, peri-, or postnatal medical history rather than directly observed, and the validity of diagnoses of brain injury from medical histories is very poor (Werry, 1979b). Even the link between PBCs and brain damage is tenuous. Prospective studies of large populations suggest that if PBCs have any effect at all on the frequency of subsequent behavioral, cognitive, and neurological abnormalities, it is to a surprisingly small degree (Davie, Butler, & Goldstein, 1972; Douglas & Gear, 1976; Niswander & Gordon, 1972). Therefore, unless brain damage is of gross proportions, its diagnosis is highly unreliable and, for the majority of children with psychiatric disorders, the diagnosis of brain damage is "no more than an enlightened guess" (Werry, 1979b, p. 98).

Given the often unreliable diagnosis of brain damage in some children, one strategy has been to study the prevalence of psychopathological disorder in children, all of whom have clear evidence of organic damage to the brain, such as cerebral palsy or epilepsy. Rutter, Graham, and Yule (1970), in an epidemiological study, identified 186 children on the Isle of Wight between 5 and 14 years of age with definite neuro-epileptic disorder. This group constituted 1.3 percent of the child population in the age range of concern. The rate of psychiatric disorder of all types within this brain disordered subgroup was 34.3 percent, compared with a prevalence rate for psychiatric disorder of 6.6 percent in the general population of children 10 and 11 years of age on the Isle of Wight, and a rate of 11.5 percent for children 5 to 14 with chronic physical disorders not involving the brain (Rutter, 1977). The rate of psychiatric disorder is thus about five times greater in the neuro-epileptically disordered group than it is in the general child population, and three times greater than among children with chronic physical handicaps. Using Rutter's figures and assuming level rates of psychiatric disorder from 5 to 14 years and a population of 12,000 children on the Isle of Wight, the rate of neuro-epileptic disorder among psychiatrically disordered children can be estimated at 6.8 percent, a rate considerably higher than the base rate of 1.3 percent for neuro-epileptic disorder in the child population. A correlation thus does exist between organic brain dysfunction and psychiatric disorder. Given brain damage, the probability of psychiatric disorder is 34.3 percent, and given psychiatric disorder, the probability of brain damage is 6.8 percent. Brain damage is thus a better predictor of psychiatric disorder than psychiatric disorder is a predictor of brain damage.

The idea has been current in the literature on child psychopathology that there is a distinctive syndrome of behavior that is characteristic of brain-damaged children (cf. Wender, 1971), a pattern consisting of hyperactivity, distractibility, impulsiveness, irritability, clumsiness, and poor school work. Although the majority of studies suggest that this syndrome is associated with certain pre- and perinatal, neurological, EEG, and physical abnormalities, the relationship between these variables and brain damage is uncertain (Werry, 1979b). Since the majority of children who exhibit this syndrome have no signs suggestive of cerebral dysfunction, therefore, in no sense can hyperactivity be taken in itself as diagnostic of brain damage (Werry, 1979b). More importantly, the empirical evidence shows that the hyperactive syndrome (attention deficit disorder, with hyperactivity) is not a characteristic outcome of brain damage. In a study of 50 preschoolers with confirmed lesions and IQs above 70, there was no modal or characteristic personality (Ernhart, Graham, Eichman, Marshall, & Thurston, 1963). Although adjustment problems and hyperactivity were more common in the brain-damaged group than in controls, there was a wide range of unfavorable personality characteristics and, furthermore, the impairments of the brain-damaged group were more severe in the cognitive and perceptual-motor domains than in the personality domain. On the Isle of Wight, of the psychiatrically disordered children, 47 percent had neurotic/emotional disorder, 35 percent had conduct or conduct and emotional disorder, and 17 percent had other disorders consisting primarily of psychoses and hyperkinesis. For non-brain-damaged psychiatrically disturbed children, 60 percent had emotional disorder, 38 percent conduct, and 2 percent had other disorders. Furthermore, rates of neuro-epileptic disorder (61 percent male, 39 percent female), and rates of psychiatric disorder in the neuro-epileptically disordered (69 percent male, 31 percent female) were only slightly disparate for males and females on the Isle of Wight, whereas hyperactivity is five to eight times more prevalent in males than females. Therefore, brain damage is not a likely cause of the majority of the cases of hyperactivity.

Rutter (1977) addressed the question of how brain damage leads to psychiatric disorder in children by discussing direct effects and effects mediated by the social consequences of cognitive and temperamental deviance. The highly elevated rates of psychiatric disorder among the neuro-epileptically disordered in the Isle of Wight study are not easily explained in terms of social acceptance and rejection because the chronically physically handicapped with neural lesions below the brain stem (who were, if anything, more stigmatized by their symptoms) had significantly lower rates of disorder (Rutter et al., 1970). Elevated rates of psychiatric disorder were observed in children with active lesions above the brain stem and especially psychomotor epilepsy (see also Holdsworth & Whitmore, 1974). These data suggest that an active neural disruption may hamper social adjustment. Among cerebral palsyed children, psychiatric disorder was associated with specific reading retardation, language retardation, and strabismus. Rutter asked whether the elevated rate of psychiatric disorder in the neuro-epileptically impaired could be explained on the basis of IQ alone, since low IQ is related to higher prevalence of psychiatric disorder in non-brain-damaged individuals and since subjects with brain damage above the brain stem did have markedly lower IQs. Even when the neuro-epileptic group was restricted to individuals with IQs above 85, the rate of psychiatric disorder was 24 percent versus 9 percent for a comparable group of physically handicapped children, and still four times the rate of disorder in nonhandicapped children with IQs above 85. In a separate study of children with head injuries resulting in localized but gross cortical damage, despite average IQ after recovery, the rate of psychiatric disorder was twice that of the control group; however, no association could be detected between the locus of the lesion and the type of psychiatric disorder (Shaffer, Chadwick, & Rutter, 1975). Factors in addition to general intelligence thus mediate the effect of brain damage on psychiatric disorders; and although the locus of the injury in the cortex may not be very important, the specific cognitive deficit may be important.

Data from the North London study (Seidel, Chadwick, & Rutter, 1975) were used to test whether the influence on psychiatric disorder of brain damage in combination with a composite index of psychosocial disadvantage (low social class, discord or broken homes, etc.) was additive or interactive. The effect proved to be additive; brain damage increased the rate of psychiatric disorder a substantial and equal magnitude among children from good and poor backgrounds. Although interaction was not observed, Rutter (1977) suggests that brain damage may evoke trans-actions with the social environment that dispose the child toward psychiatric disorder. First, the greater variation in temperament induced by brain damage may, for those children with difficult and nonadaptive temperaments, yield a higher risk of social stress. Second, family responses of either scapegoating or overprotection that are in direct response to the neurologically induced handicaps may also raise the risk of psychiatric disorder. Finally, an important role of self-appraisal and goal-setting in the development of psychiatric disorder is suggested by the frequent observation that psychiatric disorder is more likely in the child with mild or moderate physical disabilities than in the severely crippled child (Rutter et al., 1970; Seidel et al., 1975). These data suggest that stress may be greater in those children who compete with and evaluate themselves by the same standard as nonhandicapped children.

To summarize, brain damage, although not yielding a modal pattern of psychiatric disorder, does greatly increase the risk of psychiatric disorder in general. Just how brain damage contributes to psychiatric disorder is not well understood. Most strongly supported by evidence is the hypothesis that intelligence and other more specific cognitive functions, when diminished by brain damage, dispose the child toward failure in academic settings, and the stress of failure leads to psychopathology. Also supported is the hypothesis that active brain lesions disrupt psychological functioning directly. Less well-supported but plausible hypotheses include the effects of damage-induced changes in temperament, the families' overprotection or the abuse elicited by handicap, and the child's own negative self-evaluative response.

Social Influence in Childhood Psychopathology

Personality Predisposition and Caretaker Child Interaction

Despite the ubiquitous evidence for the significant heritability of many psychopathological disorders, less than half of the total variation in schizophrenia, emotional disorder, and conduct disorders can be explained by genetic differences. This leaves the greater proportion of variation to social or physical environmental influences and to classification error. In the section immediately following, I present my views of how genetic predispositions may interact with parental behavior to influence the development of personality and psychopathology in infancy and childhood (Schwarz, 1979).*

The personality tree. The development of a child's style of relating to the social world is analogous to climbing a tree whose branches, as they reach higher, may cross and recross through three styles; *cooperation,* which I arbitrarily place in the center, *fearful-avoidance* to one side, and *antagonism* to the other. As one goes higher in the tree, farther out on a limb, the harder it is to get from one side of the tree to the other. However, at every fork, change in direction is possible.

The first fork is traversed in the second half of the first year of life. This fork places the child in one of the three areas of the tree. The child will pass to the cooperative style at the center of the tree if the caretaker is sensitive and responsive to the infant's needs and the infant is biologically sound. The infant will learn to signal his or her needs with increasing competence and learn to anticipate with confidence the satisfying responses of the caretaker (Ainsworth, 1979; Clark-Stewart, 1973). If the caretaker is insensitive, unresponsive, or ineffective and repeatedly frustrates the infant, the infant will associate the caretaker with painful emotional arousal and will respond with anger or exaggerated independence (Egeland & Srouf, 1981; Farber & Egeland, 1982; Main & Londerville, 1979). The infant's personality predispositions influence the form of the response to painful interactions with the caretaker (Crockenberg, 1981; Egeland & Sroufe, 1981). Some infants, especially males, are more likely to respond with high levels of activity and strenuous, angry protest; other infants may become passive, apathetic, and self-absorbed (Moss, 1967, 1974). If the child is genetically disposed to fear strangers and the caretaker deals insensitively with the child's responses to strangers and separation in novel situations, the infant may become "clingy," dependent, socially avoidant, and reluctant to separate from the caretaker. Temperamental differences among infants and the skill and patience of the caretaker in coping with the infant's potentially erratic behavior determine whether a cooperative interaction will develop (Chess, Thomas, Rutter, & Birch, 1963; Sameroff & Chandler, 1975; Thomas, Chess, & Birch, 1970).

Even though an antagonistic relationship may have developed between an infant and caretaker, another fork in that limb of the tree lies

---

*Adapted by permission of the publisher. Copyright 1979 by the American Psychological Association.

ahead. If the parents patiently persist in encouraging the child's coop-eration, he or she may be moved toward cooperation (Whitt & Casey, 1982). On the other hand, if the parents meet antagonism with antag-onism, the child may intensify his or her resistance to influence, thereby setting a course toward conduct disorder. If the parents consistently capitulate to antagonistic, stubborn refusals, this style of interpersonal control may interfere with the child's development of more cooperative behaviors and may set a course toward oppositional disorder or narcis-sistic interpersonal exploitation. In parallel fashion, parental responses to the socially avoidant behavior of the fearful young child may exac-erbate, ameliorate, or leave unchanged this behavioral style. Gentle en-couragement and predictable parental behavior may build the child's tolerance of novelty and separation. The trauma of unannounced aban-donment by parents in strange situations will intensify the fear; and overly empathetic indulgence may solidify the avoidant pattern, predis-posing the child toward avoidant disorder or other neurotic styles of adjustment. An initially cooperative, secure relationship with the care-taker, although generally predictive of future peer adjustment (Sroufe, 1979a; Waters, Wippman, & Sroufe, 1979), is no guarantee of smooth sailing; it can be disrupted at any level. Unrelenting shame, embarrass-ment, and criticism will move the child toward social avoidance; painful, unreasonable punishment will move the child in the direction of antag-onism. Opportunities for change persist through childhood; however, the longer a child practices a particular behavioral style, the harder it will be to modify.

Attachment and the developmental tasks of infancy and toddler-hood. Although there are indications that severe social deprivation has a devastating effect on language development (Goldfarb, 1945; Spitz, 1965), the lesser variations in interactive harmony and quality of attach-ment found in mother-infant dyads have little or no effect on language development (Bretherton, Bates, Benigni, Camaioni, & Volterra, 1979; Clarke-Stewart, 1973; Connell, 1977; Pentz, 1975). However, the se-curely attached infant exhibits a higher level of gestural communication (Bretherton et al., 1979) and symbolic play that is more frequent, richer, and varied, and of longer duration than that of the insecurely attached infant and toddler (Bretherton et al., 1979; Harmon, Morgan, & Gaens-bauer, 1978; Matas, Arend, & Sroufe, 1978). The one-year-old infants of accepting, attentive, and cooperative mothers, infants who also tend to be securely attached, have been shown to be more obedient to parental requests, although as yet unskilled in expressive language (Stayton, Ho-gan, & Ainsworth, 1971).

Pentz (1975) suggested that language development is buffered against variations in mother-child interaction within a fairly wide range. It is plausible that the quality of the relationship to the caretaker may make the difference in the case of an infant who, for genetic or neurologic reasons, has less aptitude for language acquisition. Congenitally aphasic children at 2 and 3 years of age (Cohen, Caparoulo, & Shaywitz, 1976), like normal children, are skilled in gestural communication, are sociable and cooperative, and engage in imitative play; however, nonaphasic pre-school-age males who are delayed primarily in expressive language tend to be uncooperative and disobedient (Wulbert, Inglis, Kriegsmann, & Mills, 1975). The mothers of such language-delayed boys, relative to mothers of normal and Downs syndrome control boys, were found by Wulbert et al. to be less involved with the child, less emotionally and verbally responsive, and more punitive and restrictive. These data suggest that a warm and cooperative relationship with the caretaker may play a part in language development. It is frequently noted in the clinical setting that when resistance, mutual hostility, and uncooperativeness pervade the relationship between the mother and the toddler-age child, not only is expressive language delayed, but in addition there may be struggles over bladder and bowel control, eating, and other care routines. The securely attached infant at 2 years of age approaches problem-solving tasks with longer attention span, less frustration, more positive affect, and uses the mother's help more effectively (Farber & Egeland, 1982; Matas et al., 1978). Warmth in the relationship between mother and son at age 2 1/2 years is positively correlated with compliance to maternal commands (Lytton & Zwirner, 1975). The quality of the care-taker-child relationship thus affects progress on the developmental tasks of infancy and toddlerhood.

Social Influences on Conduct Disorder

Early childhood. In a further analysis of data from the New York Longitudinal Study (Thomas, Chess, & Birch, 1968), Cameron (1977) found that maternal intolerance, maternal inconsistency, and parental conflict/confusion over child handling (obtained from parent interviews at child's age of 3 years) were correlated with lack of adaptability in the child at ages 3 and 4. In this same age range, 3 to 4 years, mother's (but not father's) mood was found to be significantly, although modestly, correlated with the adjustment of both boys and girls as rated by nursery school teachers (Scholom, Zucker, & Stollak, 1979). In a more comprehensive study of adjustment in 3- and 4-year-olds involving interview and direct observation of parent-child interaction in the home and teacher ratings of child adjustment, Baumrind (1967) noted several meaningful relationships. Mothers of well-adjusted children, compared with mothers of poorly adjusted children, exerted more control and were less affected by coercive demands based on whining and crying. They also made more demands for mature behavior but accompanied demands with verbal explanation; they gave the child a hearing and accommodated to the child when reasonable. Mothers of impulsive-aggressive children were the least persistent in getting the child to meet their requests. They made few maturity demands and tended to be more nurturant. These studies suggest that maternal behavior may influence the adaptability of preschoolers.

Several studies of young children have examined specifically the relationship between parental behavior and the child's aggressive, aversive, or noncompliant behavior. Studies by Sears, Whiting, Nowlis, and Sears (1953) and Becker, Peterson, Luria, Shoemaker, and Hellmer (1962) both found for 5-year-old boys a positive linear relationship between parent reports of severity of punishment and level of aggression in school; however, for girls, both studies found a curvilinear relationship; intermediate severity of punishment was associated with a higher level of aggression than punishment of either very high or very low severity. Several observation-based studies indicate that mothers of aggressive children, in comparison with control mothers, have higher rates of aversive and commanding behaviors in interaction with their child (Delfini, Bernal, & Rosen, 1976; Forehand, King, Peed, & Yoder, 1975; Reid & Taplin, 1978; Snyder, 1977). In home observations of both clinical and normal samples correlations of .58 and .53, respectively, were found between rates of aversive parent behavior and rates of aversive child behavior (Lobitz & Johnson, 1975). Mothers who were aversive to their own preschoolers in a nursery school setting also tended to be aversive in interacting with other children in the setting (Halverson & Waldrop, 1970). In a comparison study of problem and nonproblem children using direct observation in the home, Patterson (1980) found little difference in the behavior of fathers toward children in the two groups; whereas, the mothers of families with problem children exhibited more disapproval and normative commands and less talking, laughter, and approval. There is thus a correlation between parental behaviors of demandingness, punitiveness, and disapproval and young children's aggressive, noncompliant, and aversive behavior.

Does the high level of maternal disapproval and demandingness cause the child to be aggressive, or does the child's unacceptable behavior elicit the mother's disapproval and demandingness? Patterson (1980) notes that the problem child and his or her mother often get involved in extended chains of reciprocal aversive behaviors. Unlike their younger and older siblings, the problem children immediately escalate to intensely aversive responses. Mothers of problem children, on the other hand, escalate the aversiveness of their responses more slowly than either the problem child or his older or younger siblings. Only after repeated attacks is the mother likely to reciprocate. Patterson (1980), in his statement of coercion theory, assumes that the mother's inability to control her child leads to the disruption of the family and to her increased rate of aggression and concomitant feelings of despair and low self-esteem. When she shifts to a predominance of punishment, the practiced child aggressor counter-aggresses and may continue to do so until the mother gives in. The irritated father jumps into the disciplinary breach and applies drastic emergency treatment in the form of severe punishment. This may result in a lax and inconsistent mother and a severely punitive father, a combination frequently observed in families with aggressive children (Hetherington & Martin, 1979). According to Patterson (1980), the increased effectiveness of parental punishment after training alters the coercive interchanges, whereas training parents to be nonpunitive and to ignore aggression is ineffective. Also consistent with Patterson's view is the finding that, irrespective of the criminality of the parents, the lowest crime rates in their offspring occurred when both parents were punitive but consistent during the early years (McCord, McCord, & Zola, 1959) (See also Lytton, 1979.). These data suggest that it is not punishment that leads to conduct disorder but inconsistent or delayed and ineffective discipline.

Two recent British studies (Dixon, 1979; Tizard, 1977; Tizard & Hodges, 1978) used modern research methods to provide evidence that institutional care by multiple caretakers during the first year of life and beyond may predispose children toward conduct disorder. This finding supports similar findings by Goldfarb (1945) and Bowlby, Ainsworth, Boston, and Rosenbluth (1956) from less methodologically adequate studies. In Tizard's study, institutional children in a school setting at age 8 were more attention-seeking, restless, disobedient, and unpopular than control children. Using direct behavioral observation, Dixon found that institutional children more often called out in class, disregarded teachers' directives, and exhibited off-task behavior. They were also more disruptive and attention-seeking, they fought more with other children, and they were less well liked. Tizard's longitudinal study showed continuities between excessive clinging in infancy, attention-seeking and indiscriminant friendliness at age 4, and impaired relationships with adults and children in middle childhood. This pattern is similar in some respects to the social behavior of children in maternal care who have experienced extensive infant group day care (for review see Barton and Schwarz, 1982). Rutter (1979) points out that it is uncertain whether institutionally reared children lack fundamental social qualities as a result of atypical early bonding or whether they have merely learned patterns of interaction that are adaptive in the institution but maladaptive in other settings.

Middle and late childhood. Most of the literature relating to social influences on conduct disorder focuses on influences operating during middle childhood, since the data on either the family or the child were gathered when the child was of school age. By examining child guidance clinic records, Roff (1974) provided a clinically rich picture of the childhood family characteristics of former clients whose conduct disorder evolved into a pattern of severe bad conduct in young adulthood, a picture that in several respects is similar to the developmental dynamics of aggression described by Patterson. Parents of the conduct-disordered former clients, compared with parents of former clients who were socially adequate as adults, had a higher frequency of contact with the law, of "running around," and of divorce. Mothers were reported as having no control. Also higher for the bad conduct cases was the frequency of illegitimacy, broken homes, desertion by either parent, maternal abandonment, and residence in more than one foster home. Roff characterizes these case histories as indicating neglect intensified to repudiation and intensified even beyond that to abandonment of the subject and his siblings by the mother. Roff suggests that the dynamic begins with lack of normal parental affection and care coupled with the use of overvigorous physical violence in an attempt to assert control over a misbehaving boy, control that the parent had not acquired by working at being a parent.

Roff's summary agrees with other studies recently surveyed by Hetherington and Martin (1979). For example, Becker, Peterson, Hellmer, Shoemaker, and Quay (1959) reported that parents of children with conduct disorder are typically inconsistent, arbitrary, and given to explosive expressions of anger. Most predictive of conduct-disorder symptoms on the five-year follow-up of the Manhattan Family Research Project (Langner, Gersten, & Simcha-Fagan, 1983), listed in order of predictive power, were parental punitiveness, maternal excitability and inconsistency, lack of parental affection, and emotional and physical illness of the mother. Extremes of restrictiveness and permissiveness, hostility, rejection, severe physical punishment, and inconsistency have all been found to be associated with high levels of antisocial behavior and low levels of self-control, internalization, and prosocial behavior in children (Martin, 1975). Evidence reviewed by Quay (1979) indicates that the undersocialized (psychopathic) subgroup of delinquents is predominately at Kohlberg's stages one and two of moral development and, in general, show less mature moral reasoning than socialized delinquents. Since the parents of delinquents also show a lower level of moral reasoning (Hudgins & Prentice, 1973) in addition to impulsive aggressiveness, both of these characteristics observed in many conduct-disordered children may have been influenced by the parental model, by genetic predisposition, and/or by specific prenatal childrearing behaviors. The study on adopted children by Hutchings and Mednick (1977) suggests that the separate influences of genetic predisposition, parental model, and social milieu combine additively in their contribution to the development of conduct disorder.

Social Influences on Hyperactivity

Compared with conduct disorder, there is a minuscule body of generalizable information on the early social development correlates of hyperactivity (Ross & Ross, 1982). Thomas et al. take the view that although the temperamentally difficult child is more likely to develop hyperactivity (Thomas & Chess, 1977), this is by no means an inevitable outcome. The outcome, in their view, is more a function of the patience, adaptability, and consistency of the child's caretakers.

Like Thomas et al., Bettelheim (1973) subscribes to a diasthesis-stress model that states that the genetically predisposed child responds to stress with increased restlessness and activity. A caretaker who is patient and has a high tolerance for restlessness could avoid exacerbating this difficult temperament; however, an irritable caretaker would precipitate an unhappy dyadic relationship that could deteriorate into a continuing battle, with the predisposed infant fighting back through increased restlessness. There are no adoption studies that permit the separation of genetic and rearing influences in a way that would test this model.

Another view, one more consistent with observations from the Isle of Wight study (Schachar, Rutter, & Smith, 1981), is that activity level is a biological given, and that what changes in response to social influence is whether the child develops social or antisocial behaviors of high frequency. Antisocial behaviors were much more likely to develop in children who were both hyperactive and low in social class than in either children of lower social class who were not hyperactive or hyperactive children who were not of lower class. In a controlled prospective study, Hetherington et al. (1979b) noted the emergence of symptoms of hyperactivity (impulsiveness, inattentiveness, high distractability) in 4- to 5-year-olds one year following the parents' divorce. Two months after the divorce, mothers of these children with hyperactive symptoms had been erratic and inconsistent, they had little control over their children, and they had disorganized, chaotic households. The effect was stronger for boys than for girls and was more likely to occur when conflict between the parents continued beyond the divorce.

A glimpse at possible sex differences in the developmental dynamics of hyperactivity in a middle-class setting is provided by Battle and Lacey (1972) who analyzed data from the Fels Longitudinal Study. Motor activity (clinically rated from protocols of observations at home, nursery school, and day camp, separately for ages 0–3, 3–6, 6–10) was correlated (within each sex) with ratings of maternal and child behaviors from each age level and with assessments at adolescence and adulthood. Activity was found to be uncorrelated with IQ for either males or females. The stability of hyperactivity over time was moderate for males and slight for females, decreasing with the distance between assessments for both sexes. Only the activity level of males showed consistent relationships with maternal behavior. High activity in male toddlers was associated with maternal criticality and disapproval at toddler age, and was predictive of low maternal protectiveness, absence of babying, and high disapproval in the preschool period, and of low intensity of contact and high severity of penalties at school age. High activity in preschool-age males was associated with low maternal protectiveness and high disapproval at that age, and was predictive of low clarity of policy and low restrictiveness of regulation at school age. Mothers of school-age hyperactive boys were low in restrictiveness and high in occupational attainment. Hyperactive males and females were similar in toddlerhood in both being low in concern with physical harm, and in the preschool period in being physically aggressive with and attempting to dominate peers, and in the school-age period in attempting to dominate both peers and adults and in being attention-seeking toward peers. Hyperactive males (but not females) as toddlers and at preschool age were low in compliance, at preschool and school age were high in attention-seeking from adults, and at each age were low in achievement-striving. Hyperactive females (but not males) at preschool age were high in achievement-striving and at school age were high in peer acceptance.

These data are consistent with the view that the low achieving, impulsive, noncompliant style of the hyperactive male toddler may elicit more punitive reactions from some mothers than the more compliant style of the hyperactive female toddler. In anger and frustration, mothers may be more likely to withdraw nurturance from hyperactive boys in retaliation for their indifference. That these maternal responses are not strictly a function of hyperactivity is supported by the fact that female toddlers, who were just as hyperactive as male toddlers, did not elicit them. The more punitive treatment received by the male hyperactive child may interfere with the socialization process, as manifested by the male's lower compliance and low achievement strivings. Their lower rates of compliance may further discourage their mothers from regulatory efforts, advancing mutual disengagement between mother and son. Maternal indifference may be the fuel that fires the high level of attention-seeking in the school-age hyperactive male.

Social Influences on Emotional Disorder

Early childhood. The three emotional disorders that are likely to appear in early childhood are avoidant disorder, separation anxiety disorder, and, as a transient disorder, depression. The primary symptom of avoidant disorder, fear of strangers, develops in nearly all children between 5 and 10 months of age (Schaffer & Emerson, 1964; Sroufe, 1979b). The likelihood of crying when confronted by strangers increases thereafter and reaches a peak between 12 and 18 months on the average, and then gradually subsides. It is the lack of abatement, or more rarely, the later intensification of the fear and avoidance of strangers that constitutes disorder. Fear of strangers is less marked in infants who have had extensive exposure to many different individuals (Sroufe, 1979b). Research on quality of attachment indicates that the more secure and sociable the infant and toddler is with the mother, the more sociable and competent he or she is with both adults and peer strangers (Clarke-Stewart, VanderStoep, & Killian, 1979; Easterbrooks & Lamb, 1979). Anxiously attached infants who have had less sensitively responsive mothers in the first year of life tend to show more intense fear of strangers (Ainsworth, Blehar, Waters, & Wall, 1978, p. 152). Also, 2-year-olds who were fearful of strangers had more difficult temperaments and had mothers who were rated as less effective in giving emotional support and in teaching coping strategies (Baker, 1981). The patterns of results from Baker's comprehensive study also suggested that the parents' abilities to set appropriate controls over negative behavior and to foster skills for coping with stress even at a very early age are crucial for overcoming stressful, fear-provoking situations.

Extending the developmental path yet another step, Liberman (1977) observed that discouraging autonomy correlates positively with 3-year-old children's ineffective behavior with peers and negatively with responsiveness to peers. Similarly, Baumrind and Black (1967) in their study of preschoolers reported that a marked lack of disciplinary control, and a failure to set realistic limits, are associated with immature behavior, and a high degree of control through nonrational, nonnurturing methods is associated with dysphoric and withdrawn "disaffiliated" behavior. A lack of nurturance, support, encouragement, and firm guidance is thus associated with immature behavior, failure to cope with mildly aversive conditions, and ready complaint. On the other hand, highly restrictive, autonomy-discouraging, nonnurturing methods are associated with fearful withdrawal from social interaction. The former pattern may be a precursor to separation anxiety disorder and the latter to avoidant disorder or depression.

Separation anxiety and school phobia. Psychodynamically oriented theorists (Eisenberg, 1958; Johnson, 1957; Kelly, 1973) have conceptualized school phobia and separation disorders as the result of an overdependency fostered by the mother. Eisenberg (1958) observed mother-child separations in 11 preschoolers with separation anxiety disorder in a nursery school setting and concluded that separation was as difficult for the mother as for the child. As the child began to move toward the play area and to look less at the mother, she moved closer to the child and occasionally intruded into the child's play. As infants, these children were treated with apprehensive oversolicitude: they were not trusted to babysitters outside of the immediate family and, after infancy, they were constantly warned of hazards if they ventured away from home. Although the reasons for the mothers' overprotection and/or over-involvement seemed diverse, the self-imposed burden in many cases generated ego-alien resentment toward the child. The frustration imposed on the child by the intrusions of an overprotective mother may, in turn, evoke hostility on the part of the child toward the mother. Reid (1976) found that last-born children from sibships of more than three were overrepresented among nursery school children with separation difficulties, a fact that provides at least circumstantial evidence for overinvolvement on the part of the mother.

In a comparison of school phobics and other children with neurotic symptoms, Waldron, Shrier, Stone, and Tobin (1975) observed that in addition to having a higher frequency of overinvolved mothers who had difficulty separating from the child, the school phobics were more often scapegoated children whose demands were resented by the parent. In addition, there was a higher rate of loss, threatened loss, or diminished relationship with parents for the school phobic children in the preceding year. This set of conditions suggests that insecure attachment and threat to an important parental attachment are etiological factors in the development of school phobia.

Depression and withdrawal in young children. Other studies of young children suggest that angry, critical, and rejecting parental behavior is associated with emotional lability and depression in young children. Baker (1981) also noted that parents who experienced high life stress and reported themselves to be controlling and detached in their child care also described their 2-year-olds as emotionally labile and difficult. Similarly, Milliones (1978) found that the more temperamentally difficult the mother rated the child, the lower were the ratings of the mother's contingent responsiveness in home observations. However, studies in which mothers provide ratings of their infants' temperament must be interpreted with caution, since Campbell (1977) noted that observers detected no systematic difference in the behavior of infants whose mothers rated them as irritable, irregular, and unadaptable. Through a sophisticated path analysis, Dibble and Cohen (1978) found evidence that stress affects young children primarily through its influence on parenting style. When parents were under stress they were more likely to provide less child-centered and more angry care. These parents who by and large were young and had young children, reported their children to be less attentive, zestful, and outgoing than parents reporting less stress. The combination of parental hostility and restrictiveness was associated with inhibition, anxiety, and constriction in 4- to 6-year-old girls (but not boys) from intact homes (Hetherington et al., 1979b). Clinical reports indicate that the parents of depressed children are often themselves depressed. They may have serious problems handling aggression and are often rejecting or detached and impersonal (cf. Poznanski, Kranhenbuhl, & Zrull, 1976).

Although the fabric of evidence is patchy and susceptible to diverse interpretation, taken at face value it suggests multiple and interactive determinants of childhood depression: A negative feedback system operates between a temperamentally difficult child and an environmentally stressed and irritable caretaker. The caretaker becomes depressed, detached, and impersonal, providing few emotionally gratifying interactions with the child, and the child, in response to the rejection, becomes depressed and apathetic. A depressive response to this set of instigating conditions may be more likely in the child who has experienced helplessness in earlier interactions with the caretaker. In other words, a child who has had little prior control in the relationship may be more inclined to become apathetically depressed (Goldberg, 1977), whereas the child who has had success at commanding attention via coercive methods may become irritably depressed or, if successful once again, may succeed in avoiding depression. Hyperactivity, more common in males, may be learned in this manner.

Cytryn and McKnew (1972) suggest that acute depressive reactions in children, although typically resulting from parental loss through separation, may also involve losses more subtle in form such as withdrawal of interest or affection by some important individual in the child's environment (cf. Coleman & Provence, 1957). The degree of distress at the loss of a caretaker is a function of the quality and the extent of the interaction between the child and the caretaker (Hetherington, Cox, & Cox, 1979a; Rutter, 1980; Spitz, 1946) and the ability of substitute caretakers to emulate the interaction patterns of the absent caretaker (Robertson & Robertson, 1971). The background of children with chronic depressive reactions, according to Cytryn and McKnew, is characterized by a long history of frequent separations and loss rather than a single major precipitating event.

Interparental conflict. Rutter noted in 1971 in a review of the effects of parent-child separation, that maladjustment was more common among the children of divorce than among children who had lost a parent to death, and that maladjustment was more common in children from homes high in marital conflict. Rutter concluded that it was the stress of parental conflict rather than loss of a parent per se that contributed to child maladjustment. Emery (1982) has recently reviewed the now more extensive literature on the effects of interparental conflict and divorce on children and observed that every investigation, whether of questionable or of sound methodology, found marital turmoil to be related to some form of undercontrolled behavior. An outcome of anxious overcontrol (emotional disorder) was noted consistently. Emery also noted that marital turmoil is more often reported as having negative effects on boys than on girls from both divorced and intact discordant marriages. The greater susceptibility of male than female children to this negative effect of marital turmoil may be more apparent than real for the following reasons: Marital turmoil frequently is associated with conduct disorder in males and with emotional disorder in females (Block, Block, Morrison, 1981; Hess & Camara, 1979; Hetherington et al., 1979a, 1979b; Whitehead, 1979). Females are more likely to become anxious, withdrawn, and overly compliant, and males, aggressive, noncompliant and attention-seeking. Studies using teacher ratings seldom yield negative effects for females, presumably because teachers are more aware of conduct disorder, the characteristic male response to marital turmoil, and less aware of emotional disorder, the more common response pattern in females. Parent ratings and peer ratings are more likely to reveal unfavorable effects for females (cf. Whitehead, 1979). Clinic samples are more likely to yield relationships between discord and negative behavior for males than for females, again because conduct disorder (which is more typical of males) is more likely to lead to treatment referral than is emotional disorder. Furthermore, since the mother retains custody of the children following separation or divorce in 90 percent of cases, male children may experience more frustration and deprivation than females due to the male child's loss of an appropriate sex-role model and of the customary agent of social control. Two studies indicate that males in father custody after divorce (Santrock & Warshak, 1979) or death of the mother (Gregory, 1965) fair better than do females in father custody. The manner in which females show distress and the typical condition of mother-custody after divorce may thus have muted the evidence available for a negative impact of marital turmoil on females.

The longitudinal study by Hetherington et al. (1978, 1979a, 1979b) provides the most objective data on the responses of young children to divorce and separation from father. When observed at play in the nursery school setting two months after divorce, both male and female 4-year-olds from divorced families were rated as more aggressive by peers and showed less happy, affectionate, and task-involved affect and more depressed, anxious, guilty, and apathetic affect than did children from nondivorced families. One year following divorce, 5-year-old boys showed more hostile affect than boys from nondivorced families and two years after divorce they were still less happy and more anxious (Hetherington et al., 1979a). Aggression and noncompliance, which reached a peak one year after divorce, were both more marked and more enduring for males than for females in home and nursery school settings. These data suggest that both emotional and conduct disorder symptoms are the legacy of divorce for male and female young children. The increase in aggressive behavior in young males was correlated with deterioration in maternal childrearing behaviors. Frustration at the loss of the father's companionship may, however, be an additional instigating factor. Hetherington et al. (1979b) noted that immediately following the divorce, boys in nursery schools where there were male adults made efforts to follow, touch, and seek praise or affection from these male adults. In contrast, they directed negative demands and aversive opposition toward female adults in the nursery school setting. These results, however, may not be applicable at all ages, since Wallerstein and Kelly (1975), who studied children after divorce at a wide range of ages, found that the adjustment of younger children, rather than older children, was more strongly related to the emotional adjustment of the mother.

Anxiety-withdrawal in middle childhood. The empirical literature says little about the social influences that contribute to the development of an overanxious, self-denegrating, insecure child. One treads less solid ground in attempting to generalize from adult to child anxiety disorder than in the case of conduct disorder, because of the lower predictive relationship from child to adult emotional disorder. Older individuals with anxiety symptoms tend to come from homes in which a higher proportion of parents have anxiety symptoms than in the general population (cf. Noyes, Clancy, Crowe, Hoeuk, & Slymen, 1978), and male children fitting this syndrome of disorder have a higher proportion of intact families than those from any other syndrome (Neuchterlein, Soli, Garmezy, Devine, & Schaefer, 1981). In a study of guidance clinic records of men whose neurotic adjustment persisted into young adulthood, Roff (1974) noted two patterns of maternal-child interaction: in one the child is giving in or forcing the mother to give in to the child's neurotic demands, and, in the other, the mother is anxiety inducing or does not discourage the child's anxiety, and the child is correspondingly anxious. In most cases it was impossible to tell how the neurotic interaction got started, but both parties seemed to be feeding into it. The first pattern seems parallel to the circumstances of the conflicted-irritable preschool children in Baumrind's (1967) study, whose mothers, although moderately restrictive, were less persistent and succumbed more often to the child's nuisance value. This pattern is congruent with Mowrer's (1960) view of the neurotic as undersocialized, and it fits a developmental model in which negative instrumental reinforcement plays a prominent role, as it does in Patterson's coercive system (1980). In my clinical experience, it is the insecure, guilt-avoiding, and somewhat perfectionistic mother who is most vulnerable to shows of distress and suffering (i.e., one-down manipulations) by the young child or accusations of cruelty and unfairness by the older child. The guilt and anxiety that these displays and accusations evoke in the mother are terminated when she relents in her demands. The child's one-down manipulations are negatively reinforced when they terminate the mother's mildly aversive requests, thereby increasing their frequency. In frustration with the child's inadequacy, the mother may occasionally explode with denigrating anger directed at the child and, as part of the defense against her own guilt, she may self-righteously demand of the child self-incrimination, self-punishment, or apology as a prerequisite for ending her anger and restoring her love. Thus the child is reinforced both positively and negatively for self-abasement but not for compliant behavior. Consistent with this model, LeVine (1961) noted that mothers who continued discipline (regardless of its nature) until the child verbalized that he or she was sorry, were more likely to have children who confessed wrong-doing and expressed remorse. Also consistent is Sears' (1961) evidence that mothers who were restrictive and punishing when their sons were age 5, had sons who at age 12 were inclined to self-aggression (self-punishment, suicidal tendencies, and accident proneness).

Although there is evidence that the parents of withdrawn-neurotic children are more restrictive than the parents of aggressive or delinquent children, there is little direct evidence that the former are more restrictive than parents of nondeviant children. Martin and Hetherington (1971) made a special effort in their study to have ratings of restrictiveness be independent of parental hostility and found no relationship between ratings of restrictiveness for either parent and withdrawal in 9- to 12-year-old boys or girls. Their study did indicate, however, that withdrawal was associated with the configuration of low acceptance by the same-sex parent and at least average acceptance by the opposite-sex parent. Perhaps dislike by the same-sex parent, they suggest, exerts an especially crippling effect on the self-confidence and assertiveness of children. Similar cross-sex effects have been found in other studies. Santrock and Warshak (1979) assessed the adjustment of boys and girls, 6- to 11-years-of-age, in mother versus father custody two or more years after divorce. Children living with the opposite-sex parent (fathers with custody of girls, and mothers with custody of boys) were less well adjusted than children living with the same-sex parent. The children in cross-sex custody were less mature, sociable, and independent, and more demanding. Klein, Plutchik, and Conte (1973) assessed, via therapist ratings, the adjustment problems of children and the passivity-dominance of the mothers and fathers of families in family therapy. Sons exhibited the fewest problems when the father was dominant and daughters exhibited the fewest problems when the mother was dominant. The configuration of a dominant mother and a passive father resulted in the greatest number of problems for sons and the fewest for daughters.

The thread of consistency running through these studies is their common implication that a positive interaction with the same-sex parent plays in important role in forging good adjustment. The same-sex parent provides both a model of and direct tuition in sex-appropriate behavior, as well as stricter discipline and companionship in sex-correlated interests. Several studies show that the opposite-sex parent is more benevolent, less strict, and more autonomy-granting than the same-sex parent (see review by Martin, 1975). If the same-sex parent is nonaccepting (Martin & Hetherington, 1971), passive (Klein et al., 1973), or absent (Santrock & Warshak, 1979), he or she is likely to do a poor job at all of the socializing functions normally performed by the parent of the same sex. The importance of the disciplinary role of the same-sex parent is underscored by evidence that delinquency is higher in both males and females who have lost the same-sex parent whether by divorce or by death (Gregory, 1965). On the other hand, responsibility and leadership are facilitated by the relatively greater disciplinary salience of the same-sex parent (Bronfenbrenner, 1961a, 1961b). The importance of the companionship role played by the same-sex parent is underscored by evidence that remarriage of the widowed same-sex parent is associated with an increased risk of mental disorder in the child (Langner & Michael, 1963). These data suggest that the functions of the same-sex parent are relatively more important to the child's healthy psychological development than those of the opposite-sex parent. The relationship with the same-sex parent is perhaps the primary vehicle for teaching the child how to be a good representative of his or her sex, whereas, the relationship with the opposite-sex parent may provide primarily confirmation or discomfirmation of the child's success.

In the study by Martin and Hetherington (1971), the family constellation associated with the majority of withdrawn-neurotic males consisted of a dominant, nonpunitive mother and a punitive, inconsistent, nonaccepting, and permissive father. This pattern is highly congruent with studies by Roff (1974), who found that mothers of neurotic males, in addition to being infantilizing, were assertive, nervous, and guilt inducting. Fathers were passive, had a negative evaluation of the child, and were nervous. The parents of neurotics were higher in conflict than the control families but had a lower rate of separation and divorce. A somewhat similar pattern has been observed in the family dynamics of homosexual males (Bieber, Bain, Dince, Drellick, Grand, Grundlach, Kremer, Ritkin, Wilbur, & Bieber, 1962; Evans, 1969). Other studies of children (Gassner & Murray, 1969) and of adolescents (Schwarz & Getter, 1980) agree that neurotic males more often come from homes high in parental conflict, and in which the mother is relatively more dominant than the father. These two studies plus the Schwarz and Zuroff (1979) study provide evidence that parental conflict is a powerful moderating variable: in all three studies relatively greater dominance in the opposite-sex parent in the context of high parental conflict was associated with anxious depressive symptoms.

As stated previously (Schwarz, 1979), these studies, incorporating measures of parental conflict and dominance, suggest the following dynamics for the family origin of neurotic conflict. When the marital relationship is harmonious, a son may model his father's behavior, espouse his values, and follow his interests with reasonable assurance that he will be loved and respected by both parents. His gender-appropriate behaviors will lead to affection from his mother. Likewise for a daughter, her femininity will be instrumental to acceptance by both parents. In each case emulating parental values carries few/risks. When the marital relationship is torn by strife, however, the stakes are suddenly raised. The child gets caught in a double approach-avoidance conflict; gaining the approval of the mother may mean losing the approval of the father, and vice versa. The child, so ensnarled, who can neither leave the field nor choose between the two parents, may be more likely to become disordered. The child who can stably ally himself or herself with the same-gender parent, although "normal" and unconflicted, may become defensively chauvinistic and alienated from the opposite gender. The child who becomes an ally of the opposite-gender parent is seldom free of conflict and, furthermore, risks cross-gender identification, discomfort

with peers, and diminished self-esteem. The child who avoids entangle-
ment by disaffiliation from both parents risks antisocial development as
a result of the weak socialization experience that follows rejection of
adult models. If both parents are unattractive as objects of identification,
an antisocial outcome is more likely. If the opposite-sex parent is highly
attractive as an object of identification and the same-sex parent is not,
a neurotic outcome is more likely.

Social Influences in Childhood Psychosis

Infantile autism. Many psychogenic theories have been proposed
for infantile autism (see review by Werry, 1979a); however, none can be
regarded as having any significant support. While the gross similarity
between the syndrome of infantile autism and the social-deprivation
syndrome in infrahuman primates (Harlow & Harlow, 1962; Mason,
1970) would suggest a similar origin, the data do not support the parallel.
Elevated rates of infantile autism do not come from deprived institutional environments, but rather from the higher social classes (Cox, Rutter, Newman, & Bartak, 1975). The picture of a cold, overintellectual-
ized, nonstimulating parent painted in the early literature on the basis
of clinical impressions (e.g., Eisenberg & Kanner, 1956) has not been
supported by properly controled research published since 1960 (Werry,
1979a). Later studies, for the most part, have included four methodologic improvements: more objective and systematic assessment of parent
attitudes, behaviors, and personality; proper control groups for the stress
of rearing a disabled child, such as groups of retarded, handicapped,
brain-damaged or aphasic children; separation of infantile autistic and
schizophrenic children; and matching of families on demographic variables. Two methodologic flaws remain in many of these studies: failure
to subdivide the infantile autistic children according to the likelihood of
brain damage, and reliance on the parents' retrospective reports of their
caretaking behaviors during the child's infancy. The first flaw can be
remedied with some effort, whereas the second, for all practical purposes, may be irremediable. Prospective studies provide the only hope
for obtaining uncontaminated data on parent behavior, and the base
rate of the disorder is so low that the prospective method is unfeasible.

Knobloch and Pasamanick (1975) suggest that infantile autism represents a global aphasia, in which central nervous system dysfunction is
so severe that the complexities of social stimulation cannot be integrated
or interpreted by the child, and that social interaction only produces
further interference. In their follow-up of 50 autistic infants, most of
whom had been diagnosed before 2 years of age, when observed 3 to
10 years later, three fourths had established social responsiveness ap-

propriate to their age in the absence of treatment. The mental deficiency noted at the initial assessment was, however, as great or greater at follow-up. The view of Knobloch and Pasamanick that the social avoidance and indifference of the infantile autistic child is a function of an integrational deficit is consistent with observations by Churchill (1971) and Koegel and Egel (1979), that seemingly unmotivated autistic children will respond positively when the task is made simple enough for them to comprehend. Koegel and Egel note that the child's cognitive deficiencies and inadequate responses result in few and inconsistent rewards for attempting to respond, thus decreasing the child's motivation. They recommend treatment procedures designed to keep the child responding until the task is completed correctly so that perseverance will be reinforced co-incidentally. These views suggest that consistency, simplicity, and predictability in the behavior of the caretaker during infancy may facilitate the social responsiveness of the infant biologically disposed toward autism, and that prompting to aid correct response and careful attention to the reinforcement of effort both may help to maximize the child's potential by increasing the motivation to try.

Several studies suggest that the concordance rate for infantile autism among siblings is about two percent, a rate 50 times higher than the population base rate for the disorder (0.04 percent) (Minton et al., 1982). This fact has several implications. First, this low rate rules out a powerful role for social-environmental influences. If social factors were crucially important, one might logically expect more siblings, and especially those close in age, to be affected by the same social environmental factors. Second, the rate is too low to be compatible with single-gene Mendelian models of inheritance. Third, this low but significant family concordance is consistent with a polygenetic or multifactorial explanation. Fourth, it would also be compatible with a minor role for social environmental factors as one of many substitutable factors in a multifactorial model of causation. Taken in total, the evidence suggests at most a minor role in the aggregate for social environmental influences, a role that is neither necessary nor sufficient to cause the disorder, and one that could be substantial in some cases and irrelevant in others.

Childhood schizophrenia. The clearest evidence that environmental factors play a role in the etiology of schizophrenia is the fact that the concordance rate for monozygotic twins reared together is only .46 (Gottesman & Shields, 1976). If environment were irrelevant, the reliability of diagnosis for schizophrenia could permit a concordance rate as high as .80 between identical twins. It seems likely that some of this environmental influence eminates from the physical/biochemical environment in the form of pre-, peri-, or postnatal brain damage (Stabenau, Pollin, Mosher, Frohman, Friedhoff, & Turner, 1969); however, children fitting the adult criteria of schizophrenia as a disorder distinct from infantile autistism have been the focus of little research from the neurological standpoint (Werry, 1979a). Other recent evidence suggests that the offspring of schizophrenic parents may have a genetically determined neurointegrative deficit, detectable in the first year of life in the form of poor motor and sensorimotor functioning (Marcus, Auerbach, Wilkinson, & Burack, 1981; Fish, 1977).

Earlier studies of family correlates of childhood schizophrenia have not made a distinction between autism and childhood schizophrenia, and since the former is more prevalent than the latter, these studies provide a poor basis for inferences about chlidhood schizophrenia. Faced with a dearth of controled studies on family and social correlates of childhood schizophrenia, and given the evidence of a functional similarity between childhood, adolescent, and adult schizophrenia, research on the family dynamics prodromal to the adolescent and young adult schizophrenic may have relevance to schizophrenia of childhood onset as well.

Three styles of parent-child communication that have been proposed as pathogenic in schizophrenia are the double bind, communication deviance, and the negativity of expressed emotion or affective style. First proposed as causal by Bateson, Jackson, Haley, and Weakland (1956), a double-bind communication is a message delivered in one modality, (e.g., verbal-semantic), that is negated simultaneously in another modality (e.g., intonation or gesture) or by a second message in the same modality (see Ch. 8). Communication deviance refers to a deficiency in the ability to maintain and share a focus of attention on a designated task, and it is operationally measured on Thematic Apperception Test (TAT) protocols by behaviors such as lack of commitment to ideas or percepts, disruptive speech, and closure problems (Singer & Wynne, 1966). Communication deviancy has been found to be high in the parents of schizophrenics (Wynne, 1981). Negativity of expressed emotion, first examined by Brown, Birley, and Wing (1972) and found to be predictive of relapse following remission of schizophrenic symptoms, is reflected in high criticism, weak support, guilt induction, and intrusive presumption. Two family dynamic patterns have also been reported frequently as associated with schizophrenia and poor prognosis in schizophrenia (Roff & Knight, 1981): The first is that of an intrusive, overprotective mother in combination with a passive, uninvolved father. This pattern, which may include communication deviance, is of course restricted to intact families and is reported to be associated more often with schizophrenia in sons rather than daughters (cf. Lidz, 1973). The second pattern, more often found in nonintact families, is that of family disorganization with maternal irresponsibility and indifference.

Empirical research has failed to support Bateson's assumptions and predictions that parental double-bind communications are a correlate of schizophrenia (Schuham, 1967). Several questions can be raised about the other parental communication styles and family patterns that have been found to be associated with schizophrenia. Are they causes or consequences of the emerging pathology evident in the child, or are they perhaps neither causes nor consequences but merely correlates of the genotype shared by the parents and the child who develops schizophrenia? If they are causal, are they specific to schizophrenia or are they family stress patterns that dispose children to other forms of psychiatric disorder as well?

Prospective longitudinal studies and archival studies in which data are gathered before the child develops schizophrenia avoid the problem of reactivity to the child's disorder and, therefore, may help to unravel this Gordian knot. Although several prospective studies of samples at high risk are underway, some of which have assessed these family variables, few have matured sufficiently to provide reports (Garmezy, 1978a). One prospective study (Doane, West, Goldstein, Rodnick, & Jones, 1980) has shown that communication deviancy and negativity of affective style of the parents of disturbed but nonpsychotic adolescents are predictive of their development of schizophrenic spectrum disorder five years later. Communication deviancy and affective style independently and additively contributed to the prediction of schizophrenic spectrum disorder. Clearly these communication styles were not merely reactive to schizophrenic behavior in the child; nonetheless, one or both could be noncausal correlates of a common genotype that the parents share with the schizophrenic child. A causal role for communication deviancy seems unlikely since adoption studies have shown that being reared by a schizophrenic parent does not raise the likelihood of schizophrenic spectrum disorder unless the child is genetically at risk for schizophrenia (Rosenthal et al., 1975; Wender et al, 1974).

Two archival studies provide support for the first family pattern, that of a dominant mother who was overinvolved with the child. McCord, Porta, and McCord (1962) examined family data that they had collected on 12 boys who had been in their delinquency prevention study and later became psychotic (10 schizophrenic). While only eight percent of the mothers of carefully matched controls were "smothering" (i.e., the dominant person in family, controling of the son, and affectionate toward the son), 58 percent of the mothers of the psychotic boys fit this pattern. Waring and Ricks (1965) studied the child guidance clinic records of children with chronic schizophrenia, remitting schizophrenia, or no schizophrenia. Symbiotic union with an intrusive, overcontroling parent was most frequent in chronic cases (35 percent) and least frequent in the controls (12 percent). Symbiotic union between parent and child was strongly associated with emotional divorce between the parents. Two other patterns found with substantial prevalence among the subsequently schizophrenic were the chaotic-disorganized family and the repudiated-rejected child. The former was equally prevalent in the disturbed (but not subsequently schizophrenic) controls, and the latter was especially high among the remitted schizophrenic group.

These data suggest that the two family patterns are not reactive to schizophrenic symptoms in the child, although it is possible that a child's neurointegrative deficits dispose him or her for selection as a child to be smothered by the parent (Mosher, Pollin, & Stabenau, 1971). Nor are they uniquely associated with schizophrenia. The first pattern, intrusive mother and uninvolved father, is associated in males with emotional disorder (Martin & Hetherington, 1971) and homosexuality (Bieber et al., 1962; Evans, 1969). The second pattern, that of maternal neglect and family disorganization, has been repeatedly associated with conduct disorder (cf. Roff, 1974). It seems likely that these family patterns produce maladaptive styles in the child that cause social stress. Perhaps in genetically vulnerable individuals the stress leads to schizophrenic symptoms. Congruent with this view is evidence from Watt (1978) that increases in aggressive-disruptive behavior (especially in males) and in emotional lability and introversion (especially in females) are prodromal to schizophrenia by several years. It would appear that any particular pattern of family dynamics may have, at best, only a weak association with the development of schizophrenic disorder, since, according to Matthysse and Kidd (1976), the strength of the genetic disposition to schizophrenia can vary widely.

PREVENTION

This chapter has concentrated on the etiology of the more salient forms of childhood psychopathology. With these facts and theories freshly in mind, one can hardly resist or avoid commenting on their implications for the prevention of childhood disorder. Three types of prevention can be considered: primary, secondary, and tertiary (Caplan & Grunebaum, 1967). The goal of primary prevention is elimination of the cause of a problem and thus prevention of its occurrence. This is only possible when the causes are clearly identified and understood, and even then only when the causes are potentially controlable. Secondary prevention consists of the early detection of problems so that interventions will prevent the development of more serious disorders. The feasibility of secondary prevention depends upon, first, having the knowledge and the organization to detect incipient disorder in early stages of its development; second, having the authority and consent to intervene; and third, having the knowledge about how to intervene successfully. Tertiary prevention consists of limiting the duration, consequences, or aftereffects of a disorder; it is closely related to the concept of rehabilitation. The following discussion will focus on primary and secondary prevention (see Chs. 9 and 10).

Primary Prevention

To prevent psychopathological development, the first point of intervention must be during the period of fetal development, and the intervention should be directed at reducing brain damage and other crippling defects. Since major physical disability triples the risk, and neuroepileptic disorder quintuples the risk of psychopathological disorder, maximizing the biological integrity of the newborn will reduce disorder. Furthermore, the forms of psychological disorder that are more strongly associated with brain damage (retardation and infantile psychoses) are quite burdensome to the individual, the family, and the community. Congenital brain damage could be reduced by programs that educate prospective mothers with regard to their dietary needs and to the dangers of alcohol and other drugs to the fetus during pregnancy; that provide accessible and affordable pre-, peri-, and postnatal medical care; and that eliminate biological hazards, such as excessive lead, from the environment.

Proceeding ontologically, the second point of primary intervention is during the preschool years. A feasible mode of intervention is that of training prospective and current parents to interact constructively with their infants, toddlers, and young children. An apprenticeship in parenting supervised by an expert would be ideal, because it affords the conditions of appropriate motivation to learn juxtaposed with the opportunity for modeling, feedback, and reinforcement. Other mechanisms include teaching infant and child care as part of the public school curriculum, and establishing a network of community support groups for new parents, a free neighborhood developmental clinic, and a 24-hour telephone information service to answer questions about child care and to make appropriate referrals.

A third target of primary preventive intervention should be that of improving the integrity of the family and the conditions of rearing. Since parental conflict, separation, divorce, and single-parent households are all associated with higher rates of child psychopathology, any change in the society and its institutions that will increase the stability and compatibility of marriages will reduce the rate of childhood psychopathology. The provision of sex education in the school prior to puberty may reduce the rate of teenage pregnancy and single-parent households. Governmental policies concerning taxation and the administration of public assistance should be designed with incentives to promote and maintain two-parent households. The ready availability of effective birth control methods and advice will enable couples to plan childbearing and to test the viability of their relationship before assuming the responsibilities of parenthood. With sufficient numbers of trained and affordable counselors, conflicting parents can be taught conflict-resolution skills; they can develop interpersonal skills that will help restore love, understanding, tolerance, and intimacy to their relationship. Within intact families, a greater involvement of the father in tasks of child management, especially with sons, is likely to reduce conduct disorder. More interaction with the father will increase the son's identification and self-esteem and reduce the likelihood of his gaining the upper hand through coercive means with the mother or younger siblings. Because of the increased numbers of families in which two parents work full-time, community-wide after-school programs of supervised recreation for school-age children may also be helpful in reducing the rate of conduct disorder in the community.

A fourth area for preventive change is the manner in which divorce is handled by the state and by the respective parents. When parental conflict is intractible and divorce becomes the lesser of two evils, the period of vulnerability for the children continues and, in some cases, increases. This inevitably painful transition could be made less destructive if the society were to develop appropriate institutions for mediating divorce settlements so that divorce can be removed from the adversarial traditions of the legal system. Mediation (Haynes, 1981) has the chance of reducing, rather than exacerbating the conflict between the parents and, if successful, will yield for the child benefits of reduced stress on the custodial parent (or parents), increased access to the noncustodial parent, and a general reduction in the intensity of the double approach-avoidance conflict experienced by most children when their parents are in conflict. Another legal tradition whose alteration would improve the postdivorce adjustment of children is that of awarding custody predominantly to the mother. Joint custody carries the benefit of keeping the father involved in the child's life, a condition that has been shown to be related to later adjustment, especially in boys. It will also lighten the mother's burden of responsibility. Divorce counseling can help minimize the destructive force of the increased parental rivalry that frequently attends divorce. Divorced parents need to be made aware of the potentially negative effect that continued conflict with and denigration of the former spouse can have on the child, especially a child identified with that parent.

Secondary Prevention

Adjustment problems typically develop gradually until they reach a threshold of family or community tolerance, at which point professional guidance is sought. Then the pattern of interaction may be so well practiced that it is very difficult to change. Some symptoms, such as unmanageability during the preschool years, are sufficiently predictive of conduct disorder, a condition quite refractory to later treatment, that intervention in the preschool years before the behavior exceeds the threshold of tolerance seems prudent. An outreach program that offers child management consultation to parents of unmanageable preschoolers may prevent the establishment of hardened postures of coercive control on the part of both parent and child. Since steady influence is required to change behavior, parents may need contact with professionals who can provide periodic, expert guidance, and who can motivate parents to sustain their efforts over long periods.

Problems of low self-esteem and withdrawal may also be more malleable if they receive attention during childhood in the context of their development. The interdependent quality of the influences of family members calls for conjoint family assessment and for treatment that may involve the whole family together, the sibling subsystem alone, or the parent subsystem alone (Minuchin, 1974). In family therapy, children caught in damaging alliances with parents can be restored to affiliation with their siblings, and the conflicts between the parents can be addressed directly. While the parental rift is under repair, the severely scapegoated child may benefit from placement with relatives, with foster parents, or in individual therapy.

Finally, the work of Watt and others (Watt, 1978; Watt, Grub, & Erlenmeyer-Kimling, 1982) suggests that by plotting changes in adjustment over time, it may be possible to identify early those children otherwise headed toward schizophrenic disorder. Eventually, by combining genetic, biologic, and behavioral risk-factors, forecasts may be developed with sufficient accuracy to justify prescribing preventive intervention to specific children.

Knowledge is an important element in the development of effective strategies of prevention, and with each passing decade, the precision of our knowledge about the origins of psychopathology seems to increase at a more rapid rate. One hopes also that, with each succeeding decade, the investment of this knowledge will yield a harvest of reduced rates of behavioral disorder. Then, to the intrinsic joy of discovery will have been added the enduring satisfaction of having served mankind.

REFERENCES

Achenbach, TM, & Edelbrock, CS. The classification of child psychopathology: A review and analysis of empirical efforts. *Psychological Bulletin*, 1978, *85*, 1275–1301

Achenbach, TM, & Edelbrock, CS. Behavioral problems and competencies reported by parents of normal and disturbed children aged four through sixteen. *Monographs of the Society for Research in Child Development*, 1981, Serial No. 188

Ainsworth, MDS. Infant-mother attachment. *American Psychologist*, 1979, *34*, 932–937

Ainsworth, MDS, Blehar, MC, Waters, E, & Wall, S. *Patterns of attachment.* Hillsdale, NJ: Erlbaum, 1978

Albee, GW. Emerging concepts of mental illness and models of treatment: The psychological point of view. *American Journal of Psychiatry*, 1969, *125*, 870–876

American Psychiatric Association. *Diagnostic and statistical manual of mental disorders (DSM-I).* Washington, DC.: American Psychiatric Association, 1952

American Psychiatric Association. *Diagnostic and statistical manual of mental disorders (DSM-II).* Washington, DC.: American Psychiatric Association, 1968

American Psychiatric Association. *Diagnostic and statistical manual of mental disorders (DSM-III).* Washington, DC.: American Psychiatric Association, 1980

Baker, EJ. *Temperament and child-rearing correlates of two-year-olds' reactions to strangers.* Unpublished doctoral dissertation, The University of Connecticut, 1981

Bakwin, H. Reading disability in twins. *Developmental Medicine and Child Neurology.* 1973, *15*, 184–187

Barton, ML, & Schwarz, JC. *The effects of infant daycare experience on personality development: A review of research.* Unpublished Manuscript, University of Connecticut, 1982

Bateson, G, Jackson, DD, Haley, J, & Weakland, J. Toward a theory of schizophrenia. *Behavioral Science*, 1956, *1*, 251–264

Battle, ES, & Lacey, B. A context for hyperactivity in children, over time. *Child Development*, 1972, *43*, 757–773

Baumrind, D. Child care practices anteceding three patterns of preschool behavior. *Genetic Psychology Monographs*, 1967, *75*, 43–88

Baumrind, D, & Black, AE. Socialization practices associated with dimensions of competence in preschool boys and girls. *Child Development*, 1967, *38*, 291–327

Becker, WC, Peterson, DR, Hellmer, LA, Shoemaker, DJ, & Quay, HC. Factors in parental behavior and personality as related to problem behavior in children. *Journal of Consulting Psychology*, 1959, *23*, 107–118

Becker, WC, Peterson, DR, Luria, Z, Shoemaker, DJ, & Hellmer, LA. Relations of factors derived from parent-interview ratings to behavior problems of five-year-olds. *Child Development*, 1962, *33*, 509–535

Behar, L, & Stringfield, A. A behavior rating scale for the pre-school child. *Developmental Psychology*, 1974, *10*, 601–610

Bender, L. The life course of children with schizophrenia. *American Journal of Psychiatry*, 1973, *130*, 783–786

Bettleheim, B. Bringing up children. *Ladies Home Journal*, 1973, *90*, 28

Bieber, I, Bain, H, Dince, P, Drelleck, M, Grand, H, Grundlach, R, Kremer, M, Ritkin, A, Wilbur, C, & Bieber, T. *Homosexuality: A psychoanalytic study of male homosexuals.* New York: Basic Books, 1962

Blashfield, R. An evaluation of the DSM-II classification of schizophrenia as a nomenclature. *Journal of Abnormal Psychology*, 1973, *82*, 382–389

Blashfield, RK. Propositions regarding the use of cluster analysis in clinical research. *Journal of Consulting and Clinical Psychology*, 1980, *48*, 456–459

Block, JH. Issues, problems and pitfalls in assessing sex differences: A critical review of *The psychology of sex differences. Merrill-Palmer Quarterly*, 1976, *22*, 283–308

Block, JH, Block, J, & Morrison, A. Parental agreement-disagreement on child-rearing orientations and gender-related personality correlates in children. *Child Development,* 1981, *52,* 965–974

Borland, BL, & Heckman, HK. Hyperactive boys and their brothers. *Archives of General Psychiatry,* 1976, *33,* 669–675

Bowlby, J, Ainsworth, M, Boston, M, & Rosenbluth, D. The effects of mother-child separation: A follow-up study. *British Journal of Medical Psychology,* 1956, *29,* 211–247

Brady, RC. *Effects of success and failure on impulsivity and distractibility of three types of educationally handicapped children.* Unpublished doctoral dissertation, University of Southern California, 1970

Bretherton, I, Bates, E, Benigni, L, Camaioni, L, & Volterra, V. Relationships between cognition, communication and quality of attachment. In EA Bates (Ed.), *The emergence of symbols.* New York: Academic Press, 1979

Bronfenbrenner, U. Some familial antecedents of responsibility and leadership in adolescents. In L Petrullo & BM Bass (Eds.), *Leadership and interpersonal behavior.* New York: Holt, 1961a

Bronfenbrenner, U. Toward a theoretical model for the analysis of parent-child relationships in a social context. In JC Glidewell (Ed.), *Parental attitudes and child behavior.* Springfield, Ill.: Charles C Thomas, 1961b

Brown, GW, Birley, JLT, & Wing, JK. Influence of family life on the course of schizophrenic disorders: A replication. *British Journal of Psychiatry,* 1972, *121,* 241–258

Cadoret, R, & Winokur, G. Genetic studies of affective disorders. In FF Flack & SC Draghi (Eds.), *The nature and treatment of depression.* New York: Wiley, 1975

Cameron, JR. Parental treatment, children's temperament, and the risk of childhood behavioral problems: 1. Relationships between parental characteristics and changes in children's temperament over time. *American Journal of Orthopsychiatry,* 1977, *47,* 568–576

Campbell, SB. *Maternal and infant behavior in normal, high risk, and "difficult" infants,* Paper presented at the biennial meeting of the Society for Research in Child Development, New Orleans, March 1977

Campbell, SB, Schleifer, M, & Weiss, G. Continuities in maternal reports and child behaviors over time in hyperactive and comparison groups. *Journal of Abnormal Child Psychology,* 1978, *6,* 33–45

Cantwell, DP. Psychiatric illness in the families of hyperactive children. *Archives of General Psychiatry,* 1972, *27,* 414–417

Caplan, G, & Grunebaum, H. Perspectives on primary prevention. *Archives of General Psychiatry,* 1967, *17,* 331–346

Carey, G. Genetic influences on anxiety neurosis and agoraphobia. In RJ Mathew (Ed.), *The biology of anxiety.* New York: Brunner/Mazel, 1982

Carey, G, & Gottesman, II. Twin and family studies of anxiety, phobic, and obsessive disorders. In DF Klein & J Rabkin (Eds.), *Anxiety: New research and changing concepts.* New York: Raven Press, 1981

Chess, S, Thomas, A, Rutter, M, & Birch, HG. Interaction of temperament and environment in the production of behavioral disturbances in children. *American Journal of Psychiatry,* 1963, *120,* 142–148

Christiansen, KO. A preliminary study of criminality among twins. In SA Mednick & KO Christiansen (Eds.), *Biosocial basis of criminal behavior.* New York: Gardner Press, 1977

Churchill, DW. Effects of success and failure in psychotic children. *Archives of General Psychiatry,* 1971, *25,* 208–214

Clarke-Stewart, KA. Interactions between mothers and their young children: Characteristics and consequences. *Monographs of the Society for Research in Child Development*, 1973, *38*, Serial No. 153

Clarke-Stewart, KA, VanderStoep, LS, & Killian, GA. Analysis and replication of mother-child relations at two years of age. *Child Development*, 1979, *50*, 777–793

Cohen DJ, Caparulo, B, Shaywitz, SE. Primary childhood aphasia and childhood autism. *Journal of the American Academy of Child Psychiatry*, 1976, *15*, 604–645

Coleman, RW, & Provence, S. Environmental retardation (hospitalism) in infants living in families. *Pediatrics*, 1957, *19*, 285–292

Collins, LF, Maxwell, AE, & Cameron, K. A factor analysis of some child psychiatric clinic data. *Journal of Mental Science*, 1962, *108*, 274–285

Connell, DB. *Individual differences in attachment behavior: Long-term stability and relationships to language development.* Unpublished doctoral dissertation, Syracuse University, 1977

Cox, A, Rutter, M, Newman, S, & Bartak, L. A comparative study of infantile autism and specific developmental receptive language disorder. II. Parental characteristics. *British Journal of Psychiatry*, 1975, *126*, 146–159

Crockenberg, SB. Infant irritability, mother responsiveness, and social support influences on the security of infant-mother attachment. *Child Development*, 1981, *52*, 857–865

Crowe, RR. An adoption study of antisocial personality. *Archives of General Psychiatry*, 1974, *31*, 785–791

Cytryn, L, & McKnew, DH. Proposed classification of childhood depression. *American Journal of Psychiatry*, 1972, *129*, 63–68

Cytryn, L, McKnew, DH, & Bunney, WE. Diagnosis of depression in children: A reassessment. *American Journal of Psychiatry*, 1980, *137*, 22–25

Davie, R, Butler, N, & Goldstein, H. *From birth to seven: A report of the National Child Development Study*, London, Longman, 1972

Delfini, L, Bernal, M, & Rosen, P. Comparison of deviant and normal boys in home settings. In EJ Mash, LA Hamerlynck, & LC Handy (Eds.), *Behavior modification and families* (Vol. 1). *Theory and research.* New York: Brunner/Mazel, 1976

DeMyer, M, Barton, S, DeMyer, W, Norton, J, Allen, J, & Steele, R. Prognosis in autism: A follow-up study. *Journal of Autism and Childhood Schizophrenia*, 1973, 199–246

Dibble, ED, & Cohen, DJ. *Biological endowment, early experience, and psychosocial influences in child behavior: A twin study.* Paper presented at the 9th Congress of the International Association for Child Psychiatry and Allied Professions, Melbourne, Australia, August 1978

Dixon, P. Paper in progress. Reported in M Rutter, Maternal depreciation 1971–1978. *Child Development*, 1979, *50*, 283–305

Doane, JA, West, KL, Goldstein, MJ, Rodnick, EH, & Jones, JE. Parental communication deviance and affective style: Predictors of subsequent schizophrenia spectrum disorders in vulnerable adolescents. *Archives of General Psychiatry*, 1980, *38*, 679–685

Douglas, J, & Gear, R. Children of low birthweight in the 1946 National cohort—behavior and educational achievement in adolescence. *Archives of Diseases in Childhood*, 1976, *51*, 820–827

Eagly, AH. Sex differences in influenceability. *Psychological Bulletin*, 1978, *85*, 86–116

Easterbrooks, MA, & Lamb, ME. The relationship between quality of infant-mother attachment and infant competence in initial encounters with peers. *Child Development*, 1979, *50*, 380–387

Edelbrock, C, & Achenback, TM. A typology of child behavior profile patterns: Distribution and correlates for disturbed children aged 6–16. *Journal of Abnormal Child Psychology*, 1980, *8*, 441–470

Egeland, B, & Sroufe, LA. Attachment and early maltreatment. *Child Development*, 1981, *52*, 44–52

Eggers, C. Course and prognosis of childhood schizophrenia. *Journal of Autism and Childhood Schizophreniz*, 1978, *8*, 21–36

Ehrhardt, AA, & Meyer-Bahlburg, HFL. Prenatal sex hormones and the developing brain: Effects on psychosexual differentiation and cognitive function. In WP Creger (Ed.), *Annual review of medicine* (Vol. 30). Palo Alto, Calif: Annual Reviews, 1979

Eisenberg, L. School phobia: A study in the communication of anxiety. *American Journal of Psychiatry*, 1958, *114*, 712–718

Eisenberg, L, & Kanner, L. Early infantile autism 1943–1955. *American Journal of Orthopsychiatry*, 1956, *26*, 556

Eme, RF. Sex differences in childhood psychopathology: A review. *Psychological Bulletin*, 1979, *86*, 574–595

Emery, RE. Interparental conflict and the children of discord and divorce. *Psychological Bulletin*, 1982, *92*, 310–320

Ernhart, C, Graham, F, Eichman, P, Marshall, J, & Thurston, D. Brain injury in the preschool child: Some developmental considerations. II. Comparison of brain injured and normal children. *Psychological Monographs*, 1963, *77*, 17–33

Evans, RB. Childhood parental relations of homosexual men. *Journal of Consulting and Clinical Psychology*, 1969, *33*, 129–135

Farber EA, & Egeland, B. Development consequences of out-of-home care for infants in a low-income population. In E Zigler & E Gordon (Eds.), *Day care: Scientific and social policy issues*. Boston: Auburn House Publishing Company, 1982

Feighner, JP, Robins, R, Guze, SB, Woodruff, RA, Winokur, G, & Munoz, R. Diagnostic criteria for use in psychiatric research. *Archives of General Psychiatry*, 1972, *26*, 57–63

Fish, B. Neurobiologic antecedents of schizophrenia in children: Evidence for an inherited, congenital neurointegrative defect. *Archives of General Psychiatry*, 1977, *34*, 1297–1313

Fisher, L. Dimensions of family assessment: A critical review. *Journal of Marriage and Family Counseling*, 1976, *2*, 367–382

Folstein, S, & Rutter, M. Infantile autism: A study of 21 twin pairs. *Journal of Child Psychology and Psychiatry*, 1977, *18*, 297–321

Forehand, R, King, HE, Peed, S, & Yoder, P. Mother-child interactions: Comparisons of a noncompliant clinic-group and a nonclinic group. *Behaviour Research and Therapy*, 1975, *13*, 79–84

Forness, SR, & Cantwell, DP. DSM III Psychiatric diagnosis and special education categories. *Journal of Special Education*, 1982, 49–63

Freedman, DG. Genetic influences on development of behavior. In GSA Stoelinga & Van Der Werff Ten Bosch (Eds.), *Normal and abnormal development of behavior*. Leiden, The Netherlands: Leiden University Press, 1971

Frodi, A, Macaulay, J, & Thome, PR. Are women always less aggressive than men? A review of the experimental literature. *Psychological Bulletin*, 1977, *84*, 634–660

Garmezy, N. Current status of a sample of other high-risk research programs. In LC.Wynne, RL. Cromwell, & S. Matthysse (Eds.), *The nature of schizophrenia: New approaches to research and treatment*. New York: Wiley, 1978a

Garmezy, N. DSM-III: Never mind the psychologist; is it good for the children. *Clinical Psychologist*, 1978b, *31*, 3–6

Gassner, S, & Murray, EJ. Dominance and conflict in the interactions between parents of normal and neurotic children. *Journal of Abnormal and Social Psychology*, 1969, *74*, 33–41

Gersten, JC, Langner, TS, Eisenberg, JB, Simcha-Fagen, O, & McCarthy, ED. Stability and change in types of behavioral disturbance of children and adolescents. *Journal of Abnormal Child Psychology*, 1976, *4*, 111–127

Glueck, S, & Glueck, E. *Unraveling juvenile delinquency*. New York: Commonwealth Fund, 1950

Glueck, S, & Glueck, E. *Delinquents and nondelinquents in perspective*. Cambridge: Harvard University Press, 1968

Goldberg, S. Social competence in infancy: A model of parent-infant interaction, *Merrill-Palmer Quarterly*, 1977, *23*, 163–177

Goldfarb, W. Psychological privation in infancy and subsequent adjustment. *American Journal of Orthopsychiatry*, 1945, *15*, 247–255

Gorenstein, EE, & Newman, JP. Disinhibitory psychopathology: A new perspective and a model for research. *Psychological Bulletin*, 1980, *87*, 301–315

Gottesman, II, & Shields, J. A critical review of recent adoption, twin, and family studies of schizophrenia: Behavioral genetics perspectives. *Schizophrenia Bulletin*, 1976, *2*, 360–401

Graham, P. Epidemiological studies. Chap. 5. In HC Quay & JS Werry (Eds.), *Psychopathological Disorders of Childhood*. New York: Wiley, 1979

Gregory, I. Anterospective data following childhood loss of a parent: Delinquency and high school dropout. *Archives of General Psychiatry*, 1965, *13*, 99–109

Group for the Advancement of Psychiatry. *Psychopathological disorders in childhood: Theoretical considerations and a proposed classification*. New York: Author, 1966

Hall, JA. Gender effects in decoding nonverbal cues. *Psychological Bulletin*, 1978, *85*, 845–857

Hall, JA. *Nonverbal sex differences*. Baltimore, MD: Johns Hopkins University Press, 1984

Hallgren, B. Specific dyslexia. *Acta Psychiatrics et Neurologica*. 1950, Suppl. No. 65, pp. 1–287

Halverson, CT, & Waldrop, MF. Maternal behavior toward own and other preschool children: The problem of "ownness." *Child Development*, 1970, *41*, 839–845

Halverson, CF, Jr, & Waldrop, MF. Relations between preschool activity and aspects of intellectual and social behavior at 7-1/2. *Developmental Psychology*, 1976, *12*, 107–112

Hanson, DR, & Gottesman, II. The genetics, if any, of infantile autism and childhood schizophrenia. *Journal of Autism and Childhood Schizophrenia*, 1976, *6*, 209–234

Harlow, HF, & Harlow, MK. Social deprivation in monkeys, *Scientific American*, 1962

Harmon, RS, Morgan, GA, & Gaensbauer, TJ. Infants' spontaneous play with objects. *Psychiatric Spectator*, 1978, *11*, 18–19

Haynes, JM. *Divorce mediation: A practical guide for therapists and counselors*. New York: Springer Publishing Co, 1981

Hess, RD, & Camara, KA. Post-divorce family relationships as mediating factors in the consequences of divorce for children. *Journal of Social Issues*, 1979, *35*, 79–96

Hetherington, EM, Cox, M, & Cox, R. The aftermath of divorce. In JH Stevens, Jr, & M Matthews (Eds.), *Mother-child, father-child relations*. Washington, DC.: NAEYC, 1978

Hetherington, EM, Cox, M, & Cox, R. Family interaction and the social, emotional, and cognitive development of children following divorce. In V Vaughn & TB Brazelton (Eds.), *The family: Setting priorities*. New York: Science and Medicine Publishing Co., 1979a

Hetherington, EM, Cox, M, & Cox, R. Play and social interaction in children following divorce. *The Journal of Social Issues*, 1979b, *35*, 26–49

Hetherington, EM, & Martin, B. Family interaction. In HC Quay & JS Werry (Eds.), *Psychopathological disorders of childhood* (2nd ed.). New York: Wiley, 1979

Hobbs, N. *Issues in the classification of children*. San Francisco: Jossey-Bass, 1975

Hoffman, ML. Sex differences in empathy and related behaviors. *Psychological Bulletin*, 1977, *84*, 712–722

Holdsworth, L, & Whitmore, KA. A study of children with epilepsy attending ordinary schools. I. Their seizure patterns, progress and behavior in school. *Developmental Medicine and Child Neurology*, 1974, *16*, 746–758

Hudgins, W, & Prentice, MN. Moral judgement in delinquent and nondelinquent adolescents and their mothers. *Journal of Abnormal Psychology*, 1973, *82*, 145–152

Hutchings, B, & Mednick, SA. Criminality in adoptees and their adoptive and biological parents: A pilot study. In SA Mednick & KO Christiansen (Eds.), *Biosocial basis of criminal behavior*. New York: Gardner Press, 1977

Jenkins, RL. Psychiatric syndromes in children and their relation to family background. *Journal of Orthopsychiatry*, 1966, *36*, 450–457

Jersild, AT, & Holmes, FB. Children's fears. *Child development monographs*. No. 20. New York: Teachers' College, Columbia University, 1935

Johnson, AM. Discussion on school phobia. *American Journal of Orthopsychiatry*, 1957, *27*, 307–309

Johnson, SB, & Melamed, DG. The assessment and treatment of children's fears. In B Lahey & AE Kazdin (Eds.), *Advances in clinical child psychology* (Vol. 2). New York: Plenum Press, 1979

Judd, LL. Obsessive compulsive neurosis in children. *Archives of General Psychiatry*, 1965, *12*, 136–143

Kallman, FJ, & Roth, B. Genetic aspects of preadolescent schizophrenia. *American Journal of Psychiatry*, 1956, *112*, 599–606

Kanner, L. Autistic disturbances of affective contact. *Nervous Child*, 1943, 2, 217–250

Kanner, L. Do behavior symptoms always indicate psychopathology? *Journal of Child Psychology and Psychiatry*, 1960, *1*, 17–25

Kanner, L, Rodriguez, A, & Ashenden, B. How far can autistic children go in matters of social adaptation? *Journal of Autism and Childhood Schizophrenia*, 1972, *2*, 9–33

Kelly, EQ. School phobia: A review of theory and treatment. *Psychology in the Schools*, 1973, *10*, 33–41

Kelsey-Smith, M, & Beavers, WR. Family assessment: Centripetal and centrifugal family systems. *The American Journal of Family Therapy*, 1981, *9*, (4), 3–12

Kennedy, WA. School phobia: Rapid treatment of fifty cases. *Journal of Abnormal Psychology*, 1965, *70*, 285–289

Kessler, S. The genetics of schizophrenia: A review. *Schizophrenia Bulletin*, 1980, *6*, 404–416

Kidd, KK, Oehlert, G, Heimbuch, RC, Records, MA, & Webster, RL. Familial stuttering patterns are not related to one measure of severity. *Journal of Speech and Hearing Disorders*, 1980, *23*, 539–545

Kidd, KK, Prusoff, BS, & Cohen, DJ. The familial pattern of Tourette. *Archives of General Psychiatry*, 1980, *37*, 1336–1339

Klein, DF, & Gittelman-Klein, R. Problems in the diagnosis of minimal brain dysfunction and the hyperkinetic syndrome. *International Journal of Mental Health*, 1975, *4*, 45–60

Klein, MM, Plutchik, R, & Conte, HR. Parental dominance-passivity and behavior problems of children. *Journal of Consulting and Clinical Psychology*, 1973, *40*, 416–419

Knobloch, H, & Pasamanick, B. Some etiological and prognostic factors in early infantile autism and psychosis. *Pediatrics*, 1975, *55*, 182–191

Koegel, RL, & Egel, AL. Motivating autistic children. *Journal of Abnormal Psychology*, 1979, *88*, 418–426

Kolvin, I. Psychoses in childhood—a comparative study. In M Rutter (Ed.), *Infantile autism: Concepts, characteristics and treatment*. London: Churchill, 1971

Ksacke, KR. A survey of procedures for assessing family conflict and dysfunction. *Family Therapy*, 1981, *8*, 241–253

Lambert, NM, Sandoval, J, & Sassone, D. Prevalence of hyperactivity in elementary school children as a function of social system definers. *American Journal of Orthopsychiatry*, 1978, *48*, 446–463

Langner, TS, Gersten, JC, & Simcha-Fagan, O. The relative roles of early environment and early behavior as predictors of later child behavior. In D Ricks & BS Dohrenwend (Eds.), *Origins of psychopathology: Problems in research and public policies.* New York: Cambridge University Press, 1983

Langner, TS, & Michael, ST. *Life Stress and mental health.* New York: Free Press of Glencoe, 1963

Lefkowitz, MM. Childhood depression: A reply to Costello. *Psychological Bulletin,* 1980, *87,* 191–194

Lefkowitz, MM, & Burton, N. Childhood depression: A critique of the concept. *Psychological Bulletin,* 1978, *85,* 716–726

Leslie, SA. Psychiatric disorder in the young adolescents of an industrial town. *British Journal of Psychiatry,* 1974, *125,* 113–124

LeVine, BB. *Punishment techniques and the development of conscience.* Unpublished doctoral dissertation, Northwestern University, 1961

Liberman, AF. Preschoolers' competence with a peer: Relations with attachment and peer experience. *Child Development,* 1977, *48,* 1277–1287

Lidz, T. *The origin and treatment of schizophrenic disorders.* New York: Basic Books, Inc., 1973

Lobitz, GK, & Johnson, SM. Normal versus deviant children: A multimethod comparison. *Journal of Abnormal Child Psychology,* 1975, *3,* 353–374

Loeber, R. The stability of antisocial and delinquent child behavior: A review. *Child Development,* 1982, *53,* 1431–1446

Loehlin, JC, & Nichols, RC. *Heredity, environment, and personality: A study of 850 sets of twins.* Austin: University of Texas Press, 1976

Loney, J, Langhorne, JE, Paternite, CE, Whaley-Klahn, MA, Blair-Broeker, CT, & Hacker, M. *The Iowa HABIT: Hyperactive/aggressive boys in treatment.* Paper presented at the meeting of the Society for Life History Research in Psychopathology. Fort Worth, Texas, October 1976

Loranger, AW, & Levine, PM. Age at onset of bipolar affective illness. *Archives of General Psychiatry,* 1978, *35,* 1345–1348

Lotter, V. Epidemiology of autistic conditions in young children. I. Prevalence. *Social Psychiatry,* 1966, *1,* 124–137

Lotter, V. Epidemiology of autistic conditions in young children. II: Some characteristics of the parents and children. *Social Psychiatry,* 1967, *1,* 163–173

Lotter, V. Follow-up studies. In M. Rutter & E. Schopler (Eds.) *Autism: Reappraisal of concepts and treatment.* New York: Plenum Publishing Co., 1978

Lovaas, OI, Koegel, RL, Simmons, JQ, & Long, JS. Some generalization and follow-up measures on autistic children in behavior therapy. *Journal of Applied Behavior Analysis,* 1973, *6,* 131–165

Lytton, H. Do parents create, or respond to, differences in twins? *Developmental Psychology,* 1977, *13,* 456–459

Lytton, H. Disciplinary encounters between young boys and their mothers and fathers: Is there a contingency system? *Developmental Psychology,* 1979, *15,* 256–268

Lytton, H, & Zwirner, W. Compliance and its controlling stimuli observed in a natural setting. *Developmental Psychology,* 1975, *11,* 769–779

Maccoby, E, & Jacklin, C. *The psychology of sex differences.* Stanford: Stanford University Press, 1974

MacFarlane, JW, Allen, L, & Honzik, MP. *A developmental study of the behavior problems of normal children between twenty-one months and fourteen years* (Vol. 2). Berkeley: University of California Press (University of California Publications in Child Development), 1954

Main, M, & Londerville, SB. *Compliance and aggression in toddlerhood: Precursors and correlates.* Paper in preparation, 1979

Marcus, J, Auerbach, J, Wilkinson, L, & Burack, CM: Infants at risk for schizophrenia: The Jerusalem infant development study. *Archives of General Psychiatry,* 1981, *38,* 703–713

Marks, IM. *Fears and phobias.* New York: Academic Press, 1969

Marks, IM, & Gelder, MG. Different onset ages in varieties of phobia. *American Journal of Psychiatry,* 1966, *123,* 218–221

Martin, B. Parent-child relations. In FD Horowitz (Eds.), *Review of child development research* (Vol. 4). Chicago: University of Chicago Press, 1975

Martin, B, & Hetherington, EM. *Family interaction and aggression withdrawal, and nondeviance in children.* Progress Report, 1971, University of Wisconsin, Project No. MN 12474, National Institute of Mental Health

Mason, WA. Motivational factors in psychosocial development. *Nebraska Symposium on Motivation,* 1970, *18,* 35–67

Matas, L, Arend, RA, & Sroufe, LA. Continuity of adaption in the second year: The relationship between quality of attachment and later competence. *Child Development,* 1978, *49,* 547–556

Matthysse, SW, & Kidd, KK. Estimating the genetic contribution to schizophrenia. *American Journal of Psychiatry,* 1976, *133,* 185–191

McCord, J. Some child-rearing antecedents of criminal behavior in adult men. *Journal of Personal and Social Psychology,* 1979, *39,* (9), 1477–1486

McCord, W, McCord, J, & Zola, IK. *Origins of crime.* New York: Columbia University Press, 1959

McCord, W, Porta, J, & McCord, J. The familial genesis of psychosis. *Psychiatry,* 1962, *25,* 60–71

McGuiness, D, & Pribram, KH. The origins of sensory bias in development of gender differences in perception and cognition. In M Bortner (Ed.), *Cognitive Growth and Development.* New York: Brunner/Mazel, 1979

McLemore, CW, & Benjamin, LS. Whatever happened to interpersonal diagnosis? A psychosocial alternative to DSM-III. *American Psychologist,* 1979, *34,* 17–34

Mendelewicz, J, & Rainer, JD. Adoption study supporting genetic transmission in manic depressive illness. *Lancet,* 1977, *268,* 327–329

Menkes, M, Rowe, J, & Menkes, J. A twenty-five year follow-up study on the hyperkinetic child with minimal brain dysfunction. *Pediatrics,* 1967, *39,* 393–399

Milich, RS, Loney, J, & Landau, S. *The independent dimensions on hyperactivity and aggression: A replication and further validation.* Unpublished manuscript, University of Iowa, 1981

Miller, LC. Q-sort agreement among observers of children. *American Journal of Orthopsychiatry,* 1964, *34,* 71–74

Miller, LC, Barrett, CL, & Hampe, E. Phobias of childhood in a prescientific era. In A. Davids (Ed.), *Child personality and psychopathology* (Vol. 1). New York: Wiley, 1974

Miller, LC, Hampe, E, Barrett, CL, & Noble, H. Children's deviant behavior within the general population. *Journal of Consulting and Clinical Psychology,* 1971, *37,* 16–22

Miller, R. Childhood schizophrenia: A review of selected literature. *International Journal of Mental Health,* 1974, *3,* 3–46

Milliones, J. Relationship between perceived child temperament and maternal behaviors. *Child Development,* 1978, *49,* 547–556

Minton, J, Campbell, M, Green, WH, Jennings, S, & Samit C. Cognitive assessment of siblings of autistic children. *Journal of the American Academy of Child Psychiatry*, 1982, *21*, 256–261

Minuchin, S. *Families and family therapy*. Cambridge: Harvard University Press, 1974

Mischel, W. On the interface of cognition and personality: Beyond the person-situation debate. *American Psychologist*, 1979, *34*, 740–754

Morrison, JR. Adult psychiatric disorders in parents of hyperactive children. *American Journal of Psychiatry*, 1980, *137*, 825–827

Morrison, JR, & Stewart, MA. A family study of the hyperactive child syndrome. *Biological Psychiatry*, 1971, *3*, 189–195

Mosher, LR, Pollin, W, & Stabenau, JR. Families with identical twins discordant for schizophrenia: Some relationships between identification, thinking styles, psychopathology, and dominance-submissiveness. *British Journal of Psychiatry*, 1971, *118*, 29–42

Moss, HA. Sex, age and state as determinants of mother-infant interaction. *Merrill-Palmer Quarterly*, 1967, *13*, 19–36.

Moss, HA. Early sex differences and mother-infant interaction. In RC Friedman, RN Richart, & RL Van de Wiele (Eds.), *Sex differences in behavior*. New York: Wiley, 1974

Mowrer, OH. *Learning theory and behavior*. New York: Wiley, 1960

Neuchterlein, KH, Soli SD, Garmezy, N, Devine, VT, Schaefer, SM. A classification system for research in childhood psychopathology: Part II. Validation research examining converging descriptions from the parent and from the child. In BA Maher, & WB Maher (Eds.), *Progress in experimental personality research* (Vol. 10). New York: Academic Press, 1981

Niswander, K, & Gordon, M. *The collaborative perinatal study of the National Institute of Neurological Diseases and Stroke: The women and their pregnancies*. Philadelphia: Saunders, 1972

Noyes, R, Clancy, J, Crowe, R, Hoenk, PR, & Slymen, DJ: The family problems of anxiety neurosis. *Archives of General Psychiatry*, 1978, *35*, 1057–1062

O'Connor, M, Foch, T, Sherry, T, & Plomin, R. A twin study of specific behavioral problems of socialization as viewed by parents. *Journal of Abnormal Child Psychology*, 1980, *8*, 189–199

Olweus, D. Stability of aggresive reaction patterns in males: A review. *Psychological Bulletin*, 1979, *86*, 852–875

Paternite, CE, & Loney, J. Childhood hyperkinesis: Relationships between symptomatology and home environment. In CK Whalen & B Henker (Eds.), *Hyperactive children: The social ecology of identification and treatment*. New York: Academic Press, 1980

Patterson, GR. Mothers: The unacknowledged victims. *Monographs of the Society for Research in Child Development*, 1980, *45*, (5), (Serial No. 186)

Patterson, GR, Littman, RA, & Bricker, W. Assertive behavior in children: A step toward a theory of aggression. *Monographs of the Society for Research in Child Development*, 1967, *32*, (5 and 6)

Pauls, DL, & Kidd, KK. Genetics of childhood behavior disorders. In BB Lahey & AE Kazdin (Eds.), *Advances in Clinical Child Psychology* (Vol. 4). New York: Plenum Press, 1981

Pauls, DL, & Kidd, KK. Genetic strategies for the analysis of childhood behavioral traits. *Schizophrenia Bulletin*, 1982, *8*, 253–266

Pentz, T. *Facilitation of language acquisition: The role of the mother*. Unpublished doctoral dissertation, The Johns Hopkins University, 1975

Peterson, DR. Behavior problems of middle childhood. *Journal of Consulting Psychology*, 1961, *25*, 205–209

Pfeiffer, SI. The influence of diagnostic labeling on special education placement decisions. *Psychology in the Schools*, 1980, *17*, 346–350

Plomin, R, DeFries, JC, & McClearn, GE. *Behavior genetics: A primer*. San Francisco: WH Freeman and Co., 1980

Plomin, R, & Rowe, DC. Genetic and environmental etiology of social behavior in infancy. *Developmental Psychology*, 1979, *15*, 62–72

Pond, D. Psychiatric aspects of epileptic and brain-damaged children. *British Medical Journal*, 1961, *2*, 1377–1382, 1454–1459

Poznanski, ED, Krahenbuhl, U, & Zrull, JP. Childhood depression: A longitudinal perspective. *Journal of the American Academy of Child Psychiatry*, 1976, *15*, 491–501

Pringle, MLK, Butler, NR, & Davie, R. *11,000 seven-year-olds*. London: Longmans, 1966

Puig-Antich, J. Major depression and conduct disorder in prepuberty. *Journal of the American Academy of Child Psychiatry*, 1982, *21*, (2), 118–128

Quay, HC. Dimensions of personality in delinquent boys as inferred from the factor analysis of case history data. *Child Development*, 1964, *35*, 479–484

Quay, HC. Patterns of aggression, withdrawal, and immaturity. In HC Quay & JS Werry (Eds.), *Psychopathological disorders of childhood*. New York: Wiley, 1972

Quay, HC. Classification. In HC Quay & JS Werry (Eds.), *Psychopathological disorders of childhoood*. (2nd ed.) New York: Wiley & Sons, 1979

Quay, HC, Sprague, RL, Shulman, HS, & Miller, AL. Some correlates of personality disorder and conduct disorder. *Psychology in the Schools*, 1966, *3*, 44–47

Rae, WA. Childhood conversion reactions: A review of incidence in pediatric settings. *Journal of Clinical Child Psychology*, 1977, *6*, 66–72

Reid, JB, & Taplin, PS. *A special interactional approach to the treatment of abusive families*. Unpublished manuscript, Oregon Social Learning Center, Eugene, 1978

Reid, K. *Determinants of separation reaction in preschoolers*. Unpublished master's thesis, the University of Connecticut, 1976

Richman, N, Stevenson, J, & Graham, P. Prevalence of behaviour problems in 3 year old children: An epidemiological study in a London borough. *Journal of Child Psychology and Psychiatry*, 1975, *16*, 272–287

Robertson, J, & Robertson, J. Young children in brief separation: A fresh look. *Psychoanalytic Study of the Child*, 1971, *26*, 264–315

Robins, E, & O'Neal, P. Clinical features of hysteria in children. *Nervous Child*, 1953, *10*, 246–271

Robins, LN. *Deviant children grown up*. Baltimore: Williams & Wilkins, 1966

Robins, LN. Follow-up studies. In HC Quay & JS Werry (Eds.). *Psychopathological disorders of childhood*. (2nd ed.) New York: Wiley, 1979

Robins, LN, West, PA, & Herjanic, B. Arrest and delinquency in two generations: A study of black urban families and their children. *Journal of Child Psychology and Psychiatry*, 1975, *16*, 125–140

Roff, JD, & Knight, R. Family characteristics, childhood symptoms, and adult outcome in schizophrenia. *Journal of Abnormal Psychology*, 1981, *90*, (6), 510–520

Roff, M. Childhood antecedents of adult neurosis, severe bad conduct, and psychological health. In D Ricks, A Thomas, & M Roff (Eds.), *Life history research in psychopathology*, (Vol. 3). Minneapolis: University of Minnesota Press, 1974

Rosenthal, D. Heredity in criminality. *Criminal Justice and Behavior*, 1975, *2*, 3–21

Rosenthal, D, Wender, PH, Kety, SS, Schulsinger, F, Welner, J, & Reider, RO. Parent-child relationships and psychopathological disorder in the child. *Archives of General Psychiatry*, 1975, *32*, 466–476

Ross, AO. *Psychological disorders of children: A behavioral approach to theory, research, and therapy* (2nd ed.). New York: McGraw-Hill Book Company, 1980

Ross, DM, & Ross, SA. *Hyperactivity: Current issues, research, and theory,* (2nd ed.) New York: Wiley, 1982

Rutter, M. Sex differences in children's responses to family stress. In EJ Anthony & C Koupernick (Eds.), *The child in the family* (Vol. 1). New York: Wiley, 1970

Rutter, M. Parent-child separation: Psychological effects on the children. *Journal of Child Psychology and Psychiatry,* 1971, *12,* 233–256

Rutter, M. The development of infantile autism. *Psychological Medicine,* 1974, *4,* 147–163

Rutter, M. Brain damage syndromes in childhood: Concepts and findings. *Journal of Child Psychology and Psychiatry,* 1977, *18,* 1–21

Rutter, M. Maternal deprivation 1972–1978: New findings, new concepts, new approaches. *Child Development,* 1979, *50,* 283–305

Rutter, M. Separation experiences: A new look at an old topic. *Journal of Pediatrics,* 1980, *95,* 147–154

Rutter, M, Graham, P, Chadwick, O, & Yule, W. Adolescent turmoil: Fact or fiction. *Journal of Child Psychology and Psychiatry,* 1976, *17,* 35–56

Rutter, M, Graham, P, & Yule, W. A neuropsychiatric study of childhood. *Clinics in Developmental Medicine.* No. 35/36. Philadelphia: JB Lippincott Co., 1970

Rutter, M, & Lockyer, L. A five to fifteen year follow-up study of infantile psychosis. I. Description of sample. *British Journal of Psychiatry,* 1967, *113,* 1169–1182

Rutter, M, & Shaffer, D. DSM-III: A step forward or back in terms of the classification of child psychiatric disorders? *Journal of the American Academy of Child Psychiatry,* 1980, *19,* 371–394

Rutter, M, Shaffer, D, & Shepherd, M. *A multiaxial classification of child psychiatric disorders.* Geneva: WHO, 1975

Rutter, M, Tizard, J, & Whitmore, K. (Eds.) *Education, health, and behaviour.* London: Longmans, 1970

Rutter, M, Tizard, J, Yule, W, Graham, P, & Whitmore, K. Isle of Wight studies, 1964–1974. *Psychological Medicine,* 1976, *6,* 313–332

Sameroff, AJ, & Chandler, MJ. Reproductive risk and the continuum of caretaking casuality. In FD Horowitz (Ed.), *Review of child development research* (Vol. 4). Chicago: University of Chicago Press, 1975

Sandberg, ST, Wieselberg, M, & Shaffer, D. Hyperkinetic and conduct problem children in a primary school population: Some epidemiological considerations. *Journal of Child Psychology and Psychiatry,* 1980, *21,* 293–311

Santrock, JW, & Warshak, RA. Father custody and social development in boys and girls. *Journal of Social Issues,* 1979, *35,* 112–125

Sassone, D, Lambert, NM, Sandoval, J. *The adolescent status of boys previously identified as hyperactive.* Unpublished manuscript, University of California, 1981

Scarr, S. Genetic factors in activity motivation. *Child Development,* 1966, *37,* 663–673

Scarr, S. Environmental bias in twin studies. *Eugenic Quarterly,* 1968, *15,* 34–40

Schachar, R, Rutter, M, & Smith, A. The characteristics of situationally and pervasively hyperactive children: Implications for syndrome definition. *Journal of Child Psychology and Psychiatry,* 1981, *22,* (4), 375–392

Schacht, T, & Nathan, PE. But is it good for the psychologists?: Appraisal and status of DSM-III. *American Psychologist,* 1977, *32,* 1017–1025

Schaffer, HR, & Emerson, PE. The development of social attachments in infancy. *Monographs of the Society for Research in Child Development,* 1964, *29,* (3, Serial No. 94)

Scholom, A, Zucker, RA, & Stollak, GE. Relating early child adjustment to infant and parent temperament. *Journal of Abnormal Child Psychology,* 1979, *7,* (3), 297–308

Schopler, E, Mesibov, G, Baker, A. Evaluation of treatment for autistic children and their parents. *Journal of the American Academy of Child Psychiatry,* 1982, *21,* 262–267

Schuham, AI. The double-bind hypothesis a decade later. *Psychological Bulletin,* 1967, *68,* 409–416

Schulsinger, F. Psychopathy: Heredity and environment. In SA Mednick & KO Christiansen (Eds.), *Biosocial bases of criminal behavior.* New York: Gardner Press, Inc., 1977

Schwarz, JC. Childhood origins of psychopathology. *American Psychologist,* 1979, *34,* 879–885

Schwarz, JC, & Getter, H. Parental conflict and dominance in late adolescent maladjustment: A triple interaction model. *Journal of Abnormal Psychology,* 1980, *89,* 573–580

Schwarz, JC, & Zuroff, DC. Family structure and depression in female college students: Effects of parental conflict, decision-making power, inconsistency of love. *Journal of Abnormal Psychology,* 1979, *88,* 398–406

Schwartz, S, & Johnson, JH. *Psychopathology of childhood: A clinical-experimental approach.* New York: Pergamon Press, 1981

Sears, RR. Relation of early socialization to aggression in middle childhood. *Journal of Abnormal and Social Psychology,* 1961, *63,* 466–492

Sears, RR, Whiting, JWM, Nowlis, V, & Sears, PA. Some child-rearing antecedents of aggression and dependency in young children. *Genetic Psychology Monographs,* 1953, *47,* 135–234

Seidel, UP, Chadwick, OFD, & Rutter, M. Psychological disorders in crippled children. A comparative study of children with and without brain damage. *Developmental Medicine in Child Neurology,* 1975, *17,* 563–573

Serbin, LA. Sex-role socialization: A field in transition. In BB Lahey & AE. Kazdin (Eds.), *Advances in clinical child psychology* (Vol. 3). New York: Plenum Press, 1980

Serbin, LA, O'Leary, KD, Kent, RN, & Tonick IJ. A comparison of teacher response to the preacademic and problem behavior of boys and girls. *Child Development,* 1973, *44,* 796–804

Shaffer, D. Suicide in childhood and early adolescence. *Journal of Child Psychology and Psychiatry,* 1974, *15,* 275–292

Shaffer, D, Chadwick, O, & Rutter, M. Psychiatric outcome of localized head injury in children. In *Outcome of severe damage to the central nervous system* (Ciba Foundation Symposium, No. 34). Amsterdam: Excerpta Medica, 1975

Shepherd, M, Oppenheim, B, & Mitchell, S. Childhood behavior disorders and the child guidance clinic: An epidemiological study. *Journal of Child Psychology and Psychiatry,* 1966, *7,* 39–52

Shirley, M, Baum, B, & Polsky, S. Outgrowing childhood's problems: A follow up study of child guidance clinic patients. *Smith College Studies in Social Work,* 1940–41, *11,* 31–60

Singer, MT, & Wynne, LC. Principles for scoring communication defects and deviances in parents of schizophrenics: Rorschach and TAT scoring manuals. *Psychiatry,* 1966, *29,* 260–288

Smith, R, & Daglish, L. Sex differences in parent and infant behavior in the home. *Child Development,* 1977, *48,* 1250–1254

Smith, SD, Pennington, BF, Kimberling, WJ, & Lubs, HA. Investigation of subgroups within specific reading disability utilizing neurological linkage analysis. *American Journal of Human Genetics,* 1979, *31,* 83A (Abstract)

Snyder, JJ. A reinforcement analysis of interaction in problem and nonproblem children. *Journal of Consulting and Clinical Psychology,* 1977, *86,* 528–535

Soli, SD, Neuchterlein, KH, Garmezy, N, Devine VT, & Schaefer, SM. A classification system for research in childhood psychopathology: Part I. An empirical approach using factor and cluster analyses and conjunctive decision rules. In BA Maher & WB.Maher (Eds.), *Progress in experimental personality research. Vol. 10.* New York: Academic Press, 1981

Spitz, RA. Anaclitic depression. *Psychoanalytic Study of the Child,* 1946, *2,* 313–342

Spitz, RA. *The first year of life.* New York: International Universities Press, 1965

Spitzer, R. Nonmedical myths and the DSM-III. *APA Monitor,* 1982. August/September issue, p. 3–33

Sroufe, LA. The coherence of individual development: Early care, attachment, and subsequent developmental issues. *American Psychologist,* 1979a, *34,* 834–841

Sroufe, LA. Socioemotional development, In JD Osofsky (Ed.), *Handbook of Infant Development.* New York: Wiley, 1979b

Stabenau, JR, Pollin, W, Mosher, LR, Frohman, C, Friedhoff, A, & Turner, W. A study of monozygotic twins discordant for schizophrenia: Some biological variables. *Archives of General Psychiatry,* 1969, *20,* 145–158

Stayton, DJ, Hogan, R, & Ainsworth, MDS. Infant obedience and maternal behavior: The origins of socialization reconsidered. *Child Development,* 1971, *42,* 1057–1065

Stein, J. (Ed.), *The Random House college dictionary (revised edition).* New York: Random House, Inc., 1982

Stevens, SS. Mathematics, measurement, and psychophysics. In SS Stevens (Ed.), *Handbook of experimental psychology,* New York: Wiley, 1958

Stewart, MA, deBlois, CS, & Cummings, C. Psychiatric disorder in the parents of hyperactive boys and those with conduct disorder. *Journal of Child Psychology and Psychiatry,* 1980, *21,* 283–292

Thomas, A, & Chess, S. *Temperament and development.* New York: Brunner/Mazel, 1977

Thomas, A, Chess, S, & Birch, HG. *Temperament and behavior disorders in children.* New York: New York University, 1968

Thomas, A, Chess, S, Birch, HG. The origins of personality. *Scientific American,* 1970, *223,* 102–109

Tizard, B. *Adoption: A second change.* London: Open Books, 1977

Tizard, B, & Hodges, J. The effect of early institutional rearing on the development of eight-year-old children. *Journal of Child Psychology and Psychiatry,* 1978, *19,* 99–118

Ullmann, LP, & Krasner, LA. *A psychological approach to abnormal behavior* (2nd ed.). Englewood Cliffs, NJ: Prentice-Hall, 1975

Vandenberg, SG. The hereditary abilities study: Hereditary components in a psychological test battery. *American Journal of Human Genetics,* 1962, *14,* 220–237

Waldron, S. The significance of childhood neurosis for adult mental health: A follow-up study. *American Journal of Psychiatry,* 1976, *133,* 532–538

Waldron, S., Shrier, DK, Stone, B, & Tobin, F. School phobia and other childhood neuroses: A systematic study of the children and their families. *American Journal of Psychiatry,* 1975, *132,* 802–808

Wallerstein, JS, & Kelly, JB. The effects of parental divorce: Experiences of the preschool child. *Journal of the American Academy of Child Psychiatry,* 1975, *14,* 600–616

Waring, M, & Ricks, D. Family patterns of children who become adult schizophrenics. *Journal of Nervous and Mental Disease,* 1965, *140,* 351–364

Waters, E, Wippman, J, & Sroufe, LA. Attachment, positive affect and competence in the peer group: Two studies in construct validation. *Child Development,* 1979, *50,* 821–829

Watt, NF. Patterns of childhood social development in adult schizophrenics. *Archives of General Psychiatry,* 1978, *35,* 160–165

Watt, NF, Grubb, TW, & Erlenmeyer-Kimling, L. Social, emotional, and intellectual behavior at school among children at high risk for schizophrenia. *Journal of Consulting and Clinical Psychology,* 1982, *50,* (2), 171–181

Weiss, B, Minde, K, Werry, J, Douglas, W, & Nemeth, E. Studies on the hyperactive child, VIII. Five-year follow-up. *Archives of General Psychiatry,* 1974, *24,* 409–418

Welner, Z. Childhood depression: An overview. *Journal of Nervous and Mental Disease*, 1978, *166*, 588–593

Welner, Z, Welner, A, Steward, MA, Palkes, H, & Wish, E. A controlled study of siblings of hyperactive children. *Journal of Nervous and Mental Disease*, 1977, *165*, 110–117

Wender, PH. *Minimal brain dysfunction in children*. New York: Wiley, 1971

Wender, PH, Rosenthal, D, Kety, SS, Schulsinger, F, & Welner, J. Cross-fostering: A research strategy for clarifying the role of genetic and experimental factors in the etiology of schizophrenia. *Archives of General Psychiatry*, 1974, *30*, 121–128

Werry, JS. The childhood psychoses. In HC Quay & JS Werry (Eds.), *Psychopathological disorders of childhood (2nd ed.)*. New York: Wiley, 1979a

Werry, JS. Organic factors. In HC Quay & JC Werry (Eds.), *Psychopathological disorders of childhood*. New York, Wiley, 1979b

Werry, JS, & Quay, HC. The prevalence of behavior symptoms in younger elementary school children. *American Journal of Orthopsychiatry*, 1971, *41*, 136–143

Whitehead, L. Sex differences in children's responses to family stress: A re-evaluation. *Journal of Child Psychology and Psychiatry*, 1979, *20*, 247–254

Whitt, JK, & Casey, PH. The mother-infant relationship and infant development: The effect of pediatric intervention. *Child Development*, 1982, *53*, 948–956

Willerman, L. Activity level and hyperactivity in twins. *Child Development*, 1973, *44*, 288–293

Wulbert, M, Inglis, S, Kriegsmann, E, & Mills, B. Language delay and associated mother-child interactions. *Developmental Psychology*, 1975, *11*, 61–70

Wynne, LC. Current concepts about schizophrenia and family relations. *Journal of Nervous and Mental Disorders*, 1981, *169*, (2), 82–88

Yule, W. The epidemiology of child psychopathology. In BB Lahey & AE Kazdin (Eds.), *Advances in clinical child psychology* (Vol. 4). New York: Plenum Press, 1981

Andrea L. Starrett

4

Medical Aspects of Developmental Disabilities

The term "developmental disabilities" groups together the major handicapping conditions that impair the mental, motor, communication, social, and emotional development of the infant and young child. Usually this diagnostic term includes mental retardation, cerebral palsy, hearing impairments, blindness or visual limitations, infantile autism, and speech and language disorders. Developmental disorders occur along a continuum of central nervous system dysfunction (Palmer & Capute, 1980) and include the less severe developmental deviations, so-called low severity/high prevalence disorders (Levine, 1982): learning disabilities, motor coordination difficulties and attentional and behavioral problems that may occur singly or in combination in the school-age child.

Care of the child with a developmental disability requires the cooperation of professionals from many disciplines including medicine, psychology, speech pathology, education, social work, occupational therapy, physical therapy, dentistry, nutrition, and nursing. The standard mode of delivery of care for the multihandicapped child has become the multidisciplinary team. Although this method may not be the most efficient in terms of professional time or expense, this approach probably leads to the optional habilitation of the handicapped child (Pearson, 1983; Pfeiffer, 1982). In the course of the care of the developmentally disabled child, many medical questions arise. The most important medical questions concern the diagnosis of the child's disability and the medical etiology of this condition. Both of these will greatly influence the child's prognosis for adaptive functioning and the counseling given to parents about the nature of their child's problems and his future potential. Medical treatment for specific problems is frequently necessary as part of the child's overall management. This chapter will introduce the psychologist, or other nonphysician, to the pediatric approach to these three important medical issues—diagnosis, etiology, and medical treatment—as well as the components of the medical evaluation of the developmentally disabled child. It is hoped that an understanding of the contributions of the physician to the multidisciplinary management of the handicapped child will help the psychologist use consultation with the physician over common areas of concern most effectively.

Before beginning to consider these issues, we will first discuss which doctor to consult. In this country most children receive their primary medical care from pediatricians, family practitioners, or general practice physicians. Although most pediatric training programs in the United States include exposure to pediatric neurology and developmental pediatrics in their curriculum, the major emphasis in pediatric education continues to be the treatment of acute medical disorders. The lack of information and expertise in the care of the handicapped child has been realized by many pediatric practitioners in recent years (Dworkin, Shonkoff, Leviton, & Levine, 1979) and the American Academy of Pediatrics has made a national effort in continuing education for pediatricians (American Academy of Pediatrics, 1980) to improve this situation. Although information about the child's current health status and general pediatric illnesses will be available from the child's pediatrician or primary physician, the psychologist might want to refer the child and family to a pediatric subspecialist with more expertise in the care of handicapped children to address questions of diagnoses, etiology, and the role of medical treatment in the child's overall habilitation program.

Two subspecialists are most likely to concern themselves with the issues above, a pediatric neurologist and a developmental pediatrician. Both are competent in the care of the developmentally disabled child with cerebral palsy, mental retardation, learning disorders, and other nonprogressive neurologic conditions (Rapin, 1982). The pediatric neurologist has completed residency training in adult neurology with one or more subspecialty years in pediatric neurology. A developmental pediatrician has completed residency training in pediatrics with further training in child development or handicapping conditions. Although the diagnostic evaluation of the child by these two specialists may be similar, their orientation and goals will be different. The child neurologist attempts to make a specific diagnosis of the neurologic dysfunction with an orientation to the care of acute neurological disorders or the diagnosis of rare conditions. The developmental pediatrician's main concern is comprehensive management of a child and his handicap. He is likely to have facility and familiarity with other disciplines and an orientation toward the multidisciplinary management of the complex, interacting dysfunctions of the handicapped child (Vining, Accardo, Rubenstein, Farrell, & Rozien, 1976). Referral to either medical consultant will depend primarily upon the question to be answered. If the child presents with developmental delay, and possibly a deterioration in function, a pediatric neurologist could pursue the medical etiology of a progressive neurologic disorder with comprehensive neurodiagnostic tests including electroencephalogram (EEG), computerized axial tomography (CAT) scan, evoked responses, and metabolic tests. If the infant presents a developmental delay, the developmental pediatrician would evaluate the etiology of the child's problem, but he would also document the child's level of function with developmental testing, counsel parents about necessary stimulation programs for the child, and facilitate the family's adaptation to a handicapped child. Outside of university medical centers, the choice of specialist at this time may depend upon availability and convenience for the family.

Several other medical specialists may make valuable contributions to the medical care of a handicapped child. A clinical geneticist may be able to identify a particular syndrome, if the child has several unusual physical features. The geneticist can counsel parents about recurrence risks in future pregnancies, if a diagnosis is known, and can give advice concerning prenatal diagnostic procedures, such as amniocentesis or ultrasonography, for future pregnancies. The child psychiatrist may be helpful in unraveling and managing complex behavior problems or in helping parents work through their emotional adjustment problems to their child's disability. Several surgical subspecialties such as orthopedics, ophthalmology, and urology also can make valuable contributions to a child's medical management.

Components of a Medical Evaluation

Let us now consider the components of the medical evaluation of a child with a developmental disorder (Table 4-1). The most important part of the medical evaluation is the medical history obtained by interview with the parents or other caretaker of the child. Older children are questioned about their problems, so that the physician can address their concerns as well as establish rapport. The physician will review the reason for the referral and the parents' concerns and questions about the child. An in-depth review of the child's current status will vary with the age of the child and the presenting problem. In an infant or preschooler, it

Table 4-1
Components of the Medical Evaluation
of a Child With a Known or Suspected
Developmental Disorder

Reason for referral
Present illness or status
Perinatal history
Developmental history
Emotional/social adjustment
Past medical events
Family history
Physical examination
Sensory screening
Neurological examination
Developmental testing
Laboratory tests

will address the presence of significant delays in gross motor, fine motor, adaptive and communication skills; behavioral problems; feeding and sleeping disturbances; and nursery or preschool experiences. In a school-age child, focus is on physical complaints; present medication; school grade placement and achievement; behavior at home and at school; and peer and family relationships.

A detailed review of the pregnancy, labor and delivery, and perinatal events is necessary. Whenever possible the delivery and nursery records of the infant and the maternal obstetrical record should be obtained. The developmental history covers the time of achievement of pertinent developmental milestones; however, the time devoted to this will vary according to the age of the child. In older children of normal intelligence, parents may only remember age of attainment of major milestones, such as walking, talking, or toilet training. In a younger child or in a child with mental retardation, documentation of age of attainment of skills in gross motor, fine motor, personal, social, and communication areas is possible and may go a long way toward delineation of the child's current status. This review of the child's developmental status can be approached in general history taking, structured questions (Accardo & Capute, 1979), screening (Frankenberg, van Doorninck, Liddel, & Dick, 1976), or comprehensive questionnaires (Knobloch, Stevens, Malone, Ellison, & Risenberg, 1979).

Attention is directed toward deviations in temperament and behavior that may indicate a developmental disorder. Many children with mental retardation are described as excessively placid infants who sleep excessively and rarely cry. Likewise, many infants with documented brain injury at birth are excessively irritable; cry constantly; never establish regular feeding, sleeping, or waking routines; and have marked feeding difficulties during infancy. The "difficult baby" syndrome is also described in children with attention deficit disorder. Many of these children achieve their gross motor milestones early and are constantly "on the go" as toddlers.

A negative history of developmental deviations is also important. Most parents of learning-disabled children remember no unusual difficulty with their children as infants, toddlers, or preschoolers. Concerns about the child's development will only emerge when he reaches the demands of the formal education system in kindergarten or the primary grades. The onset of academic or behavioral problems in a school-age child after the early elementary school years usually points to a psychosocial etiology of the child's problems instead of a medical or developmental one.

The child's current emotional and social adjustment is reviewed with questions concerning behavior at home and school, independence and responsibilities, relationship with peers, and participation in extracurricular activities or sports. Attention is given to certain behavioral problems such as enuresis, pica, sleep disturbance, or the parents' perception of the child as "hyper," which may reflect a developmental deviation or an emotional problem. The parents' method of discipline and responses to problem behaviors often reflect their overall understanding of their child, as well as their information on normal child development and cultural and social values.

In reviewing the child's past medical history, the occurrence of head injuries, seizures, or central nervous system infections may indicate diseases or events that bear directly on the child's current status. The history of hospitalizations or surgeries, recurrent early infections, allergies, and visual disorders may lead to consideration of medical conditions that influence the child's general health and require consideration in planning habilitation programs.

Finally, the family history covers the age, medical history, and educational attainments of the child's parents and siblings. The history of a developmental, neurologic, or psychiatric illness in the first degree relatives (parents, siblings, grandparents, aunts, uncles, or first or second cousins) may point to an autosomal mode of inheritance important in genetic counseling.

The general physical examination begins with the ascertainment of the patient's current growth status by measurements of height, weight, and head circumference, which are plotted on normative growth graphs. Both microcephaly (head circumference less than two standard deviations below the normal) and macrocephaly (head circumference greater than two standard deviations above the mean) are associated with a variety of genetic, metabolic, infectious, and toxic disorders that produce mental retardation and other developmental disorders. During the physical examination, careful attention is given to the examination of the skin, since neurocutaneous syndromes and some congenital anomaly syndromes are associated with particular skin defects or an altered distribution of more common skin lesions. For example, *café au lait* spots are flat brown discolorations of the skin that occur commonly in normal individuals. The presence of nine or more *café au lait* spots should prompt the physician to search carefully for other signs of neurofibromatosis.

Throughout the examination, care is taken to discover congenital anomalies of major organ systems (heart, lungs, kidneys, etc.), as well as minor physical anomalies that usually involve the scalp, skin, ears, eyes, face, or palmar skin creases. In a child with mental retardation, the presence of a single major congenital anomaly or three or more minor ones suggests a chromosomal or a prenatal etiology for the child's mental retardation (Cohen, 1982). In a child whose disorder leads to orthopedic complications, such as spina bifida or cerebral palsy, examination of range of motion in all large body joints and the alignment of the spine is essential, since joint contractures and scoliosis of the spine can severely impair the child's function.

In all children, an assessment of the primary senses of vision and hearing should be done as part of the physical examination. In young infants, screening may consist only of the observations of visual pursuit of objects or the localization of sounds in the environment. Children with a mental age above three years can generally cooperate with a formal testing procedure. Visual acuity may be screened using Allen cards, which consist of pictures of common objects, or the illiterate E test, until the school-age children can read a standard Snellen chart with letters. Many 3-year-old children can cooperate with screening audiometry using a standard audiometer. Whenever there is any doubt about a child's visual or hearing acuity, referral to an ophthalmologist or an audiologist is indicated. It is sound practice to refer all children less than five years of age to an audiologist or ophthalmologist to confirm screening results in the office.

After the physical examination is completed, a complete neurological examination is conducted. Again, the format of the examination will vary with the age of the child (Baird & Gordon, 1983; Paine & Oppe, 1966). In younger children, much information will be deduced from observation of the child's behavior, manipulation of objects, and locomotion in the office. Children above the age of five years can cooperate with the same type of complete neurological testing conducted with adults, although performance of some sensorimotor tasks will reflect the child's neuromaturational age. Of great importance is determination of the child's mental status, including his affect, level of cooperation, general information, and level of understanding. Many children with developmental disabilities present behavioral problems that are readily observed in the office including hyperactivity, distractibility, perseveration, bizarre, self-injurious, or self-stimulatory behavior. Mildly retarded children frequently exhibit socially inappropriate behavior, since they behave in line with mental age instead of chronologic age expectations. Spontaneous speech is observed for intelligibility as well as abnormal patterns that reflect a neurologic problem, such as dysarthria, or a communication problem, e.g., echolalia. Examination of cranial nerve function includes examination of the optic fundus, ocular movements; facial, oral, and tongue movements; cutaneous sensation of the face and head; as well as examinations of vision and hearing, discussed previously.

Examination of motor function is extremely important in all children. Muscle strength and tone are assessed in all four extremities. Percussion of the deep tendon reflexes with the reflex hammer reflects the tones maintained in the muscles by the myotactic stretch reflex. In cerebral palsy and in neuromuscular disorders, significant alterations in muscle strength, tone, and reflexes occur. In infants or retarded younger children, motor evaluation includes examination of the primitive reflexes (Capute, Accardo, Vining, Rubenstein, & Harryman, 1978) and neonatal automatisms (Illingsworth, 1980), and the general level of postural control and gross motor skills (Milani-Comparetti & Gidoni, 1967). In older ambulatory children, observations of gait when walking normally and in stressed conditions (walking on heels, toes, and in tandem) are more important. The attainment of gross motor skills appropriate to the child's age, such as the ability to hop on one foot or throw a ball overhand, as well as the child's general coordination in these tasks are recorded. Fine motor movements are tested specifically in tasks such as alternating pronation and supination of the forearm or sequential opposition of the fingers to the thumb of one hand. Ascertainment of hand and foot preference is usually part of the examination. Marked lateral preferences may point to a subtle hemiparesis but the role of mixed lateral preferences for eye, hand, and foot use (mixed dominance) in learning disabilities continues to be controversial (Knights & Bakker, 1976). Grossly abnormal movement patterns carry major diagnostic significance in cerebral palsy syndromes and neurological disorders, while minor immaturities in movement control or coordination constitute the "soft signs" seen in learning disabled or hyperactive children.

Examination of the sensory system includes responses to simple cutaneous sensations such as pen prick, light touch, or pain, which are usually intact in children with developmental disabilities. However, responses on tasks that require complex integration of one or more sensory modalities, which are mediated by the parietal cortex, may be deficient in children with mental handicaps that reflect global cerebral impairment or in children with focal cortical injury. Again, less severe difficulties in performance in cortically mediated sensory tasks, such as two point discrimination or right-left orientation, are "soft signs," when seen in isolation in children who are otherwise neurologically intact.

Finally, abnormal or bizarre behavior is carefully noted during the examination. Abnormal behaviors may form part of the symptom complex that defines a child's developmental disability, such as in an autistic child, or neurological disorder, e.g., Tourette's syndrome.

In young children, evaluation of the child's developmental status is part of the neurologic examination. In children less than five years of age, the Denver Developmental Screening Test (Frankenberg, Fandal, Sciarillo, & Burgess, 1981; Frankenberg, Goldstein, & Camp, 1971) is an accepted initial screening tool, although it has serious limitations for use in the developmentally disabled population (see Chap. 5). The child will not be rated as abnormal in cognitive, speech, and language development because of the limited number of items scored by direct observation of infants unless he also has motor delay. Many children with mild cognitive and/or speech and language delays in the preschool age range will also be missed by this test. Most developmental pediatricians and child neurologists rely more on a standard infant development scale, such as the Revised Gessell Developmental Schedules (Knoblock & Pasamanick, 1974; Knoblock, Stevens, & Malone, 1980) or on the Bayley Scales of Infant Development (Bayley, 1969), to obtain both qualitative and quantitative assessments of the child's development. When the physician is unable to test the child himself because of time constraints or lack of training, this standardized information may be obtained by referring the child to a psychologist or other professional with appropriate diagnostic skills.

The assessment of the developmental status of the older child is usually done informally by the physician. The child's general fund of information and his ability to engage in social interactions reflect his language skills and overall intelligence. Visual motor skills are judged by sampling the child's handwriting and having him copy simple line drawings or draw a human figure. Some physicians use the Bender-Gestalt Test to rate visual motor developmental age. Most physicians who deal with children with learning disabilities use some formal or informal assessments of academic skills in reading, spelling, or math, although these are not interpreted as educationally diagnostic or prescriptive. The role of more detailed assessments of developmental skills, academic precursors, and educational achievement by physicians is a matter of debate at present. Most physicians do not have the time or training necessary for the administration of standard psychological or educational tests and usually leave these responsibilities to the appropriate multidisciplinary team members. Levine (Levine, Brooks, & Shonkoff, 1980; Levine, Meltzer, Busch, Palfrey, & Sullivan, 1983) advocated a greater role for the pediatrician in the diagnostic assessment and prescription of intervention strategies for children with learning disabilities. His formalized assessment procedure covers many areas of neurodevelopmental and academic function and requires considerable time and training. Its use and efficacy in educational intervention has not been evaluated at this point, although this may become a significant future development in pediatrics.

Having established the components of the medical evaluation of children with developmental disabilities, let us now consider in children with the developmental disorders the three major medical issues set forth at the beginning of the chapter—diagnosis, etiology, and medical treatment.

Diagnosis

A medical diagnosis is based upon a synthesis of information and findings from the medical history, physical and neurological examinations, laboratory tests, and developmental evaluations. In diagnosing a developmental handicap, the pediatrician assesses three aspects of the child's developmental pattern—delay, dissociation, and deviancy (Accardo & Capute, 1979). This method of analyzing development along various streams or areas was first used by Gessell (Knoblock & Pasamanick, 1974) in assessing younger children's development; however, the same pattern of differentials in developmental attainment is applied to older children with some heuristic value (i.e., the potential/achievement discrepancy in learning disabled students). Delays in development occur when a child's attainment in an area is below that expected for his age. Analyzing the pattern of delay and dissociations among areas of development is the key to formulation of developmental diagnosis. An example of this scheme is shown in Table 4-2. In the young child with mental retardation, there is often no dissociation among the major areas; however, in the cerebral palsied child with normal intelligence, the motor/language dissociation is striking. In cerebral palsied children with mental retardation, this differential may be less striking but will continue to be relected in assessment.

A pattern of deviancy in certain areas of development is also helpful in diagnosis. Deviancy is the nonsequential appearance of skills within a single stream of development. For example, a young infant with cerebral palsy frequently has increased extensor muscle tone throughout

Table 4-2
Dissociation Phenomena in Developmental Disabilities

Developmental Area	Mental Retardation	Cerebral Palsy	Deafness
Motor			
Gross	V[a]	D[b]	N[c]
Fine	V	D	N
Problem solving	D	V	N
Language			
Receptive	D	V	D
Expressive	D	V	D
Personal-Social	D	V	V

Reprinted from Accardo, PJ, & Capute AJ. *The pediatrician and the developmentally delayed child.* Baltimore, Maryland, University Park Press, 1979, p. 124. With permission.

[a]V, variable.
[b]D, delayed.
[c]N, normal.

the axial musculature. The normal tone pattern allows the infant to "flip over" from the prone to the supine position in bed at a few weeks of age, so the infant will be reported to roll over early instead of at the normal age of four months. This same abnormal tone pattern will, however, cause the infant great difficulty in achieving steady head control in the sitting position, a skill usually acquired at three to four months of age, prior to rolling over. Deviant patterns of language and communication development are characteristic of children with infantile autism and take many forms including echolalia, perseverative speech, and abnormal pronoun and syntax usage.

After the developmental diagnosis is clearly established, the physician insures that all of the child's associated deficits are clearly delineated. Although separated for diagnostic and, frequently, for educational purposes, the developmental disabilities are interrelated chronic neurodevelopmental handicaps that occur along a continuum of central nervous system dysfunction. A child with a diagnostic label that implies a specific dysfunction may have delay or deviant development in another area (Capute & Palmer, 1980). For example, in a child with mental retardation the diagnostic label calls attention to the overall cognitive handicaps of the child; however, this child might also show delays in motor development, socialization skills, and sustained attention, as well as have an associated seizure disorder. Attention by professionals to the narrow issue of the level of cognitive function of the child would lead to neglect of many important areas for which intervention is needed for the optimal overall adaptation. Among the moderately to severely re-tarded population, forty percent or more (Gustavson, Hagberg, Hagberg, & Sars, 1977a) will have one or more associated central nervous system (CNS) handicaps. Among the mildly retarded population, a similar number will have CNS handicaps, and about one third will have psychiatric or behavioral problems (Hagberg, Lindberg, & Lewerth, 1981). The child with a developmental disability should be considered multi-handicapped until the physician has conducted examinations that assure the parents and other professionals that the vital functions of vision, hearing, and communication ability are intact and that associated problems such as seizures, orthopedic problems, or behavior disturbances have been addressed.

Seizure disorder is the associated deficit that occurs most frequently in the developmentally delayed population (Hagberg, 1978). The term seizure is used to describe any clinical event that arises from abnormal paroxysmal electrical discharge in the brain, whereas the term epilepsy is usually reserved for individuals with seizure disorders on an idiopathic basis and who therefore have no other associated central nervous system handicap (Rapin, 1982). However, these terms are frequently used interchangeably by both the lay and medical public. In general, in the developmentally handicapped population, the seizure disorder is produced by the organic injury to the brain. Seizures may be precipitated by a variety of factors in a susceptible individual including fever; metabolic disturbances, such as hypoglycemia or hypocalcemia; fatigue; emotional stress; or particular activities, such as looking at flashing lights or listening to music.

The main types of seizures in children are: generalized (grand mal) tonic-clonic; focal motor; myoclonic (including infantile spasms and minor motor seizures); psychomotor; and absence (staring spells). The first three types involve clearly abnormal motor behavior that is easily recognized by the patient, parents, or other observers. Psychomotor seizures and absence spells produce brief lapses of consciousness without a loss of postural tone. The staring may be accompanied by brief fluttering of the eyelids, or occasionally by more complex automatisms, such as facial grimacing, shoulder shrugging, etc. They are not preceded by an aura and may not be followed by a postictal state of drowsiness or confusion; so, these seizures may be very difficult to diagnose, since they only briefly alter the child's normal behavior. Good discussions of seizure disorders written for nonphysicians are included in the works of Batshaw and Perret (1981), and Buda (1981).

The diagnosis of a seizure disorder is based on the occurrence of the clinical event itself. Since seizures are rarely observed in the office, the diagnosis usually rests upon the historical description given by the observer of the seizure (parent, teacher, etc.) (Menkes, 1974). The EEG is the laboratory test used to confirm the diagnosis of seizures and is sometimes helpful in classifying various types of seizure. However, between paroxysmal events the EEG may be normal, so a negative record does not rule out a seizure disorder. Twenty-four-hour EEG monitoring is a helpful tool in the evaluation of equivocal cases (Holmes, McKeever, & Russman, 1982).

Etiology

Once a diagnosis of developmental disability is made, the physician will go on to establish a medical etiology, if possible. The etiologies of developmental disorders are always heterogeneous, since any disease or condition that affects the developing brain may result in neurodevelopmental handicaps. Medical etiologies are usually classified as prenatal, perinatal, or postnatal in origin (Table 4-3). An in-depth review of the multitude of individual disorders is not possible in this introductory chapter; therefore the reader is referred to the previously cited works by Batshaw and Perret (1981) and Buda (1981) for reference in the future. A brief review of the epidemiology of developmental disabilities will be used to introduce the psychologist to the process of establishing a medical etiology in many individual cases.

The epidemiology of developmental disorders has been studied most fully in children wtih mental retardation and cerebral palsy. The total prevalence rate of mental retardation is around one to three percent in developed countries, while the prevalence rate for children with moderate to severe mental retardation is usually about one sixth of that (0.2 to 0.3 percent). The incidence of moderate to severe mental retardation is actually greater than that predicted by a Gaussian distribution of intelligence (Moser & Wolf, 1971) because of organic causes of mental handicap. In a recent epidemiologic survey from Sweden, the overall prevalence rate of moderate to severe mental retardation was 2.88 per 1,000 over an 11-year period (Gustavson, Hagberg, Hagberg, & Sars, 1977a; 1977b) and in 86 percent of these children, a specific medical diagnosis was possible. Seventy-three percent were due to prenatal causes, ten percent to perinatal causes, and three percent to postnatal causes. This preponderance of prenatal causes of mental retardation has also been confirmed by surveys of retarded individuals in institutions (Kaveggia, Durkin, Pendleton, & Opitz, 1975; Moser & Wolf, 1971).

The conventional wisdom has held that mild to borderline mental retardation is usually due to sociocultural influences as well as an artifact of (the lower end of) the normal distribution of intelligence within the population. However, a recent epidemiological study from Sweden chal-

Table 4-3

Etiologic Classification of Mental Retardation

Type	Example
Prenatal	
Genetic	
Chrosomal abnormalities	Down's syndrome, trisomy 21, trisomy 18, Fragile X syndrome
Disorders of amino acid metabolism	Phenylketonuria, maple syrup urine disease
Disorders of mucopolysaccharide metabolism	Hunter or Hurler's syndrome
Disorders of lipid metabolism	Tay-Sachs disease
Disorder of carbohydrate metabolism	Galactosemia
Disorder of purine metabolism	Lesch-Nyhan syndrome
Hereditary degenerative disorders	Schilder's disease, Batten's disease
Hormonal deficiency	Congenital hypothyroidism
Hereditary syndromes or malformations	Primary microcephaly, X-linked hydrocephalus
Neuroectodermatoses	Neurofibromatosis, tuberosus sclerosis
Nongenetic	
Infection	Rubella, toxoplasmosis, cytomegalovirus
Irradiation	Microcephaly
Toxins	Alcohol, phenytoin
Unknown	Malformations, intrauterine growth retardation
Perinatal	
Prematurity	Respiratory distress syndrome
Anoxia	Birth trauma, asphyxia
Cerebral damage	Interventricular hemorrhage, trauma, hypoglycemia
Infection	Meningitis, encephalitis
Hyperbilirubinemia	Kernicterus
Postnatal	
Brain injuries	Accidents, cerebrovascular accidents, thrombosis, hemorrhage
Infection	Meningitis, encephalitis, brain abscess
Anoxia	Cardiac arrest, respiratory illness
Poisons	Lead, mercury, carbon monoxide
Hormonal insufficiency	Hypothyroidism
Metabolic	Hypoglycemia, hypernatremia
Postimmunization encephalopathy	Pertussis, smallpox
Sociocultural	Deprivation
Epilepsy	

Adapted from Milunsky, A. *The prevention of genetic diseases and mental retardation.* Philadelphia: WB Saunders, 1975, p 20. With permission.

lenges this assumption. In one northern county, the prevalence of mild mental retardation in the school age population was 0.4 percent (Hagberg, Hagberg, Lewerth, & Lindberg, 1981). Among the group with an IQ in the range of 50 to 75, medical etiologies could be elucidated in nearly half (Hagberg, Lindberg, & Lewert, 1981). Perinatal problems, including prematurity, asphyxia, and intrauterine growth retardation, contributed almost as many cases as did the prenatal causes (18 percent vs 23 percent). In 55 percent of children the etiology could not be established; but in about one half of these cases, the parents were of below average intelligence.

In children with cerebral palsy, perinatal factors have always played a relatively larger role (Hagberg, Hagberg, & Olow, 1975a; 1975b) so the major advances in obstetrical and neonatal care over the past 20 years have led to a decrease in the overall rate of cerebral palsy in developed countries (Hagberg, Hagberg, & Olow, 1982). At present, prenatal and postnatal factors contribute as significantly to this problem as perinatal ones (Hagberg, et al., 1975a; 1975c).

In all epidemiological studies on causes of severe developmental disorders, there are always a significant number of cases (usually around 10–20 percent) for whom no obvious medical etiology can be established in spite of exhaustive evaluation. This group of patients continues to offer considerable frustration to clinicians and to parents.

In establishing the medical etiology, the physician relies upon findings from the medical history, physical and neurological examinations, and laboratory tests. Unfortunately, although medical etiologies as a group are common, specific medical conditions that cause mental retardation or cerebral palsy may be rare. The most common chromosomal disorder, trisomy 21, which results in Down's syndrome, occurs at a rate of about 1.46 per 1000 live births (Gustavson, et al., 1977a). Other chromosomal disorders are much more rare. Phenylketonuria, the most common inborn error of metabolism, occurs at an incidence of about 1 in 4,000 live births and other metabolic disorders occur much less frequently. Indeed, many syndromes are known only as isolated case reports in the medical literature, or the individual child may present a new, undescribed constellation of congenital abnormalities. Therefore, arriving at a medical etiology for a child's condition requires considerable "detective work" on the part of the physician.

The role of diagnostic laboratory testing will vary in each case. In some instances, laboratory tests serve only to confirm the medical diagnosis. In a child with characteristic physical features of Down's syndrome (epicanthal folds, flat face, flat occiput, micrognathia, hypotonia, heart disease, and Simian creases) the chromosomal analysis only confirms the medical diagnosis suggested by the findings on physical examination. In some situations, no laboratory procedures are necessary because the etiology is clear from the history alone. In a child who was a small premature infant with a complicated perinatal course including hyaline membrane disease and interventricular hemorrhage, the etiology of his spastic diplegia is not in doubt. However, in a child with a less clearly delineated syndrome, extensive laboratory evaluation may be necessary. In an infant with developmental delay, macrocephaly, abnormal neurological signs, and a seizure disorder, a wide variety of central nervous system developmental anomalies or progressive disorders are etiologic possibilities. This child's medical work-up would be extensive, involving CAT scan of the brain, EEG, quantitative amino acids analysis, lyzosomal enzyme assays, and possible chromosomal analysis.

Most authorities caution against use of a standard battery of laboratory or neurodiagnostic tests in evaluating the child with mental deficiency (Beaudet, 1978; Lingam, Read, Holland, Wilson, Brett, & Hoare, 1982; Smith & Simons, 1975) because of expense and possible injury to the patient. Smith and Simons (1975) present a rational approach to diagnostic evaluation based on the determination of the prenatal and postnatal timing of noxious events. However, this rational, scientific approach to the use of laboratory tests must be balanced against the parents' need to know all that is possible about the origins of their child's handicap. Most physicians who deal with handicapped children have had the experience of discovering a metabolic or chromosomal disorder when tests were only done to reassure parents that these were not the problems.

Many prenatal and perinatal conditions that cause major handicapping conditions can be diagnosed at birth or shortly after that time. This had led to the concept of the "high risk infant" (Parmelee & Haber, 1973) who has sustained a known biological insult but whose long-term developmental outcome cannot be clearly predicted on the basis of biomedical factors alone in the perinatal period. Included in this category are premature infants; term infants with perinatal asphyxia, trauma, or infection; or newborns with multiple congenital anomaly syndromes. The variation in outcome of the very small premature infant with interventricular hemorrhage will be discussed to illustrate this concept more completely. In premature infants with birth weight less than 1500 g, a significant proportion will experience an intracranial hemorrhage into the subependymal germinal matrix, which may extend into the lateral and third ventricles and/or the brain parenchyma. Anatomic localization of the hemorrhage by CAT scan of the brain or cranial ultrasound allows clinical rating of the severity of the hemorrhage during the perinatal period. However, most recent follow-up studies suggest a heterogenicity of outcome among clinical groups. The overall incidence of moderate to severe developmental handicaps is 30 percent, but not all children with handicaps have severe hemorrhage and some infants with severe clinical hemorrhage seem developmentally intact at follow-up (Williamson, Desmond, Wilson, Andrew, & Garcia-Prats, 1982). Among groups with mild delay or normal development, socioeconomic and family factors significantly influence the overall level of intellectual status at age three years (Williamson, Desmond, Wilson, Murphy, Roselle, & Garcia-Prats, 1983). Because of the current inability to predict long-term outcome, the American Academy of Pediatrics currently recommends routine developmental follow-up of certain high risk groups as shown in Table 4-4.

The role of medical etiologic factors in the less severe developmental disorders of learning, cognition, language, and attention is less clear. The concept of "minimal brain damage" or "minimal brain dysfunction" has been debated in the neurologic and pediatric literature for many years. The reader is referred to the excellent reviews by Rutter (1982) and Golden (1982) that address this issue. Since an increased incidence of deficits in cognitive, language, motor, and attentional function has been documented in children with adverse prenatal and perinatal problems (Brown, 1983), in children treated from infancy for genetic and metabolic disorders such as PKU (phenylketonuria) (Berry, Grady, Perlmutter, & Bofinger, 1979; Dobson, Kushid, Williamson, & Fredman, 1976) and congenital hypothyroidism (Birrell, Frost, & Parkin, 1983; MacFaul, Donner, Brett, & Grant, 1978), and in children with postnatal cerebral injury (Rutter, 1981), organic brain pathology or "cerebral dysfunction" must play a role in the genesis of these problems in some children. In children with hyperactivity, or attention deficit disorder, the search for a biochemical deficit has been persistent (Shaywitz, Cohen, & Shaywitz, 1978). The dramatic response of the symptoms of attention

Table 4-4
Conditions Associated With "High Risk" for Developmental Disabilities

Weight less than 1500 grams at birth or gestation less than 34 weeks
Small-for-gestional age status
Perinatal asphyxia
Neurologic depression at delivery
Central nervous system abnormalities, e.g. seizures, hypotonia, or interventricular hemorrhage
Excessive jaundice
Specific genetic, dysmorphic, chromosomal, or metabolic disorders
Prenatal or perinatal infection of the central nervous system
Psychosocial disorders, e.g., maternal alcoholism or drug addiction

deficit disorder to central nervous system stimulant drugs (dextroamphetamine and methylphenidate) has led to many theories based upon altered dopaminergic systems in the brain; however, recent research documenting similar clinical responses in both normal and "hyperactive" children receiving equivalent dosages of stimulant drugs (Rapaport, Buschbaum, Zahn, Ludlow, Weingartner, Ludlow, & Mikkelsen, 1978; Rapaport, Buschbaum, Weingartner, Zahn, Ludlow, Bartko, Mikkelsen, Langer, & Bunney, 1980) has led to serious questioning of these biochemical hypotheses.

Recurrent otitis media and serous otitis media with concomitant mild conductive hearing loss are a definite cause of speech and language delay. Recently, the possible role of these disorders in causing some learning disabilities has been appreciated (Howie, 1980; Paradise, 1981). Systematic studies on the genetics of reading disabilities and on the developmental implication of specific genetic disorders that do not produce mental retardation, such as sex chromosome aberrations (Pennington & Smith, 1983), have shown clearly that some learning disabilities and speech and language disorders occur on a genetic basis. At present, however, the physician must be cautious in drawing conclusions about etiology of milder developmental dysfunctions unless they are clearly supported by the results of the medical examination.

In a child with a learning disability or attention deficit disorder, current medical technology offers little in the way of diagnostic or prognostic information, so medical tests such as CAT scans or EEGs should be avoided. The development of computerized analyses of brain electrical activity from standard EEG and cerebral cortical evoked responses (EP) in resting and in activity states may offer specific neurodiagnostic tests for these disorders in the future. Brain electrical activity mapping (BEAM) developed by Duffy and others (Duffy, Denckla, Bartels, Sandini, & Kiessling, 1980a; 1980b) presents spectral analysis of EEG and EP topographically on a color television screen. Differences have been shown between normal and learning disabled children. The neurometric system developed by John and associates (Princhep, John, Ahn, & Kay, 1983) generates a series of regression equations that compare electrical activity from different regions of the brain and has been used to compare learning disabled, underachieving, and normal populations. The applicability of these methods to clinical practice must await further research studies that demonstrate clinical usefulness in diagnosis and treatment.

Treatment

Medical treatment for children with developmental disabilities is aimed at significantly increasing the current level of functioning and the concomitant level of social adaption of the individual (Stark, 1983). Al-

though a "cure" for developmental disorders has remained elusive, there
has been significant progress in many medical fields that allows us to
talk of curative interventions for the handicapped. Stark (1983) delin-
eates care for the mentally retarded on three levels of prevention (see
Table 4-5). Primary prevention is aimed at the total prevention of handicapping conditions and includes measures such as rubella immunization
and prenatal diagnosis of chromosomal disorders, neural tube deficits,
and an increasing number of metabolic disorders (Milunsky 1976; Stephenson & Weaver, 1981). Secondary prevention involves the early diagnosis of medical conditions that leads to early medical treatment and
a reversal to the normal state. This type of intervention may involve
dietary restriction of a toxic substance in a metabolic disorder to prevent

Table 4-5
Preventive Treatment of Mental Retardation

Primary Prevention (i.e., Total prevention of the handicapping condition):
  Rubella vaccination
  Rho-Gam for Rh ($-$) mothers following first pregnancy
  Vitamin B_{12} treatment of pregnant mothers with an amniocentesis positive
    fetus (methylmalonic acid deficiency)
      Intrauterine fetal surgery: Hydrocephaly
      Maternal serum alpha-protein determination during early pregnancy:
  Neural tube disorders
  Secondary Prevention (i.e., Very early diagnosis and reversal to normal
  state—cure):
      Craniostenosis
      Congenital hypothyroidism
      Phenylketonuria
      Lead intoxication
      Galactosemia
      Maple syrup urine disease
      Homocystinuria
      Early and comprehensive treatment of meningitis and encephalitis
  Tertiary Prevention (i.e., Minimizing residual handicaps and maximizing
  future development):
      Enhanced seizure management
      Parental support and guidance
      Effective psychiatric care
      Infant and child development programs
      Special sensory treatment and/or prognosis
      Physical therapy and/or prosthesis for motor handicaps

Reprinted from Starks JA, The search for cures of mental retardation. In Menolascino,
FJ, Neman, R, & Stark, JA. (Eds), *Curative aspects of mental retardation. Biomedical and
behavioral advances.* Baltimore: Paul H. Brooks Publishing Co., 1983, p. 3. With permission.

ongoing brain damage (i.e., PKU and galactosemia) or replacement of a metabolically necessary substance that allows normal brain development (i.e., congenital hypothyroidism). The success of these forms of medical treatment has lead to the development of perinatal screening programs for congenital hypothyroidism, PKU, and an increasing number of other metabolic defects in most states (Fernoff, Fitzmaurice, Milner, McEwen, Dembure, Brown, Wright, Acosta, & Elsas, 1982). In the future, this approach to treatment may expand because of the great advances in cellular biology, neurochemistry, and genetic engineering. The reader is referred to the recent book by Menolascino, Neman, and Stark (1983) that reviews the implications of these discoveries for "curing" mental retardation in the future.

At present, most physicians involved with the care of handicapped children use treatments that are tertiary prevention measures aimed at minimizing residual handicaps and maximizing future development. In many efforts in this area, such as provision of early intervention programs, the physician will refer the child and his family to professionals in other disciplines, such as special education, occupational and physical therapy, speech and language therapy, and psychology. Often in the case of infants and young children with moderate to severe disabilities, the physician will become the de facto (Bennett, 1982) leader of the team, since both the broad range of biomedical knowledge and influence with the family will allow him to be a most effective advocate for the child's overall development. There are, however, some areas in the management of a developmentally disabled child where direct medical treatment in the form of administration of medication plays a role. Two of these—seizures and behavioral problems—will be discussed briefly to acquaint the psychologist with modes and appropriate goals of medical treatment.

Seizures may interfere with programming for the handicapped child, prohibit recreation or vocational activities, and produce social and emotional disturbances, at the very least, so their control is desirable. In general, major seizure disorders are treated with a variety of anticonvulsant drugs including barbiturates, phenytoins, carbazepine, and valproic acid. All of these drugs can cause potentially serious side effects and most can produce excessive sedation or cognitive impairment at toxic, or even therapeutic levels (Menkes, 1974). Their administration should therefore be carefully monitored by the prescribing physician with frequent office visits and determination of blood medication levels as necessary. In certain situations, drug usage must be carefully weighed against potential side effects. The reader is referred to the books by Batshaw and Perret (1981) and Buda (1981) for a more in depth review for the nonphysician of the use of anticonvulsant medications.

The use of medication for behavioral problems in children is more controversial. Since the 1930s, stimulant medications have been prescribed for children with problems of hyperactivity, distractibility, and short attention span. In spite of the extensive documentation of short-term clinical effects on activity level and behavior and almost 50 years of clinical practice, few long-term positive effects due to drugs alone have been documented for hyperactive children in terms of social adjustment, academic achievement, or cognitive performance (Barkley, 1977). Instead, outcome studies tend to indicate that psychosocial factors, particularly family socioeconomic status and adjustment, are the major influences on the outcome of the adolescent and young adult with hyperactivity (Weiss & Hechtman, 1979). Stimulant medication should therefore be prescribed best as an adjunct to educational, behavioral, and psychological interventions for children with attention deficit disorder symptoms. Parents and teachers should be educated carefully about expected effects and side effects of stimulant drugs; and when medication is used, clinical follow-up is necessary for dosage adjustment, monitoring growth, and adaptation of overall management plans.

Among the developmentally handicapped population more severe behavioral problems including aggressive, self-injurious, and self-stimulatory behaviors are common. The antipsychotic drugs (phenothiazines and haloperidol) and lithium have been used with some effect in these disorders (Campbell, Cohen, & Small, 1982; Durand, 1982): however, drug treatment must always be used as an adjunct to behavior modification and environmental control.

Good medical treatment of other pediatric conditions, such as allergies or heart disease, and routine well child care, including surveillance of growth and nutrition and immunization against childhood infectious diseases, will be necessary if the developmentally handicapped child is to participate maximally in all habilitation programs. Among the mentally retarded and cerebral palsied population, deficiencies of growth are especially common. The etiology of this in an individual child is complex and may be due to inadequate intake, motor coordination disorders, behavioral problems, or possibly neuroendocrine disturbances secondary to organic brain pathology. The severely physically handicapped child is a frequent victim of respiratory illnesses because of poor positioning, inability to handle oral secretions, or gastroesophageal reflux, all of which must be treated aggressively.

Finally, counseling for parents about the nature of their child's disability, the medical etiology, its possible genetic implications, and appropriate interventions is an important activity in the overall biomedical management of the handicapped child. As the psychologist is well aware, even the most sophisticated and educated parents (Butler, 1983) encounter great emotional distress when they learn of the diagnosis, or possible diagnosis, of a handicap in their child; and the physician who works with the parents must have skill and training in answering the questions and understanding their reactions (Meyers, 1983). A clear statement about the etiologies of the child's problems is vital to parents because it can allay parental guilt (MacKeith, 1973). An understanding of the biomedical basis for the child's disability helps the physician and the child's family plan productive intervention efforts. Ready access to accurate medical information from the physician can guide both parents and nonmedical professionals away from the all too numerous "nonstandard" medical treatments (American Academy of Pediatrics 1976; 1982; Golden, 1980; Silver, 1975) that waste the parents' emotional and financial resources and divert them from beneficial treatments for the child. Preventive counseling, in collaboration with a clinical child or pediatric psychologist, about the social and emotional stresses to the child and family in raising a handicapped child (Denhoff, & Feldman, 1981; Murphy, 1982) will help to decrease behavioral problems and to maintain the family home as the most supportive and enhancing environment for the child in the future.

REFERENCES

Accardo, PJ, & Capute, AJ. *The pediatrician and the developmentally delayed child.* Baltimore: University Park Press, 1970

American Academy of Pediatrics. Megavitamin therapy for childhood psychosis and learning disability. *Pediatrics,* 1976, *58*, 910–911

American Academy of Pediatrics. New directions in the care for the handicapped child. Inservice Training Project, 1980

American Academy of Pediatrics. The Doman-Delacato treatment of neurologically handicapped children. *Pediatrics,* 1982, *70*, 810–811

American Academy of Pediatrics, American College of Obstetricians and Gynecologists. *Guidelines for perinatal care,* 1983

Baird, HW, & Gordon, EC. Neurological examination of infants and children. *Clinics in Developmental Medicine, 84/85,* 1983

Barkley, RA. A review of stimulant drug research with hyperactive children. *Journal of Child Psychology and Psychiatry and Allied Disciplines,* 1977, *18,* 137–165

Batshaw, ML, & Perret, YM. *Children with handicaps—A medical primer.* Baltimore: Paul H. Brookes, 1981

Bayley, N. *Bayley scales of infant development.* New York: Psychological Corporation, 1969

Beaudet, AL. Genetic diagnostic studies for mental retardation. *Current Problems in Pediatrics,* 1978, *8(5),* 1–47

Bennett, FC. Pediatrician and the interdisciplinary process. *Exceptional Children,* 1982, *48,* 306–314

Berry, HK, Grady DJ, Pertmutter, LJ, & Bofinger, MK. Intellectual development and academic achievement of children treated early for phenylketonuria. *Developmental Medicine and Child Neurology,* 1979, *21,* 311–320

Birrell, J, Frost, GJ, & Parkin, JM. The development of children with congenital hypothyroidism. *Developmental Medicine and Child Neurology,* 1983, *25,* 512–519

Brown, CC. Childhood learning disabilities and prenatal risk. *Johnson and Johnson Pediatric Round Tables:9* Skillman, N.J.: Johnson and Johnson Baby Products Company, 1983

Buda, FB. *The neurology of developmental disabilities.* Springfield, Ill., Charles C Thomas, 1981

Butler, A. There's something wrong with Michael: A pediatrician—mother's perspective. *Pediatrics,* 1983, *71,* 446–448

Campbell, M, Cohen, IL, & Small, AM. Drugs in aggressive behavior. *Journal of the American Academy of Child Psychiatry,* 1982, *21,* 107–117

Capute, AJ, Accardo, PJ, Vining, EPG, Rubenstein, JE, & Harryman, S. *Primitive reflex profile.* Baltimore: University Park Press, 1978

Capute, AJ, & Palmer, FB. A pediatric overview of the spectrum of developmental disabilities. *Developmental and Behavioral Pediatrics,* 1980, *1,* 66–68

Cohen, MM. *The child with multiple birth defects.* New York: Raven Press, 1982, pp. 18–21, 139–141

Denhoff, E, & Feldman, SA. Behavior perspectives in children with chronic disabilities: a pediatric viewpoint. *Developmental and Behavioral Pediatrics,* 1981, *3,* 97–104

Dobson, JC, Kushid, E, Williamson, M, & Feldman, EG. Intellectual performance of 36 phenylketonuria patients and their nonaffected siblings. *Pediatrics,* 1976, *58,* 53–68

Duffy, FH, Denckla, MB, Bartels, PH, Sandiri, G, & Kiessling, LS. Dyslexia: Regional differences in brain electrical activity by topographic mapping. *Annals of Neurology,* 1980a, *7,* 412–420

Duffy, FH, Denckla, MB, Bartells, PH, Sandini, G, & Kiessling, LS. Dyslexia: automated diagnosis by computerized classification of brain electrical activity. *Annals of Neurology,* 1980b, *7,* 421–428

Durand, VM. A behavioral/pharmacological intervention for the treatment of severe self-injurious behavior. *Journal of Autism and Developmental Disorders,* 1982, *12,* 243–251

Dworkin, PH, Shonkoff, JP, Leviton, A, & Levine, MD. Training in developmental pediatrics. How practitioners perceive the gap. *American Journal of Diseases of Children,* 1979, *133,* 709–712

Fernoff, PM, Fitzmaurice, N, Milner, J, McEwen, CT, Dembure, PP, Brown, AL, Wright, L, Acosta, PB, Elsas, LJ. Coordinated system for comprehensive newborn metabolic screening. *Southern Medical Journal,* 1982, *75,* 529–532

Frankenberg, WK, Fandal, AN, Sciarillo, W, & Burgess, D. The newly abbreviated and revised Denver Developmental Screening Test. *Journal of Pediatrics,* 1981, *99,* 995–999

Frankenberg, WK, Goldstein, AD, & Camp, BW. The Revised Denver Developmental Screening Test: Its accuracy as a screening instrument. *Journal of Pediatrics,* 1971, *769,* 988–995

Frankenberg, WK, van Doorninck, WJ, Liddel, TN, & Dick, NP. The Denver Prescreening Developmental Questionnaire (PDQ). *Pediatrics,* 1976, *57,* 744–753

Golden, GS. Nonstandard therapies in developmental disabilities. *American Journal of Diseases of Children,* 1980, *34,* 487–491

Golden, GS. Neurobiological correlates of learning disabilities. *Annals of Neurology,* 1982, *12,* 409–418

Gustavson, KH, Hagberg, B, Hagberg, G, & Sars, K. Severe mental retardation in a Swedish country. I. Epidemiology, gestational age, birth weight, and associated CNS handicaps in children born 1959–1970. *Acta Paediatrica Scandinavica,* 1977a, *66,* 373–379

Gustavson, KH, Hagberg, B, Hagberg, G, & Sars, K. Severe mental retardation in a Swedish country. II. Etiologic and pathogenic aspects of children born 1959–1970. *Neuropadiatrie*, 1977b, *8*, 293–304

Hagberg, B. The epidemiological panorama of major neuropaediatric handicaps in Sweden. *Clinics in Developmental Medicine*, 1978, *67*, 111–124

Hagberg, B, Hagberg, G, Lewerth, A, & Lindberg, U. Mild mental retardation in Swedish school children. I. Prevalence. *Acta Paediatrica Scandinavica*, 1981, *70*, 441–444

Hagberg, B, Hagberg, G, & Olow, I. The changing panorama of cerebral palsy in Sweden, 1954–1970. I. Analysis of general changes. *Acta Paediatrica Scandinavica*, 1975a, *64*, 187–192

Hagberg, B, Hagberg, G, & Olow, I. The changing panorama of cerebral palsy in Sweden. II. Analysis of the various syndromes. *Acta Paediatrica Scandinavica*, 1975b, *64*, 193–200

Hagberg, B, Hagberg, G, & Olow, I. The changing panorama of cerebral palsy in Sweden. III. The importance of foetal deprivation of supply. *Acta Paediatrica Scandinavica*, 1975c, *65*, 405–408

Hagberg, B, Hagberg, G, & Olow, I. Gains and hazards of intensive neonatal care: an analysis from swedish cerebral palsy epidemiology. *Developmental Medicine and Child Neurology*, 1982, *24*, 13–18

Hagberg, B, Lindberg, U, & Lewerth, A. Mild mental retardation in swedish school children. II. Etiologic and pathogenetic aspects. *Acta Paediatrica Scandinavica*, 1981, *70*, 445–452

Holmes, GL, McKeever, M, & Russman BS. Prolonged EEG and videotape monitoring in children. *American Journal of Diseases of Children*, 1982, *136*, 608–611

Howie, VM. Developmental sequelae of chronic otitis media: a review. *Development and Behavioral Pediatrics*, 1980, *1*, 34–38

Illingworth, RS. *The development of the infant and young child*, (7th ed). New York: Churchill Livingstone, 1980

Kaveggia, EG, Durkin, MV, Pendleton, E, & Opitz, JM: Diagnostic/genetic studies in 1,224 patients with severe mental retardation. In DA Primrose (Ed.). *Proceedings of the Third Congress of the International Associations for the Scientific Study of Mental Deficiency*. Warsaw, Polish Medical Publishers, 1975

Knights, RM, & Bakker, DJ. *The neuropsychology of learning disorders*. Baltimore: University Park Press, 1976

Knobloch, H, & Pasamanick, B. *Gessell and Amatruda's developmental diagnosis* (3rd Ed). Hagerstown, Md.: Harper and Row, 1974

Knobloch, H, Stevens, F, & Malone, AF. *Manual of developmental diagnosis*. Hagerstown, Md.: Harper and Row, 1980

Knobloch, H, Stevens, F, Malone, A, Ellison, P, & Risemberg, H. The validity of parental reporting of infant development. *Pediatrics*, 1979, *63*, 872–879

Levine, MD. The high prevalence-low severity developmental disorders of school children. *Advances in Pediatrics*, 1982, *29*, 529–554

Levine, MD, Brooks, R, & Shonkoff, JP. *A pediatric approach to learning disorders*. New York: Wiley, 1980

Levine, MD, Meltzer, LJ, Busch, B, Palfrey, J, & Sullivan, M. The pediatric early elementary examination for 7- to 9-year old children. *Pediatrics*, 1983, *71*, 894–903

Lingam, SA, Read, S, Holland, IM, Wilson, J, Brett, EM, & Hoare, RD. Value of computerized tomography in children with nonspecific mental subnormality. *Archives of Disease in Childhood*, 1982, *57*, 381–383

MacFaul, R, Donner, S, Brett, EM, & Grant, DB. Neurological abnormalities in patients treated for hypothyroidism from early life. *Archives of Disease in Childhood*, 1978, *53*, 611–619

MacKeith, R. The feelings and behavior of parents of handicapped children. *Developmental Medicine and Child Neurology*, 1973, *15*, 524–527

Menkes, JH. Paroxysmal disorders. In *Textbook of child neurology*. Philadelphia: Lea and Febiger, 1974, pp 420–462

Menolascino, FJ, Neman, R, & Stark, JA. (Eds.). *Curative aspects of mental retardation. Biomedical and behavioral advances*. Baltimore: Paul H. Brooks, 1983

Meyers, B. The informing interview. *American Journal of Diseases of Children*, 1983, *137*, 572–577

Milani-Comparetti, A, & Gidoni, EA. Routine developmental examination of normal and retarded children. *Developmental Medicine and Child Neurology*, 1967, *9*, 631–638

Milunsky, A. Prenatal diagnosis of genetic disorders. *New England Journal of Medicine*, 1975, *295*, 202–205

Moser, HW, & Wolf, PA. The nosology of mental retardation: Including the report of a survey of 1378 mentally retarded individuals at the Walter E. Fernald State School. *Birth Defects*, 1971, *7*, 117–134

Murphy, MA. The family with a handicapped child: A review of the literature. *Developmental and Behavioral Pediatrics*, 1982, *3*, 73–81

Paine, RS, & Oppe, TE. Neurological examination of children. *Clinics in Developmental Medicine 21/22*. Lavenham, Suffolk, England, Apastics International Medical Publishers, 1966

Palmer, FB, & Capute, AJ. A pediatric overview of the spectrum of developmental disabilities. *Developmental and Behavioral Pediatrics*, 1980, *1*, 66–69

Paradise, JL. Otitis media during early life: how hazardous to development? A critical review. *Pediatrics*, 1981, *68*, 869–873

Parmelee, AH, and Haber, P. Who is the risk infant? *Clinical Obstetrics and Gynecology*, 1973, *16*, 376–387

Pearson, PH. The interdisciplinary team process, or the professional tower of Babel. *Developmental Medicine and Child Neurology*, 1983, *25*, 390–395

Pennington, BF, & Smith, SD. Genetic influences on learning disabilities and speech and language disorders. *Child Development*, 1983, *54*, 369–387

Pfeiffer, SI. Special education placement decisions made by teams and individuals: A cross-cultural perspective. *Psychology in the Schools*, 1982, *19*, 335–340

Princhep, L, John, ER, Ahn, H, & Kaye, H. Neurometrics: quantitative evaluation of brain dysfunction in children. Chap. 11 in Rutter, M. (Ed.), *Developmental neuropsychiatry*. New York: Guidford Press, 1983, pp 213–238

Rapin, I. *Children with brain dysfunction*. New York: Raven Press, 1982

Rapaport, JL, Buschbaum, MS, Weingartner, H, Zahn, TP, Ludlow, C, Bartko, J, Mikkelsen, EJ, Langer, DH, and Bunney, WE. Dextroamphetamine: cogitive and behavioral effects in normal and hyperactive boys and normal adult males. *Archives of General Psychiatry*, 1980, *37*, 933–943

Rapaport, JL, Buschbaum, MS, Zahn, TP, Weingartner, HJ, Ludlow, C, & Mikkelsen, EJ. Dextroamphetamine: cognitive and behavioral effects in normal and prepubertal boys. *Science*, 1978, *199*, 560–563

Rutter, M. Psychological sequelae of brain damage in children. *American Journal of Psychiatry*, 1981, *138*, 1533–1544

Rutter, M. Syndromes attributed to "Minimal brain dysfunction" in childhood. *American Journal of Psychiatry*, 1982, *139*, 1–33

Shaywitz, SE, Cohen, DJ, & Shaywitz, BA. The biochemical basis of minimal brain dysfunction. *Journal of Pediatrics*, 1978, *92*, 179–187

Silver, L. Acceptable and controversial approaches to treating children with learning disabilities. *Pediatrics*, 1975, *55*, 406–415

Smith, DW, & Simons, ER. Rational diagnostic evaluation of the child with mental deficiency. *American Journal of Diseases of Children*, 1975, *129*, 1285–1290

Stark, JA. The search for cures of mental retardation. In FJ Menolasino, R Neman, & JA Stark (Eds.), *Curative aspects of mental retardation. Biomedical and behavioral advances.* Baltimore: Paul H. Brookes, 1983, pp 1–6

Stephenson, SR, & Weaver, D. Prenatal diagnosis—a compilation of diagnosed conditions. *American Journal of Obstetrics and Gynecology*, 1981, *141*, 319–343

Vining, EPG, Accardo, PT, Rubenstein, JE, Farrell, SE, & Rozien, NJ. Cerebral palsy: a pediatric developmentalist overview. *American Journal of Diseases of Children*, 1976, *130*, 643–649

Weiss, G, & Hechtman, L. The hyperactive child syndrome. *Science*, 1979, *28*, 1348–1354

Williamson, WD, Desmond, MM, Wilson, GS, Andrew, L, & Garcia-Prats, JA. Early neurodevelopmental outcome of low-birth-weight infants surviving neonatal interventricular hemorrhage. *Journal of Perinatal Medicine*, 1982, *10*, 34–41

Williamson, WD, Desmond, MM, Wilson, GS, Murphy, MA, Roselle, J, Garcia-Prats, FA. Survival of low-birth-weight infants with neonatal interventricular hemorrhage. *American Journal of Diseases of Children*, 1983, *137*, 1181–1184

Gordon Ulrey

5

The Screening, Assessment, and Intervention of Children With Developmental Disabilities

Public awareness of the potential benefits of early intervention programs with young developmentally disabled children has increased substantially in the past decade. Demands from educators and parents have led to changes in federal legislation (Public Law 94-142, 1975) as well as state laws that require periodic developmental screening and provision of appropriate treatment programs. Knowledge of how biologic and environmental factors contribute to developmental disorders is now making possible the prevention of many developmental disabilities through medical and educational programs. The increased demand for prevention and treatment of handicapped children has led to an increased need for the services of child psychologists to help screen, diagnose, and treat children with developmental disabilities.

Psychologists who work with handicapped children are aware of numerous possible pitfalls in the identification (Ulrey, 1981b) and labeling of young children (Hobbs, 1975). One possible scenario is the lowered expectations by the parent for a child's progress when told their child is developmentally delayed. The reduced expectations of the parents may lead to fewer opportunities for the child to learn or overprotection of the child. The parents may talk less to the child and handle the child physically less often. The news of a developmental delay may also depress the parents and further reduce their interactions with the child or lead to expectations for less mature behaviors. The medical focus on a child as defective, such as a premature infant who is unusually small and "fragile" appearing, may be inadvertently reinforced by frequent visits to the pediatrician. For example, an infant's head size and other growth parameters are monitored closely, which may perpetuate the parent perception of the child as defective. The possibility of a child's learning and development being depressed by attention from professionals has been described by Kearsley (1979) as "iatrogenic mental retardation." The term "iatrogenic" in medicine is used for disorders caused inadvertently while treating a different disorder. Often far too little attention is given to the impact of the news on the parents and family system of a child being handicapped. The caregiver's reaction to news of a defect in their child is often underestimated and not dealt with properly by professionals.

There are two major reasons that many professionals assume early intervention is not needed. One reason is the feeling that there is little that can be done to change the child's level of functioning when a child is developmentally delayed. The second reason is the "wait and see if he will outgrow it" attitude when a mild handicap such as a language delay is identified. In fact, both positions serve only to delay treatment and in some cases seriously interfere with the effectiveness of an intervention program. Studies support the contention that children do not outgrow delays. For example, Camp, Van Doorninck, and Frankenburg (1977) found that 89 percent of a group of young children showing developmental delays on preschool screening were failing in school 5 and 6 years later.

Whether or not a child who is identified as handicapped during the first six years of life will remain handicapped is a complex question. Using mental retardation as an example, one can appreciate the importance of accurate assessment and the need for early intervention. It is useful to conceptualize mentally retarded populations into two general categories with an IQ of less than 50 as a severe handicap and from 50 to 70 as a mild handicap. Severely impaired children have a high incidence of brain abnormalities, but there is no difference among socioeconomic, sociocultural, or racial groups. In contrast, the mildly impaired group, which represents 89 percent of all children classified as mentally retarded, consists of a disproportionate representation of lower socioeconomic and minority groups (Bennett, 1981). The differences in incidence suggest that severely impaired functioning relates primarily to organic factors, while mildly impaired functioning may have significant familial and sociocultural factors contributing to the handicap. Numerous studies have demonstrated that early intervention with both groups leads to higher later/subsequent levels of functioning (Consortium for Longitudinal Studies, 1978; Koch & de la Cruz, 1975; Zigler & Valentine, 1980), and many children in the mildly handicapped groups subsequently not needing special education when in elementary or high school (Lazar & Darlington, 1978). Although there are some risks and expenses involved with early intervention, it is a mistake to adopt a "wait-and-see" attitude with children identified as handicapped during the first six years of life (Feuerstein, 1980).

The appropriate use of screening, diagnosis, and treatment with developmentally disabled children requires specialized skills of the clinical child psychologist. This chapter discusses several issues related to providing psychological services to handicapped children. These include prevention, classification of handicapping conditions, focus on an understanding of interactions between handicapped children and caregivers, review of recent screening and diagnostic procedures, treatment of developmental disabilities and discussion of training needs of clinical child psychologists.

PREVENTION

There are many estimates of how many handicaps could be reduced or eliminated through preventive medicine and educational intervention. The conservative estimate suggests 25 percent of all developmental disabilities could be eliminated while others are as high as 50 percent (Begab, 1982). There are two levels of prevention of developmental handicaps. The primary level of prevention attempts to eliminate a potential handicap or reduce the risk through genetic counseling, improving pre- and postnatal care, immunizations for childhood illnesses such as measles, reducing poverty, malnutrition, and adverse socioemotional factors. The secondary level of prevention attempts to identify a child who is "at risk" for developmental handicaps and then develop programs to eliminate or ameliorate the problem. It is generally assumed that developmental disabilities result from biologic and environmental factors. Therefore, earlier identification and treatment leads to more clinically effective, and cost-beneficial interventions. Most of the first level of prevention is managed by public health administrators and physicians. Clinical child psychologists impact on the primary prevention level by working mostly through agencies and service delivery systems. They also provide preventive treatments with high-risk families using counseling and therapy strategies. For example, Field, Goldberg, Stern and Sostek (1980) have recently reviewed several programs that focus on primary prevention of child abuse in high risk families with anticipatory guidance and treatment of parent-child interactions by psychologists. This chapter emphasizes the secondary level of prevention in which psychologists often play an important role.

The assumption that it is best to identify a handicapped child as early as possible has been questioned by several authors (McCall, 1981; Ramey, MacPhee, & Yeates, 1981). McCall argues that the optimal time for cognitive intervention is during the toddlerhood to preschool period (2 years to 6 years) rather than infancy. He views infant cognitive development as discontinuous with later preschool and school age cognition and as less susceptible to cultural and socioeconomic factors during the first two years of life. Generally, relatively lower performance on cognitive tests is not seen in culturally different or lower socioeconomic groups until preschool age. The impact of poverty and socioeconomic factors is not detected by most screening or diagnostic psychological tests before 24 months. McCall argues that it appears to be more appropriate to provide environmental intervention during the preschool period when important mental skills are developing such as symbolisms, verbal fluency, and concept formation, and logical reasoning is first emerging. His argument is supported by the fact that few, if any, variables identified during infancy have been shown to relate to later handicaps (Sameroff & Chandler, 1975), unless the handicap is severe. It is well known that infant tests are not predictive of later cognitive functioning for nonhandicapped children (Bayley, 1969), although there is predictive validity when the child scores two or more standard deviations below the mean (Honzik, 1976). The other potential concern about early identification of handicapped children is the problem of labeling the handicapped discussed earlier.

While it may not always be wise to simply begin intervention at the earliest possible time, there is still substantial need for early screening to detect handicaps. McCall's (1981) arguments are most applicable to children who will develop mild cognitive handicaps, and to sociocultural, and familial causes that are not detectable during infancy. In cases of identifiable visual, auditory, motoric, or cognitive impairment, however, the earlier the detection the better the chances are for implementing a program to prevent or decrease the long-term negative impact. For example, children with sensory handicaps such as blindness or deafness are at a much higher risk for developing emotional and behavioral disturbances (Fraiberg, 1977). Clearly, the disabilities that are evident during the first two years of life need the earliest possible intervention.

With our current knowledge of biologic and environmental factors that contribute to handicapping conditions there is a wide range of things the clinical child psychologist can do to help decrease the incidence of developmental disabilities or minimize the impact of a handicap on a child and family. The primary role of the clinical child psychologist is to be an advocate for the welfare of children. The advocacy role of the psychologist in prevention efforts involves issues of clinical, community, and educational psychology. For example, the support for secondary intervention such as large scale developmental screening and early intervention (e.g., Project Head Start) has made progress but has also met with resistance because of theoretical, political, and economic factors. Much more research of assessment and treatment outcomes is needed to provide data indicating the relative effectiveness and ways of improving intervention programs. The economic recession of the early 1980's has increased pressure for accountability in prevention procedures. The challenge is for psychologists to provide evidence that intervention programs are cost effective and to communicate these findings to legislators and the public.

CLASSIFICATION OF HANDICAPPING CONDITIONS

What is a developmental disability? Under the Education for All Handicapped Children Act of 1975 (P.L. 94-142), developmental disabilities include emotional disturbance, mental retardation, learning disabilities, physical disabilities, and hearing and visual impairments. The terms "developmentally handicapped" and "developmental disabilities" are used synonymously. The law emphasizes noncategorical programming for the handicapped since children frequently have more than one of the above handicaps. Noncategorical prgramming also encourages development of remedial education programs that are tailored to the individual child rather than a type of disorder and facilitates mainstreaming the handicapped child into regular programs. Historically, there have been many euphemisms for mental retardation and, therefore, professionals and the lay public often assume developmental disabilities or handicapping conditions are simply other terms for mental retardation. However, the current emphasis on grouping all handicaps together is important conceptually both in terms of diagnosis and treatment. A frequent problem for clinical psychologists has been difficulties in finding appropriate services for a child who "falls between the cracks" in terms of services because of multiple handicaps. A difficult example is locating services for a child who presents the particular constellation of behaviors characteristic of both emotional disturbance and mental retardation.

Perhaps the most complex and controversial handicap to classify is the "specific learning disability." An historical lack of agreement among professions on the criteria for various learning disabilities (LD) has hindered the assessment, treatment and research (Quay, 1979). The most common definition of LD is the presence of a "perceptual processing deficit" (Chruickshank, 1977), which prevents or interferes with educational achievement in spite of at least low-average intelligence. Children with a learning problem associated primarily with mental retardation or hearing impairment would not be labeled as having a specific learning disability (P.L. 94-142, 1975). However, many children who are labeled as mentally retarded or emotionally disturbed will also show behaviors that suggest a perceptual processing disorder. Emphasis on noncategorical treatment programs is important to insure that children with multiple handicaps are not excluded from appropriate individualized treatment.

The etiology of LD can range from underlying neurological factors, maturational differences and motivational problems in the child (Quay, 1979). The heterogeneity of children with LD makes it difficult to generalize about the disorder and makes highly individualized treatment strategies essential. The clinical child psychologist must be aware of the wide range of individual differences as well as the implications for psychological development of the child. How may the presence of a learning disability alter a child's emotional development and interaction with others? An assessment of learning disabilities should always include an assessment of the emotional development of the child. The implications for how the presence of a handicap may alter a child's development is discussed in the following section.

INTERACTIONS BETWEEN HANDICAPPED CHILD AND CAREGIVERS

Children with a wide range of developmental disabilities are found to have a higher incidence of emotional and behavioral disorders than nonhandicapped peers. Several recent studies have indicated an increased incidence of emotional problems among children with such handicaps as minimal brain dysfunction (Graham, Chir, & Rutter, 1968), mild mental retardation (Chess & Hassibi, 1970), hearing impairment (Schlesinger & Meadow, 1972), or visual impairment (Fraiberg, Smith, & Adelson, 1969). Reviews of several longitudinal studies of handicapped children by Thomas and Chess (1977) concluded that the presence of a developmental disability increases the stress of accomplishing normal developmental tasks. A sensory or physical disorder may actually impede or interfere with the child's emotional development, but is not necessarily the cause. The child with a hearing impairment, for example, will receive limited auditory feedback from caregivers during infancy when the attachment process and development of a basic sense of trust are being established. Since the child's responsiveness to auditory input is reduced there may be less response in general to the parents. In simple terms the child may be less "fun" or "playful" with the parents for unexplained reasons. The parents' responses will vary according to their own expectations and attitudes about child rearing as well as their own emotional needs. Obviously, even a mild hearing loss present from birth can potentially influence a child's emotional development, although it usually does not. Bell (1974) has reviewed the complex ways infants actively shape and change their world by reciprocal influences on caregivers. The cognitive abilities such as visual recognition of the human face and auditory discrimination of preference for the human voice (Kagan, Kearsley, & Zelazo, 1978) provide substantial cues to caregivers that shape early parent-child relationships and attachment behaviors. Emde and Harmon (1982) emphasize the development of attachment and "affilitative systems" because of the complex interrelationship of a wide range of behaviors interacting reciprocally to influence early socialization and emotional development.

The impact of an undetected and untreated hearing loss may lead to delayed language during the preschool period. A language delay will impact on the child's general communication system (verbal and nonverbal) in ways that may lead to withdrawal or acting-out behaviors. A common clinical example is the "hyperactive" preschooler who behaves and attends significantly less well when asked to perform language tasks and is attentive and appropriate when doing a task with minimal language demand, such as the draw-a-person test. Hearing loss is particularly insidious because congenital hearing loss and intermittent hearing loss are thought by some investigators (Downs & Blager, 1982) to be among the most frequently overlooked handicaps in young children.

It appears that a handicap in a single modality can impede development in several other developmental areas. One can imagine a kind of "sensory synergism" that occurs across different systems. A visual handicap will slow down socioemotional and cognitive development because of reduced input of certain types of information that other modalities need. A child with the "capacity" for normal emotional functioning may develop an emotional or behavioral disorder secondary to a developmental handicap and/or environmental stresses (Ulrey, 1981a). It is difficult to determine what percentage of emotional difficulties derive from an interaction between a handicap and environmental factors. However, much can be learned about behavioral disorders from an understanding of how they develop in the handicapped. An excellent example is from Selma Fraiberg's work, entitled *Insights from the Blind*

(1977), which describes the socioemotional development of blind children from birth and compares it to that of normal children.

When a child has a developmental disability such as blindness, the family system is affected. The expectations and behavior of the parents and siblings will be influenced by having a child with special needs. Recent research that has focused on the impact of the child on caregivers (Field et al. 1980; Lewis & Rosenblum, 1974) and the influences of a child's temperament on development (Thomas & Chess, 1977) help professionals appreciate how a child's handicap may influence emotional development (Ulrey & Rogers, 1982). The evaluation and treatment of all types of developmental disorders must take into account the support system available to the child and how each system impacts upon, as well as has been influenced by the child.

The emphasis on systems is useful because it provides a framework for understanding the child's interactions with the environment and reciprocal influences. It is assumed that development results from a complex interaction between the child and caregivers. The role of the child in eliciting responses from the caregiver and the attitudes and expectations of the parents interact and change as the child matures. The one important implication from this model is that a given handicap, such as hyperactivity, will have a very different implication depending on the environmental context. A parent who expects certain behavior and sets consistent limits will have a very different impact on the child's behavior than a situation in which the family is chaotic and inconsistent in setting limits. In either case the child's behavior will influence the expectations and attitudes of the parents, which will change over time. Thomas and Chess (1977) and Thomas (1982) have described the relative compatibility of parental style and a child's behavior as "goodness of fit." The results of several longitudinal studies suggest that knowing a young child's temperament is not useful unless it is observed in the context of the temperament of caregivers. A similar rationale can be used to make the important point that a young child's handicap and the implications are most meaningful when there is knowledge of the familial and sociocultural support for that child. The clinical child psychologist working with a family of a handicapped child must assess the temperamental style and expectations of parents as well as the behavior of the child. The psychologist must be sensitive to different ways individuals in a family respond to having a handicapped child. The assessment and treatment of the child should include observations of parent-child interactions and feedback to parents that will facilitate a positive and nurturing parent-child relationship. How the child makes the parent feel when he or she behaves in certain ways can be used for treatment and/or anticipatory guidance of parents of a handicapped child.

The screening, diagnosis, and treatment of children with developmental disabilities must take into consideration each child's unique family system and supports. We know, for example, from follow-up studies of Head Start programs (Lazar & Darlington, 1978) that treatment must include the parents in some capacity to achieve the most lasting results. A more dramatic finding is that abused and neglected children from low socioeconomic backgrounds show more than a 50 percent incidence of developmental disabilities (Martin, 1972). The basis for much of the developmental handicaps is assumed to relate to the pattern of parenting the child has experienced. Treatment of the parents in these cases is essential to resolve the child's handicaps. For an excellent review of the impact of abuse and neglect on child development, one should see Martin (1976).

DEVELOPMENTAL SCREENING

How can one detect which children need treatment for a developmental disability? Children with severe developmental handicaps are generally identified by concerned parents, family, or professionals by 2 years of age. However, children with mild and moderate handicaps are often not identified until they begin public education. Developmental screening can be used to identify children who are "at risk" for developmental disorders by means of a quick and easily administered test procedure. Screening tests make it possible to examine large numbers of children in the presumably normal population who may need a more in-depth evaluation. The screening procedure should never be used to substitute for a comprehensive diagnostic assessment, since screening, by definition, only samples to a limited extent the factors that one must more extensively evaluate when diagnosing a developmental disability. It cannot be emphasized enough that there are many different reasons for developmental delays that include environmental, biologic, and usually complex interactions of a number of contributory factors. Screening procedures cannot possibly yield enough information to justify placement in a treatment program. The screening procedure must be standardized to provide objective criteria for identification of a child who is "at risk" for a developmental disorder. Once a child has been detected by developmental screening there must be a system for providing a more comprehensive evaluation of the child and family to determine the most appropriate intervention strategies as well as identification of likely etiological factors.

Screening tests vary according to the scope, depth of behavior(s), and disorder(s) that are measured. A screening program must consider both the time and cost along with the range of possible developmental disorders that can be screened. Screening tests that measure many behaviors may take too long and be too costly. The important consideration is to determine what is to be screened for and what type of test will be most appropriate. Available tests can be scrutinized according to the number of false positives and false negatives the test is known to produce with a certain population. False positives are children who fail a screening test but are found not to have the disorder in question. False negatives are children who pass a screening test but are found later in fact to have the specific disorder. Any commercially available screening test should make available in the manual the percentages of false positives and negatives, along with other pertinent psychometric information such as standardization of population, reliability, and validity.

Many professionals feel that they would notice if a young child has a developmental delay without the benefit of formal test data. In the case of mentally retarded preschool children, Bierman, Connor, Vaage, and Honzik (1964) observed that of 681 children, pediatricians correctly identified only 3 of 11 retarded children. A study by Korsch, Cobb, and Ashe (1961) found that physicians consistently overestimated the IQs of their retarded patients, which suggests that without screening tests physicians do not reliably identify mentally retarded children. The use of standardized screening tests generally decreases the number of false positives resulting from well child visits but many physicians still do not use screening tests (Frankenburg, Thornton, & Chors, 1981). A psychologist should not assume that a child has had developmental screening because there has been regular pediatric care.

After a screening program has defined what potential problem(s) will be screened and the most appropriate instrument(s) has been selected, there are still some pitfalls to avoid. The labeling of a young child as "at risk" for a developmental disability may be stressful to the family and increases the possibility of iatrogenic disabilities that were discussed earlier. The issue is particularly important when results of screening tests have indicated that the child is a false positive. A good screening program must have a sensitive follow-up procedure to insure that services are provided to children as well as families. A "sensitive" follow-up procedure means an awareness of the potential impact on the care-givers when a disorder is suspected. The system should include working with families to facilitate their coping with the stresses involved with the child's behavior as well as the parent's response to this news of handicap, which may range from anger, denial, overprotection, etc. (Schnell, 1982).

Most psychologists and educators agree that early screening and referral for evaluation and treatment are important for severely handicapped children. As a general rule, the more severe a child's handicap, the more predictive tests are of later learning and behavior problems. For example, even infant tests have predictive validity of .70 to .90 when the child scores two or more standard deviations below the mean (Honzik, 1976). A diagnostic assessment is needed to insure that a physical handicap (e.g., motoric) or sensory (e.g., visual) is not mistaken for a cognitive deficit (Kearsley, 1979; Ulrey & Rogers, 1982). In the case of infants who are between 1 and 2 standard deviations below the mean (borderline delay), the current infant tests are inadequate to justify a recommendation for treatment during infancy. However, infant screening programs should not be expected to detect children who will show mild developmental delays secondary to socioeconomic and culturally different experiences before 2 years of age. There is clearly a need for an infant screening test that detects cognitive competencies during the first two years of life that is more predictive of later cognitive functioning. Recent developments of piagetian scales such as the Infant Psychological Development Scale (Uzgiris & Hunt, 1975) may provide alternative screening models. Our screening tests for the first year of life may be too simplistic to detect important differences in cognition. An innovative approach for infant assessment is currently being developed by Zelazo (1981) and his colleagues in Boston, that measures infant reactivity to perceptual-cognitive events that is not dependent on motor behaviors of the infant. Perhaps less reliance on engaging the cooperation and gross and fine motor skills of infants will make possible a valid screening of very young children who are not severely handicapped.

Based on our understanding of early development, it is important to screen for significant developmental delays from birth and to screen for developmental delays a second time at about the 24- to 36-month age level. There is general agreement that waiting until a child fails in school is not acceptable! There is ample evidence that identification and treatment of children during the preschool period is cost-effective and reduces subsequent special education and special service costs during the school age period (Consortium for Longitudinal Studies, 1978). To ensure equal opportunity for children of all socioeconomic levels and to reduce the cost of special education, all young children should be screened by at least 24 months of age.

There are many existing screening tests from which to choose when planning a screening program. Some child development centers simply compile items from existing diagnostic tests that seem to provide the needed information. A comprehensive review of principles of screening and properties of existing tests has been done by Frankenburg and Camp (1974). They stress the importance of knowing the psychometric prop-

erties of the instruments. Screening tests should be scrutinized for reliability and validity to estimate the probability of false positives or negatives. Few of the existing screening tests have been developed with large
representative samples, and lack adequate reliability, validity, and/or
normative data.

Denver Developmental Screening Test

Among the well standardized and validated screening tests, the Denver Developmental Screening Test (DDST) is the most commonly used
test. The DDST was standardized on a cross-sectional sample of 1,036
Denver area children representing minorities and socioeconomically varied groups. The popularity of the scale has resulted from the high levels
of reliability and validity. Reliability is reported to be .90 and above (test-
retest .97; interobserver .90) and both predictive and concurrent validity
are .85 or higher (Kemper & Frankenburg, 1979). The DDST in effect
will identify at least 85 percent of all infants and preschool-age children
who are developmentally delayed. A longitudinal study of the predictive
validity of the DDST indicated 89 percent of all children with abnormal
DDST results were showing school failure problems 5 years later (Frankenburg, et al. 1981). The DDST has been adopted for use in 26 countries and restandardized (translated forms) in 10 countries including
China.

The DDST yields results in four categories including: pass, fail,
questionable, and untestable. The DDST measures behaviors in four
areas of development, which include: personal social, fine motor adaptive, language, and gross motor. A "pass" indicates the child demon-
strates skills within normal range for his or her age level. A "fail" means
the child failed to demonstrate behaviors in at least two items in any one
of the four developmental areas. A "questionable" means the child failed
to demonstrate only one item in any of the four categories and the child
should be reevaluated on the DDST within one month. The "untestable"
category means the test was not completely reliable because of poor
cooperation with the examiner and a reevaluation should be conducted
within one month. A result of failure or questionable results should
always be followed up by a more comprehensive evaluation. The untestable child should be assessed another time or day to determine if a
more in-depth evaluation is needed. A major concern is the misuse of
the test for diagnostic purposes.

There are several other screening tests that have been standardized
and reviewed by Kemper and Frankenburg (1979). These include the

following: The Rapid Developmental Screening Checklist (Giannini, 1972), Guide to Normal Milestones of Development (Haynes, 1967), and CCD Developmental Progress Scale (Boyd, 1974).

The behavioral assessment of newborns is unique and offers innovative procedures for screening young children. The most widely used scale is the Neonatal Behavioral Assessment Scale (NBAS) developed by Brazelton (1973). A comprehensive review of the uses of the NBAS was recently discussed by Als, Tronick, Lester, and Brazelton (1979). The scale is used as a broad-based newborn behavioral and neurological test. Emphasis on ways in which the child interacts with people and a variety of stimuli make it useful for evaluating a neonate's responsiveness to the environmental and temperamental style.* The scale is also unique because it assesses different behaviors depending on the "state" or level of arousal of the child. The major screening use is for teaching parents about the responses of their child and special handling procedures (Erickson, 1976). Although predictive validity has not been established, the emphasis on the child's response to the environment and unique interactions with parents makes it a valuable procedure for professionals working with very young children.

Several of the major cognitive tests have been revised and shortened to serve as screening tests including the McCarthy Scale of Children's Ability (Kaufman & Kaufman, 1977), Stanford-Binet (Hallahan, Ball, & Payne, 1973; Terman & Merrill, 1973), Wechsler Intelligence Scale for Children—Revised (WISC-R) (Kaufman, 1976), and Wechsler Preschool and Primary Scale of Intelligence (WPPSI) (Kaufman, 1972). There are advantages and pitfalls when using short forms of existing tests. There is substantial evidence to indicate that none of the short forms are as valid as the entire test and should never be used to make decisions about classifications of a child without other valid supportive data (Sattler, 1982). The major advantage of the short form screening tests derived from the major intelligence tests is the size of the standardization sample. However, children have been misclassified when even short forms with a high level of validity have been used. For example, Goh[†] found that when a short form of the WISC-R was used 45 percent of a group of 142 children were misplaced. The relative strengths and weakness of

---

*Bakow, H, Sameroff, A, Kelly, P, & Fax, M. Relation between newborn and mother-child interactions at four months. Presented at Meeting of the Society for Research in Child Development, Philadelphia, 1973

†Goh, D.S. New method in design of intelligence test short formsthe WISC-R example. Paper presented at American Psychological Association, Toronto, Canada, 1978.

Binet, WPPSI and WISC-R short forms have been discussed in more depth by Kaufman (1979) and Sattler (1982).

DIAGNOSTIC TESTS

Diagnostic test procedures are useful to determine the relative strengths and weaknesses of a child as well as to differentiate specific handicapping conditions. The diagnostic process should also facilitate the generation of a number of remedial strategies for the developmentally disabled. The assessment techniques used by psychologists vary in their utility for answering diagnostic questions. The most common issue is a referral for a psychological test for which information is received about what is wrong but minimal suggestions are given about what to do about the disorder.

The primary reason that diagnostic testing does not lead to interventions as beneficial as possible is because the referral question lacks specificity and then is not clarified and made operational by the psychologist. For example, just having a child referred for a psychological evaluation is obviously not specific enough. Many school systems and clinicians, however, evaluate children with little more definition of the problem than "what is the level of cognitive functioning?" or "please do a psychological work-up," "I wonder what the psychologist will think about this child." A familiar scenario is for a child to be referred because of concerns about learning problems in school and to have the diagnostic testing confirm that the child has a learning problem. Infant stimulation programs refer developmentally delayed children to a psychologist and often receive confirmation that the child is developmentally delayed, but without the remedial educational program they had wanted. A more subtle referral question is to see if the clinician sees the child as having underlying emotional problems, when the referral simply asks for a cognitive assessment. The psychologist must always spend some time with the referring source (including teachers and parents) to determine what diagnostic procedures will be most helpful in answering the questions of interest. Diagnosis of a developmental disability must always take into account information from the family, school, and the family physician; the ecology of the child (Pfeiffer & Tittler, 1983).

The selection of appropriate assessment procedures is the next important step after the background information and specifics of a referral question are known. The three major types of assessment procedures include: norm-referenced tests, criterion-referenced tests, and informal and formal observations of the child and family. There are some important differences in how these procedures should be used.

Norm-referenced Tests

Norm-referenced tests are those that yield scores that allow a comparison of an individual child's performance to a compatible group. The comparison allows the clinician to determine the degree of similarity or difference in the obtained/observed performance. However, the scores have meaning only to the extent that the child is similar to the comparison group. If a child has not had similar opportunities for learning because of environmental, sociocultural, and/or biologic reasons, the use of the test norms may be misleading or inappropriate. A common example is when the child lives in a home where English is not the primary language, and yet the test has been standardized on a group of children who are from English-speaking homes. The use of the norms in the above example would only be useful to determine how the child's skills compare to other primarily English-speaking children, but would not provide information about the child's general ability or intelligence.

The most common norm-referenced tests that are used with developmentally handicapped children are the several cognitive tests such as the Bayley, Stanford-Binet, and the Wechsler Scales. The Binet and Wechsler tests continue to be the best available tests for determining a child's level of general ability and predicting how a child will do in academic achievement (Anastasi, 1982; Sattler, 1982). Very few children with handicaps have been included in the norms for the best known intelligence tests. These intelligence tests are useful for determining the relative strengths and weaknesses or degree of handicap for an individual child by comparing a handicapped youngster's profile to a nonhandicapped child's performance. The Wechsler Intelligence Scale for Children—Revised Performance Scale has recently been adapted for hearing impaired children (Sisco & Anderson, 1978). The norm-referenced tests must be used with caution with handicapped children when interpreting a handicapped child's performance to test norms based on a nonhandicapped sample. Will a certain norm-referenced test be useful in helping answer the referral question? If the handicapped child is placed with nonhandicapped children, the norms will help predict how well (successfully) the child will be able to compete. If the handicapped child is placed with other handicapped children, the use of norms for nonhandicapped will not be useful.

The Stanford-Binet Scale has been used with handicapped children by adapting the administration procedures. When procedures for test administration are altered, they must be interpreted cautiously because variations in the standardized item administration often alter the level of difficulty. The results of a modified administration of the Binet should be viewed as only an estimate of performance level and additional tests should be given, when possible, to compare outcomes. Sattler (1982) has reviewed most of the published adaptations of Binet items. One example is the enlargement of visual stimuli that does not appear to alter test score outcome (Sattler, 1982). The Binet scale continues to be used frequently as a criterion measure for determining concurrent validity of other scales because of its high level of prediction. The Binet is the test of choice for young handicapped children between 2 and 6 years (Ulrey & Rogers, 1982) for determining a level of general intelligence. The Binet tests a wide range of cognitive skills (verbal and nonverbal) in the younger child (Hallahan et al., 1973). In contrast, the upper age levels measure largely verbal skills (Stormer, 1966), making the WISC-R a better test for school-age handicapped children.

The WISC-R provides a profile of a wide range of cognitive processes that allow the clinician to make judgements about the child's cognitive style as well as strengths and weaknesses. Kaufman (1976) has outlined the one behavioral and two cognitive factors measured by the WISC-R, which include verbal comprehension, freedom from distractibility, and perceptual organization. Although the WISC-R is high in predictive validity for school achievement, it must always be used with other measures to diagnose developmental disabilities such as mental retardation or specific learning disabilities.

Measures of self-help and adaptive behaviors such as the Vineland Scale of Social Maturity (Doll, 1965), or the Developmental Profile (Alpern & Boll, 1972) are often used, along with intelligence scales to compare the level of intelligence with adaptive behavior. Although the adaptive scales are important supplementary tests, they must be interpreted cautiously because of the limited sample in the test norms and reliance on parental report. Parental report measures generally are lower in reliability and depend on the parent's subjective impression of the child's behavior. The use of adaptive measures is reviewed in depth by Meyers, Nihra, and Zetlin (1979).

A recently published norm-referenced test for children is the Kaufman Assessment Battery for Children (KABC), which was developed by Kaufman and Kaufman (1983). The scale appears to have been well developed with a representative sample of children from minority groups and regions of the country. It is designed to measure both intelligence and achievement of $2\frac{1}{2}$- to $12\frac{1}{2}$-year old children. The test has several innovations that allow for assessment of special abilities that could make the scale very popular and useful. Preliminary studies of validity are encouraging and suggest that the KABC may be a useful new assessment procedure for clinical child psychologists.

While norm-referenced tests are useful for measuring degrees of handicaps or delays, they do not suggest what to do about the handicap. Questions about what should be done tomorrow are better answered by using the criterion-referenced measures.

Criterion-referenced Tests

Criterion-referenced tests are based on profiles of a child's developmental functioning. The criterion tests measure a child's current skills (independent of age levels) and provide guidelines for what skills will be emerging in the future. For example, a norm-referenced test would indicate the expected age level for number concepts, whereas a criterion-referenced test would indicate the hierarchy of skills and subskills required for understanding numbers without reference to age level. The most popular application of criterion-referenced tests has been for educational programming. A few of the more widely used scales include the Learning Accomplishment Profile (LAP), Portage Project Checklist, and the Developmental Profile (Alpern & Boll, 1972), and Marshalltown (see Black, 1979, for a review of criterion-referenced tests).

When a diagnostic referral is made extensive for program planning it is more appropriate to use a criterion-referenced test. However, when further clarification of the referral question also indicates that it is unclear as to what type or degree of handicap a child may have, it is advisable to administer both types of test.

The application of norm-referenced and criterion-referenced tests with children have been discussed elsewhere by Begnato and Neisworth (1982) and Ulrey and Rogers (1982). The criterion-referenced measures have been invaluable for helping educators and clinicians link assessment with educational interventions.

In general, the diagnosis and treatment planning for handicapped children must always take into account four major areas. The disorder must be evaluated in terms of the following: developmental levels, behavior of child, psychometrics of assessment procedures, and ecology of the child. Overreliance on test scores, evaluation of the handicap without consideration of the family context, or the use of instruments of poor reliability or validity are just a few of the major pitfalls one must avoid in diagnosing a handicapping condition. Evaluators must be trained and sensitized to take into account the multitude of variables that contribute to a child's development and learning. Although critics have frequently focused on the limitations of our present test instruments, it is more accurate to say that the actual problems with assessing handicapped children occur because of how the tests are used, rather than with any inherent weaknesses in the tests themselves.

TREATMENT OF DEVELOPMENTAL DISABILITIES

Consider the case of 7-year-old David, who was referred for a psychological evaluation because of poor school attendance, temper tantrums in school, and poor peer relations. The mother was concerned because she wanted to intervene early before David's behavior became worse. There is some evidence for genetically based learning disabilities in familial dyslexia (specific reading disability). A recent study by Smith, Pennington, Kimberling, and Lubs[‡] indicates a type of familial dyslexia caused by a gene or group of genes on chromosome 15. A family history of reading problems is important to note also because the feelings the parent had about school learning will be important in the intervention process. His mother was also concerned because she separated from David's father 2 years earlier. The time of separation and divorce that occurs during the preschool period has been reported to be perhaps the most difficult time for the child with the highest risks for behavior adjustment problems (Heatherington, 1979). Changes occur in the parent-child relationship and also impact on school functioning and generally, changes occur within the family system (Wallerstein & Kelly, 1975). The teacher felt that David was bright and capable but didn't seem motivated to learn how to read. Did David have an emotional problem or another type of developmental disorder?

Interviews with the parent and the teacher as well as a psychological assessment revealed several important factors. The mother reported that she had always had difficulty with reading (was she also "turned off" to reading?) and that she feared that David would develop a dislike for reading. She also reported that David spent weekends with his father and that they appeared to be getting along very well. Her major concern was that he would become a behavior problem and dislike attending school. The teacher reported that David's behavior was only a problem when he was asked to read or when demands were made for speaking

---

‡Smith, SD, Pennington, BF, Kimberling, WJ, & Lubs, HA. An investigation of familial dyslexia using both genetic and cognitive analyses. Presented at Society for Research in Child Development, Boston, 1981

in front of the class. At other times he was cooperative and attended well, particularly to tasks that required minimal verbal output.

The psychological testing and observation of his behavior indicated that he had some specific language deficits (e.g., word finding problem and auditory sequential processing disorder), whereas his general intellectual competence and nonverbal skills were well above his age level. When David had difficulties using appropriate words to express needs or became confused if more than a two-step direction was given him, his behavior became more active and disruptive. A careful assessment of David's behavior problem revealed a pattern of communication disorder, which led to disruptions of his academic achievement as well as in peer relations. Treatment of David's language disability during second grade led to a dramatic decrease in his school behavior problems and increased his involvement with peers and his enjoyment of reading.

A focus on the emotional or behavioral problems without an appreciation for how a developmental disability may engender behavior problems can be short-sighted. This case illustrates the need for the clinical child psychologist to have expertise in the recognition and assessment of developmental disorders, and an appreciation for working with other professionals such as speech and language therapists, developmental pediatricians, child neurologists, and special educators. Psychologists who focus primarily on behavior problems, family stress, and emotional disorders may underestimate or fail to appreciate how a specific developmental disability may influence emotional development.

David's case brings up multiple issues including the impact of divorce, possible familial reading disorder, minimal brain dysfunction, and disrupted emotional development. There is clearly need for a multidisciplinary evaluation that considers the impact of a wide range of possible developmental factors, as well as environmental stresses. For this case it was important to understand both David's emotional problem and his learning handicaps to formulate an effective treatment. A focus on one or the other would have been insufficient.

Treatment of developmentally disabled children must include a consideration of the child's interactions with others in the school and the home. Treatment of the handicapped child outside the context of the family and cultural systems is likely to achieve only short-term benefits. The most conclusive data for the effectiveness of treatment that includes parents come from experience with the Head Start programs (Consortium for Longitudinal Studies, 1978).

A comprehensive review of early intervention programs (Lazar & Darlington, 1978) concluded that involvement of the parents greatly increases the long-term effects of programs. Programs that included parents and those that did not include them were compared. While short-term gains are reported when parents are not involved, the longitudinal follow-up data show clearly that parental involvement helps diminish losses when programming has stopped. Lazar's conclusion after an in-depth study is that early intervention with handicapped children does work!

TRAINING CLINICAL CHILD PSYCHOLOGISTS

The role of the psychologist working with handicapped children has been addressed by the APA Council (Schaar, 1979). The psychologist should ensure that appropriate assessments of handicapped children are completed and that the children's treatment programs meet their needs. The problem is that psychologists often have not received training in working with developmentally handicapped children and/or children under the age of 6 years (Bardon & Wenger, 1976; Mowder & Demartino, 1979; Ulrey, 1981b). Most clinical psychology training programs do not include courses in developmental disabilities in the core requirements. When clinical child psychologists have a special interest in developmental handicaps, they often must take courses from other programs or continuing education workshops. One additional avenue is to obtain an internship or postdoctoral fellowship in a medical center where there is a university-affiliated child development center, or department of pediatrics.

Requirements for course work and practicum need to expand the clinician's understanding of child development and behavior across a wider spectrum of childhood disorders. Direct supervision of experience with handicapped children would add depth to the clinical training by increasing awareness of the diversity of etiologies and intervention strategies within the fields of special education and pediatric psychology. In the field of pediatrics there has been an attempt to increase requirements for training in child development because of a previous need to have pediatricians address some concerns about child behavior and developmental problems (Frankenburg et al., 1981). Historically, pediatric training has been focused primarily on acute medical diseases and severe disorders that require hospitalization. In an analogous way clinical child psychology may be overly focused on treatment of children within a narrow range of psychiatric disorders and individual psychotherapy.

The child psychologist with expertise in assessment and treatment of children with a wide range of developmental disabilities is better able to understand the impact of the child on caregivers and how a handicap may influence other areas of development. An appreciation of developmental issues and the reciprocity of environmental transactions is essential for relevant assessment and effective treatment procedures.

The current popularity of internships housed in medical settings, and the recent attraction of health psychology, medical psychology, behavioral medicine, and pediatric psychology all suggest a growing interest in the impact of chronic disorders on development and behavior. Psychologists with extensive training in child development and developmental disabilities are better able to develop valuable skills for working with physicians and related disciplines in medical settings. The graduate level training programs need to respond to the growing and changing demands of clinical child psychologists as well as trends in child development research. The training programs should expand their involvement in professional education to ensure the relevance of psychologists' skills. Continuing education requirements for licensing, for example, will encourage and support in-service training programs for practicing psychologists.

SUMMARY

The role of the psychologist in the early detection and treatment of developmental disabilities has been discussed. Interaction of environmental factors that influence handicapped young children must be taken into account to insure valid assessment and relevant treatment programming (Thomas, 1982). Many developmental disabilities can be prevented; and early intervention is more effective and less expensive in terms of money and human suffering when implemented during early childhood. Psychologists working with developmentally disabled children must have special training to ensure that appropriate procedures are implemented and that the child receives the best possible services. A variety of screening, diagnostic, and treatment issues related to serving handicapped children exist and must be addressed by the clinical child psychologist.

The position of this author is that clinical child psychology training should place more emphasis on child development and developmental disabilities. The clinician who has expertise in child development is better able to identify and treat a wide range of behavioral and emotional disorders of childhood.

REFERENCES

Alpern, GD, & Boll, TJ. *Developmental profile manual.* Aspen, Col.: Psychological Development Publishing, 1972

Als, H, Tronick, E, Lester, B, & Brazelton, TB. Specific neonatal measures: Brazelton Neonatal Behavior Assessment Scale. In J Osofsky, (Ed.), *Handbook of infant development.* New York: Wiley, 1979, 185–195

Anastasi, A. *Psychological testing (5th ed.).* New York: MacMillan, 1982

Bardon, JI, & Wenger, RD. School psychology training trends in the early 1970s. *Professional Psychology,* 1976, *7,* 31–37

Bayley, N. *Bayley scales of infant development manual.* New York: The Psychological Corp., 1969

Begab, M. (Ed.). *Psychosocial influences and retarded performance: strategies for improving social competence.* Baltimore: University Park Press, 1982

Begnato, S, & Neisworth, J. *Linking developmental assessment and curricula: prescription for early intervention.* Rockville, Md.: Aspen Corp., 1982

Bell, RQ. Contributions of human infants to caregiving and social interactions. In M Lewis & L Rosenblum (Eds.), *The effect of the infant on its caregivers.* New York: Wiley, 1974, 1–19

Bennett, F. Rationale for early identification and treatment. In WK Frankenburg, S Thornton, & M Cohrs (Eds.), *Pediatric Developmental Diagnosis.* New York: Thieme-Stratton, 1981, 30–38

Bierman, JM, Connor, A, Vaage, M, & Honzik, M. Pediatricians' assessments of intelligence of two-year-olds and their mental test scores. *Pediatrics,* 1964, *34,* 680–690

Black, T. (Ed.), *Perspectives on Measurement: A Collection of Readings for Educators of Young Handicapped Children.* Proceedings of Measuring Child Progress at TADS, Nashville, Tennessee, 1979

Boyd, RD. *The Boyd developmental progress scale.* San Bernardino, Ca.: Inland County Regional Ct., 1974

Brazelton, TB. *Neonatal behavioral assessment scale:* Clinics in Developmental Medicine No. 50. Philadelphia: Lippincott, 1973

Camp, BW, Van Doorninck, W, & Frankenburg, WK. Preschool developmental testing as a predictor of school problems. *Clinical Pediatrics,* 1977, *16*(3), 257–263

Chess, S, & Hassibi, M. Behavior deviations in mentally retarded children. *Journal of American Academy of Child Psychiatry,* 1970, *9,* 282–297

Consortium for Longitudinal Studies. *Lasting Effects After Preschool.* Washington, DC.: US Government Printing Office (017-090-00047-0), 1978

Cruickshank, WM. Myths and realities in learning disabilities. *Journal of Learning Disabilities,* 1977, *10,* 51–58

Doll, E. *The Vineland social maturity scale: condensed manual of directions.* Circle Pines, Mn.: American Guidance, 1965

Downs, M, & Blager, F. Children with chronic otitis media. *Behavioral Developmental Pediatrics,* 1982, *2,* 44–48

Emde, RN, & Harmon, RJ. (Eds.), *The development of attachment and affiliative systems.* New York: Plenum, 1982

Erickson, ML. *Assessment and management of developmental changes in children.* St. Louis: Moseby, 1976

Feuerstein, R. *Instrumental enrichment: an intervention program for cognitive modifiability.* Baltimore: University Park Press, 1980

Field, T, Goldberg, S, Stern, D, & Sostek, A. (Eds.). *High-risk infants and children: adult and peer interactions.* New York: Academic Press, 1980

Fraiberg, S. *Insights from the blind.* New York: Basic Books, 1977

Fraiberg, S, Smith, M, & Adelson, E. An educational program for blind infants. *The Journal of Special Education,* 1969, *3*(2), 121–139

Frankenburg, WK, & Camp, B. *Pediatric screening tests.* Springfield, Ill.: Charles C Thomas, 1974

Frankenburg, WK, Thornton, SM, & Cohrs, ME. *Pediatric developmental diagnosis.* New York: Thieme-Stratton, 1981

Giannini, M. *The rapid developmental screening checklist.* American Academy of Pediatrics, New York, 1972

Graham, P, Chir, B, & Rutter, M. Organic brain dysfunction and child psychiatric disorder. *British Medical Journal,* 1968, *3,* 395–700

Hallahan, DP, Ball, DW, & Payne, JS. Factorial composition of the short form of the Stanford-Binet with culturally disadvantaged Head Start children. *Psychological Reports,* 1973, *32,* 1048–1050

Haynes, U. *A developmental approach to casefinding with special reference to cerebral palsy, mental retardation and related disorders.* Washington, DC.: Government Printing Office, 1967

Heatherington, M. Divorce: A child's perspective. *American Psychologist,* 1979, *34*(10), 851–855

Hobbs, N. *The futures of children.* San Francisco: Jossey-Bass, 1975

Honzik, M. Value and limitations of infant tests. In M Lewis (Ed.), *Origins of intelligence: infancy and early childhood.* New York: Plenum, 1976

Kagan, J, Kearsley, RB, & Zelazo, PR. *Infancy: its place in human development.* Cambridge, Ma.: Harvard Press, 1978

Kaufman, AS. A short form of the Wechsler Preschool and Primary Scale of Intelligence. *Journal of Consulting and Clinical Psychology,* 1972, *39,* 361–369

Kaufman, AS. A four test short form of the WISC-R. *Contemporary Educational Psychology,* 1976, *1,* 180–196

Kaufman, AS. *Intelligence testing with the WISC-R.* New York: Wiley, 1979

Kaufman, A, & Kaufman, N. *Clinical evaluations of young children with the McCarthy scales.* New York: Grune & Stratton, 1977

Kaufman, AS, & Kaufman, NO. *KABC Kaufman Assessment Battery for Children.* Circle Pines, Mn.: American Guidance, 1983

Kearsley, R. Iatrogenic retardation: A syndrome of learned incompetence. In R Kearsley & I Sigel (Eds.), *Infants at risk: assessment of cognitive functioning.* Hillsdale, Nj.: Erlbaum, 1979, 153–170

Kemper, M, & Frankenburg, WK. How do measurements differ from screening and diagnosis? In T Black (Ed.), *Proceedings of measuring child progress at TADS.* Nashville, Tn.: 1979, 3–25

Koch, R, & de la Cruz, F (Eds.). *Down's Syndrome (Mongolism): research, prevention and management.* New York: Brunner/Mazel, 1975

Korsch, B, Cobb, K, & Ashe, B. Pediatricians' appraisals of patient intelligence. *Pediatrics,* 1961, *27,* 990–1003

Lazar, I, & Darlington, R (Eds.). *Lasting effects after preschool.* Final report, HEW Grant 90C-1311 to the Education Commission of the States, 1978

Lewis, M, & Rosenblum, L (Eds.). *The effect of the infant on its caregiver.* New York: Wiley, 1974

Martin, HP. The child and his development. In C Kepme & R Helfer (Eds.), *Helping the battered child and his family.* Philadelphia: Lippincott, 1972, pp 125–131

Martin, HP (Ed.). *The abused child: an interdisciplinary approach to developmental issues and treatment.* Cambridge, Mass.: Ballinger, 1976

McCall, R. The process of early mental development: Implications for prediction and intervention. In N Anastasiow & WK Frankenburg (Eds.), *Early identification of at-risk children.* Baltimore: University Park Press, 1981, 38–51

Meyers, CE, Nihira, U, & Zetlin, A. The measurement of adaptive behavior. In Ellis, NR (Ed.), *Handbook of mental deficiency, psychological theory and research.* Hillsdale, Nj.: Erlbaum, 1979

Mowder, BA, & Demartino, RA. Continuing education needs in school psychology. *Professional Psychology,* 1979, *6,* 827–833

Pfeiffer, SI, & Tittler, BI. Utilizing the multidisciplinary team to employ a school-family systems orientation. *School Psychology Review*, 1983, *12* (2),168–173

Public Law 94–142, Education for All Handicapped Children Act. 94th Congress, S.G. (1975)

Quay, HC. Classification. In H Quay & J Werry (Eds.), *Psychopathological disorders of childhood (2nd ed.)*. New York: Wiley, 1979

Ramey, CT, MacPhee, D, & Yeates, K. Preventing developmental retardation: A general systems model. In L Bond & J Joffe (Eds.), *Facilitating infant and early childhood development*. Hanover, Nh.: University Press of New England, 1981

Sameroff, AJ, & Chandler, MJ. Reproductive risk and the continuum of caretaking casuality. In FD Horowitz (Ed.), *Review of child development*. Chicago: University of Chicago Press, 1975

Sattler, J. *Assessment of children's intelligence and special abilities (2nd ed.)*. Boston: Allyn & Bacon, 1982

Schaar, V. Council adopts statement: Handicapped law best beset with problems. *APA Monitor*, March, 1979

Schlesinger, H, & Meadow, K. Development of maturity in deaf children. *Exceptional Children*, 1972, *38*, 461–467

Schnell, R. The psychologist's role in the parent conference. In G Ulrey & S Rogers, (Eds.), *Psychological assessment of handicapped infants and young children*. New York: Thieme-Stratton, 1982, 179–190

Sisco, FH, & Anderson, RJ. Current findings regarding the performance of deaf children in the WISC-R. *American Annals of Deaf*, 1978, *123*, 115–121

Stormer, GE. *Dimensions of intellect unmeasured by the Stanford-Binet*. (Doctoral dissertation, University of Illinois, Champagne, Il.), 1966

Terman, LM, & Merrill, M. *Stanford-Binet Intelligence Scale: 1972 norms*. Boston: Houghton-Mifflin, 1973

Thomas, A. Current trends in developmental theory. In S Chess, & A Thomas (Eds.), *Annual progress in child psychiatry and child development*. New York: Brunner/Mazel, 1982

Thomas, A, & Chess, S. *Temperament and development*. New York: Brunner/Mazel, 1977

Ulrey, G. Emotional development of young handicapped children. In N Anastasiow (Ed.), *New directions for exceptional children*, 1981a, *5*, 33–51

Ulrey, G. The challenge of providing psychological services for young handicapped children. *Professional Psychology*, 1981b, *12*(4), 483–491

Ulrey, G, & Rogers, S (Eds.). *Psychological assessment of handicapped infants and young children*. New York: Thieme-Stratton, 1982

Uzgiris, I, & Hunt, JMcV. *Infant assessment: toward ordinal scales of psychological development*. Champaign, Ill.: University of Illinois Press, 1975

Wallerstein, JS, & kelly, TB. The effects of parental divorce: experiences of the preschool child. *Journal of the American Academy of Child Psychiatry*, 1975, *14*, 600–616

Zelazo, P. An information processing approach to infant cognitive assessment. In Lewis M, Taft L (eds.): *Developmental disabilities: theory, assessment and intervention*. New York: S.P. Medical and Scientific Books, 1981

Zigler, E, & Valentine, J (Eds.), *Project Head Start: a legacy of the war on poverty*. New York: Free Press, 1980

Jack A. Naglieri
Judy L. Genshaft

6

Recent Advances in the Psychological Assessment of Children

The aim of this chapter is to present some recent advances in assessment that incorporate new concepts and theories and that, hopefully, will mark a new generation of techniques and approaches in the psychological evaluation of children. The tests presented in this chapter are discussed as examples of the state of the art and are not meant to be an exhaustive list of new assessment devices. Our aim, however, is to bring attention to the types of innovations in the assessment of children's intellect, personality, and adaptive behavior.

PSYCHOLOGICAL TESTING

The psychological tests presented in this chapter are all systematic methods of obtaining objective information about an individual's performance in some specific area. These tests are designed to obtain an objective sample of behavior, from which generalizations to a larger realm of performance may be made. It is the process of generalization to some area of performance, which in the case of psychological tests is usually some hypothetical construct, that is the basis of test theory.

It is important to understand that, while psychological tests may cover a range of functions, there is no direct correspondence between

CLINICAL CHILD PSYCHOLOGY
ISBN 0–8089–1680–7

227

scores on given tests and certain people's characteristics in which one might be interested. Thus, there is no direct test that measures "creativity" nor any that measures "intelligence," "depression," or "personality." Tests are only samples of behavior that are obtained under well-defined conditions. Test interpretation theory assumes that the behavior being sampled has generalized to other aspects of a person's behavior.

Generalizations from test behaviors must be made cautiously, because these behaviors are viewed as an end product of a complex system of functioning. Inferences about nontest behavior should, therefore, be made only after several samples of behavior converge on one hypothesis. Patterns of behavior samples must be brought into a scheme from which generalizations may be formulated.

The various structured sampling techniques that follow are all ways in which the psychologist develops hypotheses, so that statements about some larger area of performance can be made. Although these different measures are designed to evaluate varied concepts, such as intelligence, adaptive functioning, and personality attributes, they are all systematic data collection techniques.

TESTS OF INTELLIGENCE

Psychology is a relatively new science, and as such it has only begun the developmental process of theoretical development, experimentation, synthesis, and refinement. If one were to consider that psychology began with the development of Wundt's experimental laboratory in the 19th century, then the field is only about 150 years old. In relation to other branches of science, such as physics, which dates back to the third century B.C. with Archimedes' concept that an object displaces its weight in water, psychology is barely in its infancy. Physics was about 500 years old when the Alexandrian astronomer Ptolemy put forth the view that the earth was the center of the universe. It was another 1400 years until the Polish astronomer Copernicus placed the sun at the center of our solar system. Hence, physics and psychology are at vastly different levels of scientific development. We must therefore guard against being too critical of the field of psychological assessment, since it is still quite young. Psychologists have only begun the task of understanding the "universe" within, the human mind.

In order to obtain a perspective on the area of intellectual assessment, one must first examine the historical evolution of the field of psychometrics. Although DuBois (1970) writes that civil service examinations were employed by the Chinese Empire some three thousand years ago, the major developments that have influenced cognitive assessment as we know it today began during the 1800s. It was in the early nineteenth century that individuals, such as Esquirol (1838) and Seguine (1866), began examination of mental retardation and remediation of this condition, and some of their approaches are still used today (e.g., Seguine Form Board in the Stanford Binet Scale). About this time, Galton's interest in human heredity led to his need to measure individual differences in his anthropometric laboratory. Galton's measurement of physical traits such as keenness of hearing and vision and discrimination of pitch, weight, and length of objects served as a system for measuring intellectual ability. With the application of Galton's statistical techniques for the measurement of individual abilities, the field of psychometrics was established (Anastasi, 1982).

Galton was joined by others, such as Cattell, Krapelin, and Ferrari, who were experimenting with sensory tasks as measures of intellectual ability. These tasks that measured sensory discriminations were, unfortunately, found to relate little to other estimates of intellectual ability (Bolton, 1891–1892; Gilbert, 1894; Wissler, 1901). Binet and Henri criticized these attempts at measuring intellectual ability via tasks of sensory discrimination and special abilities, because they viewed intellectual ability as complex. They offered an alternative approach (Anastasi, 1982).

With the publication of the 1905 Binet-Simon Scale (Binet & Simon, 1905), the basis of intelligence testing as we know it today was formed. After several revisions and an adaptation that included translation into English, under the direction of Terman, the Stanford-Binet emerged as the most viable instrument of its day. About 25 years later another major individual test of intelligence emerged, the Wechsler-Bellevue (Wechsler, 1946). Wechsler's subsequent development of the WAIS, WISC, and WPPSI marked a change in the concept of ability from the notion of a "g" factor to a dichotomous theory (i.e., verbal and nonverbal intelligence). Apart from incorporating nonverbal tests developed around the time of WWI (Kaufman, 1979), Wechsler's approach was not that different from Binet's.

Since the early 1900s, improvements in our intelligence tests have largely centered around better standardization samples, reliability coefficients, and test manuals rather than advances in the concept of intelligence and the system of measuring ability. For all practical purposes, the means by which we assess intellectual ability today has changed very little from the process employed around the turn of the century.

Many theories of intelligence have been developed, elaborated upon, and researched during the 100 years after Binet and Simon. Piaget (1952), Guilford (1967), Horn and Cattell (1966), Luria (1966), and recent information processing approaches, presented by researchers such as Feuerstein (1979) and Sternberg (1981), have expanded our knowledge of human functioning, but the number of intelligence tests has not grown with these developments in cognitive psychology and neuropsychology. While many potentially viable theories of intelligence have been developed, test publishers and practitioners have been resistant to embark upon alternative approaches to intellectual assessment (Kaufman, 1979). More professionals are beginning to recognize that our present system of assessment needs to be reconceptualized and redeveloped in light of these current advances.

Research in the areas of cognitive psychology and neuropsychology has contributed much to our understanding of mental abilities and it provides many possible avenues for assessment (i.e., the work of Gazzaniga [1977], Bogen [1977], Das, Kirby, and Jarman [1979], Sternberg [1981], and Feuerstein [1979]). Researchers like Sternberg (1981) who have investigated information-processing models of mental ability suggest that this approach "may enable us to diagnose and eventually remediate deficiencies in intellectual function" (p. 1188). Assessment based on such an approach will demand that previously employed intelligence tests be deemphasized and new ones developed specifically to measure processing rather than content. One such test built on an information-processing model of intellectual abilities is the recently published Kaufman Assessment Battery for Children (K-ABC; Kaufman & Kaufman, 1983).

The K-ABC: A New Generation of Intelligence Tests

The K-ABC is an individually administered measure of ability and achievement for children between 2½ and 12½ years of age. This new test differs from traditional IQ tests, such as the Binet and Wechsler scales, in several ways. In contrast to traditional measures of intelligence and achievement the K-ABC: (1) was built from psychological theory with factorial support for its construction, (2) measures intelligence apart from achievement, (3) is designed so that language plays a minimal role in the assessment of processing abilities (intelligence), (4) is designed to measure ability on the basis of the processing style required to solve tasks rather than on the basis of the task's content, (5) measures achievement in nonverbal as well as verbal domains, and (6) is constructed with attention to the developmental needs of children.

The K-ABC is comprised of two major scales—a Mental Processing Scale, which includes Simultaneous and Sequential Processing Scales, and the Achievement Scale. The Achievement Scale is designed to measure factual knowledge acquired from school and other means. In contrast, the Mental Processing Scale is intended to measure current level of intellectual functioning, as reflected by the child's performance on the Simultaneous and Sequential Scales. The tasks included in the Simultaneous Processing Scale are holistic, spatial, or analogic in nature and require that the child integrate and synthesize several pieces of information simultaneously to arrive at the correct solution. The Sequential Processing Scale tasks must be solved by arranging stimuli in some specific linear order where there is little prospect for viewing the activity in its entirety. Tasks are included on either the Simultaneous or Sequential Scales on the basis of the problem solving skills required, not according to content or modality of the material. A description of the subtests included in each K-ABC Scale is given in Table 6-1.

A Test Built From Theory

Perhaps the most important way in which the K-ABC differs from most intelligence tests is that it is derived from theoretical models of intelligence. The test's scales (two processing and one achievement) and subtests were designed to measure specific abilities based upon a dichotomous theory of intelligence. The theoretical underpinnings of the K-ABC derive strength from the fact that the test is not built on any one theorist's model of intelligence but, rather, is based on the convergence of many cognitive and neuropsychological theories that have much in common. The development of the test was inspired by theories presented by researchers such as Luria (1966) and Das, Kirby, and Jarman (1979), with their work on simultaneous and successive processing, cerebral specialization theorists such as Bogen (1977), Gazzaniga (1977), Ornstein (1972), and Sperry (1968), and cognitive psychologists such as Neisser (1967), as well as research on the Wechsler and McCarthy scales in general (see Kaufman, 1979). All of these theorists, despite their different orientations, have in common a recognition of two abilities, one that involves sequential, temporal, and analytic skill and one that requires simultaneous, spatial, synthetic, and gestalt ability. The K-ABC subtests were designed to measure simultaneous processing similar to tasks used to measure holistic (Ornstein), multiple (Neisser), right hemisphere (Gazzaniga), occipitol-parietal (Luria) ability, while the sequential scale is comprised of tasks used to measure successive processing (fronto-temporal, Luria), left hemisphere (Gazzaniga), analytic (Ornstein), and sequential (Neisser) ability.

The K-ABC and Nonbiased Assessment

The K-ABC has several features that suggest it may have potential as a nonbiased assessment device. While many IQ tests in use today, such as the Stanford-Binet, require the use of English language directions and responses to maintain standardized administration conditions, the K-ABC allows for explanation in any verbal or nonverbal manner.

Table 6-1
K-ABC Subtests

Sequential Processing Scale Subtest
1. Hand Movements (administered at ages 2½–12½)
   Requires that the child imitate a series of simple hand movements in the same sequence demonstrated by the examiner.
2. Number Recall (administered at ages 2½–12½)
   Requires the child to repeat orally presented digits in the same sequence presented by the examiner.
3. Word Order (administered at ages 4–12½)
   Requires the child to touch a series of silhouettes in the same sequence as they were named by the examiner.

Simultaneous Processing Scale Subtests
4. Magic Window (given at ages 2½–4)
   Requires the child to identify a picture that the examiner exposes by moving it past a narrow slit or "window."
5. Face Recognition (administered at ages 2½–4)
   Requires the child to select from a group photograph the one or two faces briefly viewed on a previous page.
6. Gestalt Closure (given at ages 2½–12½)
   Involves naming of an object pictured in an only partially completed black and white drawing.
7. Triangles (given at ages 4–12½)
   Requires the child to assemble blue and yellow colored triangles into an abstract pattern to reproduce models of varying sizes and shapes.
8. Matrix Analogies (given at ages 5–12½)
   Requires the child to select a picture or abstract design that best completes a visual analogy.
9. Spatial Memory (given at ages 5–12½)
   Requires the child to recall the placement of pictures on a page that was briefly exposed.
10. Photo Series (given at ages 6–12)
    Involves placement of photographs into serial order.

Achievement Scale Subtests
11. Expressive Vocabulary (given at ages 2½–4)
    Requires the child to verbally identify objects pictured in a photograph.
12. Faces & Places (given at ages 2½–12½)
    Requires the child to name the well-known person, fictional character, or place pictured in a photograph or cartoon-like drawing.
13. Arithmetic (given at ages 3–12½)
    Requires the child to demonstrate knowledge of numbers and mathematics concepts, counting and computational skills, and related tasks.

14. Riddles (administered at 3–12½)
    Requires the child to infer the name of something when given a list of its characteristics.
15. Reading/Decoding (administered at ages 5–12½)
    Requires naming letters and reading words.
16. Reading/Understanding (administered at ages 7–12½)
    Requires the child to demonstrate reading comprehension by acting out commands that are presented in print.

This is accomplished through two teaching items that appear at the beginning of every subtest on the intelligence scale, where the examiner is free to explain the task requirements and, in effect, teach the task using any language or any kind of technique. Hence, bilingual children who fail a teaching item because of a lack of verbal (English) comprehension of the directions can be instructed in their preferred language by the examiner without violation of standardized administration guidelines. The involvement of language in the assessment of intelligence is also diminished by eliminating subtests such as vocabulary as a test of ability, and moreover, requiring little more than a few words or no verbalizations at all on each subtest on the processing scale. Through the elimination of long verbal responses to earn credit, children whose culture or environment has not emphasized verbosity (e.g., Native American and lower SES groups) may not be at the disadvantage such children are when given a Binet or WISC-R, for example (Naglieri, 1984).

A second aspect of the K-ABC that suggests it may prove to have value in nonbiased assessment is related to the norming of the instrument. In addition to the national standardization sample of about 2000 children ranging in age from 2½ to 12½ years (stratified by geographic region, parents' education, community size, sex, and race and including representative proportions of gifted, learning disabled, mentally retarded, and other exceptional populations), the K-ABC has separate sociocultural norms tables. These conversion tables are provided so that the obtained raw score can be converted to a percentile rank on the basis of race (black or white) and level of socioeconomic status. This percentile rank will serve to further explain the child's relative level of performance in comparison with similar individuals. For Hispanic individuals, the K-ABC Spanish Edition (Kaufman & Kaufman, 1984), normed in Mexico, or the K-ABC translated into Spanish is recommended by the authors.

In addition to the sociocultural norms, the K-ABC has also been standardized on a sample that overlaps substantially with the Vineland Adaptive Behavior Scales' (Sparrow, Balla & Cicchetti, 1984) normative sample. This scale is a revision of the Vineland Social Maturity Scale (Doll, 1965). The similar standardization sample will allow comparison of ability and adaptive function to a highly similar norm group. In addition, the Vineland Adaptive Behavior Scales has an excellent standardization sample, unlike other measures of adaptive functioning.

Another aspect of the K-ABC that may contribute to its potential as a less biased instrument is the separation of achievement from the measurement of intelligence. Although traditional IQ tests include arithmetic, vocabulary, and general information tasks or subtests, none of these kinds of questions appear on the processing scales of the K-ABC. The authors have included such tasks on the Achievement Scale instead. All the tasks of every scale are designed to have a high level of interest through the use of colorful, child-oriented, and game-like materials to enhance rapport and therefore facilitate valid administration for children whose willingness or motivation to perform may be low. In order to avoid any items that may be objectionable to a minority examinee, the K-ABC items were carefully examined by Hispanic and Black reviewers and excluded or modified based on their critical comments. In addition, data from psychometrically derived item bias statistics (the procedures suggested by Angoff & Ford, 1973 and Wright, Meed, & Draber, 1976) were used to delete items with objectively determined bias. These, and the previously mentioned aspects suggest that the K-ABC holds promise as a measure of intelligence that will be less influenced by the intervening variables that typically spoil assessment of ability when traditional tests are used. What remains, of course, is the empirical demonstration of its effectiveness.

Assessment of Exceptional Children with the K-ABC

The K-ABC was designed so that tasks intended to measure intellectual processing ability would not contain knowledge attained through formal or informal teaching. For example, no vocabulary or general information subtests (as in the Wechsler Scales) are included in the K-ABC Mental Processing Scale, but similar tasks appear in the Achievement Scale instead. This separation of ability and achievement was of prime importance during the development of the subtests and items; and the effectiveness of the distinction was verified by factor analytic investigation of the standardization sample (Kaufman & Kaufman, 1983). The distinction between achievement and ability presented by the K-ABC is an important innovation in individual assessment, especially when learning disabled (LD) children are identified on the basis of an ability/achievement difference.

The K-ABC and LD assessment. An ability/achievement discrepancy is a common criteria for identification of a learning disability and one put forth by the U.S. Office of Education as part of the Education for All Handicapped Children Act, Public Law 94-142 (1975). Although a "severe discrepancy between achievement and intellectual ability" (p. 65083) sounds straightforward, actual usage of this system has both practical and statistical problems. While an ability/achievement discrepancy may be conceptually acceptable, practical application has proven to be flawed because past intelligence and achievement tests have considerable overlap in content (Kaufman, 1979). The result is that the ability/achievement discrepancy criteria become clouded when the tests used to find a difference have communality. When two tests have shared content there is a good chance that the scores they produce for any individual will be similar and any differences between such tests may be influenced by errors of measurement of the instruments.

A second practical problem, inherent when one uses current tests to uncover an ability/achievement discrepancy, is that these tests are normed on very different samples. For example, the WISC-R (Wechsler, 1974) standardization sample is highly representative of the 1970 U.S. population according to variables such as age, sex, race, geographic location, occupation of head of household, and urban-rural residence. In contrast, the Wide Range Achievement Test's (Jastak & Jastak, 1978) normative sample was collected without the controls used by Wechsler. Differences among WISC-R and WRAT standard scores may, therefore, reflect the differences in the compositions of the standardization samples. Whenever tests of ability and achievement are compared when these measures have different standardization samples, this concern applies.

Since the K-ABC has ability and achievement scales that were normed on exactly the same sample and these scales do not overlap in terms of content, these practical problems are circumvented. This does not guarantee that the K-ABC is highly accurate at identification of a learning disability when an achievement/ability discrepancy model is employed, as future research will have to validate the instrument's utility in terms of differential diagnosis.

Concluding Comments

Kaufman and Kaufman (1983) present a considerable amount of research that provides empirical support for their instrument. These results generally suggest that the K-ABC has adequate construct, concurrent, and predictive validity and that the test appears to be more fair to minority children such as Blacks, Hispanics, and Native Americans.

The clinical validity of the K-ABC for these populations, however, warrants further investigation and corroboration. The usefulness of the scores obtained through comparison with the sociocultural norms must be tested, and the diagnostic utility of the K-ABC for groups of exceptional children, such as learning disabled, needs careful examination. Additionally, an area of research of major importance will be the success of remedial activities based upon the simultaneous-sequential dichotomy.

It is clear that the K-ABC is a well-constructed and well-normed instrument with excellent psychometric qualities that holds promise as an important measure of intelligence and ability. Perhaps the K-ABC will stimulate the development of a new wave of innovative tests of intellectual functioning in children.

MEASUREMENT OF ADAPTIVE BEHAVIOR

Assessment tools designed to measure adaptive behavior, social maturity, social development, or whatever label one may place on the skills necessary to function on a day to day basis, are not as psychometrically advanced as most current tests of intelligence. The reliability and validity of the American Association on Mental Deficiency's Adaptive Behavior Scale (Lambert, Windmiller, Cole, & Figueroa, 1975) has been questioned (Givens & Ward, 1982; Sattler, 1982); the generalizability of the California norms for the Adaptive Behavior Inventory for Children (Mercer & Lewis, 1978) is suspect (Buckley & Oakland, 1977); and the oldest and perhaps most widely used measure of adaptive behavior, the Vineland Social Maturity Scale (Doll, 1953), contains outdated items from another era in time and is very poorly standardized. Despite these shortcomings, practitioners have had to rely on such tests of adaptive functioning when important placement decisions were required. In fact, measurement of adaptive behavior is critical in the assessment of mental retardation.

While the asessment of adaptive behavior for mentally retarded individuals has been and appears to be gaining in importance, there has been little basic theoretical work on the concept, and viewpoints vary considerably (Barnett, 1983). In many cases, adaptive behavior is largely defined by the content of the text employed and related concepts presented by the test's author, rather than a carefully articulated theory of personal functioning. Additionally, tests of adaptive functioning have historically been limited in psychometric qualities.

Perhaps the best alternative to current measures of adaptive behavior is a recently available revision of the Vineland Social Maturity Scale, called the Vineland Adaptive Behavior Scales (Sparrow, Balla, & Cicchetti, 1984). This new measure of adaptive functioning is a major revision and expansion of the 1953 Vineland, with an excellent standardization sample and promising psychometric qualities.

The Vineland Adaptive Behavior Scales

The Vineland Adaptive Behavior Scales, like its predecessor, is a system of obtaining information about an individual's level of functioning through an interview administered to the primary caregiver of a child or adolescent (ages birth to 19 years) or mentally retarded adult. The Vineland interview is an organized exploration designed to elicit information from an informant regarding the subject's performance. The interviewer's task is to determine, through extended questioning, how the subject behaves on a daily basis. This process of identifying what an individual does on a daily basis requires a sophisticated level of interviewing skills and has as a prerequisite appropriate training.

Sparrow, Balla, and Cicchetti (1984) have adopted the construct of adaptive behavior used by Doll (1953), which is the functional ability of individuals for exercising personal independence and social responsibility. Further, they extend this concept to include the developmental assessment of nonhandicapped individuals as well as handicapped or developmentally disabled persons (Sparrow, Balla, & Cicchetti, 1984). Therefore, the Vineland Adaptive Behavior Scales (VABS) may be used in a variety of settings, whenever assessment of an individual's level of social development in various areas is needed; this may include the learning disabled, emotionally disturbed, developmentally delayed, gifted, speech impaired, and hearing impaired as well as the mentally retarded.

The VABS is considerably more complete than the 1953 Vineland Social Maturity Scale. While the latter test contained 117 items organized into eight categories, which were not assessed at every age level, the revised Vineland is very thorough. The new scale contains three forms: a Survey Form, Expanded Form, and Classroom Edition. Both the Survey and Expanded Forms are norm referenced and will yield standard scores and individual profiles of adaptive behavior strengths and weaknesses. The Classroom Edition is a criterion-referenced measure designed to provide considerable material for educational planning. Within these forms, adaptive functioning is organized into several areas called domains and subdomains. These domains are measured at every age level and the item scores are combined to yield separate standard scores as well as an overall standard score of adaptive behavior. These standard scores have a mean of 100 and SD of 15. The domains and the three forms are described below:

The Five Vineland Adaptive Behavior Domains

The communication domain. Involves questions about how the individual uses verbal, nonverbal, symbolic, and written means of interacting with his or her environment. The range of questions varies from basic responses, such as smiling in response to the primary caregiver, to use of prepositions, reading and writing of simple words, to use of reference materials and communication of long range goals.

The daily living skills domain. Examines the individual's behavior in a number of areas vital to performance of everyday activities. Included in this domain are skills such as eating and food preparation, dressing, toileting and grooming, awareness of day, date, and time, use of money, performance on a job, and general maintenance of one's self and one's household.

The socialization domain. Examines the individual's interaction with those he or she encounters in various situations. Behaviors such as the kinds of interaction with peers and adults, willingness to follow rules in games and one's environment, control of one's anger, participation in social events, use of social amenities, and dating behaviors are included.

The motor skills domain. This is administered only to children ages eight and younger and aims to determine how the child physically acts on his or her environment. In this section, questions are explored about how the child manipulates objects, walks, writes, runs, and performs similar activities. The items range from simple tasks such as holding the head erect to complex use of scissors.

The maladaptive domain. This is intended to measure the kinds of behaviors commonly viewed as inappropriate for children above four years of age. Included here are behavior topics such as bed-wetting, eye contact, level of activity, truancy, and aggressiveness.

The Three Vineland Adaptive Behavior Forms

The survey form. This form is comprised of 140 items (Sparrow, et al, 1984) organized into each of the five adaptive behavior domains. The examiner administers items in each of the five domains according to the child's chronological age. Since this form is norm referenced and will yield standard scores that are comparable to tests of intelligence such as the Wechsler Scales and the Kaufman Assessment Battery for Children (Kaufman & Kaufman, 1983), it will likely be used most often in individual psychological and psychoeducational assessment.

The expanded form. This form is the longest version of the new Vineland and contains over 500 items in the five domains. Although the Expanded Form yields standard scores and is normed, it is primarily intended to gather a maximum amount of information for use in planning in educational, vocational, rehabilitation, and other settings. This Expanded Form covers the five domains, as does the Survey Form, and is administered in the same interview fashion.

The classroom edition. This is a checklist of behaviors that the individual performs on a daily basis according to the classroom teacher. This edition is subdivided into two questionnaires according to the age of the child: Level I for preschool, kindergarten grades, and first grade, and Level II for grades 2–6. Each questionnaire contains about 200 items that the teacher scores according to what he or she has observed, and estimates the individual's level of performance. Both versions of the Classroom Edition contain all but the Maladaptive Domain and are designed so that they can be completed in 20–30 minutes. Like the Survey Form and the Expanded Form, item scores can be converted to standard scores, percentile ranks, and age equivalents.

Both the Survey and Expanded Forms of the VABS were standardized on a sample of about 4500 individuals between the ages of birth and 19 years of age selected from 33 communities across the United States. The normative group was stratified by sex, race, community size, parents' education, and geographic region according to the 1980 United States Census Bureau Statistics. In addition to the normal individuals, gifted, speech impaired, learning disabled, mentally retarded, emotionally disturbed, and other children with handicaps were included in the normative sample in proportions that approximate their percentage in the general population. Supplementary norms tables are also provided for mentally retarded adults, emotionally disturbed adolescents, hearing impaired children, and visually impaired children selected from residential and nonresidential facilities in each region of the country.

An additional feature of the VABS's standardization sample is that it overlaps substantially with the normative sample of the Kaufman Assessment Battery for Children (Kaufman & Kaufman, 1983). The similarity in normative samples allows the derivation of norm-referenced scores on tests of intelligence, achievement, and adaptive behavior in comparison to virtually the same group of representative individuals, something that has not been possible with tests such as the WISC-R (Wechsler, 1974), Wide Range Achievement Test (Jastak & Jastak, 1978), and Vineland Social Maturity Scale (Doll, 1953).

Concluding Comments

Practicing psychologists have long recognized the limitations of the Vineland Social Maturity Scale and will likely find the Vineland Adaptive Behavior Scales to be a welcomed revision. The excellent standardization, supplementary norms, careful attention paid to reliability, as well as the three forms of the revised Vineland may prove to be valuable assets in the assessment of adaptive functioning. What remains is the series of research investigations designed to assess the new test's effectiveness and psychometric qualities under many clinical conditions. Only through extensive, empirical investigations will the ultimate usefulness of the revised Vineland Adaptive Behavior Scales be validated.

NEUROPSYCHOLOGICAL ASSESSMENT

Neuropsychological assessment stems from the need that neuroscientists have for behavioral evaluations to aid in neurological diagnosis, and to document brain disorders as well as recovery from brain trauma. While the evolution of adult neuropsychology was linked to military needs and wartime activities (much of the noted Soviet neuropsychologist A. R. Luria's work was done with soldiers), child neuropsychology grew with advances in areas such as mental retardation and learning disabilities (Lezak, 1976). Some recent authors, such as Gaddes (1981), suggest that diagnostic decisions about children, such as a learning disability, should be made with the help of neuropsychological assessment. Mykelbust (1967) and Cruickshank (1977) further suggest that specific diagnosis of a learning disability be defined in terms of a minor disturbance in brain function, either diagnosed or inferred. Golden and his associates extend this concept further to suggest specific neurological dysfunctions for various exceptionalities.

Golden (1981) suggests that brain injury to specific neurological areas could explain childhood disorders such as hyperactivity, mental retardation, and learning disabilities. Hyperactivity may be the result of dysfunction of the Reticular Activating System (RAS), which leads to under- or over-arousal of the child. Mental retardation is seen as dysfunction of many different kinds of injuries to the brain including Luria's

Unit I, which transmits input to the cortex; the primary areas of the brain, so that the processing of sensory input is inhibited; and injuries to only one hemisphere. Learning disabilities are viewed as being of three types according to neurological involvement—first, disorders in a specific modality, second, dysfunction in cross-modality integration, and third, disorders of motor function. Golden and his associates (1980) extend this psychoneurological model to build models that further explain other exceptionalities and have constructed tests to measure specific brain functions.

Neuropsychological Assessment using the Luria-Nebraska

The Luria-Nebraska Neuropsychological Battery Children's Revision (Golden, 1981) is a version of the Luria-Nebraska Neuropsychological Battery (Golden, Hammeke, & Purisch, 1980), which is designed to measure children's neuropsychological functioning. The instrument strives to "identify children with cortical impairments, to distinguish them from children with normal cerebral functioning, and to point to appropriate rehabilitation strategies based on the nature and extent of impairment" (Gustavson, Golden, Wilkening, Hermann, Plaisted, & MacInnes*). The Luria-Nebraska Children's Revision is designed for use with children between the 8 and 12 year age range. Based upon Luria's work in brain behavior relationships, the Luria-Nebraska's format reflects the developmental differences between children and adults. This developmental model assumes that both quantitative and qualitative differences in behavior are related to various maturational schedules of the different cortical areas. In this respect, Luria's framework for development is similar to that of other developmental theorists, such as Jean Piaget. The Luria-Nebraska Children's Revision is organized into eleven subtests covering the following topics.

Motor. Included in this area are items requiring simple hand movements, reproduction of hand positions, hand tapping, and more complex motor activities such as design drawing and following involved directions.

Rhythm. This subtest is comprised of items such as pitch discrimination and reproduction of sounds, a song, and rhythmic patterns.

---

*Gustavson JL, Golden CJ, Wilkenning GN, Herman BP, Plaisted JR, & MacInnes WD. *The Luria-Nebraska Neuropsychological Battery-Children's Revision: Validation with brain damaged and normal children.* Manuscript submitted for publication. 1982

Tactile. This section measures tactile discrimination skills (e.g., "Am I touching your hand with the point or blunt end of the pencil?"), identification of objects by feeling only, strength and shape discrimination, and detection of movement.

Visual functions. This subtest measures visual identification of actual objects, pictures of objects, visual discrimination, visual memory, and comparisons of rotated figures.

Receptive speech. Included in this subtest are items involving oral and written reproduction of sounds, following directions, and comprehension of logical grammatical structures.

Expressive speech. Tasks in this section include reading and repeating words and sentences, describing pictures, and naming objects from oral and visual descriptions.

Writing. This subtest includes letter copying, writing of letter combinations and words, and analysis of letter sequences.

Reading. Tasks in this area require reading of letters, words, sentences, and a paragraph, as well as nonsense words.

Arithmetic. This section measures number writing, reading, identification, as well as simple mathematical processes.

Memory. The items of this subtest require recall of words, designs, hand positions, and paired associate learning.

Intellect. This subtest is comprised of tasks similar to those found on the Stanford-Binet (e.g., Picture Absurdities), and Wechsler Scales (how are X and Y alike, different?), as well as elementary arithmetic problems presented orally.

The eleven subsections of the Luria-Nebraska Children's Revision are intended to measure different response capabilities and are therefore scored separately. Each subtest yields a *T*-score value (mean of 50 and *SD* of 10) where above average scores represent performance noteworthy of possible neurological dysfunction. Gustavson, et al. suggest that identification of brain-damaged subjects may be most efficiently accomplished by using a criterion based on the number of subsection scores above 60. These authors suggest using less than two T scores above 60 as indication of normal function and three or more T scores above 60 as indicative of clearly abnormal functioning. Two scores above 60 would suggest marginal performance and should indicate further testing is needed. Since the test is still in developmental stages, these criteria should be considered tentative and therefore subject to revision. This is especially important given the limited size and composition of the normative sample.

The normative sample for the current revision of the Luria-Nebraska Children's version consisted of 125 normal children between the ages of 8 and 12. The 25 children at each year level were selected from regular classes and none had any history of neurological, psychiatric, or behavioral disturbances. All of these children were functioning within two years of their grade placement and the mean Wide Range Achievement Test scores were 108 in Reading, 104 in Spelling, and 94 in Arithmetic. The sample's WISC-R Full Scale IQs were all above 80 with a mean of 108 and SD of 11, indicating slightly above average intellectual ability and some restriction in the range of intelligence levels (Gustavson et al, see footnote page 241; Wilkening, Golden, MacInnes, Plaistead, & Hermann[†]). Additional specifics on the sample are unavailable.

Research on the Luria-Nebraska Children's Revision is sparse at the present time because the test is so recently developed. Preliminary investigations indicate that the Luria "is effective in predicting IQ and WRAT reading levels," with multiple correlations across the eleven Luria scales of .70 to .85 (p = .05) (Golden, 1981). Golden also reports that a sample of brain injured children (N = 50) performed significantly poorer than matched normal controls on the scale.

Gustavson et al (see footnote page 241) report two validation studies involving normal and brain injured children. The first investigation compared 76 neurologically impaired children (diagnosis based on several medical criteria) with a normal control sample, Initial differences emerged using a multivariate analysis of variance, and a discriminant analysis accurately predicted group membership for 91 percent of the normal and 65 percent of the brain-damaged subjects. The second experiment employed a sample of 91 normal and 58 brain-damaged subjects (mean age = 10.6) and resulted in similar findings; group membership was accurately predicted 93 percent of the time for normal and 78 percent of the time for brain-damaged subjects.

The Luria-Nebraska Children's Revision has been compared to other measures of intelligence and achievement in a few additional investi-

---

[†]Wilkenning GN, Golden CJ, MacInnes WD, Plaisted JR, & Herman B. *The Luria-Nebraska Neuropsychological Battery Children's Revision: A preliminary report.* Manuscript submitted for publication, 1982

gations. Geary, Jennings, and Schultz‡ found that the Luria Intelligence Scale correlated significantly (p < .001) with the WISCR-R Verbal ($r = -.54$), Performance ($r = -.65$), and Full Scale ($r = -.64$) IQs. Pfeiffer and Naglieri§ report similar correlations between the Luria Intelligence Scale and WISC-R Verbal ($r = -.45$) and Full Scale ($r = -.43$) standard score but no significant correlation with the Performance Scale ($r = -.21, p > .10$).

Concluding Comments on the Luria-Nebraska Children's Revision

Use of the Luria-Nebraska Children's Revision in clinical settings will require more than the acquisition of administration techniques and scoring standards. The psychoneurological investigative approach is very complex for adults and compounded when applied to children due to varying development of neurological systems. These factors demand that thorough training in the theory and application of the Luria-Nebraska approach is absolutely necessary if the model is to be used appropriately. Despite the amount of training required for use of this model, the Luria-Nebraska assessment approach may prove to be a viable alternative to instruments presently available.

The Luria-Nebraska Children's Revision is an important advance in the field of psychological assessment. What remains are the many empirical investigations designed to assess the psychometric qualities of the instrument, such as its factorial structure, and the effectiveness of this approach in differential diagnosis and remediation. Little evidence is currently available to substantiate theoretical hypotheses in the area of child neuropsychology and clinicians need to exercise scientific caution and be tentative about their conclusions. This is especially vital given the relatively poor standardization sample upon which not only the Luria-Nebraska but other major neuropsychological tests were normed. Through a systematic and thorough examination of the usefulness of the model and the effectiveness of the techniques, our understanding of various human conditions may be expanded.

PERSONALITY ASSESSMENT

The use of psychological tests for purposes of personality assessment constitutes one effort to apply scientific methodology to the understanding of individual functioning. Its development was involved with critical

---

‡Geary DC, Jennings SM, & Schultz DD. *The diagnostic accuracy of the Luria-Nebraska Children's Battery for 9–12 year old learning disabled children.* Manuscript submitted for publication, 1984.

§Pfeiffer SI, & Naglieri JA. *Comparison of the WISC-R and Luria-Nebraska Children's Battery.* Manuscript submitted for publication, 1984

aspects of nineteenth century philosophical thought. The development of various psychometric techniques between 1850 and 1900 occurred within the philosophical framework of Descartes' doctrine of dualism. As the materialistic determinism of physics became dominant in the biological and physiological sciences, there was an increased effort on the part of the dualists to safeguard the scientific status of the mind. There was a need to demonstrate that psychological processes could be examined within the same general scientific framework as that advocated by physics.

Early mental testers (e.g., Cattell, Titchener) were interested in measuring overt behavioral characteristics, focusing primarily on cognitive processes, i.e., memory, problem solving, etc. While Wundt in the later 1870s had directed some attention to the measurement of affect, the new testers found the classical efforts to examine emotion to be of little use in their work. The concept of emotions, used in the sense of visible reaction or self-report of one's feelings, was quite different from the concepts of motivation that were later to become incorporated into the framework of psychodynamics.

Testing in the area of "depth" or motivational understanding of the individual was influenced from an entirely separate stream of thinking. In view of the forces in scientific psychology up to the 1920s and 1930s, it is not strange to find that testing ideas related to motivation entered the field from foreign sources; that is, outside of America and outside of psychology. Jung integrated the developing dynamic orientation of psychoanalysis with scientific methodology through the use of the word association technique to study personality.

In American universities the behavioral rebellion rejected the European mentalistic orientation. Behaviorism was marked by a sharp rejection of the "mind" and even of consciousness as appropriate objects of psychological study. Clinical assessment of the "whole man" was scorned by academic psychology, which focused on S-R units. Later developments in clinical testing in America gave rise to and were influenced by various theoretical conflicts (i.e., nomothetic vs. idiographic, clinical vs. actuarial prediction, molar vs. molecular). In retrospect, such conflict represented the lack of integration between academic and clinical psychology. While these conflicts were never adequately resolved, they became overshadowed by new influences and ideas. Within academic psychology, emphasis changed from the study of basic drives and basic principles of learning to culturally relevant variables in behavior acquisition and change.

Concurrent with the growth of interest in cognitive development, there has developed acceptance of direct attacks on problems of concern to society, such as those involved in the mental health and anti-poverty programs. Currently, psychological research in educational methods, in teacher training, and in modes of rehabilitation of disturbed or delinquent children is surprisingly accepted, considering the attitudes prevalent 10 to 15 years ago. The impact of these developments has changed test usage considerably.

The Nature of Personality Assessment

One difference between cognitive psychological testing and other methods of clinical assessment is the increased distance between the examiner and the patient. In the less structured evaluative procedures, such as interviews, it is often desirable to develop and evaluate hypotheses about the patient that are based upon the immediate interaction. These hypotheses guide the direction of the interview. The psychologist follows his own immediate hypothesis about the patient rather than the more structured data-collecting operations imposed by cognitive tests.

A second difference between cognitive psychological testing and personality testing is that the latter is based upon a composite of operating assumptions of which empiricism is but one. Personality testing involves an accumulation of information about the individual from several perspectives. The psychologist needs to gain an understanding of how the individual perceives the world, how this perception impacts behavior, and how the individual responds to the demands of the test materials. The psychologist must then integrate these data into a theoretical framework to comprehend the individual's personality structure.

Personality Tests

Developments in personality testing typically do not reflect the premises of personality theory or the directions or results of experimental personality research (Maloney & Ward, 1976). The personality devices have come from three primary sources: the projective hypothesis, the construct approach, and the empirical approach.

The projective hypothesis approach considers behavior as a manifestation of underlying processes. When a person responds to unstructured or ambiguous stimuli, the content of the response will be a reflection of the person's characteristics. Thus, projective tests (e.g., Rorschach, Thematic Apperception Test) put as few restrictions as possible on the person's mode of response. The construct approach is not based upon integrated personality theory, but rather employs tests that are designed to measure a single attribute or trait such as anxiety or depression. While these tests are designed to measure the specific phenomenon in question, empirically based personality tests are atheoritical and employ a criterion referenced approach to the assessment of personality. These empirically based personality tests are developed by testing a group of persons with known characteristics and selecting items that reflect these characteristics (e.g., MMPI).

The personality tests covered in the following sections reflect the empirically based approach to assessment for children. These inventories or scales also appear to be the most influential in the 1980s and have been accompanied by an increase in usage for children, particularly in educational settings (Carlson & Lahey, 1983).

Issues in Empirically Based Personality Assessment

There are a number of problems and issues related to the empirically founded approach to the study of personality. Obtaining valid and reliable descriptions of children's behavior is a complex process involving the interplay of many factors (Edelbrock, 1983). Only a few major considerations can be reviewed in this chapter. More comprehensive discussions may be found in the writings of Achenbach (1982), Kazdin (1980), O'Leary & Johnson (1979), and Mash and Terdal (1981).

A number of variables such as the child's age and sex have been shown to have an impact on the prevalence of certain behaviors in childhood. There is little information, however, concerning the effects of race on dimensions of childhood disorders (Carlson & Lahey, 1983). The research on the variable of race has been controversial. Kim, Anderson, and Bashaw (1968) reported obtaining identical factors for Blacks and Whites; others report that their factor scores correlated significantly with race (Miller, 1972; Swift & Spivack, 1968). A higher proportion of Blacks than Whites were identified as hyperactive (Spring, Blunden, Greenberg & Yellin, 1977). Clearly this is an area where additional research is needed.

A major controversy existing in the factor analytic literature concerns the "correct" number of extractable factors related to childhood disorders (Carlson & Lahey, 1983). Although there is general agreement on two factors, conduct disorders and anxiety disorders, disagreement exists beyond this point (Miller, 1967). While some believe a two-factor solution is best for grouping childhood disorders (Achenbach, 1966; Peterson, 1961), others argue for more complex solutions (Connors, 1969, Lachar, 1982). This controversy is further complicated by other issues such as which type of rotation is most appropriate.

The degree to which items reflect global behavior characteristics or more specific behavioral actions is also an area of controversy. Some researchers argue that global items provide meaningful and reliable information, while others claim that it is difficult to determine exactly what these item behaviors represent (Kazdin, 1980). Extremely specific items (e.g., taps foot lightly while watching TV) may not seem relevant to informants and can be interpreted in a variety of ways, whereas global items may be too vague.

Controversy also arises in determining how informants should respond to items (Edelbrock, 1983). Instruments such as the Personality Inventory for Children (PIC) employ a dichotomous scoring system (e.g., True/False). Because other researchers believe this method is too concrete to capture subtle yet important differences (many behaviors are present to some degree in all children), they have utilized a three-point response scale, such as never, sometimes, always (Achenbach & Edelbrock, 1979; Quay, 1983). More differentiated responses have been used, but caution is levied, since the more complex the rating task, the less reliable are the data (Kazdin, 1977).

Another problem facing empirically based personality assessment is that informants differ in many ways that are known to influence the behavioral ratings. Teacher, mother, father, stepparent, or treating therapist all may claim to have knowledge of the child's behavior, but this knowledge is frequently confined to a particular setting or situation. Informant's perspectives, biases, motivation, extent of observation time, and expectations when responding to the questionnaire are related to the data received about the child. Although the problem of informant differences may seem obvious, few attempts have been made to tailor rating scales to the unique qualifications of different informants (Edelbrock, 1983).

In summary, a great many characteristics of children are potentially relevant to the measurement of psychopathology. In order to identify these characteristics, an immense variety of behaviors need to be examined. The diversity of potentially relevant behaviors, complicated by the variability of each child's behavior, poses a massive information collecting task. The empirically founded approaches that follow are two systems designed to summarize children's problem behaviors.

Personality Inventory for Children

The recent publication of the Personality Inventory for Children (Wirt, Lachar, Klinedinst, & Seat, 1977) has introduced an approach to child personality assessment with characteristics compatible with current diagnostic practices. The PIC yields multidimensional data for children and adolescents, which the authors suggest may result in increased validity over current assessment practices (Lachar, Butkus, & Hryhorczuk; 1978).

The original creators of the Personality Inventory for Children were Wirt and Broen (1958), who published an initial test that contained items in booklet form. The early 600 item inventory was developed for use with children using the successful strategy of the MMPI (Hathaway & McKinley, 1951). Wirt and Broen utilized parents as respondents to measure knowledge of a child's behavior and devleopment. The inventory was further refined using an empirical approach to construct and to validate scales for the discrimination of specified criterion groups from a norm group of 2390 children (DeKrey & Ehly, 1981).

Content of the PIC

The PIC questionnaire contains 600 true-false items, which are completed by the primary informant, usually the child's mother. These responses yield 3 validity scales, which are designed to detect response tendencies toward exaggerating or minimizing symptoms, 1 screening scale for measuring general adjustment, 12 clinical scales to evaluate the presence of pathology in the child, and 17 supplemental scales created to provide additional information in areas of parental concern. Significant elevation on one of the clincal or supplemental scales indicates that the child is likely to manifest the pathological symptoms or behaviors measured by that scale (Greene, Martin, Bennett, & Shaw, 1981).

The PIC was normed on a sample of 2390 children between the ages of 6 and 16 and a sample of 192 between the ages of 3 and 5. There were about equal numbers of males and females at each age level. This sample was not systematically selected so as to be nationally representative and little information about the norm groups is provided in either the 1977 or 1982 PIC Manuals. Reliability data are reported for portions of the normative group and some specific clinical and normal samples. Coefficient alpha internal consistency estimates range considerably for both the Original Format (range = $-.03$ to .86, median = .75) and Revised Format (range = .14 to .86, median = .78) for a clinical sample of 1226 children (Lachar, 1982, p. 26). These internal consistency estimates range from very poor to moderate. Standard errors of measurement are also reported for the Revised Format (range = 3.29 to 7.70, median = 5.7). Overall, information about the performance of the normative sample on the PIC is sparse.

PIC scales were reconstructed through several item-analytic procedures. Where appropriate, the PIC item pool has been tested against criterion groups, and has been proven of value in the identification of children classified as psychotic, hyperactive, delinquent, retarded, and learning disabled (Lachar & Wirt, 1981). It is reported to be equally effective for boys and girls and for children and adolescents (Lachar &

Gdowski, 1979). A description of the PIC scales follows (Wirt & Lachar, 1981, p. 366–367):

1. The Lie scale (L) identifies a defensive response set on the part of the respondent who tends to ascribe the most virtuous of behavior and to deny minor, commonly occurring behavior problems.
2. The F Scale (F) was constructed to identify possible deviant response sets, such as deliberate exaggeration of symptoms or random responding because of an uncooperative attitude or poor reading ability.
3. The Defensiveness scale (DEF) measures the tendency of a parent to be defensive about the child's behavior during an evaluation.
4. The Adjustment scale (ADJ) aims to identify children who are in need of psychological evaluation and as a general measure of poor psychological adjustment.
5. The Achievement scale (ACH) was constructed to assist in the identification of children whose academic achievement is significantly below age expectation though they may possess adequate intellectual capacity.
6. The Intellectual Screening scale (IS) may be used to identify children who have intellectual impairment.
7. A high score on the Development scale (DVL) suggests deficits in motor coordination, language skills, or cognitive functions that may be reflected in poor classroom performance.
8. Elevation on the Somatic Concern scale (SOM) suggests frequent concern with physical symptoms that generally have a functional etiology or component.
9. The Depression scale (D) was designed to measure the importance of that component for a particular child, following the definition of depression in children formulated by the Group for the Advancement of Psychiatry (1966).
10. The Family Relations scale (FAM) measures family effectiveness and cohesion. High scores may indicate parental maladjustment, marital discord, unhappiness in the home, lack of appropriate discipline, or lack of appreciation for the rights of a child.
11. The Delinquency scale (DLQ) correctly identifies 95 percent of youths who are adjudicated delinquent.
12. The Withdrawal scale (WDL) identified children who avoid social contact, desire to remain isolated, have few friends, and distrust others.
13. The Anxiety scale (ANX) indicates that a child manifests symptoms of anxiety, such as a limited frustration tolerance, exaggeration of problems or concern, worries that reflect parental concerns, be-

havioral and physiological correlates of anxiety, irrational fears and worries, and nightmares.

14. The Psychosis scale (PSY) was constructed to discriminate children with psychotic symptomatology from normal, behaviorally disturbed nonpsychotic, and retarded children.

15. The Hyperactivity scale (HPR) was constructed to identify children who display characteristics frequently associated with "Attention Disorder with Hyperactivity" (American Psychiatric Association, 1980).

16. The Social Skills scale (SSK) is composed of items that reflect effective social relations in childhood: ability to lead and to follow, level of active participation in organized activities, self-confidence and poise in social situations, tact, and interpersonal relations.

The Revised Format Administration Booklet of the Personality Inventory for Children presents the original 600 inventory items in a different order so as to provide greater flexibility in clinical and research applications (Lachar, 1982). The rearrangement of items allows the clinician to administer fewer than the 600 original items while still allowing interpretation of the results.

In the revised PIC items are placed in one of four sections or parts of the administration booklet (Lachar, 1982). Part I is to be used as a screening device. It is comprised of the first 131 items of the Revised Format and provides a measure of informant defensiveness (Lie Scale) and four broad-based factor-derived scales: (1) Undisciplined/Poor Self-Control; (2) Social Incompetence; (3) Internalization/Somatic Symptoms; and (4) Cognitive Development. Part II consists of the first 280 items of the Revised Format and allows the scoring of the 4 factor scales, the Lie scale, the Development scale, and shortened versions of the remaining 14 clinical profile scales. Part III or the first 420 items include all the items of the 4 factor scales, 16 profile scales, and the critical item set. Part IV (items 420 to 600) includes the remaining inventory items and is used for research purposes (Wirt, Lachar, Klinedist, & Seat, 1977).

Concluding Comments

The PIC has the potential to make a meaningful contribution to an intake or a screening procedure, particularly when integrated with the idiographic procedures currently used in child and adolescent assessment. The instrument is controversial, however, and criticisms have been levied against the PIC. One major drawback often raised is the amount of time required to give the original PIC questionnaire and to hand score a single protocol. Handscoring the 16 clinical scales and 17 supplemental scales requires the use of 66 templates. This may lead to a high error rate when a large number of protocols must be scored (Greene, et al, 1981). In addition, the original clinical profile cannot be used to plot the scores obtained from the revised format profile scales due to new T-score conversions. Use of a computer scoring system is available and certainly reduces time and error. However, computer interpretation "masks the difficulty of appraising the true value of these interpretations; many of them appear to be reiterations of what the parent says on the PIC" (Achenbach, 1981).

Although the empirically derived scales of the PIC may have diagnostic utility, their value is reserved for the identification of specific disorders similar to those of the criterion group (DeKrey & Ehly 1981). Criticisms have focused upon the PIC's limited generalizibility to other settings (Achenbach, 1981). Conversely, the authors of the PIC have documented its generalizibility by referring to research in assessment of learning disabled seen for neuropsychological assessment (Porter, 1980), determination of classroom placement (DeKrey & Ehly, 1981), and the study of childhood depression (Leon, Kendall, & Garber, 1980). Additional study is necessary to document the utility and unique applications of the PIC.

Child Behavior Checklist and Child Behavior Profile

Unlike the Personality Inventory for Children, the Child Behavior Profile (CBP; Achenbach & Edelbrock, 1979) evaluates how the child has adjusted to the environment rather than personality structure or the organization of the underlying processes that determine behavior. The CBP avoids categorizing children solely on the basis of a particular syndrome and instead has been used to generate a taxonomy of behaviors. Through the use of the checklist, the examiner obtains parents' reports of their children's competencies and problems in a standardized format. The adaptive competencies and behavior problems of the child are the central concerns of the CBP as well as the assessment of behavior change. Using the profile, the examiner can obtain an overview of the specific behaviors reported by the parent. A comparison can be made as to how the child's problems and competencies cluster and how the child scores in relation to normal children of similar age and sex. The profile format preserves more information than does classification into mutually exclusive categories, and profiles are suitable for multidimensional classification (Achenbach, 1982).

The CBP yields patterns of behavioral competencies and problems scored from the Child Behavioral Checklist (138 items). It can also be used to assess changes in reported behavior over time (Achenbach and Edelbrock, 1979). Profiles are standardized separately for each sex at ages 4–5, 6–11, and 12–16 years and expressed as T scores (mean of 50 and standard deviation of 10).

The behavior problem dimensions and the norms reflect the pattern and prevalence of behaviors characteristic of the child's age and sex. The Behavioral Problems Scales form two broad-band groupings, which have been labeled Internalizing and Externalizing. The behavior scales also reflect 8 or 9 specific disorders for each age/sex group. They were empirically identified (multivariate approaches) and have located factors or clusters of items that were most robust. The behavior problem items loading highest on a factor were used to define the syndrome represented by the factor (Achenbach, 1982).

The narrow band behavior problem syndromes are analogous to syndromes found within such DSM III categories (American Psychiatric Association, 1980) as attention deficit disorders, conduct disorders, and anxiety disorders. The syndromes of both the DSM III and the Profile are intended to depict naturally occurring groups of behavior problems (Achenbach, 1982). The DSM III and Profile comprise a hierarchy of general and more specific syndrome categories. Within the DSM III's overall category of attention deficit are many specific syndromes. The Profile is similar in that the broad bands Internalizing and Externalizing incorporate three or more narrow band syndromes (Achenbach, 1982). The Internalizing and Externalizing bands are described in Table 6-2.

The Child Behavior Checklist also looks at children's competencies as well as deficits in determining their developmental progress. These competencies are represented by three scales listed below:

1. Activities: This scale taps the amount and quality of the child's activities through items such as number of sports, extent of participation and skill in sports, number of jobs, etc.
2. Social: This scale taps the amount and quality of the child's socialization through such items as: number of organizations, number of friends, behavior with others, behavior alone, etc.
3. School: This scale taps the amount and quality of the child's school experiences through such items as scholastic performance, special class placement, repeated grade(s), school problems, etc.

The norms of the Child Behavior Checklist are limited. There were 450 parents of boys being evaluated in 20 East Coast mental health settings (guidance clinics, health maintenance organizations, private practice). Of the group, 79.9 percent were White, 18.7 percent Black, and 1.5 percent other. The norms for the profile were computed from the Child Behavior Checklists of 300 normal boys from the Washington, D.C. area. Those boys received no mental health services in the previous year. Matching for race, sex, and SES was achieved. Comparison of

Table 6-2
Internalizing and Externalizing Bands of the CBP

Internalizing

Schizoid
This syndrome measures schizoid behaviors through items such as fears, fears school, auditory hallucinations, nightmares, anxious, shy, timid, etc.

Depressed
This syndrome measures the child's degree of depression through such items as lonely, cries much, harms self, feels unloved, feels worthless, sulks, nervous, anxious, guilty, etc.

Uncommunicative
This syndrome measures the child's uncommunicative behavior through such items as confused, won't talk, secretive, stares blankly, stubborn, shy, etc.

Obsessive Compulsive
This syndrome measures the child's degree of obsessive compulsive behaviors through such items as confused, daydreams, sleeps little, strange behavior, walks or talks in sleep, etc.

Somatic Complaints
This syndrome measures the child's degree of somatic problems through such items as headaches, nausea, stomach problems, pains, overtired, much sleep, etc.

Social Withdrawal
This syndrome measures the child's degree of social withdrawal through such items as poor peer relations, feels persecuted, likes to be alone, prefers young kids, slow moving, withdrawn, etc.

Externalizing

Hyperactive
This syndrome measures the child's hyperactive behavior through such items as can't concentrate, impulsive, poor schoolwork, clumsy, prefers young kids, confused, etc.

Aggressive
This syndrome measures the child's aggressive behavior through such items as argues, cruel to others, disobedient, fights, jealous, unliked, shows off, stubborn, excess talk, loud temper tantrums, etc.

Delinquent
This syndrome measures the degree of the child's delinquent behaviors through such items as destroys own things, destroys others' things, lies, cheats, runs away, steals, sets fires, vandalism, truant, etc.

disturbed and normal boys showed differences (p = .001) on all behavior problem and social competence scores. Achenbach (1982) reported correlations for the Profile reliabilities. Rank ordering of scores using the Pearson product moment correlations revealed an average correlation of .69 for agreement between mothers' and fathers' ratings and an average correlation of .88 for test-retest reliability of mother's rating across a one-week interval.

The major validity analyses conducted with the Profile have pertained to discriminant validity. Children diagnosed as being disturbed according to one feature have more features of the syndromes than children considered normal. Those children referred for mental health services were compared to demographically matched normal children. The referred children were found to have significantly higher scores on all the narrow band and broad band syndromes (Achenbach, 1978).

Concluding Comments

The CBP is a promising new test for evaluating behavior problems of children. The profile may prove to be valuable for describing children's behavior in a concise but comprehensive and meaningful fashion in a short amount of time. The strength of the profile is that it discriminates among children who may benefit from different kinds of treatment but its shortcoming is a limited norm sample. The profile appears to be sensitive to stabilities as well as changes in children's behavior. Because the profile utilizes a maximum amount of information about the child's behavior, the profile pattern may provide a better classification scheme than do typical diagnostic categories.

REFERENCES

Achenbach, T. The classification of children's psychiatric symptoms: A factor-analytic study. *Psychological Monographs*, 1966, *80* (7, Whole No. 615)

Achenbach T. The Child Behavior Profile: I. Boys aged 6–11. *Journal of Consulting and Clinical Psychology*, 1978, *46*, 478–488

Achenbach, T. The Child Behavior Profile: An empirically based system for assessing children's behavioral problems and competencies. *International Journal of Mental Health*, 1979, *7*, 24–42

Achenbach T. A junior MMPI? Review of multidimensional description of child personality. A manual for the Personality Inventory for children by RD Wirt, D Lachar, JK Kleindinst, & PL Seat, and Actuarial assessment of child and adolescent personality: An interpretive guide for the Personality Inventory for Children profile by D Lachar & CL Gdowski. *Journal of Personality Assessment*, 1981, *45*, 332–333

Achenbach, T. *Developmental Psychopathology, (3rd ed.).* New York: John Wiley & Sons, 1982

Achenbach, T, & Edelbrock, C. The Child Behavior Profile: II. Boys aged 12–16 and girls aged 6–11 and 12–16. *Journal of Consulting and Clinical Psychology*, 1979, *47*, 223–233

American Psychiatric Association. *Diagnostic and statistical manual of mental disorders DSM-III (Third ed.).* Washington: APA, 1980

Anastasi, A. *Psychological testing* (5th ed.). New York: MacMillan, 1982

Angoff, WH, & Ford, SF. Item-race interaction on a test of scholastic aptitude. *Journal of Educational Measurement,* 1973, *10,* 95–106

Barnett, DW. *Nondiscriminatory multifactored assessment.* New York: Human Sciences Press, 1983

Binet A, & Simon T. Methods nouvelles pour le diagnostic du niveau intellectual des anormaux. *Annee psychologigue,* 1905, *11,* 191–244

Bogen, JE. Some educational implications of hemispheric specialization. In MC Wittrock (Ed.), *The human brain.* New Jersey: Prentice-Hall, 1977

Bolton, TL. The growth of memory in school children. *American Journal of Psychology,* 1891–1892, *4,* 362–380

Buckley, KJ, & Oakland, TD. *Contrasting localized norms for Mexican-American children on the ABIC.* Paper presented at the meeting of the American Psychological Association, San Francisco, August 1977

Carlson, C, & Lahey, B. Factor structure of teacher rating scales for children. *School Psychology Review, 1983, 12,* 285–292

Conners, C. A teacher rating scale for use in drug studies in children. *American Journal of Psychiatry,* 1969, *126,* 884–888

Cruickshank, WM. *Learning disabilities in home, school, and community.* Syracuse: Syracuse University Press, 1977

Das, JP, Kirby, J, & Jarman, RF. *Simultaneous and successive cognitive processes.* New York: Academic Press, 1979

DeKrey, S, & Ehly, S. Factor cluster classification of profiles from Personality Inventory for Children in a school setting. *Psychological Reports,* 1981, *48,* 843–846

Doll, EA. *The measurement of social competence.* Minneapolis: American Guidance Service, 1953

Doll, EA. *Vineland Social Maturity Scale: Manual of directions (rev. ed.).* Minneapolis: American Guidance Service, 1965

DuBois, PJ. *A history of psychological testing.* Boston: Allyn and Bacon, 1970

Edelbrock, C. Problems and issues in using rating scales to access child personality and psychopathology. *School Psychology Review,* 1983, *12,* 293–299

Education for All Handicapped Children Act (P.L. 94–142), 1975

Esquirol, JED. *Des maladies manetales consideree sous les rapports medical, hygienique, et medico-legal (2 vols.).* Paris: Bailliere, 1838

Feuerstein, R. *The dynamic assessment of retarded performers.* Baltimore: University Park Press, 1979

Gaddes, WH. Neuropsychology, fact or mythology, educated help or hindrance? *School Psychology Review,* 1981, *10,* 322–330

Gazzaniga, MS. Review of the split brain. In MC Wittrock (Ed.), *The human brain.* New Jersey: Prentice-Hall, 1977

Gilbert, JA. Researches on the mental and physical development of school children. *Studies from the Yale Psychology Laboratory,* 1894, *2,* 40–100

Givens, T, & Ward, LC. Stability of the AAMD Adaptive Behavior Scale, Public School Version. *Psychology in the Schools,* 1982, *19,* 166–169

Golden, CJ. The Luria-Nebraska Children's Battery: Theory and Formulation. In GW Hynd & JE Obrzut (Eds.), *Neuropsychological Assessment of the School-Age Child.* New York: Grune & Stratton, 1981

Golden, CJ, Hammeke, TA, & Purish, AD. *The Luria-Nebraska Neuropsychological Battery Manual.* Los Angeles: Western Psychological Services, 1980

Greene, R, Martin, P, Bennett, S, & Shaw, J. A computerized scoring system for the Personality Inventory for Children. *Educational and Psychological Measurement*, 1981, *41*, 233–235

Group For the Advancement of Psychiatry. Psychopathological disorders in childhood: Theoretical considerations and a proposed classification. GAP Report No. 62, 1966

Guilford, JP. *The nature of human intelligence.* New York: McGraw-Hill, 1967

Hathaway, S, & McKinley, J. *The Minnesota Multiphasic Personality Inventory manual.* New York: Psychological Corporation, 1951

Horn, JL, & Cattell, RB. Refinement and test of the theory of fluid and crystallized general intelligence. *Journal of Educational Psychology*, 1966, *57*, 253–270

Jastak, JF, & Jastak, S. *The Wide Range Achievement Test* (rev. ed.). Wilmington, Del.: Jastak Associates, 1978

Kaufman, AS. *Intelligence testing with the WISC-R.* New York: Wiley-Interscience, 1979

Kaufman, AS & Kaufman, NL. *Kaufman Assessment Battery for Children.* Circle Pines, Min.: American Guidance Service, 1983

Kaufman, AS, & Kaufman NL. *Kaufman Assessment Battery for Children—Spanish Edition.* Circle Pines, Min.: American Guidance Service, 1984

Kazdin, A. Artifact, bias and complexity of assessment: The ABC's of reliability. *Journal of Applied Behavior Analysis*, 1977, *10*, 141–150

Kazdin, A. *Research design in clinical psychology.* New York: Harper & Row, 1980

Kim, Y, Anderson, H, & Bashaw, W. Social maturity, achievement, and basic ability. *Educational and Psychological Measurement*, 1968, *28*, 535–543

Lachar, D. *Personality Inventory for Children: Revised format manual supplement.* Los Angeles: Western Psychological Services, 1982

Lachar, D, Butkus, M, & Hryhorczuk, L. Objective personality assessment of children: An exploratory study of the Personality Inventory for Children (PIC) in a child psychiatric setting. *Journal of Personality Assessment*, 1978, *42*, 529–536

Lachar, D, & Gdowski, C. *Actuarial assessment of child and adolescent personality: An interpretive guide for the Personality Inventory for Children profile.* Los Angeles: Western Psychological Services, 1979

Lachar, D, & Wirt, R. A data-based analysis of the psychometric performance of the Personality Inventory for Children (PIC): An alternative to the Achenbach review. *Journal of Personality Assessment*, 1981, *45*, 614–616

Lambert, NM, Windmiller, M, Cole, L, & Figueroa, RA. Standardization of a public school version of the AAMD Adaptive Behavior Scale. *Mental Retardation*, 1975, *13*, 3–7

Leon, G, Kendall, P, & Garber, J. Depression in children: Parent, teacher and child perspectives. *Journal of Abnormal child Psychology*, 1980, *8*, 221–235

Lezak, MD. *Neuropsychological assessment.* New York: Oxford University Press, 1976

Luria, AR. *Higher cortical functions in man.* New York: Basic Books, 1966

Maloney, M, & Ward, M. *Psychological Assessment: A conceptual approach.* New York: Oxford Press, 1976

Mash, EJ, & Terdal, LG. (Eds.). *Behavioral assessment of childhood disorders.* New York: Guilford, 1981

Mercer, JR, & Lewis, JF. *System of Multicultural Pluralistic Assessment.* New York: Psychological Corporation, 1978

Miller, L. Dimensions of psychopathology in middle childhood. *Psychological Report*, 1967, *21*, 891–903

Miller, L. School Behavior Checklist: An inventory of deviant behavior for elementary school children. *Journal of Consulting and Clinical Psychology*, 1972, *38*, 134–144

Mykelbust, HR. (Ed.). *Progress in learning disabilities, Vol. I.* New York: Grune & Stratton, 1967

Naglieri, JA. Concurrent and predictive validity of the Kaufmann Assessment Battery for Children with a Native American Navajo sample. *Journal of School Psychology*, 1984, in press

Neisser, V. *Cognitive psychology.* New York: Appleton-Century-Corfts, 1967

O'Leary, K, & Johnson, S. Psychological assessment. In HC Quay, & JS Werry, (Eds.), *Psychopathological disorders of childhood* (2nd ed.) New York: Wiley, 1979

Ornstein, R. *The psychology of consciousness.* San Francisco: WH Freeman, 1972

Peterson, D. Behavior problems of middle childhood. *Journal of Consulting Psychology*, 1961, *25*, 205–209

Piaget, J. *The origins of intelligence in the child.* New York: International Universities Press, 1952

Porter, J. *Identification of subtypes of learning disabled children: A multivariate analysis of patterns of personality functioning.* Doctoral dissertation, University of Windsor, 1980

Quay, H. A dimensional approach to behavior disorder: The Revised Behavior Problem Checklist. *School Psychology Review*, 1983, *12*, 244–249

Sattler, JM. *Assessment of children's intelligence and special abilities* (2nd ed.). Boston: Allyn and Bacon, 1982

Seguine, E. *Idiocy: Its treatment by the psychological method.* (Reprinted from original ed. of 1866). New York: Bureau of Publications, Teachers College, Columbia University, 1907

Sparrow, SS, Balla, DA, & Cicchetti, DV. *Vineland Adaptive Behavior Scales.* Circle Pines, Minn.: American Guidance Service, 1984

Sperry, RW. Hemisphere deconnection and unit in conscious awareness. *American Psychologist*, 1968, *23*, 723–733

Spring, C, Blunden, D, Greenberg, L, & Yellin, A. Validity and norms of a hyperactivity rating scale. *Journal of Special Education*, 1977, *11*, 313–321

Sternberg, RJ. Testing and cognitive psychology. *American Psychologist*, 1981, *36*, 1181–1189

Swift, M, & Spivack, G. The assessment of achievement-related classroom behavior. *Journal of Special Education*, 1968, *2*, 137–154

Wechsler D. *Wechsler-Bellevue Scale of Intelligence.* New York: Psychological Corporation, 1946

Wechsler, D. *Manual for the Wechsler Intelligence Scale for Children-Revised.* New York: Psychological Corporation, 1974

Wirt, R, & Broen, W. *Booklet for the Personality Inventory for Children.* Minneapolis: Authors, 1958

Wirt, R, & Lachar, D. The personality inventory for children: Development and clinical applications. In P McReynolds (Ed.), *Advances in psychological assessment.* San Francisco: Jossey-Bass, 1981

Wirt, R, Lachar, D, Klinedinst, J, & Seat, P. *Multidimensional description of child personality: A manual for the Personality Inventory for Children.* Los Angeles: Western Psychological Services, 1977

Wissler, C. The correlation of mental and physical traits. *Psychological Monographs*, 1901, *3*, (6, Whole No. 16)

Wright, BD, Meed, RJ, & Draber, RE. *Detecting and correcting test item bias with a logistic response model.* University of Chicago Research Memorandum #22, 1976

Alan E. Kazdin

Recent Advances in Child Behavior Therapy

Child behavior therapy is an approach toward treatment and evaluation of therapeutic change. The central characteristic of behavior therapy is an empirical approach toward the investigation of clinical problems and therapy techniques. There is no single substantive position, etiological view, narrow set of techniques, or codified series of propositions to which one can point that encapsulates the field. Consequently, the scope of the field is extraordinarily broad and includes many different, and often competing, conceptual views and treatment techniques that are applied to the full gamut of problems seen in clinical settings.

The purpose of the present chapter is to identify the characteristics of child behavior therapy and the range of conceptual views and treatment approaches. Recent advances in identifying effective treatments and factors that contribute to their efficacy are emphasized. Also, complexities in evaluating treatment outcome in child behavior therapy are addressed. Along with advances in outcome research, the present chapter discusses issues and limitations raised by current research in child behavior therapy.

CHARACTERISTICS OF CHILD BEHAVIOR THERAPY

Behavior therapy has been difficult to characterize with any singular definition or delimited focus (Kazdin & Wilson, 1978). In child behavior therapy, few characteristics can be identified that uniformly encompass all of the field. Even so, several characteristics can be identified tentatively. Any single characteristic does not necessarily capture all of the conceptual views, clinical techniques, or treatment foci. Yet, as a whole, several features convey why child behavior therapy can be meaningfully delineated as an approach that departs from traditional models of child treatment.

Conceptual Views

Child behavior therapy draws heavily from diverse conceptual models regarding the bases for behavior and therapeutic change. At the most general level, abnormal child behavior is assumed to be on a continuum with, or qualitatively similar to, normal behavior. The task for behavior therapy is thus to understand behavior per se and the factors that account for its emergence, maintenance, and alteration. Knowledge of the factors within the context of behavior therapy, of course, is ultimately applied toward therapeutic ends. The assumption of the continuity of normal and abnormal behavior does not commit one to any particular conceptual position. Indeed, within behavior therapy, psychology serves as the broad basis from which many different theoretical views are drawn.

For years, within behavior therapy the conceptual positions were cast largely as extensions of alternative types of learning including classical conditioning, operant conditioning, and vicarious learning. There are difficulties in adhering too closely to particular paradigms or models despite their initial heuristic value. Within the realm of basic psychological theory and research, learning paradigms are undergoing basic reconceptualization and consideration. The above paradigms are not necessarily exhaustive and in many instances are not entirely distinct. Also, when learning paradigms are extended to explain child behavior problems or clinical techniques, they are often stretched to the point that their utility is unclear.

For expository purposes, current views within child behavior therapy can be cast generally as mediational and nonmediational. Nonmediational views focus on the connections between environmental or situational events and behaviors. Operant conditioning, which views behavior as a function of its consequences, represents a nonmediational view. Child behavior problems can be viewed as deficits or excesses in performance and altered directly through the application of antecedent and consequent events. Mediational views emphasize the cognitive underpinnings of behavior. Environmental events exert influence in mediational views but are processed by the child whose perceptions, plans, goals, beliefs, expectations, self-statements, and attributions influence their effects. It is largely the cognitive processes that imbue the event with meaning and determine the impact the event will have.

The dominant view within child behavior therapy can be referred to as a social learning theory of behavior. Rather than a theory that makes concrete predictions, social learning reflects a broad orientation that recognizes the importance of both cognitive and environmental influences and their reciprocal interaction (Bandura, 1977). Social learning theory has as its hallmark the integration of diverse types of learning processes. Primacy has been given to cognitive processes as the underlying basis for the acquisition and persistence of behavior. The primacy of cognitive mechanisms is, however, by no means universally endorsed within the field.

Primacy of Behavior

Within child behavior therapy, overt behavior is given primacy in different ways. Clinical problems are operationalized in terms of overt behavioral referents whenever possible. Child problems such as fear and avoidance, autism, depression, enuresis, and others are viewed primarily as problems in behavior. This does not mean that problems are viewed solely in terms of overt actions. Many clinical problems encompass subjective experience and psychophysiologic concomitants, as for example, in anxiety reactions. However, overt behavior is emphasized as the basis for seeking treatment, identifying the treatment focus, and evaluating treatment outcomes.

Typically, evaluation of child behavior therapy relies on multiple channels of assessment and may include self-report, overt behavior, psychophysiologic responses, and other modalities, as relevant to the problem (Mash & Terdal, 1981). Overt behavior usually is emphasized, especially samples of performance that reflect the child's functioning in everyday situations. For example, it may be important to show that impulsive children have changed in their approach to problems on laboratory measures or feel differently about themselves after treatment. However, the major criterion to evaluate the impact of treatment is the effect on performance in the situations in which behavior was identified initially as problematic.

Use of Paraprofessionals

Many applications of treatment involve meeting with children in individual therapy sessions, similar to traditional models of treatment. More commonly, therapy involves working directly with and training those persons who are responsible for the care, management, education, and training of children. Parents and teachers in particular, frequently serve as the agents of change within child behavior therapy.

Several different factors have pointed to the need to train those who are in contact with children. First, parents, teachers, institutional staff, and peers have been shown to develop and support many of the problem behaviors identified as worthy of intervention (e.g., obstinacy, tantrums, antisocial behavior). Hence, changing the behaviors of those in contact with the child is often critical to effective treatment. Second, treatment effects often can be more readily accomplished in the naturalistic setting than in the therapist's office. Parents and teachers have immediate access to the problems as they occur and can bring to bear potent events (e.g., their own attention and affection) to promote appropriate behaviors. Third, behavioral problems are often situation specific. For example, a child who is "hyperactive" at home may not be so at school or vice versa. Consequently, treatments need to be designed for and implemented in those situations in which behavior is a problem. Application of treatment in the home or at school is designed to focus on the behavior-situation unit to effect the requisite change. When treatment is conducted in a special setting, the attempt is made to encourage extension of the treatment outside of settings where the behaviors ultimately need to be performed.

In passing, it is worth noting that peers may also be involved in the treatment of the target child. Peers represent an important source of influence and are often incorporated into treatment directly. In diverse applications of behavior therapy, peers have been trained to help develop behaviors (e.g., social interaction) in group situations where their impact can be harnessed. As direct agents of change, peers have been effective in altering a variety of behaviors including deportment at home and at school, social interaction, and academic performance (Kazdin, 1984; Strain, 1981).

Directive and Active Treatment Prescriptions

A common feature among child behavior therapy techniques is the use of directive and active treatment prescriptions. Treatments provide prescriptions about what children and/or their caretakers need to do to produce therapeutic change. Techniques do not rely heavily on such therapeutic processes as catharsis, insight, the therapeutic relationship, and attributional processes to produce change over the course of treatment. To be sure, any of these processes might be important during the course of therapy and contribute specific beneficial effects in their own right. Such processes, however, are not viewed as carrying the major burden of producing change in the problem behaviors. Rather, explicit training experiences are prescribed in treatment. Therapy sessions are frequently used as the context in which actions for change are planned and even rehearsed.

The treatment model for many child behavior therapy techniques is that the child or persons who are responsible for his or her care must do something (behave) differently to develop the desired behaviors. Often extensive opportunities for rehearsal and practice are included in treatment. Alternatively, opportunities to provide consequences for performance of the desired responses are arranged in everyday situations. Therapeutic change is conceptualized as learning new behaviors that are to be performed in the natural environment.

Scope of Child Behavior Therapy

Research in child behavior therapy represents an area of tremendous growth and breadth. A wide range of techniques, clinical problems and settings have been studied (Ollendick & Cerny, 1981; Ross, 1981). The clinical problems for which outcome research is available include hyperactivity, fears and phobias, social skills deficits, antisocial behavior and delinquency, habit disorders, autism and schizophrenia, mental retardation, and a variety of physical illnesses and health-related problems. Within particular clinical problem areas, multiple techniques often exist with their own literature. Treatments are based on multiple variations of reinforcement, punishment, modeling, desensitization, flooding, rehearsal, cognitive therapy, self-control strategies, and others. Finally, treatments are applied in diverse settings that include the home, school, group living arrangements, institutions, and the community at large. The diversity of child behavior therapy and the scope of outcome research preclude adequately covering the field in depth.* To convey the range of techniques and the diverse conceptual positions they reflect, the present chapter reviews one major area of research, namely, the treatment of conduct problems. The area encompasses many specific behavioral problems and the application of a variety of treatment techniques.

TREATMENT OF CONDUCT PROBLEMS: A CASE STUDY IN CHILD BEHAVIOR THERAPY

The term "conduct problems" has no uniform definition within behavior therapy but refers generally to children who act out and evince aggressive or oppositional behaviors, tantrums, excessive whining, teas-

---

*For further elaboration of child behavior therapy, its techniques and breadth of applications, the reader is referred elsewhere (e.g., Lahey & Kazdin, 1977, 1979, 19′ 1981, 1982; Ollendick & Cerny, 1981; Pikoff, 1980; Ross, 1981). Also, research in the is published in several behavior therapy journals. A journal devoted exclusively topic is *Child and Family Behavior Therapy*.

ing, arguing, and so on. Such behaviors obviously can vary greatly in severity from mild forms, which try the patience of parents and teachers in the "normal" home or classroom, to severely aggressive behavior leading to serious injury to others.

Within the mental health professions, one framework for delineating severity of aggressive behavior is the description of conduct disorder children, as defined by the *Diagnostic and Statistical Manual of Mental Disorders* (DSM III) (American Psychiatric Association, 1980). Conduct disorder represents a constellation of symptoms or behaviors that has been delineated in several clinical and multivariate diagnostic systems (e.g., Achenbach, 1978; Group for the Advancement of Psychiatry, 1966; Quay, 1979). The major characteristic of conduct disorders is violation of the basic rights of others or rules and societal norms. In DSM III, aggressive and nonaggressive subtypes are distinguished. The aggressive subtype refers to children who engage in physical violence against other persons and property, including vandalism and firesetting. The non-aggressive subtype refers to children who consistently break rules as reflected in truancy, running away, stealing and substance abuse, but who are not physically violent with others. Diagnosis of conduct disorder depends on a repetitive and persistent pattern of antisocial behavior, operationalized for at least six months' duration.

Antisocial behavior in children and adolescents represents an extremely important treatment focus. First, aggressive, oppositional, and antisocial behaviors in general represent the most frequent referral problems for outpatient clinics; they encompass from one third to one half of referrals (Gilbert, 1957; Herbert, 1978; Robins, 1981). Second, among the many childhood disorders, antisocial behaviors tend to be relatively stable over time (Graham & Rutter, 1973; Olweus, 1979; Robins, 1966). The stability of conduct problems departs from other disorders that often are age specific (e.g., many fears). Third, antisocial behaviors portend other problems of adulthood including psychoses, alcoholism, and criminal behavior (e.g., Robins, 1979; Wolfgang, Figlio, & Sellin, 1972). Finally, the long-term effects of severe conduct problem behavior not only have untoward consequences for the persons themselves, but also for their children (Robins, 1981). Conduct problem males father as many children as other men (despite their higher rates of marital disruption), and their children have increased risks for childhood deviance and antisocial behavior.

From a clinical perspective, the prevalence, persistence, and prognosis of conduct problems make identification of effective treatment an especially important area for investigation. From a social perspective, treatment for conduct problems is also critical because antisocial behavior may be the most costly of childhood disorders to society (Robins, 1981).

Because a significant proportion of severely aggressive children eventually is in contact with adult mental health and criminal justice systems, the monetary costs of managing or containing these persons as adults are high.

Within child behavior therapy, many different techniques have been developed to treat aggressive and oppositional behavior. The techniques illustrate the diversity of conceptual approaches within the field and the manifold settings in which treatment is conducted. Major treatment approaches include operant conditioning, parent management training, social skills training, and cognitively based therapy.

Operant Conditioning

Operant conditioning approaches to the treatment of conduct problems focus on the application of positive reinforcement and/or punishment techniques. The goal of the treatment is to eliminate inappropriate behavior while concomitantly developing prosocial behavior. Positive reinforcement procedures, or the delivery of consequences that increase behavior, are frequently used to enhance socially desirable behaviors of children. Positive reinforcement usually consists of delivering praise or material goods, such as candy or toys, contingent upon socially appropriate behavior.

Grieger, Kauffman, and Greiger (1976) provide a good example of a positive reinforcement program in which the major reinforcer was peer praise. In their program, kindergarten children were encouraged by their teacher to report the cooperative ("friendly") behaviors of their classmates. The reporting of friendly behavior was considered to be reinforcing because of the positive peer and class attention. The identified children also received a badge with a happy face that they selected on their own. In the next phase, the teacher asked the children to report unfriendly acts instead of positive behaviors. No specific punishment was provided. In the final phase, friendly acts were again reported by the children but at this point no happy-face badges were given. The results indicated that when peer attention and praise were provided for friendly behavior, aggressive behavior decreased markedly. When unfriendly behavior was reported the aggressive behavior returned to preintervention levels. Thus peer attention for cooperative behavior was an effective consequence for decreasing aggressive behavior.

Token reinforcement often is used to alter conduct problems in children at home and in the classroom. Tokens consist of generalized conditioned reinforcers in the form of points, tickets, money, or stars that can be exchanged for various rewards, privileges, and activities, referred to as back-up reinforcers. For example, Bristol (1976) reported a program for an 8-year-old boy in a second grade classroom who constantly engaged in fighting. The program involved the cooperation of parents, the teacher, and the child who agreed to the contingencies and signed a contract to that effect. Each morning the child received a card with a smiling face on it. In the morning, at lunch, and at the end of the day, the teacher signed the card if the boy had not engaged in fighting. The teacher's signatures served as points that could be accumulated toward back-up rewards such as being a student helper in class, going to the library for free reading, or staying up 15 minutes later at bed time. Fighting decreased markedly when the program was in effect and was no longer evident for the last three weeks of the program. A report obtained seven months after the program was terminated indicated that the boy was doing well without any special program.

The above programs illustrate two different general approaches in using reinforcement to reduce aggressiveness. First, reinforcement can be delivered directly for appropriate behavior that is incompatible with the undesired behaviors. Examples would include providing reinforcing consequences for engaging in cooperative behavior or appropriate social interaction. Alternatively, reinforcement can be delivered for periods of time in which the undesired behaviors fail to occur. Both types of programs have been very effective in altering conduct problems.

In many instances, operant techniques have focused primarily on decreasing inappropriate behaviors through the application of various punishment techniques such as time out from reinforcement, response cost, and overcorrection. Time out usually refers to a social isolation procedure in which the child is removed from the situation and placed where little environmental stimulation is available for a brief, fixed period of time contingent on some undesirable behavior. Many other variations of time out exist including withdrawal of attention, physical restraint, withdrawal of specific reinforcers such as music or toys, and contingent observation, in which the child is required to watch further activities without being premitted to participate (Kazdin, 1984).

For example, Drabman and Spitalnik (1973) applied a social isolation program to a class of 9- to 11-year-old aggressive boys in a residential psychiatric setting. When a target behavior such as hitting another child occurred, a classroom observer unobtrusively signaled the teacher. The teacher immediately named the child and said, "You have misbehaved. You must leave the class." The child was then escorted without further comment to a small, dimly lit isolation room (a music practice room). After 10 minutes, the child was returned to the class, where observations began again. This procedure resulted in a marked decrease in aggressive acts after 16 days of the program.

Response cost is another type of punishment used to decrease unwanted behavior and is often used in conjunction with a token system. Response cost involves taking away a previously acquired reinforcer contingent upon an undesirable response. The child is given a set of reinforcers (usually points or tokens) at the beginning of specified periods, such as once each day. For every performance of the undesired behavior, the child is required to forfeit some of the reinforcers. In some cases, accumulated points from token reinforcement programs may be forfeited. At the end of the time period, the child exchanges his or her remaining points for back-up reinforcers.

Burchard and Barrera (1972) used a response-cost token program with 11 mildly retarded adolescents who had a history of antisocial behavior. Swearing, disobedience, and aggression were identified as behaviors to be eliminated. If a child engaged in one of the target behaviors, this was immediately verbalized by supervisors, and the child was required to give up either 5 or 30 of his tokens, or take 5 or 30 minutes of time out. Each child experienced each type of penalty over the course of the program. Response cost and time out were both effective in reducing aggressive behaviors, with the more severe penalties resulting in greater behavior change.

Overcorrection has also been used to eliminate aggressive behaviors. As originally conceived, overcorrection for disruptive behavior incorporated two components, positive practice and restitution (Foxx & Azrin, 1972). The goal is to punish unwanted behavior while providing practice opportunities for more appropriate behavior. This technique consists of requiring the child to repeat and/or elaborate upon a response that he or she failed to make or gave incorrectly.

An illustration of a typical overcorrection procedure is one applied by Ollendick and Matson (1976). The child was an aggressive preschool boy who engaged in frequent hitting and temper tantrums. During baseline observations, the boy's mother involved him in a play activity and used her usual methods of discipline. The child repeatedly engaged in aggressive behavior. The boy was required to make restitution for aggressive acts by patting the hit area for 30 seconds and apologizing 10 times each time he struck his mother. With this strategy, aggression decreased slightly. Finally, the child was asked to engage in the above restitution and then raise and lower the arm he had used for hitting 40 times. This final overcorrection method eliminated all of the child's hitting behaviors.

Several other reinforcement and punishment procedures have been used effectively to alter aggressive and oppositional behavior in the classroom, the home, and institutional settings. Characteristically, the techniques establish relatively rapid control over behavior. However, they are not always effective. For aggressive and oppositional behavior, investigators have occasionally reported that reinforcement techniques do not work (Herbert, Pinkston, Hayden, Sajwaj, Pinkston, Cordua, & Jackson, 1973; Wahler & Fox, 1980). Typically, reinforcement is more effective when supplemented with mild punishment procedures to suppress deviant behavior.

Although reinforcement and punishment techniques often produce dramatic results while they are in effect, the treatment gains are often lost when the program is terminated or the child leaves the setting. Additional evidence is needed that treatment effects can be sustained. Several procedures have been identified to promote long-term maintenance of treatment effects and their transfer to other settings (Kazdin, 1984; Stokes & Baer, 1977). However, research has yet to emerge demonstrating that specific techniques guarantee long-term maintenance.

Parent Management Training

Parent management training has received the greatest attention and empirical support among alternative behavioral techniques for conduct problems. Parent management training consists in large part in the application of operant techniques in the home. The parents alter the contingencies of reinforcement and punishment that influence child behavior. However, the basis for parent management training is broader and reflects the restructuring of the more pervasive maladaptive parent-child interaction patterns that may foster sustained deviance in the child.

Patterson and his colleagues have observed interaction in families with conduct problem children and have identified patterns of coercive exchanges among family members. Typically, the child performs a coercive behavior (e.g., manipulative or aggressive act) that is aversive to the parents. The parents unwittingly support this behavior. They comply or succumb to the demands of the child in an effort to terminate the child's aversive behavior. Through continued exchanges, coercive behaviors increase in frequency and escalate in magnitude. In addition, little parent reinforcement is provided for prosocial child behavior (Patterson, 1976). The problematic interaction of parents with their conduct problem children, their inappropriate use of reinforcement and punishment, and the correlation of these interaction patterns with deviant child behavior have been demonstrated in several investigations (Farrington, 1978; Hetherington & Martin, 1979).

Parent management training alters the pattern of parent-child interaction to promote prosocial behavior in the child. In the usual training program, parents are provided with a written manual on parent management practices or basic readings on the topic. Typically, parents are then assisted by the therapist in the identification, observation, and re-cording of undesirable behaviors. When these areas are mastered, par-ents are finally aided in applying operant techniques to the problems for which they have sought help. This may occur through parental in-teraction with the child in the clinic or in the home, or training may be provided through role-play. Application of the techniques is sometimes modeled by the therapist. Parents bring their recorded data to training sessions so that progress may be monitored by the therapist, and sug-gestions are made to improve treatment.

Several different parent training programs have been implemented (Conger, 1981). The program by Patterson and his colleagues has re-ceived considerable attention and nicely illustrates parent training to manage aggressive and antisocial children (ages 5 to 13 years) (Patterson & Fleischman, 1979). The program includes three main stages. First, parents are required to read a programmed text about child manage-ment and to pass a test demonstrating knowledge of the material. Second, they are taught to identify, observe, and graph both desirable and un-desirable behaviors of the child. Finally, they are guided in the imple-mentation of operant techniques (time out, positive reinforcement, and response-cost) to alter the child's behaviors. Follow-up is conducted for periods of up to two years, with booster treatment provided as needed. Observations of parent-child interactions are conducted by independent raters in the home before, during, and after treatment.

Reviews of the literature on parent training strongly support its efficacy for reducing a wide range of problem child behaviors (Bernstein, 1982; Patterson & Fleischman, 1979). Parents have been successfully taught to use contingency management procedures with their children using such techniques as differential reinforcement of other behavior, time out, and giving more effective verbal commands. The behaviors that parents have been able to modify include temper tantrums, non-compliance and oppositionalism, and aggression against persons or property.

Parent management training has not been effective in all applica-tions. Single parents or parents in marital distress, and parents who are poorly educated or of low socioeconomic status have often been unre-sponsive to parent management training (e.g., Patterson, Cobb, & Ray, 1973; Wahler & Afton, 1980). Families of severely disturbed children often have a variety of problems other than the behavior of the child including poor living conditions, marital discord, psychopathology or incarceration of one or more of the parents, and so on. These other factors have marked impact on the functioning of the family and im-portant implications for the efficacy of parent management training

(Griest, Forehand, Rogers, Breiner, Furey, & Williams, 1982; Patterson & Fleischman, 1979; Wahler & Graves, 1983), a topic dealt with in greater detail later.

Social Skills Training

Social skills training refers to a variety of interventions that focus on deficits in interpersonal behaviors including social withdrawal, inassertiveness, and aggressive behavior. Generally, the goal of training is to develop positive social behaviors. The specific behaviors that are trained vary as a function of the individual child's specific deficits. Training usually combines multiple procedures to develop the desired behavior. The procedures include instructions on how to perform the responses, modeling of appropriate behavior on the part of the therapist, direct rehearsal by the child, therapist feedback to improve the child's response, and reinforcement by the therapist for correct performance. The sequence is completed repeatedly within the context of treatment sessions until the large set of target behaviors is acquired across several different interpersonal situations.

For example, Bornstein, Bellack, and Hersen (1980) conducted social skills training with four aggressive child psychiatric inpatients. The children were assessed for appropriately responding in small group interactions and role-play situations before treatment. They were rated on eye contact, tone of voice, requests, facial expression, and overall assertiveness. During training, each target behavior was modeled by the therapist in a role-play scene. The child then role-played the scene and received verbal feedback about his performance on the target behavior. The therapist and child discussed the feedback to ensure the child's understanding. Rehearsal was continued until the therapist was satisfied with the child's response, which was then highly praised. Then a new situation was introduced. Target behaviors were treated one at a time until their mastery, with booster training given as necessary during the training of other behaviors. The social skills training program improved the specific target behaviors. Also, overall assertiveness improved by the end of training when the target behaviors had been improved.

The model of training illustrated in a social skills treatment regimen is important to highlight in passing. Treatment provides multiple opportunities for the child to rehearse and practice the requisite behaviors. The purpose of the sessions is to develop specific skills across a large number of situations. Different antecedent events (prompts, instructions, exemplars through modeling) and consequences (feedback, reinforcement) are used to develop the behaviors. The treatment model is active and directive and relies heavily on repeated practice on the part of the child.

Social skills training has received a great deal of empirical support. Most of the applications have been with children who evince deficits in the form of social withdrawal and inassertiveness (Combs & Slaby, 1977; Michelson, Sugai, Wood, & Kazdin, 1983; Rinn & Markle, 1979). Thus, whether the techniques can eliminate severe acting out behaviors such as repetitive aggressive acts remains to be well established.

Cognitive Therapy

Conduct problems such as impulsiveness and aggressive behavior have been treated with a variety of techniques that are based on teaching children cognitive strategies to control their behavior. Several variations are available and are referred to in various ways including cognitive therapy, self-instruction training, problem-solving therapy, and others (Kendall & Williams, 1981; Kennedy, 1982; Spivack, Platt, & Shure, 1976). The techniques share as a common theme the focus on cognitive processes believed to underlie aggressive behavior.

Cognitive therapy has been influenced greatly by the work of several investigators who have focused on the development of the self-regulatory functions of speech (see Zivin, 1979). Self-regulatory speech refers to those aspects of language used by the child to monitor, control, organize, and plan behavior. The work of Luria (1981) has been especially influential. Luria proposed that young children first learn to perform acts based on the verbal instructions of others. They then begin to use their own speech aloud to guide their behavior. Finally, children learn to fade overt statements into covert self-instructions, a strategy that is continued throughout adulthood.

Meichenbaum (1977) drew on the work of Luria to develop a program of self-statements to aid in the self-control of behavior. A self-instruction program with aggressive children consists of five components (Meichenbaum & Goodman, 1971). First, an adult model performs a task such as a maze or puzzle, while making certain statements aloud. The self-instructions include identifying the problem, labeling alternative solutions, evaluating solutions, choosing one solution, correcting errors, and providing self-reinforcement. The model may address specific aspects of the task at hand, or he or she may talk in more general terms. Following this demonstration, the child is guided by the model in performing the task. In the next two steps, the child completes the task on his or her own, first pronouncing the self-statements aloud and then whispering them. Finally, the child performs the task while making the statements covertly. Training begins with simple perceptual tasks and proceeds to more complex problems as basic skills are mastered. The child is given positive reinforcement for correct performance. In addition, a response-cost procedure may be used to decrease impulsive, incorrect behaviors (e.g., Kendall & Finch, 1978).

Camp, Blom, Herbert, and van Doorninck (1977) developed a "think-aloud" program of cognitive therapy for use with aggressive, impulsive children. The therapy program used modeling and behavioral rehearsal to teach the use of self-instructions for solving problems. Children were taught to ask and answer four basic questions: What is my problem?, What is my plan?, Am I using my plan?, How did I do? The therapists employed cognitive problems, interpersonal problem-solving games, and games requiring inhibition of impulses to teach self-instructional skills. After a 6-week period of treatment, cognitive therapy children improved significantly more than no-treatment control children on a variety of measures of impulsivity. However, no differences were evident on teacher ratings of classroom aggressive behavior.

Evidence supporting the efficacy of cognitive therapy is mixed (Hobbs, Moguin, Tyroler, & Lahey, 1980). Most studies hae been conducted with impulsive or hyperactive children. Meichenbaum and Goodman's (1971) cognitive training program with second graders displaying behavior problems resulted in decreased impulsivity, but error rates and classroom disruptive behaviors remained high. Kendall and Finch (1978) reported decreased impulsivity after their cognitive training program with emotionally disturbed children, but reanalysis, while controlling for initial level of impulsivity, failed to show significant behavior change (Abikoff, 1979). Taken together, the research to date indicates that the efficacy of cognitive training has yet to be established (Kennedy, 1982). Basic questions remain to be addressed about the contribution of cognitive processes and the success of treatment in altering performance on non-laboratory measures.

General Comments

The procedures discussed illustrate major techniques within child behavior therapy as they are applied to diverse conduct problems. The techniques represent different models and treatment procedures. Operant conditioning procedures emphasize the importance of environmental consequences in altering conduct problems. Parent management training extends the application of operant consequences, but is explicitly concerned with alteration of larger interaction patterns within the family. Social skills training focuses on the importance of direct rehearsal, practice, and feedback. Finally, self-instructional and problem-solving approaches emphasize the cognitive bases of performance.

Even though sharp distinctions might be drawn between the conceptual bases of the different techniques, considerable procedural overlap exists. For example, positive reinforcement procedures find their way into each of the techniques. In reinforcement techniques in applied settings, of course, consequences delivered by parents and teachers provide the major basis for developing prosocial behavior. In cognitively based techniques, reinforcement is used primarily within the treatment sessions to develop the child's use of problem-solving strategies. Essentially, reinforcement procedures are used as a means toward developing use of the strategies. It is the strategies, however, that are considered to promote prosocial behavior.

Although several techniques for diverse conduct problems currently exist, at this point there is no single procedure that can be recommended unequivocally for widespread use. Basic questions are still being asked about the effects of alternative procedures and their breadth of application. Parent management training, as noted earlier, is one of the more well-investigated treatments; its efficacy has been demonstrated in a large number of studies. Yet many parents—especially those whose children are extremely deviant—may not be viable candidates for parent management training, due in large part to their own problems of adjustment and stressful living conditions. Cognitive therapy may not be a viable alternative treatment for many children because of intellectual, cognitive, and reading difficulties that are beyond the boundary conditions for effective training of cognitive strategies. At this point, for all of the techniques, the family and child variables that dictate their optimal outcome warrant further attention.

RECENT ADVANCES

Within child behavior therapy, research has made several advances. Three areas where advances seem especially evident include the consideration of the role of parent and family variables in child behavior therapy, the broad effects treatment has on behavior, and expansion of the outcome criteria to evaluate therapeutic change.

Parent and Family Variables in Child Treatment

Child behavior therapy has been characterized by a relatively molecular level of analysis of child behavior, Typically, clinical problems are translated into discrete target behaviors of the child. In addition, treatment has tended to center on the child and his or her problems.) In different ways, through individual treatment sessions or by restructuring environmental contingencies, the child is the center of the focus. For many clinical problems, the focus on a molecular level of analysis and treatment of the "child's problem" has been extremely effective, perhaps especially for those problems that may be relatively circumscribed (e.g., many cases of enuresis, feeding problems). Recently, child behavior therapy has accorded greater attention to more molar variables and to the parents and family. The recent shift in focus in child behavior therapy to the broader parent, family, and system variables in which child behavior emerges can be seen in the treatment of conduct problem children. For such problems, as noted earlier, parent management training often has been applied effectively to alter contingencies to which the child is exposed at home. Researchers in this area have long recognized the importance of maladaptive interactions in the home in families of conduct problem children (Patterson, 1976). Even so, the impact of family variables in the identification and treatment of child problems has recently received increased attention. Parent and family variables are now recognized as playing a major role in the identification of childhood disorders as well as their effective treatment.

Increased evidence has suggested that parents' perception of child deviance, a critical step in identifying the target child and obtaining pretreatment assessment, may depend heavily on factors other than the child's actual range and level of deviance. In several studies, clinic-referred and nonclinic-referred children have been compared. As might be expected, parents of clinic-referred children perceive their children as more deviant than parents of their nonclinic counterparts (Doleys, Cartelli, & Doster, 1976; Lobitz & Johnson, 1975). Direct observation of the children has shown that parent perceptions of deviant behavior are reflected in differences between the two child groups. However, in terms of overt performance of deviant behavior, clinic and nonclinic samples overlap (Griest & Wells, 1983). Parent perceptions of deviance seem to discriminate the populations more sharply than do measures of overt behavior. Thus, these findings suggest the possibility that parent perceptions may depend on other factors than child behavior in the initial assessment of the child's problems (Rickard, Forehand, Wells, Griest, & McMahon, 1981).

Parent attitudes and expectancies seem to play a critical role in their reports of child deviance. For example, Cahill (1978) found that the behavior of normal children was more likely to be identified as problematic if the child's behavior and developmental progress did not meet the parent's level of expectations. Other studies have found that parent attitudes, expectancies, and beliefs discriminate among clinic-referred and nonclinic children (see Griest & Wells, 1983). Further work has revealed that parent psychopathology, such as depression and anxiety, and perceptions of marital discord influence parent perception of deviant child behavior (Griest, Forehand, Wells, & McMahon, 1980; O'-Leary & Emery, in press; Rickard et al., 1981). The above research has pointed to the critical nature of considering parent variables in identifying and assessing childhood problems. Interpretation of parent reports of the child's difficulties needs to be viewed in light of characteristics of the parents.

Beyond the initial identification of the child's problems, family variables have been shown repeatedly to be important in different aspects of treatment administration and evaluation. For example, pretreatment levels of maternal depression have been identified as a significant predictor of attrition in parent management training (McMahon, Forehand, Griest, & Wells, 1981) and the failure of parents to participate in follow-up assessment (Griest, Forehand, & Wells, 1981). However, much broader implications have been associated with investigation of parent variables in child behavior therapy.

Advances have been made as a result of some researchers devoting their attention to selected variables that mediate child treatment effects. Prominent among such work has been the research of Wahler and his colleagues who have focused their attention on the construct of *insularity* (Wahler & Afton, 1980). Insularity refers to characteristics of the parent(s) and entails both the quantity and quality of contact that the parents have with extrafamily members and community helping agencies. Insular parents tend to have relatively few contacts with extrafamily members and social agencies and the contacts they have generally are aversive to them. As might be expected, insularity is associated with several other characteristics including living at or near the poverty level, low educational attainment, residence in high crime areas, single-parent family, and others.

Insularity has been shown to have important implications for child behavior problems in the home. For example, Leske, Afton, Rogers, and Wahler[†] found an inverse relationship between the number of extrafamilial interactions of the mothers and parent-child problems in the home. The quality of the interactions outside the home has been shown to relate to parent-child problems as well. In fact, evaluation of per-

---

[†]Leske, G, Afton, A, Rogers, ES, & Wahler, RG *The interpersonal functioning of insular and noninsular families: Factors related to treatment success and failure.* Unpublished manuscript, University of Tennessee, Knoxville, 1978

formance on a daily basis has revealed that higher rates of positive friendship contacts that parents experience outside of the home are associated with lower rates of oppositional child behavior in the home. And negative contacts of the mother outside the home are associated with more aversive behavior of the mother in the home and greater coercive parent-child interaction (Wahler, 1980; Wahler, Hughey, & Gordon, 1981). Apparently, maternal insularity has important implications for parent-child interaction and the likely effects that treatment will have. In fact, insular mothers who have completed parent management training are less likely to maintain the gains over the course of follow-up (Wahler, 1980).

Increasingly, researchers have acknowledged the importance of family variables in child treatment. Parents of conduct problem children are more likely to be experiencing personal problems including psychopathology, environmental life stressors, marital discord, and others. Treatment of the deviant child behavior may need to address the associated parent and family problems. For example, Griest et al. (1982) compared the effectiveness of parent management training alone versus parent management training combined with an additional therapy component for the parents' problems. The additional therapy component focused on parent perception of the child's behavior, parent psychological adjustment, marital problems, and extrafamilial relationships. Parents who received training with the additional therapy component maintained their parent management training skills better at a 2-month follow-up than did parents who received parent training alone. Additional work of this sort will no doubt increase in the future to determine the ways in which marked and durable changes in family systems can be achieved.

In general, a major advance in child behavior is the consideration of the broader range of variables in conceptualizing clinical problems and the focus of treatment. The child is not the only source of the problem nor the only benefactor of treatment. An effective treatment that alters the behavior of the conduct problem child in the home is likely to produce broad changes. Indeed, parent management training does not merely alter specific contingencies applied to the child but major communication patterns in general. The effects of treatment often are evident well beyond the target child as, for example, reflected in improved behavior in siblings of the target child (Arnold, Levine, & Patterson, 1975), decreases in maternal psychopathology (Patterson & Fleischman, 1979), and improved marital adjustment (Forehand, Wells, McMahon, & Griest, in press). The broad focus and evaluation of treatment have only begun in child behavior therapy but already represent an important departure and advance from previous work.

Response Covariation

Assessment of child problems in behavior therapy recently has revealed important information about the organization of behavior. Research has demonstrated that alteration of one area of performance may have impact on several other areas as well, a phenomenon referred to as response covariation. For example, Sajwaj, Twardosz, and Burke (1972) observed multiple behaviors of a disturbed and mentally retarded preschool child who exhibited gross inattentiveness in class and poor academic skills. The teacher systematically ignored talking out, which effectively reduced its frequency. Seemingly unrelated behaviors changed when talking out was decreased. Specifically, initiation of conversations to other children and playing cooperatively increased. Yet, disruptive behaviors at other times of the day than when the program was conducted also increased.

Similarly, Becker, Turner, and Sajwaj (1978) found multiple effects of treating a 3-year-old girl with a history of ruminative vomiting. The child was well below her normal weight because of vomiting her meals. Rumination was decreased with a mild punishment contingency (squirt of lemon juice in the child's mouth when behavior that preceded regurgitation occurred). When rumination decreased, crying decreased, and smiling and spontaneous social interaction increased. Stereotypic play with objects and headslapping, however, increased as well.

The above examples illustrate that changes in selected target behaviors are often associated with a variety of other changes (for reviews, see Kazdin, 1982; Voeltz & Evans, 1982). The bases for the changes are unclear. The changes include some side effects that might be regarded as desirable and others that might be regarded as undesirable.

Within the context of child behavior therapy, Wahler and his colleagues have systematically investigated response covariation‡ (e.g., Kara & Wahler, 1977; Wahler, 1975). Wahler has examined the organization of behavior in deviant children who were treated in different settings. The work has revealed that behaviors are organized into clusters, i.e., a variety of responses that systematically covary (Wahler, Berland, & Coe, 1979). For example, Wahler (1975) observed children over an extended period (approximately 3 years) who were referred for treatment because of disruptive behavior. Observations were made of several behaviors at home and at school to determine correlations among different classes

---

‡Wahler, RG, & Fox, JJ. *Response structure in deviant child-parent relationships: Implications for family therapy.* Paper presented to the Nebraska Symposium on Motivation, University of Nebraska, Lincoln, October 1980

of responses. As an illustration, working on assignments at school for one child was positively correlated with engaging in self-stimulatory behaviors and negatively correlated with fiddling with objects, staring into space, and not interacting with others. The interrelationships among the behaviors could not be accounted for simply by the fact that the behaviors were incompatible with working. For this same child at home, several other behaviors were intercorrelated. Specifically, sustained play with toys was inversely associated with compliance with adult instructions, social interactions with adults and self-stimulation.

In general, Wahler found stable clusters of behavior that could be identified in the repertoires of individual children. The clusters differed among children, and for a given child, the clusters differed across settings. For two children studied by Wahler (1975), interventions that altered specific problem behavior at school affected other behaviors with which that behavior was correlated. Also, changes at school were associated with changes in behaviors at home. In one case, for example, improvements at school (e.g., decreases in oppositional behavior) were associated with increases in peer interactions at home. Both desirable and undesirable changes thus were evident. The major finding of the above research is that changes in behavior can alter correlated behaviors even though these latter behaviors are not focused on directly. Behavior changes that are positively correlated with the altered response are likely to change in the same direction; behaviors that are negatively correlated with the altered response are likely to show changes in the opposite direction (see Kara & Wahler, 1977).

Research on response covariation has potentially important implications for administering treatment. Changes in problems presented in treatment can be achieved in different ways. The most obvious way is to focus directly on the problem, the usual thrust of treatment, even though the presenting problem is defined quite differently across treatments. Alternatively, a particular problem area may be altered by focusing on a correlated area of performance. At first glance, there may be no obvious value in attempting to treat a problem indirectly by focusing on a correlated response. For some clinical disorders, however, the correlated behaviors that may influence the target problem may be more readily accessible or responsive to the intervention.

The clinical utility of focusing on correlates of performance was demonstrated by Wahler and Fox (1980), who treated children who were oppositional and engaged in aggressive and generally unruly behavior at home. Initial attempts to alter oppositional behavior directly by training parents to reward approprite social behavior and cooperative play failed. Indeed, oppositional behavior became worse when a program was developed to reinforce appropriate social interaction. Positive reinforcement for solitary play, which was negatively correlated with oppositional behavior, led to systematic and marked reductions in oppositional behavior.

Knowledge of responses that covary may provide important leads for treatment. In complex clinical cases, it is unlikely that treatment should focus either on the clinical problem or on concomitant behavior. Treatment effects may be accelerated by focusing on the problem behavior as well as on those behaviors with which it is correlated. Clinical outcomes may be improved to the extent that the constellation of behaviors is considered in the treatment plan.

Assessment of Treatment Outcome

The major focus of assessment in child behavior therapy is on the direct observation of overt problem behavior. Assessment of overt behavior is usually conducted in the clinic or at home. For example, in the clinic parents and children may be given a task (e.g., playing a game), while observers record parent behavior (e.g., use of comments, punishment) and child reactions (e.g., compliance). Alternatively, observations may be conducted at home. A major question is the extent to which assessment of overt behavior under clinic and home conditions reflects performance outside of the restricted assessment situation. Assessment introduces special conditions that may influence performance. For example, when observers record behavior in the home, all family members may be instructed to be present, to remain within a few rooms, not to make phone calls, to answer incoming calls only briefly, and not to watch television. Behaviors under these conditions may correlate minimally with family interaction under ordinary conditions.

The presence of observers in the home may introduce a significant infuence on performance of family members. Tape recordings sometimes are used in place of observers to provide a less obtrusive assessment procedure. Even so, recordings made at randomly selected times have yielded different results from those obtained when families are aware that they are being recorded (Johnson, Christensen, & Bellamy, 1976). The assessment of overt behavior in the home has been an important breakthrough in expanding on traditional methods of psychometric assessment. Yet, questions remain to be answered about the representativeness of the samples of overt behavior under the conditions in which they are ordinarily obtained.

Treatment evaluation usually includes parent and/or teacher ratings in addition to measures of overt behavior. The use of multiple measures raises other questions about treatment effects. For example, Forehand, Griest, and Wells (1979) examined several different measures of overt behavior of the child at home, parent recorded data, and parent questionnaire ratings. Within a given assessment method, changes in the different measures were moderately to highly correlated. However, across methods (e.g., overt behavior, parent questionnaire), there were no significant correlations. The conclusions reached about therapeutic change might vary depending on the measures that were used. As an example, Bernal, Klinnert, and Schultz (1980) compared parent management training and client-centered therapy in altering the behavior of conduct problem children. No differences at posttreatment or follow-up were found on the overt behavioral measures in the home, including the target behavior (noncompliance). However, on mother ratings, parent training was more effective in altering treated and untreated child problems.

Apart from different types of measures, different perspectives need to be included in assessment procedures. For example, teacher and parent perceptions of a given child's problem or maladjustment are often discrepant (Rutter, Tizard, & Whitmore, 1970). Thus, for treatment evaluation, it is critical to include measures that sample different perspectives, modalities, and settings. Conceivably, some measures may change and others may not. The effects of alternative treatments need to be evaluated not only on the magnitude of change within a particular measure, but also on the breadth of change across different measures. In child behavior therapy, the importance of evaluating treatment outcomes by multiple criteria has been increasingly recognized.

Assessment within child behavior therapy has reflected increased concern with the clinical significance of treatment effects. Clinical significance refers to evidence that changes produced in treatment are not just statistically significant but also have important social impact. For example, for conduct problem children, it is important to evaluate if treatment effects are evident on such measures as subsequent contact with the police or mental health system, adjudication, expulsion and truancy from school, and similar measures. These measures, usually derived from institutional or archival records, are critical because they reflect areas where the impact of treatment to society can be evaluated. From an assessment standpoint, however, archival records raise a variety of problems, not the least of which is their interpretation once the data are obtained. For example, contact with police is not simply a measure of deviant behavior, but has to do with a variety of conditions related to being discovered. Despite their imperfection, socially relevant measures are essential. Conceivably, alternative treatments could reflect significant therapeutic change on parent and teacher checklists and overt behavior in the home, but not lead to reductions in recidivism. The gains might be clinically important nevertheless, because parent and teacher evaluations play a major role in treatment referrals. The impact of treatment on socially relevant measures, however, is critical.

The need to include socially relevant criteria in treatment evaluation has been illustrated in recent child behavior therapy work with predelinquent youths. One of the more well-researched programs has stemmed from Achievement Place, a group home-style living facility for predelinquents (Wolf, Phillips, Fixsen, Braukmann, Kirigin, Willner, & Schumaker, 1976). Treatment is based on a teaching-family model that encompasses several strategies including a reinforcement program for adaptive behavior in the group-home setting and at school, a skills training curriculum, and a relationship with the teaching parents. Evaluation of the program has repeatedly shown the impact of treatment on behavioral measures obtained in the setting. Additional studies have shown that the program is superior to alternative residential procedures for delinquent youths, as reflected in such measures as school attendance and reinstitutionalization (Kirigin, Wolf, Braukmann, Fixsen, & Phillips, 1979).

A more recent investigation compared multiple group homes devised on the teaching-family model with other residential homes that did not rely on this model (Kirigin, Braukmann, Atwater, & Wolf, 1982). While the different programs were in effect, children who participated in teaching-family homes showed greater reductions in the number of offenses, derived from police and court records. However, one year after completion of the program, differences in the number of offenses or reinstitutionalization from the different programs were no longer evident.§ Research on the teaching-family program presents a model for assessment by its inclusion of socially relevant criteria. However, the results also convey the critical nature of extending evaluation beyond changes in specific target behaviors while the program is in effect.

The clinical significance of treatment effects in child behavior therapy has also been evaluated by comparing persons who have received treatment with others who appear to be functioning normally (Kazdin, 1977). If the behaviors of children depart from a normative group before treatment and fall within the range of the comparative group after treatment, the magnitude of change is often considered to be clinically significant. Essentially, on the dimensions assessed, treatment has moved the clients to within the realm of acceptable ("normal") behavior.

For example, Patterson (1974) compared the behavior of deviant

---

§Jones, RR, Weinrott, MR, & Howard, JR. *The national evaluation of the teaching-family model.* Final report to the National Institute of Mental Health, Center for Studies in Crime and Delinquency, June 1981

children and their nondeviant peers matched on such variables as socioeconomic status and age. Before treatment, deviant behavior of the clinical sample was greater than for their nondeviant peers. However, after treatment and up to a one-year follow-up assessment, the deviant behavior of the treated children at home and at school had decreased and fell within the range of their peers who had been considered to be functioning normally.

The use of normative data to provide a basis for judging treatment effects is an extremely important advance in treatment evaluation. The advance is especially important in child treatment because normative levels of behavior may vary greatly as a function of developmental stage and chronological age of the child. Normative data provide the necessary baseline to judge the initial deviance of the target problem and the impact of treatment in returning children to nondeviant levels of functioning.

CRITICAL EVALUATION

Major advances have been made in developing and evaluating specific treatment techniques for clinical problems of children. Important research has emerged identifying factors that contribute to clinical problems and their effective treatment. Notwithstanding the important gains, issues and limitations can be identified as well that stem in part from the approach within child behavior therapy.

Who Is the Client/Patient?

A major difficulty in child behavior therapy is evaluation of the populations to whom treatments have been applied. Characteristics of the children and their families usually are not fully described unless the information is available from existing institutional records. The primary focus of behavior therapy is on relatively isolated presenting problems or a set of circumscribed target behaviors. The target behaviors are often assessed with extreme care to evaluate the effects of the program. Typically, additional information to describe the child more generally is omitted.

The restricted assessment focus of current child behavior therapy introduces great ambiguity in identifying the populations to which treatments can be applied effectively. Different characteristics of the population might be of interest including the severity, breadth, chronicity, and type of onset of the children's dysfunction. The different dimensions of dysfunction, apart from the specific target behaviors that might be treated, have important implications for developing treatments and for evaluating existing findings (Kazdin, 1983).

Consider some of the implications of the absence of information on the dimensions mentioned above. Many child behavior therapy studies have focused on conduct problems where children are treated primarily for their aggressiveness and noncompliance. In any given treatment application, it would be extremely useful to know a great deal about the children, beyond the specific maladaptive behaviors that serve as the treatment focus. For example, in some studies children are selected for inclusion because of their aggressiveness, inattention, impulsiveness, lack of motivation, and academic difficulties (e.g., Kent & O'Leary, 1976). The severity of the problem is not clear from the information provided. Indeed, the primary presenting complaints of most of the children may not be stated. And the prognoses of different sorts of problems that serve as the basis for inclusion (e.g., academic difficulties, aggression) vary.

Apart from severity, information is needed about the breadth of childhood problems. For example, children identified as aggressive may vary in their record of arrest, truancy, use of alcohol and drugs, and type of peer relations, all of which predict antisocial behavior in adulthood (Robins, 1978). Apparently, the variety of different types of antisocial behavior (breadth of symptoms) in children is a better predictor of severe antisocial behavior in adults than is any single child behavior yet investigated. The specific types of other problems that children evince along with the primary treatment focus may also have important prognostic implications. For example, follow-up of aggressive children who have been seen in parent management training showed that those who also had stealing problems at the time of referral were significantly more likely to have subsequent contact with the courts than those referred for aggressive behavior alone (Moore, Chamberlain, & Mukai, 1979). Evaluation of treatment studies without additional information about the breadth of symptoms is problematic because populations may respond differently as a function of dimensions not encompassed by the target focus.

Contextual factors such as family characteristics and living conditions may be important to consider as well but are infrequently included in evaluations of child behavior therapy. For example, information about the father's record of offense, mother or father psychopathology, marital discord, and similar factors are related to child psychopathology (e.g., Hersov, Berger, & Shaffer, 1978). In behavior therapy, basic information on the families of children who are treated is infrequently reported.

Greater attention is needed in behavior therapy to delineate the population of children who are included in treatment. One alternative might be to use current psychiatric diagnostic nomenclature to help describe the population, as reflected in DSM III (American Psychiatric Association, 1980). Proponents of behavior modification tend to eschew traditional diagnosis and the model it embraces. Nevertheless, DSM III provides a standardized set of descriptive criteria that identifies a population defined on the basis of severity, breadth, chronicity, and onset of different disorders. Use of psychiatric diagnosis might greatly reduce the existing ambiguity about the populations who participate in treatment studies. For example, for studies in which conduct problems are treated, it would be useful to know if the children meet DSM III criteria for conduct disorder, noted earlier.

Psychiatric diagnosis by no means exhausts the relevant information that might be obtained to identify the clinical population seen in treatment. Yet it would still be helpful to learn if the populations treated in behavior therapy studies meet the criteria of DSM III. The use of a standardized diagnostic system such as DSM III need not alter the assessment and treatment approaches within behavior therapy. It would merely provide a uniform way of describing the poulations to facilitate comparison of subject populations across samples.

Psychiatric diagnosis is not the only alternative for reporting information about the subject populations. Alternative systems could be used based on multivariate techniques that identify childhood disorders empirically (Quay, 1979). For example, a recent effort using parent checklist data has identified different factors that reliably emerge in parent ratings of children, segregated by age and gender (Achenbach, 1978). Profile types of children have been further identified using cluster analyses (Edelbrock & Achenbach, 1980). Diagnostic systems based on factor or cluster analyses provide an empirically based alternative to psychiatric diagnosis. Use of a multivariate system provides information about the target population on a variety of diverse but common dimensions and also would facilitate communication about the populations.

Different arguments might be advanced to promote the use of psychiatric diagnostic systems or various multivariate approaches to classification. An attractive feature of DSM III is that it is the current system in wide use in clinical settings. Also, psychiatric diagnosis is sensitive to a variety of dimensions of dysfunction that are likely to be important in identifying effective treatments. Of course, clinical and multivariate diagnostic methods are not necessarily incompatible, and the use of multiple systems of diagnosis has much in its favor. However, the central issue in child behavior therapy is the failure to adopt any particular diagnostic system that elaborates the nature of the child's dysfunction and the context in which it appears.

What Is the Focus of Treatment?

Child behavior therapy is characterized by intensive assessment of the behaviors targeted for treatment. Despite the benefits of a specific treatment focus, ambiguities exist about the behaviors that are often treated. A major source of ambiguity pertains to what should be focused on in treatment and the significance of that focus. Consider as an illustration social skills training with children, an area that has been the subject of considerable research. As noted earlier, social skills training includes many different procedures (e.g., modeling, coaching, reinforcement, behavioral rehearsal) as applied to a variety of social behaviors (social withdrawal, inassertiveness, aggressiveness). One of the problems in child behavior therapy is the failure to examine the basis of the target focus prior to training.

Children may evince social skills problems for a variety of reasons. One reason may be anxiety when the child is placed in social situations. The child may appear timid, embarrassed, and inhibited, especially in unfamiliar situations. The child may interact with familiar persons but be extremely reticent in overcoming initial barriers to social interaction or be overly sensitive in the face of mild peer rejection. Alternatively, another child may show social withdrawal because of a lack of interest in social interaction. Such children may prefer to play by themselves and appear socially inept when social activities are foisted upon them as in game or group activities. In this case, there may be no evidence of social anxiety but rather a lack of interest when opportunities for solitary activities arise. In yet another case, a child may interact aggressively with his or her peers. After social interaction begins, the child may quickly become argumentative and physically aggressive.

In the above three instances, behavior therapists have often applied social skills training as a general treatment, because children are viewed as having "social skills deficits," i.e., they do not have the requisite skills in their repertoires. Social skills deficits are based on preconceptions of the problem or are often inferred from performance on such measures as a behavioral role-play test, where molecular responses are measured in situations that simulate ordinary interaction. Yet, whether treatment should focus on developing a standard set of particular social behaviors can be questioned. For children who are anxious, the skills might be readily displayed if anxiety could be inhibited. Active practice of the skills might be useful to overcome anxiety, and hence an anxiety or social skills deficit model may not have different treatment implications. Alternatively, for the child who withdraws by preference, skills training and active practice may not be very helpful. For such children, a focus on peers to help develop the social network of reinforcement from others may be a more useful tactic. Peers who are trained to initiate interaction and to support maintenance of the child's participation may be helpful. Essentially, the target child has the skills, but they have not been activated sufficiently. For the aggressive child, social skills training may need to focus on problem-solving skills in interpersonal situations where aggressive behavior is likely to emerge. The possibility exists that a general social skills training package applied to children with all sorts of social skills problems will have some beneficial effects. But it is more likely that the specific benefits will accrue from making distinctions among social skills problems even when the presenting problems seem to fall under the same general rubric.

Part of the problem of providing standardized treatments may come from the assessment procedures that do not permit differentiation among children who seem to fall within the class, "social skills problems." For example, behavioral role-play test performance typically is measured in which a variety of molecular responses are identified such as eye contact, speech duration, voice volume and intonation, facial expression, number of words spoken, request of others, and so on. Dramatic changes can be achieved in these behaviors with children who are identified with diverse social skills problems (see Combs & Slaby, 1977; Michelson et al., 1983; Rinn & Markle, 1979). Unfortunately, little evidence exists that changes in these behaviors have important implications for the short- or long-term social adjustment of these children. Indeed, recent studies have suggested that changes on role-play measures of social behavior can be achieved in clinical samples and normal children without any treatment (Kazdin, Esveldt-Dawson, & Matson, 1983; Kazdin, Matson, & Esveldt-Dawson, 1981).

The appropriate focus of social skills training needs to be determined empirically. One approach has been to obtain normative data from peers of the children who are seen in treatment, as discussed previously. Presumably, if the target children differ from their peers prior to treatment and are brought to within normative levels after treatment, clinically significant changes have been achieved. However, such evidence does not necessarily attest to the relevance of the target behaviors. The behaviors that are brought to within normative levels may not be critical to the adjustment of the children in everyday life. For example, it is unclear that increases in eye contact, initiation of requests, voice volume, and other behaviors effectively treated are consistently related to social interaction in everyday situations or to child adjustment as reflected in child, parent, or teacher ratings.

Overall, in child behavior therapy, problems are often treated without a clear understanding or analysis of the requisite focus. Dramatic intervention effects often distract one from asking the basic question, should these behaviors have been the focus of treatment to begin with? Of course, different areas of treatment may require varying amounts of advance research to determine the appropriate focus. Areas where highly specific and circumscribed behaviors appear to be the problem (e.g., self-injurious behavior) may require less of an analysis of the relevance of specific target behavior to the child's adjustment. Many areas such as social skills deficits and conduct problems, however, require clearer evidence that the behaviors assessed and treated have impact on the areas of functioning known or suspected to have implications for the child's present and future adjustment in everyday situations.

Maintenance of Treatment Effects

The maintenance of therapeutic changes is obviously important in treatment outcome in general. Changes evident during or immediately after treatment assume reduced significance if they are no longer evident a few months after treatment has been terminated. The goal of most treatments is to produce significant long-term changes. As many authors have noted, treatment research infrequently evaluates follow-up performance (Keeley, Shemberg, & Carbonell, 1976). Within child behavior therapy, only sporadic evidence exists on the long-term effects of treatments. To sample the literature more systematically, the present discussion will highlight parent management training for conduct problem children where the assessment of follow-up has been more systematic than in many other areas.

Follow-up data have been reported from a number of parent management training programs. Evidence suggests that children still continue to show significant reductions in deviant behavior up to one year after treatment relative to initial pretreatment levels (see Fleischman, 1981; Fleischman & Szykula, 1981; Patterson & Fleischman, 1979). The magnitude of change evident at follow-up has been impressive as well. In Patterson's program, for example, deviant behavior in the homes of over 80 percent of the children whose parents received training fell within the range of their nondeviant peers who were functioning adequately up to one year after treatment.

Longer term follow-up assessment has led to different results. For example, Christophersen, Barnard, Barnard, Gleeson, and Sykes (1980) compared parent training and a more traditionally based outpatient treatment at a child guidance clinic. Although parent management training led to greater changes immediately after treatment, at a five-year follow-up assessment, group differences were no longer evident. Children who received more traditional treatment improved over the course of follow-up to the level of the parent management training group. Similarly, Bernal et al. (1980) compared parent training and client-centered therapy. At posttreatment, parent reports and paper-and-pencil measures of child deviance indicated greater gains for the parent training group. However, at a two-year follow-up, groups were no longer different. Even studies with shorter follow-up have occasionally found that posttreatment differences attenuate over time (Kent & O'Leary, 1976).

Overall, maintenance of treatments has been evident in a few studies, but the data are difficult to evaluate because of different child populations, versions of treatment, and family characteristics. Also, in some studies, booster sessions are provided to families during the follow-up interval (Patterson, 1974; Wahler, 1975). Long-term effects (e.g., beyond two years) have been rarely evaluated. Evaluations up to a year later rarely include groups assigned to different treatments or no-treatment; thus they do not permit evaluation of durability of treatment effects associated with a particular intervention (see Fleischman & Szykula, 1981).

The maintenance of intervention effects with children is likely to depend on a variety of factors beyond characteristics of the treatments themselves. The living conditions to which the child returns may contribute greatly to maintenance of change. Although this area has only received empirical attention recently, the diversity of factors that influence maintenance has already been evident. For example, deviant parents in the home may affect the maintenance of changes in children. Stewart, Cummings, and Meardon (1978) observed the progress of hospitalized aggressive boys after discharge from an inpatient treatment program. The follow-up status of the children between one and one half and two years after hospitalization depended on departure from the child's home of a deviant parent or the child's separation from such a parent through placement in a foster home. Greater antisocial behavior was evident for boys who had returned to families where an antisocial or alcoholic father was present.

In parent management training, Wahler, Leske, and Rogers (1979) demonstrated that treatment effects and maintenance were less likely, if evident at all, among high risk families, as defined by marked poverty, low rate of parent contacts with others outside the home, poor education, single parent families, and similar adverse living conditions. As noted earlier, the maintenance of treatment effects can be improved by including in parent management training opportunities to help parents with their personal, marital, and extrafamilial problems (Griest et al., 1982). Current evidence suggests that both treatment and maintenance in children may require addressing the larger problems of the families from which these children emerge.

At this point, relatively little is known about the factors that contribute to maintenance of therapeutic change. It is still the case that techniques to produce change are not well established for most clinical problems. Thus the question of maintenance has naturally received less attention. Future work needs to examine alternative technique variations and their interaction with child and parent variables that contribute to initial change and long-term maintenance.

CONCLUSIONS AND FUTURE DIRECTIONS

The hallmark of child behavior therapy is the strong commitment to empirical research. The field is relatively young and research has only made a modest beginning. Nevertheless, important work has been completed in identifying procedures that can be applied to a large number of clinical problems.

Several obstacles confront the clinician or researcher interested in the investigation of childhood disorders and their treatment. First, a great deal of information is needed about normal behavior over the course of child development. Child behavior needs to be evaluated in the context of age-related norms. Many behaviors might be viewed as problematic or normal (e.g., aggressive acts toward siblings and peers, enuresis) depending on the child's age. The absence of a well-elucidated set of age-related behavioral norms makes evaluation of clinical problems difficult. Second and related, the course of problematic behaviors needs to be better understood. Many behaviors might be expected to diminish in frequency or change in quality over the course of normal development. Interventions may be useful in facilitating the process of change, but various behavioral problems may wax and wane over the course of development. Third, caution must be exercised in evaluating changes over time because of the developmental metamorphoses of behavior. Specific behaviors that are treated at one age may be successfully eliminated. Their elimination may hide the fact that other related behaviors emerged. For example, aggressive acts or social skills deficits may be manifest in different ways over time merely as a function of developmental and social sphere changes of the child. Assessment of the identical behaviors over time may suggest improvement, when in fact the primary change is the manner in which the problem behaviors are manifest.

In general, the implications of a developmental perspective have not been sufficiently well incorporated into child behavior therapy (see Harris & Ferrari, 1983). Clinical problems, their amenability to intervention, and the efficacy of particular treatments are likely to vary as a function of age, cognitive development, gender, and other factors. Future research in child behavior therapy will need to merge more closely with developmental psychology and developmental psychopathology to address the above issues.

Apart from developmental considerations, future research is likely to pursue more vigorously the parent and family variables that have direct impact on treatment. Epidemiological research on childhood disorders has demonstrated a variety of parent and family variables that may place the child at risk for psychiatric and behavioral dysfunction (Graham, 1977). Some of the variables identified as risk factors in children have recently emerged in the treatment literature as moderators of therapeutic change. As a case in point, such variables as family living conditions, marital discord, and psychopathology in the parent have been associated with antisocial behavior in children. Current evidence suggests that treatment of antisocial behavior requires consideration of these family variables. Because of the child's dependence on the family, efforts need to be directed toward the child and family. In many cases, treatment of family dysfunction may be a precondition for the application of effective treatment of the child. The need to focus on the family for childhood disorders is not exactly a revelation; many theoretical views have repeatedly emphasized a family systems approach in one form or another. The special feature of child behavior therapy is the empirical scrutiny of family variables in the context of treatment outcome.

Although increased research on the treatment of childhood disorders is obviously essential, more research on child development, family interaction, epidemiology, and other related areas is required as well. Little is known about the emergence of many childhood problems and the manner in which they can be averted. Behavior therapy has been applied to problems that have reached a particular level of severity or concern to those in contact with children. It would be desirable to intervene before this, so that where possible mild problems do not become severe, or more importantly, problems are prevented altogether. The application of existing knowledge toward early intervention warrants additional attention.

ACKNOWLEDGMENT

Completion of this chapter was facilitated by a Research Scientist Development Award (MH00353) and a grant (MH35408) from the National Institute of Mental Health.

REFERENCES

Abikoff, H. Cognitive training interventions in children: Review of a new approach. *Journal of Learning Disabilities*, 1979, *12*, 65–77

Achenbach, TM. The child behavior profile: I. Boys aged 6–11. *Journal of Consulting and Clinical Psychology*, 1978, *46*, 478–488

American Psychiatric Association. *Diagnostic and statistical manual of mental disorders* (3rd ed.). Washington, DC.: American Psychiatric Association, 1980

Arnold, JE, Levine, AG, & Patterson, GR. Changes in sibling behavior following family intervention. *Journal of Consulting and Clinical Psychology*, 1975, *43*, 683–688

Bandura, A. *Social learning theory*. Englewood Cliffs, NJ.: Prentice-Hall, 1977

Becker, JV, Turner, SM, & Sajwaj, TE. Multiple behavioral effects of the use of lemon juice with a ruminating toddler-age child. *Behavior Modification*, 1978, *2*, 267–278

Bernal, ME, Klinnert, MD, & Schultz, LA. Outcome evaluation of behavioral parent training and client-centered parent counseling for children with conduct problems. *Journal of Applied Behavior Analysis*, 1980, *13*, 677–691

Bernstein, GS. Training behavior change agents: A conceptual review. *Behavior Therapy*, 1982, *13*, 1–23

Bornstein, M, Bellack, AS, & Hersen, M. Social skills training for highly aggressive children. *Behavior Modification*, 1980, *4*, 173–186

Bristol, MM. Control of physical aggression through school- and home-based reinforcement. In JD Krumboltz & CE Thoresen (Eds.), *Counseling methods*. New York: Holt, Rinehart, & Winston, 1976

Burchard, JD, & Barrera, F. An analysis of time out and response cost in a programmed environment. *Journal of Applied Behavior Analysis*, 1972, *5*, 271–282

Cahill, MF. A search for the meaning of the "difficult" child. *Dissertation Abstracts International*, 1978, *39* (1-B), 154

Camp, BW, Blom, GE, Herbert, F, & van Doorninck, WJ. "Think aloud": A program for developing self-control in young aggressive boys. *Journal of Abnormal Child Psychology*, 1977, *5*, 167–169

Christophersen, ER, Barnard, SR, Barnard, JD, Gleeson, S, & Sykes, BW. Home-based treatment of behavior disordered and developmentally delayed children. In MJ Begab, HC Haywood, & HT Garber (Eds.), *Prevention of retarded development and psychosocially disadvantaged children*. Baltimore: University Park Press, 1980

Combs, ML, & Slaby, DA. Social-skills training with children. In BB Lahey & AW Kazdin (Eds.), *Advances in clinical child psychology* (Vol. 1). New York: Plenum, 1977

Conger, RD. The assessment of dysfunctional family systems. In BJ Lahey & AE Kazdin (Eds.), *Advances in clinical child psychology*, (Vol. 4). New York: Plenum, 1981

Doleys, DM, Cartelli, LM, & Doster, J. Comparison of patterns of mother-child interaction. *Journal of Learning Disabilities*, 1976, *9*, 42–46

Drabman, R, & Spitalnik, R. Social isolation as a punishment procedure: A controlled study. *Journal of Experimental Child Psychology*, 1973, *16*, 236–249

Edelbrock, CS, & Achenbach, TM. A typology of Child Behavior Profile patterns: Distribution and correlates for disturbed children aged 6–16. *Journal of Abnormal Child Psychology*, 1980, *8*, 441–470

Farrington, DP. The family backgrounds of aggressive youths. In LA Hersov, M Berger, & D Shaffer (Eds.), *Aggression and anti-social behaviour in childhood and adolescence*. Oxford: Pergamon, 1978

Fleischman, MJ. A replication of Patterson's "Intervention for boys with conduct problems." *Journal of Consulting and Clinical Psychology*, 1981, *49*, 343–351

Fleischman, MJ, & Szykula, SA. A community setting replication of a social learning treatment for aggressive children. *Behavior Therapy*, 1981, *12*, 115–122

Forehand, R, Griest, D, & Wells, KC. Parent behavioral training: An analysis of the relationship among multiple outcome measures. *Journal of Abnormal Child Psychology*, 1979, *7*, 229–242

Forehand, R, Wells, KC, McMahon, RJ, & Griest, DL. Side effects of parent counseling on marital satisfaction. *Journal of Counseling Psychology*, in press

Foxx, RM, & Azrin, NH. Restitution: A method of eliminating aggressive-disruptive behavior of retarded and brain-damaged individuals. *Behaviour Research and Therapy*, 1972, *10*, 15–27

Gilbert, GM. A survey of "referral problems" in metropolitan child guidance centers. *Journal of Clinical Psychology*, 1957, *13*, 37–42

Graham, PJ (Ed.). *Epidemiological approaches in child psychiatry*. New York: Academic Press, 1977

Graham, P, & Rutter, M. Psychiatric disorder in the young adolescent: A follow-up study. *Proceedings of the Royal Society of Medicine*, 1973, *66*, 1226–1229

Grieger, T, Kauffman, JM, & Greiger, RM. Effects of peer reporting on cooperative play and aggression of kindergarten children. *Journal of School Psychology*, 1976, *14*, 307–313

Griest, DL, Forehand, R, Rogers, T, Breiner, J, Furey, W, & Williams, CA. Effects of parent enhancement therapy on the treatment outcome and generalization of a parent training program. *Behaviour Research and Therapy*, 1982, *20*, 429–436

Griest, DL, Forehand, R, & Wells, KC. Follow-up assessment of parent behavioral training: An analysis of who will participate. *Child Study Journal*, 1981, *11*, 221–229

Griest, DL, Forehand, R, Wells, KC, & McMahon, RJ. An examination of the differences between nonclinic and behavior problem clinic-referred children and their mothers. *Journal of Abnormal Psychology*, 1980, *89*, 497–500

Griest, DL, & Wells, KC. Behavioral family therapy with conduct disorders in children. *Behavior Therapy*, 1983, *14*, 37–53

Group for the Advancement of Psychiatry, Committee on Child Psychiatry, *Psychopathological disorders in childhood: Theoretical considerations and a proposed classification* (Vol. 6). New York: Group for the Advancement of Psychiatry, 1966

Harris, SL, & Ferrari, M. Developmental factors in child behavior therapy. *Behavior Therapy*, 1983, *14*, 54–72

Herbert, EW, Pinkston, EM, Hayden, M, Sajwaj, TE, Pinkston, S, Cordua, G, & Jackson, C. Adverse effects of differential parental attention. *Journal of Applied Behavior Analysis*, 1973, *6*, 15–30

Herbert, M. *Conduct disorders of childhood and adolescence: A behavioural approach to assessment and treatment*. Chichester, England: Wiley, 1978

Hersov, LA, Berger, M, & Shaffer, D. (Eds.). *Aggression and anti-social behaviour in childhood and adolescence*. Oxford: Pergamon, 1978

Hetherington, EM, & Martin, B. Family interaction. In HC Quay, & JS Werry (Eds.), *Psychopathological disorders of childhood* (2nd ed.). New York: Wiley 1979

Hobbs, SA, Moguin, LE, Tryoler, M, & Lahey, BB. Cognitive behavior therapy with children: Has clinical utility been demonstrated? *Psychological Bulletin*, 1980, *87*, 147–165

Johnson, SM, Christensen, A, & Bellamy, GT. Evaluation of family intervention through unobtrusive audio recordings: Experience in "bugging" children. *Journal of Applied Behavior Analysis*, 1976, *9*, 213–219

Kara, A, & Wahler, RG. Organizational features of a young child's behaviors. *Journal of Experimental Child Psychology*, 1977, *24*, 24–39

Kazdin, AE. Assessing the clinical or applied significance of behavior change through social validation. *Behavior Modification*, 1977, *1*, 427–452

Kazdin, AE. Symptom substitution, generalization, and response covariation: Implications for psychotherapy outcome. *Psychological Bulletin*, 1982, *91*, 349–365

Kazdin, AE. Psychiatric diagnosis, dimensions of dysfunction, and child behavior therapy. *Behavior Therapy*, 1983, *14*, 73–99

Kazdin, AE. *Behavior modification in applied settings* (3rd ed.). Homewood Ill.: Dorsey, 1984

Kazdin, AE, Esveldt-Dawson, K, & Matson, JL. Changes in children's social skills performance as a function of preassessment experiences. *Journal of Clinical Child Psychology*, 1983, *12*, 174–180

Kazdin, AE, Matson, JL, 7 Esveldt-Dawson, K. Social skills performance among normal and psychiatric inpatient children as a function of assessment conditions. *Behaviour Research and Therapy*, 1981, *19*, 145–152

Kazdin, AE, & Wilson, GT. *Evaluation of behavior therapy: Issues, evidence, and research strategies.* Cambridge, Mass.: Ballinger, 1978

Keeley, SM, Shemberg, KM, & Carbonell, J. Operant clinical intervention: Behavior management or beyond? Where are the data? *Behavior Therapy*, 1976, *7*, 292–305

Kendall, PC, & Finch, AJ. A cognitive-behavioral treatment for impulsivity: A group comparison study. *Journal of Consulting and Clinical Psychology*, 1978, *46*, 110–118

Kendall, PC, & Williams, CL. Behavioral and cognitive-behavioral approaches to outpatient treatment with children. In WE Craighead, AE Kazdin, & MJ Mahoney (Eds.), *Behavior modification: Principles, issues, and applications.* Boston: Houghton Mifflin, 1981

Kennedy, RE. Cognitive-behavioral approaches to the modification of aggressive behavior in children. *School Psychology Review*, 1982, *11*, 47–55

Kent, RN, & O'Leary, KD. A controlled evaluation of behavior modification with conduct problem children. *Journal of Consulting and Clinical Psychology*, 1976, *44*, 586–596

Kirigin, KA, Braukmann, CJ, Atwater, JD, & Wolf, MM. An evaluation of teaching-family (Achievement Place) group homes for juvenile offenders. *Journal of Applied Behavior Analysis*, 1982, *15*, 1–16

Kirigin, KA, Wolf, MM, Braukmann, CJ, Fixsen, DL, & Phillips, EL. Achievement Place: A preliminary outcome evaluation. In JS Stumphauzer (Ed.), *Progress in behavior therapy with delinquents.* Springfield, Ill.: Charles C Thomas, 1979

Lahey, BB, & Kazdin, AE. (Eds.), *Advances in clinical child psychology* (Vols. 1–5). New York: Plenum, 1977–1982

Lobitz, GK, & Johnson, SM. Normal versus deviant children: A multimethod comparison. *Journal of Abnormal Child Psychology*, 1975, *3*, 353–374

Luria, A. *The role of speech in the regulation of normal and abnormal behavior.* New York: Liveright, 1961

Mash, EJ, & Terdal, LG. (Eds.). *Behavioral assessment of childhood disorders.* New York: Guilford, 1981

McMahon, RJ, Forehand, R, Griest, DL, & Wells, KC. Who drops out of therapy during parent behavioral training? *Behavior Counseling Quarterly*, 1981, *1*, 79–85

Meichenbaum, DH. *Cognitive-behavior modification: An integrative approach.* New York: Plenum, 1977

Meichenbaum, DH, & Goodman, J. Training impulsive children to talk to themselves: A means of developing self-control. *Journal of Abnormal Psychology*, 1971, *77*, 115–116

Michelson, L, Sugai, DP, Wood, RP, & Kazdin, AE. *Social skills assessment and training with children.* New York: Plenum, 1983

Moore, DR, Chamberlain, P, & Mukai, LH. Children at risk for delinquency: A follow-up comparison of aggressive children and children who steal. *Journal of Abnormal Child Psychology*, 1979, *7*, 345–355

O'Leary, KD, & Emery, RE. Marital discord and child behavior problems. In MD Levine & P. Satz (Eds.), *Middle childhood: Developmental variation and dysfunction between six and fourteen years*. New York: Academic Press, in press

Ollendick, TH, & Cerny, JA. *Clinical behavior therapy with children*. New York: Plenum, 1981

Ollendick, TH, & Matson, JL. An initial investigation into the parameters of overcorrection. *Psychological Reports*, 1976, *39*, 1139–1142

Olweus, D. Stability of aggressive reaction patterns in males: A review. *Psychological Bulletin*, 1979, *86*, 852–875

Patterson, GR. Interventions for boys with conduct problems: Multiple settings, treatments, and criteria. *Journal of Consulting and Clinical Psychology*, 1974, *42*, 471–481

Patterson, GR. The aggressive child: Victim and architect of a coercive system. In EJ Mash, LA Hamerlynck, & LC Handy (Eds.), *Behavior modification and families*. New York: Brunner-Mazel, 1976

Patterson, GR, Cobb, JA, & Ray, RS. A social engineering technology for retraining the families of aggressive boys. In HE Adams, & IP Unikel, *Issues and trends in behavior therapy*. Springfield, Ill.: Charles C Thomas, 1973

Patterson, GR, & Fleischman, MJ. Maintenance of treatment effects: Some considerations concerning family systems and follow-up data. *Behavior Therapy*, 1979, *10*, 168–185

Pikoff, H. Behavior modification with children: An index of reviews. *Journal of Behavior Therapy and Experimental Psychiatry*, 1980, *11*, 195–201

Quay, HC. Classification. In HC Quay & JS Werry (Eds.), *Psychopathological disorders in childhood* (2nd ed.). New York: Wiley, 1979

Rickard, KM, Forehand, R, Wells, KC, Griest, DL, & McMahon, RJ. A comparison of mothers of clinic-referred deviant, clinic-referred nondeviant, and nonclinic children. *Behaviour Research and Therapy*, 1981, *19*, 201–205

Rinn, RC, & Markle, A. Modification of social skills deficits in children. In AS Bellack & M. Hersen (Eds.), *Research and practice in social skills training*. New York: Plenum, 1979

Robins, LN. *Deviant children grown up*. Baltimore: Williams & Wilkins, 1966

Robins, LN. Sturdy childhood predictors of adult antisocial behaviour: Replications from longitudinal studies. *Psychological Medicine*, 1978, *8*, 611–622

Robins, LN. Follow-up studies. In HC Quay & JS Werry (Eds.), *Psychopathological disorders of childhood* (2nd ed.). New York: Wiley, 1979

Robins, LN. Epidemiological approaches to natural history research. Antisocial disorders in children. *Journal of the American Academy of Child Psychiatry*, 1981, *20*, 566–580

Ross, AO. *Child behavior therapy: Principles, procedures and empirical basis*. New York: Wiley, 1981

Rutter, M. Tizard, J, & Whitmore, K. (Eds.), *Education, health and behaviour*. London: Longmans, 1970

Sajwaj, T, Twardosz, S, & Burke, M. Side effects of extinction procedures in a remedial preschool. *Journal of Applied Behavior Analysis*, 1972, *5*, 163–175

Spivack, G, Platt, JJ, & Shure, MB. *The problem solving approach to adjustment*. San Francisco: Jossey-Bass, 1976

Stewart, MA, Cummings, C, & Meardon, JK. Unsocialized aggressive boys: A follow-up study. *Journal of Clinical Psychiatry*, 1978, *39*, 797–799

Stokes, TF, & Baer, DM. An implicit technology of generalization. *Journal of Applied Behavior Analysis*, 1977, *10*, 349–367

Strain, PS. (Ed.). *The utilization of classroom peers as behavior change agents.* New York: Plenum, 1981

Voeltz, LM, & Evans, IM. The assessment of behavioral interrelationships in child behavior therapy. *Behavioral Assessment,* 1982, *4,* 131–165

Wahler, RG. Some structural aspects of deviant child behavior. *Journal of Applied Behavior Analysis,* 1975, *8,* 27–42

Wahler, RG. The insular mother: Her problems in parent-child treatment. *Journal of Applied Behavior Analysis,* 1980, *13,* 207–219

Wahler, RG, & Afton, AD. Attentional processes in insular and non-insular mothers: Some differences in their summary reports about child problem behavior. *Child Behavior Therapy,* 1980, *2,* 25–42

Wahler, RG, Berland, RM, & Coe, TD. Generalization processes in child behavior change. In BB Lahey & AE Kazdin (Eds.), *Advances in clinical child psychology* (Vol. 2). New York: Plenum, 1979

Wahler, RG, & Fox, JJ. Solitary toy play and time out: A family treatment package for children with aggressive and oppositional behavior. *Journal of Applied Behavior Analysis,* 1980, *13,* 23–39

Wahler, RG, & Graves, MG. Setting events in social networks: Ally or enemy in child behavior therapy? *Behavior Therapy,* 1983, *14,* 19–36

Wahler, RG, Hughey, JB, & Gordon, JS. Chronic patterns of mother-child coercion: Some differences between insular and non-insular families. *Analysis and Intervention in Developmental Disorders,* 1981, *1,* 145–156

Wahler, RG, Leske, G, & Rogers, ES. The insular family: A deviance support system for oppositional children. In LA Hamerlynck (Ed.), *Behavioral systems for the developmentally disabled: I. School and family environments.* New York: Brunner-Mazel, 1979

Wolf, MM, Phillips, EL, Fixsen, DL, Braukmann, CJ, Kirigin, KA, Willner, AG, & Schumaker, JB. Achievement Place: The teaching-family model. *Child Care Quarterly,* 1976, *5,* 92–103

Wolfgang, MW, Figlio, RM, & Sellin, T. *Delinquency in a birth cohort.* Chicago: University of Chicago Press, 1972

Zivin, G. (Ed.). *The development of self-regulation through private speech.* New York: Wiley, 1979

Bennett I. Tittler

8

Family Systems Intervention Applied to the Problems of Children

The intent of this chapter is to present family systems theory as an evolving body of thought, and discuss its application in the treatment of emotional and social disorders in children. Emphasis will be placed on the contributions of Bowen and those who have extended his work. In this tradition, clinical practice grows out of theory and research. The discussion that follows will reflect the interplay between articulated principle and systematic investigation that serves as a backdrop for family systems therapy. While the author has found this to be an eminently practical and teachable approach, the reader will note relatively little attention to clinical technique. It is assumed that treatment is guided by a small number of principles, more than by specific techniques. Finally, it should be pointed out that the theoretical base described here applies to total family systems, and not only to children. While there are certain practical matters that arise particularly in the treatment of children, no attempt will be made to suggest a sharp distinction between children's problems and other family problems. In the multigenerational perspective that will be presented here, children, like adults, are seen to be subject to the ongoing influence of prior generations.

CLINICAL CHILD PSYCHOLOGY
ISBN 0–8089–1680–7

THE ADVENT OF FAMILY THERAPY

A variety of opinions have been offered as to when and at whose hands family therapy was born. There is little argument that it has important roots in the earlier forms of individual and group psychotherapy. Clearly, Freud was profoundly aware of the significance of the family, and his report on the treatment of childhood phobia by means of interviews with the child's father presaged later development in the area of family treatment (Freud, 1963). A second precursor to family therapy appears in the work of Moreno, whose observations on the significance of group phenomena incorporated an awareness of the family and the possibility of including family in treatment (Compernolle & Moreno, 1981). Early forms of family therapy can also be seen in the traditions of social work and marriage and sex counseling (Broderick & Schrader, 1981).

Family therapy as an articulated and discrete treatment form came into being in the decade between 1950 and 1960. To a very significant degree, its development during this time emerged out of a number of independent research projects, all concerned with the phenomenon of schizophrenia, and all arriving at the idea of treating entire families. Notable among these early clinical studies were the independent projects of Bowen (Bowen, Dysinger, Brody, & Basamania, 1957) and Wynne (Wynne, Ryckoff, Day, & Hirsch, 1958) at National Institutes of Mental Health (NIMH), Lidz (Lidz, Cornelison, Fleck, & Terry, 1957) in Baltimore and then at Yale, and Bateson (Bateson, Jackson, Haley, & Weakland, 1956) in Palo Alto. All of these researchers were struck by the possibilities for greater understanding and new therapeutic leverage by focusing on the family of the schizophrenic individual.

One interesting new direction spawned by this research on the families of schizophrenics had to do with observations on the communication patterns among family members. A communications framework was especially evident in the writings of Bateson and his co-workers. Their double bind hypothesis was an explanation of the etiology and maintenance of schizophrenia based on the quality of communication between the schizophrenic offspring and the parents or parent substitutes (Bateson et al., 1956). In brief, it stated that schizophrenia was born out of continual contradictory communication toward the child in which acknowledgment of the contradiction was not permitted. Subsequent work by this group (e.g., Haley, 1963; Jackson, 1965) expanded the communications framework to the understanding and treatment of all levels of psychiatric and life adjustment problems. The focus on communication patterns represented a reasonably cogent frame of reference with which one could look beyond the behavioral dysfunction of an individual to the influence of the family and other components of the social context.

The family systems approach, as proposed by Bowen, also departed from the individual model, using biological systems as its reference point. Bowen argued that to move the study of the family in the direction of biology was a good investment in terms of long-term progress. For one thing, biology was an established science with a distinct body of knowledge, and for another, it had an obvious place in the study of human functioning. Bowen viewed families as emotional systems, and saw emotional disturbance as existing in and emanating from the larger family system. In order to encompass the full phenomenon, his early research included hospitalizing not only the identified patient but the entire family for extended periods of time. In addition, an effort was made to divest the language with which observations were recorded of all traditional psychiatric terminology. In these ways, the methods employed by Bowen resembled the naturalistic observations of a field biologist.

Following those initial formative years, family therapy has gradually burgeoned into a new field, taking the form of a kind of subspecialty in the mental health professions. A variety of different approaches have been articulated and described (Gurman & Kniskern, 1981b). Minuchin's (1974) structural approach and Haley's (1976) strategic approach grew out of the earlier work on communications. Whitaker (Napier & Whitaker, 1978) and Satir (1972) developed experiential models of family therapy. Ackerman (1958) and others who have followed in his footsteps employed psychoanalytic theory as a basis for family treatment. Behavioral techniques have been expanded to encompass family interventions (e.g., Gordon & Davidson, 1981; Jacobson, 1981). And finally, Bowen (1974) and Boszormenyi-Nagy (Boszormenyi-Nagy & Ulrich, 1981) have pioneered working on relationships across several generations of a family.

Recent reviews (Committee on the Family, 1970; Guerin, 1976) have suggested a number of dimensions along which the different approaches to family therapy can be ordered and distinguished. From the perspective of the present author, three dimensions appear to most saliently define and distinguish Bowen's family systems approach. The first dimension is the extent to which an individual perspective is retained in contradistinction to a systems view. The notion that an individual's expressing himself emotionally will directly facilitate that individual's cure is an example of an individual concept. A systems view would pay more attention to the possibilities and limitations inherent in the interpersonal context of the person's life.

A second dimension has to do with the extent to which the therapeutic process depends on a heightening of the relationship with the therapist. Family systems therapy aims to keep this relationship at a relatively low level of intensity. The emphasis is on the emotional process in the client's life rather than on his or her relationship with the therapist. Bowen goes so far as to repudiate the title of therapist. He has described his recent approach as playing the role of a coach (Bowen, 1976). A term generally preferred by the present author is that of consultant. This title deemphasizes the mystique of the role while remaining reasonably familiar and acceptable to professionals and the lay public.

A final dimension that defines the family systems approach concerns the emphasis on building and working from theory. Technique in family systems therapy is seen as an outgrowth of and as secondary to theory. As theory develops, new techniques become apparent. The approach is defined more by theory than by technique.

BOWEN'S FAMILY SYSTEMS THEORY

Bowen's efforts toward theory grew out of his early research on schizophrenia. The theory has been communicated in the form of a set of concepts that first appeared in written form in 1965 (Bowen, 1965), and has been added to periodically since that time. Other writing and teaching has been devoted to the clarification and application of these concepts (Bowen, 1976; Kerr, 1981).

Differentiations of Self

This is perhaps the single most important idea around which the theory is organized. It bridges the gap between the individual and the social environment and reflects Bowen's attempt to move beyond the individual orientation into a systems framework.

Differentiation of self is a quality both of the individual and of the family. It refers to the achievement of a particular degree of autonomy, and also to the process involved in this achievement. Differentiation of self is conceived as the key ingredient that permits an individual to function successfully, even in the face of stress and adversity. On an organismic level, it is defined as the ability to distinguish thinking from feeling, and the ability to use thinking to gain perspective on one's own emotionality. In terms of group behavior, it represents the capacity of the individual to be a participating member of the family or group, while retaining an independence of action and thought.

In this theory, the two most important factors in determining human functioning are differentiation of self and level of stress. Though all people are vulnerable to loss of optimal functioning when stress is high enough, the more differentiated individual will recover functioning more quickly and more completely. To assess differentiation of self, it is necessary to ascertain a history of functioning over time and in relation to a record of stressful life events.

An increase in level of differentiation is difficult to achieve, and will only occur in small increments. Even such a small increment, however, has major implications for style of life and ability to cope with life's challenges. Movement toward greater differentiation is a central guiding principle in family systems therapy.

Triangles

The dyadic relationship appears to be inherently unstable, and automatically seeks third persons or activities to achieve some balance. Once a triangle has been established, it is difficult for two of the members to communicate personally without some overt or unstated reference to the third. The existence of a triangle gets in the way of two people discussing and renegotiating their relationship. Triangles are activated by stress and anxiety. In general, the greater the stress in a system, the greater the number of triangles evoked.

If a person is to achieve greater independence from his or her relationship network, it is necessary to achieve some independence from the key triangles. Key triangles are defined by the importance of the other members in a triangle. A primary example involves one's relationships to one's parents. Achieving independence from a triangle requires the attainment of a less anxious, more flexible manner of relating with each of the other members of the triangle.

Since triangles tend to exist in interdependent networks, it is generally necessary to take into consideration the reactions of the larger system when trying to grow more independent of a particular triangle. For the therapist or consultant, an understanding of triangles can help keep him or her from becoming intensely triangled with the client family. Even when meeting with only one family member, the consultant can use this concept to keep from taking sides in the family.

Nuclear Family Process

Every family exists with a certain amount of fusion or unresolved emotional attachment to previous generations. This is the opposite or reciprocal of their level of differentiation. Fusion in a family represents an allotment of chronic anxiety that gets expressed in any of four distinct forms.

One such manifestation of fusion is a chronically distant marriage. A distant marriage may be reasonably satisfactory for one or both spouses but has a tendency to result in the dissolution of the marriage if it continues unchecked over an extended period of time: A second form that fusion takes is that of the conflictual marriage. In these marriages, the spouses are intensely focused on each other. They tend to fluctuate dramatically between conflict and closeness. Both chronic distance and the conflict and closeness cycle represent relatively inflexible forms of marriage.

A third result of fusion may be a vulnerability to personal dysfunction in one or both spouses. This refers to the full range of emotional, social, and physical problems. As stress in the family increases, the vulnerable spouse will become symptomatic. In many such cases, the nonsymptomatic spouse compensates by overfunctioning, which eventuates in a dramatic disparity in the functioning levels of the two spouses.

Finally, and most importantly for the present discussion, fusion can be passed on to the children to varying degrees. This has been called the family projection process. If there are several children, one child typically absorbs a larger portion of fusion than the others. This child is then most vulnerable to childhood disorders and more of a candidate for dysfunction when older. Family therapy aims to alter the process whereby one child becomes heir to a disproportionately large share of the family's fusion.

The Multigenerational Transmission Process

The influence of family fusion on the offspring is a multigenerational phenomenon. People tend to choose a spouse who is at about the same level of differentiation. Children tend to take on roughly the same level of differentiation or fusion as their parents, with one child generally faring a little better than the rest of the family, and one a little worse. Over several generations, there will be one branch of the family tree that gradually increases in general coping ability and another that decreases, while others fall somewhere in between. In every family there is thus a tendency across multiple generations to spawn both relatively high and relatively low levels of functioning. From this perspective, dysfunction or symptomatic behavior in a child is seen to reflect not only the adjustment level of the parents but also the adjustments of the parents' parents and the generations before them. To the extent that treatment succeeds in addressing the multigenerational context of family functioning, progress is more likely to be pervasive and enduring.

Cut-offs

As children get older, there is a tendency for them to relinquish emotional contact with the family in which they grew up. If such cut-offs continue and become fixed, they represent a significant vulnerability in the life of the family. Ongoing, meaningful contact between generations allows for a more rapid dissipation of stress and leaves open avenues for continued emotional growth and differentiation. Though it is often described as an effort toward greater autonomy, the cut-off is a product of family fusion. People who cut off from their parents tend to focus excessively on their own children who are, in turn, prone to cut off from them as they grow up.

The concept of cut-off has opened up a series of new directions in family treatment, related to the possibility of reawakening unresolved issues with the previous generations. Along with the central importance of one's parents, contact with and developing relationships with other family members of the parental generation and the previous one can help to elucidate and make more workable the relationships with parents. Cut-offs are a key in understanding what keeps the family and its members from increasing their vitality and emotional flexibility.

Sibling Constellation

Based on the work of Toman (1969, 1976), this concept provides a scheme for understanding relationship behavior based on factual, life history data. In particular, Toman has demonstrated that the sex and birth order of oneself in relation to that of one's siblings are major determinants of later relationship behavior. Other life history data of special importance concern the loss of parents, especially when the child is young. Early trauma such as these tend to distort predictions of relationship style based on sibling constellation and to increase vulnerability to dysfunction.

According to Toman, oldest siblings will tend to take on the greatest share of responsibility among the children, and youngest siblings will be the most playful and carefree. Children with opposite sex siblings will relate easily to the opposite sex and children with the same sex siblings will relate easily to members of the same sex. These tendencies lend themselves toward certain kinds of life activities and away from others. When persons or families are in a state of dysfunction, predictions based on sibling constellation are apt to appear in an exaggerated form or to remain latent so that they are not immediately recognizable in the behavior of the individual.

Societal Regression

This concept refers to the larger societal context in which the family exists. It is hypothesized that society undergoes long-term cycles in which the movement is either progressive or regressive. In regressive times, the ongoing stress on families and individuals is greater and the overall level of functioning of society is at a lower level. This cycle is affected by large scale demographic phenomena such as population density.

FAMILY SYSTEMS THERAPY

Growing out of the concepts of Bowen's theory are a number of corollaries and an evolving approach to the treatment of families.

A central focus of the family systems approach concerns how the family or individual is functioning. Level of functioning is, to a significant degree, the product of three factors: differentiation of self, stress, and meaningful contact with extended family and prior generations.

Stress emanates from major shifts and losses in the physical and social environment. As stress increases, the functioning of the family tends to decline. However, families at higher levels of differentiation are less vulnerable to the effects of stress, and are quicker to recover their functioning following such disruptions. In addition, regular contact with extended family tends to dissipate and lessen the influence of stress. Family systems therapy proceeds by assessing the current functioning of the family and the family's resources for increasing its functioning.

Functioning level is manifested behaviorally in myriad forms. All aspects of emotional, social, and physical functioning are included. How one responds to important life events such as an accident or death in the family is involved. The major realms of life activity such as family, work, and relationship to the community are likewise included.

Successful functioning is grounded in the ability to act more from a thinking than an emotional base. The term thinking, as it is being used here, is distinguished from IQ or verbal facility. It has to do with the capacity to step back from emotionally triggered, automatic patterns of behavior. As the thinking process is able to act on and modulate the emotional process, a greater array of adjustments and solutions are made possible when faced with life's various challenges.

The aim in family therapy or any other helping procedure that is grounded in family systems theory is to activate and optimize the capacity for thinking. To accomplish this, the consultant attempts to operate in terms of his own thinking and to communicate with reference to the thinking of the client. Emotionality is not seen as a goal of treatment, but rather as a fact of living that one can learn to recognize and act on, given certain conditions. The consultant is of value to the extent that he can bring thinking to an area that heretofore has been dealt with mainly through emotion. This contribution is grounded in the functioning capacity of the consultant.

Progress in psychotherapy is viewed in terms of two components or stages of change. The first of these has to do with forming a relationship with an outside helper. By providing a new circuit to receive excess family anxiety, the helper relieves the system, and the symptom or disorder often subsides at this point. However, this initial change is apt to be temporary and relapse will often occur when the helper withdraws from the system or becomes so involved in the system that he or she loses the capacity to draw off any further family tension.

More permanent change resides in the family's attainment of an increased capacity for thinking. By emphasizing the thinking capacity of the family, rather than the curative powers of the therapeutic relationship, the consultant optimizes the possibility of a more lasting change.

As family systems theory has evolved, certain technical innovations or directions in therapy have emerged. Since therapeutic change or progress is seen as an activation of the more functional features of the family, the greatest effort in therapy is with those persons who are in the best positions to effect a shift in family patterns. For this reason, the emphasis is on working with adults rather than children, even though a child may be the main symptom bearer in the family. Movement is sought initially with the more functional rather than the less functional members of the family. A shift in the thinking of an influential family member will predictably affect the functioning of other family members.

In order to make visible and highlight crucial life history information, a multigenerational family diagram is typically used by family systems therapists (Guerin & Pendagast, 1976; Pendagast & Sherman, 1979). This diagram includes information on sibling constellations and major aspects of functioning across several generations of recent family history. Figure 8-1 illustrates the skeleton of a four-generation family diagram as Bowen has used it. Empty space on the diagram is used to make notes about the style and level of functioning of crucial individuals and relationships. The diagram helps direct the therapy to facts about the family, rather than the relationship with the therapist. It also serves as a backdrop for the subsequent therapy process through which developments in therapy can be evaluated and new directions sought.

In keeping with the concept of differentiation and the multi-generational framework, therapy guides participants in considering the significance of the families in which they grew up and the generations that went before (Anonymous, 1972; Bowen, 1974). By reapproaching the family of origin in a more thinking and less emotional state, progress toward greater differentiation becomes possible. An understanding of the theory helps the family members to approach this project constructively and to sustain the differentiating effort. In general, a confrontational or too rapid approach to the family of origin will often evoke a rebuff that makes future approaches all the more difficult.

An additional implication for therapy derives from the emphasis on theory. Since functional understanding is the goal, the parallel between therapy and an educational process is pertinent. Bowen (1971) has experimented with a multiple family therapy format in which fam-

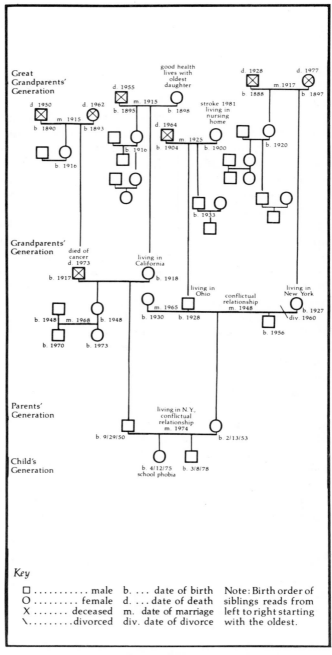

Fig. 8-1. Example of a multi-generational family diagram. (Used with permission of Murray Bowen.)

306

ilies learn by observing each other in treatment. He and his colleagues at Georgetown University have also pioneered the use of short courses on family systems theory to be offered to the interested lay public or as an adjunct to therapy (Meyer, 1977). By making his own clinical work available for observation to selected audiences, Bowen has demonstrated the treatment of clients as associates in a research enterprise. One practical implication of the emphasis on education and research in therapy was the realization that once the initial inductive phase was completed, treatment did not need to continue at very frequent intervals. Therapeutic consultations might occur monthly or even less frequently. Family systems treatment can thus be viewed as an induction into an ongoing process of learning about self and family that becomes increasingly self-directed.

Finally, the effectiveness of the consultant or therapist is grounded both in an understanding of the family systems theory, and in personal experience with the differentiating process in his or her own family. Specific traits of the therapist that are traditionally considered effective ingredients in treatment—such as the capacity for empathy—are viewed here as effective to the extent that they are outgrowths of differentiation. Because the family systems approach is predicated on the capacity of the therapist to maintain an objective perspective, formal training is emphasized as an important prerequisite in the successful application of the theory.

FAMILY SYSTEMS THERAPY WITH CHILDREN

Child Focus in the Family

The central observation that a family systems perspective has contributed to understanding psychological disorders in children is the child focus. As the family concentrates on a problem or other special quality in a child, that aspect of the child tends to become accentuated and fixed in place. This tendency is inherent in the family projection process, the mechanism whereby family fusion and anxiety is passed on to the next generation. Several authors have written about the child focus in some detail (Barragan, 1976; Bradt & Moynihan, 1971).

The Therapeutic Focus on Functioning

The family systems approach views children's functioning in the context of the family. The child's functioning is seen as one aspect of current conditions in the larger family system.

Families, like individuals, can be approached mainly in terms of their difficulties, or they can be approached in a more comprehensive way that places difficulties in a context of functioning. The assumption of family systems therapy is that progress with difficulties emanates more readily from the larger perspective of functioning. A practical corollary of this assumption states that progress results from an activation of the more functional, rather than the less functional, elements in the family.

This principle would hold whether or not formal help was sought. The chances of improvement are maximized when the more functional members of the family remain involved and when they proceed in terms of a functional plan instead of a primary focus on the problem.

Dysfunction in a family member tends to be associated with an intense focus on that person and on his or her dysfunction. Child focus is a special case of this phenomenon. As the parents and other family members set their focus on the dysfunction in a particular child, that child becomes more fixed in dysfunction. In the majority of cases, this focus emanates most strongly from the mother, and is supported by a lack of successful intervention on the parts of others in the family (Bateson et al., 1956; Bowen, 1959).

One aspect of successful functioning in a family involves the ability to employ good judgment in a variety of circumstances. This question of judgment will lie at the heart of any psychiatric complaint or life problem. Intense and continual focus in a relationship tends to promote the loss of good judgment in regard to that relationship. When an intense child focus is concerned, the parent tends to lose perspective as to when and how much to guide the child and when to leave the child alone or in the hands of others. Rigidly distant relationships with children are recognized as a manifestation of child focus in the same way that overly close relationships are (Blotcky, Tittler, & Friedman, 1982; DeCarlo, Sandler, & Tittler, 1981).

Such observations about loss of judgment are one way to understand the link between child focus and dysfunction. Conversely, improvement in the child's condition, if it is to continue, will generally be accompanied by a decrease in focus and an increase in perspective in relation to the child.

A Model of Motivation for Change

One aspect of functioning in families concerns the family's approach to change and to the future. An important special case is the motivation for seeking help.

Functioning exists as an overall description of the family over time, but it also exists in regard to specific issues at a particular time. When concrete difficulties arise in a family, such as dysfunction in a child, the family's response to these difficulties represents a specific instance of their functioning at that time. The decision to seek help and the way it is employed, here called the motivation for help, is a reflection of the style and quality of the family's functioning capacity.

Motivation for change can be described in terms of four dimensions. First, the degree of discomfort, or the activation level, is a kind of driving force. Second, the level of overall functioning is the context that influences the quality and flexibility of motivation. A third dimension has to do with the focus of concern or interest that designates the direction of the motivation and its efforts. An example would be the focus on a child's school performance. Finally, the leadership pattern has to do with who is directing or governing the family's motivation.

These four dimensions suggest a model of motivation for change. They can serve as a guide for assessing the quality and style of a family's problem solving ability in the context of the family's current life circumstances. A set of standards for evaluating shifts in a family's motivation for change will be presented below.

The Significance of the Father and the Multigenerational Perspective

In the case of a fixed, intense focus on a child, the central players in this phenomenon are the child and the main parenting person, usually the mother. However, the notion of child focus implies the involvement of the larger family system. An exploration of the father's position in a child focus provides the most immediate example of the larger system's influence.

It appears that the accessibility and involvement of the father is one factor that moderates the intensity of a child focus. Researchers report that the prognosis for children in treatment is better when both the mother and father become involved in the treatment (LaBarbera & Lewis, 1980). Families where the father is emotionally unavailable or actually missing appear to be at a disadvantage.

Not only does the father represent a second major relationship for the child that can relieve some of the pressure on the mother-child relationship, but the father also represents a significant attachment for the mother in the same sense that she was attached to her own parents. As is the case in any relationship system, there is a tendency for the relationships among mother, father, and child to overlap and become confused with one another. This triangling phenomenon is especially likely to happen during periods of stress. An intense mother-father-child triangle often signals that the child is experiencing difficulties. In such instances, the relationship between the parents becomes confused with each parent's relationship to the child. The fixed focus on child serves to maintain the lack of clarity between parents. This problem of contaminating the relationship system seems to exist under stress even when one spouse is missing. Prototypical examples are the mother who relates to one child in terms of a resemblance to the father, or the father who backs off from the children because they are considered mother's domain.

Clinical experience reveals the centrality of the father when treating children's problems. The major finding in this regard can be summarized as follows: When possible, a shift of focus to the spouse relationship can help lessen the intense focus on the child.

The clinical vignettes that follow represent examples of the various ways in which a focus on the mother-father relationship can help to set loose the child focus.

Family 1. A father, who was an oldest brother in his family of origin, and a mother, who was a youngest sister, were experiencing a lot of difficulty with their 13-year-old son. In keeping with the style of their sibling positions, the mother was treated with caring by the rest of the family but the father's words carried more weight. The father was very involved in business and stopped coming to our sessions after the second meeting. The mother continued with the sessions but in an ambivalent, approach-avoidance fashion. Finally, after missing a session, she attributed her doubts about the treatment to her husband. That led me to the question, raised at our next meeting, as to what extent she felt she needed her husband's help in order to calm down her relationship with her son. Her answer was clear: "I don't need his help." Within weeks she had jumped forward in her ability to maintain perspective with her son which was reflected in an almost immediate improvement in his functioning. He raised his failing school marks enough to be promoted into the next grade, and began making constructive plans for the summer. The father then returned for one session during which it appeared that he had begun exploring his own relationship to the family.

The turning point in this treatment came about when the mother became aware of her tendency to wait for her husband's help. By turning her attention to the overlap between her relationships with her husband and her son, she was able to take a firm, independent position with her son. Even though it was dealt with only briefly in treatment, the mother's consideration of her relationship with her husband helped her to clarify her relationship with her son.

Family 2. The 17-year-old son of a respectable family was tangled up in drug and alcohol use and had begun to get in trouble with the law. His mother, who was herself a youngest sister, talked a tough, limit-setting game with her son, but that policy was invariably preempted by the soft-hearted, overresponsible father. Finally, the mother broke a long-standing agreement that she should stay at home and went to work to help offset the debt incurred due to the extravagances of the children. Along with her increased role of responsibility in the family, her stand toward her irresponsible son took on greater weight. The boy escalated his antisocial behavior and the parents moved to more clearly let him go in the sense of no longer bailing him out. Though they discontinued treatment rather early, the mother informed me of the course of these events over a period of time after we terminated our meetings. The parents came to feel that the best thing they could do was to focus less energy on their problem child and more on their own lives and the rest of the family. Their son would suffer more of the negative consequences of his behavior and possibly be able to relate to them some day on a more independent footing.

Family 3. A mother sought help because of the noncompliant behavior of her diabetic 12-year-old daughter and the general unruliness of all four of her children. The father was an immigrant from the Middle East who had met his wife while attending college in the United States. He declined the invitation to take part in the consultation with me. The mother worked over a period of months on how she could gain come control in her relationships with her children. Something of a breakthrough occurred following the question "Is your difficulty in controlling your children somehow related to your husband?" Though she did not have a definite answer to this question, it elicited an exploration of her relationship with her husband that had seemed irrelevant to her until that time. She began to see a parallel between her overresponsible attitude toward her husband and her behavior toward her children. Her approach toward her husband had been an ongoing series of concessions to his desire to be shielded from domestic tensions. One possibility that emerged for her was the idea that less concessions might increase the possibility of meaningful interaction with her husband as well as increasing her effectiveness with her children. An action suggested to her in therapy that would necessarily redefine her relationships at home was the possibility of visiting her parents unaccompanied by her husband or children, something she had never done since being married. This kind of action often serves as a statement of differentiation from one's nuclear family, and a way to separate and clarify one's most significant relationships. Continued exploration elucidated the overlapping difficulties she was having with her children, her husband, and her parents. She reacted in an emotionally disorganized manner toward her children in the context of her mother's chiding her about her "bad" marriage. Though the child focus for this woman remained predominant, she began to give more attention to possible readjustments to the areas of her marriage and her family of origin. Her diabetic daughter became less of a behavior problem and started to make progress in her relationships with peers and with the rest of the family.

The last vignette illustrates how shifting the focus to the marital sphere can sometimes lead directly back to unresolved issues in the family of origin. The following examples reflect how a shift to family of origin can be used in the treatment of childhood symptoms.

Family 4. A 9-year-old boy had been losing ground in school and otherwise showing signs of lethargy and depression. The family history revealed that the mother was significantly cut off from her family of origin. A series of recent deaths among friends and family had been treated in a rather taciturn fashion by this mother and father, as if to protect the children from such harsh realities. In addition to his other symptoms, their son seem preoccupied with questions about death. Following the initial assessment, it was suggested that the mother consider reestablishing contact with her original family. This was a complex undertaking, since her natural mother had died when she was quite young and she had been brought up by an adoptive family. Though both parents seemed edgy about becoming so centrally involved in the treatment, mother followed through by expanding her contacts with her own family. Within about four months time, their son began to brighten up and his school performance returned to a respectable level. When there was a subsequent death in the neighborhood, the children were included in discussions about it and were given the choice to attend the funeral, which they did. The parents were pleased not only by their son's renewed energy but also by his increased ability to stand up for himself at school and among friends.

Family 5. A successful professional and his wife were concerned about their 12-year-old son, who was underachieving in school and seemed socially immature. Over a period of time, the father worked at easing the pressure he was putting on his son. The mother began to recognize her tendency to become involved in fighting for her son. As the need to do this lessened, she faced the problem of how to negotiate more directly with her husband about their own relationship. In an effort to confront her sense of fear and fragility, she began returning to her family of origin in which her mother had become prematurely senile and her father had remained somewhat detached and self-interested. Key themes that emerged from this effort were the need to relate to father in a less indulgent manner and to overcome her revulsion and avoidance of her mother. Her husband also made a few approaches toward his family, though in a less systematic fashion. As the focus of treatment moved from the child to the parents, to the parents' families of origin, there was a reduction in the youngster's symptomatic behaviors, and his positive qualities began to emerge. Though still not performing at the level predicted by his high IQ, his grades were more consistently above average. He definitely was making friends and was elected a school officer. Also, he was very proud of and diligent about a part-time job he had obtained.

Over the course of the treatment, which lasted $3\frac{1}{2}$ years, the focus periodically returned to the youngster. Though the parents continued to have some concern for their son, they had achieved a significant increase in their perspective on him and on the limits of their responsibility for him. Subsequently, they were able to effectively approach new challenges and concerns about him with little or no outside consultation.

Change as a Shift in Family Motivation

What happens when a family is able to diminish its child focus? One way to understand this kind of development is in terms of a shift in motivation. If motivation is seen as the immediate, situation-specific manifestation of the family's functioning, then obtaining a reading of current motivation should indicate something about recent developments in the family.

This notion suggests a model of change in which motivation is not only an antecedent that influences the course of treatment, but is also a meaningful consequence of change. According to this view, if change has occurred, it should be reflected in some modification of the way in which the family approaches future change.

An examination of how families orient to change will reveal a variety of styles. This would be true whether the family were seeking professional help or coping with life's challenges without formal assistance. A distinction can be made between those approaches that emphasize "change as relief" and those that emphasize "change as process." Roughly speaking these concepts correspond to a focus on the problem in contrast to a focus on the functioning of the larger system. While most efforts toward change would combine these contrasting approaches, the emphasis would tend to be on one or the other in varying proportions. The relative emphasis on relief versus ongoing process will, in part, depend on the capacities and motivation of the family and the orientation of the outside consultant. The contrast between these two orientations toward change is demonstrated in Table 8-1 using the four dimensional description of motivation for change that was presented earlier.

To begin with the first component, discomfort can be approached solely in terms of relief, or it can be approached with an eye to the future by also increasing the capacity to bear discomfort. Second, shifts in overall functioning are not a primary goal of relief and are more likely to occur through a consistent, long-term emphasis on process. Third, while the intensity of focus on the problem will lessen in both cases, there is greater likelihood of a lasting shift of focus to other areas of responsibility and interest when process is pursued. The shift of focus helps to insure against a return of focus to the old problem at the original level of intensity.

With regard to the final component, when the emphasis is on relief, leadership will tend to come from people outside the family, with or without the explicit invitation of the family. An example of this would be a psychotherapist taking on a leadership role in the family. Another hallmark of the emphasis on relief would be for the leaders in the family to exempt themselves from the efforts toward change. In contrast, change

Table 8-1
Levels of Change in Terms of Motivation

Components of Motivation	Change as Relief	Change as Process
Degree of discomfort	Relief accomplished	Discomfort becomes more bearable
Overall functioning	Does not address long-term change	Opens up the possibility of long-term change
Focus of concern	Decrease in intensity	Less intensity, shift of focus to other areas
Leadership pattern	Leadership from outside the system, temporary internal shifts in leadership	Current leadership extended, new leadership patterns emerge

as process is more apt to extend the current leadership arrangement, not to supersede it, but also to allow the emergence of new leadership patterns. As the current family leadership clarifies its relationship to the tasks at hand, new leadership is enabled to come forth. This last point is of sufficient importance to warrant an example.

Family 6. A 16-year-old adolescent girl and her parents came into treatment following a series of events in which the youngster got pregnant by her boyfriend, underwent an abortion, and attempted suicide by taking an overdose of sleeping pills. The mother was aware that she overfunctioned in the family, and made an attempt to relinquish some of the many responsibilities she carried for the family. Subsequently, the adolescent began to take initiative in the treatment and clarified her desire to establish a more independent approach to her boy-friend and her family. In addition, she and her father found that they now had more access to each other, and the father took on a more active parenting role. After six months of treatment, this youngster had established a significantly more robust orientation toward her relationships with others and toward the future. Her parents were invited to return for further consultation if they found that they needed some help in reorienting themselves as their youngest child approached the age of leaving home.

In the case of child dysfunction, how the family accomplishes greater perspective toward the child is reflected in how their motivation toward change has shifted. It is a premise of family systems therapy that an emphasis on process, rather than relief, will maximize the solidness and durability of the family's accomplishments and the child's gains.

Orienting Therapy around the Observable Aspects of Functioning

If the motivation of the family represents its current functioning capacity, then solid change can only evolve as far and as fast as this motivation permits. The therapist's or consultant's job is to keep track of the family's motivation, and to keep from side-tracking it with his or her own extraneous motivations. For the present author, this lesson evolved as a way of decreasing the number of families who disengaged prematurely from treatment. For others, there will be other implications of the tendency to get side-tracked.

By orienting around observable facts about the family's functioning, the consultant is better able to maintain his perspective and to let the family move under its own steam. For one thing, observable phenomena are more likely to have a common meaning among the various people involved. For another, they help maintain a constructive focal point. Motivation, as one form of functioning, is grounded in observable facts. It asks the questions: How strong is the press for change? What is the history or background of functioning from which the motivation emanates? Where are the efforts directed? And by whom?

Thus the emphasis in family systems theory is not on trying to identify the primary cause of the problem. Rather, the emphasis is on how the family has approached the problem and on how they might broaden and shift their approach. Background and contextual information are important, not because they provide a single etiological explanation, but because they help broaden the perspective of the therapeutic effort.

Research on psychotherapy has generally found that success in treatment is unrelated to the theory of therapy adhered to by the therapist (Parloff, 1980). Rather, the functioning capacities of the client and the therapist tend to be the key factors. By maintaining a clear focus on functioning, family systems theory holds promise as a more relevant guide to the fields of clinical child psychology and child psychotherapy. In this framework, the symptomatic child becomes the beneficiary of the family's ability to activate their potential for increased functioning. The therapist's contribution lies in the ability to relate to this process.

Loss of Parent and Other Special Problems of Children

Loss of a parent, whether by death, divorce, or some other cause, is a significant source of vulnerability for the child. The emotional risk involved is heightened when the child is younger and when the lost adult was the more functional of the two parents. According to Toman (1976), the liability is all the more when the child never knew a second parent, either prior to or following birth. Early loss can adversely affect a child, even when it occurred in a previous generation, as in the early experience of one or both parents.

Marital separation and divorce represent a special kind of loss and disruption for a child. People in the midst of these events often lose sight of certain basic realities about relationships. Of particular importance is the fact that marital and parent-child relationships do not generally dissolve with the physical removal of one parent. Even after the custodial parent has remarried, the child will continue to experience a relationship with the departed parent. Denial of this reality can seriously exacerbate the sense of discontinuity and disturbance that the children will experience. Step-parents can not fully replace real parents and will only gain importance to the child gradually. A common problem in forming remarried families stems from unrealistic expectations about the ability of the step-parent to rapidly move into a full-fledged parental relationship with the child (McGoldrick & Carter, 1980).

Foster placement and adoption represent additional special circumstances of childhood. The earlier the age of the child at adoption, the more the relationship between child and parents can resemble that of a natural child. Serial placements in a number of different families represent a circumstance of serious jeopardy for the child, especially when this occurs at an early age. Adopted children who have grown up and enter therapy often pose an interesting question: should they attend more to their natural family or their adoptive family? The greater the amount of time with a family the greater its significance to the individual. When it is possible, the adopted individual can benefit from maintaining relationships with and learning more about each of the families with whom a significant amount of time was spent.

It should be kept in mind that underlying each of the special circumstances described here is the issue of overall functioning level of the family. The higher the functioning level, the better able the family is to help the child recover from these disruptions of normal family life. Steady, mature contact with extended family is one source of family coping ability during such times of upheaval.

RESEARCH: THE STUDY OF FAMILY FUNCTIONING

Research is an integral part of a systems approach. To remain vital, theory must be open to new information. An understanding of the differentiation of self concept provides some clues to the significance of research in family systems theory.

The differentiation concept proposes that effective functioning is grounded in the ability to distinguish the objective from the subjective. Here objectivity is seen as an ongoing process of formulating and testing reality, something akin to the scientific method. Subjectivity is always with us, but it may be monitored and transformed by the capacity for objectivity. In terms of family systems theory, subjectivity emanates from an emotional process and objectivity is a product of the thinking process.

This metaphor can be further developed. Research represents the application of objectivity to the subjective field. Theory may be thought of as the refinement of subjectivity to a point that is maximally responsive to the operations of objectivity. A central tenet of this section is that research and theory properly exist in a reciprocal relationship and that each can only thrive as a result of this mutual contact. To elaborate, research gains relevance by its connection to theory and theory retains its utility and flexibility to the extent that it makes contact with an ongoing series of empirical tests and inputs. In terms of the present metaphor, the highest forms of subjectivity guide and are guided by the regular application of objectivity.

Sometimes subjectivity takes on such strength and vividness that it obliterates or even poses for objectivity. People tend to become submerged in subjectivity around important relationships, for example, when in the family. People may also become submerged in subjectivity while pursuing important activities. This is true even when striving for objectivity, as in the case of the behavioral scientist. By maintaining contact with theory, the behavioral scientist can stay in touch with a larger constellation of objective facts while planning and interpreting research

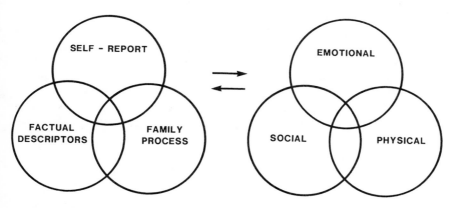

The Range of Family Variables   Realms of Human Functioning

Fig. 8-2. Research scheme used to organize the field of family research.

undertakings. When effective, theory helps transcend the more limited and insulated forms of subjectivity.

Figure 8-2 presents the research scheme used here to organize the field of family research. The focus is on the whole phenomenon of human or animal functioning, rather than just the specifics of treatment techniques. The research question being asked concerns the relationship of family behavior to indices of functioning in the family. By varying the family behavior and aspects of functioning under investigation, this scheme provides a strategy for organizing a wide array of possible research projects. The ultimate goal is a greater understanding of family functioning.

Aspects of Functioning

Quality of functioning may be thought of as existing in three spheres: the emotional, the social, and the physical. Dysfunction is an individual or family is manifested by symptom development in one or more of these spheres.

Some of the earliest research in family functioning involved investigation of the family's role in serious emotional disturbance, especially schizophrenia (e.g., Bateson et al., 1956; Bowen, Dysinger, Brodey, 1957; Lidz et al., 1957; Wynne et al., 1958). These studies demonstrated the association of schizophrenia with particular and distinct ways in which family members interacted among themselves.

There is now evidence that some of the same interactional phenomena observed in schizophrenia are also apparent to a lesser degree in families with other forms of emotional disturbance. For example, double bind communication has been demonstrated in the families of children with moderately severe behavior problems (Blotcky, Tittler, & Friedman, 1982) and hyperactive children (Weakland, 1979). Issues of family interaction have also been cited in cases of learning disability (Weakland, 1977). In a recent study, Barnett* demonstrated a greater family focus on the learning-disabled child and his problem than in a control group of families with non-learning-disabled children. This focus was shown to influence the larger relationship patterns of the family as well as relationships with the symptomatic child himself. In addition, improvement in the learning-disabled children was most likely in those families whose focus on the child was somewhat less extreme.

Social dysfunction refers to problems in functioning such as delin-

---

*Barnett, LL. Observed relationships between children's reading difficulties and patterns of family involvement. Unpublished doctoral dissertation, George Peabody College of Vanderbilt University, 1981

quency, substance abuse, and an impaired sense of responsibility toward work, family, and other aspects of interchange with the external world. Several researchers have found evidence of family patterns that tend to distinguish between families prone to emotional dysfunction and those prone to social dysfunction. Reiss (1971) found that families with a schizophrenic member tend to place a great emphasis on consensus in their communication, while families with a child manifesting a conduct disorder tend to engage in relatively little communication about matters of mutual interest.

Minuchin and his colleagues (Minuchin, Montalvo, Guerney, Rosman, & Schumer, 1967) found that families with delinquents tended to lack leadership and other organizational characteristics that permit a group to function interdependently. Minuchin has also noted a distinction between families in terms of boundary disturbances. He refers to the two types of family dysfunctions as enmeshment, an overinvolvement among family members, and disengagement, a state of underinvolvement within the family (Minuchin, 1974). Though they are distinct, both patterns serve to interfere with the family's ability to effectively resolve differences and solve problems of mutual concern. Disengagement is particularly associated with antisocial kinds of behavior.

Finally, dysfunction may take the form of physical symptomatology. Though not necessarily a "primary cause" of physical illness, evidence is beginning to accumulate that family factors contribute to the incidence and continuation of physical problems in children. Based on work with anorexia nervosa, asthma, and diabetes in children, Minuchin (Minuchin, Rosman & Baker, 1978) posits an enmeshed family pattern that is conductive to psychosomatic illness. In these families, there is a marked tendency for members to take responsibility for one another and to treat the symptomatic child as devoid of age-appropriate responsibility or competence.

Other authors have addressed the larger field of physical illness. The study of the family has lent impetus to the emergence of a new field in medicine—family practice (Jackson, 1965; Smilkstein, 1980). Blotcky (1981) has provided data suggesting that level of family functioning is a significant predictor of the time required for recovery from illness. Kerr (1980) has been accumulating evidence of multigenerational factors in physical illness, and the parallel between serious emotional disturbance and physical illness. He has written in particular about the family and emotional context of cancer.[†]

[†]Kerr ME. Cancer and the family emotional system. Unpublished manuscript, Department of Psychiatry, Georgetown University Medical Center, 1981

The Range of Family Variables

Self-report Scales

The earliest and perhaps simplest way to study the family was to have family members report about the family along certain specified dimensions. A reasonably exhaustive review of these and other kinds of family measures has been provided by Cromwell, Olson, and Fournier (1976). Self-report scales are limited in that they rely entirely on the perceptions of the family and tend not to provide a systemic view of the family. An example of such a scale that has been validated against observational measures and clinical data is the Family Characteristics Inventory (Lewis, Beavers, Gossett, & Phillips, 1976).

Life History Descriptors

These include all the demographic and life history data that have been explored by the clinical sciences over the years. Toman's (1969, 1976) contribution has been to systematize this approach and to demonstrate its utility. In addition to documenting the relationship between sibling constellation and interpersonal style, he has highlighted the significance of early loss in the family as a major source of disruption in personality development. Additional factors that he mentions include characteristics of residence, frequency of moves, existence of family friends, social class, religious affiliation, and intellectual, physical, and temperamental attributes of family members. An interesting study described by Love and Kaswan (1974) found that the most effective style of intervention around school and behavior problems varied depending on the social class of the client family. A study on adjustment in black adolescents (Calhoun)‡ reported that clinic and non-clinic groups could be distinguished by the number of people in the household, and by the number of fathers missing for reasons other than a legal divorce. In general, the use of factual descriptors appears to have been underutilized in the study of family functioning.

Family Process Variables

With the advent of family therapy and assessment, a new methodology was revealed, the observation of family interaction patterns. This approach gave the clinician and researcher a clearer view of the family as a system, and a sizeable number of studies resulted. There have been several major reviews on the topic of family process research (Bodin, 1968; Doane, 1978; Haley, 1972; Jacob, 1975; Riskin & Faunce, 1972).

---

‡Calhoun PD. Family factors in black adolescent mental health. Unpublished doctoral dissertation, George Peabody College of Vanderbilt University, 1981

The major limitation of this work has been a difficulty in tying family interaction variables to theory (Riskin & Faunce, 1972). It has been difficult to know which of the nearly infinite number of possible interaction variables were meaningful and worthy of continued study.

Two classes of family process variables suggested by family systems theory seem to lend themselves to a direct association with indices of functioning. The first concerns the frequency and quality of family members' contacts outside of the immediate family, especially with extended family. According to theory, a well-functioning family will tend to have a substantial amount of contact with family of origin and other extended family members, along with at least a moderate amount of contact with friends and acquaintances. A small number of studies have begun to approach this kind of measurement, as it applies to different levels of normality and disturbance in the family (Pattison, DeFrancisco, Wood, Frazier, & Crowder, 1975; Tolsdorf, 1976; Wahler, 1980).

A second type of variable of particular relevance has to do with the family's capacity for thoughtful behavior. The quality of a family's thinking may be considered a direct derivative of their differentiation level. Tittler (1980) was able to identify several characteristics of family thinking in families with disturbed children which correlated with pretreatment functioning and treatment outcome. This study concluded that more effective thinking in families emanated from the ability to step back somewhat from the problem and take an objective view, in contrast to simply gathering closer together. Other research models that bear a resemblance to the study of family thinking are the study of problem-solving behavior (e.g., Reiss, 1967) and the study of task effectiveness in families (e.g., Lieber, 1977; Solvberg & Blakar, 1975).

Family Functioning in Treatment

A special case in the study of family functioning has to do with the family's performance in treatment. (See Gurman and Kniskern, 1981a, for a recent review of research on family therapy outcome.) In the present framework, gains in treatment process and outcome are seen as an outgrowth of the reparative capacities of the family. A number of studies have focused on the family's ability to engage in treatment (e.g., Shapiro & Budman, 1973; Trotzer, 1982). Other researchers have demonstrated an association between the family's initial behavior in therapy and later outcome (Seeman§; Tittler, Friedman, Blotcky, & Stedrak, 1982). One factor that appears to play a positive role in the engagement

---

§Seeman L. Early improvement in family therapy and its relationship to engagement and outcome. Unpublished doctoral dissertation, George Peabody College, 1977

phase of treatment is the presence and cooperation of the father (LaBarbera & Lewis, 1980; Shapiro & Budman, 1973).

More generally, evidence is accumulating that the involvement of the family in treatment significantly enhances outcome in cases of child and adolescent dysfunction (Alexander & Parsons, 1973; Langsley & Kaplan, 1968; Masten, 1979; Ro-Trock, Wellisch, & Schoolar, 1977; Tittler et al., 1982). Future approaches to treatment will be guided by an increasing understanding of how families make use of outside resources to bring about change.

Profiles of the Healthy Family

A number of contributors to the field of family research have attempted to construct a model or profile of the healthy family. For example, Lewis et al. (1976) identified dimensions on which to evaluate the functional level of the family. These dimensions included an affiliative attitude about human encounter, respect for subjective views, a belief in complex motivation, high levels of initiative, a healthy level of structure, room for personal autonomy, a methodology congruent with objective reality, openness to the expression of affect, and involvement with people and activities outside of the family. The McMaster Model of Family Functioning (Epstein & Bishop, 1981) focuses on the dimensions of problem-solving, communication roles, affective involvement, and behavior control. These authors note that theirs is an incomplete list that may be subject to new additions and further refinement. In a review on the healthy family, Kaslow (1982) mentions these and other approaches and provides examples of healthy family functioning.

In some contrast to the above, Bowen's family systems' approach to family functioning is guided by an understanding of the differentiation of self concept. While different methods of operation of this concept are possible, we do not yet know enough to isolate the most critical dimensions with which to describe the healthy family. Depending on the circumstances and descriptive characteristics of the family, particular dimensions might be more relevant for some families than others (Tittler, Friedman, & Klopper, 1977). More importantly, indices of successful functioning are more likely to be found in clearly defined, observable phenomena than in subjective scales. Three general categories of data are recommended for this undertaking: factual life history descriptors of the family and their circumstances (e.g., a history of losses and other significant events), the amount and quality of contact with extended family, and samples of thinking behavior with regard to emotional issues in the family. The assessment of family functioning is more exact and secure when based on observations over an extended period of time.

IMPLICATIONS AND NEW DEVELOPMENTS

The Interface between Family and Community

The family is the natural mediator between the child and society. As children mature, they gain some direct access to the community. The principal avenue of entry into the larger community is through the school. A second important contact that children sometimes have with the institutional structure of the community is through medical and other human service agencies.

When working with children's problems, it is important to be aware of the other major community involvements that the family has on behalf of the child. Disturbances in the smooth functioning of these community involvements may reflect some malfunctioning on the part of the family, the community agency, or both. Family systems theory guides the clinician in being aware of and working with the overlapping relationships between the family and the various community agencies.

The school provides a primary example (Tittler & Cook, 1981). The ease or difficulty with which children's problems are remediated will depend, in part, on the intensity of focus on the child. Intense focus on the child will tend to foster a triangle including child, school, and family. In these cases an overly close affiliation or, more commonly, a state of alienation between family and school contributes to the intransigence of the problem. In other words, a disturbance in the relationship of the family and school will compound the child's problem and interfere with its remediation. The consultant in this situation must avoid becoming party to the triangle. This is achieved by establishing some degree of emotional contact with both family and school. By being in touch with both parties, and presenting as objective a view as possible, the consultant can help to modify the rigidity that has developed in the relationship between family and school. The better this relationship is functioning, the more able the school and family will be to respond effectively in the event of future difficulties involving the child (Pfeiffer & Tittler, 1983).

The same principle holds when multiple agencies are involved with the child. By anticipating and counteracting the tendency to triangle among family and agencies, the consultant can help to calm the system and to keep the positions of each party reasonably clear and objective.

This can make the difference between the helping system being a constructive factor in contrast to becoming part of the problem.

In order to gain entry into a family, it is sometimes useful for the consultant to temporarily join a triangle. In such cases, the consultant allies with another agency in order to make use of the leverage that the agency has with the family. The agency is motivated to endorse the consultant in the belief that his or her skill with families will contribute to the agency's goals. For example, by working through a school and meeting in the context of the school setting, the consultant can attain credibility with a family who otherwise would not have sought his services. To say this in another way, family involvement can often be obtained when it is associated with or made contingent on some other kind of service desired for the child. Other examples might be family components attached to therapeutic nurseries or juvenile probation programs. Here again, the consultant initially gains importance with the family through a strong recommendation from the agency. In all such cases, it is important to establish a relationship to the family with some independence from the host program as soon as possible. If the consultant becomes too rigidly triangled, which is to say, strongly identified with one side of the relationship between the family and agency, he or she loses the ability to have influence as an independent party.

The Research Frame of Mind

An understanding of natural systems implies a way of thinking that maintains perspective and a level of openness to new information. This can be characterized as the research frame of mind. It is a mode of functioning that prevents premature closure and points to areas where greater understanding and clarity are needed. For example, to assume that we know precisely how to treat psychological problems in children is generally a statement that goes beyond the facts. That we have a level of knowledge about certain aspects of children's problems and hypotheses about other aspects is closer to the factual truth.

On one level, client families may be thought of as research associates. In turn, the therapist is a person with specialized training who is guided by a set of professional standards, but he is not one who can provide definitive answers beyond the state of current knowledge. This partial understanding and the quest for further understanding should define the therapist-client relationship. Because of the natural inclination to imbue the therapist with greater understanding than he has, the therapist must actively work at defining his role. The therapist will have informed suggestions to make at times but he must also represent the incompleteness and imprecision of collective knowledge. His goal is to keep the family's major focus on themselves as subjects of interest, rather than on the therapist.

In the sense that is intended here, opportunities for relevant research are available to anyone who is interested. For the therapist, principal laboratories exist in the form of his clinical practice and in the study of his own family. Another significant laboratory for increasing understanding of natural systems is the larger realm of biology and the study of animal behavior. Recent advances in these areas (e.g., MacLean, 1978; Wilson, 1975) hold promise for contributing to a greater understanding of human functioning and the amelioration of human difficulties. The goal in all of this is to bring fresh data to bear on the problems of functioning.

As with the therapist, the family in treatment can learn to apply the research attitude to themselves. Their efforts can be supplemented by educational inputs and by the experience of the therapist which is offered as a guide. By taking on the mind set of the scientist, the family is empowered in their problem-solving and in their sense of how to approach the future.

On Treating Future Generations

Family treatment for children's problems is based on the idea of human dysfunction being transmitted down through the generations. Successful treatment raises the possibility not only of improving the lot of the present generation and the next generation but also of succeeding generations. This preventive aspect of family treatment has not received much notice thus far. One interesting study that is relevant here was reported by Klein, Alexander, and Parsons (1977). By treating a family with a delinquent adolescent, it was demonstrated that the delinquent and his siblings were less likely to get in future trouble with the law, as compared with control families. The implications of these results for the generalized influence of family therapy are manifold.

Two premises of this chapter bear highlighting. By treating children in terms of their natural environment, the possiblity for positive results is significantly enhanced. Furthermore, the effects of a family systems approach increases the probability that others in the child's present and future environments will also benefit.

In family systems treatment, the family is encouraged to view itself as a subject for study, and to take increasing responsibility in this endeavor as time goes on. When successful, the result is a clearer definition of the individual within the family, and the attenuation of the conditions that support dysfunction. By taking responsibility for itself, the present generation clears the way for future generations.

As the science of human functioning evolves, its contribution can be seen to extend beyond the psychotherapy relationship. Progress takes place both in the increase of collective knowledge, and in those gains in functioning that are passed on through the family.

SUMMARY

Bowen's family systems theory has been described as one development of the early family research on schizophrenia during the 1950s. It grew from an attempt to bring the study of human functioning more in line with the methods and knowledge base of the biological sciences. The approach to family therapy that emerged from Bowen's theory is distinguished by its emphasis on theory and research rather than technique, and by its evolving, open-ended nature.

The application of family systems therapy to children is based on a theoretical understanding of how families function. As with other human problems, the problems of children are understood to involve a fixed and inflexible focus on the part of the family that works against their efforts to solve the problem. Family systems therapy proceeds as the family is enabled to modify the way it focuses on the symptomatic child. The capacity to shift focus in the family is grounded in motivational characteristics of the family and the therapist.

Research plays a central role as a vehicle for expanding and refining theory. A framework has been suggested for organizing the growing body of research on human functioning in the context of the family. Research on family therapy is viewed as one aspect of the larger study of how families function. With regard to the problems of children, a number of recent studies have documented the significance of the family's involvement in treatment.

The family systems approach holds promise as a source of new ideas concerning the welfare of children. In addition to providing treatment of immediate problems, the family systems framework opens up the possibility of constructively influencing the families, the communities, and the descendants of today's children.

REFERENCES

Ackerman, NW. *The psychodynamics of family life.* New York: Basic Books, 1958

Anonymous. On the differentiation of self. In JL Framo (Ed.), *Family interaction: A dialogue between family researchers and family therapists.* New York: Springer, 1972 (Also papers in Bowen, M. *Family therapy in clinical practice.* New York: Jason Aronson, 1978, Chap. 21.)

Alexander, JF, & Parsons, BV. Short-term behavioral intervention with delinquent families: Impact on family process and recidivism. *Journal of Consulting and Clinical Psychology*, 1973, *81*, 219–225

Barragan, M. The Child-centered family. In PJ Guerin (Ed.), *Family therapy: Theory and practice*. New York: Gardner Press, 1976

Bateson, G, Jackson, DD, Haley, J, & Weakland, J. Toward a theory of schizophrenia. *Behavioral Science*, 1956, *1*, 251–264

Blotcky, AD. Family functioning and physical health: An exploratory study with practical implications. *Family Therapy*, 1981, *8*, 197–202

Blotcky, AD, Tittler, BI, & Friedman, S. An investigation of the conditions of the double-bind situation in families of disturbed children. *Journal of Genetic Psychology*, 1982, *141*, 129–142

Bodin, AM. Conjoint family assessment. In P McReynolds (Ed.), *Advances in psychological assessment* (Vol. 1). Palo Alto: Science and Behavior Books, 1968

Boszormenyi-Nagy, I, & Ulrich, DN. Contextual family therapy. In AS Gurman & DP Kniskern (Eds.), *Handbook of family therapy*. New York: Brunner/Mazel, 1981

Bowen, M. The role of the father in families with a schizophrenic patient. *American Journal of Psychiatry*, 1959, *115*, 1017–1020 (Also in Bowen, M. *Family therapy in clinical practice*. New York: Jason Aronson, 1978, Chap. 2.)

Bowen, M. Intrafamily dynamics in emotional illness. In A D'Agostino (Ed.), *Family, church, and community*. New York: PJ Kennedy and Sons, 1965. (Also appears in Bowen, M. *Family therapy in clinical practice*. New York: Jason Aronson, 1978, Chap. 7.)

Bowen, M. Principles and techniques of multiple family therapy. In J Bradt & C Moynihan (Eds.), *Systems therapy*. Washington, DC.: Groome Child Guidance Center, 1971 (Also appears in Bowen, M. *Family therapy in clinical practice*. New York: Jason Aronson, 1978, Chap. 11.)

Bowen, M. Toward the differentiation of self in one's family of origin. In F Andres & JP Lorio (Eds.), *Georgetown Family Symposium* (Vol. 1). Washington, DC: Department of Psychiatry, Georgetown University Medical Center, 1974. (Also appears in Bowen, M. *Family therapy in clinical practice*. New York: Jason Aronson, 1978. Chap. 22.)

Bowen, M. Theory in the practice of psychotherapy. In PJ Guerin (Ed.), *Family therapy: Theory and practice*. New York: Gardner Press, 1976. (Also appears in Bowen, M. *Family therapy in clinical practice*. New York: Jason Aronson, 1978, Chap. 16.)

Bowen, M, Dysinger, RH, Brodey, WM, & Basamania, B. Treatment of family groups with a schizophrenic member. Paper presented at the annual meeting of the American Orthopsychiatric Association, Chicago, 1957 (Also appears in Bowen, M. *Family therapy in clinical practice*. New York: Jason Aronson, 1978, Chap. 1.)

Bradt, O, & Moynihan, CJ. Opening the safe: A study of child-focused families. In JO Bradt & CJ Moynihan (Ed.), *Systems Therapy*. Washington, DC: Groome Child Guidance Center, 1971

Broderick, CB, & Schrader, SS. The history of professional marriage and family therapy. In AS Gurman & DP Kniskern (Eds.), *Handbook of family therapy*. New York: Brunner/Mazel, 1981

Committee on the Family. *The field of family therapy*. New York: Group for the Advancement of Psychiatry, 1970

Compernolle, T, Moreno JL. An unrecognized pioneer of family therapy. *Family Process*, 1981, *20*, 331–335

Cromwell, RE, Olson, DH, & Fournier, D. Tools and techniques for diagnosis in marital and family therapy. *Family Process*, 1976, *15*, 1–49

DeCarlo, T, Sandler, HM, & Tittler, B. The role of personal space in family theory. *Family Theory*, 1981, *8*, 255–266

Doane, JA. Family interaction and communication deviance in disturbed and normal families: A review of research. *Family Process*, 1978, *17*, 357–376

Epstein, NB, & Bishop, DS. Problem-centered systems therapy of the family. In AS Gurman & DP Kniskern (Eds.), *Handbook of family therapy*. New York: Brunner/Mazel, 1981

Freud, S. *The sexual enlightenment of children*. New York: Collier Books, 1963. (Originally published, 1909.)

Gordon, SB, & Davidson, N. Behavioral parent training. In AS Gurman & DP Kniskern (Eds.), *Handbook of family therapy*. New York: Brunner/Mazel, 1981

Guerin, PJ. Family therapy: The first twenty-five years. In PJ Guerin (Ed.), *Family therapy: Theory and practice*. New York: Gardner Press, 1976

Guerin, PJ, & Pendagast, EG. Evaluation of family system and genogram. In PJ Guerin (Ed.), *Family therapy: Theory and practice*. New York: Gardner Press, 1976

Gurman, AS, & Kniskern, DP. Family therapy outcome research: Knowns and unknowns. In AS Gurman & DP Kniskern (Eds.), *Handbook of family therapy*. New York: Brunner/Mazel, 1981(a)

Gurman, AS, & Kniskern, DP. (Eds.). *Handbook of family therapy*. New York: Brunner/Mazel, 1981(b)

Haley, J. *Strategies of psychotherapy*. New York: Grune & Stratton, 1963

Haley, J. Critical overview of present status of family interaction research. In JL Framo (Ed.), *Family interaction*. New York: Springer, 1972

Haley, J. *Problem-solving therapy*. San Francisco: Jossey-Bass, 1976

Jackson, DD. The study of the family. *Family Process*, 1965, *4*, 1–20

Jacob, T. Family interaction in disturbed and normal families: A methodological and substantive review. *Psychological Bulletin*, 1975, *82*, 33–65

Jacobson, NS. Behavioral marital therapy. In AS Gurman & DP Kniskern (Eds.), *Handbook of family therapy*. New York: Brunner/Mazel, 1981

Kaslow, FW. Profile of the healthy family. *The Relationship*, 1982, *8*, 9–24

Kerr, ME. Emotional factors in physical illness. *The Family*, 1980, 7, 59–66

Kerr, ME. Family systems theory and therapy. In AS Gurman & DP Kniskern (Eds.), *Handbook of family therapy*. New York: Brunner/Mazel, 1981

Klein, NC, Alexander, JF, & Parsons, BV. Impact of family systems intervention of recidivism and sibling delinquency: A model of primary prevention and program evaluation. *Journal of Consulting and Clinical Psychology*, 1977, *45*, 469–474

La Barbera, JD, & Lewis, S. Fathers who undermine children's treatment: A challenge for the clinician. *Journal of Consulting and Clinical Psychology*, 1980, *9*, 204–206

Langsley, DG, & Kaplan, DM. *The treatment of families in crisis*. New York: Grune & Stratton, 1968

Lewis, JM, Beavers, WR, Gossett, JJ & Phillips, YA. *No single thread: Psychological health in family systems*. New York: Brunner/Mazel, 1976

Lidz, T, Cornelison, AR, Fleck, S, & Terry, D. The intrafamilial environment of the schizophrenic patient: II. Marital schism and marital skew. *American Journal of Psychiatry*, 1957, *114*, 241–248

Lieber, DJ. Parental focus of attention in a videotape task as a function of hypopthesized risk for offspring schizophrenia. *Family Process*, 1977, *16*, 467–475

Love, LR & Kaswan, JW. *Troubled children: Their families, schools and treatment*. New York: Wiley, 1974

MacLean, P. A mind of three minds: Educating the triune brain. In *Seventy-seventh yearbook of the national society for the study of education*. Chicago: University of Chicago Press, 1978

Masten, AS. Family therapy as a treatment for children: A critical review of outcome research. *Family Process*, 1979, *18*, 323–335

McGoldrick, M, & Carter, EA. Forming a remarried family. In EA Carter & M McGoldrick (Eds.), *The family life cycle: A framework for family therapy.* New York: Gardner Press, 1980

Meyer, PA. The educational process: A vehicle for bringing change. In JP Lorio & L McClenahan, *Georgetown Family Symposia* (Vol 2) (1973–1974). Washington, DC: Georgetown University Family Center, 1977

Minuchin, S. *Families and family therapy.* Cambridge, Mass.: Harvard University Press, 1974

Minuchin, S, Montalvo, B, Guerney, BA, Rosman, BC, & Schumer, F. *Families of the slums: An exploration of their structure and treatment.* New York: Basic Books, 1967

Minuchin, S, Rosman, BL, & Baker, L. *Psychosomatic families.* Cambridge, Mass.: Harvard University Press, 1978

Napier, AY, & Whitaker, CA. *The family crucible.* New York: Harper & Row, 1978

Parloff, MB. Psychotherapy and research: An anaclitic depression. *Psychiatry,* 1980, *43,* 279–293

Pattison, EM, DeFrancisco, D, Wood, P, Frazier, H, & Crowder, J. A psychosocial kinship model for family therapy. *American Journal of Psychiatry,* 1975, *132,* 1246–1251

Pendagast, EG, & Sherman, CO. A guide to the genogram. In EG Pendagast, (Ed.), *The best of the family,* 1973–1978). New Rochelle, NY: The Center for Family Learning, 1979, pp 101–112

Pfeiffer, SI, & Tittler, BI. Adopting a family systems orientation to providing psychoeducational services in the schools. *School Psychology Review,* 1983, *12,* 168–173

Reiss, D. Individual thinking and family interaction. I. Introduction to an experimental study of problem-solving in families of normals, character disorders, and schizophrenics. *Archives of General Psychiatry,* 1967, *16,* 80–93

Reiss, D. Variations of consensus and experience III: Contrasts between families of normals, delinquents, and schizophrenics. *Journal of Nervous and Mental Disorder,* 1971, *152,* 73–95

Riskin, J, & Faunce, EE. An evaluative review of family interaction research. *Family Process,* 1972, *11,* 365–455

Ro-Trock, GK, Wellisch, PK, & Schoolar, JC. A family therapy outcome study in an inpatient setting. *American Journal of Orthopsychiatry,* 1977, *47,* 514–522

Satir, V. *Peoplemaking.* Palo Alto, Calif.: Science and Behavior Books, 1972

Shapiro, RJ, & Budman, SH. Defection, termination, and continuation in family and individual therapy. *Family Process,* 1973, *12,* 55–67

Smilkstein, G. The cycle of family function: A conceptual model for family medicine. *The Journal of Family Practice,* 1980, *11,* 223–232

Solvberg, H, & Blaker, R. Communication efficiency in couples with and without a schizophrenic offspring. *Family Process,* 1975, *14,* 515–534

Tittler, BI. Qualities of family thinking with regard to family change. *The Family,* 1980, *7,* 70–75

Tittler, BI, & Cook, VJ. Relationships among family, school, and clinic: Toward a systems approach. *Journal of Clinical Child Psychology,* 1981, *10,* 184–187

Tittler, BI, Friedman, S, Blotcky, AD, & Stedrak, J. The influence of family variables on an ecologically-based treatment program for emotionally disturbed children. *American Journal of Orthopsychiatry,* 1982, *52,* 123–130

Tittler, BI, Friedman, S, & Klopper, EJ. A system for tailoring change measures to the individual family. *Family Process,* 1977, *16,* 119–121

Tolsdorf, CC. Social networks, support and coping: An exploratory study. *Family Process,* 1976, *15,* 407–417

Toman, W. *Family constellation.* New York: Springer, 2nd ed., 1969, 3rd Ed., 1976

Trotzer, JP. Engaging families in therapy: A pilot study. *International Journal of Family Therapy,* 1982, *4,* 4–19

Wahler, RG. The insular mother: Her problems in parent-child treatment. *Journal of Applied Behavior Analysis,* 1980, *13,* 207–219

Weakland, JH. OK—you've been a bad mother. In P Papp (Ed.), *Family therapy: Full-length case studies.* New York: Gardner Press, 1977

Weakland, JH. The double-bind theory: Some current implications for child psychiatry. *Journal of the American Academy of Child Psychiatry,* 1979, *18,* 54–66

Wilson, E. *Sociobiology: The new synthesis.* Cambridge, Mass.: Harvard University Press, 1975

Wynne, LC, Ryckoff, IM, Day, J, & Hirsch, SI. Pseudo-mutuality in the family relations of schizophrenics. *Psychiatry,* 1958, *21,* 205–220

Valerie J. Cook
George W. Howe
Bertha G. Holliday

9

Community Psychology for Clinical Child Psychologists: Perspectives and Roles

The administrative and consultative role demands of clinical child psychologists are increasing but there is a commensurate absence of preparatory training for these new roles. With this in mind, we write this chapter in the spirit of "professional coping." We believe that psychologists will more effectively solve those problems emerging in consultative and administrative work to the extent they recognize various options in their professional roles. In order for child clinicians, in particular, to recognize such options, they first must become more aware of those existing knowledge bases on techniques and problems in designing and implementing community intervention programs.

This chapter seeks to promote such awareness by introducing clinical child psychologists to a set of principles and procedures that might be subsumed under the label of "community psychology." Because many child clinicians are unfamiliar with such principles, we shall attempt to identify those conceptual and research themes that seem most critical in the works of community psychologists. We will also suggest how knowledge of these themes might better inform the work of clinical child psychologists by describing community-influenced intervention for use by child clinicians and discussing exemplary strategies and programs for child intervention.

331

MAJOR THEMES IN COMMUNITY PSYCHOLOGY

Rappaport (1977) suggests that community psychology is defined by its set of values, its field of inquiry, and its applied procedures.

Community Psychology as a Set of Professional Values

Dominant among the values of community psychology is its emphasis on viewing psychopathology and deviant behavior as culturally bound and value bound. Deviant behavior is thus not viewed as a particular entity universally meaningful in and of itself, but as an entity that is meaningful only in relation to the culture in which it occurs. A major corollary of this theme is that positive mental health and social competence also must be considered within the context of a particular culture. Consequently, community psychologists focus on the concept of "person-environment fit" wherein an emotional disorder cannot be identified solely in terms of individual intrapsychic indicators, but, instead, must be identified in terms of peoples' adaptation to particular environments.

This theme leads directly to a second value: the valuing of cultural relativity, diversity, and pluralism. As Rappaport (1977) observes, "a major political social question for the rest of this century will involve the ability of diverse groups to 'live and let live,' and this will mean understanding that there are neither sick persons (in a social psychological sense) nor invariant cultures" (p. 52).

A third common value of community psychologists is an emphasis on providing services to the disadvantaged, disempowered, and disenfranchised. People from outside the mainstream culture are not only more often labeled as pathological, but are almost always less empowered in the society (Rappaport, 1977). Community psychology holds that much of the work performed by psychologists involves such disenfranchised people, and many psychological techniques of assessment and intervention do not take into account the cultural matrix of such disempowered people. For example, as Lachar (1981) has noted, although psychological assessment techniques such as the Minnesota Multiphasic Personality Inventory (MMPI) are commonly administered to nonwhite clients, the predictive validity of such techniques is based almost entirely on the white-majority-culture population.

A fourth general value theme in community psychology involves the expansion of appropriate roles for psychologists. While the Boulder model of clinical training prescribed that psychological roles include those of researcher and clinician, community psychology further expanded this range of roles along three dimensions. First, in addition to research and clinical practice, community psychologists have suggested that community action and advocacy for disenfranchised groups are acceptable roles for psychologists. Second, community psychologists have suggested that in addition to individual approaches to intervention, such as psychotherapy, psychologists might expand their repertoire to include group, agency, institution, and community interventions. Finally, community psychology recognizes that psychological intervention includes not only tertiary prevention involving rehabilitative approaches such as psychotherapy, but also includes prevention involving enhancement of competence and stress resistance building.

Community Psychology as a Field of Inquiry

Coherent scientific disciplines are fields of inquiry restricted to studying a selected range of phenomena. This range is often defined by the units of analysis or observation and methodology most commonly used in a particular discipline. As scientific disciplines expand, they tend to break up into subfields or more narrowly defined areas of inquiry. For example, biology has developed subfields focusing primarily on such aspects of the biological world as physiology, anatomy, or genetics. Although a single level of analysis tends to oversimplify the nature of phenomena, such simplicity is necessary in order to study phenomena intensively. As fields of study develop and proliferate subfields, however, the inherent limitations of narrow focus and a single level of analysis become more and more pronounced. At a certain point, disciplines may emerge that attempt to bridge two related areas of inquiry. For example, biochemistry has linked the study of chemical processes to the development of biological organisms. As a field of inquiry, community psychology may be seen as such a bridging discipline between psychology and sociology, for much of what is studied in community psychology involves units of analysis at both the individual and the social group level. In this sense, community psychology is definitely an emerging discipline (Elias, Dalton, & Howe, 1981).

A cursory glance at journals of community psychology suggests that community psychology is a "borrower" of theory and method. The tradition within American clinical psychology bears certain similarities to this pattern. Clinical psychologists tend to be borrowers from a range of different psychological theories. Indeed, the majority of clinicians view themselves as pragmatically adopting an eclectic approach in their use of theories of human behavior. Community psychology has extended this clinical tradition, borrowing heavily from a variety of fields of inquiry, for pragmatic reasons.

However, the inquiry method of community psychology has begun to coalesce around what has been termed "action research." The concept of action research predates community psychology by many years. Collier, in 1945, suggested that collaboration between administrators, researchers, and laypersons could be used to improve ethnic relations between majority culture and American Indian subcultures (Collier, 1945). Kurt Lewin (1946) was the most well-known advocate of action research. More recently, Ketterer, Price, and Politser (1980) suggested that action research has five characteristics: it is problem-focused; its activities are closely linked to significant social problems; it involves collaboration between researchers, practitioners, and lay people; its two major goals are the development of knowledge and the solution of practical problems; and it emphasizes the utilization and dissemination of research products.

Community Psychology as a Field of Practice

Goodstein and Sandler (1978) view the practice of community psychology as one point on a continuum of practices that psychologists use to promote human welfare. They suggest that in addition to clinical psychology, which focuses on providing individual assessment and behavior change intervention for troubled individuals, psychologists also may promote human welfare through the practice of community mental health, community psychology, and public policy psychology. Others, such as Heller and Monahan (1977), do not take such a restricted view of community psychology, suggesting that community approaches can be applied in a variety of ways, at different levels of the community, in a variety of settings, and by persons in varied professional roles. Thus, community psychologists have pressured for the expansion of professional roles of psychologists, far beyond the traditional ones of academic scientist and clinician. These expanded roles include those of the ecologically oriented case consultant, the program planner/administrator/evaluator, the organization development consultant, the community activist/advocate/consultant, and the legislative lobbyist.

Although community psychology may press for psychologists to undertake these roles, it is our opinion that psychologists have, in general, been pushed into consultative and administrative roles by the needs of agencies, the current political circumstances, or simply as part of the psychologist's professional career development. As far as we can tell, however, few psychology training programs appear to include courses in administration or consultation skills. Consequently, community psychology holds out much promise to those professionals who find themselves caught up in these less traditional roles.

Community Psychology Concepts and Principles of Intervention

The primary theoretical principle that guides community psychology as a "bridging discipline" is that of person-environment fit. This principle views human behavior as defined not solely by characteristics of the individual, but as the transaction between individuals and their environments. The unit of analysis becomes the transaction, and, therefore, must include elements of both the individual and the environment without reducing the level of analysis to one or the other exclusively. People are viewed as active transactors with their environments, and an individual's behavior cannot be separated from the context in which it occurs. Kelly (1969) states this succinctly in his definition of adaptation:

"Adaptation is viewed as specific to a particular social setting, and as dependent upon the congruence between particular coping styles, that is, individual preferences for mastering the environment, and the normative requirements of the environment. Thus, a particular set of coping styles will be relevant to adaptation in one environment but not in another" (Kelly, 1969, p. 184).

People thus may act to change their environments or to adapt to them, and these active transactions between person and environment are a joint function of characteristics of each.

While this notion of the "indivisibility" of transactions is basic to community psychology, the field has borrowed from theoretical models that bring either the person or the environment side of the transaction into focus as the figure of study. The theories of person most often used appear to be those subsumed under the general title of cognitive social learning theories; those focusing more on the environment side of the transaction include systems theory and theories of social psychology (Rappaport, 1977).

While community psychology has utilized operant theories of behavior modification (Jason, 1977), issues have been raised that the strict operant view frames human behavior as under the control of environmental stimuli. This view is in contradiction to the model of human behavior described above, which holds that people are active, self-initiating transactors with their environments. Cognitive social learning models are more congruent with this latter view, suggesting that people both shape and are shaped by their environments in complex patterns of mutual influence (Mischel, 1973). The work of Elias, Larcen, Zlotlow, and Chinsky (1978)* provides an excellent example of this framework. Elias and his colleagues have studied how children actively formulate and solve problems in their social world, and have developed a series of training methods to help children develop productive strategies for dealing with problematic social situations. Although such studies primarily focus on person variables in the form of individual problem-solving styles, they by no means ignore the environment. Instead, they tend to focus on specific environmental domains as the settings for individual behavior, rather than studying the characteristics of those domains as the primary topic of research (Krasner & Rubin, 1981).

In a similar fashion, environmental models do not ignore the contribution of the individual to the transaction. Through use of such models, regularities and recurrent characteristics of environments are investigated as specific behavioral domains. The work of Roger Barker and his colleagues provides an excellent example of this approach. Barker (1964) introduced the concept of "behavior settings," defined as "standing patterns" of behavior that occur with a great deal of regularity in particular physical settings, independent of the specific people in that setting. A setting characteristic studied intensively by Barker and colleagues is school size. After several years of studying a range of schools in Kansas, these researchers reported that small schools were more likely to follow the pattern of "undermanned behavioral settings," in which students actively participated in more types of activities than students in large schools, although the larger schools had more than four times as many types of activities available (Barker & Gump, 1964). Barker hypothesized that smaller organizations enable greater participation of more members in a variety of key roles, and that such participation is instrumental in creating a sense of community in the organization.

Although environmental models may include very general structural variables such as organizational size or aspects of the physical environment (Proshansky, Ittelson, & Rivlin, 1970), most emphasize the study of the "social environment." Examples of social environmental models include: the organizational climate models Rudolph Moos (1981) used to assess environmental variables in various organizations as perceived by organizational members; systems theory as applied to both social systems in general (Murrell, 1973), and such specific systems as the family (Hoffman, 1981), formal organizations (Cummings, 1980), and communities (Bernard, 1973).

Although a detailed description of person-environment theories is

---

*Elias, M, Larcen, S, Zlotlow, S, & Chinsky, J. *An innovative measure of children's cognitions in problematic interpersonal situations.* Paper presented at the Annual Meeting of the American Psychological Association, Toronto, 1978

beyond the scope of this chapter, several of their underlying principles seem particularly relevant for clinical child psychologists. These are: transactions as social exchange, systems as self-correcting patterns of transactions, and boundaries as the point of cross-system transactions. We will define each of these principles briefly, then suggest how they might fit into a general model of child functioning and development that can guide the efforts of clinical child psychologists.

Transactions as Social Exchange

The social exchange perspective of person-environment transactions assumes that a transaction involves the exchange of something of value between two people. The rules of this social exchange are governed by an explicit or implicit set of expectations that have been called a social contract. This contract involves a set of rules for how individuals will act toward one another, what they will provide for each other, and what they can expect from each other. Barker's behavior settings probably represent settings where behavior is guided by such social contracts.

Systems as Self-Limiting Patterns of Transaction

The rules that govern behavior under a social contract are by no means always explicit, and may not even be accessible to the awareness of those who are following them. Systems theory suggests that such implicit rules are maintained by the behavior of those involved in the transaction. The behavior of one party to a transaction thus functions to restrict the behavior of the other party. For example, a crying child may distract arguing parents, restricting the options the parents have for settling their differences. In a similar fashion, a teacher may note that a child's poor performance on a test is due to unchangeable characteristics of the child, and therefore the teacher may be unmotivated to help the child with remediation, thus perpetuating the child's failure. Families and classrooms may be conceptualized as small social systems that develop such "contracts" of behavior and expectations among members that function to limit and direct future behavior and expectations. These patterns of expectation and behavior define the social environment that the developing child both adapts to and helps to shape.

Boundaries as the Point of Cross-system Transactions

If family and school systems provide social settings where things of value are exchanged in transactions among members, then the "boundaries" of these systems are those points at which one system transacts business with another. People may be members of a variety of systems without providing any substantive point of exchange between systems. A child's school functioning may follow the rules of the classroom and school, and be unaffected by the rules and patterns of transactions experienced by the child in the home. Alternatively, the child may be the family member entrusted with transacting the family's business with the school. Emigrant children whose parents speak the majority culture language poorly are very likely to be put in the role of negotiator with teachers or school personnel, when and if either system feels the need to transact business with the other.

A COMMUNITY PSYCHOLOGY INTERVENTION MODEL FOR CLINICAL CHILD PSYCHOLOGISTS

The community psychology themes and principles that we have discussed are the basis for a model of human functioning that both incorporates several levels of analysis, and is useful in guiding the efforts of child clinicians in their roles as researchers, assessors, and intervenors. This model assumes that psychological practice involves an implicit or explicit contract between the psychologist and a member(s) of some social system. The level of the social system (in terms of size, complexity, and relationships to other systems) shapes the role and behavior of the psychologist by determining his or her unit of analysis and intervention focus. Table 9-1 provides a summary of this model, including implications for intervention focus and roles.

When the social contract has been negotiated at the child level, the child is conceptualized as an active learner of social transaction in various social environments. This is the level of traditional clinical assessment and intervention. For example, cognitive social learning approaches involve assessment of the child's cognitions and behavioral repertoire, and interventions aimed at helping children develop skills and strategies in dealing with a range of social transactions (Krasner & Rubin, 1981).

The second level of the model involves social contracts within those naturally occurring small social groups that both provide the most immediate social systems for the child and most directly affect the child's development. Examples of such systems include the family, the classroom, and in mental health or special needs settings, the treatment unit. These systems involve transactions that facilitate or hinder the child's learning skills of social competence and adaptation. Accordingly, these systems set "boundary conditions" on how and in what direction the child may develop. This process is by no means unidirectional; child development and child behavior patterns in turn may have a major impact on how these systems operate (Margolin, 1981; Sameroff, 1975). Research on family functioning suggests that family patterns of conflict resolution within the family may have a major effect on a child's social

Table 9-1
A Community Psychology Intervention Model for Clinical Child Psychologists

Level of System	Model of Functioning	Unit of Analysis	Focus of Intervention	Intervention Role
Child	Child as proactive learner of social transaction in various social environments.	Child's behavior and cognitions.	Child's skills and strategies.	Therapist, special educator, traditional case consultant.
Small Group, e.g., family, classroom, treatment unit	System as integrated unit for established transactions of value.	System's patterns of interaction. General expectations of contract in system.	Systemic patterns of negotiation, problem solving, and adjustment to stress.	Ecologically oriented case consultant, family therapist, program consultant, program administrator.
System-System, e.g., family-school transactions, agency-agency transactions, unit-unit transactions within school or agency	Integrated service system of transacting agencies, schools, consumer groups and families.	Boundary transactions. Implicit and explicit contracts among various systems.	Patterns of negotiation between agencies, schools, consumer groups and families. Development of new programs and resources. Resource exchange networks.	Case manager, liaison specialist, organizational consultant, program planner/developer, community activist.
Sociopolitical, e.g., communities, states, federal government	Occasionally integrated system, with multiple interest groups trying to control resources.	Policy as boundary condition for lower-level contracts. Processes of political change and resource allocation.	Laws, policy, and procedures for allocating resources	Expert witness, legislative advisor, lobbyist, political activist.

and emotional development (Rutter, 1971), and may even affect the child's ability to maintain physical health (Minuchin, Rosman, & Baker, 1978). Interventions at this level may include family therapy, or program consultation in those systems such as the classroom, where particular children are not being served adequately. Such consultation might be case focused, as when the classroom setting is not working well with a particular child. It may be program centered, as when a school needs help in developing more efficient and effective programming for its students with special needs.

At the third level, the psychologist effects a contract to work at the intersection(s) of the child's immediate social systems. For example, families and schools may be seen as units that transact business within a larger system. This transaction process may break down at times, and a child may become caught in the war between parents and school system in much the same way that children get caught between warring parents. Reiss (1981) has suggested that families develop very consistent patterns for transacting business with the outside world. Some families keep the boundaries very permeable, seeking information in order to adjust or adapt to new conditions. Some families are more likely to work well with task-oriented institutions such as schools or hospitals. Other families maintain very rigid boundaries—transacting with agency personnel only minimally, and closing communication pathways very quickly.

Similarly, when a child has multiple special needs, the lack of co-ordination among multiple service providers can cause confusion for the child and his or her family, as well as undermine any set of inter-ventions by individual service providers. Such a pattern even can occur within agencies. Stanton and Schwartz (1954) described how patients in a mental hospital became upset when they were the objects of unack-nowledged conflict among staff regarding treatment approaches. These researchers also reported "their [the patients'] excitement terminated, usually abruptly, when the staff members were brought to discuss se-riously their points of disagreement with each other" (Stanton & Schwartz, 1954, p. 345). Such conflict involves implicit contracts related to staff behavior. Service programs for children need to seriously consider the possible presence of such organizational issues. Psychologists who are involved in a case may become organization consultants in such instances. And psychologists who are developing or administering child treatment programs need to be aware of the process and content of their implicit contracts for transacting with other agencies or schools.

At the fourth level, schools, agencies, and treatment programs are affected by boundary conditions existing among larger sociopolitical sys-tems such as communities, state governments, or federal governments.

General policies established explicitly through law or implicitly through regulation and operating procedures have a major effect on the availability of resources for child treatment. For example, Public Law 94-142 (Education for all Handicapped Children Act), which mandates services for children with special education needs, has significantly affected the roles of school psychologists by emphasizing testing activities to the exclusion of activities related to problem-oriented case consultation. Such efforts additionally have been intensified by cutbacks in school funding. Intervention at this level involves controlling the flow of resources among multiple interest groups. Although this process is often described as adversarial, it also can be conceptualized as a process of negotiation and bargaining regarding transactions of valued social resources. Psychologists may be involved in this process as expert witnesses and legislative advisors to various groups involved in decision making, or as lobbyists and political activists engaged in organizing interest groups for legislative change.

EXEMPLARY STRATEGIES AND PROGRAMS

Just as we may look at person-environment transactions from a number of levels, so may we define roles for clinical child psychologists associated with intervention at each of these levels. And just as different principles of human functioning are assumed at each level, so may intervention roles require different skills at different levels.

In this section of the chapter, we will impose our community psychology intervention model on the work of clinical child psychologists by describing existing exemplary programs of intervention at various system levels. We will also define the related social contracts and professional roles implicit in these programs. The section will culminate with a description of a comprehensive program that integrates intervention at all levels of the system.

The Child Level: The Traditional Clinical Child Psychologist

The traditional roles of the clinical child psychologist, emphasizing assessment or therapy with an individual child, are characteristic of this level of our model. Traditionally, the child clinician who functions as a case consultant works at this level. Such a consultant typically accepts a psychoeducational referral and then seeks, through testing and assessment, to delineate characteristics and attributes of the child. Following this, consultation focuses on identifying and implementing strategies for enhancing the child's learning processes and changing the child's behavior.

However, a community psychology perspective suggests limitations of professional role activities at this level. First, the content of such an assessment would be better directed at the child's transactions in a range of systems. Second, transactions between these systems in which the child is involved may have major implications for treatment or remediation, and as such need to be included in the assessment. Finally, the role of assessor presupposes that psychologists are somehow separated from referring social systems, and thus do not need to negotiate or develop the social contracts between themselves and other members of the systems in which referred children are involved.

The Small Group Level: The Ecologically Oriented Case Consultant

When the small group is the level of intervention, a variety of professional roles may emerge. At this level, the psychologist focuses on the child's system as an integrated unit with which problem solving is negotiated. Consequently, the psychologist may function as a family therapist, program consultant or administrator, or an ecologically oriented case consultant. Differences between intervention at the levels of the child and small group can be noted by the example of psychological activities at the Peabody Child Study Center (CSC).

The Organization and Operation of the CSC

The Child Study Center is an interdisciplinary (clinical and school psychology, and special education) training, service, and research unit of George Peabody College of Vanderbilt University. The "presenting client problems" span the range of learning and/or behavior problems that are ascribed to the children. The training function and rationale for services have been described in detail by Tittler and Cook (1981). At the CSC, psychological activities are ecologically oriented and influenced by the work of Bowen (1978) and Hobbs (1966). The emphasis of this description will be on the clear articulation of the social contract, and the ecological orientation to assessment and consultation.

The typical referral to the CSC involves a request for assessment of a child. Assessment is viewed as a problem identification and problem-solving process and as the first phase of consultation. Assessment and consultation roles are thus viewed as inextricably intertwined. The consultant begins the process, not by doing any assessment, but by defining the needs and goals of all parties involved in the referral. These personal agendas are by no means always obvious. Children have been referred with "reading problems" who exhibit no intellectual or learning difficulties, but instead are embroiled in covert family conflicts that overtly center around the school achievement (see Cook, in press). Children have been referred by special education teachers whose real agenda is to have an ally in confronting the school board concerning the need for help in an overcrowded resource room. Organizational consultants have written frequently about the need to clarify the goals of the consultation prior to jumping in and collecting data; this step is also important for case consultants. Such goal clarification leads to defining the social contract and expectations under which the consultant will operate, as he or she enters into the child's various social environments.

CSC Intervention Strategies

After the contract is tentatively defined, the consultant begins to identify which aspects of the child's "ecology" require detailed assessment. This ecological survey involves: scanning the various social environmental settings in which the child is involved, getting some sense of how the various settings might involve systems that help or hinder the child's development, and determining how these systems are interacting with each other (i.e., the third level of our model). This usually entails surveying, at the minimum, family functioning, school functioning, and interactions between family members and school personnel. A variety of ecological survey techniques are used, but emphasis is placed on interview and observation. The ecological survey is conducted to identify possible problem situations in which the child finds him or herself. Simultaneously, each of those situations is evaluated in light of potential resources for problem resolution.

To assist in the conceptualization of the problem situation, an "Ecological Assessment: Initial Survey" form has been developed. The unit of analysis for this survey is the child-in-transaction, with emphasis on the functional meeting point, or match, between child and the ecological characteristics. Examples of transactions surveyed include those of child-curriculum, child-school personnel, child-peers, child-parents, child-family, family-school personnel, parent-parent, and occasionally, transactions of the family or parents with extended family and/or other aspects of the community. Each transaction is surveyed along three dimensions: intensity varying from deficit to strength, affect varying from distress to joy, duration varying from chronic or general to acute or flexible. Human transactions include the fourth dimension of conflict to cooperation.

This focus on transactions is consistent with the community psychology value of the person-environment fit. Deviance or deficits are not seen so much as belonging to the individual child; rather, a "problem situation" is identified. From this perspective, the child who is in need of special education needs special instructional services, not only because he or she is "handicapped," but also because of such circumstances as the lack of appropriate content in the regular curriculum or lack of appropriate training of the regular teacher.

In the third phase of consultation at the CSC, the psychologist narrows the field of inquiry, using assessment techniques to provide a detailed view of functioning within those areas of transaction that seemed most problematic. This might involve additional family interviews, classroom observation, or more traditional forms of assessment, e.g., intellectual and educational assessment. In the final phase, the consultant writes reports of findings and shares information and uses these as intervention tools, that is, as vehicles for effecting change in child-systems transactions.

Dissemination of the CSC Model

This ecologically oriented case consultation model of service delivery can be implemented by private clinics, community mental health centers, or schools. Indeed, in the past year, the CSC has moved from the university-based clinic into the public schools with a new name more reflective of its orientation and services: The Child and Family Consultation Service. But regardless of the setting in which this model is implemented, it is important that the clinical child psychologist recognizes that the difference between traditional case consultation and ecologically oriented case consultation extends beyond a difference in the ordering of activities. The shift from a child-centered model to a small group focus requires: a shift of thinking regarding the locus of problems, from individuals to transactions or situations; an understanding of systems theory and patterns of interaction; and experience in collaborative, rather than expert, consultation in which all major actors in the child's primary ecologies are viewed as both valued sources of information and significant agents of change.

The System-System Level: The Program Developer/Planner

Emory Cowen and his colleagues have engaged in exemplary intervention at the system-system level. Cowen, a clinical psychologist, was influenced by the changing views of mental health, especially those regarding: the cause of dysfunction, psychology's failure with profound disorders (e.g., schizophrenia) and the concomitant need for prevention, the limits of psychotherapy and the resulting shift to psychoeducational perspectives, the differential demographic distribution of disorders, and the mismatch between the supply of mental health professionals and the demand for their services.

In the 1950s, unlike the situation nationally, Cowen and his colleagues found an unusual richness and strength in the mental health services available to children in Rochester, New York. However, the bulk of such efforts were directed to responding to crises situations and/or already dysfunctional children. Cowen and his colleagues at the University of Rochester responded to this situation by developing the Primary Mental Health Project (PMHP).† Although this program has changed over the years, the primary thrust remains the same: The early identification of and intervention with children likely to have problems of school adaptation (learning or behavioral). From its inception, the PMHP has had two interdependent components: service and research. The research has been used to develop screening procedures and to conduct evaluations, which, in turn, inform the intervention designs of the service component.

The Organization and Operation of the PMHP

Shortly after the beginning of the school year, the school psychologist administers a battery of intellectual and personality screening tests to small groups of all first graders. Teachers complete behavior rating scales for each of their students. The school social worker interviews the parent(s) of those children considered "at risk" from the screening procedures. All of this information is brought to bear on the decision to refer a child to the program.

Upon acceptance in the program, an initial conference is held in which goals are set and the child is assigned to a nonprofessional aide. The aide then works with the child, usually individually, in 30- to 40-minute sessions twice a week. A mid-year conference is held (including parent and teacher, PMHP and school personnel) in which the child's progress is evaluated and the decision to terminate, continue, or revise the intervention is made. If continued, an end-of-the-year conference is held to decide whether to terminate or continue the child in the program next year, or to "wait and see" how the child adjusts to school the next year.

While the direct service component is being administered in the schools, the PMHP core staff, usually clinical psychologists, is involved in ongoing consultation with school personnel. Two thirds of the consultation is likely to be case consultation regarding individual children. The remaining consultation is consultee-centered (staff or school per-

---

†This description of the Primary Mental Health Project is based on the numerous writings of Emory L. Cowen and his colleagues from 1966 to 1983.

sonnel) regarding problems pertaining to PMHP responsibilities, or program consultation regarding the effectiveness of the program in the eyes of school personnel.

PMHP Intervention Strategies

The indirect, or ecological, interventions implemented by the consultants are targeted toward the junction of children and school personnel and toward collaboration between home and school. In the process, teachers become exposed to mental health professionals and develop a better understanding of children, thus enabling them to be more effective in day-to-day activities and situations. The children served in the PMHP include those having learning problems as well as those who are acting-out or are shy and withdrawn. The goals and psychoeducational strategies may thus vary widely. Three general goals, however, emerge: to strengthen the child's academic background, to build a relationship with the child, and to free-up the child's behavior (e.g., active decision making).

PMHP Staffing

The nonprofessional aide is the backbone of the PMHP. Care is taken to select women who have good helping skills, and experiences, personalities, and interests that qualify them for helping roles with young children. Training is provided to the aides to help them conceptualize the psychological and educational needs of children and to alleviate their own anxieties about assuming the helping role. Furthermore, the aides are supervised by school mental health professionals and/or PMHP staff.

The PMHP staff generally consists of a program director responsible for the integration of the service and research components, a chief psychologist and chief social worker sharing responsibility for the supervision of personnel and the service operation, a research coordinator, and a community liaison whose functions include public relations, budgeting, and administrative planning. This core staff is augmented, whenever possible, with doctoral and postdoctoral trainees in the mental health professions. The composition of the core staff varies across schools from entirely university based to entirely school based.

The involvement of existing school mental health professionals is integral to the PMHP. The role of these school psychologists and school social workers changes, however, to one of reduced direct service and increased educational, consultative, supervisory, and resource functions.

Clinical child psychologists are also involved in multiple and expanded roles. At the small group level, they serve as ecologically oriented case consultants, consultee-centered (i.e., focused on parents and school personnel) consultants, program consultants, trainers of nonprofessional aides, and, perhaps, as any one program administrator. At the system-to-system level, clinical child psychologists are involved in enhancing home-school collaboration and community liaison activities. The roles of clinical child psychologists in the PMHP are markedly different from the direct service roles and functions for which they are traditionally trained.

PMHP Sponsorship

The original PMHP in the Rochester schools was funded by NIMH as a demonstration project. While NIMH and other federal sources have continued to provide funding for some projects or aspects of projects, the public schools also have provided financial support to their individual projects.

Evaluation, Dissemination, and Cost-effectiveness of the PMHP

Over 50 research studies have been conducted on the PMHP or its components. Most recently, Weissberg, Cowen, Lotyczewski, and Gesten (1983) reported the results of seven consecutive years of program outcome research. The child's adjustment was measured from three different perspectives: the teacher and child in the classroom, the aide and child in the individualized session, and the mental health professional's overall view based on contacts with adults in the child's ecosystem. Children involved in the PMHP were judged (by all three perspectives) to be improved in their school adjustment. "[T]he intervention reduced acting-out, shy-anxious, and learning problems, and promoted competencies such as adaptive assertiveness, peer sociability, and frustration tolerance" (p. 103). While improvement for all kinds of children was seen, the PMHP was judged to be more effective with shy-anxious children compared with acting-out children. These long-term findings were consistent with earlier reported findings of more limited time and scope.

Further testimony to the success of the PMHP is indicated by the extent of its dissemination. The PMHP has grown from a demonstration project in one Rochester school to a full-scale service/research project in 20 Rochester-area schools and in more than 300 schools in 80 school districts nationwide (Cowen, Spinell, Wright, & Weissberg, 1983). The PMHP serves approximately 11 percent of the primary graders in each of its schools.

The dissemination of PMHP has proven to be highly cost-effective. In fact, for about a 40 percent increase in program cost, a 1,000 percent increase in effective services is realized (Cowen, Trost, Lorion, Dorr, Izzo, & Isaacson, 1975). The PMHP has thus stood the test of time and growth pains associated with dissemination while providing cost-effective services that have been amply documented as effective in preventing school maladjustment.

Summary

The PMHP is one example of how community psychology perspectives can be brought to bear in providing psychological services to children. The functions or activities of the clinical child psychologist as program developer/planner were implicit in all project activities. As exemplified by Cowen and his colleagues, the necessary attributes for successful performance of the developer/planner role are: the ability to collaborate with other professionals (e.g., school personnel) to gain their involvement in the development and implementation of the program, the ability to communicate the need and vision of the program to obtain financial support, and a commitment to research and evaluation as a means by which to further refine the program.

The System-System Level: The Multisystem Developer/Coordinator

The creation and implementation of a program to supplement ongoing services is a challenge, but this challenge is magnified when one is faced with the prospects of developing an entirely new program of service delivery. Such was the situation in the early 1960s when Leon Lebovitz, a clinical and school psychologist, was hired (half-time) as the sole psychological services provider for the entire Memphis, Tennessee, school system. Lebovitz's challenge was compounded by the general paucity of mental health services for children in Memphis. Faced with such predicaments, Lebovitz and his associates drew upon principles of mental health consultation and developed the following tenets of the Memphis City Schools Mental Health Center (MCSMHC):‡

a. Mental health services need to be preventive in nature.
b. A great deal of primary and secondary prevention can be accomplished within the context of a school system.
c. Services are best provided where the people are.
d. Optimal use of resources can be achieved by "piggy-backing" mental health services on an existing system such as the Memphis City Schools.

---

‡This description of the Memphis City Schools Mental Health Center is based on Paavola (1983, March; 1983, June).

Paavola, JC. *The Memphis City Schools Mental Health Center.* A paper presented at the annual convention of the National Association of School Psychologists, Detroit.

Paavola, JC. (1983, June). Telephone interview, personal communication.

e. Creative use of mental health services in this way is further enhanced by the fact that the Memphis City Schools has a "captive" population. (Paavola, 1983, p. 1).

The MCSMHC was incorporated as a nonprofit mental health agency in the fall of 1969. By the fall of 1972, the MCSMHC began to take its present form.

The MCSMHC, now under the directorship of school psychologist James Paavola, is unique in that "it blends the talents, orientation, and philosophies of the professions of psychology, social work, education, mental health, and public welfare."‡ The MCSMHC provides a broad range of services within the Memphis City Schools, an urban district covering 290 square miles having a population of 675,000. The student population of 107,000 is 74.9 percent black, and has a poverty index of 62 percent.

The established goals of the MCSMHC are:

a. to provide therapeutic, consultative, and preventive mental health services to youngsters and their families residing in the Memphis/Shelby County area.

b. to promote an educational climate within the Memphis City Schools conducive to fostering mentally healthy growth and development.

c. to provide substance abuse related therapeutic, consultative, and preventive services to youngsters and their families residing in the Memphis/Shelby County area.

d. to establish and maintain effective relationships within the community as a component of the network of helping agencies within Shelby County.‡

The Organization and Operation of the MCSMHC

The majority of the approximately 5,000 annual referrals to the MCSMHC are made by school faculty. While this referral pattern is typical of school psychological services, it is unusual in mental health centers. However, this pattern has the advantage of bringing a captive adult who has daily contact with the child into the service delivery plan, thus enhancing procedures from referral to follow-up. Furthermore, faculty identify students for services prior to the time they would seek services for themselves. The provision of services through the schools also reduces the stigma associated with "mental health."

A referral is responded to by 1 of 19 clinical teams. Each team includes a school psychologist, a social worker, and a psychometrist under the coordination of a doctoral school or clinical child psychologist. After reviewing available information, the team determines the nature and extent of the intake workup. This workup may vary from observation and interview to formal testing and psychiatric consultation. Within 30 days after referral, the team develops a formal treatment plan for the youngster and/or family members. Cases are closed only when the team has determined that the goals have been achieved as best possible.

MCSMHC Intervention Strategies

While 55 percent of the referrals are special education related, over half of the MCSMHC staff's time is devoted to treatment, namely, individual, group, or family therapy. The typical annual treatment caseload for the program includes 175 abused/neglected children and their families, 150 youngsters in the alcohol and drug treatment program and their families, 75 emotionally disturbed students, and 400 to 500 other youngsters and their families. Approximately 12 percent of the staff's time is devoted to such consultation and education activities as teacher consultation; workshops for teachers, counselors, principals, and parents; school consultation regarding, for example, discipline and race relations; program and policy-centered consultation with the superintendent's staff and board members; participation in local, state, and federal agencies and planning groups; and provision of a speaker's bureau. The MCSMHC has the largest children and youth programs in the state of Tennessee in the areas of general outpatient treatment, outpatient alcohol and drug treatment, alcohol and drug prevention, and abuse and neglect treatment.

The principles and values of community psychology especially are apparent in the MCSMHC consultation activities. The Memphis City Schools, for example, had a grave "white flight" problem, private schools attracted many of the potential white students. The school board wished to attract these students back to the public schools and the MCSMHC staff provided consultation. Teams of eight to ten people (principal, four or five teachers, parents, business people) were developed for each of the eight targeted schools. The MCSMHC staff helped each team develop action plans for the school year. Hundreds of hours were devoted to staff development necessary for upgrading the quality of the schools. The electronic and print media were used to inform the public of the good things happening in the schools. And each school team developed its own public information strategy. As a result of such efforts, the eight target schools attracted 648 white students from private schools, a rate three times that of the system average of new students. The private-to-public school pattern is now so well established that some of the private elementary schools are viewed as "feeder schools" for the public junior highs. Further evidence of community support for the schools was realized in a referendum increasing taxes for the schools.

MCSMHC Staffing

The MCSMHC has a professional staff of 95, consisting of doctoral (clinical and school) supervising psychologists, school psychologists, school social workers, psychometrists, alcohol and drug counselors, homemakers, and psychology interns.

Of course, the staffing of a mental health center in the schools poses unique challenges. Psychologists must possess a systems perspective, knowledge of the school as a system, understanding of children in a developmental context, and skills in assessment, therapy, and consultation. Consequently, it is unusual for a psychologist to come "fully equipped" to the MCSMHC. The strengths and weaknesses of each psychologist thus are outlined, and supervision is provided accordingly. The MCSMHC commitment to continuing education is reflected in the allocation of 30 percent of one doctoral psychologist's time to coordinating staff development.

The clinical child psychologist in the MCSMHC is likely to have multiple roles, including case and program consultation, provision and supervision of therapy, coordination and management of the clinical teams, and usually directorship of one of the specially funded (e.g., child abuse, alcohol and drug prevention) programs. The MCSMHC clinical child psychologist thus must have the orientations and skills to work at three levels of the system described in our model: the child level, the small group level, and the system-system level.

MCSMHC Sponsorship

The MCSMHC was originally established with a direct allocation from the Tennessee legislature, supplemented by Title I (federal education) funds. School social workers were added with Title IV-A funds (Social Security Act). The MCSMHC presently receives funding from several sources: city and county tax revenues, the Tennessee Department of Mental Health and Mental Retardation (TDMHMR), the Tennessee Department of Human Services (TDHS), the U.S. Education Department, the Tennessee Department of Education, and the Ford Foundation. Services are provided at no charge to all youngsters and their families who are residents of Shelby County, regardless of school attendance.

MCSMHC Evaluation and Dissemination

Little formal research has been completed on the overall effectiveness of the MCSMHC program. There are, however, several indices of success. The child abuse and neglect treatment programs were cited by the TDHS as model programs to be replicated in other areas of the state.

When Title XX programs were being eliminated, the TDHS found secure funding for the program, including a 5 percent increase. The alcohol and drug abuse prevention program has been identified as a model program by the TDMHMR, additional funding has been allocated, and state-wide dissemination is being planned. Similarly, the U.S. Education Department selected the program as one of five in the nation to receive discretionary funds for additional activities. When the TDMHMR eliminated the funding of almost all noncommunity mental health centers, the MCSMHC funding was cut by only 50 percent. The five community mental health centers in Shelby County have reduced their children and youth components to only a handful of staff, and are now referring children and youth to the MCSMHC for outpatient treatment. Over the past two years, the Memphis City Schools eliminated millions of dollars in program and staff, yet increased the local funding to the MCSMHC. Finally, in 1982, the MCSMHC received the first national Award of Excellence for School Psychological Services from the American Psychological Association, Division 16 and the National Association of School Psychologists.

Summary

Although Lebovitz was a clinical and school psychologist, community psychology values formed the very basis of his goals and plans for the MCSMHC. These values are reflected in his emphasis on: prevention, meeting the needs of the underserved, and maximizing resources by using the schools as a natural organizing force in the community. His vision, unlike Cowen's focused prevention program, was comprehensive in nature. The multisystem developer/coordinator must share the characteristics of the single-program developer, but, along all dimensions, the need for those characteristics is magnified. Additionally, Lebovitz and the successive program directors have been creative and excellent grantsmen in seeking funding for multiple programs from local, state, and federal agencies as well as private foundations. Their administrative task involves more than running several programs at one time; it involves coordinating various programs into one organized service delivery model.

The Sociopolitical Level: The National Advocate

It is not unusual for the American Psychological Association (APA) to take policy positions regarding issues in American society, although these positions seldom result in more than discussion among psychologists. However, in 1976, Irwin Hyman responded to the APA Council of Representatives' resolution opposing the use of corporal punishment in the schools by establishing the National Center for the Study of Corporal Punishment and Alternatives in the Schools[§] at Temple University. The center seeks to eliminate the use of corporal punishment in the schools. Two principles seem to guide the center's efforts: the arguments against corporal punishment must come from a firm data base, and the efforts to eliminate one form of discipline in the schools must be accompanied by the efforts to provide positive alternatives for discipline, which must also be data based.

Organization and Sponsorship of the Center

The center was established with small grants from the American Civil Liberties Union and the Randen Foundation. Also, it is affiliated with and partially supported by the Department of School Psychology at Temple University. The department's graduate students (some volunteers) are a major source of research and advocacy assistance in support of the center's goals.

Research

The center has developed and maintains extensive collections of research literature on corporal punishment and alternative methods of discipline, and nationwide press clippings regarding corporal punishment cases (since 1976). These materials are used for advocacy, policy analyses, and related research. The center's program of research is focused equally on the effects of corporal punishment and the effectiveness of positive alternatives to discipline in the schools. (For example, Bogacki, 1981;[||] Clarke, Liberman-Lascoe, & Hyman, 1980;[#] Dennehy, 1981;[**] Kreutter, 1982;[††] Lally, 1982,[‡‡] McDowell-Friedman, 1979.)

[§]This description of the National Center for the Study of Corporal Punishment and Alternatives in the Schools is based on the reports of Hyman and his colleagues (Hyman & Fina, 1983; Hyman & Wise, 1979).

[||]Bogacki, D. Attitudes toward corporal punishment: Authoritarian personality and pupil control ideology of school personnel. Unpublished doctoral dissertation, Temple University, 1981

[#]Clarke, J, Liberman-Lascoe, R, & Hyman, IA. An analysis of corporal punishment cases as reported in nationwide newspapers: Types, incidents and outcomes. Paper presented at the Annual Meeting of the National Association of School Psychologists, Washington, DC., 1980

[**]Dennehy, SN. An assessment of teacher effectiveness training on improving the teacher-student relationship, maintaining classroom discipline and increasing teacher and student capacity for problem solving. Unpublished doctoral dissertation, Temple University, 1981

[††]Kreutter, K. Student and teacher attitudes toward disciplinary practice in a junior high school setting. Unpublished doctoral dissertation, Temple University, 1982

[‡‡]Lally, D. Administrators' perceptions of the effectiveness of discipline codes in New Jersey high schools. Unpublished doctoral dissertation, Temple University, 1982

One of the Center's comprehensive research projects was spurred by a 1977 United States Supreme Court decision that ". . . school children do not enjoy constitutional protection from paddling under the Eighth Amendment" (Hyman & Fina, 1983, p. 258). Following a series of literature reviews and original research, Hyman (1979) was able to refute many of the statements appearing in the written majority opinion. Examples of such statements are: (a) that corporal punishment seldom results in physical injury, (b) that there is no trend towards its elimination in schools, and (c) that corporal punishment promotes positive student attributes and maintains group discipline. Later, Hyman and Fina (1983, p. 258) mused, "Perhaps if this evidence had been available preceding the opinion, there might have been a different outcome."

This sought after connection between research and policy formation is the guiding force of the center's activities.

> The Center's research efforts are not conducted solely for scholarly use, but also provide a growing data base to support the elimination of corporal punishment. In addition, these findings have been used extensively to support advocacy efforts (Hyman & Fina, 1983, p. 258).

Advocacy

Paralleling their research efforts, center personnel place equal emphasis on advocacy against corporal punishment and advocacy for positive alternatives for discipline in the schools. The center has undertaken a variety of advocacy activities. Affidavits and expert testimony have been presented to several state legislatures, other state bodies, and organizations. Hyman, Director of the Center, has provided depositions and expert testimony in individual cases. One such case reached the West Virginia Supreme Court. The Court, in this case, refused to abolish corporal punishment, but prohibited school personnel from using instruments in their application of such punishment (Hyman & Fina, 1983).

In addition to targeting their advocacy toward policy makers, the center provides "education" on school discipline issues to parents, school personnel, and the lay population at large. A media campaign has been undertaken involving appearances on local and national television shows, radio show interviews, and articles translating research findings for lay publications. Numerous inservice programs on a variety of positive alternatives to corporal punishment have been prepared and delivered to school personnel. The center has also accepted a consultation contract with the New Jersey State Department of Education to assist the efforts of an urban school district to improve discipline. Additionally, the center publishes a newsletter and makes available reports regarding school discipline. Their advocacy efforts have been enhanced by involvement in a network of over 30 concerned organizations.

Summary

There are hundreds of advocacy groups attempting to influence policy development within the United States. The National Center for the Study of Corporal Punishment and Alternatives in the Schools is an exemplary model for child clinicians because it is directed by a psychologist, and it is adamantly committed to a research base for its advocacy efforts. The center's activities suggest that psychologists who accept a professional advocate role must have skills necessary for converting "psychological theory and research into messages with audience appeal" (Hyman & Fina, 1983, p. 259).

A Comprehensive, Multi-level Example

In 1953, the Southern Regional Education Board pointed out that emotionally disturbed children and their families were confronted with either a lack of services, inappropriate services, or prohibitively costly services. It was this predicament that was addressed by Nicholas Hobbs, a clinical psychologist, at George Peabody College for Teachers in Nashville, Tenn. Hobbs and his Peabody colleagues worked with mental health officials and developed an innovative approach that became known as Project Re-ED,[§§] an acronym for "a project for the re-education of emotionally disturbed children".

As Hobbs (1979) observed, "Just what re-education meant was not at all clear at the outset" (p. 6). Nevertheless, Hobbs and his colleagues, who were influenced by the then emerging field of community psychology, preferred concepts of education over those of psychiatry (Cook & Plas, 1984). The Re-ED model was initiated at Cumberland House (in Nashville, Tenn.) and Wright School (in Durham, N.C.) in 1962–63. Since then, the model has been refined and replicated. There currently are 23 Re-ED schools throughout the nation,[||||] yet no Re-ED orthodoxy exists. What these schools share are the following intervention principles and values.

The child is an inextricable part of his or her ecosystem, including family, school, and community. The child is considered disturbed because his or her behavior is disturbing to others (e.g., parents, teachers) in the child's ecosystem. Thus, equal attention is given to the child and the ecosystem in assessment and intervention. The goal is not the cure of the child, but rather enablement of the child's ecosystem to function reasonably well.

[§§]This description of Project Re-ED is based on the numerous writings of Nicholas Hobbs from 1966 to 1982.

[||||]A directory of the RE-ED schools is published in Hobbs, 1982.

Intervention strategies take into account the whole child and serve to emphasize the natural strengths of childhood, i.e., growth and development of competencies. The development of educational competencies is considered crucial; thus, individualized instruction is included. Other activities are oriented to the arts, camping, sports, and life skills. Time (i.e., natural development of children) is considered an ally.

Human relationships are valued and encouraged. The development of trust is the first step in re-education. Through the use of peer group processes and immediate discussion of problematic situations, troubled children are encouraged to express their feelings in socially appropriate ways.

The Organization and Operation of Re-ED

The children served by Re-ED have been previously diagnosed as moderately to severely emotionally disturbed. Although the original schools were designed to serve children ages 6 to 12 years, additional schools have been developed for adolescents (e.g., Pine Breeze School in Chattanooga, Tenn., and Crockett Academy in Nashville, Tenn.). Upon entering the program, a child is usually assigned to a group of eight to ten children on the basis of sex and age. Thorough individual and ecological assessments are conducted and an individual "enablement plan" is developed for each child. The development of the enablement plan reflects collaborative efforts among the principal members of the child's ecosystem. Specific steps are outlined toward the goal of restoring the ecosystem to a level of functioning that is satisfactory to all members, including the Re-ED staff. Each ecosystem member's responsibilities toward the fulfillment of the enablement plan are specified (Hobbs, 1982), thus formalizing the social contract.

Re-ED Intervention Strategies

Direct intervention services or "psychological strategies" of Re-ED include: individualized educational programs, behavior modification for control of symptoms and development of social competencies, and peer group process sessions. The types of psychological strategies used in Re-ED vary across schools and ages of children served (e.g., more individual therapy is provided to teenagers).

"Ecological strategies [are] ways of working with child, family, neighborhood, school, and community" (Hobbs, 1979, p. 18) and include a variety of indirect services (Apter, 1982). The primary intervention techniques are consultation and the development of networks and covenants (Rhodes & Paul, 1978). Parent involvement in the intervention process is integral to ecological intervention. Minimally, parents are involved in goal setting and are committed to work with Re-ED staff. Parent consultation may be enhanced by formal contracts involving commitments to participate in specific interventions including, but not limited to, parent training or family therapy. Some Re-ED schools directly provide these services, while other schools refer parents to other mental health professionals or services in the community. School consultation is considered essential both to the development of intervention strategies and educational plans in Re-ED, as well as to the development of the program for reintegrating the child in the home school.

Re-ED Staffing

Each group of children is assigned to a three-person Re-ED team consisting of a day teacher-counselor, night teacher-counselor, and liaison teacher-counselor. The teacher-counselors usually hold a master's degree in special education supplemented by on-the-job training in Re-ED techniques. The day and night teacher-counselors are responsible for the psychological intervention strategies, while the liaison teacher-counselor coordinates the ecological intervention component. The functioning of the Re-ED teams is enhanced by the use of psychological consultants. As Hobbs (1982, p. 19) explained, "A cardinal principle in Re-ED from its inception has been that the knowledge of specialists should be brought to bear in the day-to-day operation of programs as well as in their general design." As consultants, clinical child psychologists have provided support to Re-ED related to program design and management, assessment, assignment of children to groups, training and support for teacher-counselors, and research and evaluation (Hobbs, 1982, Chap. 5).

Re-ED Sponsorship

The two original Re-ED schools were established as part of an eight-year demonstration project funded by NIMH and the states of Tennessee and North Carolina. Nationwide dissemination of the Re-ED model was assisted by a contract with the United States Office of Education (Alwes, 1978). Currently, the majority of the Re-ED schools are under public mental health auspicies, although some are associated with psychiatric hospitals, public schools, universities, philanthropic foundations, and private for-profit agencies.

Evaluation, Dissemination, and Cost-effectiveness of Re-ED

The average length of residence in Re-ED is four to six months, as compared with an average of 18 months in traditional programs. Hobbs (1966) reported an 80% success rate based on comparing enrollment observations with six-month postdischarge observations of approximately 100 children. Re-ED children showed higher academic performance, better adjustment, more positive self-concepts, and greater confidence in their ability to control their environment, than did a group of equally disturbed children receiving a variety of other (traditional) services (Weinstein, 1969, 1974). Furthermore, 87% (of 223) students returned to their homes and regular classrooms (Hermann, 1979). Finally, the costs associated with Re-ED are about one-half that of custodial programs and one-fourth less than other active treatment programs.

Project Re-ED has stood the test of time (over 20 years) and the discontinuance of federal funds (since 1968). The Tennessee program has expanded to the extent that most (200 of 225) children and adolescents in public residential care are in Re-ED programs, and all but two traditional wards in state mental hospitals have closed (Hobbs, 1979). Both the 1969 "Panel of Visitors" and the 1970 Joint Commission on Mental Health of Children concluded that Re-ED was sound and effective, and recommended the establishment of two programs in every state.

Hobbs (1982) expressed his regret that Re-ED has not been disseminated more widely, and attributed the situation to a lack of communication about the model and its successes. He emphasized the need for application of Re-ED principles and techniques to prevention programs aimed at keeping children out of Re-ED schools and other residential programs. Some steps have been taken in this direction. The Regional Intervention Project in Tennessee serves disruptive preschoolers and their families. And, the Central Kentucky Re-ED Program (in Lexington) has a successful ten-county prevention-outreach program.

Summary

Project Re-ED was chosen as an exemplary program involving intervention at all levels of our model. At the child level, "psychological interventions," including prescriptive individual education plans, are implemented. More attention, however, is given the small group level—with emphasis on the functioning of the Re-ED unit, the child-in-group processes, and working with families of the children in the Re-ED programs. A full one third of staff efforts are devoted to the system-system level: the liaison teacher-counselor conducts "ecological interventions" specifically aimed at bringing together various components of the child's ecosystem to work toward the goal of the healthy development of the child. At the sociopolitical level, Re-ED has changed the total mental health service delivery system for children in many states.

EPILOGUE: NEW CHALLENGES AND ROLES FOR CLINICAL CHILD PSYCHOLOGISTS

As indicated by the 1972 Presidential veto of the Comprehensive Child Care Development Bill (Ross, 1972a, 1972b), cutbacks in funding of community mental health centers (CMHC) and declines in CMHC dollars spent on children (Knitzer, 1982, Ch. 5), and erratic implementation of P.L. 94-142 (Knitzer, 1982, Chap. 4), during the past 12 years, federal and state initiatives in support of child mental health have been neither exceptionally dramatic nor innovative. We believe such patterns of initiatives suggest that this is not an era in which major new kinds of child-serving institutions and institutional arrangements will be created. Improved child mental health services will occur only through innovative collaborations among existing child-serving institutions and expansion of professional roles.

We believe that the foregoing descriptions of the Peabody CSC, the PMHP, the MCSMHC, the National Center for the Study of Corporal Punishment and Alternatives in the Schools, and Project Re-ED demonstrate how clinical child psychologists can use community psychology in attempting to forge collaborations and expand professionals roles. We take this opportunity to identify both the major commonalities of these exemplary programs, and the major directions they suggest for the practice of clinical child psychology.

All of these programs have been designed and are targeted at levels beyond that associated with the traditional child level of clinical child psychologists. Nevertheless, several of these programs formally intervene at that level. The psychologists at the CSC often identify the child's cognitive strengths and weaknesses (associated with traditional psychoeducational assessment and consultation) in order to effect a more compatible child-curriculum transaction. The aides in the PMHP work directly with the child as a means of increasing child competencies. The MCSMHC provides individualized educational and therapeutic services. RE-ED has a clearly articulated "psychological interventions" component.

No one program is a "pure" example of intervention at any one level of the model. Even the staff of our model advocacy program became involved in intervention at the small group level. Indeed, activities of our exemplary programs suggest that as psychologists target their interventions at "higher" levels of the system, all levels "below" are affected. It is also the case that systems-oriented psychologists will attend to the potential impact of lower-level interventions on higher levels of the system. For example, Re-ED, which started with one school, eventually became the statewide mental health model throughout Tennessee.

The school is the major organizing structure. All of these programs view the school, a system in which all children are captive, as both a major organizing structure in the child's ecosystem and a locus for collaboration.

Higher levels of intervention are associated with increasingly expanded roles for clinical child psychologists. While clinical child psychologists in these programs may call upon their traditional skills in assessment and therapy, they may also need other skills. Thus, a concern with the "community," especially at higher levels of intervention, results in dramatically expanding the roles for clinical child psychologists.

Collaborative consultation is a key skill used for nontraditional clinical purposes. In contrast to more traditional "expert" consultation, collaborative consultation requires that the child clinician establish and maintain equal status relationships with a broad spectrum of professionals and community members. Such relationships are characterized by psychologists' willingness to: share their skills and knowledge with others, forego treatment responsibility, and adopt eclectic theoretical orientations and procedures (cf. Hobbs, 1982, Chap. 5).

Other skills were used in support of collaborative consultation by psychologists in our exemplary programs. For example, when child clinicians target their intervention to levels beyond the individual child, treatment is frequently the responsibility of nonpsychologists and nonprofessionals. Psychologists are expected to provide training and supervision for these personnel. Similarly, effective collaboration with other child-serving institutions and policy makers often requires that psychologists develop skills related to public relations and public information dissemination. Of course, psychologists functioning as program administrators need far more than clinical and research skills. They also must have specific skills related to program development, personnel and fiscal management, policy analyses, and grantsmanship.

In this chapter, we have sought to suggest those specific orientations, attributes, and skills that clinical child psychologists must adopt if they are to meet new challenges in providing mental health services to children by expanding their roles. We believe that these increasing challenges can be best addressed through the adoption of a community psychology perspective.

REFERENCES

Alwes, DR, Sr. Re-ED School: A model for serving emotionally disturbed children. *Behavioral Disorders*, 1978, *3*, 67–79
Apter, SJ. *Troubled children: Troubled systems.* New York: Pergamon Press, 1982
Barker, RG. *Ecological psychology.* Stanford, Calif.: Stanford University Press, 1964
Barker, RG, & Gump, PV. *Big school, small school.* Stanford, Calif.: Stanford University Press, 1964
Bernard, J. *The sociology of community.* Glenview, Ill.: Scott, Foresman & Co., 1973

Bernard, J. *The sociology of community.* Glenview, Ill.: Scott, Foresman & Co., 1973

Bowen, M. *Family therapy and clinical practice.* New York: Jason Aronson, 1978

Collier, J. United States Indian Administration as a laboratory of ethnic relations. *Social Research,* 1945, *12,* 275–276

Cook, VJ. Formal family systems assessment: Rationale and case study. *Journal of Psychoeducational Assessment,* in press

Cook, VJ, & Plas, JM. Systematic intervention with disturbed children: Ecological viewpoint. In MJ Fine (Ed.), *Systematic intervention with disturbed children.* Boston: Spectrum, 1984, 157–178

Cowen, E. Prevention in the public schools: Strategies for dealing with school adjustment problems. In SJ Apter (Ed.), *Focus on prevention: The education of children labeled emotionally disturbed.* Syracuse, NY.: Syracuse University, 1978

Cowen, EL, Gesten, EL, & Weissberg, RP. An interrelated network of preventively oriented school based mental health approaches. In RH Price & P Politzer (Eds.), *Evaluation and action in the community context.* New York: Academic Press, 1980

Cowen, EL, Lorion, RP, Kraus, RM, & Dorr, D. Geometric expansion of helping resources. *Journal of School Psychology,* 1974, *12,* 288–295

Cowen, EL, Spinell, A, Wright, S, & Weissberg, RP. Continuing dissemination of a school-based mental health program. *Professional Psychology,* 1983, *13,* 118–127

Cowen, EL, Trost, MA, Lorion, RP, Dorr, D, Izzo, LD, & Isaacson, RV. *New ways in school mental health: Early detection and prevention of school maladaptation.* New York: Human Sciences Press, 1975

Cowen, EL, Zax, M, Izzo, LD, & Trost, MA. The prevention of emotional disorders in the school setting: A further investigation. *Journal of Consulting Psychology,* 1966, *30,* 381–387

Cummings, TG (Ed.), *Systems theory for organization development.* New York: John Wiley, 1980

Education for all Handicapped Children Act (P.L. 94–142)

Elias, MJ, Dalton, JH, & Howe, GW. Studying community psychology as a community of professionals: An empirical approach. *Professional Psychology,* 1981, *12,* 363–376

Goodstein, LD, & Sandler, I. Using psychology to promote human welfare: A conceptual analysis of the role of community psychology. *American Psychologist,* 1978, *33,* 882–892

Heller, K, & Monahan, J. *Psychology and community change.* Homewood, Ill.: The Dorsey Press, 1977

Hermann, A. *An analysis of public policies affecting project Re-ED: An educationally-oriented program for emotionally disturbed children.* Nashville, Tenn.: Vanderbilt Institute for Public Policy Studies, 1979

Hobbs, N. How the Re-ED plan developed. In NJ Long, WC Morse, & RG Newman (Eds.), *Conflict in the classroom.* Belmont, Calif.: Wadsworth Publishing, 1965

Hobbs, N. Helping disturbed children: Psychological and ecological strategies. *American Psychologist,* 1966, *21,* 1105–1115

Hobbs, N. Project Re-ED: New ways of helping emotionally disturbed children. In Joint Commission on Mental Health of Children, *Crisis in child mental health: Challenge for the 1970's.* New York: Harper & Row, 1970

Hobbs, N. In JM Kauffman & CD Lewis (Eds.), *Teaching children with behavior disorders: Personal perspectives.* Columbus, Ohio: Charles E. Merrill Publishing, 1974

Hobbs, N. *The futures of children.* San Francisco, Calif.: Jossey-Bass, 1977

Hobbs, N. Perspectives on Re-Education. *Behavioral Disorders,* 1978, *3,* 65–66

Hobbs, N. *Helping disturbed children: Psychological and ecological strategies, II: Project Re-Ed, twenty years later.* Nashville, Tenn.: Vanderbilt University Institute for Public Policy Studies, 1979

Hobbs, N. An ecologically oriented, service-based system for the classification of handicapped children. In S Salzinger, J Antrobus, & J Glick (Eds.), *The ecosystem of the "sick" child: Implications for classification and intervention for disturbed and mentally retarded children.* New York: Academic Press, 1980

Hobbs, N. *The troubled and troubling child.* San Francisco: Jossey-Bass, 1982

Hoffman, L. *Foundations of family therapy.* New York: Basic Books, 1981

Hyman, IA. Social science analysis of evidence cited in litigation on corporal punishment. In IA Hyman & JH Wise (Eds.). *Corporal punishment in American education.* Philadelphia: Temple University Press, 1979, 394–404

Hyman, IA, & Fina, A. The National Center for the Study of Corporal Punishment and Alternatives in the Schools: Moving from policy formation to implementation. *Journal of Clinical Child Psychology,* 1983, *12,* 257–260

Hyman, IA, & Wise, JH (Eds.). *Corporal punishment in American education.* Philadelphia: Temple University Press, 1979

Jason, LA. Behavioral community psychology: Conceptualizations and applications. *Journal of Community Psychology,* 1977, *5,* 303–312

Kelly, JG. Naturalistic observation in contrasting social environments. In EP Willems & HL Raush (Eds.), *Naturalistic viewpoints in psychological research.* New York: Holt, Rinehart, & Winston, 1969, 188–199

Ketterer, RF, Price, RH, & Politser, PE. The action research paradigm. In RH Price & PE Politser (Eds.), *Evaluation and action in the social environment.* New York: Academic Press, 1980

Knitzer, J. *Unclaimed children: The failure of public responsibility to children and adolescents in need of mental health services.* Washington, DC.: Children's Defense Fund, 1982

Krasner, LR, & Rubin, KH. The assessment of social problem-solving skills in young children. In TV Merluzzi, CR Glass, & M Genest (Eds.), *Cognitive assessment.* New York: Guilford Press, 1981, 452–478

Lachar, D. *The MMPI: Clinical assessment and automated interpretation.* Los Angeles: Western Psychological Services, 1981

Lewin, K. Action research and minority problems. *Journal of Social Issues,* 1946, *2,* 34–46

Margolin, G. The reciprocal relationship between marital and child problems. In JP Vincent (Ed.), *Advances in family intervention, assessment and theory* (Vol. 2). Greenwich, Ct.: JAI Press, 1981, 131–182

McDowell, E, & Friedman, RH. An analysis of editorial opinion regarding corporal punishment: Some dynamics of regional differences. In IA Hyman & JH Wise (Eds.), *Corporal punishment in American education.* Philadelphia: Temple University Press, 1979, 329–334

Minuchin, S, Rosman, BL, & Baker, L. *Psychosomatic families: Anorexia nervosa in context.* Cambridge, Mass.: Harvard University Press, 1978

Mischel, W. Toward a cognitive social learning reconceptualization of personality. *Psychological Review,* 1973, *80,* 252–283

Moos, RH. *The social climate scales: An overview.* Palo Alto, Calif.: Consulting Psychologists Press, 1981

Murrell, SA. *Community psychology and social systems.* New York: Behavioral Publications, 1973

Proshansky, HM, Ittelson, WH, & Rivlin, LG (Ed.), *Environmental psychology: Man and his physical setting.* New York: Holt, Rinehart & Winston, 1970

Rappaport, J. *Community psychology: Values, research and action.* New York: Holt, Rinehart & Winston, 1977

Reiss, D. *The family's construction of reality.* Cambridge, Mass.: Harvard University Press, 1981

Rhodes, WC, & Paul, JL. *Emotionally disturbed and deviant children: New views and approaches.* Englewood Cliffs, NJ.: Prentice-Hall, 1978

Ross, AO. Forecasting the future: An attempt to second guess the probable social impact of the Joint Commission on programs for children and youth. *Journal of Clinical Child Psychology*, 1972, *1*(3), 8–10(a)

Ross, AO. Four years after the forecast. *Journal of Clinical Child Psychology*, 1972, *1*(3), 11(b)

Rutter, M. Parent-child separation: Psychological effects on the children. *Journal of Child Psychology and Psychiatry*, 1971, *12*, 233–260

Sameroff, AJ. Transactional models in early social relations. *Human Development*, 1975, *18*, 65–79

Stanton, A, & Schwartz, M. *The mental hospital.* New York: Basic Books, 1954

Tittler, BI, & Cook, VJ. Relationships among family, school, and clinic: Toward a systems approach. *Journal of Clinical Child Psychology*, 1981, *10*, 184–187

Weinstein, L. Project Re-ED schools for emotionally disturbed children: Effectiveness as viewed by referring agencies, parents, and teachers. *Exceptional Children*, 1969, *35*, 703–711

Weinstein, L. *Evaluation of a program for re-educating disturbed children: A follow-up comparison with untreated children.* Washington, DC.: U.S. Department of Health, Education, and Welfare (ERIC ED-141-966), 1974

Weissberg, RP, Cowen, EL, Lotyczewski, BS, & Gesten, EL. The Primary Mental Health Project: Seven consecutive years of program outcome research. *Journal of Consulting and Clinical Psychology*, 1983, *51*, 100–107

William E. Stilwell
Stephen T. DeMers
Garland F. Niquette

10

Mental Health Programs in the Schools: Primary, Secondary, and Tertiary Interventions

The historical connection between mental health programs for children and educational institutions is both long and controversial. Many observers trace the beginnings of applied professional psychology to the early involvement of psychologists with the schools (Bardon & Bennett, 1972, 1974; Tindall, 1979; White & Harris, 1961). For example, in 1896, Witmer established a laboratory clinic at the University of Pennsylvania considered to be the first child guidance clinic in America because of its focus on solving children's learning problems. By the turn of the century, large city school systems like New Haven and Chicago employed psychologists to evaluate and treat children with learning and adjustment difficulties. Long before psychologists in America established a role for themselves in hospitals, business, or private practice, the application of psychological knowledge was underway in the schools.

Since nearly all children attend school in America for a major portion of their youth, and since schools provide a naturalistic laboratory for the detection and remediation of problems (Bardon & Bennett, 1972), this early marriage of psychology and education seemed promising. However, as early as 1928, differences in the perspectives and orientation of educational and mental health personnel were noted (Wickman, 1928). Several investigators (Hunter, 1957; Thompson, 1940; Wickman, 1928) have concluded that while teachers seem more concerned with "exter-

CLINICAL PSYCHOLOGY
ISBN 0–8089–1680–7

nalizing" aggressive or antisocial behaviors like fighting, lying, disobeying, and learning difficulties, mental health specialists are more concerned with "internalizing" behaviors such as social isolation, depression, and anxiety.

Clarizio (1979) suggests that these differences in perspective reflect a more basic underlying conflict of values with clinicians favoring warmth, spontaneity, noncompetitiveness, and individual attention. Such values often clash with the teachers' focus on the group over the individual, intellect over emotion, and academic competitiveness. Consequently, teachers often view clinicians' recommendations to provide individual attention, make exceptions to rules, and encourage the expression of inner feelings, as unrealistic or inappropriate for the school setting. Clinicians view teachers' nonacceptance of their recommendations as callous disregard for the mental health needs of children.

The purpose in describing these differences in perspectives is not to discourage the implementation of mental health programs in schools. Rather, school-based mental health programs must be designed and implemented with due regard to these different perspectives if these programs are to succeed. Many successful programs have been developed and schools have continued to employ psychologists, social workers, and counselors who can blend their mental health goals with the value system of the educational organization.

This chapter describes a variety of mental health programs and services available in schools and the mental health and educational professionals who typically provide these services. The descriptions are organized into sections or categories reflecting a model of comprehensive, multifaceted, and, it is hoped, integrated levels of service (Stilwell, Buffington, DeMers, & Stilwell, 1984). One way to conceptualize and categorize mental health programs in schools is to use the notion of primary, secondary, and tertiary intervention (Albee, 1967; Clarizio, 1979; Cowen, Gardner, & Zax, 1967; Lambert, 1964; Wonderly, Kupersmid, Monkman, Deak, & Rosenberg, 1979).

Primary intervention, or prevention.   This refers to the adoption of strategies or procedures designed to reduce the likelihood of psychological maladjustment prior to the manifestation of any symptoms or signs of psychological difficulties (Kessler & Albee, 1975). According to Caplan (1964), primary prevention seeks to lower the risk of maladjustment for a whole population rather than any one individual. Probably the best examples of primary intervention or prevention programs come from community medicine where vaccination, prenatal care, and nutrition programs have successfully reduced the risk of later illness for targeted populations.

Secondary intervention. This refers to programs aimed toward children at risk, that is, those who may be manifesting some early signs or precursors of problems, but whose difficulties are not yet serious or debilitating. Examples of secondary intervention include screening programs, group counseling for children of divorce, mental health consultation with teachers, and parenting courses for high school students.

Tertiary intervention. Tertiary intervention refers to programs designed for children with significant learning or emotional difficulties where the goal is to remediate the problem so the child can function normally in his natural environment (Clarizio, 1979). Schools often provide some intensive counseling and special education programs that are described later. Schools also can serve as a link beween parents of emotionally handicapped students and the various nonschool mental health programs, agencies, and service providers in the community.

Comprehensive mental health services in schools require action at each of these three levels of intervention; however, the line separating the levels is often vague. For example, a program to reduce drug abuse might have aspects of general drug education (primary), early detection of potential abusers (secondary), as well as counseling or referral of current abusers (tertiary). While some programs clearly fit one category or another, it may be most appropriate to view each level as a continuum with a degree of overlap with other levels. The sections that follow describe representative programs at each level of intervention. The final section discusses the need for integration across the three levels both to avoid duplication and to maximize effectiveness.

PRIMARY PREVENTION

The traditional role of American elementary and secondary schools has been the preparation of citizens for adequate functioning in their day-to-day environment. This preparation for life involves not only imparting skills and knowledge and enculturation of certain values, but also the prevention and/or remediation of various learning or adjustment difficulties, preferably well in advance of their occurrence (Aubrey, 1978; Gordon & Snyder, 1983; Sprinthall, 1980). To various degrees, elementary and secondary schools have succeeded in balancing the three Rs with student needs for the fourth R, i.e., relationships (affective-social skill development), and for the fifth R, i.e., reality (life-career preparation). The degree of success has been a function of at least three factors: the availability of federal funds for innovative or enriched programs; the professional staff's commitment to the five Rs; and, the community's support for all five Rs, rather than just the three more traditional Rs.

Although an optimal comprehensive mental health service system would seem to be obviously desirable for every school system, widespread implementation of such an educational philosophy has been limited because of decreasing finances, dwindling human resources, and a dearth of effective models. Shortages in federal, state, and local dollars for education are persistent problems. However, shortages in trained personnel and in effective models of preventive mental health programs are slowly being reversed by various changes in the educational community. The following sections describe these changes, which can serve to improve both the commitment of the school staff and community to preventive mental health programs in schools. The changes are seen in four major areas: teacher training, system-focused consultation, curricular modifications to include affective education programs, and ecological analyses that focus on the psychological climate of schools.

Teacher Training: Preservice, Inservice, and Postgraduate Levels

Teacher training has been viewed as the special domain of the teachers' colleges for many years. In this domain future teachers completed four undergraduate years by taking mostly education courses (e.g., the history of American education, human development and learning, methods courses, State history, and student teaching). The "liberating arts" were present in these four-year programs, but in small amounts. Over time the expectations for classroom teachers have changed to include primary mental health efforts within the schools. In turn, the Colleges of Education have changed their curricula.

Fortunately, in the last 15 years, professional education associations, parent pressure groups, legislators, and state departments of certification have stimulated, often dramatically, changes in teacher training, certification, and skill maintenance. Examples of changes in teacher training include competency-based teacher education, in which preservice teachers demonstrate predetermined competencies; and a master of arts approach in teaching, in which the student earns a liberal arts bachelors degree before committing a full year to graduate course work in education and student teaching. Innovations in teacher certification have included a full year's precertification internship in which the full-time teacher is employed, monitored, and closely supervised before obtaining a permanent certificate. These and similar innovations have been controversial; however, many of the changes at all three levels of teacher education have contributed to the increasing readiness for acceptance of preventive mental health efforts. Some of these changes by level of teacher education are described below.

Preservice Teacher Training

In many preservice training programs a strong effort is made to lay the groundwork for preventive mental health activities. For many students, the classroom teacher is their first preventive mental health experience. Preservice training programs have thus been changed to reflect this expectation. In particular, the teacher education program faculties try to prepare their graduates for the ongoing issues of the Back-to-Basics movement. The pressure to return to the three Rs comes from conservative social and political groups who argue that the school has the sole responsibility for academic skills mastery, while the family has the complete responsibility for all other kinds of learning.

Despite the Back-to-Basics movement, many teacher-educators are committed to helping preservice professionals learn how to promote mental health in the schools by creating an awareness of the multitude of available school-based mental health programs. Miller (1976) has summarized 27 mental health curricula for use in the schools. In the literature, one might find these mental health curricula listed under such titles as "confluent education," "humanistic education," "psychological education," and "affective education," which include such curricula as Developing Understanding of Self and Others (DUSO) (Dinkmeyer, 1970), Toward Affective Development (Dupont, Gardner, & Brody, 1974), values clarification (Simon, Howe, & Kirschenbaum, 1972), transactional analysis (Freed, 1973),* and Magic Circle (Bessell & Palomares, 1970). Unfortunately, preservice students typically are provided only a brief exposure to these mental health programs and curricular materials in such texts as Miller (1976) and Worell and Stilwell (1981), rather than a more extensive and experiential exposure.

Other changes in the preservice preparation of teachers that may result in teachers who are better equipped to implement preventive mental health efforts include the following:

Fewer students are entering teacher education programs. In the last 10 to 15 years many colleges of education have noted an abrupt drop in enrollments (e.g., at the University of Kentucky, the College of Education enrollment dropped from a little over 2500 in 1972 to a little over 1000 in 1982). Reduced enrollments mean that classes are smaller and faculty

---

*Copeland, PS. Affective education: Effects of transactional analysis training in seventh grade students. Unpublished doctoral dissertation, Texas A&M University, 1975

can provide more individual attention. The focus in teacher education has shifted from quantity to quality since the teacher shortage in the 1960s.

Having fewer students in programs has allowed faculty to assess and improve teacher-education programs.   A long-needed change has been the creation of more rigorous admission procedures. For example, many colleges of education have established entrance requirements that include a structured interview, an expository writing test, and standardized reading and math tests with minimum "passing scores."

Special education preservice has been a bright spot in colleges of education.   The impact of the Education for All Handicapped Children Act (also known as P.L. 94-142) has caused changes in all preservice, inservice, and postgraduate programs. Under this legislation, the classroom teacher, the guidance counselor, and other human service personnel, as well as the school-building administrators are being required to learn how to "mainstream," that is, to educate children with handicapping conditions with children without handicaps wherever possible. To prepare teachers for mainstreaming, many teacher-educator programs have expanded their psychology course requirements to include six credits of educational psychology, as well as six credits of personality and developmental psychology.

In short, despite less financial support and pressures to limit educators to teaching the three Rs, preservice teacher training has improved because of higher admission standards, lower enrollments, more emphasis on quality preparation, and both the realization and requirements to educate all children to their full potential.

Inservice Training

Inservice training refers to workshops and programs provided to teachers on the job and typically occurs during the school year. Not to be confused with postgraduate training, inservice training is similar to the Continuing Education Unit program required by psychologists, social workers, and rehabilitation counselors.

The instructors for inservice training are typically consultants from the State Department of Education, faculty members from colleges and schools of education, and/or human service professionals (e.g., clinical child psychologists, social workers) who can address topics of current concern. The usual list of topics for inservice training includes classroom management, student motivation, self-concept, reading, and a plethora of more specific topics such as substance abuse, student pregnancies, single parenting, and occasionally, affective education. Inservice training programs aimed at primary prevention activities in the schools must be closely interwoven with traditional educational concerns to be effective.

An effective inservice mental health program was implemented in the Stuttgart Arkansas School District No. 26 in the late 1970s. Grade level teacher teams were identified within the program school. Consultants conducted monthly inservice training in human relations skill development and the use of the Magic Circle program (Bessell & Palmores, 1970). The inservice days were financed by special funds administered by the Arkansas Department of Education for demonstration projects. In the second year of the project these more experienced teachers became the inservice trainers for the teachers who were new to the program. When the funding was no longer available and the district was unable to pick up the differences due to a shortfall in the taxes, the experienced teachers continued on with the program without extramural support. Evaluations of the efficacy of this exemplary program can be found in the ERIC Documentation System (Stilwell & Barclay, 1977a, 1977b, 1978).

Postgraduate Training

Postgraduate training for teachers is required by nearly all State Departments of Education to maintain certification in the teaching area and/or to acquire additional professional endorsements (e.g., guidance counselor, principal) above the basic teaching certificate. The postgraduate programs may vary in terms of length, classroom activities, mental health-related courses, and practicum/field work, depending upon professional goals. Elective courses in mental health, mental hygiene, or affective education are typically available and may be recommended to any postgraduate teacher-education student. However, most postgraduate training in preventive mental health occurs within the typical pupil personnel areas of guidance, school psychology, and school social work.

Guidance counselors. Guidance counselors (who may also be licensed counseling psychologists trained to perform within a school district's guidance system) are expected to complete 36 to 42 planned credits in their program leading to certification. Mental health per se might be taught as a content area in some programs, but all programs appear to place a high value on screening for mental health among the potential and current students. In the guidance counselor's masters' degree program the typical student completes extensive prepracticum, experiential coursework, as well as approximately 250 hours of supervised practicum experience. The emphasis in the skill development portion of the training program is applied mental health, e.g., mastery of self-regulation, self-management, and/or self-control. Guidance counselors, in order to maintain their professional endorsement, are expected to enroll in a planned post-master's program in advanced counseling, advanced practicum, guidance system management (which includes referral to comprehensive mental health delivery systems and private agency settings), and an additional practicum with an emphasis upon supervision.

School psychologists. Traditionally, school psychologists begin their psychology training as Arts and Science undergraduate psychology majors. In their postgraduate training programs, students are admitted typically to either a 60 to 66 credit hour program required for entry level certification in most states, or a doctoral program, which leads to licensure as a psychologist as well as certification as a school psychologist. Over one third of the approximately 60 doctoral training programs in school psychology are fully accredited by the American Psychological Association (1982). Preadmission interviewing and supervised practice are the usual means for ensuring that the students can practice mental health in the schools. Typically, the professional training program includes extensive coursework on learning, human development, counseling theories and techniques, assessment, special education program development and evaluation, teacher and systems consultation, and an orientation to the role and function of school psychologists. Usually part-time practicum experience (approximately 500 hours) precedes the full-time, full-year internship (2000 hours). In some states the training of school psychologists is not as well integrated, is less oriented toward building a professional identity, and amounts to a 30-credit program added on to the guidance counselor training.

School social workers. They may be trained at the BA or master's level and graduates of a Council on Social Work Education (CSWE) accredited program. As a rule, these accredited programs place a strong emphasis upon experiential learning such that approximately half of the master's level training is completed in field work. Persons who are planning on becoming school social workers typically complete 6 to 12 specified credit hours in a college of education. The state department of education reviews transcripts prior to determining whether the social worker may serve as a school mental health worker.

System Focused Mental Health Consultation

Primary prevention in the schools may be delivered through a type of mental health consultation that focuses on improving the effectiveness and particularly the communication skills of the school system as a whole. A popular sign or indicator of the need for system-wide consultation is teacher "burn-out." System-focused consultation seeks to identify and remove unnecessary stresses using an organizational development approach (Schmuck, 1982) in order to prevent the otherwise inevitable increase in student learning and behavior problems.

In an effort to develop effective consultation models based upon various psychological theories, four general consultative approaches have emerged: behavioral (Bergan, 1977), mental health (Caplan, 1970), organizational development (Schmuck, Runkel, Saturen, Martell, & Derr, 1972), and team (Stilwell & Santoro, 1976). Essentially, these consultative approaches have shared a common, basic philosophy that espouses a largely preventive as well as remedial purpose. By definition, consultation is an indirect approach to service delivery in which care-giver or consultee (e.g., teacher(s), parent(s), or administrator(s)) seeks the help of a professional colleague or consultant (e.g., counselor, psychologist, social worker) because of a difficulty with a client (e.g., student(s), class). The consultant provides the climate whereby the consultee can voluntarily explore alternatives and innovative solutions for the dual purpose of both alleviating the present problem and preparing the consultee to be better equipped to deal with future similar problems (Meyers, Martin, & Hyman, 1977; Meyers, Parsons, & Martin, 1979). Effective consultation services to schools, whether system focused (primary intervention) or focused on particular teachers and students (secondary intervention), thus have a preventive aspect to the extent that they prepare educators to cope more effectively with similar problems in the future.

Affective or Mental Health Education in the School Curriculum

Primary prevention in the schools can be effectively managed through district/system-wide mental health programs integrated into the normal school curriculum. Successful implementation of such an integrative approach to preventive mental health requires that the planning, organization, coordination, and direction of the program take the whole school system into account; that is, mental health programs cannot be simply added to the regular curriculum (Durlak, 1983; Ryan, 1973; Silvern, 1969; Stilwell, 1976a), rather the teachers need to be made aware of mental health and the curriculum needs to be expanded to include mental health. Elsewhere, a seven-function, general implementation model has been presented for affective education on a district-wide basis (Stilwell, 1976b) and a specific implementation model has been prepared for human abuse service teams on a local area basis (Emener, Stilwell, & Witten, 1981). It is important to emphasize a systems perspective and to encourage potential users/managers to work toward an interdependent, multidiscipline comprehensive model of mental health education integrated with the normal school program.

Existing Components of a Comprehensive Program

A number of system-wide educational programs are available from commercial publishers (Worell & Stilwell, 1981). Essentially, these packages include learning objectives, instructional strategies, evaluation materials, and inservice training materials for teachers, administrators, and parents. Embedded within these educational programs are attempts to address primary mental health concerns. For example, Individually Prescribed Instruction has been implemented in more than 270 schools in 38 states for the basic language arts, social studies, math, and science, and has recently added a humanizing learning component. This "preventive" mental health program is designed to help educate students for living.

Another example is Project PLAN (Program for Learning in Accordance with Needs), which has embedded "guidance" learning activities within the regular curriculum. Guidance activities in PLAN include organizing and providing career planning information, scheduling small problem-solving groups, integrating life-career information into the math, science, and social studies curriculum, under the supervision of a learning consultant. A third example is Individually Guided Education, a comprehensive curriculum developed by the University of Wisconsin, which has been growing over the last 20 years, while gathering program monitoring and evaluation data on student achievement and such important preventive mental health topics as inservice teacher training and parent-community relationships. Sample mental health programs have been developed both with and without external support and have enjoyed extemely encouraging results (Stilwell & Barclay, 1978). Still, it remains for the preventive mental health activists to stimulate system/district-wide program implementation.

Packaged Minicurricula

A number of commercially available free-standing minicurricula have been developed for use within a school system on a school-by-school or on a classroom basis. Each program can be characterized as "user friendly" with stimulus stories, discussion guidelines, and prescriptions for students, teachers, and/or parents. These mental health minicurricula are usually accompanied by a carefully thought out training program. The intention is for these mental health minicurricular packages to be integrated within the classroom learning activities. For example, using Adlerian principles, Dinkmeyer and his associates have developed two levels of DUSO and a preventive program for teachers, Sequential Teacher

Education Program (STEP) (Dinkmeyer, 1970; Dinkmeyer & McKay, 1974). Corsini has also devised an Adlerian-based school-wide individually guided education program that has been very successful (Corsini, 1979). Still another example of a mental health minicurriculum is the one developed by Dupont and his associates. The Toward Affective Development (TAD) curriculum contains 191 lessons on such topics as self-concept and group relations. Teachers may select the appropriate lesson from a domain by grade-level matrix. In this manner, TAD can be used in a primary as well as in a secondary mental health mode (Dupont, Gardner & Brody, 1974). Successful experiences with these minicurricula, as evidenced by student, parent, and teacher feedback, can be used to stimulate a school district to adopt/adapt a system-wide preventive mental health program.

Thus far, the systematic research on mental health-related curriculum development has been infrequently reported in the literature for a number of reasons. The complex research issues include examining the curricular objectives, the reading level of the materials, the alternative instructional strategies, and the methods of evaluation for each program. The general, four-part, research question on curriculum development takes the form: What curricular strategy can mental health professionals use to help this unique student reach the particular learning objective? Development of better answers to this general question involve multimethod, multisource data collection, e.g., paper-and-pencil, interview, and observation data collected from students, teachers, and parents. Thus, the professional psychologist involved in selecting, adapting, or adopting preventive mental health curricula will want to weigh carefully the curricular package's goals, activities, and multimethod, multisource empirical evidence, before making recommendations to the schools.

Ecological Analysis

Primary prevention in the schools can be facilitated by use of appropriate ecological analysis techniques. The topic has been studied for the last 25 years since Pace and Stern (1958) applied their "environmental press" model to college settings. More recently, three major environmental assessment strategies have been developed for three distinctive purposes: understanding the perceived institutional structure (e.g., Insel & Moos, 1974; Moos, 1974, 1979), understanding educational outcomes (e.g., Ellett & Walberg, 1979; Walberg, 1969), and understanding the classroom environmental process (Barclay, 1966, 1983b). Moos' and Walberg's strategies have been amply reviewed by Fraser and Fisher (1982) and by Anderson (1982) who identified nearly 200 references on school climate. In contrast with the thrust of those ecological analysts who studied institutional structure and the educational outcomes, Barclay's work has presented a heuristic three-part model for understanding, describing, and evaluating classroom climates. Barclay collects information on the individual student, on peer support, and teacher expectations. He has studied primarily elementary school age children with the Classroom Climate Inventory (BCCI), recently renamed the Barclay Classroom Assessment System (Barclay, 1983a). The individual and classroom assessment report recommends interventions for changing either the student's or the classroom teacher's behaviors and expectations.

Barclay's system suggests that the interaction among teacher expectations, peer support, and the student's learning history contribute to performance on standardized achievement tests (Barclay, 1966, 1982; Barclay, Covert, Scott, & Stilwell, 1978; Barclay & Kehle, 1979; Barclay, Phillips, & Jones, 1983). The system also offers strategies for changing an individual student's peer support within the classroom (Stilwell & Barclay, 1979) and for modifying teacher expectations (Buffington & Stilwell, 1981). The thrust of this section on ecological analysis is that psychologists must establish primary prevention programs within the classroom and school environments, based upon data obtained from a thorough ecological analysis of the classroom, school system, and the host community.

SECONDARY INTERVENTIONS

Whereas primary prevention efforts focus on the mental health of all of a school's population, secondary intervention strategies respond to the needs of children who are beginning to exhibit social deficits or emotional problems. These problems may be manifested as poor peer relationships, deficient motivation, declining scholastic performance, and/or rapidly diminishing or inappropriate behavior or affect. Secondary interventions are designed to identify and ameliorate such problem behaviors before they become chronic or more debilitating.

Since a child's socioemotional well-being is interrelated with both his academic competence and environmental circumstances, secondary interventions are also targeted for children with current or potential learning problems. Children who have been identified as having problems with reading, writing, calculating, remembering, or understanding may need secondary mental health interventions as much as those who are culturally disadvantaged, handicapped, abused, or suffering from situational stresses such as parental divorce or a family move. Educators are attempting to address this population's needs by developing a system that focuses on the early identification of these children, and provides interventions designed to enhance personal adjustment and academic growth. This system has been implemented at both the preschool and school levels.

Early Identification and Intervention at the Preschool Level

Federal legislation and subsequent funding have stimulated secondary intervention practices. At the preschool level, Project Head Start has continued to be one of the best known examples of a preschool program based on an early intervention premise. Designed to provide culturally disadvantaged children with a "head start" in school, this objective has been realized in a variety of federally funded preschool programs.

In 1974 Head Start was mandated to make available at least ten percent of its enrollment spaces to children with handicaps. Further impetus for preschool programs has been prompted by the 1968 Handicapped Children's Early Assistance Act (PL 90-538), and most recently the 1975 Education for All Handicapped Children Act (PL 94-142), which assures the rights of school-age children as well. Spurred by this legislation, "child find" efforts to identify and provide services to children at risk have been developed.

Many programs have also incorporated the tenets of early identification and intervention. One of these, the Sumter Child Study Project (Newton & Brown, 1967) represents a collaboration between a state mental health agency and a public school district. The project's goals were to identify those youngsters who would be at risk for emotional stress upon school entry and in early school years, and to provide teachers and parents with interventions for reducing this stress (Newton & Brown, 1967). The spring prior to their entering first grade, preschool children were evaluated during a 45-minute period by a psychologist, while their parents were engaged in an interview by a psychiatric social worker. The identified children, whose problems included immaturity, speech difficulties, and deficits in social and adaptive skills, were targeted for individual and group implemented interventions. These provided for medical and nutritional care, parent-guided speech therapy and group experiences, and placement in a school-based summer enrichment program.

The positive effects of the Sumter Project (Newton & Brown, 1967), in addition to other preschool programs, suggests that early intervention efforts may reduce or eliminate the problems that may later affect a child's socioemotional well-being (Kershman, 1981; Zigler, Kagan &

Muenchow, 1982). Furthermore, the Sumter Project, as a collaborative venture between professionals both within and external to a school district, illustrates that mental health programs are not the exclusive purview of any one professional group. These programs can be effectively planned, coordinated, and implemented by a variety of mental health professionals including clinical child psychologists, social workers, and school psychologists.

Secondary Intervention at the School Level

Screening efforts for the early identification of children with problems are further conducted at the school level, particularly in kindergarten and first grade. Young children's repertoires of adjustment and academic competencies are examined to determine their "readiness" for the demands of subsequent grades. Much of this screening is conducted by classroom teachers, and some school districts have developed specific instruments for this purpose. Bower (1961), for example, investigated the effficacy of several screening instruments used to identify maladjusted elementary school children. He found a triad of instruments that combined teacher, peer, and self perceptions to be the most discriminating index, while still economical of teacher time. In one validation study of this screening battery, clinical psychologists determined that 89 percent of a group of 225 children identified as maladjusted by the screening devices had emotional problems (Bower, 1961).

Findings from screening devices or teacher observations of a child experiencing exceptional difficulty may lead to the child's referral for a more comprehensive assessment. Many school systems have available a multidisciplinary team who conduct indepth evaluations (Pfeiffer & Heffernan, 1984). These specialists may include a language pathologist, school psychologist, social worker, principal, nurse or doctor, occupational or physical therapist, counselor, and special education teacher. The integration of the team's diagnostic findings takes place at a team meeting where problem solving and group decision making occur (Catterall & Gazda, 1978; Pfeiffer, 1981; Pfeiffer & Tittler, 1983; Stilwell & Santoro, 1976).

The team's recommended interventions will be contingent upon the child's needs and the resources available in the school, home, and community. Frequently these interventions require educational components aimed at remediating academic deficits that may have resulted from or contributed to the child's emotional problem(s). Public Law 94-142 has required that such intervention activities take place in the least restrictive environment possible, with a particular emphasis on the regular classroom. Schools have generated a wide range of intervention alternatives that may include teacher consultation, parent involvement and counseling, child aides, individual, group or family counseling, and participation in special education services. Each of these will be addressed in more detail below.

Teacher Consultation

As discussed earlier, consultation refers to the process by which an adult's behavior with a child is modified in order to change the child's behavior (Monroe, 1979). Although consultation as a primary prevention strategy typically focuses on system-wide organizational development, consultation as a secondary intervention focuses on specific problem behaviors evidenced by particular students; with the goal being both to ameliorate the child's present problem and also to reduce the likelihood that the teacher will experience similar problems in the future (Meyers et al., 1977; Meyers et al., 1979). Consultation may involve only one teacher who has raised questions regarding one or more students, or may include a group of teachers with similar concerns. While consultation usually involves an interaction between teachers and school-based specialists, the Yale Psychoeducational Clinic project (Sarason, Levine, Goldenberg, Cherlin, & Bennett, 1966) illustrated how psychologists external to the school can provide consultation services to teachers. These psychologists observed children with teacher-identified problems at school, and then explored strategies to modify the classroom in order to alter the problematic behaviors with the teachers. Although consultation services in general vary according to consultant characteristics, orientation, and the nature of the problem, research has substantiated its success in changing teacher and pupil behaviors and attitudes (Medway, 1979). Consultation continues to be used, therefore, as an early intervention strategy in the schools (Cook & Patterson, 1977; Gutkin & Curtis, 1982; Meachem & Peckham, 1978; Sarason, 1982).

Parent Involvement and Counseling

Public Law 94-142 requires that parents of handicapped children be actively involved in their children's placement decisions and in the development of their individual education programs (IEP). The IEP is a written contract of the projected goals to be attained by the child during the school year and the methods by which these objectives will be measured. The involvement of parents in this process increases their understanding of the child's program, and may enhance their commitment toward the program, as well as enhance their attitude toward (or expectation of) their child (Bersoff, 1982; McLoughlin, 1981; Turnbull, Leonard & Turnbull, 1981; Weisberg, 1983).

Frequently, intervention strategies include a parent counseling component that seeks to modify parental behavior to positively influence a child's development. The St. Louis School Mental Health Project (Gildea, Glidewell, & Kantor, 1967), for example, reported the success of a parent counseling program. The project involved the parents of children, whom teachers had identified as maladjusted, in group therapy sessions. These sessions provided parents the opportunity to begin exploring their effect on their child's behavior and ways to change the dysfunctional parent-child interaction.

Other intervention strategies have similarly focused on the impact of dysfunctional parent-child interactions and initiated therapy sessions to modify these. Klein, Altman, Dreizen, Friedman and Powers (1981a, 1981b) have explored four dysfunctional parental attitudes that may adversely influence a child's learning or behavior in school. These attitudes may be directed toward "authority, responsibility for learning, the child, or based on cultural factors" (Klein et al., 1981 (a), p. 15). Therapeutic interventions, guided by a psychotherapist and a psycho-educational therapist, are designed to restructure these dysfunctional attitudes, and thus enhance the child's performance at school.

Aponte (1976) has described another intervention, which in addition to focusing on the parent-child interaction, incorporates the school. In this intervention, known as the "family-school interview," the child's problem is examined and addressed through an ecological perspective. All systems relevant to the presenting problem, such as the child, the child's parents, and school personnel, are engaged in collaborative sessions in which the problem is explored and subsequent interventions planned and coordinated.

Child Aides

An intervention strategy developed by the Primary Mental Health Project (PMHP) has used direct interactions between child aides and students with school adjustment problems such as learning, withdrawal, and aggression (Cowen, Orgel, Gesten, & Wilson, 1979). The program has maintained several emphases throughout its nearly 25-year history including the early identification of young children with problems that are not yet chronic, and the use of nonprofessional child aides to provide services to identified children (Cowen et al., 1979). The child aides are chosen for employment based on personal characteristics such as "warmth, interpersonal effectiveness, caring about children and skills for working with them" (Cowen, 1980, p. 137). Aides are assigned to work with identified children either individually or in groups, and meet their personal and academic needs through unstructured help sessions or formal lessons. Evaluation data (Cowen et al., 1979) suggest that the program has been more effective for the withdrawn pupils than for either the aggressive students or children with learning difficulties. A recent investigation has focused on the development of specific interventions targeted for children with acting-out behaviors, and incorporation of these interventions into child aide training (Cowen et al., 1979). The aggressive children with whom these interventions were implemented made significantly greater gains than those aggressive children with whom the nondifferentiated interventions were used. This study may herald a new trend in the training of child aides in the PMHP in the future. Two general sources of evaluative data, consumer perceptions and objective studies, demonstrate the overall effectiveness of the PMHP program, which has been replicated in over 300 schools across the United States (Cowen, 1980).

Counseling

Regular and special classroom placement may need to be supplemented by individual or group counseling that is targeted at children experiencing typical developmental or situational conflicts. Counseling sessions may address "crisis" issues such as adjustment to a new family member (e.g., blended families, new siblings), the loss of a parent through death or divorce, or even physical or substance abuse (Justice & Justice, 1976; Kameen & Thompson, 1983; Visher & Visher, 1979). Furthermore, counseling may focus on more long-term problems such as difficulty in relating to others, making decisions, or value conflicts (Catterall & Gazda, 1978). It should be noted that the type of counseling described here is generally short term and focused on ameliorating mildly maladaptive behaviors in the natural environment before these same problems require long-term or intensive treatment.

Participation in Special Education Services

The "least restrictive environment" provision of PL 94-142 holds schools responsible for educating handicapped children in settings most appropriate for them. In response to this charge, school systems have developed a continuum of services that varies according to "degree of restrictiveness" (e.g., time spent in a setting other than the regular classroom).

Of all placement alternatives, obviously the least restrictive environment available is the regular classroom. Many presenting problems can be effectively handled in the regular classroom. For example, a child who frequently falls behind in classwork can be provided with additional aide time or peer tutoring that is structured to compensate for missed or difficult assignments. Environmental changes may also assist a child who is having difficulty. Moving a distractible child away from a doorway, or implementing a behavioral management system may prove sufficient for producing a desired behavioral change. Having a student remain in the regular classroom also provides the child with appropriate models to emulate.

Despite these classroom-based interventions, some children are still unable to compensate and successfully function within the regular classroom. They fall further and further behind academically and socio-emotionally. These children are consequently recommended for placement in remedial programs, resource rooms, or special classes. These more intensive services are discussed in the section on tertiary interventions.

In summary, secondary mental health interventions focus primarily on preschool and early elementary years for the detection, evaluation, and remediation of children's learning and adjustment difficulties. These interventions are accomplished through the use of various school-based professionals such as counselors, psychologists, special educators; paraprofessionals such as child aides; and parents. Mental health professionals who may be external to the school district may ensure effective coordination of services with these school-based specialists in several ways. An external professional should first secure an understanding of the role of each professional (including himself or herself) in the assessment/intervention process. Clarification of each team member's role will minimize duplication of effort, and thus facilitate the process. An external mental health professional should also acquire a knowledge of the school district's existing resources for meeting the needs of emotionally handicapped children. This prerequisite knowledge will enable the external professional to recommend the most facilitative, and most likely to be implemented, intervention alternative. Recommendations based on unavailable or unfeasible interventions are unlikely to be implemented, and thus the child's mental health needs are unlikely to be met. Furthermore, the external mental health professional should communicate frequently with team members in order to glean further insight into the roles of these professionals as well as to ensure the ongoing coordination of services to children.

TERTIARY INTERVENTION

Despite the educational community's limited attempts to provide effective primary and secondary intervention programs for the mental health needs of students, some children still require relatively intensive mental health services. Special programs, schools, or services that are provided to remediate significant learning and/or adjustment difficulties due to emotional causes constitute tertiary interventions (Clarizio, 1979).

Balow (1979) notes an interesting discrepancy in reviewing empirical studies of the incidence of severe emotional maladjustment in school children. He describes how state and federal education officials cite expectancies of two percent to three percent of school populations as being significantly emotionally disturbed, while studies reporting data from local school personnel (e.g., teachers, counselors, school psychologists, and social workers) suggest rates as high as 15% to 30%. It is our belief that these higher estimates result, in part, from the lack of effective and comprehensive primary and secondary level interventions in the typical school program. To the extent that schools fail to implement such early intervention programs, a predictably high percentage of students will thus need more intensive and costly treatment for emotional problems. Even the implementation of model primary and secondary level services, however, will not totally eliminate the need for some special services for emotionally disturbed children, although the number of children needing such services should be closer to the two percent to three percent estimate.

Education's involvement in providing intensive or tertiary interventions has consisted of two aspects. First, are those special programs or services offered within the public school environment, e.g., counseling groups or special education classes. Second, the public schools can serve a liaison or integrative function, that is, a link between the family and those special schools, programs, or services that exist in the community.

School-Based Tertiary Services

Schools vary widely in the nature and extent of programs and services available to children with significant learning and adjustment difficulties. These differences typically result from such variables as the number of competent mental health professionals on staff and their particular philosophies and expertise (i.e., human resources), the level of budgetary support (i.e., financial resources), and the school system's and community's commitment to providing such services. In general, most school districts offer some type of each of the following services.

Short-term Individual and Group Counseling

Perhaps one of the oldest controversies in the field of school psychology concerns whether psychotherapy should occur in school settings (Bardon & Bennett, 1972; Smith, 1967; Woody, 1969). These authors suggest that while short-term therapy that focuses on rather circumscribed and nondebilitating problems may be appropriate, long-term, intensive treatment of more serious and chronic emotional problems is best not handled within the school setting. In addition, most school-based mental health professionals are considerably overworked and understaffed with ratios of 1 psychologist or counselor for anywhere from 1,500 to 10,000 children (Bardon & Bennett, 1974) making long-term treatment an inefficient and cost-ineffective luxury. As a result, a move toward increased indirect service delivery systems such as mental health consultation (Caplan, 1970; Meyers et al., 1979) has become imperative.

Despite this general trend away from direct therapeutic services in the schools, some specific types of short-term individual and small group therapies have persisted in the schools. Most notable perhaps is the wealth of evidence for the effectiveness of behavior therapy in educational settings (Kazdin, 1982; O'Leary & O'Leary, 1972). While behavioral techniques with children originally appeared limited to social problems like fighting and out-of-seat behavior, and learning problems such as attentional deficits and incomplete homework (Krumboltz & Krumboltz, 1972), current behavioral strategies are also effective with fears and phobias (Johnson, 1979), motivational deficits (Krumboltz & Krumboltz, 1972), and even self-management of problem behaviors (Kazdin, 1982) (see Chapter 7 in this volume for a more detailed discussion of the range of behavioral techniques available to the child therapist).

Several aspects of behavioral techniques are particularly well suited for application in school settings: they are typically consistent with educators' emphasis on setting specific, practical objectives; they "teach" correct behavior as well as seek to eliminate problem behaviors; they work best when applied in the natural setting where the problem exists and not in the private office where one must depend on transfer and generalization of learned behaviors; they offer a variety of specific techniques to apply to different problems allowing teachers to select a strategy that complements their style; and they fit with education's current emphasis on accountability and demonstrable results (Clarizio, 1979). Educators quickly became disenchanted with the practice of referring children with emotional problems out to child guidance clinics or private service providers for treatment and then impatiently waiting to see changes in classroom behavior. Even though it typically meant more effort on their part, teachers generally preferred the direct, immediate, and measurable results of behavior modification over traditional therapeutic methods (Woody, 1969).

Another therapeutic approach popular with educators is Glasser's (1969) reality therapy, where again the emphasis is on the remediation of current problems in the natural setting of the school. Glasser's approach relies on the dual principles of children taking responsibility for and suffering the natural consequences of their actions. Studies of the success of reality therapy in terms of reduced maladaptive behavior and improved self-concept have resulted in mixed reviews with, unfortunately, the more rigorously controlled studies typically showing few significant benefits (Shearn & Randolph, 1978).

More traditional insight-oriented individual and group counseling, while less prevalent than either behavior or reality therapy, is still practiced in the schools, particularly where staff mental health professionals have received specific training in a particular technique (Barbanel, 1982; Claiborn & Strong, 1982). Ruth Newman has been a leading advocate of small group counseling techniques in the schools. In her book, *Groups in Schools* (1974), Newman explains that since the source of many children's inappropriate or unsuccessful behaviors is the interaction of that individual with his or her parents, teachers, and peers, these problems must be explored, understood, and corrected in a group context involving all the relevant system members. Andronico and Guerney (1967) suggested a similar approach that focused on parents, called filial therapy, which sought to bring parents of problem children to school for training in how to relate to their disturbed children at home. Interestingly, Fine and Holt (1983) and Pfeiffer and Tittler (1983) have recently suggested an updated version of filial therapy based on a family systems perspective whereby the parents, school personnel, and child all collaborate within a therapeutic context. Claiborn and Strong (1982), in a recent review of group counseling in schools, note that many varieties of group treatment are being practiced. School-based group psychotherapy has included behavioral, encounter, awareness, and play therapy, depending on the training and orientation of the leader, objectives of the group, age, and type of students.

Special Education Services for Emotionally Disturbed Children

Federal and state special education regulations recognize learning and adjustment handicapping conditions, which are primarily the result of an emotional dysfunction. Variously referred to as emotionally disturbed/handicapped and/or conduct/behavior disordered, these categories of children are eligible for assessment and treatment services under Public Law 94-142. As with all other psychoeducational services, the provision of specific special education services will depend on the availability and talent of local school staff, and school and community resources. However, most school systems have some combination of the following special services: crisis intervention program; resource room or partial day placement in a special class for disturbed children; and self-contained or full-time placement in a special class or school for emotionally disturbed children (Reynolds & Birch, 1982). The emphasis is to serve the child in the least restrictive or most normal environment in which he or she can benefit.

Crisis intervention is a type of special education service whereby a child is helped through a sudden, disruptive, or confrontational situation without being labeled or placed in a routine special education program (Reynolds & Birch, 1982). The goal in crisis intervention is to intervene prior to a child's self-destructive or other destructive act, to remove the child to a calm, "safe" environment, and then return the child to the regular classroom once the source of the crisis has been reduced or eliminated (Morse, 1971). Grotsky, Sabatino, and Ohrtman (1976) describe the process of crisis intervention as first, separating the people involved; second, assuring each party of a full hearing of all views involved; third, a careful piecing together of the events or influences leading to the confrontation, and finally, arriving at an equitable resolution of the dispute including applying consequences where appropriate. Reynolds and Birch (1982) suggest that crisis intervention is most appropriate for children with infrequent but serious disruptions in behavior and thus capitalizes on the fact that many children with emotional problems need only intermittent or sporadic services.

Anderson, Martinez, and Rich (1980) describe the partial-day or resource room model as an approach where handicapped students maintain a continuous enrollment in a regular class, but leave that class for supportive or corrective instructional services for some regularly scheduled portion of their school day or week. Anderson et al. (1980) suggest that pupils served under the resource room model are best grouped according to educational needs (e.g., reading, math, or writing deficits) rather than disability labels like learning disabled or emotionally disturbed. Morsink (1981) notes that these categorical distinctions between disabilities are pragmatically arbitrary since most of these children share common learning problems that include attentional deficits, limited motivation, and low frustration tolerance.

In a national survey conducted prior to implementation of P.L. 94-142, Shultz, Hirshoren, Manton, and Henderson (1971) found that special classes for the emotionally disturbed or conduct disordered was the most prevalent special education option with resource rooms the next most prevalent. Although no more recent data are reported in the literature, Blackhurst and Berdine (1981) suggest that the resource room model is currently more prevalent than special classes since more children experience the less severe problems typically handled by the partial day approach. However, these same authors suggest that since passage of P.L. 94-142 more school systems are providing programs for severely emotionally handicapped children (e.g. psychotic, autistic) in a self-contained special classroom. School systems differ as to whether these special classes are housed within the regular school building or in separate, special schools for handicapped children. Regardless of the logistical arrangements, the self-contained special education class is based on the belief that some emotionally handicapped students can only function in a more supportive and structured environment provided by the special class and teacher on a full-time basis (Reynolds & Birch, 1982).

What actually transpires in a self-contained class for emotionally handicapped children depends on the severity of the disability and the theoretical orientation of the teacher. Newcomer (1980) describes several therapeutic approaches used with emotionally disturbed children in school, including behavior modification, particularly the totally behaviorally engineered classroom (Hewett, 1968); art/music/sociodrama therapies; milieu therapy, where the goal is to provide a healthy, structured environment; play therapy; and the rational-emotive therapeutic approach. Woods (1982) describes still another approach called developmental therapy. Developmental therapy focuses on first identifying where in the normal sequential pattern of development the child is functioning, and then facilitating the child's progression through successive stages by remediating specific social skills and knowledge deficits.

Blackhurst and Berdine (1981) report that while in theory children should gradually move from special classes back to regular classes as they make progress, in fact, for many seriously disturbed children an "out of sight, out of mind" philosophy often exists. Taylor and Soloway (1973) describe an attempt to counteract this philosophy by dividing the special education services into four levels based on student competencies, with students moving towards regular class placement as competencies are developed.

Integration With Community-based Services

Some school children's mental health needs are more effectively and efficiently served outside of the school. Most typical of such needs would be long-term, specialized, or intensive treatment best provided by a mental health, child guidance clinic, or private practitioner, and residential placement in a public or private facility because of unstable or unfavorable home conditions, or the need for a totally controlled environment. The traditional role of the school in such situations has been to identify, refer, and then wait for the rehabilitated student to return. However, both the passage of P. L. 94-142 and the growing recognition of the need for an integrated service delivery system have pressured schools to become more actively involved in out-of-school services and placement (Mearig, 1982).

Under P. L. 94-142, public schools are both financially and legally responsible for the educationally-relevant services provided to its students in the community. Mearig (1982) notes that schools often actively discourage their staff from recognizing the need for such related services as defined by federal and state law because of the costs involved. However, school districts can be held accountable for the costs of some mental health services (e.g., individual or group counseling when recommended by the school placement team in the child's Individual Education Program) and for the educational portion of a residential placement in a private school.

In addition to the legal mandate, educators and others are beginning to recognize the need to integrate and coordinate services delivered to severely handicapped children, if that service is to be effective. Mearig (1982) describes the situation where a family bounces aimlessly from agency to agency in search of appropriate services for a handicapped child. She sees the school's responsibility as multifaceted and ongoing, including a comprehensive multidisciplinary assessment to identify all relevant needs; coordination of referral to outside service providers; continual monitoring of services provided, and then follow-up and evaluation of the placement or services. Hobbs (1966, 1978†) has been a leading proponent of the integrated services delivery model since the introduction of the RE-Ed program in 1966. Hobbs stresses an ecological and systems' perspective in the etiology and maintenance of children's maladaptive behavior and suggests the use of a written contract where the roles and responsibilities of different caregivers are described and coordinated to minimize gaps or duplication in services provided.

In summary, tertiary intervention includes a continuum of different levels of mental health services provided to children with identified, debilitating emotional problems. These services include both in-school programs and community-based services, and range from intermittent, crises-survival sessions to full-time residential placement. Where community services or placements are required, the primary obligation of the school is to see that appropriate services are identified, secured, and coordinated.

CONCLUSIONS

The foregoing sections have identified and briefly described the major mental health efforts occurring in the school setting. These educational efforts, programs, services, and service-providers were categorized as falling under one of three levels of intervention, namely, primary, secondary, and tertiary. The major difference between these

---

†Hobbs, N. *An ecologically-oriented, service-based system for the classification of handicapped children.* Unpublished paper, Center for the Study of Families and Children, Vanderbuilt Institute for Public Policy Studies, Vanderbuilt University, 1978

categories or levels of service is the extent to which school children are already evidencing maladaptive behavior, rather than the focus or content of the program. But perhaps most importantly, it is critical to emphasize that actual services provided in any particular school system depend on the human and financial resources available. Furthermore, even where schools are providing a significantly broad array of mental health services, there typically remains a lack of sufficient coordination and integration to make the programs as successful as they might otherwise be.

This lack of coordination and integration frequently results in gaps in services, duplication of efforts, "turf" battles, and frustrated educational consumers including students, parents, and members of the larger community (Mearig, 1982). Such confusion and lack of communication also frustrates mental health service providers outside of schools who often have their own coordination problems with complex mental health service systems. School-community links suffer and thus frequently result in each party focusing on the other's dysfunctional practice.

One solution to this costly dilemma has been alluded to in various statements made earlier. Comprehensive and effective mental health services for children need to be multifaceted, integrated, and continually evaluated and improved. These services need to involve qualified and dedicated mental health professionals working both within and outside the school. Mental health practitioners working in both private and public mental health agencies need to become aware of what mental health services are available in their local schools and how best to impact school systems to get coordinated services for their clients. Also the mental health needs of children must become a valued and integral part of the routine mission of schools and not a patchwork of peripheral, expendable programs.

How can such goals be accomplished? The planning, development, implementation, and evaluation of an optimal comprehensive, mental health delivery system for children involves seven independent and interdependent functions (Stilwell, 1976a; Stilwell et al., 1984). Indeed, the general model for the management of educational delivery systems has been expanded to include two additional functions (Mannebach & Stilwell, 1978). The general model for a school-based mental health program has nine functions:

Obtain community involvement. The initiation of a comprehensive mental health program is dependent upon the cooperation of many individuals and groups within the community, including city/town officials, school board members, school administrators, mental health center directors, private service providers, etc. The mental health program manager (e.g., clinical child psychologist, guidance counselor, school psychologist, or school social worker) and a consumer advisory group (e.g., other health care agency representatives, special interest group advocates, and lay persons) will want to visit exemplary, ongoing programs with the intention of identifying program elements that can be easily adopted or adapted by the school and the community. All too frequently new programs appear to be undertaken in schools without evaluation first of the necessary and appropriate physical, financial, and human resources.

Conduct needs assessment. Evidence regarding the mental health needs of persons (students, teachers, administrators, and parents) in the school district can be collected and analyzed for mental health program implications. A major effort within the needs assessment function is the selection of appropriate assessment instruments for use with students, teachers, and parents. In some settings, the assessment materials must be adapted or created for the school situation. The traditional data collection strategy is paper and pencil questionnaire. To this traditional approach the mental health worker may add the collection of observational data (frequency and variety of behaviors) and the use of structured interviews. This multimethod, multisource needs assessment can become useful in the establishment of mental health program goals.

Specify program goals. Specification of mental health program goals is a joint undertaking that occurs on multiple levels (e.g., funding agency, local institutions, and recipients, if possible). The mental health program will operate with three levels of specificity: program goals can be developed by professionals, community leaders, and the funding agencies; the school subgoals can be developed by the school level mental health committee (e.g., teachers, parents, administrators, and mental health professionals); and, individualized mental health objectives can be mutually developed by the mental health professional and the consumer (i.e., therapeutic short and long term objectives). The individual consumer's mental health objectives can be stated in a mental health plan (MHP) that addresses, minimally, behavior, attitude, and knowledge changes. These documents are reviewed periodically and used in program evaluation.

Adopt/adapt/create program materials. An assumption in this model is that a majority of the curricular materials for the mental health program are available. The recommended hierarchy of adoption, adaption, and creation of mental health program materials incorporates the most desirable elements of observed or conceptualized programs, meets the needs of the program's consumers, and reaches the specific program goals and objectives. In a sense, this function provides for preprogram-implementation evaluation of the available materials.

Prepare for program installation. The preparation of mental health program personnel in the schools occurs in three steps: orient personnel to mental health, select personnel for specific mental health activities, and train the personnel in the use of mental health concepts and practices. Inservice training for key school and community personnel can be conducted by such mental health professionals as clinical child psychologists, guidance counselors, school psychologists, and school social workers. The mental health program implementation model is intended to avoid surprise and to involve teachers, parents, and students in program development, planning, implementation, and evaluation.

Implement comprehensive mental health program. This function simply says, "do it." The mental health planning and program development provides for a thorough and efficient implementation. Essentially in the implementation function the program managers will want to answer the powerful, heuristic question, "Which mental health strategy, managed by whom, is better for that particular student who has this specific objective?" Direct service mental health workers will want to develop a primary and secondary strategy in their MHP. In the event the program has elements which function inadequately, e.g., exceeding program costs or falling below forecasted program goals, adjustments must be made to ensure program success.

Evaluate the program. Internal and external program evaluation should occur with both formative and summative evaluation aspects (Mason & Bramble, 1978). Internal continuous evaluation, conducted by the program staff, is of two types: immediate program impact (e.g., Stilwell & Barclay, 1979) and long term impact (Barclay et al., 1978). External periodic evaluations, conducted for funding agencies and consumer groups, provide community impact and accountability information. The feedback to mental health providers within the program, to surrounding community members, and to funding agencies is crucial to a viable program.

Maintain behavior change. In many areas related to mental health, students, teachers, and parents "forget" their recently mastered skills. The activities in this function might include training post-direct services support groups, sending postcard "prompts" to serve as weekly reminders, and conducting checkups to monitor the stability of the behavior change.

   Maintain mental health program reference system.   The MHP reference system is crucial to program development. The multiple inputs (program goals, assessment data, implementation strategies, and outcomes) can be used to prepare probabilistic answers for better interventions and needed inservice training.

   The general model for the school based mental health program can serve as a management document for mental health professionals. Each program manager will need to develop their own rationale for implementing such a program. However, a number of common benefits from the mental health program model can be identified: Preservice training programs can be modified to include theory and practice of mental health. The mental health program delivery system can become inexpensive. Many school systems already employ the human resources for a comprehensive mental health program. The overall system can be developmental such that information and experiences build upon each other in an orderly manner. Accountability is built into the system such that documentation for continuation funding is readily available.

   Professionals who are committed to mental health in the schools have a unique opportunity to take from the "better" programs, organize the elements for each school and system setting, and benefit parents, teachers, and students.

REFERENCES

Albee, GW. The relation of conceptual models to manpower needs. In EL Cowen, E Gardner, & M Zax (Eds.), *Emergent approaches to mental health problems.* New York: Appleton-Century-Crofts, 1967, 63–73

American Psychological Association. APA-approved programs in clinical, counseling, and school psychology: 1982. *American Psychologist,* 1982, *37,* 1374–1376

Anderson, CS. The search for school climate: A review of the research. *Review of Educational Research.* 1982, *52,* 368–420

Anderson, RM, Martinez, D, & Rich, HJ. Perspectives for change. In J Schifani, RM Anderson, & SJ Odle (Eds.), *Implementing learning in the least restrictive environment: Handicapped children in the mainstream.* Baltimore: University Park Press, 1980

Andronico, MP, & Guerney, B Jr. The potential application of filial therapy to the school situation. *Journal of School Psychology,* 1967, *6,* 2–7

Aponte, HJ. The family-school interview: An eco-structural approach. *Family Process,* 1976, *15,* 303–311

Aubrey, RF. Consultation, school intervention, and the elementary counselor. *Personnel and Guidance Journal,* 1978, *56,* 351–354

Balow, B. Definitional and prevalence problems in behavior disorders of children. *School Psychology Digest*, 1979, *8*, 348–354

Barbanel, L. Short-term dynamic therapies with children. In C Reynolds & T Gutkin (Eds.), *Handbook of school psychology.* New York: John Wiley, 1982

Barclay, JR. Sociometric choices and teacher ratings as predictors of school dropouts. *Journal of School Psychology*, 1966, *4*, 40–44

Barclay, JR. Meta-theory and meta-analysis: The possible contributions to measurement and evaluation. *Measurement and Evaluation in Guidance*, 1982, *15*, 36–39

Barclay, JR. *Barclay Classroom Assessment System.* Los Angeles: Western Psychological Services, 1983(a)

Barclay, JR. Moving toward a technology of prevention: A model and some tentative findings. *School Psychology Review*, 1983, *12*(3), 228–239(b)

Barclay, JR, Covert, RM, Scott, TW, & Stilwell, WE. Some effects of schooling: A three-year follow-up of a Title III project, 1975 ERIC Documentation Reproduction Service 1978, (ED 145 967)

Barclay, JR, & Kehle, TJ. The impact of handicapped students on other students in the classroom. *Journal of Research and Development in Education*, 1979, *12*, (4), 80–91

Barclay, JR, Phillips, GW, & Jones, T. The development of a predictive index of giftedness. *Measurement and Evaluation in Guidance*, 1983, *16*(1), 25–35

Bardon, JI, & Bennett, VC. Helping children in school. In B Wolman (Ed.), *Manual of child psychopathology.* New York: McGraw-Hill, 1972

Bardon, JI, & Bennett, VC. *School psychology.* Englewood Cliffs, NJ.: Prentice-Hall, 1974

Bergan, JR. *Behavioral consultation.* Columbus, Ohio: Charles E. Merrill, 1977

Bersoff, D. The legal regulation of school psychology. In C Reynolds & T Gutkin (Eds.), *Handbook of school psychology.* New York: John Wiley, 1982

Bessell, H, & Palmores, U. *Methods in human development: Theory manual and curriculum activity guide.* San Diego: Human Development Training Institute, 1970

Blackhurst, AE, & Berdine, WH. (Eds.), *An introduction to special education,* Boston: Little, Brown, and Co., 1981

Bower, EM. Primary prevention in a school setting. In G Caplan (Ed.), *Prevention of mental disorders in children.* New York: Basic Books, Inc., 1961

Buffington, PW, & Stilwell, WE. Teachers attitudes and affective education: An unexpected finding. *Education*, 1981, *101*, 176–182

Caplan, G. *Principles of preventive psychology.* New York: Basic Books, 1964

Caplan, C. *The theory and practice of mental health consultation.* New York: Basic Books, 1970

Catterall, CD, & Gazda, GM. *Strategies for helping students.* Springfield, Ill.: Charles C Thomas, 1978

Claiborn, C, & Strong, S. Group counseling in the schools. In GC Reynolds & T Gutkin (Eds.), *Handbook of school psychology.* New York: John Wiley, 1982

Clarizio, H. School psychologists and the mental health needs of students. In G Phye & D Reschley (Eds.), *School psychology: Perspectives and issues.* New York: Academic Press, 1979

Cook V, & Patterson, J. Psychologist in the schools of Nebraska: Professional functions. *Psychology in the Schools*, 1977, *14*, 371–376

Corsini, RL. Individual education. In E Ignas & RJ Corsini (Eds.), *Alternative educational systems.* Itasca, Ill.: FE Peacock Publishers Inc., 1979

Cowen, EL. The primary mental health project: Yesterday, today and tomorrow. *The Journal of Special Education.* 1980, *14*, 133–154

Cowen, EL, Gardner, E, & Zax, M. *Emergent approaches to mental health.* New York: Appleton-Century-Crofts, 1967

Cowen, EL, Orgel, AR, Gesten, EL, & Wilson, AB. The evaluation of an intervention program for young school children with acting-out problems. *Journal of Abnormal Child Psychology,* 1979, *7,* 381–396

Dinkmeyer, D. *Developing understanding of self and others (DUSO-I).* Circle Pines, Minn.: American Guidance Service, 1970

Dinkmeyer, D, & McKay, GD. *Systematic training for effective parenting.* Circle Pines, Minn.: American Guidance Service, 1974

Dupont, H, Gardner, OS, & Brody, DS. *Toward affective development.* Circle Pines, Minn.: American Guidance Service, 1974

Durlak, JA. Providing mental health services to elementary school children. In CE Walker & MC Roberts (Eds.), *Handbook of clinical child psychology,* New York: Wiley-Interscience, 1983

Education for All Handicapped Children Act (P. L. 94-142).

Ellett, CD, & Walberg, HJ. Principals' competency, environment, and outcomes. In HJ Walberg (Ed.), *Educational environments and effects.* Berkeley, Calif.: McCutchan, 1979

Emener, WG, Jr, Stilwell, WE, & Witten, BJ. Delivering human services for abused clients: A systems and individual approach. *Family and Community esslerHealth,* 1981, *4* (2), 71–83

Fine, M, & Holt, P. Intervening with school problems: A family systems perspective. *Psychology in the Schools,* 1983, *20,* 59–66

Fraser, BJ, & Fisher, DL. Predicting students' outcomes from their perceptions of classroom psychological environment. *American Educational Research Journal,* 1982, *19,* 498–518

Freed, AM. *T. A. for tots.* Sacramento, Calif.: Jalmar Press, 1973

Gildea, MC-L, Glidewell, JC, & Kantor, MB. The St. Louis Mental Health Project: History and evaluation. In EL Cowen, EA Gardner, & M. Zax (Eds.), *Emergent approaches to mental health problems.* New York: Appleton-Century-Crofts, 1967

Glasser, W. *Schools without failure.* New York: Harper and Row, 1969

Gordon, S, & Snyder, SU. Sex education. In CM Walker & MC Roberts (Eds.), *Handbook of clinical child psychology.* New York: Wiley-Interscience, 1983

Grotsky, J, Sabatino, D, & Ohrtman, W. (Eds.), *The concept of mainstreaming: A resource guide for regular classroom teachers.* King of Prussa, Pa.: Eastern Pennsylvania Regional Resource Center, 1976

Gutkin, T, & Curtis, M. School-based consultation: Theory and techniques. In C Reynolds & T Gutkin (Eds.), *Handbook of school psychology.* New York: John Wiley, 1982

Handicapped Children's Early Assistance Act (P. L. 90-358).

Hewett, F. *The emotionally disturbed child in the classroom.* Boston: Allyn & Bacon, 1968

Hobbs, N. Helping disturbed children: Psychological and ecological strategies. *American Psychologist,* 1966, *21,* 1105–1115

Hunter, EC. Changes in teachers' attitudes toward children's behavior over the last thirty years. *Mental Hygiene,* 1957, *41,* 3–11

Insel, PM, & Moos, RH. Psychological environments: Expanding the scope of human ecology. *American Psychologist,* 1974, *29,* 179–188

Johnson, SB. Children fears in the classroom setting. *School Psychology Digest,* 1979, *8,* 382–396

Justice, R, & Justice, B. *Abusing families.* New York: Human Science Press, 1976

Kameen, MC, & Thompson, DL. Substance abuse and child-abuse neglect: Implications for direct-service providers. *Personnel and Guidance Journal,* 1983, *61,* 269–273

Kazdin, A. Applying behavioral principles in the schools. In G Reynolds & T Gutkin (Eds.), *Handbook of school psychology.* New York: John Wiley, 1982

Kershman, SM. Early childhood education. In AE Blackhurst & WH Berdine (Eds.), *An introduction to special education.* Boston: Little, Brown, and Co., 1981

Kessler, M, & Albee, GW. Primary prevention. In MR Rosenzweig & LW Porter (Eds.), *Annual review of psychology*. Palo Alto, C.A.: Annual Reviews, 1975

Klein, RS, Altman, SD, Dreizen, K, Friedman, R, & Powers, L. Restructuring dysfunctional parental attitudes toward children's learning and behavior in school: Family-oriented psychoeducational therapy, Part I. *Journal of Learning Disabilities*, 1981, *14*, 15–19(a)

Klein, RS, Altman, SD, Dreizen, K, Friedman, R, & Powers, L. Restructuring dysfunctional parental attitudes toward children's learning and behavior in school: Family-oriented psychoeducational therapy, Part II. *Journal of Learning Disabilities*, 1981, *14*, 99–101(b)

Krumboltz, JD, & Krumboltz, HB. *Changing children's behavior*. Englewood Cliffs, N.J.: Prentice-Hall, 1972

Lambert, N. *The protection and promotion of mental health in the schools*. Washington, DC.: U.S. Government Printing Office, 1964

Mannebach, AJ, & Stilwell, WE. Developing career education programs: A team approach. *Vocational Guidance Quarterly*, 1978, *26*, 308–317

Mason, EJ, & Bramble, WJ. *Understanding and conducting research: Applications in education and the behavioral sciences*. New York: McGraw-Hill, 1978

McLouglin, TA. The role of parents. In AE Blackhurst and WT Berdine (Eds.), *Introduction to special education*. Boston: Little, Brown, and Co., 1981

Meacham, M, & Peckham, P. School psychologists at three quarters century: Congruence between training, practice, preferred role and competence. *Journal of School Psychology*, 1978, *16*, 195–206

Mearig, J. Integration of school and community services for children with special needs. In C Reynolds & T Gutkin (Eds.), *Handbook of school psychology*. New York: John Wiley, 1982

Medway, FJ. How effective is school consultation?: A review of recent research. *Journal of School Psychology*, 1979, *17*, 275–282

Meyers, J, Martin, R, & Hyman, I. *School consultation*. Springfield, Ill.: Charles C Thomas, 1977

Meyers, J, Parsons, R, & Martin, R. *Mental health consultation in the schools*. San Francisco: Jossey-Bass, 1979

Miller, JA. *Humanizing the classroom*. New York: Praeger, 1976

Monroe, V. Roles and status of school psychology. In GD Phye & DJ Reschley (Eds.), *School psychology: Perspectives and issues*. New York: Academic Press, 1979

Moos, RH. Systems for the assessment and classification of human environments: An overview. In RH Moos & PM Insel (Eds.), *Issues in social ecology*. Palo Alto, Calif.: National Press Books, 1974

Moos, RH. *Evaluating educational environments: Procedures, measures, findings, and policy implications*. San Francisco: Jossey-Bass, 1979

Morse, W. Crisis intervention in school mental health and special classes for the disturbed. In MJ Long, W Morse, & R Newman (Eds.), *Conflict in the classroom: The education of children with problems*. Belmont, Calif.: Wadsworth, 1971

Morsink, CV. Learning disabilities. In AE Blackhurst & WH Berdine (Eds.), *An introduction to special education*. Boston: Little, Brown, and Co., 1981

Newcomer, PL. *Understanding and teaching emotionally disturbed children*. Boston: Allyn & Bacon, 1980

Newman, R. *Groups in schools*. New York: Simon and Schuster, 1974

Newton, R, & Brown, RA. A preventive approach to developmental problems in school children. In EM Bower & W Hollister (Eds.), *Behavioral science frontiers in education*. New York: John Wiley, 1967

O'Leary, KD, & O'Leary, S. *Classroom management: The successful use of behavior modification*. New York: Pergamon, 1972

Pace, CR, & Stern, GG. An approach to the measurement of psychological characteristics of college environments. *Journal of Educational Psychology*, 1958, *49*, 269–277

Pfeiffer, SI. Facilitating effective team decision making. In M Gaasholt & N Haring (Eds.), *Organizing for change: Inservice and staff development in special education*. Seattle, WA.: Program Development Assistance System, 1981

Pfeiffer, SI, & Heffernan, L. Improving multidisciplinary team functions. In C Maher, R Illback, & J Zins (Eds.), *Organizational psychology in the schools: A sourcebook for professionals*. Springfield, Ill.: Charles C Thomas, 1984

Pfeiffer, SI, & Tittler, BI. Utilizing the multidisciplinary team to facilitate a school-family system orientation. *School Psychology Review*, 1983, *12* (2), 168–173

Reynolds, M, & Birch, J. *Teaching exceptional children in all America's Schools (Revised Edition)*, Reston, Va.: Council for Exceptional Children, 1982

Ryan, TA. A conceptual model of career development. *Educational Technology*, 1973, *9* (6), 28–38

Sarason, S. Community psychology, networks, and Mr. Everyman. *American Psychologist*, 1982, *31*, 317–328

Sarason, SB, Levine, M, Goldenberg, II, Cherlin, DL, & Bennett, EM. *Psychology in community settings: Clinical, educational, vocational social aspects*. New York: Wiley, 1966

Schmuck, RA. Organizational development in the schools. In C Reynolds & T Gutkin (Eds.), *Handbook of school psychology*. New York: John Wiley, 1982

Schmuck, RA, Runkel, PJ, Saturen, SL, Martell, RT, & Derr, CB. *Handbook of organizational development in schools*. Eugene, Ore.: National Press Books, 1972

Shearn, D, & Randolph, D. Effects of reality therapy methods applied in the classroom. *Psychology in the Schools*, 1978, *15*, 79–83

Shultz, E, Hirshoren, A, Manton, A, & Henderson, R. Special education for the emotionally disturbed. *Exceptional Children*, 1971, *38*, 313–320

Silvern, LS. LOGOS: A system language for flowchart modeling. *Educational Technology*, 1969, *9(6)*, 18–23

Simon, S, Howe, H, & Kirschenbaum, H. *Values clarification: A handbook of practical strategies*. New York: Hart, 1972

Smith, D. Counseling and psychotherapy in the school setting. In JF Magary (Ed.), *School psychological services in theory and practice*. Englewood Cliffs, N.J.: Prentice-Hall, 1967

Sprinthall, NA. Guidance and new education in schools. *Personnel and Guidance Journal*, 1980, *58*, 485–489

Stilwell, WE. A systems approach for social-, educational-, or institutional change. In LC Silvern (Ed.), *Applications of systems thinking to the administration of instruction*. Los Angeles, Calif.: Educational and Training Consultants, 1976, 79–88(a)

Stilwell, WE. A systems approach for implementing an affective education program. *Counselor Education and Supervision*, 1976, *15*, 200–215(b)

Stilwell, WE, & Barclay, JR. Affective education in the primary grade levels: A pilot program, 1977 (ERIC Document Reproduction Service No. ED 129 436) (a)

Stilwell, WE, & Barclay, JR. Effects of affective education through developmental guidance services: A one-year study, 1977 (ERIC Document Reproduction Service No. ED 133 077) (b)

Stilwell, WE, & Barclay, JR. Effects of an affective-social education program over two years, 1978 (ERIC Document Reproduction Service No. ED 143 425)

Stilwell, WE, & Barclay, JR. Effects of an affective education intervention in the elementary schools. *Psychology in the Schools*, 1979, *16*, 80–87

Stilwell, WE, Buffington, PW, DeMers, ST, & Stilwell, DN. Integrating psychological education programs: A comprehensive checklist. *School Counselor*, 1984, *31* (3), 249–255

Stilwell, WE, & Santoro, DA. A training model for the 80s. *Personnel and Guidance Journal*, 1976, *54*, 461–465

Taylor, FD, & Soloway, MM. The Madison School Plan: A functional model for merging the regular and special classrooms. In E Deno (Ed.), *Instructional alternatives for exceptional children*. Reston, Va.: Council for Exceptional Children, 1973

Thompson, CE. The attitudes of various groups towards behavior problems of children. *Journal of Abnormal and Social Psychology*, 1940, *35*, 120–135

Tindall, R. School psychology: Development of a profession. In G Phye & D Reschley (Eds.), *School psychology: Perspectives and issues*. New York: Academic Press, 1979

Turnbull, AP, Leonard, JE, & Turnbull, R. Defensible analyses of P.L. 94-142: A response. *The Journal of Special Education*, 1981, *15*, 25–32

Visher, EG, & Visher, JS. *Stepfamilies: A guide to working with stepparents and stepchildren*. New York: Brunner/Mazel, 1979

Walberg, HJ. Class size and the social environment of learning. *Human Relations*, 1969, *22*, 465–475

Weisberg, P. Education and enrichment approaches. In CE Walker & MC Roberts (Eds.), *Handbook of clinical child psychology*. New York: Wiley-Interscience, 1983

White, MA, & Harris, D. *The school psychologist*. New York: Harper and Row, 1961

Wickman, EK. *Children's behavior and teacher attitudes*. New York: Commonwealth Fund, 1928

Wonderly, D, Kupersmid, J, Monkman, R, Deak, J, & Rosenberg, S. Primary prevention in school psychology: Past, present, and proposed future. *Child Study Journal*, 1979, *9*, 163–179

Woods, M. Developmental therapy: A model of therapeutic intervention in the US schools. In C Reynolds & T Gutkin (Eds.), *Handbook of school psychology*. New York: John Wiley, 1982

Woody, RH. *Behavioral problem children in the schools*. New York: Appleton-Century-Crofts, 1969

Worell, J, & Stilwell, WE. *Psychology for teachers and students*. New York: McGraw-Hill, 1981

Zigler, E, Kagan, S, & Muenchow, S. Preventive intervention in the schools. In C Reynolds & T Gutkin (Eds.), *Handbook of school psychology*. New York: John Wiley, 1982

Robert Marion
Ernie Bernal

11

Working With Culturally Diverse Children and Families

The early childhood years are considered by some to be critical times in the development of the child's mental health. In this formative period the child begins to develop a sense of identity, purpose, and direction (Lee, 1973), becomes less egocentric, and expands its awareness of a world that exists outside the family circle. Moreover, the child begins to discover that his or her existence carries with it the responsibility of adhering to the rules of society (Comer & Poussant, 1975).

Although the early childhood years are considered important milestones in the lives of all children, their significance is especially crucial for the developmental tasks faced by racial and ethnic minority children. Not only do minority children have to pass through the ordinary developmental stages and tasks of childhood, but they also have to cope with the burdens that the dominant society places on them because they are considered "different." Their quality of life and the resulting state of mental health are tied inescapably to this reality.

A Cause for Alarm

The President's Commission on Mental Health (1978) has indicated that far too many Americans have no access to mental health care and that the services available to them are limited or not sufficiently responsive to their individual circumstances. Although not directed specifically toward blacks, Hispanics, and other racial or ethnic minorities, these observations underscore the dilemmas that are faced by many families and children of culturally different populations. While the majority of children in the United States are enjoying the benefits of modern medicine and science as gateways to stable mental health, too many minority children can be expected to grow up and live under less than nurturing conditions.

The vagaries that attend the quality of life experienced by minorities include both social stigmatization and poverty. The concomitant problems of these conditions include a large and ever-increasing number of households headed by working mothers with a need for quality child care; high unemployment rates, especially among females; a growing rate of child abuse; continuing outbreaks of childhood diseases; alarming upswings in pregnancies and venereal diseases among children and youth; escalating incidences of alcoholism and drug abuse among adults, adolescents, and children; declining levels of academic achievement and high dropout rates; and accelerating child and juvenile violence and crime.

In some cases descriptive statistics can be used to illustrate the comparative differences that exist between the modal mental health attainments of majority and minority populations. However, most of these numerical descriptors used alone will not convey the total picture of the quality of life experienced by many culturally different parents and their offspring. In this regard early researchers have generally tended to make use of data that presented a distressful picture of the state of mental health endured by minorities. To gain a more sensitive understanding, statistics should be buttressed by in-depth sociopsychological research that explicitly establishes the relationship of race/ethnicity and mental health. That such demographic categories should be inextricably bound up with psychodynamic processes is due to the implicit importance that society has attached to race and its intolerance of behavioral and cultural differences.

Melting Pot Syndrome

Prior to the 1960s the dominant political and social philosophy of the United States was expressed by the notion of the "melting pot," the principle of assimilation and the goal of "sameness." The culturally different person who immigrated to our country was expected to forget the old ways and acquire the characteristics of Americans (Glazer, 1977). In this way the United States would make not a single society, but a single culture out of many. Under the melting pot philosophy, parents and children who maintained a culturally different style of life were seen not merely as atypical but as backward, un-American, or pathological. Public advocates of the melting pot during the nineteenth and early twentieth centuries never really intended that blacks, Chinese, American Indians, or Mexicans be added to the cauldron. Instead, the debates centered around which Europeans were worthy of admission to the United States without "corrupting" the new American bloodline, diluting its white Protestantism, or impeding the development of its industrial ethic (e.g., Grant, 1922).

The upshot has been that the "place" of culturally/racially different peoples within American society has remained destructively ambiguous both for the nation and for individuals. For example, many minority individuals who painfully severed their ethnic ties have met only discrimination, not acceptance. The resultant psychological damage of being neither white nor minority, of having been somehow betrayed after risking so much, has devastated many culturally different persons.

But while certain individuals have sought to "make it" or "pass for white," many minority groups have characteristically maintained their cultures, or at least have tried to do so. For them, it is sufficient to embrace their citizenship loyally. Their lifestyles, they believe, should be respected, and bicultural competence is their own internal goal (Bernal, 1969). Perhaps they interpret *e pluribus unum* to mean one society, not one homogeneous culture.

The Larger Societal Fabric and Service Institutions

It can be maintained that community mental health centers (MHCs), schools, and other service organizations are enmeshed in the larger societal fabric and are dependent on the continued goodwill of the society-at-large. One might argue that these formal organizations reflect dominant cultural values and ultimately serve the society's pivotal institution, which is economic. Consciously or not, their practices thus largely supported and perpetuated a class system that is definable in no small part by race and ethnicity.

Some of the economic system's unfortunate practices have been discrimination in hiring and promotion, in housing, and in the political arena. The upshot has been the creation and perpetuation of ghettos and segregated, substandard schools (Griffin, 1971). Coupled with the melting pot myth and the notion that in America a person can "rise to the top" through individual effort despite one's origins, these actions have resulted in considerable frustration, confusion, alienation, and a sense of powerlessness among many minority youth and adults (Hulbury, 1975).

A great deal of conformity is implied by popular, mainstream notions of Americanism, and individuals have been allowed to differ only to the point of "minding their own business," speaking a standard English without an accent, and not appearing or acting in a manner that identifies them with any cultural minority. Since many minority children and families could not eliminate these characteristics, they could be treated differently. This differential treatment of minorities is perhaps best exemplified by school programs that merely diluted the standard course of studies, were staffed by improperly prepared, often demoralized teachers, and housed in substandard facilities.

Educators and mental health workers in general have tried to serve the minority student or client by assuming an assimilationist posture or orientation in their work (Banks, 1977). They have not understood the impracticality and inappropriateness of this type of intervention for many persons, have not appreciated the risks and anxieties that ordinarily accompany its implementation in real life nor its disruption of minority groups' integrity. Finally, these individuals have not realized how badly their credibility is strained in the mind of any client who has a healthy sense of the possible. Such practitioners convey the message of inadequacy or inferiority to students and clients, the feeling that somehow they are fundamentally not good enough as they are, that they must not only overcome their problem but also become more like whites (Brown, 1981).

Children and adults who have not "melted" thus place strains on the skills of educational and clinical professionals who have been trained to deal exclusively with individuals or groups who represent the dominant ethnic group.

Cultural Pluralism

By way of contrast to the idea of the melting pot, the principle of cultural pluralism has been espoused by some elements in American society in recent years. Saville-Troike (1976) has borrowed a gastronomic metaphor, the "salad bowl," to characterize the situation where different cultural ingredients are mixed in one dish. This concept is based on the realization that Americans are in fact not all of one way of thinking and living, and, furthermore, that their differences are acceptable if not actually desirable. Cultural pluralism is often discussed as a positive force in our society, rather than as a potentially devisive or separatist orientation.

There has also been a notable resurgence of ethnic pride in the last twenty years, a kind of affirmative ethnic citizenship felt at all levels within minority groups (Smith, 1981). In the 1980s, greater numbers of young ethnic leaders are emerging who have never abandoned their cultural traditions, but other minority persons continue to feel trapped and alienated by the narrowness of our society's institutions.

In the fields of education and mental health, cultural pluralism is only just beginning to find its expression. The numbers of minority persons are growing, constituting an ever larger proportion of the U.S. population. Moreover, the culturally different are beginning to insist that schools and mental health agencies serve all segments of society equitably and flexibly enough to meet their needs effectively, even if it means having to effect some internal changes and innovations (Bernal, 1969).

In clinical and other service settings, greater minority participation and more intensive inservice education have been in evidence. Although more minority professionals are being hired, it is now realized (Brown, 1981) that this practice will not ensure an ethnic orientation or sensitivity, and may place the burden of serving minority clients exclusively on an acculturated individual who would rather not do so or who would be quickly relegated by her/his colleagues to the role of the one in charge of minority problems (Bernal, 1969). It has been observed that there is more value similarity among professionals of different ethnic backgrounds than there is between professionals and nonprofessionals of the same racial or ethnic group (Milutinovich, 1976). Based on this evidence, inservice training in minority matters, especially in the effective delivery of needed services, should be seriously considered for all professionals, irrespective of their ethnicity.

Some agencies have decentralized their offices to encourage the local and even neighborhood-level participation of minority representatives on advisory boards and policy councils. True minority input has promoted mutual understanding and accountability (Chilman, 1973), and may change professional perspectives from institutionally centered to client-centered ones.*

System Realities and Reactions

According to the 1975 Special Census, the population of the United States included 22 million black Americans, 12 million Hispanic Americans, 3 million Asian and Pacific Island Americans, and 1 million Amer-

---

* Safran, D. *Preparing teachers for parent involvement.* Berkeley, Calif.: Center for the Study of Parent Involvement, October 1974

ican Indians and Alaskan Natives. The cultural diversity of the United States can readily be seen from these population data. This diversification of the American populace is expected to continue into the future. It has been postulated that Americans of non-European ancestry will constitute the majority of the United States population by the year 2000.

The average size of a family in the United States is continuing to decline according to the U.S. Census Bureau. Their data show that the average number of children under the age of 18 living with their families in the United States had declined from 2.0 in 1977 to 1.96 by 1978. For blacks and Hispanics the corresponding figures are higher than the national average. In 1978 black families contained 2.0 children under the age of 18, while the comparative number for Hispanics was 2.20.†

Family differences could also be discerned when looking at the kinds of sibling and adult pairings that constituted minority and majority families. In 1976, 84 percent of all primary families in the United States were husband and wife units. Thirteen percent were headed by females without a husband and three percent were male-headed without the presence of a wife.‡

However, between 1980 and 1982 a significant change occurred in the number of primary households. Primary families (husband and wife) accounted for only 47 percent of the 2.8 million households added during the two-year interval 1980 to 1982. This decrease in the percentage of primary households during these years can be attributed to the growth of families maintained by men or women without a spouse being present. Specifically, within some culturally different families, this trend toward single parent families increased significantly. For example, in 1976, 85 percent of all white children lived with both parents. In comparison, 75 percent of all Hispanic and only 50 percent of all black children resided with two parents. By 1980, however, 41 percent of black children under the age of 18 were living in households headed by women.

The issue of poverty is also a critical variable in assessing households headed by minority working women. In 1978, 26 percent of two-parent households had incomes over $25,000, while only four percent of the homes headed by single females received such income. More specifically, 31 percent of female-headed households had a median income of $5,000

---

† U.S. Bureau of the Census. Current Population Reports, Series P-20, No. 334, *Population Profile of the United States, 1978*. Washington, DC.: U.S. Government Printing Office, 1979, p. 2

‡ U.S. Bureau of the Census. Current Population Reports, Series P-20, No. 336, *Population Profile of the United States, 1978*. Washington, DC.: U.S. Government Printing Office, Washington, DC., 1979, p. 55

or less.§ On the other hand, black female-headed households had an annual income of only $1,268. These figures point out the difference in the quality of life enjoyed by culturally different households headed by women.

Taken within this context of poverty, more than half (52.8 percent) of the black women (with their children) who headed these households lived below the poverty level (Ladner, 1971). Of Hispanic children, 29 percent live at the low income level and 69 percent of Spanish origin children in families headed by women are subsisting in poverty conditions. Abject poverty and welfare seem to be the fate of most families headed by minority women.

Children who live in poverty are at a particularly high risk for mental health problems (Calhoun, Grotberg, & Rackley, 1980). Minority children and youth are overrepresented among the poverty population in the nation and, as such, have a greater likelihood of being raised in a one-parent, female-headed family and of experiencing higher rates of school failure and dropout, run-away, drug abuse, and unemployment/underemployment (Florez, 1978). Dohrenwend, Dohrenwend, Gould, & Wunsch-Hitzig, (1980) report that their analyses of epidemiological studies in the U.S. showed that "psychopathology" in general was found to be at least two and a half times more prevalent in lower socioeconomic status (SES) groups than in the highest classes.

Kellam, Ensminger, and Turner (1977) discovered that the rate of psychological disorders in children would change as a function of family structure. They indicated that female single-parent families had the highest risk of maladjustment in children and two-parent families the lowest risk. When these two propositions are combined, they can be directly related to a higher incidence of mental health difficulty identified in Hispanic and black children.

Habitat has also been related to high rates of mental illnesses among minority children. Since most minority children reside within metropolitan areas (87 percent of Mexican-American and 81 percent of the black populations), childhood emotional disorders in inner city and urban youth are found to be correspondingly more prevalent than in rural areas (Rutter, Cox, Tupling, Burger & Yale, 1975). Langer, Gersten, Green, Eisenberg, Herson, and McCarty (1974) found that twice as many black and Spanish speaking inner-city children showed signs of severe psychiatric disorders than Anglo children.

---

§ U.S. Bureau of the Census. Current Population Reports, Series P-20, No. 340, *Household and Family Characteristics: March 1978.* Washington, DC.: U.S. Government Printing Office, 1979, p. 3

Still, the "culture of poverty" is not homogeneous, neither in its expression nor in its effects. Shipman‖ reminds us that many socioeconomic variables only poorly predict the level of cognitive stimulation in particular homes. Zigler and Child (1969), after reviewing many pieces of seemingly contradictory findings, conclude that studies based on observed maternal behavior towards children in the home suggest that interclass differences are not as great as one would infer by looking at data derived from interviews with parents. Nor do economically disadvantaged children necessarily suffer from low self-esteem (Soares & Soares, 1969). In short, while poverty-ethnicity-ghetto life precipitates different behaviors, most persons in these conditions are surprisingly quite able to cope with the vicissitudes of their lives.

Mental Health and the Judicial System

The damaging impact of the conditions of poverty and race is also reflected in the delivery of mental health services and the extent of mental illness among minority children and youth. Black and Hispanic children in women-headed families, for instance, are admitted to outpatient mental health facilities at a rate four times as great as children from two-parent families. In addition, minority children are institutionalized in medical and educational facilities at a rate that is 20 percent higher than that of whites. When access to mental health services is limited, these minority children are four times as likely to be incarcerated in correctional facilities as white children (Calhoun et al., 1980).

Bertram Brown# describes what happens when minority youth face entry into the judicial or the mental health system. The likelihood is that minority youth will be relegated to rehabilitation, not treatment. Brown felt that this general trend of moving minority youth who exhibited truant or socially unacceptable behavior toward the criminal justice system had frightening overtones. He estimated that almost one third of black youngsters will have had some contact with the criminal justice rather than the mental health system by 1983.

The tendency to refer minorities to the judicial system rather than to waste psychotherapy on minority groups is not just limited to the courts. In education, too, blacks and Hispanics are more likely to be

---

‖ Shipman, VC. *Disadvantaged children and their first school experiences: Demographic indexes of socioeconomic status and maternal behaviors and attitudes.* (Report under Grant No. H-8256). Princeton: Educational Testing Service, June 1972

\# Brown, B. Mental health programs in Black America. Taped for radio "In Black America." Austin, Texas, 1976

referred to counselors or social workers than whites, proportionately more of whom will be referred to a psychologist or a psychiatrist regardless of their parents' financial means (Langer et al., 1974).

EDUCATION

Schools are quintessentially middle class institutions that historically have failed to deal effectively with individuals or groups whose lifestyles or ambitions are not congruent with those of community leaders or with their notions of how society should be structured (Dickerman, 1973). Rather than to focus on whatever personal strengths the poor may possess in their own right (Reissman, 1964), such as their realism, practical innovation, and interpersonal skills, educators almost automatically regard children whose behavior is identified as "different" as "disadvantaged" or "deprived" (Saville-Troike, 1976). Schools with high percentages of poor or culturally different students, as a rule, have mimicked the actions of more prestigious school, heedless of the special needs of their populations (Cardenas & Cardenas, 1973). Instead, the schools have accommodated children who are the most acculturable while stigmatizing the rest (Kelly & Piuk, 1973), thereby contributing to their maladjustment and misbehavior (Saville-Troike, 1976).

Minorities have primarily been subjected to two systems of alternative or special need education. These have been designated as compensatory and special education.

Compensatory education is clearly based on a deficiency model of learning (Baratz & Baratz, 1970), one that strives to compensate for the numerous deprivations of lower class and cultural or linguistic minority students, who are typically stereotyped, not studied. These "special" programs also deviate from the "regular" program only superficially and are thus almost assuredly doomed to fail to show significant effects (Taba & Elkins, 1966), since compensatory educators fail to identify and build upon the repertoires of the students. Instead, they concentrate on imparting information that will make minority pupils appear cognitively more like their economically advantaged Anglo counterparts in the regular school program. Unfortunately, these efforts to compensate for presumed deprivations are often to little avail, since the skills taught are not directly reinforced by the ghetto and barrio environments in which these children live. An implicit conflict between what the children need to learn and what the school then begins to unfold is a familiar plot that leads to psychological violence and sometimes physical retaliation that is played out till the maladjusted minority students drop out, alienated and brutalized, their chances for a fulfilling life dashed, or until the teachers, counselors, and administrators quit the profession in frustration and disgust.

Bilingual Education

Bilingual education can be used to illustrate the compensatory educational viewpoint. Fairly well based pedagogically and linguistically (Troike, 1978) to serve an estimated 3.6 million (Pifer, 1979) to 3.8 million (O'Malley, 1981) limited English proficient (LEP) children, bilingual education programs have grown dramatically in number, but are not ordinarily seen as having any inherent quality or any purpose other than remediation (Gonzales, 1979). For example, LEP children are seldom seen as normal, much less as bright students (Bernal, 1980). Jackson and Cosca (1974) found that teachers interacted less frequently with Mexican American students than they did with Anglo students, and that their lack of positive contact was correlated to a lack of student achievement. Segregation of LEP students has continued to be an issue (Gonzales, 1977).

Bilingual programs have generally been poorly implemented; minimal legal or regulatory requirements are seen as maximal efforts in the schools (Gonzales, 1977), and are not strongly enforced by state departments of education. Many teachers are willing to try bilingual education, but education systems apparently are not, implicitly preferring the more traditional practices that have contributed to the high dropout-pushout rate among language and culturally different children (Cardenas & Cardenas, 1973). The prevailing attitude in the schools seems to be that children should be "exited" from these programs at the earliest possible moment, and exit achievement criteria are most often arbitrarily set (Curtis, Ligon, & Weibly, 1980) to effect a quick transition to an all-English curriculum. These practices have been followed by educators who are apparently oblivious to the advantages of first language instruction, particularly during childhood, and of the importance of first language development to second language acquisition and the normal cognitive and linguistic growth so necessary for ultimate educational success (Cummins, 1981).

Special Education

Special education has also been slow to respond to the needs of nondominant ethnic students. An excessive number of minority students have been assigned to this category of intervention and nonmainstream education (Mercer, 1976; Ortega, 1971). Hispanics and blacks have historically been overrepresented in one category of special education, mental retardation (Marion, 1979). This may be changing, however, as more children (students) referred for special education services are being diagnosed as learning disabled. Hispanics, however, are underrepresented in this category**, a classification that evades the spirit of legal and regulatory proscriptions against capricious placement in MR programs. In Texas, for example, the proportion of Chicano children in special education is approximately equal to the proportion of nonminority students. This general figure, however, masks the fact that Hispanics there are overrepresented in the LD category by over 300 percent and *underrepresented* significantly in all other categories, including physical handicaps.**

It can be disputed that many such placements doubtlessly have been well-intentioned attempts to individualize instruction and bring more resources to bear on culturally or linguistically different children. However, there are negative consequences to the children that result from such misplacement (Chinn, 1979), especially the relative lack of progress in important content areas, such as reading and math, which further retards the children's ability to transition "at grade level" into the regular program, and the possible effects of labeling.

Culturally different children have been steered towards a separate school subsystem, special education, where those with any kind of vague "problem" could be segregated from regular education. This has been especially easy to do where screening is keyed to an individually administered IQ test, performance in which is unusually low even for many intellectually normal black and LEP children. The end result has been increased isolation from their fellow students, and increased dropout rates (Gay & Abrahams, 1973).

Partly because of a lack of trained personnel, professionals whose background has ill-prepared them to deal with culturally and linguistically distinctive children, special education has too often been ineffectual in dealing with minority children in general, and with LEP students in particular (Chinn, 1979).††

** Ortiz, A. Private conversation with Alda Ortiz, Director of the Bilingual Special Education Program, University of Texas, Austin, 10/12/82

†† Morrison, JA. *The relationship between bilingual education and special education.* Unpublished manuscript, Institute for Cultural Pluralism, San Diego State University, Calif., 1981

TESTING

Perhaps the issue that has been the most crucial to the status and opportunities of the culturally different has been the issue of testing. Psychological research, educational placement, job selection or promotion, and clinical diagnosis have all been affected by the charges and countercharges of test bias, court decisions restricting the use of tests, and the resurgence of the old heredity-environment controversy with, again, strong political and economic overtones.

That blacks and certain ethnic minority groups on the average score significantly below whites on IQ tests and most achievement tests has been well documented (Cleary, Humphreys, Kendrick, & Wesman, 1975; Jensen, 1980; Shuey, 1966). The reasons why this phenomenon has occurred are, however, in contention (Bernal, 1975; Sattler, 1982). Some psychologists have argued a strong hereditarian determination of ability, that heredity accounts for approximately 80 percent of the systematic variance in measured intelligence, especially of the general intellectual factor g. Others, as Matarazzo (1972) points out, have reviewed the same data and have reached conclusions that favor a strong environmentalist position. Still others have recognized the heredity-environment interaction but have contented themselves by defending the essential validity of standardized tests, affirming that the deficits in the performance of minority groups are real and that society, not the tests, is to blame (for example, Jacobson, 1977; Wechsler, 1971).

Test bias is not a unitary concept, and much of the literature defending tests is psychometrically sound. Still, the testing establishment has been slow to respond both to research and to the experience of many practitioners, which indicates that for a significant percentage of minority individuals tests simply have not tapped their true achievements or potential.[‡‡] Contrary to assumptions of Jensen (1980) and others (for example, Humphreys, 1969; Cleary et al., 1975), the scores made by minority persons are highly coachable.[§§,‡‡] It is reasonable to assume that minority children's past experience with tests has not been sufficient to teach them how to cope most effectively with these instruments. Standard testing conditions for group or individually administered tests, it should be noted, frequently violate the communication protocols (Gay & Abra-

---

[‡‡] Bernal, EM. Discussion: Intelligence tests on trial. In J. Sattler (Chair), *Intelligence tests on trial: Larry P. and PASE.* Symposium presented at the meeting of the American Psychological Association, Los Angeles, August 1981

[§§] Dyer, PJ. Effects of test conditions on Negro-White differences in test scores. Doctoral dissertation, Columbia University, 1970

hams, 1973) to which some ethnic minority students are accustomed (role-related, interactive expectations between an authority figure and children; interpretations of the verbal, tonal gestural, and postural concomitants of oral communication generally and questioning in particular). When minority children are taught to overcome these barriers to understanding and are motivated to "play the game" of testing with the same rules that middle class whites use, their scores usually increase, sometimes dramatically.[††] The validity of scores obtained under coaching conditions has not been investigated in terms of practical criteria, but at least the presumed stability of minority children's test scores can be called into question, as well as the continued use of responses that seem to be differentially effective for whites and at least some minority groups. Gay and Abrahams (1973), approaching the testing situation from a linguistic point of view, point out that the direct querying of children by adults "tends to be associated, by black children, with prospective threat in some accusation of wrongdoing" (p. 335), and that black children's style of learning by observing others, as well as their accustomed ways of soliciting and giving information, are not accommodated by standard, formal testing, where true interactions are usually precluded.

For many minority persons, of course, testing has served as a gate-keeping function used by whites to deny them access to higher education or advancement in employment. Establishing so-called cutoff scores may be justified economically or on the basis of efficiency, but many decision-makers have not tempered their use of tests with more personalized judgments about individuals' qualifications, especially when cutoffs have been established arbitrarily for the presumed prestige value attached to high marks (Astin, Astin, Green, Kent, McNamera, & Williams, 1982). Tests used for selection rarely have high correlations with criterion measures, but may be useful in selection in practical situations (Wesman, 1953). It is important to be aware of demonstrated ability and to not be blindly insistent on objective test scores alone, particularly in the case of those minority persons whose background makes them different from the groups used to develop and standardize the instruments (Bernal, 1977; Oakland & Matuszek, 1977).

Testing has also been used to control educational placements of minority persons in the public schools. For example, when traditional, test-based criteria for gifted programs are strictly set, few minority individuals are accepted (Bernal, 1980). Similarly, the general overrepresentation of minority students in special education, particularly in the more nebulous learning disabled categories, and in "special" or remedial programs has been justified in no small part by their low scores.[††] Disadvantage in a testing situation occurs when persons are asked to perform in a manner inconsistent with their backgrounds and protocol expectations; differences in experience can thus be converted to deficits (Cole & Bruner, 1971) in scores.

Because of this, many practitioners in the schools as well as in clinical settings have adopted "corrective" measures in applying tests, but unfortunately with mixed results. Constrained often by regulations that mandate formal assessment with officially adopted tests prior to placement, and knowing experientially how poorly many of these instruments predict the full course of intervention for individuals with certain cultural or demographic characteristics, some diagnosticians have devised certain practices and techniques for obtaining ostensibly more accurate or useful data.

The first such practice consisted of adding points to obtain scores of language minority students. This procedure is, of course, basically a way of making low test scores more palpable, since it does nothing to increase a test's validity. Sometimes the number of points to be added is subjectively determined; in other instances the number is based on the obtained average difference between Anglo and minority scores, a very questionable practice indeed, especially when applied to individuals. The method is wrong but it indicates that educators working with minority children often find that many of them are more capable than the normative tests scores indicate.

Instead of adding points, tests should be scored in a standard manner to obtain a measure of a person's immediate condition or estimate of short-term potential in a traditional, white-oriented educational or clinical setting. The professional, however, must keep in mind that assessment is a more inclusive concept than test scoring and reporting. He/she is thus approved to engage in some alternative assessment activities that may add information about or insight into the student's or client's functional status, potential, and specific needs.

A second and related practice involves renorming, i.e., the computation of ethnic norms, often locally. Renorming accomplishes what adding points does, but the numbers are determined empirically. The only real advantage of renorming is that it provides good descriptive statistics for a particular ethnic population, particularly a better distribution of scores. But renorming appears to the psychometrically unsophisticated to do more, to somehow make the test better. It does not.

This procedure is perhaps best exemplified by Mercer's (1976) System of Multicultural Pluralistic Assessment (SOMPA), which includes an empirically determined procedure for correcting obtained Wechsler IQ scores according to certain child characteristics of a demographic nature to yield Estimated Learning Potential scores (Mercer, 1979). This procedure has been criticized (see Sattler, 1982, for a summary of critical comments) for having geographically restricted norms and lacking demonstrated validity in practical assessment settings. Other parts of the SOMPA instrument, however, introduce additional data and perspectives for the professional's consideration, such as a measure of the child's adaptive behavior and health history.

A third and related practice is the routine use of out-of-level testing with minority children. The argument goes among some diagnosticians and evaluators that since minority children modally score so low on standardized achievement tests, some technique is necessary to generate more variance at the lower end of the scale to enhance precision and more nearly normalize the distributions. Out-of-level testing does this, but makes interpretation difficult even with the application of expanded standard scores, which extend across several age-grade groups and corresponding levels of tests. Such testing, in our opinion, is rarely used to enhance individual diagnosis. Instead, these data are summarized, and the resultant reports often becloud the problems, however lamely, with passing references to the normative standard or the introduction of grade equivalent explanations. In the hands of many practitioners, out-of-level testing becomes a statistical legerdemain for adding points.

A decision to test a child out-of-level may be good if it is based on the individual case and the results are used diagnostically. Out-of-level testing is justified basically only when accurate assessment is not possible on-level, as in the cases of the extremely gifted and the very low ability or low achieving student. For students at the lower end of the spectrum, however, the professional must first determine whether the impediments to on-level testing might be easily removed. Many students, for instance, lack test-taking skills, do not fully understand the test directions, are not basically proficient in the language of the test, do not respond to tests because they feel a lack of rapport with the examiner (Bernal, 1975; Bernal & Tucker, 1981), or find the materials uninteresting, too passive, or too artificial to sustain the motivation necessary to complete them as directed (Laosa, 1973). These impediments will not necessarily be eliminated by using a simpler form of the test in question, but are amenable to instruction, appropriate rapport, or the use of alternative instruments.

Out-of-level tests should be scored in detail, looking at clusters of items that tap some of the skills or dimensions of interest, for the explicit purpose of determining what the person knows or can do. The scores, if they are derived, are of lesser importance, and should guide our individual programming for the child. Out-of-level testing, then, finds its greatest justification as a diagnostic technique.

Another practice is the administration of selected subscales of larger diagnostic and intelligence tests to minority students. If this practice were based on empirical findings of greater reliability or validity for certain subtests, there would be little reason to object; however, this practice usually rests on the belief that minority students generally, and LEP students especially, score higher (i.e., look better) on some subscales than on others. Performance subscales, for example, are often preferred over verbal scales (Kirkpatrick, Ewen, Barrett, & Katzell, 1968), in spite of the fact that basing general interpretations on performance tests has usually yielded disappointing results, both for the Anglo population (Nunnally, 1959) and for different cultural groups as well (Anastasi, 1976). As a rule, the decision to administer only certain subtests to linguistically different students should be based on empirical studies that incorporate linguistic and demographic variables in their designs, as well as relevant diagnostic or outcome criteria.

Test translation without methodical tryout and subsequent modification and validation has also become a popular practice, whether commissioned by a testing company or done ad hoc by a practitioner, when testing LEP students. Sometimes only the directions are translated, but often the entire test is recast into another language, usually Spanish. We have witnessed individually administered tests presented in both languages, a procedure that involves the repetition of each item and that produces unsystematic practice effect on scores, depending on a child's bilingual skills and the order of presentation.

Some testing companies' brochures illustrate English and translated versions of a test in a way that suggests that they are parallel forms, when in fact no verification or equating procedure has been attempted, not even back translation, a technique that has proven so useful in equating the meanings of statements in cross-cultural research (Manaster & Havighurst, 1972). Some translated, multiple choice paper-and-pencil tests are so parallel that even the position of the correct answer is unchanged, a measurement travesty when one considers that both versions are sometimes administered to the same students in quick succession, again producing an untoward practice effect. Furthermore, some translated tests have no norms for the non-English language version; test users are left to assume that the English norms are directly applicable.

The psychometric and practical problems with test translation are many. Obviously some types of tests, such as simple psychomotor or discrimination tasks or straightforward computation problems, can usually be presented in another language with little adaptation, particularly so when no reading is required of the examinee. Even here, however, cultural content should be checked and test directions back translated, whenever appropriate, and submitted to a trial phase. Vocabulary tests or problem-solving tasks involving cultural content or internal verbal mediation cannot be simply translated without risking the alteration of item characteristics or the factor structure of the tests. In other words, translation usually changes the difficulty range of an item (e.g., if *spangle* is translated to *lentejuela,* the item changes in difficulty for Hispanic students). Translation may also change the options a student may otherwise have in answering an item (e.g., *stamp* may be a verb or a noun in English, but *timbre, estampilla,* or *sellar* in Spanish limit the usage of the word). Test scores, such as those derived from the WISC-R, which have criteria for discontinuation of a subtest (such as after five consecutive misses), could be seriously affected if the rank order of item difficulty is significantly altered by translation. Finally, a test that measures one factor for Anglos (e.g., practical intelligence: "What should you do if you cut your finger?") might be measuring another factor for Hispanics (e.g., degree of acculturation to Anglo values and practices), especially if scoring criteria have a limited range of acceptable responses.

Most often, translated tests use a relatively formal standard dialect to produce expeditiously a test that will appeal to as wide a group of potential customers as possible. The result, tragically, is that some language minority students who speak a dialect of the language and who have not had sufficient bilingual education, score low on tests in both languages. In still other cases (fortunately few), all language minority children entering school for the first time are tested exclusively in the non-English language, thereby penalizing those who are most proficient in English, a special case of test misuse that once again places certain minority students in a disadvantage situation.

In recent years some diagnosticians have adopted the practice advocated by Bernal and Tucker (1981) of administering both English and native language oral proficiency tests to LEP children suspected of having any of several language-related handicaps, to serve as cross checks to a tentative evaluation. Low scores in English combined with normal to high scores in the native language would be interpreted as a lack of English proficiency that could interfere with English-tested performance, but the child would likely be language normal, at least insofar as speech is concerned. Children scoring low on both languages might be regarded as having a language problem if the tester is satisfied that the child did not receive a low score due to her/his having mixed English and native language words and phrases in responding to the questions. Extant, commercially available tests of oral language proficiency penalize responses that are not given exclusively in one language or the other (Bernal, 1977), and thus underestimate the communicative competence and language level of those children whose native "language" is acquired normally but in environments where code switching is the rule. Language proficiency tests, properly administered by persons who can speak, read, and write the child's native language, and interpreted by an informed psychologist, can serve to confirm or contraindicate certain exceptionalities in the language domain.

Cummins (1981) suggests that the continuous assessment of bilingual students' progress in the development of native language skills is important, particularly if one wants to predict their success in an all-English educational environment. Native language achievement is an indicator of students' general academic potential in English as well. His recent theoretical work distinguishes between easy, context-embedded oral language skills and context-reduced language proficiency, the metalinguistic skill that provides the kinds of learning advantages that some bilinguals seem to enjoy, and that predicts success in the second language (L2) environment. Children who are forced to acquire L2 before developing their ability to think in L1 may not develop metalinguistic skills in either language, and thus suffer educationally as they get older and the cognitive requirements of the curriculum place greater emphasis on abstract thought.

Out-of-level testing has already been discussed as one alternative way of assessing certain minority students, provided that an intelligent decision is reached in each individual case and the results are to be used diagnostically. This practice is related to the notions of testing-of-limits and test-teach-retest, clinical procedures for estimating a person's status and ability to learn (Guerin & Maier, 1983).

In testing-of-limits the examiner wants to gain as much information as possible about the examinee's test performance, and should ideally be used only after it has been administered in a standard fashion (Sattler, 1982). Procedures that violate standard administration may then be used freely, such as providing additional cues, extending time limits, repeating the items, or rewording or translating them. The examiner may even ask the examinee how he/she solved a problem, if this is not evident. The conditions that lead to improved test performance should, of course, be noted in detail, since these may provide clues for both diagnosis and intervention. Taylor (1961) presents excellent examples of testing-of-limits for clinical use.

One of the inherent limitations of testing-of-limits is that the "coaching" involved may invalidate a standard readministration of the same test at a later time (Sattler, 1982). If a parallel form of the test is available, of course, it may be used without this risk. Similarly, at a later time the child may be tested with a more advanced or on-level form of an achievement test series.

Test-teach-retest may use both formal test items or less formal measures, such as those devised by teachers or found in student workbooks. How long does it take a student to learn or master the next sequential skill above his/her current level of attainment? What explanatory techniques and instructional materials seem to work best (by process of elimination)? Is the learning retained? Can it be transferred to other problems?

These procedures are in the repertoire of expert diagnosticians, but they require the sensitive application of clinical skills and judgments. These can be effected only if the professional is acquainted with the range of behavior of minority clients, in exactly the same way as he/she must know the dominant culture when dealing with Anglos.

It is our experience that many diagnosticians are reluctant to take this risk, feeling a lack of confidence in dealing with minority individuals on a subjective basis and retreating, instead, into rigid procedural rationalizations. What is required is an intensive inservice program and a willingness to learn from minority clients. Opportunities to hear alternative explanations from minority professionals, clients' relatives, etc., are of paramount importance to the conscientious diagnostician, and for this reason multidisciplinary team evaluations are very much in order, as is the notion of participatory decision-making for minority persons, especially the parents of minor children (Pfeiffer, 1980). Documented clinical observations and the patterns they form constitute the foundation of professional intuition, which for the protection of the client should always be open to challenge. Similarly, placement and intervention decisions should be reviewed in the light of clinical experience and later assessments. There is no need to fear the clinical judgment with non-dominant ethnic clients. Indeed, given the limitations of assessment instruments with many minority persons, such insights may be of great service.

To supplement standardized test scores and complement clinical judgments, adaptive behavior scales have been used, again with mixed results. Adaptive behavior is usually expressed as social, economic, behavioral, and affective competencies that are tied to stages in life or level of maturation. Items may usually be completed by professionals, persons familiar with the client, or by interviewing the client directly, depending on the test itself (see Chapter 6).

Sattler's (1982) compendium, the upcoming *Ninth Mental Measurements Yearbook*, and other test reference works indicate that none of these instruments is without shortcomings, especially for minority children. One known source of difficulty is the accuracy of observations. It is our belief that another source of difficulty lies in the fact that few individuals are actually in a position to observe all of the behaviors, which can be rated on the more comprehensive instruments, though they may not acknowledge this when marking their estimates.

Then, too, some minority informants may require help to understand the item, and explanations may require rewording, translation, or both, all of which may affect an item's equivalence and reliability. It is our experience that in obtaining data on children the use of adult family members exclusively as raters is not always the best practice; adolescent siblings and individuals who care for these children during the day should also be sought out, since they often observe facets of behavior that are virtually unknown to some parents. Still another problem lies with the inclusion of items that are culture or class-specific manifestations of a trait, items that may actually discriminate against lower socioeconomic status and ethnic minority clients (Cole & Bruner, 1971). Here again the professional may have to use his/her intuition in identifying these questions and in interpreting their intended meaning in terms of the client's cultural background. Notions of "independence," "initiative," and personal "use of money," for example, have more culture-specific referents than whether or not a child can drink from a cup unassisted or climb stairs without help.

Various kinds of developmental scales have also been used to assess minority students, including tests for infants based on Piagetian stages of cognitive growth. Piagetian measures would appear to have the advantage of being able to be translated without significant modification (Bernal, 1977). Parts of other developmental tests require only normal reactions (such as head turning in response to a sound) from the examinee.

The application to minority ethnic/racial persons of tests developed for use primarily with whites calls into question the test's appropriateness (Bernal, 1977). Some of these tests may even alienate the client from the intervention, since by focusing on certain arbitrarily "right" answers or looking for culturally specific behaviors they seem to imply that the client's lifestyle is wrong (Alley & Foster, 1978). The prudent practitioner, then, cannot rely on these tests to make his/her work with minority persons routine. Assessment requires the application of all of the professional's testing skills and behavioral insights.

COUNSELING CULTURALLY DIFFERENT FAMILIES AND CHILDREN

> . . . The 'melting pot' illusion is fading and people can take pride in the fact that we are a culturally pluralistic society. Cornbread, tortillas, and bagels are finally holding their own against Wonder Bread, however enriched. The recognition of diversity can lead to respect for the unique qualities as well as the unique problems of each group. (Korchin, 1980, p. 262).

Within the melting pot concept, the terms "culturally deprived," "socially and economically disadvantage," "underprivileged," and "disadvantaged" have frequently been used to describe minority families and children. These descriptions served to suggest that minority parents and children were different and not governed by the Anglo's warm human emotions or worthy motivations (Sager, Brayboy, & Waxenberg, 1972). Cultural pluralism, on the other hand, stresses the worth of cultural diversity but resists any alignment of such differences along an inferior-superior axis or any attempt to ascribe diversity to unchangeable determinants (Korchin, 1980), such as genetic heritage. From such a point of view has emerged a realistic approach to working with families of culturally different children. This can be done since the application of cross-cultural intervention therapy has been found to be as effective with minority patients as with Anglo clients (Griffith & Jones, 1979; Jones, 1974, 1978; Lorion, 1978). However, practitioners should always be sensitive to ethnic minority issues that tend to influence the initiation, the continuance, and the completion of therapeutic intervention with their clients (Sue, 1983).

Assumptions Concerning Mental Health Needs of Culturally Different Populations

Two popular assumptions have tended to be advanced as explanations of why culturally different populations have more need for and have not benefited from mental health services. Both underlie the counseling challenges that face therapists who work with minority families and children.

The first assumption holds that problems of the culturally different can be traced to the heavy social stresses imposed upon them by a racist society (Banks, 1972). It is argued that these stresses can only be ameliorated through actions geared toward social change. Moreover, from this point of view, society and not the client can be construed as sick. Therefore, the victim cannot be held responsible for troubles caused by a social order that controls and distorts his/her life. Furthermore, it is conceded that current mental health treatment procedures in effect have been developed by white, middle class professionals and that these practices have distracted our efforts from dealing with the true problem, the discriminatory practices of the dominant society (Banks, 1972).

The second assumption is predicated upon the premise that the institutions, principles, and practices of the majority mental health system are ill-equipped to deal with the problems and needs of culturally different populations. Minority persons are deemed to be misunderstood, their behaviors have been misinterpreted as pathological, and clinical procedures have tended to minimize their strengths and to maximize their weaknesses. Moreover, mental health services have been located so as to be remote and inaccessible to the minority community. Finally, the lack of therapists trained in cultural differences has been a hinderance to the therapeutic relationship because of differing expectations of professional and client. The end result has been a lack of follow-through by the client. Culturally different clients want and need more direct intervention than is afforded them in the traditional forms of psychotherapy (Korchin, 1980).

These beliefs have not helped those clinicians working with culturally different populations to find a common ground that will bridge the gap between racial realities and intrapsychic issues. To do this, mental health professionals need to see the behaviors and customs of diverse cultural groups in relation to how they affect the psychological health of individual group members. In so doing, not only would the professional therapist be sensitive to the crucial issue of understanding the functioning of particular behaviors as they relate to a different culture, but the therapist also would be prepared to evaluate and to propose change within the framework of universal standards (Korchin, 1980).

Mental Health and Intrapersonal Viewpoints

The three major theoretical viewpoints that have permeated mental health practice, namely psychoanalytic, behavioral, and humanistic, have tended to regard mental health as a largely individual problem. The state of mental health has been objectified as the result of deficient genes, inadequate parenting, or the inability to manipulate a person's environment (Smith, Burlew, Mosely, & Whitney, 1978). However, the mental health problems of minority persons cannot be completely explained from these viewpoints alone. For example, Rabkin (1979) found what at first might seem to be an unusual relationship between ethnic density in urban neighborhoods and psychiatric hospitalization. Studying New York City's 338 health areas, their data indicate that for blacks, whites, and Puerto Ricans, the lower the ethnic density the higher the hospitalization rate, in comparison to other groups in the same area and to the same group in areas where it would constitute a numerical majority. Simultaneous analyses of sociodemographic data showed that this effect cannot be accounted for by differences in poverty, family cohesiveness, or population mobility.

An awareness that the issues of race and ethnicity have permeated into the psycho-sexual, self-esteem, psychodynamic, and behavioral development processes of minority children should be incorporated into the exploration of the mental health status of culturally different persons in the United States. For these persons, mental health is in no small measure a function of the societal conditions they encounter, conditions over which they have little control, cannot choose to avoid, and to which they cannot adjust without compromising their own integrity. It has led to a questioning of the traditionally held belief that minority mental health problems are primarily intrapersonal. Moreover, the intrapersonal view has been an incomplete explanation when investigating the developmental process of the minority child since its state of mental health is unavoidably influenced by the issue of race (Smith et al., 1978). Only within this context can the personality development and behavior of the culturally different child be examined.

Minority Mental Health Providers

One significant factor affecting the mental health of minority children has been the lack of culturally and linguistically competent professionals and staff to meet their needs. For example in 1974, El-Khawas and Kinger indicated that blacks represented 4.2 percent and Spanish-surnamed students constituted 1.2 percent of the graduate students in psychology training programs in the United States. In other words, the two largest minority groups are contributing only a minute percentage of students preparing to work in the mental health field. This can be further illustrated by the fact that there are approximately 37,900 practicing psychologists in the U.S. Only 500 of these professionals can be counted as blacks (Smith et al., 1978). Corresponding figures could notably be attributed to practicing Hispanic psychologists.

The greatest concentration of minorities in mental health fields is in the area of social work. Even here the representation of black and Hispanics cannot be found to be proportional to their respective populations. The records of the Council of Social Work Education indicated that the percentage of full-time Hispanic students at the master's level ranged from 2.7 percent to 4.6 percent during the period 1969 to 1975 with a peak in 1972. In Ph.D. or D.S.W. programs Hispanic enrollment comprised 5.5 percent of the total in 1974 and 4.5 percent in 1975. These statistics can be offered as proof that the minority mental health worker is a scarce commodity.

Factors that Affect the Cross-Cultural Approach

Stereotyping

Adoption of a cross-cultural approach is tied to several factors. First, faulty, stereotyped thinking is rejected. For example, some mental health practitioners use their knowledge of different culture groups not as a basis for gauging an individual's condition but for trying to fit the person into a predetermined category. They might have established a mind-set to support the supposition that Hispanics are nonmaterialistic, noncompetitive, superstitious, passive, and dependent (Boulette, 1977). Similarly, the professional who sees blacks as nonverbal, concrete, and ill suited for therapy (Jones & Seagull, 1977) may have the preconceived notion that they are untrusting and have character disorders that are unchangeable (Pinderhughes, 1973). This stereotypic thinking on the part of therapists does not recognize the heterogeneity that exists within cultures and rather assumes that "they" fit into homogeneous molds (Banks, 1975), and thus therapists treat "them" as interchangeable units (Bernal, 1969). The enlightened therapist will have an awareness of the differences among members of culturally different populations as well as among members of the same minority group.

Therapist-Client Similarity

The adoption of the nonstereotypical attitude by the clinician is closely tied to the second factor that is important within the cross-cultural approach. The attitudinal outlook that promotes stereotypic thinking is often wedded to the issue of therapist-client similarity (i.e., You've never been black/Hispanic so how do you know how black/Hispanics feel? or only blacks/Hispanics can treat blacks/Hispanics!) Moreover, it is not just defined within the boundaries of minority client-minority therapist relationships, but has ramifications for the minority patient-majority therapist therapeutic setting.

In any therapeutic relationship, the essence of the treatment is directly linked to the interactions between client and clinician (Rogers, 1962). Therefore, therapists, majority or minority, should have an understanding of the American social system and the ways in which minorities have been the objects of discrimination, have been oppressed, and have not had access to equal opportunities. Such an understanding can be viewed as critical, since white therapists far outnumber minority clients (Jones & Seagull, 1977).

Accepting this as a given, the white psychologist working with minority clients should be willing to examine his/her feelings toward the culturally different individual. Obviously, the white therapist who has exhibited blatantly racist attitudes toward minorities should not counsel them (Jones & Seagull, 1977). However, for the clinician not in this category, self-knowledge should be given high priority in the skill-acquisition process. By talking to other professionals, organizing discussion groups, and listening to specialized experts on the topic, open-minded therapists should be effecting ways to make themselves more useful when working with culturally different clients.

In addition, the psychologist's willingness to accept change can be viewed as a positive attribute. The therapist who has been trained in a one dimensional model wherein cultural differences were lightly treated or ignored might be forced to reexamine his/her values when working with culturally different families and children. For example, the practitioner who is guided by the values of self-actualization and self-determination would need to experience a reworking of these values when confronted by a client who believes that his or her life is God-determined (Mendes, 1982). The therapist's failure to adjust, or adherence to faulty conceptualizations (Myers, 1982) would likely result in serious implications for the therapeutic process. The ability of the therapist to be open to racial and cultural differences has been shown to positively affect the ability of majority therapists to work with minority patients (Korchin, 1980).

The clinician's knowledge base can be expanded through inservice training, workshops, and reading. Books and other informative materials can be found that will give the majority therapist an informed view of the culture, aspirations, and customs shared by the culturally different clients that he/she will be working with.

Finally, the clinician's willingness to accept differences can be demonstrated early in the working relationship. Therapists should be willing to raise the issue of majority therapist-minority client relationship and the feelings and issues that accompany the fact that one is white and the other is not. Although the white therapist will not have changed racial identity, he/she will have demonstrated a familiarity and sensitivity toward culturally different peoples and their culture. This appreciation has often served to decrease the interpersonal differences between minority patient and psychologist (Jones & Seagull, 1977; Korchin, 1980).

Any discussion of client similarity would be considered incomplete without an examination of minority therapist-minority client relationships. In this case, the minority psychologist's familiarity with the patient's cultural background and verbal expressions may have the desirable effect of increasing the level of understanding between the two principal participants. On the other hand, the professionally trained minority therapist might have succumbed to the dominant middle class value system (Brown, 1981) and might be rendered immobile in the encounter.

In the case of the former, these therapists have usually maintained positive self-perceptions and have cultivated identity building experiences with a wide spectrum of minority peoples. They have "got themselves together" and have no problem knowing who they are. As a result of these actions, these therapist have the ability to serve as effective role models and clinicians in their work with culturally different clients (Banks, 1975).

Minority psychologists who have compromised their ties to culturally different populations might have to resort to a different kind of retooling process than their white counterparts. In this instance, they will have to become actively involved in the educational, political, and cultural aspects of minority life, particularly if they intend to work with people whose cultural or racial roots are similar to those of the therapist. They will have to gauge the pulse of the community by regular visitations to favorite meeting places of the several subcultures, i.e., colleges, beauty parlors/barbershops, restaurants, and churches. In many cases this may be difficult, especially for those who have deliberately or even unconsciously rejected their heritage. It should not be presumed that all minority therapists want to work with minority clients since both may suffer in the process. Psychologists should have a familiarity with the language patterns, dress and hair styles, and slang expressions. Moreover, these differences should be attended to at various class levels and in different geographical and cultural levels. By showing an understanding of these differences in counseling sessions, the minority therapist will have facilitated the process of client-therapist interaction (Banks, 1975; Jones & Seagull, 1977).

Recognition of the Importance of Religion

In addition to stereotype rejection and therapist-client similarities, a third factor that impacts the cross-cultural approach should be noted. The clinician must have an appreciation of the place of religion in the background of the black or Hispanic client. Children especially are affected by this moral force through the lives of minority parents. Dilemmas and scars left by the issue of race have weighed heavily on the black and Hispanic psyche, and relief from these traumas has often been sought in religion. Religion has been an important vehicle in relieving the frustration, anger, and helplessness that many minorities have felt in their existence in the dominant society (Cole, 1972). Thus, for blacks "to steal away to Jesus" may have a therapeutic value and should be dealt with in a constructive fashion by the attending therapist. Similarly, Hispanics, many of whom are of the Roman Catholic faith, have relied upon their religious heritage. Over 80 percent of Mexican Americans are designated as Catholic and the Church is held in high regard by most grass-roots Mexican Americans (Acuna, 1967). It should not be surprising to the therapist that many Mexican Americans, even those who are not consistent churchgoers, abide by the dictates of the church as its precepts relate to their daily lives.

Religion may influence the relationship between therapist and client. For instance, black patients have assumed that the psychologist shares the same range of experiences and values that they have concerning religion. In this case the clients are imbued with the feeling that the therapist will quickly provide magical and perhaps painless solutions to their problems (Banks, 1975). Similarly, Hispanic patients may be seeking a like remedy in their sessions with the clinician. These clients then have placed the "Doctor" in an omnipotent role and expect that the psychologist will immediately recognize and cure the affliction (Montijo, 1975).

This transference of faith to the therapist is in keeping with the importance that many minority groups attach to religious healing. The clinician who is attuned to this phenomena will not be rebuffed by the patient's adherence to religious feelings, but rather will use this dogmatic belief to further the development of a positive state of mental health within the minority client.

Clinician Variables in Therapist-Client Interactions

The essence of the therapeutic relationship is the interaction between the therapist and the patient. The success of this endeavor rests mainly on the competence of the therapist; his/her perceptual sensitivities, degree of personal awareness, analytic know-how, skillful use of technique, and clear communication and understanding of the client (Banks, 1975).

Since the success of the therapeutic relationship rests so heavily upon the sensitivites and skill of the clinician, he/she should be aware that certain fundamental concepts will influence the therapeutic process regardless of race or culture (McGuigan, 1981). Some of these principles are universal or culture related, but both sets of concepts become significant when the therapist interacts with culturally different parents and children.

Universal Principles

Sensitive clinicians have already embraced many of the universal concepts as a matter of commitment to the profession. Effective psychologists are accepting of, respectful toward, and genuinely concerned about their clients. They have the ability to listen, convey an attitude of caring, build confidence, and teach clients to take responsibility for their actions. These therapeutic qualities reflect Carl Rogers' (1962) principles of a helping relationship: a relationship characterized by sensitive and accurate empathy on the part of the clinician; by a high degree of congruence or genuineness and of respect, regard, and appreciation of the client; and by an absence of conditionality in his/her interaction with the patient.

Empathy

Empathy can be defined as the process whereby one experiences someone else's feelings as his/her own; the facility to stand in the shoes of another individual. Empathy is more fully understood as the process of identifying and incorporating one's self with another individual. Although easily said, this has not proven to be a simple task for certain psychologists who have attempted to work with culturally different clients. Their attempts to be empathetic with those unlike themselves have been made difficult because often therapists' own personal biases have prevented them from utilizing their personal skills when seeking to help their clients. Many times the difficulty has been intensified when the therapist has failed to identify with the realities of the minority client's experiences.

These differences have been further accentuated by race. The therapist must have the affinity to relate to the scars that minority persons bear because of this issue. These racial conflicts have tended to consume an extraordinary amount of the psychic energy of culturally different parents. Enterprising clinicians must have the empathetic ability to distinguish minority persons as individuals and not to view all culturally different clients as disadvantaged, underprivileged, or deprived. Therapists will have to be more inclined to separate and to understand the various modalities of behavior manifested by the various classes of minority patients.

Genuineness

Rogers (1962) has stated that personal growth is facilitated when the therapist is genuine in a relationship with the client and has not put on a front or facade. In working with culturally different individuals, this professional attribute has to be fully exploited. The therapist must have an understanding of her/his own cultural conditioning and psychodynamics. The culturally different patient probably has his detection system working and any attempts by the therapist to resort to a false front are likely to cause the professional to be branded as a phony (Banks, 1975).

Both minority and majority clinicians have been affected in their attempts to become a part of the total counseling situation (Vontress, 1970). Minority therapists who have failed to accept their racial identity have found themselves "doomed to wear a mask," especially in the presence of whites (Hare, 1965). A common phenomenon thus seen along minority clinicians has been the more punitive behavior shown by culturally different therapists toward clients of their own race than toward white patients (Brown, 1950). Therefore, many minority psychologists have been hard pressed to authenticate themselves (Broyard, 1950).

At times majority therapists have had equal difficulty allowing their genuine concern to surface. Clients' overuse of slang and unfamiliar esoteric expressions has often plagued the white therapist (Banks, 1975). On the other hand, minority clients do not appreciate majority therapists who use slang or resort to the language of the street to prove that they understand their client. Culturally different clients above all are seeking to find skilled therapists who are committed to helping them. It is reasonable to expect that this commitment will be questioned by many of the therapist's minority clients, especially during the initial encounter. The sensitive antennae of the culturally different patient have the capability to pick up all signals that disclose the white person's genuineness concerning the patient's quest for acceptance and equality (Russell, 1970).

Acceptance

Rogers (1962) has said that the client's change and growth are enhanced more when the therapist exhibits a warm, positive, accepting attitude toward the present state of the client, not as he/she could or will be. Belief in this concept has important ramifications for the therapist who would work with culturally different persons. Therapists will have surrendered the luxury of choosing those patients whom they would wish to accept completely. Under the full acceptance principle they would be beholden to accept the ugly, foul-talking minority patients as well as the angry, embittered one (Vontress, 1970).

Nowhere is this principle of total acceptance tested more than when working with culturally different patients. Social and economic conditions in the United States have caused minorities to adjust their values and attitudes toward themselves, toward others, and toward society. The tensions caused by these adjustments have made it difficult for many therapists to accept culturally different patients. For instance, the continued press by minorities for equal opportunity might be disturbing to certain middle-class individuals who feel that minorities may now be getting more than their fair share. White friends no longer feel obliged to join civil rights organizations, and their participation in such groups is declining. Moreover, the emphasis on race relations has lost its importance to many majority persons.

On the other hand, minorities confined to the ghetto are perceiving their lives as hopeless and empty; for many of them, trying to make a living is an exercise in futility. They are forced to make it the best way they can. Many other minorities living at a higher economic level have found themselves lumped together as a race, and not regarded as individuals. In the midst of all these uncertainties, therapists often find themselves hard pressed to accept all individuals (Vontress, 1970).

In spite of these life-upsetting upheavals in the lives of minority clients, clinicians can continue to maximize their use of the universal principles of empathy, genuineness, and acceptance in the therapeutic process. Research has shown that the therapist's confidence in the concepts is justified and that these clinical attributes have been found to be successful in assisting culturally different clients to restructure their lives (Banks, 1975; Korchin, 1980).

Sociocultural Factors

Family Structure

A much studied but often misunderstood factor in the assessment of the mental health of culturally different populations has been the family. Some race relations investigators have tended to characterize minority families as pathological, deficient, or deprived (Moynihan, 1965; Rainwater, 1970). Moynihan (1965) particularly saw the deterioration of the black family as the key to the disorganization and instability of the black community. He attributed much of the black family disunity to a one-parent female family head who leads the family through a deficient lifestyle (Myers, 1982). Therefore Moynihan (1965) theorized that such a radical departure from the majority culture was deviant and pathological. He saw divorce rates, illegitimacy rates, percentage of children on Aid to Families with Dependent Children (AFDC), and juvenile crime and delinquency rates as powerful determinants of a dysfunctional social institution.

Later during the 1970s proponents of the cultural diversity philosophy reexamined the variety of families found in black populations and assessed their structures in terms of those positive traits attributed to the various family configurations. Hill (1972) and Billingsley (1968) wrote about the diversity found in black families. The former was one of the first to recognize that black families were no longer to be viewed as homogeneous non-white entities but should be seen as complex multi-structured phenomena (Myers, 1982). Likewise, Ladner (1971) and Nobles (1978) argue that the familial structure of black families provides stability rather than instability and disorganizatiron. However, in spite of these advances in factual information, myths about black families that had been translated into scientific fact still continued to be perpetuated (Myers, 1982).

Hispanic families too have often suffered from comparisons to the majority nuclear family. Sometimes family size (average Hispanic family is larger than U.S. family) or machismo household head (seen in a narrow sense) has hindered the acceptance of the Hispanic family (Becerra, Karno, & Escobar, 1982). Other writers have mistakenly stereotyped Hispanic families as sloppy and dirty, lazy and avoidant of work, and stupid (Bettelheim & Janowitz, 1950; Wyatt, Powell, & Bass, 1982). In other instances, Hispanic families were plagued with the similar problem that afflicted black families. There was a point of view that promoted the belief that all Hispanic families were homogeneous within Spanish speaking groups and were similar within the different socioeconomic levels in the same racial-cultural classification.

An understanding of these views regarding black and Hispanic families is necessary for the therapist who works with culturally different families and children. For example, the clinician should have knowledge of Hill's (1972) study that stressed the strengths of black families as opposed to Moynihan's (1965) pathological model. Psychologists would recognize these traits as a strong religious orientation, strong work orientation, strong kinship bonds, adaptability of family roles, and high achievement orientation.

Clinicians also must be inclined to expect differences in Hispanic families. Therapists should consider family solidarity (Castaneda, James, & Robbins, 1974; Flores, 1972) as one strength. Another would be religious orientation cited by Bach-y-Rita (1982), Fitzpatrick and Travieso (1980), and Madsen (1964). Other positive familial factors would be high achievement (Evans & Anderson, 1973), and cooperation (Ramirez, Herold, & Castenada, 1974; Ruiz, 1982).

Psychologists would be well advised to incorporate these perceptions of the strengths of black and Hispanic families into their conceptual framework for therapeutic interaction. In this manner they will avoid letting biased ideological perspectives and faulty conceptualizations concerning the stability and function of the culturally different family negatively affect their treatment with minority clients.

Communication Differences

When addressing the needs of culturally different patients, psychologists must give consideration to the language differences that could directly or indirectly affect the diagnosis and treatment of the clients (Ruiz, 1982). There are several barriers or differences that should command the attention of therapists when treating linguistically different minority patients.

First, clinicians should be aware that blacks, Hispanics, and other culturally diverse clients have different modes of communication. Blacks have a history of oral communication that crosses all socioeconomic strata. Even the most educated black American is able, to some extent, to converse with his/her less fortunate brother or sister. This oral tradition originated in the slave spirituals where its usage was designed to express and to conceal messages for slave use only. This verbal history has been continued in the raps, blues, folk tales, and fire and brimstone sermons of every succeeding generation. These oral traditions have constituted and perpetuated the black experience (Bass, 1982).

Another aspect of the rich language heritage of black families has been the use of black dialect. Referred to as Black English (Mitchell-Kernan, 1982), it is a language that features some unique characteristics that differentiate this form of speech from all others. First, black english (BE) speakers tend to pronounce the *th* in words such as *the* and *them* as *d* resulting in "de" or "dem." The second distinguishing characteristic is the omission of the verb *to be* in certain cases. Speakers are prone to say "He come" or "She going" instead of "He is coming" or "She is going." A third phenomena of BE is the use of the possessive suffix. Thus black persons may be heard saying "Robert coat" rather than "Robert's coat."

In contrast to the oral history of blacks, Hispanic populations have used nonverbal communication methods extensively (Ruiz, 1982). Touching, especially, has been commonly used in the communication process to convey different meanings. Psychologists must thus be trained to recognize the subtle differences that this form of nonverbal communication might take when used by Hispanics.

Perhaps one of the most difficult tasks faced by clinicians when treating the Hispanic patient lies in the language domain. From a language standpoint Hispanic clients present some unique differences from both whites and blacks and these differences must be recognized and considered in the treatment process. A major factor regarding language differences is the presence of two languages within Hispanic populations. As evidence of their impact Ruiz (1982) reports that some patients may use language switching as a form of resistance to diffuse emotionally charged material. This kind of resistance can seriously affect psychotherapeutic interactions if both languages are used simultaneously to complicate the problems under consideration by the client and therapist.

Another serious language problem for Hispanic patients receiving treatment is the issue of translation. Differences in translation exist among various Hispanic groups as well as among groups in different regions. For instance the word *tostone* may refer to a quarter or fifty cents to Mexican-Americans, while to a Puerto Rican it means a squashed part of a fried banana (DeAvila, 1976).

Other problems in translation can also occur. For example the frequencies and potencies of one language often are not transferrable to the second language. The word *pet* is common in English, yet its Spanish equivalent *mascota* or *animal domestico* is used infrequently by Hispanics. Moreover, direct translation of a word can radically change its meaning. For instance there are many seemingly innocent English words that translate into Hispanic swear words (DeAvila, 1976). Finally, it is impossible to use a single translation across different geographic regions because there are important distinctions in Hispanic dialects. The word "*kite*" could be translated as *cometa, chiringa,* or *huila* depending upon country of origin (DeAvila, 1976).

It is apparent that any therapist who would seek to intervene successfully in the lives of culturally different families and children would do well to have an awareness and sensitivity to the language differences and patterns exhibited by minority patients.

Having identified with his clients, the therapist is not tempted to see them as weak if they respond in a "mumbling" manner. Nor is the therapist distressed if these clients fall back on linguistic or language differences to disguise the fact that they are reluctant to give a full disclosure of themselves because they do not fully trust the "man." In this respect, the psychologist is taking into account that various minority persons have sought to suppress their true feelings and have used atypical mechanisms to conceal their anger and resentment (Vontress, 1970). Therefore, therapists will not be rendered helpless by the differences in language that they observe in a black from rural Mississippi, a black Catholic from a New England town, a black Methodist from Albany, Georgia, and a wealthy black Episcopalian in Chicago (Banks, 1975). Likewise the clinician will have to be as much at ease with the linguistic differences of a rural Mexican-American as with the jive talk of the urban streetwise Puerto Rican.

Kinship Networks

Another important clinical variable of significance for the therapist who works with culturally different families and children is the kinship network concept. While the kinship principle seems not to be unique or culture bound, with minorities it does seem to have a universal foundation in the dynamics of excluded groups. These groups utilize the principle by coming together, forming communication networks, sharing resources, and developing support systems for survival (Myers, 1982). These kinship systems may vary among culturally different populations, but the existence of the kinship network has been essential for the survival of minority families.

In black families, particularly in low-income units, it has been a common practice for several generations of related kinfolk to live in the same home or dwelling (Smith et al., 1978). Another usual custom among black families has been the habit of extending the family circle to include neighbors and their children as additional unifying forces for protection and strength. This heavy emphasis and reliance upon relatives and friends has continued to exist in modern day society. Moreover, it has been found to be true of impoverished as well as prosperous black families (Bass, 1982; Johnson, 1982). Middle class blacks have often been sustained in their present status through the support of mutually helpful family and nonrelatives who assisted them on their rise to their present levels of achievement. These more fortunate blacks have tended to maintain close contact with families, other relatives, and nonrelatives (Johnson, 1982).

Hispanic families, too, have extended family and community networks. A strong identity and loyalty to the family is especially fostered in traditional Mexican American families (Castaneda, 1976). Escobar and Randolph (1982) have found that these closely knit networks have remained a fixture of Hispanic families at all levels in spite of generational shifts. In other words, while acculturation has modified kinship relationships in all forms of Hispanic families (traditional, dualistic, and atraditional), the dense, extended family network has endured. Thus, the *compadrazco* (act of establishing the relationship of *compadres*) is one of primary means whereby ties with other extended families (other than through marriage) are formalized and are expressed in religious ceremonies, baptism, confirmation, and marriage (Castaneda, 1976). As in the case of blacks, Hispanics have also used their extended family networks for survival and support.

In summary, black and Hispanic families have been characterized by closely knit groups with extended networks of relatives and nonrelatives. Although both of these culturally different family types have tended to maintain their differing kinship relationships for positive reasons, some researchers have warned that the networking could be potentially destructive (Escobar & Randolph, 1982; Myers, 1982). Specifically, these investigators feel that the kinship networking might be hindering the treatment modalities of minorities. For example, the family's supportive atmosphere may provide a protective force against mental illnesses, but conversely the added support and protection afforded by the family might raise its level of tolerance for psychopathology postponing the entrance of the mentally ill into therapy (Escobar & Randolph, 1982).

In summary, it would appear that extended kinship networks play a pivotal role in the perpetuation and survival of culturally different families. Therapists should be aware of the importance of these networks since the structures allow positive family characteristics to surface as strengths.

GUIDELINES FOR THERAPEUTIC INTERACTIONS WITH CULTURALLY DIFFERENT FAMILIES AND CHILDREN

Mission of the Therapist

What then can be asked of therapists? Basically, culturally different clients have expectations that the therapist will not assign them back to the world that they currently live in. Therefore, children and parents are not looking for rejection and continued frustration in a microcosm of their present environment. The minority patient is expecting the psychologist to recognize and respect him/her as an individual. Clients are holding out for therapy to fulfill its promise. Clients are asking for the right to fail, the opportunity to explore options, to learn, to hope and to dream, to try and to succeed. Wilson (1971) urges therapists to relate to minority clients in ways that will enhance their cultural identity; that will allow their cultural identities to become positive sources of pride and powerful motivators of behavior.

Counseling with culturally different parents, then, can be expected to be a personally and professionally demanding task. Therapists should be prepared to be subjected to a wide range of emotions without being devastated and without feeling the need to retaliate within the counseling framework. Clinicians must be inclined to withstand rejection, criticism, and hostility, but still feel at ease with culturally different clients. They must be able to share themselves without controlling the patient and to accept the client while maintaining the genuineness of the helping role. Therapists will have to summon the strength to be empathetic to the patient's needs and to sustain themselves through sessions that are stressful and whose effects are not dramatically apparent in the short run. Finally, clinicians must be able to understand the problems of self-image, racial and social class, and the anger that culturally different populations bring to the personal encounter.

Parents

The self-concept of culturally different parents can be enhanced by the therapeutic process. As their needs are met, they can be made to feel that they are important as human beings. As they are made to feel worthwhile, they can be helped to develop a positive state of mental health. Although the success of treatment will often be judged by what happens to the minority child, the mental health of the child will be dependent upon the well-being of the culturally different parent.

The ability of the therapist to assist the culturally different parent to translate this concept into meaningful action is the basis for working with minority parents. Clinicians must have the facility to interact with several categories of culturally different parents when addressing this issue. With black families psychologists should be aware that they are likely to be involved with parents of differing households. Therapists might find themselves interacting with single, two-parent, or the adolescent parent family. All of these families are found in other cultures but the controversies surrounding these types of black families should be well known to the clinician.

The therapist should be aware that the matriarchial single parent family fits many of the stereotyped characteristics generally ascribed to the black family due to circumstances of poverty, limited resources, and the effects of racism (Myers, 1982). However, the clinician should have the knowledge that the family might not be pathological, that the roles of family members have been adapted to fit family circumstance, and the kinship network is working to diminish the damaging effects of low socioeconomic lifestyle (Johnson, 1982; Myers, 1982).

Therapists should also realize that black parents head a variety of familial structures. Second, clinicians should be aware that the parental roles may be disproportionately affected by their employment status (last hired, first fired). Third, therapists have to accept the fact that black female parents are at risk of being deserted, separated, or divorced and left with the responsibility of child rearing. Fourth, black parents, middle class and poor, seek support and strength from extended kinship, "parakin," and nonrelative networks. Finally, the clinician should recognize that some black parents have embraced acculturation as a way of life, have altered their lifestyles accordingly, and are finding themselves at risk in urban societies (Bass, 1982; Johnson, 1982).

Hispanic parents are of special concern for two reasons. First, they head up households within a large population that is disproportionately represented in the lower socio-economic level; and second, they and their families are highly susceptible to the stresses of migration and acculturation.

Whether the Hispanic parent and family reside in the barrio or elsewhere, minority status has economic implications. In the first case, the head of the poverty stricken family in the barrio/ghetto has the stress of meeting everyday economic needs of the family. Second, sometimes parents are migrant farm workers in which case low wages and substandard living conditions cause additional family and economic strain. Third, if living in rural, isolated, and impoverished areas, parents have scant possibility of relieving their severe economic plight (Smith et al., 1978).

Perhaps even greater stress has been introduced into the Hispanic family through the acculturation process. For example, as an aftermath of this process can be found three distinct Mexican-American communities. Parents and their families may be residing in traditional, dualistic, or atraditional communities. Therapists who interact with parents of households living in traditional communities can expect to see adults who usually exhibit a lifestyle that strongly identifies with Mexican values, i.e., strong religious orientation, personalized interpersonal relationships. Clinicians who treat parents from dualistic communities can look forward to interfacing with persons who show some adoption of mainstream America as well as traditional Mexican values. Psychologists who seek to intervene in the lives of atraditional adults will face parents who have amalgamated Mexican-American and mainstream American values (Castaneda, 1976).

Within the acculturation of all Hispanic families have come problems that have caused concern and stress to parents. In an earlier work Madsen (1964b) coined the term "the alcoholic agringado" to portray the trauma associated with cultural transfer among young Mexican-American males seeking to become acculturated. He saw the young male standing alone, caught between two conflicting cultural worlds, and resorting to alcohol for anxiety relief. Ramirez, Castaneda, and Cox[||||] discussed Hispanic parents who made a practice of discouraging their children from speaking Spanish in the hopes that they (the children would not suffer) discrimination as they did. Fitzpatrick and Travieso (1980) spoke of the changes in values from first to second generation Puerto Rican families. Many Puerto Rican parents have problems adjusting to the shifting role of the child (independence). Likewise, tension may ensue between the parents. The change in the wife's economic status may cause role reversal, i.g., wife becomes principal breadwinner, resulting in familial strife.

Despite all of these cultural modifications therapists can still expect to see a majority of parents who generally place high values on religion, interpersonal relationships, family, friends and relatives, and cooperation. However, just as there is heterogeneity in black families, the same principle applies to Hispanic family units. Psychologists should not be surprised to find that they will also interact with Hispanics who exhibit mainstream American lifestyles.

The Child

For most culturally different parents, life has unraveled through trying human experiences and these in turn are impressed upon the culturally different child. With a sense of responsibility often bred in despair and desperation, minority parents are hoping that therapists will afford them the right to have an effective voice in decisions that affect them and their children.

In assessing their professional obligation, therapists have discerned that many parenting problems of culturally different parents are the result of the interaction of sociopolitical, racial, and intrapsychic issues. These problems are related to skin color, physical appearance, emotional self-awareness, and self-management. They should all be considered significant variables in the formation of the minority child's identity

---

[||||] Ramirez, M., Castenada, A., & Cox, B. A bicultural inventory for Mexican-American students. Unpublished research report, 1977

(Harrison-Ross, 1977). The therapist should be attuned to the fact that these variables will combine in creating problems unique to culturally different parents and their children. Writing in *The Black Child—A Parent's Guide*, Harrison-Ross and Wyden (1973) identified five special problems of the black child. These problems can be generalized to all culturally different children.

He (the child) bears the white man's burden. The child triggers inherited guilt and shame that makes it difficult for whites to accept (blacks) easily, to emphathize, to socialize.

He (the child) bears the minority man's burden. The child has to cope with his family's feeling of being different, of being discriminated against, of rage, pride.

He (the child) is born to face a fight. The child has to fight for his education, has to conquer white (especially adult) hostility.

He (the child) presents an exercise in frustration and helplessness to the parents. They have to learn how to instill courage, confidence, and self-esteem in the child and to help him develop a positive self-image.

With culturally different children, single treatment modalities will not be effective. In view of the fact that many of the affected minority children will come from low socioeconomic levels, from inner city areas, or from families with language or linguistical differences, different kinds of treatment modalities will have to be utilized to relieve them of psychosocial stress (Canino, 1982; Powell, 1982).

Child Treatment Inverventions

Individual psychoanalytical therapy has been found to be effective with culturally different children (Banks, 1975; Korchin, 1980). Graffagnino, Bucknam, Orgun, and Leve (1970) also successfully used this modality with lower socioeconomic black and white urban children. These were children (7 to 10 years old) who had serious emotional problems, and failed to function in a regular classroom. These authors found that children from unstable homes could benefit from individual psychotherapy when it was a part of a clinical educational setting.

Family therapy can also be utilized with culturally different children. Minuchin, Talvo, Guerney, Rosman, and Sehumer (1967) used family therapy with black and Hispanic boys who were seriously disturbed. Using conflict resolution in family therapy, he challenged their methods of communication and of experiencing affect. Canino and Canino (1980) also recommended a family therapy approach. They used an ecostructural family therapy method that included the Puerto Rican family as a resource in intervention.

Group therapy and community therapeutic approaches have also been utilized with varying degrees of success in working with culturally different children. Scheidlenger (1965) used a motivational group therapy approach that consisted of three stages: guided gratification, guided regression, and upbringing and socialization. The therapeutic community approach was put into effect by the Unitas Therapeutic Community in the Bronx, New York. They trained older Puerto Rican adolescents in basic psychological theory and clinical skills and then used them as community caretakers. They became counselors and caretakers of younger children.

CONCLUSION

Although it would be desirable for Hispanic and black patients to be treated by Hispanic and black therapists, it is not feasible due to the paucity of minority health providers. However, one of the most important components of both assessment and intervention is the therapeutic interaction. The clinician who is aware of the lifestyle of culturally different families and children can fulfill a very significant role in assuring that appropriate treatment modalities and strategies are utilized with minority patients (Becerra, Karno, & Escobar, 1982). As Vontress (1970) stated:

> Talk is easy, but action betrays verbalization of committment and dedication. If professionally responsible people do care, now is the time to show it by helping others to care. . . . Although everybody will not be psychologically capable of doing this, an effort must be made to acquaint counselors with the nature and needs of people . . . who, if something is not done and done quickly have nothing to anticipate but a life of misery and shame (p. 719).

REFERENCES

Acuna, R. *The story of the Mexican Americans.* New York: Litton Educational Publishing, 1967

Alley, G, & Foster, C. Nondiscriminatory testing of minority and exceptional children. *Focus on Exceptional Children,* 1978, 9 (8), 1–16

Anastasi, A. *Psychological testing* (4th ed.). New York: MacMillan, 1976

Astin, AW, Astin, HS, Green, KC, Kent, L, McNamera, P, & Williams, MR. *Minorities in American higher education: Recent trends, current prospects, and recommendations.* San Francisco: Jossey-Bass, 1982

Bach-Y-Rita, G. The Mexican American: Religious and cultural influences. In RM Becerra, M Karno, & JI Escobar (Eds.), *Mental health and Hispanic Americans.* New York: Grune & Stratton, 1982

Banks, HC. The black person as client and as therapist. *Professional Psychology,* 1975, 6:470–474

Banks, JA. The implications of multicultural education for teacher education. In FH Klassen & DM Gollnick (Eds.), *Pluralism and the American teacher: Issues and case studies.* Washington, D.C.: Ethnic Heritage Center for Teacher Education of the American Association of Colleges for Teacher Education, 1977

Banks, WM. The Black client and helping professions. In RL Jones (ed.), *Black Psychology.* New York: Harper & Row, 1972, pp. 205–212

Baratz, S, & Baratz, J. Early childhood intervention: The social science basis of institutional racism. *Harvard Educational Review,* 1970, *40,* 29–50

Bass, B. The validity of sociocultural factors in the assessment and treatment of Afro-Americans. In B Bass, G Wyatt, & G Powell (Eds.) *The Afro-American family: Assessment, treatment and research issues.* New York: Grune & Stratton, 1982, p. 69

Becerra, R, Karno, M, & Escobar, J. Hispanic patient: Mental health issues and strategies. In G Becerra, M Karno, & J Escobar (Eds.), *Mental health and Hispanic Americans.* New York: Grune & Stratton, 1982 pp. 2–3

Bernal, EM. Changing the structure from within and without: A common sense approach to the development and effective utilization of Mexican American professionals. In EM Bernal (Ed.), *The San Antonio Conference: Bilingual-bicultural education—Where do we go from here?* San Antonio: St. Mary's University, 1969 (ERIC Document Reproduction Service No. ED 033 777), pp. 10–12

Bernal, EM. A response to "educational uses of tests with disadvantaged subjects." *American Psychologist,* 1975, *30,* 93–95

Bernal, EM. Assessment procedures for Chicano children: The sad state of the art. *Aztlan,* 1977, *8,* 69–81

Bernal, EM. *ERIC/TM Report 72: Methods of identifying gifted minority students.* Princeton, N.J.: ERIC Clearinghouse on Tests, Measurements, and Evaluation (Educational Testing Service), 1980

Bernal, EM, & Tucker, JA. *A manual for screening and assessing students of limited English proficiency.* Paper presented at the Council for Exceptional Children's Conference on the Exceptional Bilingual Child, New Orleans, February 1981. (ERIC Document Reproduction Service No. ED 209 785)

Bettelheim, B, & Janowitz, M. *Dynamics of prejudice.* New York: Harper & Row, 1950

Billingsley, A. Black families in white America. Englewood Cliffs, N.J.: Prentice Hall, 1968

Boulette, RR. Parenting: Special needs of low-income Spanish-surnamed families. *Pediatric Annals,* September 1977, *6,* 95–107

Brown, J. Staff development: Becoming more sensitive and responsive to cultural issues. In MP Gaasholt (Ed.), *Organizing for change: Inservice and staff development in special education.* Seattle: University of Washington, Program Development Assistance System, 1981, pp. 79–97

Brown, LB. Race as a factor in establishing a casework relationship. *Social Casework,* 1950, *31,* 91–97

Broyard, A. Portrait of the inauthentic Negro: How prejudice distorts the victim's personality. *Commentary,* 1950, *10,* 56–64

Calhoun, JA, Grotberg, EH, & Rackley, WR. *The status of children, youth, and families, 1979.* Washington, DC.: U.S. Department of Health and Human Services, 1980

Canino I. The Hispanic Child. In R Becerra, M Karno, & J Escobar (Eds.), *Mental health and Hispanic Americans.* New York: Grune & Stratton, 1982, pp. 157–168

Canino, I, & Canino, G. Impact of stress on Puerto Rican family: Treatment considerations. *American Journal of Orthopsychiatry*, 1980, *50*, (3) 535–541

Cardenas, B, & Cardenas, JA. Chicago: Bright-eyed, bilingual, brown, and beautiful. *Today's Education*, February 1973, *62*, 49–51

Castaneda, A. Cultural democracy and the educational needs of Mexican American Children. In R Jones (Ed.), *Mainstreaming and the minority child*, Reston, Va.: Council for Exceptional Children, 1976, pp.181–192

Castenada, A, James, R, & Robbins, W. *The educational needs of minority groups*. Lincoln, Neb.: Professional Education Publications, 1974

Chilman, CS. Programs for disadvantaged parents. In BM Caldwell & HN Ricutti (Eds.), *Review of child development research*. Chicago: University of Chicago Press, 1973, pp. 29–37

Chinn, PC. *Special problems of handicapped minority students*. Reston, Va.: ERIC Clearinghouse on Handicapped and Gifted Children. Fact Sheet, 1979

Cleary, TH, Humphreys, L, Kendrick, S, & Wesman, A. Educational uses of tests with disadvantaged students. *American Psychologist*, 1975, *30*, 15–41

Cole, M, & Bruner, J. Cultural differences and inferences about psychological processes. *American Psychologist*, 1971, *26*, 867–876

Cole, R. God and the rural poor. *Psychology Today*. New York: Communications Research Machines, 1972, *5*, 33–40

Comer, JP, & Peussant, AE. *Black child care*. New York: Simon and Schuster, 1975

Cummins, J. The role of primary language development in promoting educational success for language minority students. In *Compendium on bilingual-bicultural education*. Sacramento: California State Department of Education, 1981

Curtis, J, Ligon, GD, & Wiebly, GW. When is a LEP student no longer LEP? *Bilingual Education Paper Series*, (Vol. 3, No. 8), Los Angeles: National Dissemination and Assessment Center, 1980

DeAvila, E. Mainstreaming ethnically and linguistically different children: An exercise in paradox or a new approach. In R Jones (Ed.), *Mainstreaming and the minority child*. Reston, Va.: Council for Exceptional Children, 1976, pp. 93–108

Dickerman, M. Teaching cultural pluralism. In JA Banks (Ed.), *Teaching ethnic studies: Concepts and strategies*. Washington, DC.: National Council for the Social Studies, 1973, pp. 5–26

Dohrenwend, BP, Dohrenwend, BS, Gould, MS, & Wunsch-Hitzig, R. *Mental illness in the United States*. New York: Praeger Publishers, 1980

El-Khawas, EH, & Kinger, JL. Enrollment of minority graduate students of Ph.D. granting institutions. *Higher Education Panel Reports*, No. 19. Washington, DC.: American Council of Education, 1974

Escobar, J, & Randolph, E. The Hispanic and social networks. In R Becerra, M Karno, & J Escobar (Eds.), *Mental health and Hispanic Americans*. New York: Grune & Stratton, 1982, pp. 41–52

Evans, F, & Anderson, JG. The psychocultural origins of achievement and achievement motivation: The Mexican American family, *Sociology of Education*, 1973, 46 (4), 396–416

Fitzpatrick, JP, & Travieso, L. The Puerto Rican family: Its role in cultural transition. In A Fantini & R Cardenas (Eds.), *Parenting in a multicultural society*. New York: Langman Inc., 1980, pp. 103–119

Flores, M. *A study of Mexican American cultural characteristics as perceived by members of 100 impoverished Mexican American families and its educational implications*. Houston, Tex.: University of Houston, 1972

Florez, J. Issues and problems affecting Hispanic youth: An analysis and blueprint for action. In M Montiel (Ed.), *Hispanic families; Critical issues for policy and programs in human services.* Washington, DC.: National Coalition of Hispanic Mental Health and Human Service Organizations, 1978, p. 57

Gay, B, & Abrahams, RD. Does the pot melt, boil, or brew? Black children and White assessment procedures. *Journal of School Psychology,* 1973, *11,* 330–340

Glazer, N. Public education and American pluralism. In JS Coleman, JE Coons, WH Cornog, DP Doyle, EB Edwards, N Glazer, AM Greeley, RK Greenawalt, M Lagerson, WC McCready, M Novak, JP O'Dwyer, R Singleton, T Sowell, SD Sugarman, & RE Wagner (Eds.), *Parents, teachers and children: Prospects for choice in American education.* San Francisco: Institute for Contemporary Studies, 1977, p. 89

Gonzales, JM. What are the research issues, needs, and capabilities that need to be identified and clarified? In National Institute of Education, *Desegragation and educational concerns of the Hispanic community: Conference report, June 26–28, 1977.* Washington, DC.: U.S. Government Printing Office, 1977, p. 12

Gonzales, JM. *Towards quality in bilingual education: Bilingual education in the integrated school.* Rosslyn, Va.: National Clearinghouse for Bilingual Education, 1979

Graffagnino, P, Bucknam, F, Orgun, I, & Leve R. Psychotherapy for latency age children in an inner city therapeutic school. *American Journal of Psychiatry,* 1970, *127,* 626–634

Grant, M. *The passing of the great race* (4th. rev. ed.). New York: Charles Scribner & Sons, 1922

Griffin, JB. Discrimination in public education. Washington, D.C.: Bulletin of the N.A.S.S.P., November 1971, pp. 89–90

Griffith, MS, & Jones, EE. Race and psychotherapy: Changing perspectives. In JH Masserman (Ed.), Current psychiatric therapies (Vol. 18). New York: Grune & Stratton, 1979

Guerin, GR, & Maier, AS. *Informal assessment in education.* Palo Alto, Calif.: Mayfield, 1983

Mare, N. *The black Anglo-Saxons.* New York: Marzani and Munsell, 1965

Harrison-Ross, P. Parenting the black child. *Pediatric Annals,* 1977, *6,* 83–94.

Harrison-Ross, P, & Wyden, B. *The Black child—A parent's guide.* New York: Peter Wyden/David McKay, 1973

Hill R. *The strengths of black families.* New York: Emerson Hall Publishers, 1972

Hulbury, WE. Race, deprivation, and adolescent self-images. *Social Science Quarterly,* 1975, *56,* 105–114

Humphreys, LG. Racial differences: Dilemma of college admissions. *Science,* 1969, *166,* 167

Jackson, G, & Cosca, G. The inequality of educational opportunity in the Southwest: An observational study of ethnically mixed classrooms. *American Educational Research Journal,* 1974, *11,* 219–229

Jacobson, RL. Standardized testing and cultural bias. *Chronicle of Higher Education,* July 25, 1977, *XIV,* 3–4

Jensen, AR. *Bias in mental testing.* New York: Free Press, 1980

Johnson, J. The Afro-American family: A historical overview. In B Bass, G Wyatt, & G. Powell, (Eds.), *The Afro-American family: Assessment, treatment, and research issues.* New York: Grune & Stratton, 1982, pp. 3–11

Jones, A, & Seagull, AA. Dimensions of the relationship between the Black client and the White therapists. *American Psychologist,* 1977, *32,* 850–855

Jones, EE. Social class and psychotherapy: A critical review of research. *Journal of Psychiatry,* 1974, *37,* 307–320

Jones, EE. Effects of race on psychotherapy process and outcome: An exploratory investigation. *Psychotherapy: Theory, research and practice,* 1978, *15,* 226–236

Kellam, S, Ensminger, M, & Turner, RJ. Family structure and the mental health of children: Concurrent and longtitudinal community wide studies. *Archives of General Psychiatry,* 1977, *3,* 1012–1022

Kelly, DH, & Piuk, WT. Social origins, school status, and the learning experience. *Pacific Sociological Review*, 1973, *16*, 121–134

Kirkpatrick, JJ, Ewen, RB, Barrett, RS, & Katzell, RA. *Testing and fair employment: Fairness and validity of personnel tests for different ethnic groups*. New York: New York University Press, 1968

Korchin, SH. Clinical psychology and minority problems. *American Psychologist*, 1980, *35* (3), 262–269

Ladner, JA. *Tomorrow tomorrow: The black woman*. Garden City, NY.: Doubleday, 1971

Langer, TS, Gersten, J, Green, EI, Eisenberg, JG, Herson, JJ, & McCarty, ED. Treatment of psychological disorders among urban children. *Journal of Consulting and Clinical Psychology*, 1974, *42*, 170–179

Laosa, LM. Cross-cultural and subcultural research in psychology and education. *Interamerican Journal of Psychology*, 1973, *7*, 241–248

Lee, DL, *From plans to planets*. Chicago: Broadside Press, 1973

Lorion, RP. Research on psychology and behavior change with the disadvantaged: Past, present, and future directions. In SL Garfield & AE Bergin (Eds.), *Handbook of psychotherapy and behavior change: An empirical analysis* (2nd ed.). New York: Wiley, 1978

Madsen, W. The alcoholic agringado. *American Anthropoligist*, 1964, 66, 355–361 (a)

Madsen, W. *The Mexican-American of south Texas*. New York: Holt, Rinehart & Winston, 1964 (b)

Manaster, GJ, & Havighurst, RJ. *Cross-national research: Social-psychological methods and problems*. New York: Houghton-Mifflin, 1972

Marion, RL. Minority parent involvement in the IEP process: A systematic model approach. *Focus on Exceptional Children*, January 1979, pp. 1–14

Matarazzo, JD. *Wechsler's measurement and appraisal of adult intelligence* (5th ed.). Baltimore: Williams & Wilkins, 1972

McGuigan, CA. Systematically planning for effective inservice training or staff development. In MP Gaasholt (ed.), *Organizing for change: Inservice and staff development in special education*. Seattle: University of Washington, Program Development Assistance System, 1981, pp. 59–78

Mendes, HA. The role of religion in psychotherapy with Afro-Americans. In A Bass, G Wyatt, & G. Powell (Eds.), *The Afro-American family: Assessment, treatment and research issues*. New York: Grune & Stratton, 1982, pp. 205–206

Mercer, J. Pluralistic diagnosis in the evaluation of Black and Chicano children: A procedure for taking socio-cultural variables into account in clinical assessment. In CA Hernandez, MJ Hang, & NN Wagner (Eds.), *Chicanos: Social and psychological perspectives*. St. Louis, Mo.: CV Mosby, 1976, p. 50

Mercer, J. *System of multicultural pluralistic assessment technical manual*. New York: Psychological Corporation, 1979

Milutinovich, JS. A comparative study of work attitudes of Black and White workers. In DL Ford (Ed.), *Readings in minority group relations*. La Jolla, Calif.: University Associates, 1976

Minuchin, S, Talvo, B, Guerney BG, Rosman BL, & Sehumer, F. *Families of the slums: An exploration of their structure and treatment*. New York: Basic Books, 1967

Mitchell-Kernan, C. Linguistic diversity in the service delivery setting: A case of Black English. In B Bass, G Wyatt, & G Powell (Eds.), *The Afro-American family: assessment, treatment, and research issues*. New York: Grune & Stratton, 1982, pp. 85–98

Montijo, J. The Puerto Rican client. *Professional Psychology*, 1976, *6*, 475–477

Moynihan, D. *The Negro family: The case for national action*. Washington, D.C.: Office of Policy Planning and Research. United States Department of Labor, March, 1965

Myers, H. Research on the Afro-American family. In B Bass, G Wyatt, & G Powell (Eds.), *The Afro-American family: Assessment, treatment and research issues.* New York: Grune & Stratton, 1982, p. 50

Nobles, WW. Toward an empirical and theoretical framework for defining black families. *Journal of Marriage and the Family,* 1978, *40,* 679–688

Nunnally, JC, Jr. *Tests and measurements: Assessments and prediction.* New York: McGraw-Hill, 1959

Oakland, T, & Matuszek, P. Using tests in nondiscriminatory assessment. In T Oakland (Ed.), *Psychological and educational assessment of minority children.* New York: Brunner/Mazel, 1977, pp. 52–69

O'Malley, JM. *Children's English and services study: Language minority children with limited English proficiency in the United States.* Rosslyn, VA: National Clearinghouse for Bilingual Education, 1981

Ortega, R. Special education placement and Mexican Americans. *El Torito,* 1971, *4,* 29–35

Pfeiffer, SI. The school-based interprofessional team: Recurring problems and some possible solutions. *Journal of School Psychology,* 1980, *18,* 388–394

Pifer, A. Bilingual education and the Hispanic challenge. In *1979 Annual Report.* New York: Carnegie Corporation, 1979

Pinderhughes, CA. Racism and psychotherapy. In C Willie, B Kramer, & Brown, BS (Eds.), *Racism and mental health.* Pittsburgh: University of Pittsburgh Press, 1973, pp. 61–121

Powell, G. Overview of epidemiology of mental illness among Afro-Americans. In B Bass, G Wyatt, & Powell, (Eds.), *The Afro-American family: Assessment, treatment and research issues.* New York: Grune & Stratton, 1982, 155–163

President's Commission on Mental Health. *Report to the President.* Superintendent of Documents, Washington, DC.: U.S. Government Printing Office, 1978

Rabkin, JG. Ethnic density and psychiatric hospitalization: Hazards of minority ethnic status. *American Journal of Psychiatry,* 1979, *136,* 1562–1566

Rainwater, L. The problem of low-class culture. *Journal of Social Issues,* 1970, *26,* 133–148

Ramirez, M, Herold, L, & Castenada, A. *Mexican-American values and culturally democratic educational environment; new approaches to bilingual, bicultural education* (2). Austin, Tex.: Dissemination Center for Bilingual, Bicultural Education, 1974

Reissman, F. Lower-income culture: The strengths of the poor. *Journal of Marriage and the Family,* 1964, *26,* 417–421

Rogers, CR. *Client-centered therapy.* Boston: Houghton-Mifflin, 1951

Rogers, CR. The interpersonal relationship: The core of guidance. *Harvard Educational Review,* 1962, *32,* 416–429

Ruiz, P. The Hispanic patient: Sociocultural perspectives. In R Becerra, M Karno, & J Escobar (Eds.), *Mental health and Hispanic Americans.* New York: Grune & Stratton, 1982, p. 17

Russell, RD. Black perception of guidance. *Personnel and Guidance Journal,* 1970, *48,* 721–728

Rutter, M, Cox, A, Tupling, C, Berger, M, & Yale, W. Attainment and adjustment in two geographical areas. The prevalence of psychiatric disorder. *British Journal of Psychiatry,* 1975, *126,* 493–509

Sager, CJ, Brayboy, TL, & Waxenberg, BR. Black patient-white therapist. *American Journal of Orthopsychiatry,* 1972, *42,* 415–423

Sattler, JM. *Assessment of children's intelligence and special abilities* (2nd ed.). Boston: Allyn & Bacon, 1982

Saville-Troike, M. *Foundations for teaching English as a second language: Theory and methods for multicultural education.* Englewood Cliffs, NJ.: Prentice-Hall, 1976

Scheidlenger, S. Three group approaches with socially deprived latency-age children. *International Journal of Group Psychotherapy,* 1965 *15,* (4), 123–128

Shuey, AM. *The testing of Negro intelligence* (2nd ed.). New York: Social Science Press, 1966

Smith, WD, Burlew, AK, Mosley, MH, & Whitney, WM. *Minority issues in mental health.* Reading, Mass.: Addison-Wesley, 1978

Smith, WE. Cultural aspects of bilingual education. *IDRA Newsletter,* December 1981, pp. 1–3, 8

Soares, AT, & Soares, LM. Self-perceptions of culturally disadvantaged children. *American Educational Research Journal,* 1969, *6,* 31–45

Sue, S. Ethnic minority issues in psychology. *American Psychologist,* 1983, *38,* 583–593

Taba, H, & Elkins, D. *Teaching strategies for the culturally disadvantaged.* Chicago: Rand McNally, 1966

Taylor, EM, *Psychological appraisal of children with cerebral defects.* Cambridge, Mass.: Harvard University Press, 1961

Troike, RC. *Research evidence for the effectiveness of bilingual education.* Rosslyn, Va.: National Clearinghouse for Bilingual Education, 1978

Vontress, CE. Counseling blacks. *Personnel and Guidance Journal,* 1970, *48,* 713–719

Wechsler, D. Intelligence: Definition, theory, and the IQ. In R Cauero (Ed.), *Intelligence: Genetic and environmental influences.* New York: Grune & Stratton, 1971, p. 54

Wesman, AG. Better than chance. *Test Service Bulletin No. 45.* New York: Psychological Corporation, 1953

Wilson, ME. The significance of communication in counseling the culturally disadvantaged. In R Wilcox (ed.), *The psychological consequences of being a black American.* New York: Wiley, 1971

Wyatt, G, Powell, G, & Bass, B. The survey of Afro-American behavior: Its development and use in research. In B Bass, G Wyatt, & G Powell, (Eds.), *The Afro-American family: Assessment, treatment and research issues.* New York: Grune & Stratton, 1982, p. 16

Zigler, E, & Child, IL. Socialization. In G Lindzey & E Aronson (eds.), *Handbook of Social Psychology* (Vol. 3, 2nd ed.). Reading, Mass.: Addison-Wesley, 1969

Index